CD-CCL-329

Taxation in the Global Economy

A National Bureau
of Economic Research
Project Report

Taxation in the Global Economy

Edited by Assaf Razin and
Joel Slemrod

The University of Chicago Press

Chicago and London

Assaf Razin is the Daniel Ross Professor of International Economics at Tel Aviv University, a research associate of the National Bureau of Economic Research, and a visiting scholar at the International Monetary Fund. Joel Slemrod is professor of economics, professor of business economics and public policy, and director of the Office of Tax Policy Research at the University of Michigan, Ann Arbor, and a research associate of the National Bureau of Economic Research

The University of Chicago Press, Chicago 60637
The University of Chicago Press, Ltd., London
© 1990 by the National Bureau of Economic Research
All rights reserved. Published 1990
Printed in the United States of America
99 98 97 96 95 94 93 92 91 90   5 4 3 2 1

Library of Congress Cataloging-in-Publication Data

Taxation in the global economy / edited by Assaf Razin and Joel Slemrod.
    p. cm.—(A National Bureau of Economic Research project report)
    Includes bibliographical references.
    ISBN 0-226-70591-9 (alk. paper)
    1. Income tax—United States—Foreign income. 2. Corporations, American—Taxation. 3. International business enterprises—Taxation—United States. I. Razin, Assaf. II. Slemrod, Joel. III. Series.
HJ4653.F65T39   1990
336.24'3—dc20   90-30262
                                            CIP

Relation of the Directors to the
Work and Publications of the
National Bureau of Economic Research

1. The object of the National Bureau of Economic Research is to ascertain and to present to the public important economic facts and their interpretation in a scientific and impartial manner. The Board of Directors is charged with the responsibility of ensuring that the work of the National Bureau is carried on in strict conformity with this object.

2. The President of the National Bureau shall submit to the Board of Directors, or to its Executive Committee, for their formal adoption all specific proposals for research to be instituted.

3. No research report shall be published by the National Bureau until the President has sent each member of the Board a notice that a manuscript is recommended for publication and that in the President's opinion it is suitable for publication in accordance with the principles of the National Bureau. Such notification will include an abstract or summary of the manuscript's content and a response form for use by those Directors who desire a copy of the manuscript for review. Each manuscript shall contain a summary drawing attention to the nature and treatment of the problem studied, the character of the data and their utilization in the report, and the main conclusions reached.

4. For each manuscript so submitted, a special committee of the Directors (including Directors Emeriti) shall be appointed by majority agreement of the President and Vice Presidents (or by the Executive Committee in case of inability to decide on the part of the President and Vice Presidents), consisting of three Directors selected as nearly as may be one from each general division of the Board. The names of the special manuscript committee shall be stated to each Director when notice of the proposed publication is submitted to him. It shall be the duty of each member of the special manuscript committee to read the manuscript. If each member of the manuscript committee signifies his approval within thirty days of the transmittal of the manuscript, the report may be published. If at the end of that period any member of the manuscript committee withholds his approval, the President shall then notify each member of the Board, requesting approval or disapproval of publication, and thirty days additional shall be granted for this purpose. The manuscript shall then not be published unless at least a majority of the entire Board who shall have voted on the proposal within the time fixed for the receipt of votes shall have approved.

5. No manuscript may be published, though approved by each member of the special manuscript committee, until forty-five days have elapsed from the transmittal of the report in manuscript form. The interval is allowed for the receipt of any memorandum of dissent or reservation, together with a brief statement of his reasons, that any member may wish to express; and such memorandum of dissent or reservation shall be published with the manuscript if he so desires. Publication does not, however, imply that each member of the Board has read the manuscript, or that either members of the Board in general or the special committee have passed on its validity in every detail.

6. Publications of the National Bureau issued for informational purposes concerning the work of the Bureau and its staff, or issued to inform the public of activities of Bureau staff, and volumes issued as a result of various conferences involving the National Bureau shall contain a specific disclaimer noting that such publication has not passed through the normal review procedures required in this resolution. The Executive Committee of the Board is charged with review of all such publications from time to time to ensure that they do not take on the character of formal research reports of the National Bureau, requiring formal Board approval.

7. Unless otherwise determined by the Board or exempted by the terms of paragraph 6, a copy of this resolution shall be printed in each National Bureau publication.

(Resolution adopted October 25, 1926, as revised through September 30, 1974)

Contents

Preface

This volume includes eleven papers that were prepared as part of a research project on International Aspects of Taxation by the National Bureau of Economic Research. The papers examine the role of taxation in cross-border flows of capital and goods, the real and financial decisions of multinational corporations, and the implications of growing economic interdependence for a country's choice of a tax system. These papers were presented at a conference attended by academics, policymakers, and representatives of international organizations. The conference was held in Nassau, the Bahamas on 23–25 February 1989.

We would like to thank the Ford Foundation for financial support of this project. The success of the project also depended on the efforts of Kirsten Foss Davis, Ilana Hardesty, Robert Allison, and Mark Fitz-Patrick.

Assaf Razin and Joel Slemrod

Introduction

Assaf Razin and Joel Slemrod

The globalization of economic activity over the past three decades is widely recognized. Despite recent indications of renewed protectionism, this trend is likely to continue. With the integration of international activity has come the awareness that countries are linked not only by the cross-border transactions of private firms and citizens but also by the cross-border ramifications of their governments' fiscal policies. The tax policy of one country can affect economic activity in other countries, and in the choice of tax policy instruments a policymaker must consider its international consequences.

Examples of the growing awareness of fiscal interdependence abound. The rate-reducing, base-broadening U.S. tax reform of 1986 has been followed by similar reforms in many countries. In some cases, such as that of Canada, the tax reform was clearly hastened by a sense of the adverse economic consequences that would follow from a failure to harmonize to the new U.S. system. In other cases, the link may have been as much intellectual stimulation as economic necessity.

The move toward European integration in 1992 has also focused attention on fiscal issues. Many observers are concerned that, as barriers to trade and investment come down, cross-country differences in the taxation of economic activity will loom larger and cause inefficient decisions and self-defeating tax competition among member nations. Initial proposals to harmonize European systems of value-added taxes and to impose a uniform withholding tax rate on portfolio investments have not met with much success, however.

Assaf Razin is the Daniel Ross Professor of International Economics at Tel Aviv University, a research associate of the National Bureau of Economic Research, and a visiting scholar at the International Monetary Fund. Joel Slemrod is professor of economics, professor of business economics and public policy, and director of the Office of Tax Policy Research at the University of Michigan, and a research associate of the National Bureau of Economic Research.

Finally, there is a growing sense that the internationalization of financial markets and the increased importance of multinational enterprises are making it increasingly difficult to administer and enforce efficient and equitable income tax systems. Tax authorities must balance, on the one hand, their desire to preserve their national revenues and, on the other hand, their unwillingness to harm the international competitiveness of their domestic business interests. Thus there is not only heightened international competition among business but also heightened awareness of the possibilities and perils of international fiscal competition.

The research presented in this volume is an attempt to lay some intellectual groundwork for an understanding of these issues, which are destined to command the increasing attention of policymakers in the years to come. It represents an unusual exercise in academia, because it brings together people from two branches of economics—taxation and international economic relations. Our hope was that our joint expertise, perspectives, and methods would be more productive than our separate efforts. Both theoretical and empirical papers are represented. All the papers share the common goal of shedding light on the role of tax policy in a more highly integrated world economy.

A pervasive problem in international taxation, and one that makes the subject so complicated, is the existence of overlapping tax jurisdictions. Every country in the world asserts the right to tax income earned within its borders, regardless of the citizenship of the wealthowner or controller of the income-earning capital. Many countries, including the largest economies in the world, also assert the right to tax the income of their residents, individuals and corporations, regardless of where the income is earned (the "worldwide" system of taxation). In order to reduce the tax burden that would result from taxation by both host and home countries, those countries that use the worldwide system of taxation generally allow taxes paid to foreign governments to be credited against domestic tax liability, but this is subject to various limitations. In addition, a network of bilateral treaties has sprung up to coordinate taxation in the case of overlapping jurisdictions. The United States is an example of a country that operates a worldwide system of taxation and is also party to a number of bilateral tax treaties. Its system of taxing foreign-source income has had a great influence on other countries. This system, though, has undergone continual change, and the Tax Reform Act of 1986 continued the process of change.

In the opening chapter of this volume, Hugh J. Ault and David F. Bradford describe the basic rules that govern the U.S. taxation of international transactions and highlight the changes brought by the Tax Reform Act of 1986. The U.S. attempts to tax the worldwide income of its residents, both individuals and corporations. It does, however, differentiate domestic-source and foreign-source income, principally by taxing foreign subsidiaries' foreign-source income only on repatriation of dividends, at which time a credit for foreign corporáte taxes paid in association with these dividends is offered. This allows a deferral advantage to foreign-source income. The Tax Reform Act lowered the statutory rate of tax applied to these dividends, but also substantially tightened the limitation of foreign tax credit by creating several additional categories of income (called "baskets") across which averaging of foreign taxes is not allowed. It also revised the rules for allocating expenses between domestic- and foreign-source income, requiring a greater allocation of expenses to foreign operations.

Ault and Bradford go on to explore the economic policies or principles that the tax system reflects. They argue that the assignment of income to a geographic location is often an ill-defined concept, and therefore any operational rules that do so must be essentially arbitrary. There are competing theoretical frameworks for analysis in the international area that lead to quite different results. Real-world phenomena, they believe, are inconsistent with any single unifying framework. They conclude that the most important task for policy analysis is to try to determine with more accuracy exactly what impact the complex system of rules has on the form and extent of international activity. That charge is taken up in the remainder of the book.

Taxation and Multinationals

Multinationals pose special problems for taxing authorities because the geographic source of income is not easily determined. Overlapping tax jurisdictions, which generally employ different tax bases and rules, add enormously to the complexity of tax compliance and administration. They also can create opportunities for multinational companies to play the national tax systems against each other to reduce their worldwide tax payments. The concern for tax minimization can create incentives for real and financial strategies that would, in the absence of taxation, make little sense.

The next set of four papers examines several ways that the tax system affects the decisions of multinational corporations. The first two papers study its impact on foreign direct investment, and the next two examine two aspects of financial behavior that are affected by taxation.

Foreign direct investment (FDI) has surged dramatically in recent years. FDI into the United States reached $57 billion in 1988, after averaging only $4.1 billion in the 1970s and $18.5 billion in the 1980–85 period. Outward foreign investment from the United States in 1987 was $45 billion compared to an average of only $10 billion in 1977–84. The FDI of some other countries, particularly Japan, has grown even more rapidly than that of the United States.

The taxation system of the potential host country of an investment and home country of the multinational can affect the after-tax return, and therefore the incentive, for foreign direct investment. Each of the following two papers uses time-series data on FDI flows to assess how important the tax effects on FDI to and from the United States have been.

The paper by Joosung Jun examines the effect of U.S. tax policy on outward FDI. He delineates the three channels through which domestic tax policy can affect firms' international investment flows. First, tax policy can affect the way in which foreign-source income is shared among the firm, the home country government, and the host country government. Second, tax policy can affect the relative net profitability of investments in different countries. Finally, it can affect the relative cost of raising external funds in different countries.

Using this three-channel framework, Jun examines the aggregate time-series data on outward flows of FDI and concludes that U.S. tax policy toward U.S. domestic investment has had an important effect on outflows of direct investment by influencing the relative net rate of return on investment located in the United States and investment located in foreign countries.

The paper by Joel Slemrod investigates how the U.S. tax system, in conjunction with the tax system of a capital exporting country, affects the flow of foreign direct investment into the United States. First, using aggregate data, the paper corroborates earlier work suggesting that the effective U.S. tax rate does influence the amount of FDI financed by transfer of funds from parent companies, but not the amount financed by retained earnings. Next, it disaggregates FDI by exporting country to see if, as theory would suggest, FDI from countries that exempt foreign-source income from taxation is more sensitive to U.S. tax rates than FDI from countries that attempt to tax foreign-source income on a residual basis. The data analysis does not show a clear differential responsiveness between these two groups, suggesting either difficulties in accurately measuring effective rates of taxation or the existence of financial strategies that render ineffective attempts by the home country to tax foreign-source income.

Two of the chapters focus on how multinationals adjust their accounting and financial policies in response to the tax system. Jean-Thomas Bernard and Robert J. Weiner present a case study of transfer pricing practices in the petroleum industry. By setting the price of interaffiliate transactions, a multinational enterprise can affect the allocation of taxable profits among the countries in which its subsidiaries operate in order to reduce the worldwide tax burden of the multinational. Using data on oil imports in the United States from 1973 to 1984, they find that the prices set in interaffiliate transactions differed from the price set by unaffiliated parties ("arm's length" prices) for oil imported from some, but not all, countries. The average difference in price was small, however, representing 2 percent or less of the value of crude oil imports. Furthermore, the observed differences across exporting countries between arm's length and transfer prices are not easily explained by average effective tax rates in the exporting countries. Their results thus provide little support for the claim that multinational

petroleum companies set their transfer prices to evade taxes. These findings
may not be readily generalizable to other industries, particularly because
petroleum is a relatively homogeneous good for which market prices are
easily observable, thus facilitating the job of tax authorities in the U.S. and
abroad concerned with transfer price manipulation.

James R. Hines, Jr., and R. Glenn Hubbard investigate how tax policy
affects U.S. multinationals' policy of repatriating dividends from subsidiaries to the parent company. The income earned by foreign subsidiaries is
subject to U.S. tax only when dividends are repatriated. At that time the
taxes deemed to have been paid to foreign governments on the earnings
behind the dividend payment may be credited against U.S. tax liability. The
credit that may be taken in any given year is limited to the amount of U.S.
tax liability on the foreign-source income. This system provides multinationals with an incentive to defer dividend repatriations that will incur a net U.S.
tax liability and to favor repatriations from firms in high-tax countries for
which the tax credit will exceed the U.S. tax liability. In order to study the
quantitative significance of these incentives, Hines and Hubbard examined
data collected from tax returns for 1984 on financial flows from 12,041
foreign subsidiaries to their 453 U.S. parent corporations. They found that,
although on average dividend repatriations composed 39 percent of
subsidiaries' after-foreign-tax profits, most subsidiaries paid no dividends at
all. The pattern of repatriations was related to the tax cost, so that in net
terms the U.S. government collected very little revenue on the foreign
income of U.S. multinationals while at the same time the tax system is
apparently distorting their internal financial transactions.

The Effect of Taxation on Trade and Capital Flows

The international ramifications of tax policy go far beyond the impact on
multinationals' behavior. The tax policy of one country can ''spill over'' to
other countries' economies thereby affecting trade patterns, the volume of
saving and investment, and the desired portfolios of wealthholders. Each of
the next set of three papers addresses one aspect of how tax policy in one
country can affect the cross-border flow of goods and claims to assets.

Jacob A. Frenkel, Assaf Razin, and Steve Symansky deal directly with the
international spillovers of taxes in a stylized two-country model. Adopting
the saving-investment balance approach to the analysis of international
economic interdependence, they emphasize dynamic effects of domestic tax
restructurings on interest rates, investment, employment, consumption, and
the current account position. They show that a domestic budget deficit,
under a consumption tax system, raises the world rate of interest and crowds
out domestic and foreign investment. It also lowers the growth rates of
domestic consumption while raising those of foreign consumption. In
contrast, under an income tax system, the same budget deficit lowers the

world rate of interest, reduces the growth rates of domestic and foreign consumption, and crowds out domestic investment while crowding in foreign investment. The analysis of revenue-neutral tax conversions in a single country and revenue-neutral tax conversions in the context of a two-country VAT harmonization reform (as planned for the European Community in 1992) highlights the crucial role played by trade imbalances resulting from intercountry differences in saving and investment propensities. Existence of such international differences implies that tax harmonization may result in output and employment expansion in some countries and contraction in others, thereby generating conflicting interests among the various countries. The analytical results are supplemented by detailed dynamic simulations which highlight the variety of mechanisms through which the effects of tax policies spill over to the rest of the world.

Martin Feldstein and Paul Krugman scrutinize the view, common among many businesspersons, that reliance on the VAT aids a country's international competitiveness since such a tax is levied on imports but rebated on exports. They claim that in practice VATs are selective and fall more heavily on internationally traded goods than on nontraded goods and services. In this case, use of a VAT causes a substitution of nontraded goods and services which reduces both exports and imports, but the trade balance can either improve or worsen. The only pro-competitive aspect of a VAT may be the fact that substituting a consumption tax for an income tax encourages saving which, by itself, tends to improve the trade balance in the short run.

A. Lans Bovenberg, Krister Andersson, Kenji Aramaki, and Sheetal Chand deal with the effects of the tax treatment of investment and savings on international capital flows. They evaluate changes in tax wedges on savings and investment in the U.S. and Japan and examine how recent reforms of capital income taxation created incentives for bilateral capital flows between these countries during the 1980s. The results reveal that the tax burden on assets located in Japan exceeded the tax burden on assets located in the U.S., while a U.S. saver faced a heavier tax burden than a Japanese saver for assets located in both countries. They suggest that these differential tax burdens could to some extent explain the pattern of bilateral flows of savings and investment between the U.S. and Japan in the 1980s.

Some Implications For Optimal Tax Policy

Much of the research reported here has suggested that taxation can exert a potentially powerful influence on both real and financial decisions about cross-border movements of capital and goods. At the same time, it is clear that the increasing internationalization of economic affairs has profoundly changed what is appropriate tax policy. The last set of papers in this volume explore the implications for optimal tax design of several aspects of openness.

Assaf Razin and Efraim Sadka address two policy issues in the context of world capital market integration: (a) the effects of relaxing restrictions on the international flow of capital on the fiscal branch of government and (b) the degree of international tax coordination needed to ensure a viable equilibrium in the presence of international tax-arbitrage opportunities.

First, Razin and Sadka show that notwithstanding the use of distortionary taxes as part of the optimal program, it requires an efficient allocation of investment between home and foreign uses so that the marginal product of capital is equated across countries. Consequently, capital-market liberalization tends to lower the cost of public funds and increase the optimal provision of public goods and services. More public goods are demanded because of the increase in real income resulting from the improved trade opportunities and because broadening the tax base lowers the marginal cost of public funds through a distortion-reducing change in the marginal tax rates.

Second, they remind us that a complete integration of the capital markets between two countries requires that the residents of each country face the same net-of-tax rate of return on foreign and domestic investments. Otherwise, there must exist profitable arbitrage opportunities. These conditions will be met only if taxes by the home country levied on domestic residents on their domestic-source income and foreign-source income, and taxes on nonresidents' income in the home country are related to the corresponding foreign country taxes in a specific way. To assure such a relationship without arbitrage opportunities, the countries must coordinate to some degree their domestic and foreign tax structures.

The net effect of a country's tax system on international trade and factor flows is only partly revealed by how it taxes international transactions. As Roger H. Gordon and James Levinsohn point out, what are ostensibly "domestic" taxes can have an important impact on international transactions. They study the optimal coordination between domestic taxation and both tariff and nontariff trade policies. When the set of tax instruments is restricted, perhaps owing to administrative cost considerations, then tax policies that distort trade patterns may be optimal, although the direction of trade loss may be of either sign.

Gordon and Levinsohn next investigate to what extent the observed use of border distortions (tariffs, export subsidies, etc.) may result from a country's attempt to offset the trade distortions created by their domestic tax structure. To examine this hypothesis, they look at International Monetary Fund financial statistics for thirty countries during the period 1970–87. The data suggest that, while for poorer countries border taxes do seem to offset the trade impact of domestic taxes, the richer countries have significant trade-discouraging distortions caused by domestic taxation that are not offset by border taxation.

The final chapter, by John Douglas Wilson, deals with the optimal tax structure for an open economy in which similar types of workers are paid different wages since worker productivity in some industries depends on the level of wages (the efficiency wage model). The first-best optimal policy, an industrial policy which subsidizes high-wage firms, is not obtainable either due to asymmetric information between the government and the firms or because employment subsidies lead to increased efficiency at the cost of a less equitable income distribution. Consequently, a second-best policy of capital-market intervention is desirable. A role for capital-market intervention as a second-best policy emerges only when there exist capital-market asymmetries. A somewhat surprising result of the analysis is that if the government does not know the identity of firms in which supervision problems lead to the dependence of labor productivity on wages, then high-wage firms should face a positive tax on capital at the margin while low-wage firms should face a positive subsidy. In this way the optimal tax policy encourages capital investment in the sector that lacks a supervision problem, the low-wage sector. This form of capital-market intervention enables the government to make greater use of employment subsidies for high-wage firms, because it discourages low-wage firms from masquerading as high-wage firms in an attempt to obtain these subsidies.

Conclusion

A major challenge to policymakers faced with a more integrated world economy lies in the area of taxation. In fact, the international effects of taxation are now attracting increased interest in both professional circles and governments. This volume provides a first attempt to deal with the complex issues associated with the taxation of internationally mobile goods, services, and factors of production. We hope that the book will stimulate further intensive research in this important new area, international taxation economics.

I An Overview of the U.S. System of Taxing International Transactions

1

Taxing International Income: An Analysis of the U.S. System and Its Economic Premises

Hugh J. Ault and David F. Bradford

International tax policy has been something of a stepchild in the tax legislative process. The international aspects of domestic tax changes are often considered only late in the day and without full examination. As a result, the tax system has developed without much overall attention to international issues. This paper is an attempt to step back and look at the system that has evolved from this somewhat haphazard process.

We will describe in general terms the basic U.S. legal rules that govern the taxation of international transactions and explore the economic policies or principles they reflect. Particular attention will be paid to the changes made by the Tax Reform Act of 1986, but it is impossible to understand these changes without placing them in the context of the general taxing system applicable to international transactions.[1] The first part (secs. 1.1–1.4) contains a description of the legal rules, and the second part (secs. 1.5–1.9) undertakes an economic analysis of the system. We have tried to make both parts intelligible to readers with either legal or economic training.

Hugh J. Ault is professor of law at Boston College Law School. David F. Bradford is professor of economics and public affairs at Princeton University and director of the Research Program in Taxation at the National Bureau of Economic Research.

The authors would like to thank Daniel Frisch, James Hines, Thomas Horst, Richard Koffey, Joel Slemrod, Emil Sunley, and participants in the NBER Conference on International Aspects of Taxation for helpful discussions of various aspects of this research, and the National Bureau of Economic Research for financial support. This paper was completed while Bradford was a fellow at the Center for Advanced Study in the Behavioral Sciences. He is grateful for the Center's hospitality and for financial support arranged by the Center from the Alfred P. Sloan Foundation and the National Science Foundation (grant #BNS87–00864). Bradford would also like to acknowledge financial support provided by Princeton University and by the John M. Olin Program at Princeton University for the Study of Economic Organization and Public Policy.

11

1.1 Basic Jurisdictional Principles

1.1.1 Domiciliary and Source Jurisdiction

U.S. persons are subject to tax on a worldwide basis, that is, regardless of the geographic "source" of their income. Traditionally, this principle has been referred to as "domiciliary"- or "residence"-based jurisdiction since it is based on the personal connection of the taxpayer to the taxing jurisdiction. In contrast, foreign persons are subject to tax only on income from "U.S. sources" and then only on certain categories of income. Individuals are considered U.S. persons if they are citizens of the United States (wherever resident) or if they reside there.[2] Corporations are considered U.S. persons if they are incorporated in the United States. The test is purely formal, and residence of the shareholders, place of management of the corporation, place of business, and so forth are all irrelevant. "Foreign persons" are all those not classified as U.S. persons.

As a result of the rules outlined above, a foreign-incorporated corporation is treated as a foreign person even if its shareholders are all U.S. persons. The foreign corporation is taxed by the United States only on its U.S.-source income, and the U.S. shareholder is taxed only when profits are distributed as a dividend. Thus, the U.S. tax on foreign income of a foreign subsidiary is "deferred" until distribution to the U.S. shareholder. A special set of provisions introduced in 1962 and modified in 1986, the so-called Subpart F rules, limits the ability to defer U.S. tax on the foreign income of a U.S.-controlled foreign corporation in certain circumstances.[3]

This pattern of taxing rules depends crucially on identifying the source of income. A complex series of somewhat arbitrary rules is used to establish source. For example, income from the sale of goods is sometimes sourced in the country in which the legal title to the goods formally passes from the seller to the buyer.

1.1.2 Overlapping Tax Jurisdiction and Double Taxation

Where several countries impose both domiciliary- and source-based taxation systems, the same item of income may be taxed more than once. For example, if a U.S. corporation has a branch in Germany, both the United States (as the domiciliary country) and Germany (as the country of source) will in principle assert the right to tax the branch income. It has been the long-standing policy of the United States to deal with double taxation by allowing U.S. taxpayers to credit foreign income taxes imposed on foreign-source income against the otherwise applicable U.S. tax liability. The United States as domiciliary jurisdiction cedes the primary taxing right to the country of source. Nevertheless, the United States retains the secondary right to tax the foreign income to the extent that the foreign rate is lower than the U.S. rate. Thus, if a U.S. taxpayer realizes $100 of foreign-source income subject to a 50 percent U.S. rate and a 30 percent foreign rate, the entire foreign tax of $30 could be credited and a residual U.S. tax of $20 would be collected on the income. If the foreign rate were 60 percent, $50 of the $60 of foreign taxes would be creditable. Thus, subject to a number of qualifications discussed below,[4] the amount of foreign taxes currently creditable is limited to the U.S. tax on the foreign income. The credit cannot offset U.S. taxes on U.S.-source income. If the U.S. taxpayer pays "excess" foreign taxes—that is, foreign taxes in excess of the current U.S. tax on the foreign-source income—the excess taxes can be carried back two years and forward five years, but they can be used in those years only to the extent that there is "excess limitation" available, that is, to the extent that foreign taxes on foreign income in those years were less than the U.S. tax. In effect, the carryforward and carryback rules allow the U.S. taxpayer to average foreign taxes over time, subject to the overall limitation that the total of foreign taxes paid in the eight-year period does not exceed the U.S. tax on the foreign-source income.

The foreign tax credit is also available for foreign income taxes paid by foreign corporate subsidiaries when dividends are paid to U.S. corporate shareholders, the so-called deemed-paid credit.[5] Thus, if a foreign subsidiary earns $100 of foreign income, pays $30 of foreign taxes, and later distributes a dividend of $70 to its U.S. parent, the parent would include the $70 distribution in income, "gross up" its income by the $30 of foreign tax, and then be entitled to credit the foreign tax, subject to the general limitations discussed above, in the same way as if it had paid the foreign tax directly itself.

It should be emphasized that the credit is limited to foreign income taxes and is not available for other types of taxes. The determination of what constitutes an income tax is made under U.S. standards, and detailed regulations have been issued to provide the necessary definitions (Treasury Regulations, sec. 1.901-2). In general, the foreign tax must be imposed on net realized income and cannot be directly connected with any subsidy that the foreign government is providing the taxpayer. Special rules allow a credit for gross-basis withholding taxes.

1.1.3 Source of Income Rules

The source rules are central to the taxing jurisdiction asserted over both U.S. and foreign persons. For foreign persons (including U.S.-owned foreign subsidiaries), the source rules define the U.S. tax base. For U.S. persons, the source rules control the operation of the foreign tax credit since they define the situations in which the United States is willing to give double-tax relief.[6] In general, the same source rules apply in both situations, though there are some exceptions. The following are some of the most important of the source rules.

Sale of Property

As a general rule, the source of a gain from the purchase and sale of personal property is considered to be the residence of the seller. Gain on the sale of inventory, however, is sourced where the legal title to the good passes. If the taxpayer manufactures and sells property, the income is allocated by a formula that in effect allocates half the income to the jurisdiction where the sale takes place and half to the place of manufacture.[7] Sales of financial assets are generally sourced at the residence of the seller, with an exception for the sale of stock in a foreign affiliate of a U.S. resident.

Interest

Interest received on an obligation issued by a U.S. resident (including the federal government) is U.S.-source income unless the payor has derived more than 80 percent of its income over the last three years from an active foreign trade or business. Interest paid by a foreign obligor in general has a foreign source, except that interest paid by a U.S. branch of a foreign corporation is U.S. source. In addition, in the case of a foreign corporation that has 50 percent or more U.S. shareholders,[8] a portion of the interest will be treated as U.S. source for foreign tax credit purposes if the foreign corporation itself has more than 10 percent of its income from U.S. sources.

Dividends

All dividends from U.S.-incorporated corporations are U.S.-source income regardless of the income composition of the corporation. Dividends paid by foreign corporations are in general foreign source unless the corporation has substantial U.S.-source business income, in which case the dividends are treated as partially from U.S. sources.[9] As in the case of interest, a special rule preserves the U.S. source (for foreign tax credit purposes) of dividends paid by a U.S.-owned foreign corporation that itself has U.S.-source income.

Rents and Royalties and Services

Rents and royalties from the leasing or licensing of tangible or intangible property have their source where the property is used.[10] If a transaction involving intangible property is treated as a sale for tax purposes, the royalty source rule applies to the extent that any payments are contingent on productivity. Services income has its source where the services are performed.

The source rules put a great deal of stress on the appropriate categorization of a particular item of income. For example, is the granting of a letter of credit the performance of a service, the extension of credit, or something else?[11]

1.1.4   Allocation of Deductions

The source rules apply only to establish the source of gross income. Gross income must be reduced by the appropriate deductions to arrive at net foreign-source income and net U.S.-source income. In 1977, the Treasury Department issued a set of specific and quite detailed rules dealing with the allocation of deductions (Treasury Regulations, sec. 861-8). In general, the regulations look at the factual relation between particular costs and the appropriate income categories.

Special rules apply for interest and for research and development expenses. Interest is allocated on the theory that money is fungible and thus that interest expense should be allocated to all categories of gross income and apportioned on the basis of foreign and domestic assets.[12] Technical changes in the allocation rules made by the 1986 Act have required more interest expense of U.S. corporate groups to be allocated to foreign-source income, thus reducing the amount of net foreign-source income and hence the ability to use foreign tax credits.[13]

Research and development costs are allocated to broad product categories and then apportioned in part on the basis of where the research took place and in part on the basis of the relative amount of sales (i.e., U.S. or foreign) involved.[14]

1.1.5 Foreign-Exchange Rules

Before 1986, there were no specific statutory rules dealing with the calculation of foreign-exchange gain or loss or the appropriate method for translating into dollars the gain or loss realized in transactions denominated in foreign currency. As a result, taxpayers had considerable flexibility in the treatment of the foreign-currency aspects of international transactions. The 1986 Act established a fairly extensive set of rules governing these matters.

All U.S. taxpayers initially must establish a "functional currency" in which their income or loss must be calculated. The dollar is presumptively the functional currency, but the taxpayer can alternatively establish as its functional currency for its "qualified business units" the currency in which the unit's activities are conducted and in which its financial books and records are kept. Thus, for example, if a U.S. corporation has a branch in Switzerland and another branch in the United Kingdom, the dollar will be the functional currency of the U.S. head office, the Swiss franc the functional currency for the Swiss office, and the pound the functional currency for the British office. The Swiss and British offices will calculate their income initially in the appropriate functional currency, and this amount will then be translated into dollars at an appropriate exchange rate to determine the U.S. tax liability.[15] For foreign-tax-credit purposes, foreign taxes are translated at the rate in effect at the time the taxes are paid or accrued.[16]

The 1986 Act also provided rules for the treatment of gain or loss arising from certain transactions undertaken by the taxpayer in a "nonfunctional currency." Generally, direct dealings in nonfunctional currency, such as borrowing or lending, can result in foreign-currency gain or loss that is

treated as ordinary income and has its source in the taxpayer's country of
residence. This means, for example, that, if a U.S. taxpayer with the dollar
as its functional currency realizes a foreign-currency gain on the repayment
of a foreign-currency loan, the gain will be taxable as ordinary income with
a U.S. source. Regulations may be issued that will treat the gain as interest
income in certain circumstances.[17] A special and complex set of rules
applies to "hedging" transactions involving foreign currency whereby the
taxpayer is seeking to reduce the risk of currency fluctuations.

1.2   Some Aspects of the Taxation of U.S. Business
Operations Abroad

The following material discusses some more specific applications of the
general principles outlined above. The focus is on the effect of the tax rules
on patterns of U.S. foreign investment. Particular reference is made to the
1986 Act's changes and perceived responses to those changes.

1.2.1   Branch versus Foreign Subsidiary Operation

In General

If foreign operations are undertaken by a branch (i.e., without the
interposition of a foreign subsidiary), any income generated will be subject
to U.S. taxation currently (with a credit for any foreign income taxes paid),
and any foreign losses will likewise be currently deductible.[18] If operations
are carried out through a foreign subsidiary, the income will be subject to
U.S. tax only when distributed[19] (with a deemed-paid credit for foreign
taxes), and operating losses will not be currently deductible. Before the 1986
Act reduction in U.S. rates, these rules favored the organization of
subsidiaries in those jurisdictions where the foreign effective rate was lower
than the U.S. rate. The potential tax attributable to the difference between
the U.S. rate and the foreign rate could be deferred until the income was
distributed as a dividend. When U.S. rates were reduced, the advantages of
deferral were obviously reduced. Since most of the tax preferences (e.g.,
investment tax credit, accelerated depreciation) that were eliminated by the
1986 reform had not in any case been available for foreign income, the effect
of the associated reductions in statutory tax rates was also to reduce the
effective rate of U.S. tax on foreign income. As a result, foreign effective
rates in general are today in excess of U.S. rates, and many U.S. taxpayers
are in "excess credit" positions.

Despite the reduction or elimination of the advantage of deferral of
income recognition, there is still a tax incentive to use foreign subsidiaries.
If operations are in the form of a branch, the "excess" foreign tax credits go
into the carryforward and carryback mechanism immediately, and, if they
cannot be used within the carryover period, they are lost completely. On the

other hand, foreign taxes paid by a foreign subsidiary and creditable under the deemed-paid rules begin to toll the carryover period only when the corresponding dividends are distributed. Thus, in the post-1986 world, use of a foreign subsidiary may allow the deferral of excess credits instead of the deferral of U.S. taxes.

Subpart F

The ability to defer current recognition of income of a U.S.-controlled foreign corporation (CFC) is limited by the Subpart F provisions.[20] Income subject to Subpart F is in effect treated as if it had been distributed as a dividend to the U.S. shareholder and then reinvested. A foreign tax credit is available for the income that is currently includible; it parallels the deemed-paid credit for dividend distributions. Later distributions of the previously taxed income can be made tax free and are "stacked" first.

The Subpart F rules apply to certain classes of income received by a CFC. In general terms, the rules affect dividends, interest, and other forms of passive or investment-type income, income from financial services, and income from certain dealings with related parties. The latter category covers situations where the foreign corporation is in effect used as a conduit to sell goods outside its country of incorporation. For example, if a U.S. parent corporation manufactures widgets with a cost of $100 and sells them to its Swiss sales subsidiary for $120 (an arm's length price) and the Swiss subsidiary sells the widgets to German customers for $150, the $30 of profit in the Swiss subsidiary will be taxed directly to the U.S. parent. On the other hand, income from sales in Switzerland would not be taxed currently. Neither would income derived by the Swiss corporation from the manufacture and sale of widgets using component parts purchased from the parent company.[21] Similar rules apply to the provision of services on behalf of related parties. The 1986 Act expanded the scope of Subpart F somewhat by extending the rules to financial services income and shipping income.

Subpart F also contains rules that in effect treat as a dividend distribution any transaction by a CFC that indirectly makes its earnings available to the U.S. shareholder. This is clearest in the case in which the CFC makes a loan to the U.S. shareholder or guarantees a loan by a third party, but the rule also applies to other investments in U.S. property by the CFC.

Note that, to the extent that the objective of Subpart F is to oblige companies to repatriate earnings not currently used in the active conduct of a business, it is not strictly sufficient to tax the passive income generated by earnings retained abroad. Thus, for example, where a foreign subsidiary defers U.S. tax by retaining active income earned abroad and investing instead in assets generating passive income (e.g., interest), subjecting the passive income to current U.S. tax is not enough to produce the equivalence of repatriation of the original active income because the passive income is itself partially earned on the initially deferred taxes.

The role of Subpart F after the 1986 Act rate reductions is somewhat unclear. The provisions were originally enacted to limit the ability to defer U.S. tax through the use of a foreign subsidiary where foreign rates were typically lower than U.S. rates. At present, however, deferral is an advantage in only a limited number of cases. In fact, in some cases CFCs are intentionally creating Subpart F income to use foreign tax credits without paying the additional foreign withholding tax that would be due on an actual dividend distribution of non–Subpart F income. Deferral is still significant in tax haven operations that slip through the Subpart F definitions and in situations where the foreign jurisdiction has a low rate of tax on certain operations (e.g., a tax holiday in a developing country).

1.2.2   Foreign Tax Credit Planning after the 1986 Act

Background

As discussed in general terms in section 1.1.2, the foreign tax credit is limited to the U.S. tax applicable to foreign-source income. But the credit does not attempt to "trace" foreign taxes to particular items of foreign income to determine if the foreign tax exceeds or is less than the corresponding U.S. tax. Rather, the credit is limited by the following fraction: ((foreign-source taxable income)/(worldwide taxable income)) × (U.S. tax liability). This approach in principle allows an averaging of foreign taxes where foreign effective rates are above and below U.S. rates. This means that a U.S. corporation with high-taxed foreign-source income (e.g., dividends from an operating subsidiary in Germany) would have an incentive to create low-taxed foreign-source income to use the excess credits it has with respect to the high-tax source income. On the other hand, a U.S. corporation with low-taxed foreign income is not deterred from investing in a high-tax country since it can absorb the high tax against the excess limitation created by the low-tax income and "average out" to the U.S. rate.

Limits on Averaging

The 1986 Act placed a number of restrictions on the ability to average high- and low-taxed foreign income. It was anticipated that the rate reductions would place many companies in an excess credit position and would encourage them to attempt to create additional low-tax foreign-source income. Accordingly, the Act adopted a sort of schedular system that requires that foreign income be classified into a number of separate "baskets" or categories and prohibits the averaging of foreign taxes across baskets. Averaging is still permitted for active business income but is otherwise substantially restricted. Thus, if a U.S. corporation has high-taxed foreign-source manufacturing income, it can average the taxes on that income with the taxes on low-taxed foreign sales income.[22] On the other hand, it could not average high-tax manufacturing income with low-tax foreign-source portfolio interest or dividend income.

In applying the basket system, dividends, interest, and royalties from CFCs (and amounts subject to the deemed distributed requirements of Subpart F) are subject to a "look through" rule, which categorizes the payments according to the character of the underlying income out of which they are made. Thus, for example, interest normally falls in the passive basket and cannot be grouped with business income.[23] But interest from a CFC that has only active business income would go into the business income basket. A special rule places interest from export financing in the business basket. Income from banking is in a separate basket and cannot be combined with other business income. In addition, dividends from foreign corporations in which the U.S corporate shareholder owns less than 50 percent go in a separate basket "per corporation" and cannot be used to average at all.

Reducing Foreign Effective Rates

A U.S. parent corporation can affect the form in which it gets its returns from its foreign subsidiaries. These income flows can take the form of dividends on equity investment, interest on loans, royalties on licenses, or payments for management services. Payments in the form of interest, royalties, or service fees can in principle reduce the foreign tax base and hence the overall effective rate of foreign tax. This is true, of course, only if the foreign fiscal authorities accept the characterization of the payments and do not treat them as disguised dividend distributions. Within certain broad limits, however, a range of deductible payments is possible. The 1986 Act rate reductions and the corresponding excess credit position of many companies have encouraged greater use of nondividend forms of returns that have the effect of reducing taxable income (and therefore tax) from the point of view of the foreign jurisdiction, but not of reducing foreign-source income for purposes of calculating the creditable portion of the foreign tax. Under the "look through" rule discussed above, the nondividend payments from a CFC still fall in the business income basket (assuming that the foreign subsidiary has active business income) and allow the U.S. company to reduce the overall effective foreign rate to the U.S. rate so that the foreign taxes are more likely to be fully creditable.

Pooling of Foreign Earnings

Before the 1986 Act, the deemed-paid foreign tax credit was calculated on the basis of an annual calculation of the earnings and taxes of the foreign subsidiaries, with the most recently accumulated earnings (and associated taxes) deemed to be distributed first. This procedure gave an incentive to make dividend distributions in years in which foreign rates were high and to skip distributions in low-tax years (assuming that the higher credits could be used currently). This was especially the case in foreign systems in which the effective tax rate could be substantially influenced by the taxpayer, for example, by taking or not taking optional depreciation deductions. The foreign subsidiary could have an artificially high tax rate in one year by taking no depreciation deductions and paying a dividend in that year and then reducing its foreign taxes in the next year through higher depreciation and paying no dividend. Through a judicious use of this so-called rhythm method of distributions, foreign tax credits could be accelerated when compared to those that would have resulted in a level distribution of the same total amount.

The 1986 Act responded to this problem by requiring a pooling of earnings for foreign-tax-credit purposes for years after 1986. In effect, foreign earnings and taxes are calculated on a cumulative rather than an annual basis for purposes of determining how much foreign tax credit a dividend distribution brings with it.

Allocation of Costs

The numerator of the foreign-tax-credit fraction is taxable foreign-source income. The more costs allocated to foreign-source income, the smaller the fraction, with a corresponding reduction in the available credit. The 1986 Act in general requires a greater allocation of expenses to foreign-source income. In the first place, expenses (in particular, interest expense) must be calculated on a consolidated basis, taking into account all the members of the U.S.-affiliated group. Previously, interest calculations were made company by company. Thus, borrowing for the group could be isolated in an affiliate corporation that had no foreign-source income, and as a result the consolidated taxable foreign-source income of the group would not be reduced by the interest expense. Similarly, other expenses could be "loaded" in affiliates that had no foreign-source income. Requiring consolidated calculations has eliminated these manipulations.

Summary and Evaluation

The present structure of the credit is extremely complex. In order to apply the credit, the following operations are necessary:

1. segregate items of gross income into U.S. and foreign sources;
2. segregate foreign-source income into the appropriate categories;
3. allocate and apportion expenses to each category;
4. determine the creditable foreign taxes attributable to each category;
5. "pass through" these attributes through the various tiers of foreign subsidiaries involved; and
6. compute a separate carryover mechanism for each category.

Even considering that the addressees of these rules are for the most part large multinational corporations with substantial resources and computer capacity, one can question whether the welter of technical complexity does not try to fine tune the system to too great an extent.

1.2.3   Some Specific Subsidy Provisions

In addition to the general structural rules outlined above, the U.S. tax system has some explicit subsidy provisions in the international area. The most important are the rules for Foreign Sales Corporations (FSCs) and so-called possessions corporations operating in Puerto Rico.

Foreign Sales Corporations

Since 1971, the U.S. tax system has contained several tax regimes intended to promote U.S. exports. The original provisions involved the tax treatment of Domestic International Sales Corporations (DISCs). In essence, a DISC is a paper U.S. company through which export sales could be channeled. If the appropriate formalities were followed, a portion of the U.S. tax normally due on the export income could be deferred. In 1976, a GATT panel found that the DISC provisions violated the prohibition on export subsidies, and as a result the provisions were effectively repealed in 1984 and replaced by the FSC rules.[24]

The FSC provisions attempt to subsidize exports while at the same time technically complying with the GATT rules. As Congress interpreted the GATT rules, an exemption from tax on export income is not a prohibited subsidy if the economic processes that generate the income take place outside the country of export. The FSC rules try to meet that test by requiring that an FSC (unlike a DISC, a foreign company) have "foreign management" and engage in certain foreign activities.[25] Special provisions in effect waive the normally applicable arm's length pricing rules in determining the amount of income attributable to the FSC and hence qualifying for the exemption. Under various complex pricing formulae, the overall tax saving from the exemption is generally not more than 5 percentage points of tax on the export income. Whether the current FSC rules are compatible with GATT principles has not yet been determined.[26]

Possessions Corporations

In order to encourage economic development in Puerto Rico, a variety of tax subsidies have been offered over the years to U.S. corporations investing in Puerto Rico and other U.S. possessions. In its present form, the subsidy consists of a tax credit that in effect eliminates the U.S. tax on income arising in Puerto Rico. In order to qualify for the credit, the corporation must derive the bulk of its income from sources within Puerto Rico and be engaged in an active trade or business there.

Special rules apply to the income from intangibles (patents, know-how, etc.) involved in the Puerto Rican activities. In the past, some of the most

important intercompany pricing issues have involved possessions corporations and the amount of intangible income appropriately allocated to them.[27]
In 1982, Congress enacted provisions limiting the amount of intangible
income that can qualify for the possessions tax credit.[28]

During the preliminary considerations of the 1986 Act, a proposal was
made to repeal the possessions tax credit and replace it with a temporary
(inexplicably, in view of the underlying policy justification for a subsidy)
credit tied to the amount of wages paid in Puerto Rico, but the proposal was
ultimately rejected.[29]

1.3   Taxation of Foreign Persons on U.S.-Source Income

The U.S. system of source-based taxation is substantially less developed
technically than the system of domiciliary-based taxation, reflecting presumably the history of the United States as a capital exporting country. The
system is essentially schedular; it distinguishes among three basic
categories of U.S.-source income: investment returns ("fixed or determin-
able annual or periodic income"), business income (income "effectively
connected with a U.S. trade or business"), and capital gains. The 1986 Act
expanded source-based taxation in several ways. It retained the prior tax rate
on investment income received by foreign persons (while reducing domestic
rates), limited the role of tax treaties in reducing U.S.-source-based taxation,
and imposed a new layer of tax on foreign branch operations in the United
States.

1.3.1   Investment Income

Investment income is taxed at a statutory 30 percent gross rate and is
collected through withholding by the U.S. payor. The rate is often reduced,
sometimes to zero, through bilateral income tax treaties in which both
contracting states agree to a reciprocal reduction in source-based taxation.
Representative types of income subject to the 30 percent rate are dividends,
interest from related parties, royalties, and rents.[30] The theory of this form
of taxation is that it is impossible administratively to calculate the deductions
of the recipient that net-based taxation would require. Accordingly, a lower
gross rate of tax is applied as a surrogate for net-based taxation. The basic
statutory rate of 30 percent, however, was not changed when rates on
domestic taxpayers were reduced in 1986, and the arguable result is
overtaxation of investment in situations in which the 30 percent rate is
applicable.[31]

Several categories of investment income are exempt by statute. The most
important is portfolio interest, essentially interest paid by U.S. borrowers
(including the U.S. government) to unrelated foreign lenders other than
banks lending in the normal course of business.[32] Interest on deposits by
foreign persons with U.S. banks is also exempt.

1.3.2 Capital Gains

In general, capital gains are not subject to tax unless the foreign taxpayer is engaged in a U.S. trade or business and the gains are "effectively connected" with that trade or business. Statutory provisions make it comparatively easy for foreign investors to avoid trade or business status for their stock-trading activities in the United States unless they are dealers in securities with their principal office in the United States.

Special rules apply to gains from the sale of real estate or the shares of U.S. corporations that have substantial investments in real estate. Such gains are taxed regardless of whether or not the foreign investor is otherwise engaged in a U.S. trade or business. The tax is enforced through a withholding mechanism that requires the buyer of a U.S. real property interest to withhold tax on the sale proceeds if the seller is a foreign person.

1.3.3 Business Income

"Normal" business income of a U.S. trade or business operated by a foreign person is taxed at the usually applicable individual or corporate rates on a net basis in the same way as corresponding income earned by a U.S. taxpayer. In the case of corporations, the income is also subject to a second layer of tax, the so-called branch profits tax.[33] Income that would usually be classified as investment income or capital gain is treated as business income if it is deemed to be "effectively connected" with the foreign taxpayer's U.S. trade or business. For example, interest income on trade accounts receivable would be taxed as business income rather than as interest income subject to 30 percent gross withholding. Similarly, the capital gain on the sale of a business asset would be taxable, but an unrelated capital gain would be exempt from tax. Complex rules define the line between effectively connected and non–effectively connected income.

1.3.4 Forms of Business Investment

Different patterns of taxation apply, depending on whether a foreign person invests in the United States through a U.S. corporation or directly through a U.S. branch. If the investment is through a U.S. corporation, all the income realized by the corporation will be subject to the normal tax rules applicable to U.S. persons because, technically, the foreign-owned U.S. corporation is simply a U.S. taxpayer subject to tax on its worldwide income. Dividends paid by the U.S. corporation to the foreign shareholder are subject to the 30 percent gross withholding tax (reduced by treaty). Interest paid by the corporation on shareholder loans is subject to withholding tax as well. The shares of the corporation could be sold without U.S. tax as long as the corporate investment was not primarily in real estate. A sale of the assets followed by a liquidation of the corporation would result in tax at the corporate level but no tax at the shareholder level.[34]

If the foreign corporate investor forms a U.S. branch, the net business income of the branch (and any investment-type income that was effectively connected) would be taxed at normal U.S. rates. Deductions would be allocated to the U.S. operations under roughly the same rules that are used to make similar allocations for purposes of the foreign-tax-credit fraction. In addition, to the extent that the branch did not reinvest its net profit in the U.S. branch operation, a second level of tax would be imposed on the corporate profits. This "branch profits tax," enacted by the 1986 Act, is intended to replicate the shareholder-level dividend tax that would have been applicable if the investment had been made through a U.S. corporation that then distributed its net profit as a dividend. The branch analog to a dividend distribution is the failure to reinvest the branch profits in the U.S. business. Thus, if a foreign-owned U.S. subsidiary has $100 of pretax profit and pays $34 of corporate level tax, a distribution of the $66 after-tax profit would be subject to the dividend withholding tax. Similarly, if the U.S. branch of a foreign corporation has $100 of pretax profit and does not reinvest the $66 of after-tax profit in the U.S. business, the branch profits tax would be applicable. If the branch profits tax has been avoided in past years through reinvestment and in a subsequent year the U.S. business investment is reduced, the tax becomes due at the time of disinvestment.

The branch profits tax replaced a largely ineffective withholding tax on dividend distributions by foreign corporations with substantial U.S. business income. It represents a more serious attempt to establish the U.S. claim to two levels of source-based taxation on U.S.-generated corporate profits. The treaty aspects of the branch profits tax are discussed below.

1.4   Other International Aspects of the 1986 Act

1.4.1   Transfer Pricing for Intangibles

Under section 482, the income arising out of transactions between related parties must be determined on an "arm's length" basis, that is, as if the various parties were not related. Thus, if a U.S. parent sells manufactured products to a foreign subsidiary, the price charged (which will determine the amount of income that the United States will tax currently to the parent) must be that which would have been charged to an unrelated third party. The same principles apply to sales by a foreign parent to its U.S. subsidiary. In the absence of any comparable third-party sales, regulations provide for a number of different methods for constructing an appropriate intercompany price. In practice, these rules have been very hard to administer and have resulted in extensive administrative and judicial disputes. Problems have arisen, in particular, with the transfer and licensing of intangibles.

In response to these difficulties, Congress in 1986 amended section 482 as it applies to intangibles by specifically providing that, in the case of a transfer or license of an intangible, "the income with respect to such transfer or license shall be commensurate with the income attributable to the intangible." This language was intended to mandate an approach that looks to the actual profit generated by the intangible and the relative economic contribution that each of the related parties involved has made to the income that has been generated. The "commensurate with income" standard applies to all intangible transactions, but it was particularly aimed at the transfer of intangibles with a high profit potential, so-called crown jewel intangibles.

A congressionally mandated Treasury Department study (1988)—the "White Paper"—has been issued in connection with the 1986 Act change in the treatment of intangibles. It contains an extensive analysis of the issues involved in developing the commensurate-with-income standard. The White Paper starts from the premise that, if an "exact comparable" in fact exists, an arm's length price should be based on that comparable. That comparison gives the best evidence of what unrelated parties would have done in the situation under examination. If, as generally will be the case, there is no exact comparable, several alternative approaches are suggested. One is to attempt to find an "inexact comparable," one that differs in significant respects from the intangible transaction in question, and then to make appropriate adjustments. The White Paper, although it in general accepts the principle of looking to inexact comparables, finds that in the past their use has led to "unpredictable outcomes" and downplays such comparisons. It stresses instead a method that looks to arm's length rates of return rather than arm's length prices.

The arm's length rate of return method begins by identifying the assets and other factors of production the related parties will be using in the line of business in which the intangible will be used. This determination involves a functional analysis of the business. Then a market rate of return is assigned to each of the identified functions, based on the rates of return in unrelated transactions. This analysis will give the appropriate amount of the income generated in the line of business that is attributable to all the quantifiable factors of production. All the remaining income is allocated to the intangible. For example, assume that P has developed a patent for the manufacture of a product that will be manufactured under a license by an affiliate. The transaction will generate $500 of income, and, at a market rate of return on the tangible assets involved, $300 of the income would be allocated to the tangible assets. The remaining $200 would be allocated to P's intangible as the commensurate amount of intangible income.

The example above assumes that the manufacturing intangible was the only intangible involved in the line of business and that the returns on the tangible assets could be determined. In more complex cases where both of the related parties have intangibles, for instance, where the foreign affiliate has marketing intangibles, the White Paper approach is to apply the arm's length rate of return analysis to the extent possible and then split the residual income based on the relative values of the intangibles involved. Thus, in the example above, the residual $200 of income would be split in some fashion between the manufacturing intangible and the marketing intangible. The White Paper recognizes that "splitting of intangible income . . . will largely be a matter of judgment" (U.S. Treasury Department 1988, 101). Nevertheless, some guidance may be got from unrelated parties that use similar intangibles.

The legislative history of the 1986 changes in the treatment of intangibles indicates that the income from the intangible subject to allocation under section 482 should reflect the "actual profit experience realized as a consequence of the [license or transfer]."[35] The White Paper takes the position that this language justifies periodic adjustments to intangible returns to reflect changes in levels of profits that occur after the original transaction. Such periodic adjustments will be required only in situations in which third parties dealing at arm's length would have normally included provision for them. In practice, this may mean that licenses for "normal" intangibles will not be subject to periodic adjustment but that such adjustment would be required in situations involving intangibles with unusually high profit potential.

1.4.2 Tax Treaties

As indicated above, bilateral income tax treaties can affect the basic pattern of domestic taxing rules. In general, the treaties typically do not have any effect on the U.S. taxation of U.S. persons but may reduce the taxes imposed by the source country treaty partner. This will be especially significant in the future, when many U.S. taxpayers will be in excess credit positions. The treaty may also provide that a foreign tax that might not otherwise be creditable as an income tax will qualify for the credit.

For foreign persons, the treaties can reduce the U.S. source-based tax that would normally be applicable. For example, many treaties eliminate the 30 percent tax on nonportfolio interest entirely and reduce the dividend tax to 15 or 5 percent in the case of parent-subsidiary dividends. Treaties may also prevent the imposition of the 1986 branch profits tax. Most treaties contain a so-called nondiscrimination clause, under which the United States agrees not to subject foreign persons to taxation "more burdensome" than the taxation imposed on similarly situated U.S. persons. As described above, the branch profits tax is imposed on foreign corporations doing business in the United States but not on U.S. corporations. This difference in treatment is viewed as violating nondiscrimination clauses and prevents the application of the branch tax in many treaty situations.[36]

A number of recent treaties contain provisions to prevent so-called treaty shopping, that is, the use of a treaty country corporation by third-country investors to obtain a reduction in U.S. source-based taxation that they could not have received directly because there was no treaty (or a less favorable treaty) between their country and the United States. In addition, the 1986 Act specifically denied treaty benefits in some circumstances to foreign corporations that are treaty shopping.[37] In particular, treaty-shopping foreign corporations are prohibited from claiming relief from the branch profits tax under a treaty nondiscrimination clause.

1.5   Recapitulation of Present Policy

The tax treatment of international income flows reflects a variety of policy objectives, so it is difficult to discern the policy principles in the actual rules—to state the optimizing problem to which the rules are the solution.[38] Broadly speaking, though, the regime for taxing international transactions can be understood as springing from a fundamental principle that U.S. citizens and residents should be taxed on all their income. Coupled with this basic premise, in a multijurisdictional system, is the principle that people should not be taxed twice on the same income. Both principles reflect notions of equity. The first reflects the conception of income as a measure of ability to pay—since the source of income has no bearing on its validity as a measure of ability to pay, the tax burden should be based on "worldwide income." But the tax burden is not simply imposed by the home government; if two people with the same income are to pay the same tax, the amount extracted by a foreign jurisdiction must be counted equally with that taken by the home government.

These simple and superficially plausible normative conclusions are buttressed by a similarly plausible efficiency criterion, that of capital export neutrality. A nation's tax rules satisfy capital export neutrality if the choice of a domestic taxpayer between foreign and domestic investment is unaffected by tax considerations and depends only on the relative level of before-tax rates of return. Of course, an efficiency criterion is itself at heart an expression of an equity objective, that of maximizing the size of the economic pie. If all the tax authorities in the international system adhere to export tax neutrality, a perfectly competitive international capital market will leave no gain from reallocation of (any *given* stock of) world capital unexploited.

In the context of real-world politics and practical tax administration, the two foundation stones of U.S. international income tax policy, taxation on the basis of worldwide income and capital export neutrality, give rise to a continually evolving set of rules. The most recent version has been described in secs. 1.1–1.4. Much as we can think of the domestic personal income tax as an accretion income tax with certain exceptions and the basic corporate tax as a "classical" second-level tax on corporations, we can broadly describe the current treatment of international business as follows:

1. U.S. corporations are taxed on their income wherever earned. The "income" of a U.S. corporation attributable to its holdings of shares in a

foreign company (even a controlled subsidiary) is basically interpreted as the dividends received, when received. Hence, there is "deferral" of U.S. tax until repatriation.

2. Sovereign governments have the first claim to tax income created within their borders. This principle applies to the taxation of U.S. corporations operating abroad and to foreign corporations operating in the United States.

3. To alleviate the "double taxation" of income arising from activities abroad, the United States allows U.S. taxpayers to credit foreign *income* taxes paid against their U.S. tax liabilities. The foreign tax credit should not be seen to reduce the tax on income created by a company in the United States; hence, the credit is limited to the amount of U.S. tax that would have been collected on the foreign income. U.S. companies should not be inhibited by tax considerations from using foreign subsidiary corporations to do business abroad. Therefore, a credit against U.S. income tax is allowed to U.S. corporate shareholders for foreign taxes actually paid by foreign corporations.

4. Certain payments to foreigners (mainly dividends and interest) are subjected to a withholding tax that mimics the tax that would be paid by a U.S. individual recipient. The withholding tax is eliminated or reduced mutually by bilateral treaty agreement with other governments.

5. Certain tax rules are intended to encourage investment in the United States (now, mainly, accelerated depreciation). Generally, these rules do not apply to investment abroad.

As the discussion of the legal rules in secs. 1.1–1.4 makes clear, implementing these general principles is far from straightforward. The present system is the result of a long process of successive "loophole closing" efforts, as the tax policy makers have discovered one way after another in which taxpayers (or foreign governments) can organize their affairs to take advantage of the U.S. rules. The 1986 changes are the latest in the series, with particular attention to the implications of the substantial lowering of U.S. tax rates incorporated in the reform.

The thrust of the 1986 changes with respect to U.S. firms operating abroad was to scale back deferral through expansion of the Subpart F provisions that require immediate taxation of "tainted" forms of income, to limit further the creditability of foreign taxes through wider use of "baskets" of income by type, and to reduce the relative attractiveness of domestic investment through elimination of the investment tax credit and slowdown of depreciation allowances.

With respect to foreign firms operating in the United States, the 1986 Act introduced a branch profits tax, whose objective was to put branches of foreign corporations and U.S. subsidiary corporations of foreign corporations on a more similar footing. The branch profits tax corresponds to the withholding tax on the dividends paid by U.S. corporations to foreign shareholders. For foreign firms, the second main thrust of the 1986 changes was the consequence of *not* changing the rate of withholding tax at the same time domestic rates were being cut; the effect was to the disadvantage of foreign relative to domestic ownership.[39]

1.6 Do the Bricks Lack Straw?

Before we turn to some of the more specific policy issues raised by these rules, it may be useful to devote a bit of critical attention to the two basic building blocks of worldwide taxation and the foreign tax credit.

1.6.1 Worldwide Taxation

The argument underlying the principle of worldwide taxation—taxation of income from whatever source—appears to be motivated by a conception of income as a given attribute of an individual or a firm. If A and B have the same income, they should pay the same tax. But income for tax purposes is not an abstract flow. Rather, it is an accounting construct built up by adding and subtracting amounts paid and received (or accrued, to make matters worse). The banal fact that an income tax is based on *transactions* (admittedly, the transactions are sometimes subjected to very complicated transformations) has destructive implications for the equity case often made for tax rules. It also has profound implications for tax design, implications that have as yet been only partially digested in academic economic thinking and that are only beginning to be felt in the making of tax policy.

The equity proposition that it is unfair for two people with equal incomes to pay different amounts in tax would perhaps be persuasive if income were an attribute with which an individual is endowed. But it is generally fallacious when income is an aggregation of transactions entered into by the taxpayer. To take an obvious example, if two people have the same amount of money to invest, it is of no equity consequence that one chooses tax-exempt bonds and pays no tax and the other chooses taxable bonds and pays tax. Since either could make the same choice as the other, no inequity can be said to result from the fact that they send different amounts of money to the tax collector.[40]

Equity arguments based on the view of income as an exogenous attribute are particularly misleading in the context of capital markets. In part, this is because the opportunities of participants are to a considerable degree unrelated to a meaningful measure of their ability to pay: people differ in their wages but not in the rate of interest that they can earn on savings. More important, as the tax-exempt interest example illustrates, is the fact that determining the actual tax burdens (in economists' jargon, the *incidence* of taxes) requires a difficult analysis of the effect of the rules in the context of strong forces tending to equate the rate of return on investment for a given taxpayer at all margins of choice. In capital markets, those margins are extraordinarily varied and simultaneously available to many participants.

The more profound consequence of the view of income as an aggregation of transactions is to place income tax policy in the framework of taxes on transactions more generally. The more complex uses of transaction data in the income tax context concern purchases and sales of claims on goods at different times or under different contingencies. In mundane terms, the hard part of income taxation is to use transactions to measure "income from capital." But, when these transactions are viewed like other purchases and sales of goods, the case for employing the peculiarly complex procedures of income accounting (rather than much more simple rules) in order to achieve various equity objectives becomes much less clear than it appears when income is viewed as an abstract attribute. A striking instance of how little it is recognized that an income tax consists of a collection of taxes on transactions is the almost total lack of connection between the making of international income tax policy and the making of international trade policy.[41]

1.6.2 Credit for Foreign Income Taxes

Recognizing that an income tax is levied on the basis of voluntary transactions, not exogenously determined attributes of individuals and firms, upsets the equity argument for crediting foreign income taxes as well. At first glance, if A and B have the same income but B is subjected to a foreign income tax, it seems fair to allow B's foreign tax to count against an overall burden. But, if B's wealth can alternatively be allocated between a foreign asset and a domestic one, it is clear that allowing or not allowing a credit for the foreign tax will affect the location of B's wealth, not B's tax burden.

1.7 International and Foreign Transactions in a System of Accretion Income Accounting

The traditional literature on income taxation begins with a discussion of the accretion income concept, generally known in the jargon of the trade as Haig-Simons or Schanz-Haig-Simons (SHS) income.[42] SHS income is defined to be the sum of consumption and the change in net worth (at market value) of a person over some specified period. A natural question is how the rules relating to international income relate to this fundamental income notion.

1.7.1 Source of Income and Allocation of Deductions

Accounting for Personal Income

The idea that income has a locatable source seems to be taken for granted, but the source of income is not a well-defined economic idea. The SHS definition describes a quantity that is, in principle, measurable, whatever the practical problems may be (and they are substantial). The emphasis placed by tax reform advocates on the objective of taxing income "from whatever source" has obscured the fact that the SHS income concept is not susceptible to characterization as to source at all. Income in this definition attaches to someone or something that consumes and that owns assets. Income does not come from some place, even though we may construct accounts to approximate it by keeping track of payments that have identifiable and perhaps locatable sources and destinations. To the extent that income describes an activity, it is not that of production but that of consumption and wealth accumulation, and its location is presumably the place of residence of the person doing the consuming and accumulating.

Naturally, calling a tax an income tax does not imply that it will or should embody the SHS norm. The fact is, however, that something like the SHS income norm does appear to motivate much of the U.S. system. More important, the objective of increasing wealth is rather persuasively the motivator of investment decisions. Large changes in wealth occur continually by virtue of changes that have no natural locational aspect. Examples are the discovery of a new drug formula or new consumer good. Even more significant are simple changes in expectations and beliefs about the future, which can result in large changes in asset values. Attaching locations to these phenomena inevitably involves arbitrary line drawing, with its attendant controversy. (See the discussion in secs. 1.1–1.4 of transfer pricing of intangibles.)

The view of income as a payment for factor services (rather than as the sum of saving and consumption) may appear to offer a firmer basis for attribution of source. The reasoning that leads to an SHS concept, however, emphasizes that the payment actually received by a person has to be interpreted in terms of some notion of accruing benefit. In crude terms, the normative notion of income must be net of the "costs of earning" any payments. That is why is seems correct to deduct employee business expenses from wages; the same line of argument may justify a deduction for medical expenses as well (they do not buy consumption in a normative sense).

As we have emphasized, an income tax in practice is built up from transactions. It would be very difficult to construct a system of accounts that would give a close approximation to SHS income. Actual income accounts do not even attempt it. When one then adds the necessity of attaching a locational label to the transactions, an operation that is not itself based on a well-defined economic question, complexity and arbitrariness are hard to avoid.

In many cases, amounts paid and received can be rather readily given a location by association with a process of production or similar activity. A practical consequence is that the transaction becomes susceptible to monitoring by a particular local jurisdiction and thereby becomes a potential basis for taxation. The association is so obvious that it is apparently taken for granted that a government has the "right" to levy a tax based on a measure of the profits earned by a production activity physically carried on within its jurisdiction. One may speculate that force majeure has been as important as any ethical conception of sovereignty in producing a general acceptance of the priority of the "source" jurisdiction to tax particular transactions.

Income of a Corporation

For a corporation, the analog of personal consumption is distributions to shareholders. The corporation tax treatment of particular transactions, such as receipt of a dividend or of the proceeds of the sale of an asset, has to be understood as a piece of a system of accounts designed to capture the sum of distributions to shareholders and increase in net worth. A dividend, itself, is not SHS income; it may be used to measure income, but, if the change in value of the stockholder's remaining claim on the corporation is ignored, the accounts will produce a bad approximation to SHS income (Bradford 1986, chap. 3). The defective accounts will either over- or understate the taxpayer's SHS income; typically, such mismeasurement sets up opportunities for tax-motivated arbitrage with balancing transactions that involve different mismeasurement.

The economist is struck by the frequency with which one encounters in the law legal and institutional distinctions without an economic difference. As a result, the rules frequently prescribe different tax consequences for economically equivalent (or nearly equivalent) transactions. Where this is the case, there is an opportunity for arbitrage profit. The efforts of the policymakers to limit arbitrage profit (without actually instituting consistency) have much to do with the evolution of the rules.

As a simple example, consider the distinction between distributed and undistributed earnings of a wholly owned foreign subsidiary. In one case, the sub sends the parent a dividend. In the second case, the sub simply retains the earnings but lends the parent money. The bundle of real claims owned by the parent is the same after the transactions are completed in both cases. Yet before 1962 the tax results were very different. It then might have made sense for the sub never to pay the parent a dividend since the exactly equivalent cash flow could have been effected with a lower tax penalty by the lending route. The policy response: a rule treating loans to the parent as dividends and a series of subrules dealing with transactions similar to loans, for example, the sub's guarantee of a loan to the parent.

This is an example of the problems created by inconsistency of the tax treatment of transactions with similar economic effects. Such inconsistency is ubiquitous in the implementation of the income tax. Although the point is a simple one and even well known, it is still insufficiently appreciated by policymakers. The difficulty of designing rules to implement equal tax treatment for economically equivalent results is severe in the case of an income tax, basically because of the difficulty of measuring accruing changes in value. These difficulties are compounded when the ill-defined criterion of location of income is added.[43]

1.7.2   Deduction or Credit for Foreign Taxes?

Discussions of the foreign tax credit are often cast in a framework in which the tax at issue is on the capital income of domestic residents. Viewed as an element of a set of accounting rules to approximate the sum of a person's consumption and increase in net worth during the period, the foreign tax credit makes little sense. True, the payment of taxes might be regarded as a use of buying power that is not consumption (although the point is arguable; see Bradford et al. 1984), and it certainly is not evidence of an increase in net worth. But SHS income tax principles would seem to imply, at most, deductibility of taxes paid to other jurisdictions by persons otherwise regarded as within the income tax net.

1.8   Economic Analytical Problems Posed by Actual Policies

In the discussion of the economics of the international tax rules so far, we have attempted to relate them to philosophical objectives. We turn now to economic issues more directly related to the actual system as it has evolved.

1.8.1   International Tax Rules as Taxes on Capital Flows

Most economic modeling related to international tax policy assumes that the implementation problems have been solved. Specifically, analysts take for granted the existence of a measurable quantity called capital (K) that can be located in a particular country and whose ownership can be observed. Also assumed observable is the measurable return (rK) accruing to capital in each country. As we have emphasized, actual tax rules depend on a variety of observable transactions, none of which corresponds neatly to the accruing return on capital.[44] Before we turn to a closer look at problems associated with particular aspects of the rules, however, we may note a troublesome problem of consistency that is likely to present itself quite apart from matters of definition and measurement. This problem, which has been emphasized by Slemrod (1988), can be described as one of tax harmonization. It arises when the tax rules applied by different countries to investors in different countries are not appropriately coordinated.

We can best express this problem in a setting in which risk is assumed away and investors are indifferent between returns arising in different countries (no bias toward returns in one's own country). Then investors will move their capital around to achieve the highest return after all taxes. A condition of equilibrium is that the rate of return after all taxes be simultaneously equal in all countries for residents of each country. In a two-country case, let r_d be the domestic rate of return before taxes and r_f the return in the foreign country. Let t_{ijk} be the tax levied by country i on investors resident in country j on returns to capital they own in country k, where i, j, and k can be either d (domestic) or f (foreign). Then there are eight possible tax rates. If we rule out the taxation by one country of the income of residents of the other country earned on capital in that country (t_{dff} and t_{fdd} are zero), there are six tax rates. If domestic investors are to be indifferent between investing at home and abroad, it must be true that

$$r_d(1 - t_{ddd}) = r_f(1 - t_{ddf} - t_{fdf}).$$

Similarly, in order for foreigners to be indifferent between investing in their own country and abroad, it must be true that

$$r_d(1 - t_{dfd} - t_{ffd}) = r_f(1 - t_{fff}).$$

Taking the ratio of the two conditions, we see that together they imply

$$\frac{(1 - t_{ddd})}{(1 - t_{dfd} - t_{ffd})} = \frac{(1 - t_{ddf} - t_{fdf})}{(1 - t_{fff})}.$$

This is one condition on six tax rates. The difficulty is that there is very little assurance that it will be satisfied by the rules chosen by any given pair of countries (much less that the corresponding generalization will be satisfied for various pairwise linkings of several countries). If the condition is not satisfied, one or the other after-tax equalization condition must fail. The difficulty that this failure creates for economic modeling is clear (we would say that the markets have no equilibrium), but the world was not created to satisfy the modelers. Actually, some process will balance the demands and supplies—probably some combination of transactions cost, nonlinearity of the tax rates (e.g., the nonlinearity that results from the fact that taxes are nonrefundable), and special "patches" in the tax rules designed to limit the arbitrage between more and less favorable jurisdictions.[45]

1.8.2 Incentives for Business Location: Form and Substance

Place of residence and even citizenship are choices. Since the U.S. tax laws make distinctions on the basis of place of residence and citizenship, we may expect the laws to influence the choices. Clearly, in exceptional cases (movie stars, for instance), taxes influence people's domicile and citizenship. But for most people, in the range of tax regimes that is typically encountered, we expect little elasticity of domicile or citizenship to changes in tax policy, and therefore distinctions based on residence of people will be of a lump-sum character.

One might expect the choice of place of incorporation to be much more responsive to variations in tax rules. The U.S. policy of distinguishing between U.S. and foreign corporations must have effects, either on the choices or on the rules enacted (having in mind their effect on place of incorporation). If the people choosing the location of incorporation are U.S. taxpayers and they want to be able to control the management of the operation located abroad, they have two basic options: to incorporate (or even not incorporate but operate in noncorporate form) in the United States and run the foreign activity as a branch or to incorporate abroad while maintaining significant ownership interest. These two forms of organization are economically virtually equivalent. In addition, there are such less perfectly substitutable alternatives as a noncontrolling interest in a foreign corporation ("portfolio investment") and royalty and similar contingent claims. Note that a capital market "imperfection" is implicit in the observation that one cannot create a perfect substitute for a controlling interest through an appropriate combination of available securities. A controlling interest in a corporation could presumably in principle be reproduced by a sufficiently complicated contract that could be marketed as a portfolio security. The cost of writing and monitoring such contracts is required for a distinction between controlling and portfolio investment.

The basic policy toward residence of corporations is an extension of the legal doctrine that the corporation is a separate person. A corollary of the distinction between U.S. and foreign persons is the deferral of tax on the earnings of foreign subsidiaries of U.S. corporations. For U.S. corporations that own other U.S. corporations, the tax accounts are consolidated. Dividends passing from the sub to the parent have no tax consequences. By the same logic, dividends paid from one company to another ought not to be taxed when both corporations are separately U.S. taxpayers but not in a relation of parent and sub. (In fact, a fraction of dividends received by a U.S. corporation from another U.S. corporation, other than a controlled sub, is included in the recipient's tax base. The fraction was increased by the 1986 Act.)

In the case of a subsidiary that is not a U.S. taxpayer, the policy that springs from the treatment of a corporation as a person is to tax the parent only on "income" as measured by dividends, that is, in the cash flow sense of income often encountered in the U.S. income tax. No one suggests "integrating" corporate and shareholder income accounts in the case of portfolio investment, so deferral, which is a much debated policy, might seem a sensible way of avoiding a sharp break in tax treatment at the point at which the shareholder's interest is regarded as crossing the boundary to "control." The main effect, however, of this extension of the metaphor of corporation as person and of the use of dividends as a measure of income arises precisely with control because the policy puts a great deal of tax weight on a decision that is under the U.S. taxpayer's control. In this connection, the critical choice is probably not between retention of funds and their distribution as dividends. More important is the choice between dividends and distribution in other forms, such as share repurchase, royalties, favorable loan terms, or manipulation of other intercompany prices ("transfer prices").

1.8.3 The Foreign Tax Credit as an Implicit International Agreement

As has been mentioned, the creditability of foreign income taxes is usually justified on the equity grounds of avoiding double taxation and on the efficiency grounds of capital-export neutrality, which requires that taxes should not influence the country of location of capital. The credit is supposed to make U.S. tax burdens independent of the location of investment, thereby assuring that a U.S. firm will not be influenced in its investment decisions by differences between U.S. and foreign taxes.

It is difficult to construct an optimizing model from a national perspective that implies capital-export neutrality, even if it could be achieved without sacrificing revenue to foreign governments. Optimal tariff considerations (whereby a large country seeks to exploit its monopoly advantage by, in effect, raising the prices of its exports and forcing down the prices of its imports through the use of tariffs) would generally imply that foreign investment should be discouraged relative to the level implied by unobstructed competitive capital markets.[46] It is even more difficult to justify crediting taxes paid to foreign governments as a method of achieving capital-export neutrality, as long as the policies of foreign governments are taken as given. The reason is simple. The foreign government collects the taxes on the investment. The yield to the domestic economy is net of foreign tax, whereas the yield of domestic investment is gross of domestic tax. National self-interest would seem to imply something like deduction of foreign taxes.

It is a serious error, though, to view the choice of policy as made in an international vacuum.[47] Since the tax policy of foreign governments cannot be taken as a given, an analysis of the national interest that neglects their reactions is fundamentally flawed. Like free trade, capital-export neutrality has to be understood as an international discipline or standard that may leave all participants better off than they would be under likely noncooperative alternatives.[48] That is, a policy of capital-export neutrality by all countries may lead to an outcome that is better for all than would obtain if policy were made separately on the assumption of no foreign interactions.

Unfortunately, this hypothetical possibility is merely that. The suggested policy that makes the economic pie as big as possible (and note that, since the taxes affect the level as well as the allocation of capital, there is no assurance that universal capital-export neutrality would be better than, for example, no taxation of capital) also affects who gets what part of the pie. Characteristically of efficiency rules in general, capital-export neutrality as a desideratum of policy makes no reference to who gets what share of the world economic pie (or even of the world's tax revenues).

We have described above the equity principle that it is unfair to tax income that has already been subjected to tax. This may be called the "intranational" equity principle in that it concerns fair treatment of two apparently similarly situated U.S. taxpayers. As has been emphasized, if we put to one side issues of transitional incidence (thereby probably putting aside the bulk of tax politics), the argument for the foreign tax credit based on the individual equity principle is surely fallacious. It is a condition of equilibrium that investors obtain the same rate of return after all taxes at all margins of investment. It therefore cannot be inequitable to subject certain forms of investment to higher or lower rates of tax, although it may be wasteful.

One encounters in this context, though, another notion of equity that is focused less on the U.S. taxpayer per se and more on the obligations of a tax jurisdiction toward the other members of the community of jurisdictions. This "international" equity principle is that each jurisdiction has an obligation to provide relief from double taxation up to the level of tax that would be levied on a taxpayer with purely domestic-source income. If we think of equity in terms of outcomes for individuals, the international equity principle seems a rather odd precept. But it is different from the intranational equity principle. For example, the international equity principle would be satisfied by exempting foreign-source income from domestic tax, provided the basic premise holds—that income is an exogenous attribute of taxpayers. Even more than the intranational equity principle, the international equity principle suffers in implementation from its definition in terms that are purely institutional rather than more fundamentally in terms of outcomes or even alternatives for individuals. For the latter purposes, it is not important whether something is taxed more than once or whether the burden is imposed by an income or by a sales tax. All the same, it is significant that the international principle carries with it a notion of obligations of good jurisdictional citizenship that is missing altogether from the intranational equity principle.

There is a further justification for the foreign tax credit suggested by the view of the corporate tax as a substitute for accrual accounting for income at the individual shareholder level. If the basic function of the "double taxation" of corporate income is to impose single taxation on the income of shareholders, something like the foreign tax credit is clearly necessary to dilute the strong incentive that would otherwise arise for individuals to hold shares directly rather than indirectly via U.S. corporations. If the nationality of the controlling corporation is a matter of indifference, such a policy as substituting a deduction for the credit would presumably result in significant shifts in portfolio form, little extra revenue, and the economic value loss that would result from inhibiting direct control.

Rather little attention has been paid to the implications of confining creditable foreign taxes to "income" taxes. The basis for the limitation is legal and institutional rather than economic. That is, the allowable credit is not determined by asking whether the incidence or other economic effect of the foreign tax or other policy is like that of the U.S. income tax. Instead, implementation depends on the foreign tax having various institutional features that make it look like the U.S. income tax (a VAT of the income type, for example, would not be creditable). As a result, it would be quite possible for a foreign government that desired to do so to implement simultaneously a capital subsidy and a formal income tax in such a way that the tax is "paid" by the U.S. government (through the credit) while the effective tax burden on investment is zero. U.S. law disallows the credit in cases where there is a direct connection between a subsidy received by a company and its tax obligations. It would not be difficult, however, to circumvent this rule (Gersovitz 1987).

So far we have not commented in detail on another important feature of U.S. law with respect to the crediting of foreign taxes, namely, the limitation of the credit, in effect, to the amount that would have been collected on the same income under U.S. law. The logic of the foreign tax credit as an intranational equity-based adjustment in a corporation's U.S. liability would imply no such limitation. Nor would the efficiency-oriented principle of capital-export neutrality. A more obvious justification has to do not with the behavior or burdens of taxpayers but with the behavior of governments. A country that is host to a large amount of activity owned by a U.S. corporation could obviously impose a tax at a virtually unlimited rate if the difference between its tax and the U.S. tax on the same income would be paid by the U.S. Treasury. Naturally, this reasoning is not confined to the issue of crediting foreign taxes in excess of U.S. rates. It applies as well to crediting taxes up to U.S. rates. Canadian tax policy analysts, for example, regard the Canadian corporate tax primarily as an instrument for absorbing the U.S. tax credit.

It is difficult to exaggerate the complexity that has been introduced to the U.S. rules by the need to limit the foreign tax credit. The present international tax rate constellation, in which a large number of U.S. taxpayer corporations find themselves with excess credits, sets up strong pressures on governments. Those with tax rates in excess of that in the United States, still an extremely important source of direct investment, will find themselves under pressure to reduce rates to the U.S. level. The stock of excess credits, though, will imply additional pressure for some countries to reduce rates below the U.S. level. Ironically, the foreign tax credit will become increasingly a source of capital-export nonneutrality, as firms find opportunities in low-tax jurisdictions artificially enhanced by the option that they provide to use up excess credits on the U.S. tax books.

1.8.4 International Taxation as Conditioned on Control

In the literature on international income taxation, most attention has been paid to the way in which the taxes influence the decision of an investing individual or firm to locate capital. Here, too, though, there has perhaps been too little focus on the actual transactions taxed, which are not flows of income in the abstract but dividend, royalty, interest, and other "payments" (perhaps just on the books), and on the distinctions that influence the amount of tax (e.g., the distinction between a portfolio and a controlling investor).

One of the more elusive aspects of the rules for taxing international business is their reliance on discrimination among degrees of *control* of activities carried on abroad. Thus, the deemed-paid credit for foreign corporate income taxes is entirely denied to corporate portfolio investors, that is, corporate shareholders owning an insignificant fraction of the stock of the foreign company. To qualify, the U.S. corporation must own at least 10 percent of the voting stock. Even at this level of control, the foreign tax credit is limited according to the various "baskets" of income types, foreign company by foreign company. When the level of control rises to the level of a CFC, the foreign tax limits are determined by aggregates of foreign income by type. (Reminder: a CFC is a foreign corporation in which U.S. shareholders owning at least 10 percent of the voting stock together own at least 50 percent of the voting stock.)

The most obvious manifestation of the importance placed by the tax law on control of a foreign business activity is the distinction between active and passive income (in its various forms). The distinction (which is found in the purely domestic tax sphere as well) has no place in the SHS income conception, nor is it readily modeled in the usual capital flow model (of the sort outlined earlier in connection with the problem of international tax harmonization). Yet control and taxes are the two most obvious bases for the existence of multinational corporations.

We have discussed at length the traditional concept of capital-export neutrality, which (among other things) can at least be understood in the context of conventional capital flow models. Introducing the notion of control as an economic phenomenon provides a context for mentioning another traditional neutrality concept. "Capital-import neutrality" refers to the nationality of ownership of firms.[49] It obtains when there is no tax-based difference in circumstances of firms operating within a given country associated with the nationality of the firm's owners. The U.S. policy of deferring income tax on the earnings of foreign subsidiaries (thereby subjecting those earnings to the local tax system alone, until repatriation) can be thought of as applying the standard of capital-import neutrality to retained foreign earnings. (Arguably, the U.S. tax that will be due on repatriation is an unavoidable toll charge that has no influence on the foreign investment decision [Hartman 1984].) The usual models of international capital flows do not allow one to address the justification for capital-import neutrality effectively. The nationality of the owners of capital is not generally associated with economically significant consequences (apart, perhaps, from portfolio diversification).

The study of control promises to be an interesting one. In particular, it appears to be the obvious place to bring the notion of international competitiveness into the analysis in a meaningful way, one different from a mere identification with capital importation. (See, e.g., Summers 1986.) Control is, however, not easily given a rigorous economic interpretation— note, for example, that the extent of control of the corporate sector of an economy can range from 0 to 100 percent according to the degree of portfolio diversification by shareholders.

1.9 Concluding Comments

The conventional analysis of the broad economic principles traditionally said to underlie the basic structure of the U.S. system for taxing foreign income is fairly straightforward. A system of worldwide taxation combined with a foreign tax credit for taxes paid to other governments is asserted to achieve capital-export neutrality and the most efficient international allocation of investment. From the perspective of the domestic investor, the choice at the margin between foreign and domestic investment should be unaffected by tax considerations and should respond to the international levels of before-tax rates of return. This system will create an efficient worldwide allocation of resources and maximize world welfare. At the same time, some assert that national welfare will also be maximized when the overall effects of foreign investment are taken into account.

Although this theoretical analysis is relatively straightforward, as the preceding sections have shown, the implementation of these general principles in the real world of tax rules is enormously complex and the results often inconsistent. Some of the sources of this complexity can be identified relatively easily. In the first place, capital-export neutrality under the current system is present only when the U.S. tax rate exceeds the foreign rate. When the foreign rate of tax exceeds the U.S. rate, the theory of capital-export neutrality in principle would require the United States to credit the taxes against the U.S. taxes paid on U.S.-source income and, if necessary, refund the excess. If this step is not taken, then investment is discouraged in countries with rates of tax higher than that of the United States. In view of the revenue cost of such a policy, however, particularly when the possible reactions of foreign governments are taken into account, the credit has historically been limited to the U.S. taxes attributable to foreign-source income, though the form of the limitation has varied over the years. The failure to refund excess foreign taxes was less significant before 1986 since most companies then could fully use their foreign tax credits. Now, however, the majority of firms are in an excess credit position, and the limitations on the availability of the credit have led to much of the complexity of the legal rules.

More important, perhaps, the present form of the limitation has led to significant "second-best" issues. For example, under the current rules, averaging of foreign taxes is allowed for active business income. This means that a U.S. company that is currently paying high foreign taxes with respect to one active business investment is encouraged at the margin to undertake a new business investment in a low-tax foreign country rather than in the United States. The excess credits on the high-tax investment can in effect shelter all (or at least some) of the U.S. tax burden on the low-tax investment. In the extreme case where the foreign country does not tax the investment at all—for example, under a tax holiday—the U.S. firm is comparing the before-tax rate of return in the foreign country with the after-tax rate of return on a domestic investment. Thus, an imperfectly pursued policy of capital-export neutrality can lead to results exactly the opposite of those the policy was intended to achieve.

Similar issues arise with respect to the taxation of income earned though U.S.-controlled foreign subsidiaries. A fully implemented policy of capital-export neutrality would tax the subsidiary income to the U.S. shareholder as it accrues. On the other hand, a fully implemented policy of capital-import or competitive neutrality would lead to the complete exemption of foreign income. Historically, Congress has accepted business arguments that current U.S. taxation adversely affects the competitive position of U.S. companies in foreign markets. It has allowed the deferral of U.S. tax on subsidiary income until repatriation, but only as long as that income fell into certain categories. On repatriation, capital-export considerations reassert themselves, and the income is then taxed, with the allowance of the "deemed" foreign tax credit for the foreign taxes paid by the subsidiary. This "hybrid" mixture of capital-import and capital-export considerations again has led to the complex dividing lines required by Subpart F to sort out income into deferral and accrual categories as well as the convoluted "pass through" of baskets for foreign-tax-credit purposes.

Another perspective from which to view the international rules is taxpayer equity. How should traditional notions of horizontal equity be applied in connection with foreign income? The exemption of foreign-source income would clearly seem inconsistent with any equity criterion based on ability to pay or well-being, assuming that income is taken to be an exogenous characteristic of taxpayers. An SHS approach to income definition would seem to imply inclusion of foreign income and a deduction for foreign taxes as a cost of producing income.

On the other hand, many have argued that a credit for foreign taxes is required by what we have called international equity considerations. The U.S. taxpayer who is subject to tax both here, because of a domiciliary connection, and in the foreign jurisdiction where the income arises is, some assert, not similarly situated when compared with a U.S. taxpayer who has income only from U.S. sources. The United States as the country of domicile has an internationally recognized responsibility to relieve the burden of international double taxation arising because of the overlapping assertions of taxing jurisdiction by the United States and the source country.

Having chosen initially to tax foreign-source income, the United States has an accompanying responsibility based on equity considerations to relieve double taxation through the credit.

On the other hand, if the responsibility of the domiciliary country to relieve international double taxation is recognized, a foreign tax credit is not the only means available. An alternative would be a "territorial" system that left out of account both foreign income and foreign taxes. Such an approach, in turn, would lead back to the question of the relative merits of capital-export and capital-import neutrality and reintroduce the appropriateness from an equity perspective of eliminating from the tax base a receipt that clearly would be included under traditional income notions.

In short, as in so many other tax policy issues, the possible theoretical starting points for analysis in the international area lead to quite different results, and the real-world phenomena are often "noisy" and inconsistent with any single overarching approach. The most important task for policy analysis at this point is to try to determine with more accuracy exactly what effect the complex system of rules has on the form and extent of international activity.

Notes

1. For a fuller exposition of the applicable U.S. tax law, see McDaniel and Ault (1981). For the details of the Tax Reform Act of 1986, see U.S. Congress (1987) and U.S. Congress, Joint Committee on Taxation (1987).

2. The Internal Revenue Code provides a series of mechanical rules for determining residence of aliens; see sec. 7701(b). Special rules exempt certain amounts of earned income received by citizens residing abroad; see sec. 911.

3. The Subpart F rules are described in more detail in sec. 1.2.1 below.

4. The foreign tax credit mechanism is discussed in more detail in sec. 1.2.2 below.

5. The U.S. shareholder must be a corporation and must own at least 10 percent of the voting stock of the foreign corporation. The deemed-paid credit is also available for taxes paid by lower-tier foreign subsidiaries under certain conditions as income is distributed up a chain of foreign corporations to the U.S. shareholder.

6. That is, the credit is limited to foreign taxes on income that is determined by the United States to be from a foreign source. If a foreign country imposed a tax on an item of income that under the U.S. source rules is determined to be U.S. source, the credit is in effect not available (unless there are other items of income from foreign sources that create excess limitation; see the discussion in sec. 1.2.2).

7. More technically, if there is no independently determined factory price, half the income is allocated to the location of the assets used in the production and sale and half to the place of sale. In practice, this means that, if property is manufactured in the United States and sold abroad with no sales assets located abroad, half the income is foreign source even though it is unlikely that any foreign jurisdiction will tax it (Treasury Regulations, sec 1.836-3(b)).

8. Treasury Regulations, sec. 904(g).

9. Such dividends are not subject to tax when received by nonresident aliens or foreign corporations if the dividend-paying corporation is subject to the branch profits tax discussed in sec. 1.3.4 below.

10. The determination of where an intangible is used is obviously not always easy.

11. See Bank of America v. U.S., 680 F.2d 142 (Ct. Cls. 1982).

12. Treasury Regulations, secs. 864(e), 1.861-9T. Special rules apply for the allocation of the interest expense of a foreign corporation with a U.S. branch that in effect try to take into account the relation between interest rates and exchange rate gain or loss (Treasury Regulations, sec. 1.882-5).

13. See the discussion in sec. 1.2.2.

14. The regulations originally provided that 30 percent of research and development costs would be allocated to the place in which more than 50 percent of the research costs were incurred. Congress enacted a moratorium on the application of the regulation and allocated all research and development expenses incurred in the United States to U.S.-source income. For 1987, 50 percent (rather than 30 percent) allocation was established by the 1986 Act and subsequently modified. Additional legislative action is anticipated.

15. For the branch operations described above, the translation rate is the average exchange rate for the year. Calculation of income under this so-called profit and loss method means that unrealized foreign-exchange gains or losses in the taxpayer's invested capital are not taken into account currently. Special rules apply to taxpayers who do business in "hyperinflationary economies," which in effect allow changes in the dollar value of invested capital to be accounted for currently.

In the case of a distribution of income from a foreign subsidiary that has a foreign currency as its functional currency, the translation rate is the spot rate in effect at the time of the distribution.

16. Appropriate adjustments are made if there is a difference between the amount accrued and the amount actually paid.

17. The legislative history of the 1986 Act recognizes the economic connection between exchange gain and interest income.

18. If the losses reduce U.S. income, i.e., if there is an overall foreign loss, adjustments are later required in the foreign-tax-credit fraction to limit the creditability of foreign taxes on an operation that, from the U.S. perspective, has not generated any net income.

19. Subject to the limitations of Subpart F discussed in sec. 1.3.2.

20. The rules apply to any foreign corporation in which "U.S. persons" own more than 50 percent of the voting power or value of the outstanding stock of the corporation. A "U.S. person" is defined as a U.S. individual or corporation that owns 10 percent or more of the voting stock of the foreign corporation.

21. The regulations have extensive rules defining the types of activities that constitute manufacturing as contrasted with mere assembly and packaging. In addition, the income would not be taxed currently if it bore a rate of foreign tax that approximated the U.S. rate.

22. This makes the source rule discussed in sec. 1.1.3 extremely important. This rule sources income from sales of inventory in the jurisdiction in which title is passed. That rule makes it possible to create income that is technically foreign source but is unlikely to attract any foreign taxes. As a result, the foreign taxes on high-tax foreign-source income can become currently creditable.

23. A special rule applies to interest that is subject to a high withholding tax. Such interest is segregated in its own basket to prevent averaging with other normally low-taxed passive income.

24. Technically, the DISC provisions were retained in a limited form, and an interest charge was imposed on the deferred tax liability. Thus, the taxpayer may still benefit from an indirect loan from the government at a potentially favorable rate of interest.

25. Treasury Regulations, sec. 924(d)-(e). In fact, since the FSC can "contract out" the foreign activities to related parties, its actual foreign presence can be minimal.

26. See U.S. Congress, Joint Committee on Taxation (1984, 1042). The European Community has "raised questions" about the FSC provisions under GATT.

27. See, e.g., Eli Lilly v. Commissioner, 84 T.C. 996 (1984).

28. See Treasury Regulations, sec. 936(h).

29. See U.S. Treasury Department (1984, 2:327–30). The Treasury analysis of the possessions tax credit estimated that the average tax benefit for corporations taking advantage of the possessions tax credit was $22,000 per employee while the average employee wage was only $14,210.

30. Rental income from real property is in principle taxed at the 30 percent gross rate, but the foreign taxpayer can elect to have the income treated as business income so that deductions such as depreciation, taxes, and interest are available. The resulting net income is taxed at normal U.S. rates.

31. As indicated below, very often the 30 percent rate is eliminated or reduced by treaty, and several important categories of income are exempt. Nonetheless, the existence of the high withholding rate can be significant in some circumstances.

32. The exemption for portfolio interest was added in 1984. Certain formalities must be complied with to ensure that the portfolio debt will not be acquired by U.S. taxpayers. Before the exemption in 1984, U.S. corporations could in effect issue tax-exempt bonds to foreign lenders through a convoluted technique involving the use of wholly owned finance subsidiaries organized in the Netherlands Antilles. The transactions took advantage of a tax treaty between the United States and the Antilles. These structures originated in the 1970s with the blessing of the Treasury Department to encourage U.S. corporations to borrow abroad during a period of balance-of-payments difficulties. The direct exemption for portfolio interest has made them obsolete, and the treaty on which they were originally based has been terminated.

33. See the discussion in sec. 1.3.4 below.

34. Although a sale of the shares would result in no current U.S. tax, presumably a purchaser would discount the purchase price for the shares to reflect the fact that it could get a stepped-up basis in the underlying assets of the corporation only by paying the corporate-level tax. Thus, the two methods of disposition would have roughly the same after-tax consequences to the seller.

35. H. Rep. 99-426, 99th Cong., 1st sess. (1985), 425.

36. The branch profits tax is only a surrogate for the tax on a dividend distribution to the foreign shareholder, but it technically falls on the foreign corporation, and thus the nondiscrimination clause is applicable.

37. A foreign corporation is deemed to be treaty shopping if more than 50 percent of its stock is owned by non–treaty country residents, with an exception for publicly traded corporations.

38. For an overview of the economics of international income taxation, see Adams and Whalley (1977), Sato and Bird (1975).

39. Grubert and Mutti (1987) present an analysis of the economic effects of the 1986 changes.

40. For a clear development of this point, see Bittker (1980).

41. In his elegantly clear exposition of tax policy in open economies, Dixit (1985) makes no mention at all of income taxes. For promising beginnings at integration of the two subjects, see the papers by Frenkel, Razin, and Symansky and by Gordon and Levinsohn in this volume.

42. For an extended discussion of income concepts and references to the literature, see Bradford (1986) or Institute for Fiscal Studies (1978).

43. Within the United States, income is typically allocated to different jurisdictions by formula. Formula apportionment solves some problems but introduces others. See Gordon and Wilson (1986).

44. Newlon's (1987) analysis of the taxation of multinationals provides a nice illustration of the importance of looking closely at the rules relating to specific transactions (such as payment of interest).

45. For a model that takes into account the imperfect substitutability of assets in different countries in investor portfolios, see Mutti and Grubert (1985).

46. This conclusion has long been recognized. See, e.g., Richman (1963) and Musgrave (1969). Feldstein and Hartman (1979) present a formal analysis.

47. For a forceful statement of this viewpoint, see Ross (1985).

48. For an analysis of tax policy determination as an international noncooperative game, see Gordon and Varian (1986).

49. Hufbauer and Foster summed up the law in 1976 as follows: "Both in legislation and in bilateral tax treaties, the United States has attempted to ensure the type of neutrality appropriate to different situations, while at the same time protecting U.S. tax revenue. Thus, United States taxation of the foreign income of U.S. owned firms embodies a mixture of capital-export neutrality, capital-import neutrality, and revenue protection clauses" (1976, 15).

References

Adams, J. D. R., and John Whalley. 1977. *The international taxation of multinational enterprises in developed countries*. Westport, Conn.: Greenwood.

Bittker, Boris I. 1980. Equity, efficiency, and income tax theory: Do misallocations drive out inequities?" In *The economics of taxation,* ed. Henry J. Aaron and Michael J. Boskin, 19–31. Washington, D.C.: Brookings.

Bradford, David F. 1986. *Untangling the income tax.* Cambridge, Mass.: Harvard University Press.

Bradford, David F., and the U.S. Treasury Tax Policy Staff. 1984. *Blueprints for basic tax reform.* 2d ed., rev. Arlington Va.: Tax Analysts.

Dixit, Avinash. 1985. Tax policy in open economies. In *Handbook of public economics,* ed. Alan J. Auerbach and Martin S. Feldstein, 1:313–74. New York: Elsevier.

Feldstein, Martin, and David Hartman. 1979. The optimal taxation of foreign source investment income. *Quarterly Journal of Economics* 93 (November): 613–29.

Gersovitz, Mark. 1987. The effects of domestic taxes on foreign private investment. In *The theory of taxation for developing countries,* ed. David Newbery and Nicholas Stern, 615–35. New York: Oxford University Press.

Gordon, Roger H., and Hal R. Varian. 1986. Taxation of asset income in the presence of a world securities market. NBER Working Paper no. 1994. Cambridge, Mass.: National Bureau of Economic Research, August.

Gordon, Roger H., and John D. Wilson. 1986. An examination of multijurisdictional corporate income taxation under formula apportionment. *Econometrica* 54 (November): 1357–73.

Grubert, Harry, and John Mutti. 1987. Taxes, international capital flows and trade: The international implications of the Tax Reform Act of 1986. *National Tax Journal* 40 (3):315–29.

Hartman, David. 1984. Tax policy and foreign direct investment in the United States. *National Tax Journal* 37:475–87.

Hufbauer, Gary, and David Foster. 1976. U.S. taxation of the undistributed income of controlled foreign corporations. In *Essays in international taxation: 1976.* Washington D.C.: U.S. Treasury Department, U.S. Government Printing Office.

Institute for Fiscal Studies. 1978. *The structure and reform of direct taxation: The report of a committee chaired by Professor J. E. Meade.* London: Allen & Unwin.

McDaniel, Paul R., and Hugh J. Ault. 1981. *Introduction to United States international taxation.* 2d rev. ed. Boston, Mass.: Kluwer.

Musgrave, Peggy B. 1969. *United States taxation of foreign investment income: Issues and arguments.* Cambridge, Mass.: Harvard Law School.

Mutti, John, and Harry Grubert. 1985. The taxation of capital income in an open economy: The importance of resident-nonresident tax treatment. *Journal of Public Economics* 27 (3): 291–309.

Newlon, T. Scott. 1987. Tax policy and the multinational firm's financial policy and investment decisions. Ph.D. diss., Princeton University.

Richman, Peggy Brewer. 1963. *Taxation of foreign investment income: An economic analysis.* Baltimore: Johns Hopkins University Press.

Ross, Stanford G. 1985. A perspective on international tax policy. *Tax Notes* 26 (18 February): 701–13.

Sato, Mitsuo, and Richard Bird. 1975. International aspects of the taxation of corporations and shareholders. IMF Staff Papers no. XII-2. Washington, D.C.: International Monetary Fund.

Slemrod, Joel. 1988. International capital mobility and the theory of capital income taxation. In *Uneasy compromise: Problems of a hybrid income-consumption tax,* ed. Henry J. Aaron, Harvey Galper, and Joseph A. Pechman. Washington, D.C.: Brookings.

Summers, Lawrence H. 1986. Tax policy and international competitiveness. NBER Working Paper no. 2007. Cambridge, Mass.: National Bureau of Economic Research, August.

U.S. Congress. 1987. *Tax Reform Act of 1986.* Washington, D.C.

U.S. Congress. Joint Committee on Taxation. 1984. *General explanation of the revenue provisions of the Deficit Reduction Act of 1984.* Washington, D.C.

_____. 1987. *General explanation of the Tax Reform Act of 1986.* Washington, D.C., 4 May.

U.S. Treasury Department. 1984. *Tax reform for fairness, simplicity, and economic growth.* Vol. 1, *Overview.* Vol. 2, *General explanation of the Treasury Department proposals.* Vol. 3, *Value-added tax.* Washington, D.C.: U.S. Government Printing Office, November.

_____. 1988. *A study of intercompany pricing.* Washington, D.C., 18 October.

Comment   Daniel J. Frisch

Tax policy debates generally take place on two levels. One concerns the broad outlines of tax structure; an example is the debate over full versus partial taxation of capital gains. This level considers the equity and efficiency effects of taxation and, at its best, is based on solid economic analysis. The second level takes the basic structure as given and debates how it should be applied to the myriad real-world situations in which taxpayers find or put themselves. For example, special treatment for capital gains spawned a vast and complex set of tax code provisions that defined capital

Daniel J. Frisch is a senior fellow at the Institute for International Economics.

gains and limited the types of income eligible for the preferential treatment. This type of debate does not typically involve economists; indeed, they are often completely unaware of it. Instead, it is usually left to lawyers.

This dichotomy is a healthy one. If economists, especially academic economists, wished to influence the second type of debate, they would have to incur a substantial investment to learn about all the line drawing and rule making that has gone on in the past. Economists and lawyers are nearly unanimous in agreeing that it would not be worthwhile for the former to do so. Further, it seems clear that those good at the detailed type of tax policy often have difficulty recalling fundamental objectives and developing fresh approaches for achieving them. In short, it is efficient for some analysts to specialize in the broad policy concerns and others to specialize in the detailed aspects of implementation.

A major problem for international tax policy is that this kind of specialization has withered away during the last decade or so. The current generation of tax policy economists, with a few exceptions, seems to have decided that, because learning all the detailed rules would be so costly, it should refrain from commenting on the field at all. This conclusion is incorrect and has led to a situation in which no one examines the basic principles. This conference will represent a major contribution, therefore, if it inspires a greater number of economists to address the basic issues in international tax policy.

The paper by Hugh J. Ault and David F. Bradford is a perfect one to start off a conference designed to achieve this goal. It surveys the current tax rules in an admirably clear and concise fashion and speculates on the economic principles on which they are and should be based. I will comment on each of these sections in turn.

Current U.S. Tax Rules

The survey of current rules that constitutes the first half of the paper (secs. 1.1–1.4) is a significant achievement. In a remarkably short span, it outlines all important aspects of current U.S. rules for taxing international activities. It starts from first principles, outlining who is subject to U.S. tax, what part of their income is taxed, and how double taxation is avoided. Despite this starting point, it encompasses all the rules, at least all U.S. rules, that any policy analyst needs to know. As is mentioned above, economists may have shied away from the field partly out of fear that they may inadvertently neglect some crucial tax detail that would undercut their analysis. This survey can cure this fear; after reading it carefully, economists will not have this reason, or excuse, for avoiding international tax policy questions any longer.

The survey would have been even more valuable, however, had it given some indication as to the relative importance of the tax issues described. This information would guide analysts in choosing the rules on which to concentrate and in identifying the ones most likely to have large effects on economic activities. One way of providing this information would have been to discuss the available empirical evidence, including IRS statistics, revenue estimates that accompany tax legislation, the tax expenditure budget, and certain other Treasury Department publications.

For example, IRS statistics show that U.S. withholding taxes on interest, dividends, and royalties paid to foreign investors raise remarkably little revenue. This fact may cast some doubt on the importance of an issue mentioned several times in the paper, that the general withholding tax rate was not lowered from 30 percent when the Tax Reform Act reduced all other rates. (The reason why this issue is unimportant empirically is that the general rate applies only when a treaty is not present, and the vast majority of investment comes from or through treaty countries.) Revenue estimates could have been used in a similar fashion to reflect on the importance of the "branch tax" instituted in 1986. The revenue estimates accompanying the Tax Reform Act of 1986 indicate that this change is an exceedingly minor one empirically; it was estimated to raise only about $25 million a year. (See U.S. Congress, Joint Committee on Taxation [1987, 1047]. Reasons include that very little foreign investment in the United States occurs through branches and that treaties reduce or eliminate the tax for investors from most important countries.)

Another example concerns the subsidies for exports provided through the tax code. The survey mentions the special source rule for sales of "inventory property" and even (in n. 22) stresses its importance. Later, in a section describing subsidy provisions, the paper outlines the FSC (formerly DISC) provision that partially exempts income from exports. However, the survey neglects to point out that the former is a much more powerful incentive for exports than the latter. The tax expenditure numbers included in Special Analysis G of each year's Budget of the U.S. Government show that the sales source rule is the largest tax expenditure in the international area by far and is estimated to cost $2.9 billion for fiscal year 1989; the FSC provison is estimated to cost only $425 million. Finally, one should note that the paper does not completely neglect empirical evidence; note 29 uses a Treasury Department report to present an intriguing statistic on the efficiency of the other subsidy provision described, the "section 936" incentive for operating in Puerto Rico.

Economic Principles

The second half of the paper (secs. 1.5–1.9) sets an ambitious goal for itself, to describe and criticize the economic principles that underlie the current system of tax rules. Perhaps because the goal is so ambitious, this section is more than a little discursive; it presents aspects of each of its arguments in several different places. Therefore, it may be worthwhile to summarize the main points in a slightly different way than they are presented in the paper. It seems to me that the section seeks to point out four types of problems with current analyses of international tax policy issues.

First, equity considerations have dominated international tax policy decision making, according to the paper. For example, the main argument for taxing worldwide income is that not doing so would violate horizontal equity. The decision to provide a foreign tax credit is more complicated, but "intranational equity" and "international equity" considerations are stressed. The problem is that, because international tax policy questions involve taxation of corporations or, more generally, return to capital, it makes very little sense to consider equity in this field. If the tax system is "unfair" to one particular channel for earning a return to capital, the amount invested in it will fall, but the properly measured net rate of return generally will not change. Thus, the relative position of individual investors, in equilibrium, will not be affected by "inequitable" taxation of corporations or other investment opportunities.

The second problem is that income, specifically the "Schanz-Haig-Simon" (SHS) concept, is a bad basis for tax policy. Actual taxation must be based on observable transactions, and it is exceedingly difficult to coax a measure of SHS income from them. Further, the SHS concept does not seem to answer several important international tax policy questions, including the fundamental one of whether specific items of income should be treated as foreign or domestic source.

The third problem has been described by Slemrod and others (as the paper acknowledges). Because tax systems vary, investors in various countries may face different after-tax rates of return on similar investments, yet we do not observe the specialization that should occur. It is very hard to construct a satisfactory economic foundation for a set of rules that, in their current form, should be causing serious arbitrage problems. There is a danger that economists' policy recommendations will end up sounding like, "The rules must be changed right away so that they are in a form that we can analyze."

The fourth problem is that we have been too narrow in our view of the ways in which income is earned abroad. Traditional models consider only the allocation of a homogenous K, capital, amoung countries. However, investors have lots of choices when deciding where and how to locate their capital. For example, U.S. investors who want to own capital abroad can buy shares in a U.S. corporation that has a foreign branch, a U.S. corporation with a foreign subsidiary corporation, or directly in a foreign corporation. A key distinction is that, in the first two alternatives, a U.S. corporation controls the foreign activities, but no U.S. investor has control in the third. Further, the U.S. tax system treats these investments very differently in several respects. The authors wonder whether control is important and, if so, how it should affect tax policy decisions. For example, it may be that repeal of "deferral" would cause U.S. investors to substitute their own foreign portfolio investment for their U.S. companies' foreign direct investment. If so, the revenue and other effects of this response should be considered.

Each of these four themes has a great deal of truth in it; however, I am not sure that they lead to the formulation of a better set of economic principles. For example, I agree with the first conclusion, that equity is basically irrelevant to international tax policy. However, I did not find the premise convincing. Although they may mention equity considerations, most traditional analyses do not spend much time on them. Instead, they depend much more heavily on concepts such as *capital-export neutrality, national neutrality,* and *capital-import neutrality.* These terms all claim to address efficiency issues; indeed, even the more modern (though hardly more satisfactory) concept of *international competitiveness* claims to address the problem of maximizing the United States' economic effectiveness and thus falls within the efficiency concern. In fact, a brief (i.e., introspective) literature search turned up only one analysis of international tax policy that turns on equity questions (Vogel 1988). Note that the authors do not cite even this many analyses of international taxation in which equity considerations are crucial.

The second theme, that income is a faulty basis for taxation, also seems to miss the point to some degree. Many participants in the conference and readers of these words would have no trouble agreeing that, as one of the authors has persuasively argued on many occasions, a consumption-based tax may be preferable. However, I do not see how this conclusion forces one to decide that an income tax can never treat international income in a rational or consistent fashion. For example, just because neither Schanz, Haig, nor Simon considered the issue of the source of income does not imply that it cannot be studied. A well-specified model should be able to analyze the incentive effects of current source rules and indicate their effects on efficiency and welfare. If so, it may yield a consistent and valuable foundation for source rules; at least, the paper did not convince me that such an analysis is not worth a try.

The third theme is the existence of arbitrage opportunities and lack of equilibrium that should exist under current tax rules. This problem is not unique to international taxation. As Stiglitz (e.g., 1983) has pointed out, the voluntary nature of realizations causes a similar problem in capital gains taxation. His conclusions may apply here, too. If arbitrage opportunities continue to exist, there must be imperfections in international capital markets or tax rules that prevent their exploitation. Further, these imperfections and rules must be key aspects of the markets, and analyses of the effects of taxation should incorporate them.

The final theme is the need to differentiate between types of investments that confer control and those that do not. A U.S. multinational corporation's decision to locate activity abroad seems fundamentally different from a U.S.

investor's decision to add foreign securities to his or her portfolio. These decisions will involve different considerations and tradeoffs, and taxation will probably affect them in different ways. Therefore, it may be important to differentiate between foreign direct investment income and foreign portfolio income in tax policy analysis.

I am not sure, however, how useful it is to analyze these activities as if they were close substitutes. It is not obvious to me that a tax change that disadvantaged foreign direct investment would cause it to disappear rapidly, along with an equal rise in foreign portfolio investment. The size of the cross-elasticity is an empirical question, of course; however, until it is measured, there are strong reasons why it may be better to assume it is much closer to zero than infinity. Internationl trade economists have long known that the existence of multinational corporations has very little to do with access to capital or other factor-based comparative advantages (see, e.g., Caves 1982, chap. 2). Instead, they exist for "industrial organization" reasons; for example, large corporations have advantages in certain activities, such as R&D-intensive industries, where large fixed costs must be incurred. Evidence to support this view includes the fact that many multinationals raise capital, along with other factors of production, in the local market. This implies that U.S. multinationals may not be affected one way or the other if the U.S. taxed international capital flows more heavily. This view also seems to predict that U.S. participation in "pure" international capital markets may be relatively unaffected by a system that taxed U.S. multinationals more heavily, such as one that contained a repeal of deferral.

Despite this conclusion, I feel that the authors' observation that foreign direct investment income and foreign portfolio income are fundamentally different is the most important point in the second half of the paper. This observation indicates to me that tax policy analyses should examine them as distinct activities. Principles that apply to one probably do not apply to the other. Specifically, traditional analyses that concentrate on net rates of return and allocation of capital may be relevant for tax policy toward international portfolio investment, but they may have little to do with multinationals' activities. Instead, a new type of analysis may be necessary to identify the proper economic principles for taxation of multinationals' overseas income.

Summary

Ault and Bradford have provided us with a perfectly suited and extremely valuable first paper for this conference. It contains a survey of current U.S. rules that is remarkably clear, complete, and concise. Tax policy economists need no longer fear that analysis of international issues must be preceded by a lengthy and painful initiation into tax law. The paper also make a number of provocative comments on the economic weaknesses of current rules and analyses but does not resolve these issues completely. Thus, the paper not only reduces the cost of studying international tax issues but also increases the benefits by indicating some important questions in need of answers.

References

Caves, Richard E. 1982. *Multinational enterprise and economic analysis.* Cambridge: Cambridge University Press.
Stiglitz, Joseph. 1983. Some aspects of capital gains tax. *Journal of Public Economics* 21:257–94.
U.S. Congress. Joint Committee on Taxation. 1987. *General Explanation of the Tax Reform Act of 1986.* Washington, D.C. 4 May.
Vogel, Klaus. 1988. The search for compatible tax systems. In *Tax policy in the twenty-first century,* ed. Herbert Stein. New York: Wiley.

II Taxation and Multinationals

2   U.S. Tax Policy and Direct Investment Abroad

Joosung Jun

The effect of tax policy on the process of capital accumulation has long been an important subject of policy debates and academic research. The tax policy debate in the 1980s has been largely motivated by a concern over the rate of capital accumulation in the United States. Tax rules can affect the nation's capital formation by influencing the return to saving and to investing in plant and equipment. However, the presence of international capital mobility requires policymakers to design tax incentives from a different perspective from that which would be taken in the case of immobile capital. Savings incentives and investment incentives can no longer be treated as alternative devices to enhance domestic capital formation. Part of domestic savings may flow into investment projects abroad, while domestic investment incentives can bring in more foreign capital. If long-term capital in particular is mobile across national boundaries, a country with higher domestic tax rates will drive domestic businesses abroad, while a country with generous investment allowances will attract more investments in plant and equipment.

Several theoretical papers have suggested that international capital mobility would have important implications for the welfare effects of tax policy (e.g., Gordon 1986; Slemrod 1987; and Giovannini 1988). Using a general equilibrium simulation model, Goulder, Shoven, and Whalley (1983) have shown that the effects of elastic foreign investment flows could dominate other effects of tax policy on welfare. Summers (1986) shows that international capital mobility can have potentially significant implications for the effects of taxes on international competitiveness and the current account.

Despite the importance of knowing the elasticity of international capital flows with respect to rates of return, however, very few attempts have been

Joosung Jun is assistant professor of economics at Yale University and a faculty research fellow of the National Bureau of Economic Research.

made to measure it. Hartman (1981, 1984) reports significant elasticities of direct investment flows with respect to U.S. net return variables. Using updated investment data and tax variables, Boskin and Gale (1987) provide estimates that also confirm the basic conclusions in Hartman's studies. While these studies represent the first serious attempts to estimate elasticities, their estimation seems to be subject to measurement problems, as discussed later.

The profit-maximizing international firm will try to optimize over the capital allocation between the parent and the subsidiaries, given different rates of returns and sources of funds between countries. An empirical analysis of the tax effects on international capital flows entails a thorough theoretical examination of international firm behavior and the intertemporal, intercountry, and intercompany nature of direct investment. The lack of rigorous theoretical frameworks from which testable implications can be drawn, combined with various data problems, has contributed to the sparseness of reliable empirical evidence in this area.

The purpose of this paper is twofold. First, I attempt to estimate the sensitivity of U.S. direct investment capital outflows to the U.S. net rate of return. The second and more general goal is to address various potential misrepresentation problems with empirical models in this area. Such problems are partly due to the absence of reliable data and to the lack of reliable theoretical underpinnings.

Section 2.1 provides a brief theoretical discussion of various channels through which domestic tax policy can affect the home country firm's direct investment abroad. Section 2.2 discusses issues related to using existing direct investment data in an empirical model and stresses the importance of a theoretical structure in choosing a proper model. Section 2.3 presents the empirical model, which is based on the theoretical framework developed in section 2.1, and the estimation of equations that relate U.S. direct investment outflows to the domestic net rate of return. A brief summary section follows.

2.1 A Theoretical Framework

The present section heuristically investigates three major channels through which domestic tax policy can affect the home country firm's international direct investment. A more rigorous treatment of this issue is presented in Jun (1988). First, the tax treatment of foreign-source income will have a direct relevance to the net profitability of foreign investment. Tax rules applied to foreign-source income include the corporate tax rate, the foreign tax credit, and the deferral of home country taxes on unrepatriated foreign-source income. Second, tax policy can affect the relative net profitability of investments between different countries. Specifically, home country tax policy instruments toward domestic investment, such as the corporate tax rate, the investment tax credit, and depreciation allowances, will affect net domestic returns and, accordingly, the relative net profitability between domestic investment and foreign investment. Third, tax policy can affect the relative net cost of external funds between different countries. Since the international firm can raise funds both at home and abroad, tax rules that affect the domestic net cost of funds, such as the tax deductibility of interest, will influence the relative net cost of funds between countries and therefore the flow of investment funds.

Tax policy toward foreign-source income has long been a subject of policy debate and political controversy. Most of the existing literature is also concerned with this aspect of the tax effects on international capital movements. One major concern regarding international investment is the possibility for foreign source income to be taxed twice, once by the host country government and again by the home country government. In many industrial countries including the United States, a credit or deduction is allowed for taxes paid to the host country government in an effort to avoid double taxation. Furthermore, the home country tax can be deferred until foreign-source income is repatriated to the domestic parent. Tax deferrals combined with the foreign tax credit can have a significant effect on the international firm's investment and financial decisions.

A central issue in evaluating tax policy toward foreign-source income concerns the firm's method of financing marginal foreign investment. Foreign operations can be financed in several ways. The most explicit form is the transfer of funds to a foreign subsidiary by the domestic parent. These parent transfers consist of equity investments and intercompany loans. The retention of earnings by the foreign subsidiary is another major source of funds. In fact, the sum of these two financing sources—parent transfers and retained earnings—is the definition of direct investment in the balance of payments data.[1]

The effect of tax policy on foreign investment is highly dependent on whether parent transfers or retained earnings are assumed to be the marginal source of funds. Traditional researchers have either ignored retained subsidiary earnings or assumed a fixed dividend payout ratio so that they can regard parent transfers as the marginal source of financing foreign investments. In this case, while the home country tax affects foreign investment, the deferral of taxes on retained earnings will reduce the effective tax rate on foreign investment below the home country rate, favoring capital outflows, if the home country tax rate is higher than the host country rate. Hartman (1985) challenges this view by demonstrating that deferred home country taxes are capitalized in the market value of the subsidiary so that those taxes can have no effect on the firm's new investment decision. Since in this case the marginal cost or the equilibrium shadow value of capital is smaller than in the parent-transfer case, Hartman argues, retained earnings must be the optimal marginal source of funds whenever feasible. This tax capitalization view has the strong policy implication that any special taxes on foreign-source income have no effect on the marginal investment decision of mature subsidiaries with after-foreign-tax earnings in excess of desired investment expenditures.

Understanding the tax effects on international direct investment requires a proper model of subsidiary behavior since foreign investment is eventually undertaken by a foreign subsidiary. One might be tempted to treat the subsidiary, as many previous studies implicitly do, like the domestic firm that maximizes its market value given the rate of return required by the shareholders. If we solve the subsidiary's maximization problem given an exogenous rate of return required by its shareholder—the parent—the resulting expressions for the cost of capital or the effective tax rate will summarize the contrasting views between the two existing positions regarding the marginal source of funds. With retained subsidiary earnings as the marginal source of funds for foreign investment, the effective tax rate is simply the host country tax rate reflecting the capitalization of the home country tax into the subsidiary value. Under the more traditional transfers regime, the effective tax rate will be a weighted average of the home and host tax rates in which the weights are the dividend payout ratio.[2]

Although the practice of isolating the subsidiary's maximization problem is a convenient way of studying foreign fixed investment undertaken by the subsidiary or of summarizing the effects of tax policy toward foreign source income on direct investment,[3] it can be quite misleading when we try to understand the overall effects of the home country tax system on direct investment flows. Tax policy can also affect direct investment through other channels, which can be best analyzed when we recognize that the subsidiary is one part of the international firm. Although the parent controls domestic operations in the home country, its major concern is the maximization of the overall profits of the international firm. Thus, to gain a proper understanding of international firm behavior and corresponding capital flows, it is imperative to integrate the subsidiary's foreign operation with the parent's domestic operation. The profit-maximizing international firm should optimize over every relevant decision variable—domestic, foreign, or intrafirm. Specifically, in addition to the marginal source of funds for foreign investment, the international firm should optimize over the location of physical investment and the location of external sources of funds.

The second major channel through which domestic tax policy influences direct investment is through its effects on the relative net rates of return between the home country and the host country. The direct investment decision of international firms can be affected by a variety of factors; for example, they establish branches and subsidiaries abroad to secure local markets, to have easy access to raw materials, and to take advantage of lower labor costs. In sum, direct investment arises from expectations of higher profitability from venturing abroad. Tax policy can influence the decision of investment location by affecting the relative net profitability between different countries.

In order to derive the criteria for intrafirm investment allocation, Jun (1988) integrates the subsidiary's foreign operation and the parent's domestic operation by explicitly recognizing the ownership chain of the international firm—the subsidiary–the parent–the domestic shareholders—and the relevant rate of return required by each party's immediate owner. Specifically, the rate of return used by the subsidiary in discounting its future profit stream is endogenously determined in the model in a way that maximizes the overall profits of the entire firm.[4] In that process, we can sum the tax effects at the foreign-source income tax and the relative net return channels and explicitly derive the criteria for intrafirm investment allocation between domestic and foreign operations under each financing regime at the margin. With retained subsidiary earnings as the marginal source of funds, for example, the model predicts that the international firm should invest abroad until the net returns in the home and host countries are equalized; in this case, the domestic tax rate affects foreign investment only by changing relative net returns. Since the relative net return channel itself is independent of the financing regime, the domestic tax system can affect direct investment even under the retained earnings regime.

The paper also shows that the intrafirm allocation criteria do not include parameters associated with domestic shareholders, while in the long run the cost of foreign capital can be expressed as a function of the rate of return required by the shareholders. This result implies that, although the foreign subsidiary is ultimately owned by the domestic shareholders through the ownership chain, the investment location decision is a purely intrafirm variable that is not directly affected by the shareholders. I call this result the "parent veil," which can be thought of as a strong form of the corporate veil. In other words, the shareholders will be concerned with the ultimate rate of return on the overall operations paid through the domestic parent but may not care about transactions within the firm. This parent-veil proposition is supported by evidence presented in section 2.3.

The third channel for tax effects on direct investment flows is related to the way taxation affects the cost of external funds for the firm. The discussion of the first two channels focused primarily on issues related to the allocation of funds available within the international firm—internal funds.[5] The parent concerned with overall profit maximization will be sensitive to any difference in the cost of external funds between countries. As long as local fund-raising in the host country is feasible and costs less than in the home country, the parent will have an incentive to let the subsidiary rely more on this source and to reduce its transfers.

Tax rules have always been a central focus of the debate regarding the real effects of corporate financial policy. Since income accruing within a firm and income accruing directly to individuals receive different tax treatments, there is an incentive at the margin for the firm to favor debt financing until the benefits from the tax deductibility of interest payments are matched by the potential bankruptcy and agency costs associated with a higher debt-equity ratio. For the international firm, the possibility of raising funds in different countries can create another opportunity for tax arbitrage. The intuition behind this can be easily illustrated by a simple example. Suppose that both the parent and the subsidiary borrow at the margin to raise funds. The cost of funds can be defined as $COF = (1 - t)i$ and $COF^* = (1 - t^*)i^*$, where i and i^* are the interest rates, with the asterisk denoting a host country variable. A reduction in the domestic tax rate t would imply that local borrowing in the host country becomes a cheaper source of external funds, other things being equal. As a result, the subsidiary is more likely to resort to local borrowing and less likely to receive transfers by the parent than before. Thus, tax policy can influence international direct investment by affecting the relative cost of funds between countries.

This relative cost of funds channel has not been recognized in the existing literature but can be quite important in practice, as exemplified in the transactions between the Netherlands Antilles finance affiliates and their domestic parents. The next section discusses this example in detail.

The preceding discussion suggests that domestic tax policy can have a significant effect on direct investment flows through various channels. What are the implications of this theoretical framework for empirical work in this area?

First, the multichannel analysis suggests that empirical work specify which tax channel, which decision of the firm, or which tax policy it focuses on. Note that the relative net return channel and the relative net cost of funds channel are concerned with the choice of location between the home country and the host country. On the other hand, the fact that U.S. international firms' global income is subject to domestic taxation implies that application of the U.S. corporate tax rate to foreign source income is related to the international firm's overall investment. Thus, while the reduction of the domestic corporate rate may increase foreign investment through its effect on overall investment (the first channel), it will have negative allocative effects on foreign investment by increasing domestic net returns and the net cost of funds (the second and third channels). In addition to emphasizing the different ways in which a given tax policy affects investment, this multichannel analysis also facilitates the evaluation of different types of tax policies. For example, the foreign tax credit, the investment tax credit or depreciation allowances, and the tax deductibility of interest payments affect international investment through different channels.[6]

Second, the choice of an empirical model and relevant data should be consistent with the implications derived from a theoretical model. In most previous studies, foreign investment undertaken by the foreign subsidiary and direct investment of the international firm are treated as equivalent.

Specifically, previous studies employ the balance of payments direct investment flows as a proxy for foreign fixed investment undertaken by the subsidiaries. In practice, however, these two concepts can deviate from each other significantly; this difference gives rise to the need to reexamine the empirical methodology employed in existing studies.

2.2 Direct Investment Data

International direct investment implies that an investor in one country has a controlling interest in, and therefore a degree of influence over the management of, a business enterprise in another country. Specifically, direct investment involves the establishment of a new enterprise or the acquisition of an existing enterprise and a lasting control of these facilities in a foreign country. What constitutes a controlling interest can vary case by case and thus is defined somewhat arbitrarily. The U.S. Department of Commerce (1985, 2) defines controlling interest as ownership or control of 10 percent or more of the voting securities or an equivalent interest of a foreign business enterprise. Any investment abroad that is not direct investment is considered portfolio investment.

The most frequently investigated data on direct investment are the Commerce Department balance of payments (BOP) direct investment flows—both U.S. direct investment abroad and foreign direct investment in the United States. The BOP items consist primarily of transactions between parents and their affiliates. Specifically, direct investment capital outflows consist of equity capital outflows, intercompany debt outflows, and reinvested subsidiary earnings. Note that the first two items are summed as parent transfers in this study.

One major reason that the recent trends in BOP direct investment flows have become an important policy concern is their implications for capital formation in the United States. Table 2.1 shows that BOP direct investment inflows in 1979 and outflows in 1981 each reached about a quarter of U.S. net domestic investment in plant and equipment. Moreover, there has been a dramatic change in the direction and magnitude of these flows in the early 1980s. Although the first half of the 1980s was a period characterized by a series of unusual economic events—high real interest rates and a deep recession, a sharp appreciation and later depreciation in the real value of the dollar, and huge budget and trade deficits—the changes in investment incentives enacted in the tax legislation both in the early 1980s and in 1986 have evoked concern over the nature and extent of the influence of tax policy on international flows.

Specifically, in the 1980s, the direction of BOP direct investment flows roughly coincides with what the relative net return channel implies. In the early 1980s, when various investment incentives were enacted in tax legislation (the Economic Recovery Act of 1981 and the Tax Equity and

Table 2.1   Ratios of International Direct Investment to U.S. Net Nonresidential Fixed Investment

	U.S. Direct Investment Abroad	Foreign Direct Investment in the United States
1960–64	.207	.021
1965–69	.155	.021
1970–74	.195	.042
1975–79	.265	.091
1980–84	.066	.239
1979	.255	.120
1980	.216	.190
1981	.098	.256
1982	−.036	.211
1983	.008	.261
1984	.042	.276
1985	.160	.152
1986	.346	.309

Note: These ratios were calculated on the basis of data in U.S. Department of Commerce (1982, 1984), various issues of *Survey of Current Business,* and the national income and product accounts.

Fiscal Responsibility Act of 1982), the ratios of direct investment outflows to domestic net nonresidential fixed investment dropped significantly while the corresponding ratios for capital inflows increased substantially.[7] Note that the conventional wisdom in the early 1980s held that, with the extremely overvalued dollar, U.S. firms would lose competitiveness and thus invest abroad instead of in the United States. The coincidence between tax changes and international investment flows occurred again in 1986. The 1986 Tax Reform Act abolished many favorable incentive provisions like the investment tax credit or the Accelerated Cost Recovery System. Seemingly in response to this tax change, U.S. direct investment abroad bounced back sharply in 1986. The similar surge in foreign direct investment in the United States may seem counterintuitive, but it occurred mainly because foreign firms tried to take advantage of the favorable incentive provisions before their expiration at the end of the year.

Notice, however, that the BOP direct investment measures may not exactly represent the foreign equivalent of domestic investment figures. Therefore, the denominator and the numerator of the ratios presented in table 2.1 may not be comparable. In fact, the BOP direct investment flows can be most accurately regarded as *financial* transactions between *affiliated* parties and therefore do not necessarily represent real capital expenditures by foreign affiliates. To the extent that foreign subsidiaries resort to unaffiliated sources of funds like local borrowing, the BOP direct investment measures underestimate real foreign investment. On the other hand, to the extent that direct investment flows do not finance real purchases of investment goods, the BOP figures overestimate real foreign investment. Therefore, these BOP figures cannot be regarded as the exact foreign equivalent of net domestic fixed investment, and, consequently, use of these numbers as a proxy for foreign investment as in table 2.1 should be viewed with caution. Nonetheless, citing the offsetting effects mentioned above, previous authors have tried to justify these figures as an alternative for true net foreign fixed investment.[8] This practice deserves a closer scrutiny.

First, as discussed in detail in Jun (1989b), the BOP flows may seriously underestimate the true degree of foreign interests in U.S. assets because of the presence of unaffiliated financing sources—most important, local borrowing in the host country. Therefore, even when the BOP flows are all used to finance real long-term investments, these figures will underestimate net foreign fixed investment to some extent. Some authors argue that local borrowing may be mostly short term in maturity and have little to do with long-term real investment. Using foreign affiliate financial and operating data, however, Jun (1989b) shows that, though on average the majority of liabilities are short term in maturity, long-term debt is as prevalent as short-term debt for many industries.[9]

Second, part of the BOP flows may have little to do with real productive investments. To the extent that BOP flows do not finance long-term physical investment, these figures will overestimate foreign fixed investment. Such overestimation may possibly offset the underestimation mentioned above. Note, however, that the BOP figures represent net, not gross, flows. Any inflows in U.S. direct investment abroad will be netted against gross outflows. This negative entry can cause no problem as long as it represents decreased foreign fixed investment. However, some foreign affiliates may raise debt capital in the host country and then transfer the proceeds to domestic parents. Such funds can be recorded as negative direct investment abroad in the BOP accounts but have little to do with productive activities. In this case, the BOP figures will underestimate net foreign fixed investment.

The most noticeable example of this is the transactions between the Netherlands Antilles finance affiliates and their U.S. parents. These finance affiliates have been established to provide U.S. parents with a means of raising funds abroad without having the associated interest payments subjected to a 30 percent U.S. withholding tax on interest payments to foreigners. Since 1977, the funds reloaned to U.S. parents have been included in the BOP accounts as negative U.S. direct investment abroad. Table 2.2 summarizes total U.S. capital outflows and the transactions with Netherlands Antilles finance affiliates for the last several years. Note that parent transfers are composed of both equity investment and intercompany debt flows. In 1982, for example, the negative debt flows vis-à-vis Netherlands Antilles affiliates can explain most of the total change in that

Table 2.2   U.S. Direct Investment Abroad and Transactions with Netherlands Antillean Finance Affiliates (total equity debt)

	Total Direct Investment				Netherlands Antilles Affiliates			
	Direct Investment Abroad		Parent Transfers		Direct Investment Abroad		Parent Transfers	
	(1)	(2)	(3)	(4)	(5)	(6)	(7)	(8)
1982	−2.4	−3.7	9.7	−13.4	−8.6	−9.4	4.2	−13.6
1983	.4	−6.8	4.9	−11.7	−3.1	−4.1	1.4	−5.7
1984	2.8	−5.7	1.7	−6.9	−2.0	−2.8	1.0	−3.8
1985	17.3	−1.1	−2.2	1.1	4.2	3.4	−.8	4.2
1986	28.0	9.1	.4	8.7	5.1	5.4	1.0	4.4

Note: Though retained earnings data are suppressed in this table, they can be obtained by subtracting parent transfers (cols. 2 or 6) from total direct investment (cols. 1 or 5).

category. It is not hard to see that these debt flows substantially contributed to reducing total BOP U.S. direct investment abroad in some years, especially in the early 1980s. The U.S. withholding tax was repealed in July 1984, and the Netherlands Antilles intercompany debt accounts began to show positive entries in 1985, implying that U.S. parents have been paying off debts to the affiliates.

Besides the reasons mentioned above, there are a host of other factors that may contribute to the skepticism about any meaningful comparison between the BOP flows and domestic fixed investment figures, including book valuation practices, depreciation calculations, changing coverage of surveys, and exchange rate fluctuations.[10]

Considering all these factors, I believe that the best strategy for utilizing existing investment data is explicitly to distinguish between the foreign investment undertaken by the subsidiary and the direct investment of the international firm and to develop empirical models based on distinct theoretical considerations in each case. First, if foreign fixed investment undertaken by subsidiaries is the major focus of a study, actual capital expenditures by subsidiaries, rather than the BOP financial flows, are the appropriate data to be used. In this case, the isolation of the subsidiary's maximization problem is a perfectly justifiable modeling strategy, but one must not forget any possible source of funds for foreign investment, especially local borrowing, which is not included in the BOP direct investment data by definition. Second, if one is interested in the effects of taxes on international investment capital flows, then the BOP figures are still the best alternative despite the suggested measurement problems. In this case, the more difficult problem is to develop a theoretical framework in which all possible channels for tax effects can be incorporated. It is this second approach that is adopted in this paper.

One caveat is that, in this case, contrary to popular belief, even the inclusion of the Netherlands Antilles transactions in the direct investment figures can be perfectly justified since those financial transactions are consistent with profit maximization by the international firm, as discussed in the context of the relative net cost of funds. In reality, in the early 1980s, the Netherlands Antilles finance affiliates could borrow at a lower cost abroad (mostly in Eurobond markets) and transfer funds to U.S. parent firms without incurring the withholding tax on subsequent interest payments. The popular argument against the inclusion of these data in the BOP accounts is based on the inappropriate identification of direct investment flows with real foreign investment undertaken by foreign subsidiaries. This Netherlands Antilles example clearly shows that an adequate theoretical framework is a prerequisite for the correct specification of an empirical model and for the proper utilization of existing data in studying the complex subject of international investment.

2.3 Estimation

The diversity of ways in which domestic tax policy can affect direct investment flows suggests that the evaluation of this subject is ultimately an empirical matter. As discussed earlier, choosing the correct specification and appropriate data for an empirical model critically hinges on proper theoretical underpinnings. Since my major focus is on the effects of taxes on direct investment flows, I use the BOP direct investment capital outflows as the dependent variable in the regression analysis. Since the BOP direct investment data basically represents intrafirm transactions between affiliated parties and the tax changes in the 1980s are largely reflected in the U.S. net rate of return, the main focus of my empirical model is on relative net rates of return. However, unlike previous studies that consider only the net return channel, this model explicitly incorporates the net cost of funds, another channel for the tax effects on the intrafirm allocation of investment funds.

In order to estimate the tax effects on investment flows through the relative net return channel, we need some measure of the net rate of return on domestic investment in the United States. The conventional method is to use the same net-of-tax return variables as employed in estimation of U.S. domestic investment equations. However, among several available alternatives, not all these variables can be a good candidate for our purposes. Again, as in the case of selecting proper direct investment data, the choice of an appropriate net return variable should also involve rigorous theoretical considerations. Specifically, two basic criteria are proposed for which a net return variable is to be evaluated.

First, the variable should capture the relevant incentive effects for firms undertaking marginal direct investment. Often, the marginal net return or effective tax rate differs from the average net return or effective tax rate since incentive provisions like the investment tax credit and accelerated depreciation allowances are relevant only to new investments, not to existing capital. Although the use of the average tax rate has some advantages, like capturing the effects of special provisions or the lack of full loss offset in the tax law, the marginal tax rate is more relevant in capturing incentive effects on marginal investment decisions.

The second and more relevant criterion is related to the intrafirm-transaction nature of direct investment. As discussed in section 2.1, one pivotal aspect of international direct investment is the ownership chain of the international firm: the subsidiary–the parent–the shareholders. The decision of investment location is a purely intrafirm variable that is not directly affected by the shareholders. Although the foreign subsidiary is ultimately owned by the domestic shareholders, the ''parent veil'' seems to be virtually impenetrable.[11] Thus, the net return measure in my model is supposed to capture the incentive effects on the part of the corporate, not the portfolio, investor. Differences in the measurement of net profitability can be used to distinguish the ''corporate- investor'' returns from the ''portfolio-investor'' returns. In a corporate-investor model, investment is explicitly made by the corporation. In a portfolio-investor model, on the other hand, the economy is treated like a black box in which the investment mechanism is obscure but that produces the plausible result that more capital flows into an asset when the rate of return on that asset is high.

The net return variables used for estimating domestic investment equations first in Feldstein (1982) and recently in Feldstein and Jun (1987) are good examples of these two types. One variable (RN) is the real net-of-tax return received by the providers of debt and equity capital. This RN variable is calculated by subtracting from the pretax return on nonfinancial corporate capital the ratio of the taxes paid by the corporations, their shareholders, and their creditors to the capital stock. Thus, RN is an example of the average net return since it measures the net return on existing corporate capital. RN is also an example of the portfolio-investor model since it measures the return to portfolio investors. Interestingly, virtually all previous regression studies used this RN variable as the U.S. net rate of return.

The other net return variable (MPNR) is the maximum net return that firms can afford to pay providers of debt and equity capital. This ''maximum potential net return'' variable can be best interpreted as the internal rate of return of a project in an economy with taxes and inflation. Changes in tax rules, inflation, and pretax profitability all alter the maximum potential net return and therefore the incentive to invest.[12] MPNR differs from RN in two fundamental ways. First, the investment decision is explicitly made by the corporation. Second, this variable measures the prospective yield on new marginal investment rather than the yield on existing capital. MPNR, therefore, represents the marginal, corporate-investor net return and, consequently, better satisfies the two criteria for the model than RN, an average, portfolio-investor net return variable.

In an attempt to test the "parent-veil" hypothesis, I also estimate equations with a marginal but portfolio-investor variable. Consider first a very simple economy in which there is no taxation or inflation. Each share of stock claims the ownership of a single unit of capital and the earnings that it produces. A simple model of share valuation implies that the price that the individual would be willing to pay per share (QM) would make the marginal product of capital ($F'[K]$) equal to the net return he would receive per dollar invested in alternative assets plus a risk premium or simply some required rate of return (R). Then the investor's indifference condition becomes $F'(K)/QM = R$. From the perspective of the corporate investor, $F'(K)$ represents the maximum return that he can pay to the providers of capital or the marginal efficiency of capital in the standard textbook model, while R represents the cost of capital or simply the rate of interest. In a more complex and realistic economy with taxes and inflation, we can calculate the marginal share value (QM) by replacing $F'(K)$ with the maximum potential net earnings (MPNRE) that can be paid out to the equity investor. Using the MPNR data and a given financial structure (the debt-capital ratio), we can derive MPNRE. As a realistic proxy for the cost of funds (R), we can use some fixed rate of return required by the equity holder or the after-tax safe interest rate plus a risk premium. Jun (1989a) discusses different types of QM series based on various tax assumptions and risk premia. The major point here is that QM uses exactly the same data on earnings, taxes, and inflation as used for MPNR but employs the perspective of the portfolio investor. Thus, comparison of estimation results for QM to those for MPNR may provide information concerning the parent-veil hypothesis.

Table 2.3 summarizes the three variables outlined above by their respective characteristics. While previous studies focus only on the RN variable, here direct investment equations are estimated using all three net return variables. Among the three variables, it is expected that the MPNR variable performs best in estimating the tax effects on direct investment flows since it is the forward-looking marginal corporate-investor net rate of return. Before reporting the results, however, a few caveats are in order.

First, a significant coefficient on the net-of-tax return itself does not necessarily mean that direct investment flows are sensitive to tax changes. Thus, we need a reasonable decomposition of the effect of net return changes into the effect of the change in tax rules and the effect of the change in the pretax rate of return. Unlike RN, which reflects changes in both the pretax return and the effective tax rate, the MPNR variable assumes a fixed pretax rate return. Thus, MPNR has a clear advantage in that it focuses on changes in the tax law and in inflation.[13]

Second, in estimating domestic investment equations, Feldstein and Jun (1987) use the difference between the maximum net return that firms can pay

Table 2.3   Alternative Net Return Variables

	Portfolio Investor	Corporate Investor
Average return	RN	. . .
Marginal return	QM	MPNR

(MPNR) and the actual cost of funds (COF). COF is taken to be a weighted average of the costs of debt and of equity funds, with the weights equal to the debt-capital ratios. In estimating direct investment, however, that specification will no longer be valid since U.S. multinational firms can raise investment funds in host countries as well as in the United States. As shown in section 2.1, tax changes can influence the intercompany flow of funds by affecting the relative net cost of funds between countries. To the extent that host country external funds (COF*) are cheaper, the parent will have an incentive to have its affiliate depend more on local funds in the host country. Therefore, the correct and complete specification would include COF-COF* and MPNR-MPNR*, which represent the relative net cost of funds channel and the relative net return channel, respectively. In the absence of the COF* and MPNR* variables, only MPNR and COF are included, of course as separate terms.

Both MPNR and COF should relay some information about the allocative effect of taxes in equations using the BOP direct investment data. However, MPNR, which represents the allocation of internal funds, is expected to explain the BOP data better than COF, which represents the allocation of external funds. The BOP flows—the sum of retained subsidiary earnings and parent transfers—can be best interpreted as representing the allocation of internal funds within the entire international firm. As discussed in detail in Jun (1989b), parent transfers may be drawn from external funds (e.g., funds borrowed by the parent from unaffiliated sources) but can be best thought of as internal funds of the parent. Therefore, while I expect a negative coefficient on the MPNR variable in an estimated equation, I do not expect the COF variable to reveal statistically significant information about the relative cost of fund channel in the absence of COF*, which is probably more directly relevant to the parent's transfer decision in practice.

Table 2.4 presents the estimated equations relating the ratio of U.S. direct investment abroad in the balance of payments accounts to GNP to the net return variables discussed above. As in previous studies, separate equations are estimated for the two components—retained subsidiary earnings and parent transfers—of direct investment. This practice allows me to compare my estimates with previous ones and also provides indirect evidence on the marginal source of funds for foreign investment. In all previous estimation studies (Hartman 1981, 1985; Boskin and Gale 1987), only the equations for retained earnings show sensitivity to net return variables.[14] This result seems

Table 2.4   **Estimates of U.S. Direct Investment Abroad Equations**

	Parent Transfers			Retained Earnings		
	(1)	(2)	(3)	(4)	(5)	(6)
Constant	.7	6.1	.9	.3	.6	.1
	(2.5)	(1.8)	(2.2)	(3.9)	(3.1)	(3.4)
RDIA	11.0	11.9	10.7	23.7	17.1	23.3
	(11.0)	(11.1)	(10.6)	(25.2)	(26.1)	(25.6)
RN	4.3	. . .	. . .	1.8	. . .	. . .
	(33.8)			(31.0)		
MPNR	. . .	−47.5	. . .	. . .	−31.9	. . .
		(33.6)			(38.1)	
COF	. . .	−7.4	. . .	. . .	42.8	. . .
		(34.6)			(38.7)	
QM	. . .	. . .	.1	. . .	. . .	.2
			(1.6)			(1.4)
u	.8	.4	.8	.4	.4	.4
	(.1)	(.2)	(.1)	(.4)	(.5)	(.4)
$\bar{R}^2$	.634	.671	.634	.398	.407	.399
Durbin-Watson	1.85	1.81	1.82	1.85	1.73	1.85

Note: Dependent variables are retained earnings × 1000/U.S. GNP and parent transfers × 1000/U.S. GNP, respectively. All explanatory variables are one-period lagged. Sample period is 1965–86 for all equations. The equations are estimated with a first-order autocorrelation correction, and the simultaneously estimated autocorrelation coefficient is presented as the coefficient of the variable u. Standard errors are shown in parentheses. RDIA: actual net return on direct investment; RN: net return on U.S. nonfinancial corporate capital; MPNR: maximum potential net return; COF: cost of funds; QM: marginal q.

consistent with the tax capitalization view that retained earnings should be the marginal source of funds for mature subsidiaries. In Jun (1989d), however, I refute this view using evidence based on individual firm data and argue that parent transfers should be the marginal source of funds for the majority of subsidiaries.

Included in each equation is the "actual net average return" (RDIA: actual after-foreign-tax direct investment earnings divided by direct investment position) to represent any specific incentives associated with foreign investment that are not to be captured by the domestic net return. This RDIA variable may be regarded as a proxy for MPNR*, possibly mitigating the missing variable bias associated with the net return channel. Since studies generally indicate a lag that peaks at twelve to eighteen months between changes in the determinants of investment and subsequent changes in investment, the explanatory variables are one-year lagged as conventionally done in estimation of domestic investment. Note that all previous works do not lag the independent variables, an omission that I believe is a major source of the problems with their estimations.

As shown in columns 1 and 4 of table 2.4, the coefficients on the average yield on existing capital (RN) are very small in size, incorrect in sign, and statistically insignificant. On the other hand, the maximum potential net return for the corporate investor (MPNR) has sizable and correctly signed coefficients, as shown in columns 2 and 4. It suggests that U.S. tax changes can have significant effects on U.S. multinational firms' investment abroad. However, the t-statistics for MPNR in the retained-earnings equation is not large enough to be significant, while the t-value in the transfer equation is relatively sizable. This fact supports the view that parent transfers are the marginal source of funds for the majority of subsidiaries. In any event, the results also confirm my initial guess that MPNR—the marginal and corporate-investor variable—is a more appropriate variable than RN—the average and portfolio-investor variable—in estimating tax effects on intrafirm investment allocation between parents and subsidiaries.

While even the best net return measure for our purposes (MPNR) fails to have significant coefficients for any retained earnings equation, the transfers equations show consistently higher $\bar{R}^2$s than their retained earnings counterparts. This result provides indirect support for the claim that parent transfers are the marginal source of funds for foreign investment.

Columns 3 and 6 show the estimated equations with the QM variable. Neither equation succeeds in producing significant coefficients. The size of the coefficients is small, as in other Q-investment equations, although my Q-variables are not based on the adjustment cost function. Considering that MPNR and QM use virtually identical data except that each model is based on different types of investors, this result provides further support to the parent-veil argument.

In all equations, the lagged RDIAs fail to produce any significant coefficients. This result can be contrasted with the significant coefficients on the corresponding variable (RDFI: actual return on foreign direct investment in the United States) in similarly defined equations regarding foreign direct investment in the United States presented in Jun (1989c). One potential explanation comes from the presumption that RDIA or RFDI is supposed to capture the return on existing investment projects. When we decompose BOP direct investment into "inflows to existing affiliates" and "funds used for acquisition and establishment,"[15] RDIA or RFDI may be more directly relevant to the first type of funds, while the host country net return (the U.S. net return in the case of studying foreign direct investment in the United States) may be related more to the latter type. Thus, the contrasting performance of RDIA and RFDI might be due to the different composition of the BOP inflows and outflows between these two types of direct investment opportunities—new and old. However, a more convincing explanation is related to the RDIA variable itself. As noticed earlier, U.S. direct investment position and income—the denominator and the numerator of RDIA, respectively—may be subject to serious valuation problems, such as book valuation of the investment position and currency-conversion effects. The data for the RFDI variable may be subject to fewer problems.

I have not obtained reliable results for the COF variable; this outcome, however, is not surprising, partly because BOP figures are more relevant to the net return channel as discussed earlier and also because most of the tax changes in question are associated with the profitability of investment rather than with the cost side.

How do these results compare with previous works? Hartman (1981) and, recently, Boskin and Gale (1987) have estimated the same specification as in columns 1 and 3 using the same type of data—both investment and tax data—but they do not lag the explanatory variables at all. For the retained-earnings equations, they typically report very large and statistically significant coefficients on RDIA and very high $\bar{R}^2$s (larger than .9 in all cases).[16] Their transfer equations show a very poor fit. These results are in sharp conflict with my theoretical predictions and empirical findings. A closer look at their estimation shows, however, that their significant results seem to be the product of spurious correlation. Specifically, for the retained earnings equations, retained earnings data are used to construct both the dependent variable (the ratio of retained earnings to GNP) and RDIA, the independent variable (retained earnings are the major component of the numerator of RDIA). My suspicion is also supported by the fact that it is hard to believe that a 90 percent $\bar{R}^2$ can be obtained from such parsimonious specification, that the same variable (RDIA) shows such drastically different results in the retained earnings and transfers equations. It is also hard to find serious theoretical arguments for their findings. One caveat is in order. Even if we believe their results, the coefficients of RDIA have nothing to do with the U.S. tax system. So, in fact, they failed to find any "tax effects" on U.S. capital outflows, contrary to their claim.

2.4 Summary

The analysis presented in this paper shows that U.S. tax policy can have a significant effect on direct investment capital flows through various channels. I stress that a sensible choice of model specification and data in an empirical model entails rigorous theoretical underpinnings. In particular, I emphasize the difference between foreign investment undertaken by the subsidiary and direct investment of the entire international firm and the need to use different theoretical frameworks to handle each problem. I present estimated equations relating the BOP direct investment outflows to various measures of the U.S. net rate of return. Specifically, the evidence shows that U.S. tax policy toward domestic investment can have significant effects on U.S. direct investment outflows by influencing the relative net rate of return between the United States and abroad. Among various specifications, the transfers equation including the maximum potential net return (MPNR) fits best, which is consistent with the implications derived from my theoretical framework. On the basis of these findings and of the estimation of a domestic investment equation with separate MPNR and COF variables presented in Feldstein and Jun (1987), we can say that a reduction of sixteen cents of transfers made by U.S. parent firms occurs for every dollar increase in U.S. domestic investment. The findings in this study also support the claims that parent transfers are the major marginal source of funds for foreign investment and that there exists a strong form of the corporate veil—the parent veil—between the foreign subsidiary and the domestic shareholders.

Notes

1. In practice, local borrowing in the host country can be an important source of financing foreign investment. The presence of local funds may also have implications for the choice between parent transfers and retained earnings at the margin. See Jun (1989d).

2. I assume that the home country rate is larger than the host country rate.

3. Note that I explicitly distinguish between foreign investment undertaken by the subsidiary and direct investment made by the parent. Foreign investment can be financed through other sources than direct investment, while direct investment may not necessarily finance foreign fixed investment.

4. In equilibrium, the denominator of marginal q for foreign capital is equal to the numerator of marginal q for domestic capital. See Jun (1988).

5. For a domestic firm, internal funds are retained earnings, while external funds are raised through new shares and bonds. Similarly, internal funds for an international firm consist of retained earnings of both the parent and the subsidiary.

6. The Tax Reform Act of 1986 includes provisions reducing the statutory corporate tax rate, repealing the investment tax credit, and restricting the foreign tax credit and tax deferral. The overall effect on direct investment is not evident since these policies can have offsetting effects. However, such a combination of policies may have implications for the composition of investment. For example, relatively more equipment investment may be undertaken by foreign subsidiaries.

7. The absolute level of direct investment flows also shows the same trend.

8. For a summary of previous arguments, see Hartman (1984, 486).

9. In finance, insurance, and wholesale industries, short-term liabilities dominate, while, in manufacturing, mining, and real estate industries, long-term debt occupies a significant portion of total liabilities (about 50 percent for manufacturing).

10. For a discussion of potential problems associated with benchmark data, see Boskin and Gale (1987). Hartman (1984) correctly argues that the BOP figures are more comparable to net investment figures since retained earnings are net of depreciation, though this is in book value. Exchange rate movements in the early 1980s may have affected the BOP figures in two ways. First, changing relative competitiveness may have influenced direct investment activities. Second, as for U.S. direct investment abroad, there may well have been a currency conversion effect. Foreign earnings may have been understated when being translated into the dollar value in the early 1980s, when the dollar was highly overvalued.

11. This point is rigorously proved in Jun (1988).

12. I constructed both the constant-profit version (MPNR) and the varying-profitability version (MPNRVP) of the maximum net return. The MPNRVP variable assumes that firms adjust their assumed pretax rate of return from year to year in proportion to that year's actual pretax profitability of capital in the nonfinancial corporate sector. In this study, I use MPNR to focus only on the tax change.

13. See n. 12 above.

14. I do not even bother to include my replication of their findings since most previous estimation studies share the same basic specification and produce the same qualitative results. I also estimated equations with total direct investment but failed to find any significant covariance effects between the two components of direct investment.

15. Jun (1989b) discusses this issue for foreign direct investment in the United States.

16. Some of their equations show small but significant coefficients on RN, but I failed to have any significant results for this variable using updated data.

References

Boskin, M., and W. Gale. 1987. New results on the effects of tax policy on the international location of investment. In *The effects of taxation on capital accumulation,* ed. M. Feldstein, 210–19. Chicago: University of Chicago Press.

Caves, R. 1982. *Multinational enterprise and economic analysis.* Cambridge Surveys of Economic Literature. Cambridge: Cambridge University Press.

Feldstein, M. 1980. Inflation and the stock market. *American Economic Review* 70: 839–47.

——. 1982. Inflation, tax rules and investment: Some econometric evidence. *Econometrica* 50 (4).

Feldstein, M., and C. Horioka. 1980. Domestic savings and international capital flows. *Economic Journal* 90: 314–29.

Feldstein, M., and J. Jun. 1987. The effects of tax rules on nonresidential fixed investment: Some preliminary evidence from the 1980s. In *The effects of taxation on capital accumulation,* ed. M. Feldstein, 101–56. Chicago: University of Chicago Press.

Giovannini, A. 1988. International capital mobility and tax evasion. Mimeo.

Gordon, R. 1986. Taxation of investment and savings in a world economy. *American Economic Review* 76: 1086–1102.

Goulder, L., J. Shoven, and J. Whalley. 1983. Domestic tax policy and the foreign sector. In *Behavioral simulation methods in tax policy analysis,* ed. M. Feldstein. Chicago: University of Chicago Press.

Hartman, D. 1981. Domestic tax policy and foreign investment: Some evidence. NBER Working Paper no. 784. Cambridge, Mass.: National Bureau of Economic Research.

——. 1984. Tax policy and foreign direct investment in the United States. *National Tax Journal* 37 (4): 475–87.

——. 1985. Tax policy and foreign direct investment. *Journal of Public Economics* 26: 107–21.

——. 1987. The effects of tax policy on the international location of investment: Comment. In *The effects of taxation on capital accumulation,* ed. M. Feldstein, 219–22. Chicago: University of Chicago Press.

Horst, T. 1977. American taxation of multinational firms. *American Economic Review* 67: 376–89.

Jun, J. 1988. Tax policy and international direct investment. NBER Working Paper no. 3048. Cambridge, Mass.: National Bureau of Economic Research.

_____. 1989a. Marginal q and average q: Taxation and corporate investment. Mimeo.

_____. 1989b. Tax policy and foreign direct investment in the U.S. Mimeo.

_____. 1989c. The true measure of foreign control of U.S. business enterprises. Mimeo.

_____. 1989d. What is the optimal marginal source of funds for foreign investment? NBER Working Paper no. 3064. Cambridge, Mass.: National Bureau of Economic Research.

Lipsey, R. 1987. Changing patterns of international investment in and by the United States. Cambridge, Mass.: National Bureau of Economic Research.

Slemrod, J. 1987. International capital mobility and the theory of capital income taxation. University of Minnesota. Mimeo.

Summers, L. 1986. Tax policy and international competitiveness. NBER Working Paper no. 2007. Cambridge, Mass.: National Bureau of Economic Research.

U.S. Department of Commerce. 1982. *Selected data on U.S. direct investment abroad, 1950–76.* Washington, D.C.: Bureau of Economic Analysis.

_____. 1984. *Selected data on foreign direct investment in the U.S., 1950–79.* Washington, D.C.: Bureau of Economic Analysis.

_____. 1985. *U.S. direct investment abroad: 1982 benchmark survey data.* Washington, D.C.: Bureau of Economic Analysis.

_____. 1987. *U.S. direct investment abroad: Operations of U.S. parent companies and their foreign affiliates, preliminary 1985 estimates.* Washington, D.C.: Bureau of Economic Analysis.

Comment   Michael P. Dooley

Jun's paper examines balance of payments data to estimate the effect of taxes on direct investment. In doing so, the author is forced to utilize "flow of funds" financial data to test the implications of a macro model. While there are circumstances where this is appropriate, these circumstances are quite special and are unlikely to be present in the data used in this paper.

Consider, for example, a basic closed-economy macro model, which relates after-tax rates of return to savings and real investment but does not set out the details of financial intermediation. In general, a complex *flow* of funds from savers to investors through financial intermediaries leaves behind a multiple set of financial assets and liabilities. Flow of funds accounts follow savings of a household or a firm to a commercial bank, then to a money-market fund, then to commercial paper, and ultimately to purchase of an investment good. The predictions of the macro model, however, are

Michael P. Dooley is chief of the External Adjustment Division, Research Department, International Monetary Fund. The views presented here are those of the author and should not be taken as representing those of the Fund.

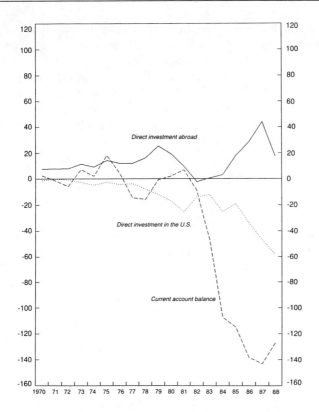

Fig. C2.1a   U.S. gross direct investment and the current account (in billions of U.S. dollars)
Sources: IMF, *Balance of Payments* and *U.S. Federal Reserve Bulletin.*

invariant to the route from households or firms to investors. One reason that flow of funds data are seldom used for economic analysis (though for the United States such data exist) is that the route savings takes to the investor can be very unstable. New financial markets open up, competitive conditions change, and, perhaps most important, taxation and regulation of financial intermediaries and financial markets provide strong incentives to reroute the flow of funds.

For an open economy, the problem of interpreting a flow of funds accounting framework is even more difficult. The counterpart to real savings in the closed economy includes for the open economy net exports of goods and services or, more conventionally, the current account balance. But the problem relating net savings flows to the flow of financial funds across national borders is truly daunting.

The capital account in the balance of payments is a flow of funds account. It measures the dollar value of gross financial transactions involving residents and nonresidents. The direct investment data are financial capital flows as reported by a subset of reporters who own more than 10 percent of the voting shares of the counterparty in that transaction.

Now, if the financial transactions reported by direct investors were representative of other investors, it might be possible to interpret foreign direct investors as contributing to capital formation. However, it is also possible that transactions reported by direct investors are systematically offset by transactions among other groups of investors. As shown in figure C2.1a, the United States has borrowed heavily from the rest of the world since 1982. It is also the case that U.S. direct investment abroad has increased, but so has foreign direct investment in the United States. Clearly, as shown in figure C2.1b, net direct investment has been dominated by net inflows through other financial markets.

Returning to a closed economy model for simplicity, we can imagine two important types of taxes that might influence the relations among various types of financial transactions. One would tax the earnings of capital at the

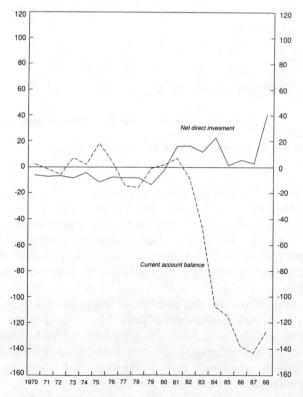

Fig. C2.1b   U.S. net direct investment and the current account (in billions of U.S. dollars)
Sources: IMF, *Balance of Payments* and *U.S. Federal Reserve Bulletin.*

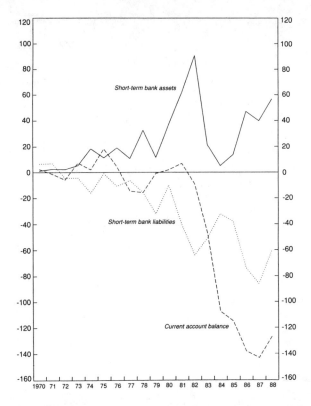

Fig. C2.2a   U.S. gross short-term bank reported capital flows and the current account (in billions of U.S. dollars)
Sources: IMF, *Balance of Payments* and *U.S. Federal Reserve Bulletin.*

source, for example, a real estate tax. Another would tax earnings from a particular type of financial position, say, bond interest. Both types of taxation might discourage savings and, in turn, investment in a given country. But suppose that, instead of directly evaluating the effect on savings (as recorded in national income accounts), we looked at the increase in direct investment reported by households as measured by purchases of equities.

The real estate tax would presumably discourage all types of investment, including that financed by equity, and, other things being equal, an increase in the tax would suggest a fall in both investment and the accumulation of equity by households. A tax on bond interest would be, in part, avoided by switching to equity claims. To the extent that bonds were still held, the tax would also discourage savings and, in turn, investment. But equity holdings would increase, and, if we were using this as a measure of investment, we would get the wrong answer.

In an international context, both kinds of taxes change frequently. Thus, the type of financial capital flows associated with a net transfer of savings

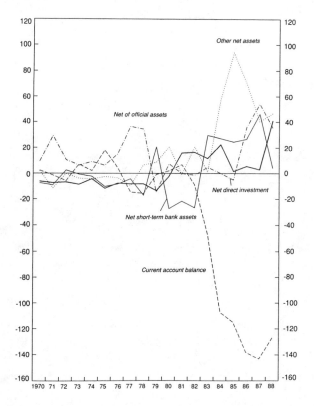

Fig. C2.2b   U.S. net capital flows and the current account (in billions of U.S. dollars)
Sources: IMF, *Balance of Payments* and *U.S. Federal Reserve Bulletin.*

has shown a great deal of instability. In addition to important financial innovations and changes in tax and regulatory incentives, governments intervene on an important scale in order to influence exchange rates. Even if one is skeptical about the power of official transactions to influence exchange rates, there is no doubt that large-scale private capital movements are the necessary counterpart to intervention. As shown in figure C2.2a, b, the changing structure for these flows in the face of a growing net capital inflow to the United States as measured by the current account balance suggests that none of these financial flows are likely to be good measures of the contribution of groups of investors to capital formation.

3 Tax Effects on Foreign Direct Investment in the United States: Evidence from a Cross-Country Comparison

Joel Slemrod

The magnitude and financing of foreign direct investment (FDI) in the United States, which totaled more than $40 billion in 1987, are potentially influenced by the tax systems of both the United States and the investor's country. Nevertheless, all recent studies of FDI in the United States have investigated only the effect of U.S. taxation. The home country's tax system has been ignored because either the appropriate data are unavailable or, on theoretical grounds, it is deemed to be irrelevant to FDI.

This paper investigates the effect of both U.S. and home country taxation on FDI in the United States. It does this by first extending and updating the standard model of aggregate FDI in the United States and then disaggregating FDI by the country of the investing firm so as to facilitate the study of home country influences, including taxation.

The results of this new empirical approach generally support a negative effect of U.S. effective rates of taxation on total FDI and new transfers of funds, but not on retained earnings. The disaggregated analysis does not, though, provide much support for several propositions about the effect on FDI in the United States of foreign countries' tax rates and systems of taxing foreign-source income.

The paper is organized as follows. Section 3.1 reviews the existing empirical literature, and section 3.2 discusses some of the important issues regarding data on FDI in the United States. The next two sections present the

Joel Slemrod is professor of economics, professor of business economics and public policy, and director of the Office of Tax Policy Research at the University of Michigan, and a research associate at the National Bureau of Economic Research.

The author is grateful to David Hartman, other conference attendees, and the participants at the NBER Summer Institute for valuable comments and suggestions. He also acknowledges the help of Leticia Fernandez and Ken Timbers in providing exceptionally able research assistance and of Julian Alworth for graciously providing critical data.

results of the data analyses—in section 3.3 for aggregate FDI and in section 3.4 separately for each of seven major investing countries. Section 3.5 provides a conclusion.

3.1 Review of the Existing Empirical Literature

It is generally accepted that FDI is primarily an issue of industrial organization. Dunning (1985, 6–7) has argued that FDI by firms of country A in country B is more likely if A's firms (i) possess ownership-specific advantages relative to B's firms in sourcing markets, (ii) find it profitable to use these advantages themselves rather than lease them to B's firms, and (iii) find it profitable to utilize their ownership-specific advantages in B rather than A. A large body of empirical literature has been addressed to testing this theory of international production, usually referred to as the "eclectic" theory. Much of this research has been cross-sectional, relating the extent of foreign investment in a given sector to characteristics of that sector that represent ownership-specific and location-specific comparative advantages. Several examples of this type of analysis are contained in Dunning (1985).

Studies of the effects of taxation on FDI have generally taken the perspective that, whatever its benefits to firms are, they must be balanced against the tax consequences of carrying out FDI. The tax systems of both the firm's home country and potential host countries can affect the incentives concerning FDI as well as how to finance a given pattern of FDI. Theoretical treatments of these questions are presented in Alworth (1988) and Gersovitz (1987). The limited empirical literature on the effect of taxes on multinationals' behavior is summarized in Caves (1982).

Empirical study focusing on the effect of taxation on the time series of FDI in the United States was pioneered by Hartman (1984). Using annual data from 1965 to 1979, he estimated the response of FDI, separately for investment financed by retained earnings and transfers from abroad, to three variables: the after-tax rate of return realized by foreign investors in the United States, the overall after-tax rate of return on capital in the United States, and the tax rate on U.S. capital owned by foreigners relative to the tax rate on U.S. capital owned by U.S. investors. The first two terms are meant to proxy for the prospective return to new FDI, the first term being more appropriate for firms considering expansion of current operations and the second more applicable to the acquisition of existing assets that are not expected to earn extraordinary returns based on production of differentiated products or possession of superior technology. The relative tax term is designed to capture the possibility that tax changes that apply only to U.S. investors will, by affecting the valuation of assets, alter the foreign investor's cost and therefore the return to acquiring the asset.[1]

Hartman does not attempt to measure either an effective withholding tax rate or the foreign income tax rate applied to the aggregate of FDI. He defends their absence by noting the likelihood that the average values of these tax rates are relatively constant over time. Furthermore, no attempt is made to measure the alternative rate of return available abroad to foreign investors.

Hartman's regression results reveal both a positive association of after-tax rate of return variables with the ratio to U.S. GNP of FDI financed by retained earnings and a negative association of the FDI-GNP ratio with the relative tax rate on foreigners compared to domestic residents. The model does not explain transfers from abroad as well as retained earnings, although coefficients of all three variables have the expected sign and are significantly different from zero. From this research, Hartman concludes that the effect of taxes on FDI, both that implied by reinvestment of earnings and that accomplished by explicit transfer of funds, is quite strong.

Boskin and Gale (1987) reestimate Hartman's equation using the updated tax rate and rate of return series from Feldstein and Jun (1987). Although the estimated elasticities of FDI to the rates of return are somewhat lower, none of the point estimates changes by more than one standard deviation. They also extend the sample forward to 1984, and in some cases backward to 1956, and experiment with a variety of alternative explanatory variables and functional forms. They conclude that, although the results are somewhat sensitive to sample period and specification, the qualitative conclusions of Hartman are fairly robust.

Young (1988) uses revised data on investment, GNP, and rates of return earned by foreigners to estimate similar equations. These changes increase the estimated elasticities with respect to the rate of return realized by foreigners and the relative rate of return. However, the equations for new transfers of funds estimated using the years 1956–84 yield very poor results, suggesting to Young that the simple Hartman model is inadequate for studying foreign direct investment through new funds when applied to the expanded sample period. Relaxing Hartman's assumption of a unitary income elasticity and including the lagged dependent variable as a right-hand-side variable does not substantially alter the conclusions for retained earnings (although the estimated responsiveness is significantly lower), but the tax responsiveness of transfer of new funds still is not supported.

Newlon (1987) reexamines the results of Hartman as well as those of Boskin and Gale. During his attempt at replication, he discovered that the series measuring the rate of return on FDI, used in all earlier papers, had been miscalculated from the original Bureau of Economic Analysis data for the years 1965–73. Using the corrected series, the equation explaining retained earnings does not fit as well, although the equation explaining transfers fits better. In explaining retained earnings, the estimated coefficients on the return to FDI and the tax ratio are slightly larger in absolute value and remain statistically significant, although the estimated coefficient on the net return in the United States is lower and is no longer statistically significant. For transfers of funds, the estimated coefficient on the return to FDI is much larger and becomes significant, although the estimated coefficient on the net return in the United States becomes smaller and insignificant. When the sample period is extended to range from 1956 to 1984, Newlon's results also differ from those of Hartman and those of Boskin and Gale. In particular, the equation explaining transfer of funds fits poorly, and no estimated coefficient is significant.[2]

It is notable that none of these studies has deviated very far from the approach taken in Hartman's (1984) paper. Although Young (1988) refers to Feldstein's (1982) dictum that, in the absence of a perfectly specified model, many alternative models should be investigated, the empirical research has been extremely one tracked. This is a sufficient reason to explore alternative methodologies. Furthermore, there are several problems with the standard approach that bear further study.

In the previous literature, the disincentive to investment caused by the tax system is implicitly measured by an average tax rate, computed as total taxes paid divided by a measure of profits. However, the incentive to undertake new investment depends on the effective marginal tax rate, which, as is well known, can deviate substantially from an average tax rate concept.

None of the existing studies attempts to estimate the effect of the home country's tax system on FDI in the United States. Of course, collecting the appropriate data is difficult, and perhaps, as Hartman argued, these tax rates have not in fact varied much. The observed stability, though, applies to statutory tax rates and not necessarily to the more appropriate effective marginal tax rates. There is also a theoretical reason to focus attention on the host country tax rate. Hartman (1985) has argued that only the host country's tax system matters for investment coming from subsidiaries' earnings, even when the home country taxes its residents on the basis of worldwide income. This is because the home country's tax equally reduces the parent's return to an investment and the opportunity cost of making an investment (remitting a dividend to the parent).[3] Thus, for any subsidiary whose desired investment exceeds earnings, the tax due on repatriation of earnings does matter. This situation would likely occur for newly formed subsidiaries. In any event, it is worthwhile to investigate empirically the effect of both the home country's rate of taxation and its system of taxing foreign-source income.

The interpretation of the estimated coefficient on the rate of return to FDI variable is also problematic, as stressed by Newlon. This rate of return is defined as the after-tax income from direct investment divided by the stock of direct investment. When the home country has a foreign tax credit with deferral, it is often optimal for the subsidiary to finance investment first by using retained earnings and then, only when these earnings are exhausted, by using funds transferred from the parent firm. This hierarchy of financing implies that, whenever a subsidiary's investment exceeds its retained earnings, its retained earnings will exactly equal its income. Thus, for these firms, we would expect a direct association between the calculated rate of return (in which after-tax income is the numerator) on FDI and retained earnings, regardless of whether the average rate of return in fact influences decisions concerning new FDI. As Newlon notes, if subsidiaries were following a fixed dividend payout rule (e.g., it pays out a fixed fraction of income), a direct association between income and retained earnings would also be observed. This argument may also apply to subsidiaries of firms residing in countries that employ territorial systems of taxation, thus rendering problematic any observed empirical association between FDI out of retained earnings and realized rate of return.

3.2 Data Issues

3.2.1 Definition of FDI

FDI, as measured by the Bureau of Economic Analysis (BEA), consists of earnings retained by subsidiaries and branches of foreign parents and transfers of funds from the foreign parents to the U.S. firms, including both debt and equity transfers. Thus, FDI does not correspond directly to any measure of real investment, as it excludes investment financed by funds raised locally (or in third countries) by the U.S. firm and includes purchases of existing assets by foreigners. It is more accurately thought of as a measure of financial flows rather than of real investment. Unfortunately, no data exist on real investment made by foreign branches and subsidiaries. Note also that the data do not distinguish between branches and subsidiaries, even though in general the tax treatment by the home country of the two forms of organization is different. Finally, only in this decade has the data on transfers of funds been disaggregated into debt and equity transfers, rendering multivariate analysis impossible at this time.

3.2.2 Drift from Benchmark Years

The data on FDI in the United States is based on benchmark surveys conducted by the BEA in 1959, 1974, and 1980. For nonbenchmark years, estimates for all series except equity and intercompany account inflows were constructed by extrapolating the benchmark data based on sample data from quarterly surveys. The 1959 benchmark data were extrapolated backward to construct estimates for 1950–58 and were extrapolated forward to construct estimates for 1960–73. The 1974 benchmark data were used to derive estimates for 1974–79, and the 1980 benchmark data were used for estimates of 1980 and thereafter. Reported equity and intercompany account flows are taken directly from the quarterly sample with extrapolation, owing to the unreliable relation between the reported and the unreported data.

Note that, except for 1959, the benchmark data are *not* used to revise the data based on the quarterly survey for earlier years. This procedure gives rise to the suspicion that data for nonbenchmark years misestimate true FDI. This suspicion has been confirmed for 1974 because the BEA has compared estimates based on the 1974 benchmark survey with estimates based on an extrapolation from the 1959 benchmark. For equity and intercompany account flows, the extrapolated total is $2.50 billion compared to $3.70 billion from the 1974 benchmark, an underestimate of more than one-third. In contrast, for reinvested earnings the extrapolated figure is $1.13 billion, actually higher than the benchmark figure of $1.07 billion. The discrepancy between the two estimates varies widely by country and by industry, however.

Other important changes in concept and definition were introduced with the 1974 benchmark survey. The minimum ownership criterion in the definition of FDI was decreased from 25 to 10 percent, a change that in 1974 accounted for $1.2 billion of the $25.1 billion total FDI position in the United States. Also in 1974 began major changes in the treatment of unrealized capital gains and losses, the classification of incorporated insurance affiliates, and the coverage of reverse equity ownership (U.S. affiliates' equity ownership in their foreign parents). Finally, starting in 1974, FDI was classified by the country of foreign parent—the first foreign person in the ownership chain of the U.S. affiliate. Before 1974, estimates for some affiliates were classified by the "ultimate beneficial owner," which is the person in the ownership chain, beginning with the foreign parent, that is not owned more than 50 percent by another person. This change in classification apparently affected several large affiliates, with the result that the geographic distribution of the estimates was significantly affected.

Some of the earlier studies of FDI ignored these data definition issues, while others included a dummy variable to differentiate pre- and postbenchmark periods. However, none of the studies directly addressed the apparent problem that, the further away from a benchmark year, the greater the survey-based numbers misreport actual FDI. To account for this tendency, in much of what follows I utilize a dummy variable whose value is the difference between the data year and the benchmark year from which the reported data are estimated. Thus, this variable has a value of zero in the benchmark years 1959, 1974, and 1980 and a positive value in all other years since 1960 (when the benchmark data are extrapolated forward). It takes on a maximum value of fourteen in 1973, when the benchmark data are extrapolated fourteen years forward. This procedure allows for a constant amount of drift between benchmarks of the reported FDI data. In addition, I consider a dummy variable for the period beginning in 1974 to account for the one-time changes in concepts, definitions, and classification of FDI by country that occurred in that year.

3.3   Total FDI in the United States

3.3.1   Trends

Figure 3.1 shows the behavior of FDI in the United States, as a ratio to U.S. GNP, for the period 1953–87. It also breaks this ratio down into two components—retained earnings and new transfers of funds, both as a ratio to U.S. GNP.

As figure 3.1 shows, the ratio of FDI to GNP shows no clear trend until approximately 1972, when it began to grow quickly. By 1974, FDI amounted to 0.32 percent of GNP, or more than four times as high as the average percentage in the two decades from 1953 to 1972. A second surge of FDI began in 1978, pushing the ratio to a record 0.83 percent in 1981 and an average of 0.48 percent from 1982 to 1984, or five times higher than the 1953–72 average and two and a half times the 1977 ratio. In 1987, FDI in the United States totaled nearly $42.0 billion, or 0.94 percent of the GNP of $4.49 trillion. Both the total FDI and the ratio to GNP in 1987 were all-time highs.

One striking aspect of FDI is the decline within the last decade in the relative importance of retained earnings compared to new transfers of funds. Through 1980, retained earnings represented a large, stable component of total FDI, composing 37.0 percent of the total. In 1977, the contribution of retained earnings relative to new transfers began to fall, and, by 1981, it began to decline in absolute terms as well. In the period 1981–87, retained earnings composed only 1.4 percent of total FDI.

Is the rapid growth of FDI in the United States since 1972 part of a worldwide trend, or does it instead represent a relative shift of FDI to the United States from other locations? Figures 3.2 and 3.3 help answer that

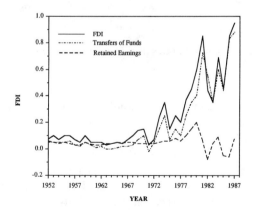

Fig. 3.1   Total FDI, retained earnings and transfers as a percentage of U.S. GNP, 1953–87

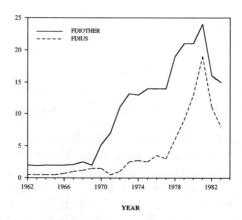

Fig. 3.2   FDI to the United States and to the rest of the world from seven countries ($billions), 1962–83

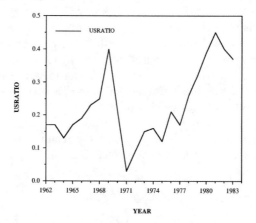

Fig. 3.3   FDI in the United States as a fraction of worldwide FDI of seven countries, 1962–83

question. Figure 3.2 shows that outward FDI from seven major investing nations to countries other than the United States was flat until 1969, when a large boom lasting until 1973 occurred, followed by relative stability and another surge from 1978 through 1981.[4] According to figure 3.3, FDI in the United States as a fraction of the seven countries' worldwide FDI reached 40.5 percent in 1969, fell sharply until 1971, and then rose steadily until an all-time high of 43.7 percent was reached in 1981. It has remained at a high level since then. Apparently, the strong growth of FDI in the United States starting in 1972 does indeed represent an increase in the relative strength of the United States as a location of FDI.

Table 3.1   **Regression Results for FDI Financed by Retained Earnings, 1956–84**

Independent Variables

τ			− .0068	.223
			(.0846)	(.141)
t		.493		
		(.608)		
t^1		− .494		
		(.835)		
r		.800	.788	
		(.105)	(.094)	
r^1		− .120	.062	
		(.302)	(.158)	
$r(1 - t)$	.766			
	(.094)			
$r^1(1 - t)$	.048			
	(.193)			
$(1 - t^1)/(1 - t)$	− .154			
	(.263)			
Intercept	2.602	2.486	2.71	.780
	(.510)	(.574)	(.422)	(.152)
Durbin-Watson statistic	1.82	2.04	1.92	1.47
$\bar{R}^2$	.734	.731	.731	.050

Note: Dependent variable is the logarithm of $[(1000 \times RE/GNP) + 1.23]$. Column 1 corresponds to eq. 2 of table II.2b in Newlon (1987). All independent variables are in logarithms. Standard errors in parentheses.

3.3.2 Analysis

Replication of Earlier Findings

As is ritual in this literature, I begin the analysis by trying to reproduce the aggregate time-series results of a predecessor in the literature, in this case Newlon (1987). In a break from precedent, I am able to reproduce his main results to three significant digits. These results are reported in the first column of tables 3.1 and 3.2. As discussed in section 3.1, they suggest a strong positive association between the after-tax return on FDI—denoted $r(1 - t)$—and FDI financed by retained earnings, but not for new transfers of funds. The relative tax rate—denoted $(1 - t^1)/(1 - t)$—variable and the overall rate of return—denoted $r^1(1 - t)$—have no significant effect on either component of FDI.[5]

Because of my uneasiness about the economic implications of a statistical association between the components of FDI and the measured average after-tax of return to capital, I next separate out as explanatory variables the average pretax rate of return earned by foreigners (r), the average pretax rate of return earned on all capital in the United States (r^1), and the two average

Table 3.2   **Regression Results for FDI Financed by Transfers of Funds, 1956–84**

Independent Variables				
τ			−.683	−.826
			(.123)	(.183)
t		−2.790		
		(.874)		
t^1		1.788		
		(1.202)		
r		.167	.367	
		(.152)	(.137)	
r^1		−1.112	−1.46	
		(.434)	(.231)	
$r(1 - t)$	−.070			
	(.283)			
$r^1(1 - t)$	−.319			
	(.582)			
$(1 - t^1)/1 - t)$	−1.011			
	(.793)			
Intercept	−.485	−2.429	−2.07	.195
	(1.541)	(.827)	(.617)	(.197)
Durbin-Watson statistic	.34	1.67	1.80	.68
$\bar{R}^2$	.104	.794	.788	.407

Note: Dependent variable is the logarithm of $[(1000 \times \text{TR/GNP}) + 1.676]$. Column 1 corresponds to eq. 4 of table II.2b in Newlon (1987). All independent variables are in logarithms. Standard errors in parentheses.

tax rate terms (t for the tax rate on foreigners, t^1 for the total tax rate including taxes paid by U.S. residents at the personal level).[6] The results are reported in the second column of tables 3.1 and 3.2. While the pretax return to FDI retains a positive association with the ratio of retained earnings to GNP, neither tax term is significantly different than zero. However, this is not the case for transfers of funds. In this case, the average tax rate faced by foreigners does have a statistically significant negative coefficient, and, as suggested by the theory, the total tax rate faced by a U.S. investor has a positive coefficient.

Note that these results concerning the tax rate variables reverse the conclusions of Hartman (1984), who concluded that the behavior of retained earnings was consistent with expectations but that the estimated response of transfers of new funds did not conform to expectations. I attribute his first finding to the inevitable relation between retained earnings and a measure of rate of return whose numerator is highly correlated with retained earnings.

I next replace the two measures of average tax rate by a measure of the marginal effective corporate tax rate on fixed investment (τ) in the United

States, as calculated by Auerbach and Hines (1988). This is arguably a better measure of the expected tax burden on a prospective new investment. These results, shown in column 3 of tables 3.1 and 3.2, suggest that the U.S. marginal tax rate has had a significant effect on transfer of funds but not on retained earnings.[7] The coefficient on the tax rate corresponds to a tax elasticity of transfers of -1.40, when evaluated at the average transfers to GNP ratio over the period.[8]

None of the previous work reports the results of equations explaining total FDI in the United States; rather, it considers only its component parts (retained earnings and transfer of funds). Table 3.3 reports the results of repeating the regressions of tables 3.1 and 3.2 for total FDI. These results strongly support the negative association of total FDI with U.S. taxation. The elasticity of response is -1.16, slightly less than that estimated for transfers alone.

In column 4 of tables 3.1–3.3, I present the results of the simplest possible formulation of this model, with only the effective marginal tax rate on new investment included as an explanatory variable. The principal reason for eliminating the rate of return variables is to investigate whether the estimated negative tax effect may be related to the definitional relation

Table 3.3   **Regression Results for Total FDI, 1956–84**

Independent Variables				
τ			-1.161	-1.281
			$(.240)$	$(.326)$
t		-5.646		
		(1.696)		
t^1		4.476		
		(2.332)		
r		$.641$	1.082	
		$(.294)$	$(.266)$	
r^1		-1.632	-2.666	
		$(.843)$	$(.449)$	
$r(1 - t)$	$.278$			
	$(.498)$			
$r^1 (1 - t)$	$-.477$			
	(1.024)			
$(1 - t^1)/(1 - t)$	-2.157			
	(1.396)			
Intercept	-1.215	-4.079	-4.18	$-.978$
	(2.712)	(1.603)	(1.198)	$(.367)$
Durbin-Watson statistic	$.46$	1.67	1.80	$.60$
$\bar{R}^2$	$.183$	$.772$	$.765$	$.332$

Note: Dependent variable is the logarithm of $(1000 \times$ FDI/GNP$)$. All independent variables are in logarithms. Standard errors in parentheses.

between the dependent variable and these measures. The results do not indicate that this problem is a real one. The tax variable still has no significant association with retained earnings, but it does have a statistically significant negative association with transfers and total FDI.

New Specifications

In this section, the robustness of the finding that both new transfers of funds and total FDI, but not retained earnings, have a significant negative association with the effective rate of U.S. capital income taxation is tested against the kinds of specification changes suggested earlier. These changes are discussed below.

Linear Specification. The simple association between either total FDI or transfers and the effective tax rate survives the replacement of the logarithmic specification with a linear one. For both transfers and total FDI, the estimated tax rate coefficient implies an elasticity similar to what is obtained in the logarithmic specification; in both cases, the estimated tax coefficient is insignificantly different from zero in explaining retained earnings.

Although there is no theoretical reason for preferring one specification to the other, because of the presence of negative dependent variables the logarithmic specification necessitates the addition to the unlogged value of an arbitrary constant. This procedure clouds the comparison of estimated coefficients across equations, which becomes important below when home country disaggregation is done.

Including Other Explanatory Variables. The vector of explanatory variables is expanded to consider potential nontax influences on FDI. In particular, I include the following.[9]

RGDP: the ratio of total GDP of the seven major investing countries to U.S. GDP, where the foreign GDPs are valued at the purchasing power parity exchange rates calculated by Summers and Heston (1988). This variable is meant to capture the effect of the changing relative size of the principal investing countries compared to the United States.

USUNEMP: the unemployment rate of prime-age males in the United States. This variable is meant to capture potential business cycle effects on FDI.

REXC: the real exchange rate of the U.S. dollar against a GDP weighted average of the seven major investing countries' currencies. Dunning (1985) and Pugel (1985) have suggested that a low dollar reduces comparative production costs in the United States, thus providing an incentive to FDI.

DRIFT: a dummy variable equal to the number of years elapsed since the previous benchmark survey of FDI conducted by the BEA.[10]

Lagged Tax Rate Terms.   Because of the time it takes to implement an investment decision, there may be a lag between changes in the effective tax rate and the effect on FDI. To allow for this possibility, not only the concurrent tax rate but also the tax rate lagged one year and two years are included as explanatory variables.[11] This procedure limits the length of the lag but imposes no structure on the time pattern of the lagged response of investment.

The results of estimating this specification are presented in the first column of table 3.4. Of the nontax explanatory variables, the estimated coefficients on USUNEMP, RGDP, and DRIFT are not significantly different than zero. The estimated coefficient on the real rate of exchange variable,

Table 3.4   **Further Regression Results for FDI**

	Sample Period and Dependent Variable				
Independent Variables	1960–87, FDI/GNP	1969–87, FDI/GNP	1960–87, RE/GNP	1960–87, TR/GNP	1960–87, FDIMF/GNP
τ	−7.11	8.81	1.40	−8.51	.660
	(7.22)	(11.35)	(1.87)	(7.08)	(1.96)
τ_{-1}	4.28	9.47	−.199	4.48	−.53
	(8.35)	(9.23)	(2.16)	(8.17)	(2.27)
τ_{-2}	−10.25	10.82	.689	−10.94	−2.27
	(6.25)	(10.87)	(1.61)	(6.11)	(1.70)
RGDP	−1.36	15.78	.551	−1.91	−3.37
	(6.63)	(20.29)	(1.71)	(6.48)	(1.80)
USUNEMP	10.24	−183.0	−14.95	25.19	13.07
	(40.32)	(77.92)	(10.41)	(39.42)	(10.94)
FUNEMP		440.61			
		(177.41)			
REXC	−6.21	−4.31	−1.49	−4.72	−2.83
	(3.30)	(3.77)	(.851)	(3.22)	(.894)
DRIFT	−.036	−.135	−.050	.014	.0412
	(.114)	(.148)	(.029)	(.111)	(.0309)
Intercept	16.18	−23.70	2.00	14.18	7.77
	(9.66)	(31.33)	(2.50)	(9.45)	(2.62)
$\tau + \tau_{-1} + \tau_{-2}$	−13.08	29.10	1.89	−14.98	−2.14
	(3.46)	(18.72)	(.89)	(3.38)	(.939)
Durbin-Watson statistic	1.30	1.29	1.87	1.24	1.39
$\bar{R}^2$	.677	.717	.455	.696	.558
Mean of dependent variable	2.85	3.91	0.54	2.31	.61

Note: FDI is measured in millions of dollars, and GNP is measured in billions of dollars, so the dependent variable is 1,000 times the actual value of FDI divided by GNP. Standard errors in parentheses.

REXC, is negative and significant, suggesting that a low dollar may in fact have stimulated FDI in the United States.[12] Though not significant, the DRIFT parameter has the expected negative sign, suggesting that FDI may be increasingly underestimated as the time elapsed since the previous benchmark survey increases.

Of the tax rate variables, both the current value and the value lagged two years have a significant negative coefficient. There is substantial multicollinearity among the three tax variables, however. The t-statistic on the estimated sum of -13.3 of the three tax coefficients is -3.67, indicating that it is different than zero at a 95 percent level of confidence. The tax rate elasticity is -1.57 when evaluated at mean values for the entire period.

That this result is not robust to all reasonable specification changes is suggested by the results shown in the second column of table 3.4. When a weighted average of the seven investing countries' unemployment rate is included (denoted FUNEMP), it is highly positively related to FDI, and the tax coefficients now sum to a positive rather than a negative number.[13] Thus, a competing alternative explanation for the time series of FDI is that it has been propelled by deteriorating economic conditions in the home countries.[14] In order to focus on the possible tax influences on FDI, the analyses that follow do not include the foreign unemployment rate variable.

The third and fourth columns of table 3.4 display the results of disaggregating FDI into retained earnings (RE) and transfers of funds (TR). The conclusion drawn from tables 3.1 and 3.2 still holds—that transfers are associated with taxes negatively but that for retained earnings no negative association is apparent.[15] Finally, in the equation shown in the fifth column of table 3.4, the dependent variable is FDI from manufacturing for four countries—Canada, Japan, the Netherlands, and the United Kingdom. The negative association with U.S. effective tax rates is still evident, although the estimated elasticity of response is about three-fifths of what it was for total FDI.

3.4   FDI in the United States by Investing Country

3.4.1   Motivation and Theory of Cross-Country Comparisons

Most countries choose one of two basic options for taxing the income earned abroad by its domestic residents. Under a residence-based (or "worldwide") system, the capital-exporting country taxes its residents' income wherever it is earned. To avoid double taxation, these countries as a rule allow their residents (individuals and corporations) to credit foreign taxes paid against the domestic tax owed on the foreign income. The credit is limited to the tax due under the home country's tax rules. Any home country tax liability in excess of the tax paid to foreign governments, sometimes termed the "repatriation tax," is generally deferred until dividends are remitted to the parent company. Under a source-based (also known as a "territorial" or "exemption") system, foreign-source income is exempt from home country taxation. Furthermore, no credit is given for taxes paid to foreign governments. Which principle applies for a given country may depend on the form that the investment income takes (e.g., dividend, interest, capital gains), the location of the investment (e.g., treaty vs. nontreaty countries), and the extent of ownership and control exercised by the domestic owner.

The effect of a host country's tax structure on inward foreign investment depends on the tax system of the capital-exporting country. For example, when the country of capital export has an exemption tax system, the effective corporate-level rate of tax on FDI is equal to the tax rate imposed by the host country. Therefore, differences among host country effective tax rates would be expected to have an effect on the location decision of investment from exemption countries. The effect of differences in host countries' tax structures would be expected to have less influence on foreign investment from countries that have worldwide tax systems with a foreign tax credit. In a simple case without deferral, unless the host country's tax rate is higher than the home country's tax rate, the effective tax rate on FDI becomes the home country's, regardless of the tax system of the host country. The effective tax rate is more complicated when there is deferral, multicountry investment, and differing definitions of taxable income in different countries. Nevertheless, for firms based in foreign tax credit countries, the effect of the host country's tax system is filtered through the tax system of the home country and may be substantially mitigated.

Of the major countries that make FDI in the United States, some operate exemption systems, while others operate a worldwide system with foreign tax credit. This fortuitous divergence of approach invites an investigation of whether the system of taxing foreign-source income is a factor in the responsiveness of FDI to host and home country taxation. In what follows, I examine the time series of FDI in the United States emanating from seven countries and investigate whether these time series are consistent with several propositions about the effect on FDI of tax rates and systems of taxing foreign-source income.

3.4.2   Trends

Figures 3.4a–3.10a and 3.4b–3.10b present the time series of FDI for each of seven major investing countries, in 3.4a–3.10a as a ratio of U.S. GNP and in 3.4b–3.10b as a ratio of total FDI in the United States by these seven countries. The figures generally show rapid growth in FDI beginning in the early 1970s. They also show the rise in the relative prominence of Japan, whose FDI was negligible in the 1960s but by 1985 represented nearly 20 percent of total FDI in the United States, and the relative decline

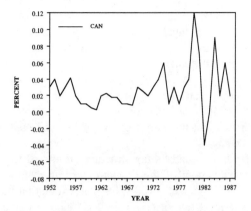

Fig. 3.4a   FDI from Canada as a percentage of U.S. GNP

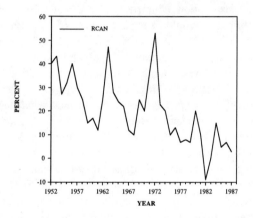

Fig. 3.4b   FDI from Canada as a percentage of total FDI in the United States

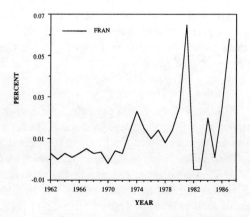

Fig. 3.5a   FDI from France as a percentage of U.S. GNP

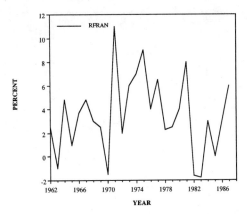

Fig. 3.5b   FDI from France as a percentage of total FDI in the United States

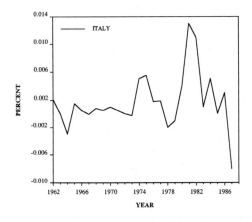

Fig. 3.6a   FDI from Italy as a percentage of U.S. GNP

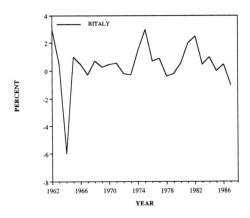

Fig. 3.6b   FDI from Italy as a percentage of Total FDI in the United States

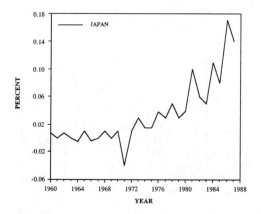

Fig. 3.7a   FDI from Japan as a percentage of U.S. GNP

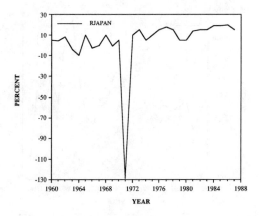

Fig. 3.7b   FDI from Japan as a percentage of total FDI in the United States

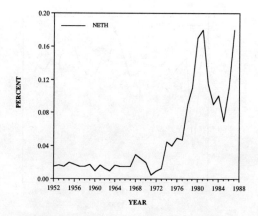

Fig. 3.8a   FDI from the Netherlands as a percentage of U.S. GNP

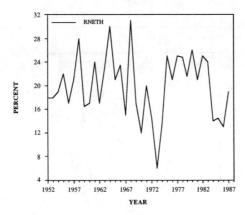

Fig. 3.8b   FDI from the Netherlands as a percentage of total FDI in the United States

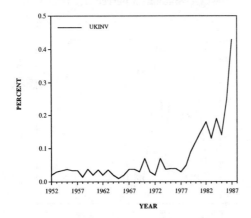

Fig. 3.9a   FDI from the United Kingdom as a percentage of U.S. GNP

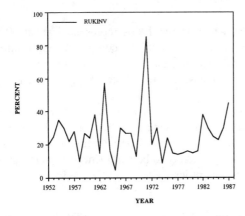

Fig. 3.9b   FDI from the United Kingdom as a percentage of total FDI in the United States

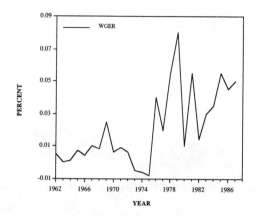

Fig. 3.10a   FDI from West Germany as a percentage of U.S. GNP

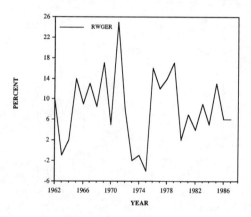

Fig. 3.10b   FDI from West Germany as a percentage of total FDI in the United States

of FDI from Canada, which in the 1960s represented about 30 percent of FDI in the United States but by the 1980s composed significantly less than 10 percent of total FDI. The largest investors for most of this period have been Canada, the Netherlands, and the United Kingdom, challenged in the 1980s by Japan.

Another message that the figures convey is that FDI, while generally (i.e., except for Canada and Italy) growing as a fraction of U.S. GNP since the early 1970s, has followed somewhat different paths in the seven countries. Therefore, no single story is likely to be sufficient to explain the behavior of FDI from each of these countries.

3.4.3   Analysis

As discussed in section 3.4.1, analysis of the FDI data disaggregated by the residence of the investing firms can shed further light on the effect of the host and home countries' tax systems on the magnitude and location of FDI. Two empirical strategies are followed. In the first, separate FDI equations similar to those of table 3.4 are estimated for each of the seven major investing countries. The differences in responsiveness in taxation are then related to the investing country's system of taxing foreign income. In particular, the response of countries with exemption systems is compared to countries with worldwide tax systems and a foreign tax credit. In the second approach, country-specific FDI equations are estimated utilizing time-series data on the statutory corporate tax rates and the effective tax rates on new investment in the home country. These results are then examined for insights into several propositions relating to the effect of taxes on FDI.

Tables 3.5–3.7 present the first set of results for country-specific FDI regressions. Ordinary least squares (OLS) is used in each case.[16] Table 3.5 contains the equations for retained earnings, table 3.6 contains equations explaining transfer of funds, and table 3.7 is concerned with total FDI, each expressed as a ratio to U.S. GNP. The explanatory variables used are identical to those used in the equations of table 3.4, except that the overall GDP ratio and overall real exchange rate are replaced by country-specific variables.

The countries are grouped by their system of taxing income from FDI in the United States. In the first group are countries that effectively exempt such income from domestic taxation—Canada, France, the Netherlands, and West Germany.[17] For these countries' firms, it is the U.S. tax rate, unfiltered by home country tax rules, that affects the attractiveness of FDI in the United States compared to alternative investment locations and compared to no investment at all.

The second group of countries—Italy, Japan, and the United Kingdom—operate a foreign tax credit system with deferral for subsidiaries. U.S. tax is due on the income as earned. When income is repatriated to the home country, the grossed-up earnings are subject to home country taxation, but taxes paid to the U.S. government are credited against tax liability, as long as this liability does not exceed the home country liability on this income.

What the effective total tax rate on investment is in this situation has been the subject of some controversy. In the absence of deferral (and assuming that both home and host country use the same definition of income), the home country tax rate applies unless the host country tax rate exceeds the home country rate, in which case the host country rate applies. With deferral, Hartman (1985) has argued that the host country tax rate is the effective tax rate on investments that are financed by retained earnings, and the above reasoning applies to investments financed by new transfers of funds.

This brief look at received wisdom suggests the following propositions.

1. FDI from exemption countries should be at least as sensitive to U.S. tax rates as FDI from foreign tax credit countries.

Table 3.5   Regression Equations Explaining Retained Earnings, by Investing Country

	Country and Sample Period						
	"Exemption" Countries				**Foreign Tax Credit Countries**		
Independent Variables	Canada, 1960–87	France, 1962–87	Netherlands, 1960–87	West Germany, 1962–87	Italy, 1962–87	Japan, 1960–87	United Kingdom, 1960–87
τ	.692	.180	−.168	−.010	.053	−.229	.479
	(.555)	(.133)	(.829)	(.331)	(.049)	(.378)	(.266)
τ_{-1}	−.324	.0076	.947	−.109	.022	−.239	−.479
	(.635)	(.142)	(.913)	(.353)	(.053)	(.437)	(.313)
τ_{-2}	.478	−.0053	−.452	−.189	−.0013	.132	.084
	(.517)	(.106)	(.675)	(.260)	(.040)	(.334)	(.273)
RGDP	8.72	.162	−36.04	5.35	.116	1.764	.200
	(3.85)	(.594)	(25.89)	(2.30)	(.374)	(.778)	(2.38)
USUNEMP	−5.55	−1.28	−1.34	−3.21	−.229	−2.18	1.34
	(2.57)	(.789)	(3.99)	(1.74)	(.275)	(2.16)	(1.17)
REXC	.307	−.026	−.283	.095	−.000047	.0010	−.535
	(.528)	(.0086)	(.122)	(.045)	(.000019)	(.0006)	(.156)
DRIFT	−.0127	−.0012	−.017	−.0015	−.00045	−.0069	.0034
	(.0076)	(.0019)	(.012)	(.0044)	(.00065)	(.0064)	(.0043)
Intercept	−1.07	.124	2.76	−1.09	.0164	−.517	.401
	(.96)	(.115)	(1.30)	(.50)	(.0567)	(.337)	(.379)
$\tau + \tau_{-1} + \tau_{-2}$	.846	.183	.327	−.398	.074	−.336	−.0012
	(.361)	(.068)	(.526)	(.244)	(.027)	(.192)	(.172)
Durbin-Watson statistic	2.08	1.05	1.44	1.87	1.25	1.26	1.95
$\bar{R}^2$	.479	.759	.304	.099	.543	.240	.390
Mean of dependent variable	.0547	−.00561	.212	.0114	−.00885	.0677	.160

Note: See notes to table 3.4.

Table 3.6   Regression Equations Explaining Transfers of Funds, by Investing Country

| | Country and Sample Period | | | | | | |
| | "Exemption" Countries | | | | Foreign Tax Credit Countries | | |
Independent Variables	Canada, 1960–87	France, 1962–87	Netherlands, 1960–87	West Germany, 1962–87	Italy, 1962–87	Japan, 1960–87	United Kingdom, 1960–87
τ	-.857	-.931	-.108	-1.93	-.219	-1.59	.186
	(1.14)	(.818)	(1.32)	(.960)	(.165)	(1.17)	(2.53)
τ_{-1}	.389	.561	.577	2.17	.126	.633	-1.69
	(1.31)	(.874)	(1.45)	(1.02)	(.178)	(1.351)	(2.98)
τ_{-2}	-.0164	-.613	-1.099	-1.57	.0287	-1.47	-2.79
	(1.065)	(.650)	(1.071)	(.756)	(.132)	(1.03)	(2.59)
RGDP	17.7	.940	-68.8	-3.72	2.53	-4.90	-.879
	(7.94)	(3.65)	(41.1)	(6.67)	(1.25)	(2.41)	(22.6)
USUNEMP	-4.90	-1.35	11.02	-1.55	-.113	5.80	13.5
	(5.28)	(4.84)	(6.33)	(5.06)	(.917)	(6.67)	11.1
REXC	1.48	-.070	-.472	-.229	.00176	-.00476	-2.79
	(1.09)	(.053)	(.194)	(.129)	(.0000655)	(.00186)	(.148)
DRIFT	-.00882	-.0018	.00992	.00265	-.00340	.0136	.0630
	(.0157)	(.0119)	(.0191)	(.0128)	(.00216)	(.0198)	(.0409)
Intercept	-2.67	.765	4.55	2.11	-.477	3.70	3.17
	(1.98)	(.709)	(2.07)	(1.45)	(.189)	(1.04)	(3.60)
$\tau + \tau_{-1} + \tau_{-2}$	-.485	-.984	-.629	-1.33	-.0640	-2.43	-4.30
	(.744)	(.416)	(.834)	(.651)	(.0888)	(.593)	(1.63)
Durbin-Watson statistic	2.07	1.20	1.30	1.32	2.09	1.76	1.12
$\bar{R}^2$	.238	.197	.608	.421	.446	.695	.600
Mean of dependent variable	.227	.113	.369	.192	.0233	.263	.597

Note: See notes to table 3.4.

Table 3.7   Regression Equations Explaining Total FDI, by Investing Country

	Country and Sample Period						
	"Exemption" Countries				Foreign Tax Credit Countries		
Independent Variables	Canada, 1960–87	France, 1962–87	Netherlands, 1960–87	West Germany, 1962–87	Italy, 1962–87	Japan, 1960–87	United Kingdom, 1960–87
τ	−.165	−.751	−.276	−2.03	−.166	−1.82	.666
	(1.33)	(.783)	(1.49)	(.965)	(.163)	(1.15)	(2.64)
τ_{-1}	.0646	.568	1.52	2.06	.148	.394	−.225
	(1.52)	(.834)	(1.64)	(1.03)	(.176)	(1.33)	(3.11)
τ_{-2}	.462	−.618	−1.55	−1.76	.0274	−1.34	−2.71
	(1.24)	(.621)	(1.21)	(.759)	(.130)	(1.02)	(2.71)
RGDP	26.4	1.10	−105	1.63	2.65	−3.13	−.679
	(9.24)	(3.49)	(46.4)	(6.70)	(1.23)	(2.37)	(23.6)
USUNEMP	−10.4	−2.63	9.67	−4.75	−.341	3.63	14.8
	(6.15)	(4.63)	(7.16)	(5.08)	(.905)	(6.56)	(11.6)
REXC	1.78	−.0960	−.755	−.134	.000128	−.00373	−3.32
	(1.26)	(.0503)	(.219)	(.130)	(.0000647)	(.00183)	(1.55)
DRIFT	−.0215	−.00299	−.0068	.00119	−.00385	−.00688	.0664
	(.0183)	(.0114)	(.0215)	(.0128)	(.00214)	(.0195)	(.0428)
Intercept	−3.75	.888	7.32	1.03	−.461	3.18	3.57
	(2.31)	(.678)	(2.33)	(1.46)	(.187)	(1.02)	(3.76)
$\tau + \tau_{-1} + \tau_{-2}$	.361	−.801	−.302	−1.72	.0101	−2.76	−4.30
	(.865)	(.398)	(.943)	(.654)	(.0877)	(.583)	(1.71)
Durbin-Watson statistic	2.02	2.04	1.22	1.60	2.10	1.84	1.09
$\bar{R}^2$	.135	.182	.673	.375	.360	.745	.606
Mean of dependent variable	.282	.112	.581	.203	.0144	.331	.757

Note: See notes to table 3.4.

2. The greater sensitivity of FDI from exemption countries for U.S. tax rates should be most apparent in the behavior of new transfers of funds.

The results shown in table 3.6 offer strong corroboration for the negative association of U.S. tax rates and FDI financed by transfers of funds. The summed tax coefficient is negative for all seven countries and significantly different from zero in four of these cases. The estimated tax effect on retained earnings, shown in table 3.5, ranges from significant positive to significant negative, with no clear trend emerging. For total FDI (shown in table 3.7), the tax effect is significantly negative for four of seven countries. The tax effect in these four countries sums to more than the tax effect shown in the first column of table 3.4.

The regression analyses do not support propositions 1 and 2 strongly. The four countries that have a significant tax effect on transfers and total FDI are evenly divided between exemption countries (Netherlands and West Germany) and foreign tax credit countries (Japan and the United Kingdom). The association of tax rates with retained earnings also has no obvious pattern according to the tax system.

Table 3.8 displays the results of repeating the regressions explaining total FDI for manufacturing investment only. These data are fully available for only four of the seven countries—Canada, Japan, the Netherlands, and the United Kingdom. The summed tax effect for Japan and the United Kingdom remains negative and significantly different from zero. The magnitude of the estimated effect shrinks substantially in the case of Japan, reducing the elasticity from -2.90 to -2.25. The estimated elasticity for the United Kingdom stays about the same as for total FDI. For Canada and the Netherlands, the summed tax effect is, as for total FDI, not significantly different from zero.

3.4.4   The Effect of Home Country Taxation on FDI in the United States

The rate of home country taxation may influence FDI in the United States through at least two different avenues. First, it affects the after-tax return to investment in the home country, which is presumably an alternative to FDI. For this reason, we would expect the home country tax rate to be positively associated with FDI in the United States.

A second avenue of influence applies only to home countries that operate a foreign tax credit system, not countries that operate an exemption system. Ignoring deferral, and assuming that the multinational operates only in at most the home country and the United States, the effective tax rate on income from FDI is the maximum of the U.S. rate and the home country rate.[18] When the home country rate exceeds the U.S. rate, it is the effective tax rate on both home country investment and FDI, and so its level does not affect the relative after-tax returns of the alternative investments, although it does depress the return of all investment alternatives. In a more general situation, when there is deferral and multicountry operation, the home

Table 3.8   **Regression Equations Explaining Total FDI in Manufacturing, by Investing Country**

	Country and Sample Period			
	"Exemption" Countries		Foreign Tax Credit Countries	
Independent Variables	Canada, 1960–87	Netherlands, 1960–87	Japan, 1960–87	United Kingdom, 1960–87
τ	.129	.356	.105	.462
	(.477)	(.874)	(.312)	(1.15)
τ_{-1}	.0419	−.232	−.231	−.723
	(.546)	(1.01)	(.343)	(1.36)
τ_{-2}	−.674	−.173	−.207	−1.21
	(.444)	(.773)	(.254)	(1.18)
RGDP	9.57	−1.19	−10.3	.0639
	(3.31)	(1.80)	(9.73)	(10.31)
USUNEMP	−2.84	2.71	.192	2.26
	(2.20)	(4.99)	(1.50)	(5.07)
REXC	.542	−.00171	−.0687	−1.69
	(.453)	(.00139)	(.0459)	(.675)
DRIFT	−.00707	.00322	.000990	.0301
	(.00656)	(.0148)	(.00451)	(.0187)
Intercept	−1.21	1.02	.839	1.65
	(.827)	(.779)	(.489)	(1.64)
$\tau + \tau_{-1} + \tau_{-2}$	.103	−.369	−.33	−1.47
	(.310)	(.444)	(.198)	(.744)
Durbin-Watson statistic	2.14	1.96	1.46	.711
$\bar{R}^2$	.197	.169	.452	.466
Mean of dependent variable	.160	.152	.0514	.267

Note: See notes to table 3.4.

country tax rate will increase the effective tax rate on FDI, though by less than it increases the tax rate on investment in the home country. Recall, however, Hartman's demonstration that, for investment out of retained earnings, only the host country's tax rate is relevant.

This review of the effects of home country taxation on FDI suggests the following propositions.

3. FDI from exemption countries should be positively related to the rate of home country taxation.

4. FDI financed by new transfers of funds from foreign tax credit countries should have a less clearly positive, or even negative, relation to home country taxation.

5. Retained earnings from foreign tax credit countries should be unaffected by, or positively related to, home country taxation.

Statutory tax rates have an influence on multinationals' decisions, independent of their effect operating through the effective tax rates on investment. A multinational has an incentive to do its borrowing through firms operating in a country with relatively high statutory rates, so as to maximize the tax benefits of the interest deductions. This would imply a negative relation between the volume of transfers and the difference between the U.S. statutory rate and the home country statutory rate. A multinational also has an incentive to set transfer prices so as to show lower income in countries with relatively high statutory rates. Holding other policies constant, this also implies a negative relation between reported retained earnings and the difference between the U.S. statutory rate and the home statutory rate. These effects should be stronger for exemption countries compared to foreign tax credit countries. They should also depend only on current statutory tax rates, with no lagged effect as in the case of investment incentives. The following proposition summarizes these incentives.

6. Both retained earnings and transfers of funds should be negatively related to the current difference between the U.S. statutory corporate rate and the home country statutory corporate rate, with the effect stronger for exemption countries.

Tables 3.9–3.11 present the results of adding four variables to each country-specific regression equation: (i) the effective corporate-level tax rate on new investment in the home country, including the current rate and two lags; and (ii) the difference between the U.S. statutory corporate tax rate and the home country statutory corporate tax rate. Note that these tax rate series are not available for the Netherlands and that therefore regression results for only six countries are presented.

The results do not provide much support for propositions 3–5. According to table 3.11, in no exemption country is the home country's tax rate positively related to FDI. Table 3.10 reveals that the effect of home country taxation on transfers is not obviously more negative for foreign tax credit countries compared to exemption countries. Table 3.9 does suggest that retained earnings are, as proposed, not usually affected by home country taxation in foreign tax credit countries. Proposition 6 fares slightly better, with a significant coefficient of the expected negative sign on the difference in statutory rates occurring for West Germany and Italy (for transfers of funds and total FDI) and no case of a significant positive sign occurring. Note also that the estimated negative effect of U.S. taxation on total FDI for West Germany and Japan disappears when the home country tax rates are included, although a negative effect of U.S. taxes on Canadian investment appears when it did not in the absence of home country tax rates.

There are several possible explanations for the lack of a clear difference in the tax responsiveness of FDI from exemption and foreign tax credit countries. One is that the data are simply not good enough to pick up the differences in behavior that do in fact exist. In particular, the effective tax rate series have well-known problems as accurate measures of the disincentives to invest. Alternatively, it may be that the ability of firms from

Table 3.9 Regression Equations Explaining Retained Earnings Using Home Country Tax Rates, by Investing Country

	Country and Sample Period					
	"Exemption" Countries			Foreign Tax Credit Countries		
Independent Variables	Canada, 1965–86	France, 1962–87	West Germany, 1962–87	Italy, 1962–87	Japan, 1972–87	United Kingdom, 1962–87
τ	.873	.223	−.0421	.0296	.239	.478
	(1.00)	(.166)	(.315)	(.0550)	(1.58)	(.326)
τ_{-1}	−.242	−.0230	.119	.0227	−.135	−.530
	(.874)	(.154)	(.333)	(.0525)	(.983)	(.402)
τ_{-2}	−.205	−.0527	−1.04	.0542	.788	−.0263
	(.795)	(.122)	(.442)	(.0546)	(1.09)	(.422)
T	−.00594	.0577	2.37	−.106	−6.17	.00948
	(.916)	(.114)	(1.14)	(.0612)	(8.59)	(.294)
T_{-1}	.291	.0793	−.658	−.0403	7.09	.0686
	(.632)	(.102)	(.804)	(.0729)	(8.06)	(.262)
T_{-2}	−.560	.0195	.433	.0761	4.73	.166
	(.693)	(.138)	(.865)	(.0533)	(6.51)	(.303)

DIFSTAT	−2.07	.464	1.72	−.0907	.419	−.0274
	(3.11)	(.373)	(1.03)	(.102)	(2.58)	(.535)
RGDP	16.6	−.0211	−1.32	.720	6.03	−.864
	(9.85)	(.937)	(3.87)	(.632)	(10.5)	(3.62)
USUNEMP	−5.66	−1.07	−.301	−.427	−13.3	1.31
	(4.85)	(.833)	(1.96)	(.394)	(9.93)	(1.48)
REXC	.323	−.0281	−.0191	−.0000549	.00181	−.439
	(.740)	(.0101)	(.0707)	(.0000206)	(.00165)	(.235)
DRIFT	−.00396	.0000356	.0115	−.00150	−.0230	.00629
	(.0183)	(.00253)	(.00641)	(.00160)	(.0244)	(.00735)
Intercept	−1.74	.0904	−.624	−.0225	−3.06	.497
	(1.43)	(.154)	(.644)	(.0652)	(2.40)	(.587)
$\tau + \tau_{-1} + \tau_{-2}$	.836	.148	−.963	.107	.891	−.779
	(1.12)	(.0855)	(.427)	(.0302)	(1.59)	(.254)
$T + T_{-1} + T_{-2}$	−.263	.157	2.15	−.0704	5.65	.244
	(1.68)	(.207)	(.897)	(.0610)	(6.57)	(.280)
Durbin-Watson statistic	2.46	1.25	1.69	1.52	1.10	2.03
$\bar{R}^2$	.361	.737	.273	.573	−.145	.219
Mean of dependent variable	.0469	−.00561	.0114	−.00885	.105	.162

Note: See notes to table 3.4.

Table 3.10   Regression Equations Explaining Transfers of Funds Using Home Country Tax Data, by Investing Country

	Country and Sample Period					
	"Exemption" Countries			Foreign Tax Credit Countries		
Independent Variables	Canada, 1965–86	France, 1962–87	West Germany, 1962–87	Italy, 1962–87	Japan, 1972–87	United Kingdom, 1962–87
τ	−1.70	−1.42	−1.63	−.369	.667	−.179
	(1.70)	(1.05)	(.897)	(.187)	(4.50)	(2.13)
τ_{-1}	−.170	.863	1.93	.140	−.239	−3.61
	(1.48)	(.965)	(.949)	(.179)	(2.81)	(2.62)
τ_{-2}	−.235	−.520	1.39	.221	−.0543	.105
	(1.35)	(.769)	(1.26)	(.186)	(3.12)	(2.75)
T	.246	.253	−6.76	−.389	16.6	1.15
	(1.56)	(.716)	(3.25)	(.208)	(24.6)	(1.91)
T_{-1}	2.24	−.0640	−1.64	.123	−17.2	2.69
	(1.07)	(.639)	(2.29)	(.248)	(23.0)	(1.71)
T_{-2}	.707	−.816	4.79	−.0671	16.1	1.55
	(1.18)	(.866)	(2.47)	(.181)	(18.6)	(1.98)

DIFSTAT	-5.82	-2.17	-7.58	-.562	5.41	2.02
	(5.28)	(2.35)	(2.95)	(.347)	(7.39)	(3.49)
RGDP	40.1	-.286	11.7	5.58	-32.1	-37.9
	(16.7)	(5.89)	(11.0)	(2.15)	(30.1)	(23.6)
USUNEMP	-11.0	-1.98	-9.87	-1.56	26.7	13.0
	(8.24)	(5.55)	(5.60)	(1.34)	(28.4)	(9.64)
REXC	1.64	-.0910	.261	.000159	-.0104	-3.08
	(1.26)	(.0635)	(.201)	(.0000701)	(.00472)	(1.53)
DRIFT	-.00938	-.00668	-.0351	-.0108	.0196	.0526
	(.310)	(.0159)	(.0183)	(.00544)	(.0697)	(.0479)
Intercept	-4.79	1.49	-1.43	-.638	9.37	8.59
	(2.43)	(.969)	(1.84)	(.222)	(6.86)	(3.83)
$\tau + \tau_{-1} + \tau_{-2}$	-1.95	-1.08	1.69	-.00784	.374	-3.69
	(1.27)	(.537)	(1.22)	(.103)	(4.55)	(1.66)
$T + T_{-1} + T_{-2}$	3.19	-.627	-3.61	-.333	15.5	5.39
	(2.86)	(1.30)	(2.56)	(.208)	(18.8)	(1.82)
Durbin-Watson statistic	2.09	1.96	2.28	2.44	1.76	1.78
$\bar{R}^2$	.304	.0818	.549	.463	.512	.760
Mean of dependent variable	.269	.113	.192	.0233	.491	.637

Note: See notes to table 3.4

Table 3.11   Regression Equations Explaining Total FDI Using Home Country Tax Data, by Investing Country

	Country and Sample Period					
	"Exemption" Countries			Foreign Tax Credit Countries		
Independent Variables	Canada, 1965–86	France, 1962–87	West Germany, 1962–87	Italy, 1962–87	Japan, 1972–87	United Kingdom, 1962–87
τ	−.829	−1.20	−1.67	−.339	.906	.299
	(2.10)	(1.01)	(.982)	(.172)	(3.88)	(2.28)
τ_{-1}	−.259	.840	2.05	.163	−.374	−4.14
	(1.83)	(.928)	(1.04)	(.164)	(2.42)	(2.82)
τ_{-2}	−.0302	−.572	.349	.275	.733	.0784
	(1.66)	(.740)	(1.38)	(.171)	(2.69)	(2.96)
T	.252	.311	−4.39	−.495	10.5	1.16
	(1.92)	(.689)	(3.55)	(.191)	(21.1)	(2.06)
T_{-1}	2.53	.0153	−2.30	.0828	−10.2	2.76
	(1.32)	(.614)	(2.51)	(.228)	(19.8)	(1.84)
T_{-2}	.147	−.797	5.22	.00902	20.8	1.72
	(1.45)	(.833)	(2.70)	(.166)	(16.0)	(2.12)

LHSTAT	-7.88	-1.70	-5.86	-.653	5.83	1.75
	(6.52)	(2.26)	(3.23)	(.318)	(6.36)	(3.75)
RGDP	56.8	-.307	10.4	6.30	-26.0	-38.7
	(20.6)	(5.67)	(12.1)	(1.97)	(25.9)	(25.4)
USUNEMP	-16.6	-3.06	-10.2	-1.99	13.3	14.3
	(10.2)	(5.34)	(6.13)	(1.23)	(24.4)	(10.4)
REXC	1.97	-.119	.242	.000105	-.00863	-3.52
	(1.55)	(.0611)	(.220)	(.0000643)	(.00406)	(1.64)
DRIFT	-.0133	-.0664	-.0235	-.0123	-.00340	.0588
	(.0383)	(.0153)	(.0200)	(.00499)	(.0600)	(.0515)
Intercept	-6.53	1.58	-2.05	-.660	6.31	9.09
	(2.99)	(.932)	(2.01)	(.203)	(5.90)	(4.11)
$\tau + \tau_{-1} + \tau_{-2}$	-1.12	-.931	.723	.0987	1.27	-3.77
	(.716)	(.517)	(1.33)	(.0942)	(3.92)	(1.78)
$T + T_{-1} + T_{-2}$	2.93	-.470	-1.47	-.403	21.1	5.63
	(3.53)	(1.25)	(2.80)	(1.90)	(16.2)	(1.96)
Durbin-Watson statistic	2.34	1.96	2.16	2.43	2.36	1.71
$\bar{R}^2$	.593	.0547	.422	.464	.661	.750
Mean of dependent variable	.0316	.112	.203	.0144	.596	.799

Note: See notes to table 3.4.

foreign tax credit countries to defer indefinitely home country taxation and to engage in sophisticated financial transactions renders insignificant the effective rate of home country taxation. If the latter hypothesis is true, then the U.S. tax rate is the important source of investment disincentives for all capital-importing countries, regardless of their system of alleviating international double taxation.

3.5 Conclusions

This research was undertaken in order to shed light on the role of both U.S. and investing country tax systems on FDI in the United States. Two distinct approaches were attempted. In the first, the standard empirical model relating total FDI in the United States to U.S. taxation was respecified to (i) eliminate the spurious bias caused by relating retained earnings to a measure of rate of return that would be behaviorally related to retained earnings, (ii) use a measure of the marginal effective rate of tax on new investment rather than an observed average or statutory tax rate, (iii) hold constant the influence of nontax variables on FDI, and (iv) take account of the data collection process, which introduces increasing underestimation of FDI as the time elapsed from the previous benchmark survey of FDI increases. The results of this new empirical approach generally support a negative effect of U.S. effective rates of taxation on total FDI and transfers of funds, but not on retained earnings. There is, however, at least one very successful alternative explanation of FDI in the United States—that it is propelled by stagnation in the home country, as measured by its unemployment rate of prime-age males—that precludes the association of U.S. tax rates with FDI.

In the second approach, I examined the time series of FDI in the United States disaggregated by the seven major investing countries. This disaggregation allows a detailed examination of the effect on FDI in the United States of the rates of home country taxation and the home country's system of taxing foreign-source income (i.e., exemption vs. worldwide taxation with a foreign tax credit). The results of these country analyses generally corroborate the aggregate analysis of the effect of U.S. taxes on FDI. However, they do not generally support several propositions about the different tax sensitivity of FDI from countries that exempt foreign-source income from domestic taxation compared to countries that tax worldwide income and offer a foreign tax credit to mitigate double taxation. The inability to support these propositions may be due to the difficulties in accurately measuring home country effective tax rates, or they may indicate that, because of deferral and the availability of sophisticated financial strategies, the home country tax rate and its system of alleviating international double taxation is not an important determinant of FDI.

Appendix
Data Definitions and Sources

1. *Foreign Direct Investment.* Taken from several issues of the *Survey of Current Business.* The most recent citation is August 1988: "Foreign Direct Investment in the United States: Detail for Position and Balance of Payment Flows," tables 12–19.

2. *U.S. Marginal Effective Corporate Tax Rates* (τ). Auerbach and Hines (1988, table 1, col. 1). The 1987 tax rate is obtained by multiplying their 1986 figure by the ratio of the post-tax-reform and pre-tax-reform effective tax rates on capital in Fullerton and Karayannis (1987, tables IV.5 and IV.6, col. 3).

3. *Foreign Marginal Effective Tax Rates* (T). For France, Italy, the United Kingdom, and West Germany, these are calculated from separate series on the effective tax rate equipment and structures provided by Julian Alworth. The overall effective tax rate is equal to

$$[a_E t_E/(1 - t_E) + a_S t_S/(1 - t_S)] / [a_E/(1 - t_E) + a_S/(1 - t_S)],$$

where t_E and t_S are the effective tax rates on equipment and structures, respectively, and a_E and a_S are the fraction of the capital stock in equipment and structures, respectively. This formula is taken from King and Fullerton (1984). The value of a_E is set to be 0.585 and a_S to 0.415. This corresponds to the fraction of capital stock in equipment and structures, respectively, in manufacturing found by King and Fullerton for both the United Kingdom and West Germany, the only two European countries they investigate.

For Japan, the tax rate series is taken from Tajika and Yui (1988, table 3, col. 4). These calculations include the effect of personal taxes. However, the personal tax parameters are either small in magnitude (the capital gains tax is zero) or unimportant (the tax on dividends is presumed to affect only the cost of capital financed by new share issues, which constitutes only 3.6 percent of total finance). The values for 1985–87 are set equal to the 1984 rate.

For Canada, the tax rate series up to 1981 is from Boadway, Bruce, and Mintz (1987, table 3.3, col. 10). Comparable values for 1982–87 were provided by Jack Mintz.

4. *U.S. and Foreign Statutory Corporate Tax Rates.* U.S. rate taken from Pechman (1987, table A-8). Foreign rates taken from same sources as above. U.S. rate is federal only.

5. *Relative GDP (RGDP).* Up to 1985, real GDP for each country is calculated by multiplying real GDP per capita in current international prices

by the population. The real GDP per capita and population measures are taken from the supplement in diskette to Summers and Heston (1988). Real GDP for 1986 for each country is calculated as the 1985 GDP calculated as above multiplied by one plus the rate of real growth as reported in the Organization for Economic Co-operation and Development's (OECD) *Main Economic Indicators* ([October 1988], 37–41). 1987 real GDP is calculated in a similar manner.

6. *U.S. Unemployment Rate (USUNEMP).* U.S. unemployment rate for males twenty years and over taken from *Economic Report of the President* (1988, table B-39).

7. *Foreign Unemployment Rate (FUNEMP).* For each country, it is the unemployment rate for males ages twenty-five to fifty-four taken from the OECD's *Labour Force Statistics* ([1966–86], 472–501; and various back issues). The overall foreign unemployment rate is a weighted average of these rates, using 1975 real GDPs as the weights.

8. *Real Exchange Rate (REXC).* For each country, it is the product of the nominal exchange rate (foreign currency/U.S.$) and the ratio of GDP deflators (U.S. GDP deflator/foreign GDP deflator). 1987 nominal exchange rates taken from the OECD's *Main Economic Indicators* ([October 1988], 30). 1987 GDP deflators are calculated using the percentage change in GDP deflators from 1986 to 1987 in the OECD's *Quarterly National Accounts* (first quarter 1988). The 1987 GDP deflator for the Netherlands was calculated using the percentage change in the CPI from the OECD's *Main Economic Indicators* ([October 1988], 140). GDP deflators up to 1986 are from the OECD's *National Accounts, Main Aggregates* ([1960–86], chart 31, pp. 138–39). Nominal exchange rates up to 1986 are taken from the same source (chart 2, pp. 150–51).

The overall real exchange rate is calculated by setting real exchange rates in 1975 levels to one and then weighting the change from 1975 real exchange rate levels by their respective shares of real GDP in 1975.

Notes

1. Hartman argues that, because the variable measuring the rate of return to domestic capital is based on replacement costs, it will not capture these valuation effects.
2. Newlon also estimates variants of Hartman's original model with several additional variables, including a quadratic time trend, dummy variables for the years when data revisions were made, and a definition of the return to direct

investment that includes the fees and royalties that accrue to the parent from its foreign subsidiary. Most of these changes do not alter the qualitative results reported earlier.

3. If, however, the home country's tax system is expected to change, then there is an incentive to time repatriations appropriately.

4. The seven countries, whose direct investment in the United States will be analyzed in more detail below, are Canada, France, Italy, Japan, the Netherlands, the United Kingdom, and West Germany.

5. There are several reasons for the striking differences between Hartman's results and the results reported in the first column of tables 3.1 and 3.2. First, all the data have been corrected and updated. That procedure itself renders the coefficient on $r^1(1 - t)$ in the retained earnings equation to be insignificantly different from zero. Second, Hartman deals with the presence of a negative retained earnings value by adding a positive constant to the *numerator* of the dependent variable. Because the denominator (GNP) is growing with time, this is tantamount to adding a gradually declining value. Following Newlon, I add a constant to the left-hand-side variable before taking the logarithm. This reduces the absolute value of most coefficients and renders $r^1(1 - t)$ insignificant in the transfers equation. Finally, the regressions of tables 3.1 and 3.2 extend the sample period back from 1965 to 1956 and forward from 1979 to 1984. The latter eliminates the significance of $r(1 - t)$ in the transfer equation and the combination of the two renders $(1 - t^1)/(1 - t)$ insignificant in both equations.

6. As Hartman (1984) notes, no separate estimate of the pretax rate of return to FDI is available. The value used for r is obtained by assuming that the average rate of corporate and property tax faced by foreigners in the United States (t) is the same as that faced by U.S. residents and solving for r using the known value of $r(1 - t)$.

7. The conclusion does not depend on the log-linear specification. A linear version of these regressions yields the same conclusion.

8. The tax elasticity is equal to $\hat{\beta}[(\bar{y} + k)/\bar{y}]$, where $\hat{\beta}$ is the estimated tax rate coefficient, $\bar{y}$ is the average ratio of transfers to U.S. GNP, and k is the constant added to this ratio before taking the logarithm.

9. See the data appendix for the definition and source of all the variables used in the analyses.

10. Other potential influences on FDI, for which I was unable to obtain reasonable indices, include the extent of current and expected U.S. tariff and nontariff barriers to imports and the degree of quantitative restrictions, such as exchange controls, on outward FDI.

11. Of course this argument also applies to the other influences on FDI. One promising direction for future work is the investigation of more general lag structures.

12. It has been argued that the strong dollar of the early 1980s was in part caused by tax incentives given to investment at that time. This suggests that an instrumental variables estimation technique may be appropriate.

13. Because of data availability, the sample period for this regression begins in 1969 rather than 1960. This is not, however, the source of the difference in results because a version of the regression without FUNEMP that begins in 1969 also shows a significant negative tax effect.

14. Another variable whose inclusion eliminates the tax effect is the dummy variable for the post-1974 era, justified above because the BEA definition of FDI was changed in 1974. Apparently, much of the estimated tax effect reflects the simple fact that the post-1974 era is characterized by high FDI and low taxes, relative to the pre-1974 era.

15. In fact, the sum of the tax coefficients has a positive sign that is significantly different from zero.

16. I also experimented with the method of seemingly unrelated regressions to estimate the seven equations as a system. Because the results were very similar to those obtained using OLS, they are not reported here.

17. By statute, Canada and West Germany operate foreign tax credit systems. However, both countries exempt from domestic taxation business-related income earned within the borders of its treaty partners, including the United States.

18. The home country effective tax rates technically apply to domestically located investment. If the tax law discriminates investment by location (as the U.S. tax law does), then the series on effective tax rates may not accurately capture the tax law's effect on foreign-source income. For example, French and Japanese corporations engaged in foreign investment are entitled to deduct from taxable income certain special reserves. Other details of the home country's tax system may also be important, particularly the degree of corporate and personal tax integration. For example, although by treaty dividends from U.S. subsidiaries to West German parent corporations are untaxed by the West German government, if and when exempt foreign-source income is distributed to shareholders by the parent, it is taxed differently than dividends from earnings on domestic-source income.

References

Alworth, Julian. 1988. *The financial decisions of multinationals*. Oxford: Blackwell.

Auerbach, Alan, and James Hines. 1988. Investment tax incentives and frequent tax reforms. *American Economic Review* 78 (2): 211–16.

Boadway, Robin, Neil Bruce, and Jack Mintz. The economic impact of capital income taxes in Canada. In *Taxes on capital income in Canada: Analysis and Policy*. Canadian Tax Paper, no. 80. Toronto: Canadian Tax Foundation.

Boskin, Michael J., and William G. Gale. 1987. New results on the effects of tax policy on the international location of investment. In *The effects of taxation on capital accumulation,* ed. Martin Feldstein. Chicago: University of Chicago Press.

Caves, Richard. 1982. *Multinational enterprise and economic analysis*. Cambridge: Cambridge University Press.

Dunning, John H., ed. 1985. *Multinational enterprises, economic structure and international competitiveness*. Clichester: Wiley.

Economic Report of the President. 1988. Washington, D.C.: U.S. Government Printing Office, February.

Feldstein, Martin S. 1982. Inflation, tax rules and investment: Some econometric evidence. *Econometrica* 50 (4): 825–62.

Feldstein, Martin S., and Joosung Jun. 1987. The effect of tax rules on nonresidential fixed investment: Some preliminary evidence from the 1980s. In *The effects of taxation on capital accumulation,* ed. Martin Feldstein, 101–62. Chicago: University of Chicago Press.

Fullerton, Don, and Marios Karayannis. 1987. The taxation of income from capital in the United States, 1980–1986. NBER Working Paper no. 2478. Cambridge, Mass.: National Bureau of Economic Research, December.

Gersovitz, Mark. 1987. The effects of domestic taxes on foreign private investment. In *The theory of taxation for developing countries,* ed. David Newbery and Nicholas Stern. New York: Oxford University Press.

Hartman, David G. 1984. Tax policy and foreign direct investment in the United States. *National Tax Journal* 37 (4): 475–88.

————. 1985. Tax policy and foreign direct investment. *Journal of Public Economics* 26: 107–21.

King, Mervyn A., and Don Fullerton, eds. 1984. *The taxation of income from capital.* Chicago: University of Chicago Press.

Newlon, Timothy Scott. 1987. "Tax policy and the multinational firm's financial policy and investment decisions." Ph.D. diss., Princeton University.

Organization for Economic Co-operation and Development. 1987. *International investment and multinational enterprises, recent trends in international direct investment.* Paris.

Organization for Economic Co-operation and Development. Department of Economics and Statistics. 1984. *Balance of payments of OECD countries, 1963–1982.* Paris.

Pechman, Joseph. 1987. *Federal tax policy.* Washington, D.C.: Brookings.

Pugel, Thomas. 1985. The United States. In *Multinational enterprises, economic structure and international competitiveness,* ed. John H. Dunning. Clichester: Wiley.

Summers, Robert, and Alan Heston. 1988. A new set of international comparisons of real product and prices for 130 countries, 1950–1985. *Review of Income and Wealth* 34 (1): 1–25.

Tajika, Eiji, and Yuji Yui. 1988. Cost of capital and effective tax rate: A comparison of U.S. and Japanese manufacturing industries. *Hitotsubashi Journal of Economics* 29 (2): 181–200.

U.S. Department of Commerce. Bureau of Economic Analysis. 1988. Foreign direct investment in the United States: Detail for position and balance of payment flows, 1987. *Survey of Current Business* 68 (8).

Young, Kan H. 1988. The effects of taxes and rates of return on foreign direct investment in the United States. *National Tax Journal* 41 (1): 109–21.

Comment   David G. Hartman

As Joel Slemrod points out, recent empirical work on foreign direct investment has been narrowly focused, making subtle changes to aggregate annual regressions. It is a reflection of the dearth of information, certainly not the elegance of the empirical work in Hartman (1984), that succeeding research has been so single tracked. With so many similar exercises now reported, the question that has to arise is whether a small and suspect information base has been used and reused beyond the limits of statistical validity.

In this paper, Slemrod pursues "two distinct approaches" for enhancing our knowledge of tax effects on foreign investment. It is his second approach that breaks with tradition, by looking at investment in the United States by home country, and truly advances the level of debate, it is to be hoped for good. But, first, Slemrod goes back over some familiar territory, extending and updating the standard model in several ways.

David G. Hartman is Group Vice President and Chief International Economist with DRI/McGraw-Hill and a research affiliate of the National Bureau of Economic Research.

His first objective is to eliminate the spurious correlation between retained earnings investment and the rate of return, which could result from the inclusion of retained earnings as part of the total return calculation. He tests for possible bias by estimating separate coefficients for taxes, $\ln(t)$, and gross rates of return, $\ln(r)$, finding that the tax effect is not confirmed.

With less than half of earnings typically reinvested in aggregate (and with reinvestment ratios quite variable), it is not generally true that investment exhausted earnings, creating an artificial rather than behavioral relation between rate of return and investment. Nevertheless, doubts should at least be raised about spurious correlation due to measurement errors in earnings. So I concur completely with Slemrod's emphasis on the problem, which I highlighted in my original paper and in my comments on Boskin and Gale. But I wish he had followed my procedure of separating of $\ln[r(1 - t)]$ into $\ln(r)$ and $\ln(1 - t)$, which had strongly confirmed the coefficient of the combination variable (using then-available data, over a shorter interval). As it stands, we cannot tell if Slemrod's results differ because of the shift in functional form or because the relation I identified was not robust across data revisions and time intervals. With the surge in international investment in the 1980s, and particularly in highly leveraged corporate acquisitions, it would be unremarkable if previous relations no longer held.

Another disturbing aspect of Slemrod's proposed remedy is that it does not really address the problem. By all logic, the spurious correlation would exist between retained earnings and the after-tax return, $r(1 - t)$, so testing whether t matters on its own cannot distinguish between a spurious and a causal relation.

Two procedures that might help were pursued in my 1984 paper: to instrument $r(1 - t)$ by its value lagged a year and to see if there is a rate of return effect on the dividend payout ratio (which, of course, has the offending earnings figure in both numerator and denominator).

Slemrod's second objective is to replace average tax rate measures by marginal rate measures. The reader tends to accept without question a statement that marginal rates are better, but in this case I am not sure. Probably more often than not, the direct investment decision of the 1980s is whether to buy a U.S. company, or at least whether to buy an existing U.S. plant, in which case the average tax rate could well be more relevant.[1] Even leaving acquisitions aside, foreign direct investment is far less likely than domestic investment to be ''purely marginal'' since it will frequently involve the development of an entire operation rather than an addition to capital alone. All that having been said, the use of the Auerbach-Hines tax terms confirms the previous conclusions.

Finally, Slemrod seeks to confirm prior results by including a variety of alternative explanatory variables. While one can always criticize such efforts, I think we too seldom employ eclectic tests of robustness.

What does concern me is that, from this point on, Slemrod abandons the model of foreign investment as a function of rates of return. Once again, the potential for spurious correlation between investment and the rate of return is Slemrod's concern, but it is far from clear what theory of investment is implied by a specification that keeps only the tax rate and then adds alternative variables. For instance, a model could be advanced to relate the relative growth rates of GNP to investment. But the results from table 3.4 are based on equations including levels of GNP.

Of even more concern than the lack of a well-specified model is the possibility that the tax rate itself might be cyclically sensitive. If so, the tax parameter could tend to proxy for the gross rate of return to investment, and all interpretations of its coefficient would be suspect.

In general, annual time-series analysis puts a premium on testing clean and parsimonious alternative specifications. Adding variables without clear theoretical justification can test robustness, but annual time series are so highly correlated that some added variable is almost bound to reduce the significance of the tax effect.

So I am not as disturbed as Slemrod that a foreign unemployment variable is highly (positively) related to direct investment in the United States to the extent of reversing estimated tax effects. As far as we can tell from the paper, the result emerges only in equations without rate of return variables. If unemployment is serving as a proxy for the return to investment, it is probably a poor one. Could it serve as a proxy for the after-tax return just as well as a proxy for the gross return? If so, the lack of an independent tax effect is not disturbing. On the other hand, unemployment as a measure of labor market conditions and not a proxy for general business conditions would surely have the opposite sign. So I would not be quick to conclude that this is an "alternative explanation." It may simply be that too many experiments are being conducted on the limited and crude information base available.

I find Slemrod's other additions more significant. His result that the dollar matters is new, interesting, and plausible. The attempt to correct for the nonlinkage of data around benchmark survey years is even more useful. Indeed, I found the fact that inclusion of a dummy variable for the post-1974 era eliminates the tax effect to be the most interesting result of the first half of the paper.[2] The discussion, relegated to a note, is certainly sobering. Nonetheless, I believe that Slemrod's conclusion that the estimated tax effects are arising solely from the recent investment surge in a low-tax environment is too harsh. Significant results such as those in my 1984 paper were produced in a period before both phenomena.

The test of any extension of similar work is what conclusions were supported or rejected. Slemrod generally finds tax effects that seem fairly robust, but he finds them in direct investment by funds transfers and not in retained earnings investment. These results are interesting in reversing many of the prior conclusions, while supporting others. Slemrod has taken considerable care to find the sources of divergence between his results and prior work, a procedure that is all too seldom followed in this field. The conclusions here are, thus, highly useful, particularly in pointing out where earlier results were not robust.

When Slemrod turns to the disaggregation by home country, he uses the formulation that includes the "other explanatory variables" but not any gross rate of return measures. My previous comments thus apply to the remainder of the paper.

That said, I think that this effort is headed in a very positive direction and that Slemrod is in many cases too tough on himself, in that he presented a difficult set of propositions for testing.

For example, he first looks at U.S. tax effects on foreign investment, hoping to see distinctions in the responsiveness of investment from "exemption countries" and "tax credit countries." All the tax effects on direct investment involving transfers of funds are of the correct sign, and four of seven are significant. Despite the fact that there is not an obvious pattern of greater significance in "exemption countries," and despite the perverse results for retained earnings investment, I find these results encouraging. There are a variety of reasons for expecting a lack of sharp results in the disaggregation by home country.

One problem is simply the identity of the home country. As Slemrod points out, the 1974 benchmark shifted from a definition that included some "ultimate beneficial owners" to a consistent "first foreign entity in the ownership chain" standard. That definitional change produced a break in each time series, sometimes with large consequences for the country identification of investors. Furthermore, it highlighted the difficulty of defining the national identity of and relating to national tax parameters the behavior of entities that are fundamentally global.

Disaggregation also emphasizes the effect of singular events in the data. For instance, one of the more striking patterns is that of Japan, shown in figure 3.7b. The extreme 1971 Japanese retreat from the United States was entirely accounted for by a $487 million disinvestment by "other industries" after a history of investment never exceeding double digits. This episode, which has all the earmarks of a single large transaction, is far from unusual in the foreign investment data. These events merely contribute to a pattern in the aggregate data but can easily overwhelm all else in disaggregated analysis. Especially in an era of large acquisitions, we are faced with very "noisy" disaggregated data.

A related point is that the industry composition of investment varies by country. In estimating tax effects, it is critical that the relevant tax parameters be identified. But, if various NBER tax projects have taught one lesson above all, it is that the variation in effective tax rates across industries may overwhelm the variations through time or across countries. Investments involving the countries analyzed by Slemrod certainly have very different sectoral compositions. For total direct investment as of 1987, manufacturing led with 35 percent, followed by trade (18 percent), petroleum (14 percent), and real estate (9 percent). Japan, by contrast, had nearly three-quarters of its U.S. investment in the trade sector as recently as 1983. The recent surge in real estate raised its share to 13 percent in 1987, with trade falling to less than half. While only about 16 percent of Japan's investment is in U.S. manufacturing, that sector accounts for about 90 percent of France's investment. The Netherlands and the United Kingdom are far more focused on petroleum investments than the average. In general, average U.S. tax rates would be expected to have varying degrees of relevance to investments by different countries. This is particularly true in light of the special U.S. tax treatment of real estate and petroleum.

In summary, the data by country are very noisy; also, it is hard to identify the relevant "home" country; and, even then, the extent to which the measured tax rates are relevant varies. For these reasons, it is no surprise that the strength of estimated tax effects cannot easily be related to the home country's treatment of foreign-source income. To me, the real surprise is the success in identifying consistent U.S. tax effects on investment by transfer of funds.

Slemrod then goes on explicitly to include measures of home country taxes; there is little confirmation of the hypotheses he wants to test. Again, the lack of significance could have been anticipated. Still relevant here are all the concerns about the singular events that dominate the data, the national identity of firms, and the industry composition of investment (the relevance of the measured tax rates is questionable for both the United States and the host country this time). A related issue is the standard against which U.S. investments are judged by a global firm. The relevant tax comparison for a U.K. subsidiary of a Dutch firm thinking of investing in the United States might be between Canada and the United States (rather than the United Kingdom and the United States as measured here). Obviously, the situations can be highly complex, but the number of parameters estimated here has already exceeded what one can probably expect from the data.

Perhaps most important, the sign of the home country tax parameter is indeterminate from economic theory. Under a foreign tax credit system, as Slemrod points out, higher home country taxes tend to favor U.S. investment over home country investment but tend to discourage both. But, even in the case of an exemption system, the case is far from clear. Recent investment research has established a theoretical role for internal cash flow, legitimizing what have long been highly robust empirical models. In such a model, foreign investment would be negatively affected by even those home country taxes that do not directly apply to operations abroad. Not only is the sign of the tax effect indeterminate, but it depends in part on each country's financial structure and on the "average firm's" situation.

So, for a wide variety of theoretical and practical reasons, it is not surprising that a crisp set of conclusions about home country tax effects fails

to emerge. It is probably enough that the U.S. tax effects identified ea[r]
generally hold up in the presence of home country tax parameters.

Like most prepared conference comments, these accentuate the neg[...]
and are more critical than my overall opinion of Slemrod's efforts. [...]
moving this area of research in a very positive direction, despi[...]
monumental data problems that he has confronted. There is still much[...]
done—I think, for example, that there is hope for analysis by indust[...]
country, despite the data being even noisier. In any case, researching fo[...]
investment and especially the effects of tax policy is a dirty job (not for t[...]
purist), but I hope that Slemrod and others keep doing it.

Notes

1. *Survey of Current Business* reports (e.g., May 1988, 50–58) imply that annual
U.S. acquisitions have typically been between 50 and 100 percent as large as total
direct investment in the 1980s. The figures are not directly comparable since
acquisitions financed by U.S. debt would not count as direct investment.

2. The dummy variable reflects the new benchmark and associated definitional
changes in the calculation of direct investment. As Commerce noted in comparing the
1974 figures under both definitions, the changes were very significant. Under the new
definitions, the 1974 direct investment stock was 21 percent higher, while direct
investment income was 29 percent lower

4 Multinational Corporations, Transfer Prices, and Taxes: Evidence from the U.S. Petroleum Industry

Jean-Thomas Bernard and Robert J. Weiner

Whenever goods cross national borders within the channels of a multinational corporation (MNC), a transfer price must be calculated for tax purposes. When corporate tax rates differ on the two sides of the border, the MNC has an incentive to set its transfer prices in a way that reduces its tax burden by reporting higher profits in the country where corporate profits are taxed more lightly.

The ability of MNCs to set transfer prices to minimize taxes, however, is circumscribed by the tax regulations of the home and host countries. In the United States, Section 482 of the Internal Revenue Code requires that transfer prices for imports and exports of goods and services be set equal to "arm's length prices."

Defining *arm's length prices* is often nontrivial. Unless the good transferred is perfectly homogeneous and has a well-functioning arm's length market, determination of "arm's length" prices will involve some arbitrariness. The process of determining arm's length prices in practice is one of negotiation with the U.S. Internal Revenue Service (IRS). The numerous court cases involving arm's length pricing (LaMont 1975) are an indication that the process is not cut and dried.

Jean-Thomas Bernard is professor of economics and director of GREEN at Université Laval, Québec. Robert J. Weiner is assistant professor of economics at Brandeis University and adjunct research fellow at the EEPC, Kennedy School of Government, Harvard University.

The authors are grateful to Danny Bélanger for able assistance and to Shantayanan Devarajan, William W. Hogan, Robert Stern, Robert Stobaugh, Raymond Vernon, and participants in the 1988 Summer Institute on International Aspects of Taxation, National Bureau of Economic Research, the 1988 "Journées du GREEN," and seminars at the Canadian Department of Finance and Brandeis, Harvard, and Laval Universities for comments. We thank the Energy and Environmental Policy Center, John F. Kennedy School of Government, Harvard University, where Bernard was visiting fellow when this paper was conceived, for hospitality. Opinions expressed, as well as any errors, are the authors'.

Allegations of "abuses" of transfer pricing are widespread, where *abuse* is loosely defined as a divergence between transfer prices and some notion of arm's length prices. These allegations are supported by some indirect evidence (Lall 1973; Vaitsos 1974; Jenkins and Wright 1975; Roumeliotis 1977; Bertrand 1981), but there have been no direct comparisons of interaffiliate and arm's length prices. This paper carries out such a study for the U.S. petroleum industry.

The main reason for choosing the petroleum industry is data availability. The main limitation in examining this industry is that its tax history in the United States, for both purely domestic companies and multinationals, has been quite different from that of manufacturing. Thus, one should be extremely cautious in generalizing results from petroleum to other industries.

Nevertheless, there is much to be said for examining petroleum, quite apart from data availability. As seen in table 4.1, in the last decade for which tax data are available, the oil and gas industry has accounted for between one-third and two-thirds of U.S. taxable income from abroad, paid well over half of foreign taxes, and earned a similar fraction of foreign tax credits. Roughly speaking, the petroleum industry from this standpoint is about as large as all other industries combined.

Table 4.1 is also useful for obtaining a rough idea of the tax position of the industry. From column 5, the average foreign tax rate is very high, more than double that for other industries. From column 6, the ratio of the foreign tax credit to U.S. taxable income from abroad is close to the U.S. statutory corporate tax rate, suggesting that there was little tax left to be paid at home. From column 7, whereas other industries were able to offset almost every dollar of foreign tax paid against U.S. tax liabilities, the petroleum industry was able to offset only half to three-quarters of the foreign taxes it paid. These figures are averages across all countries; as discussed below, situations vary from one country to another.

The U.S. petroleum industry has been alleged to be a notorious abuser of transfer pricing (see, e.g., U.S. Congress 1977; Bertrand 1981). In addition to purely political considerations, there are at least three reasons for this. First, until the mid-1970s, U.S. MNCs were permitted by the IRS to treat virtually all payments to governments for oil abroad as foreign income taxes, enabling the companies to deduct these costs directly from their U.S. tax liabilities rather than from their taxable income.[1] The incentive was thus very strong for them to make these payments appear as large as possible.

The second reason is the nature of the petroleum market. Crude oil, a raw material, accounts for most of the petroleum moving in international trade. Until the 1980s, there was virtually no spot-auction market in crude oil (see Hubbard and Weiner 1989). The arm's length market was one of long-term contracts. Crude oil is not a homogeneous product, and contract terms depend inter alia on its sulfur and gravity, size of ship transporting the cargo, and terms of credit. In addition, as Hines (1988b) points out, the contractual relation itself can have value by, for example, mitigating moral hazard problems (referred to in the contracting literature as "opportunism"; see Williamson 1975). Moreover, the market for crude oil is not competitive; rather, it has been dominated by OPEC, a cartel whose power has waxed and waned over time. Oligopolistic interaction among sellers is likely to lead to varying degrees of freight absorption in markets with geographically dispersed production, so that the arm's length price will depend on the exporting country and point of destination. In the case of petroleum, the Atlantic and Pacific markets are particularly likely to differ because moving the product between them is costly.

The final reason is the sheer size of the industry. While crude oil is not perfectly homogeneous, it is more homogeneous than other products often cited for transfer-price abuse such as pharmaceuticals. Although the scope for transfer-price manipulation may be substantially smaller as a percentage of arm's length price, when multiplied by the enormous volume of petroleum moving in international trade, the revenue transferred, and tax avoided, is potentially great.

Suspicions of tax evasion through transfer pricing by the industy have not been limited to researchers and politicians. In 1978, the IRS created a special unit, the Petroleum Industry Program, to monitor the industry and, inter alia, make determinations regarding arm's length prices. The U.S. Department of Energy (DOE) monitored transfer prices in the course of administering the regulatory program imposed on the domestic petroleum industry in the 1970s. This monitoring process is the source of the data used in this study, which were required to be submitted to the U.S. Energy Information Administration (EIA), the data-collection branch of DOE, by American companies that import crude oil.

The approach in this paper is as follows. First, we use regression methods to isolate systematic differences between third-party and interaffiliate prices, controlling for the factors discussed above. One hypothesis we examine is whether the rise of the spot market and centralization of IRS petroleum expertise at the end of the 1970s resulted in a reduced scope for creative transfer pricing. We then go on to relate these differences to the tax regimes of exporting countries.

4.1 Data

The data were obtained from EIA, which deleted any information that would allow identification of individual firms. The data are described in some detail in Weiner (1986) and Anderson (1988);[2] the discussion here is limited to attributes salient to this paper. The data cover the period October 1973–October 1984,[3] a period that encompasses tremendous variations in oil prices, changes in the structure of the petroleum industry, and tax rates. The data base contains information on dates of loading and importation,

Table 4.1   U.S. Foreign Income, Tax, and Tax Credit, Oil and Gas Industry versus all Industries ($ million)

	(1) U.S. Taxable Income from Foreign Sources	(2) Foreign Tax Paid or Accrued	(3) Foreign Tax Carryover	(4) Foreign Tax Credit Computed	(5) Foreign Tax as % of U.S. Taxable Income (2)/(1)	(6) Foreign Tax Credit as % of U.S. Income (4)/(1)	(7) Foreign Tax Credit as % of Foreign Tax (4)/(2)	(8) Foreign Tax Carryover as % of Credit (3)/(4)
1972:								
Oil and gas	6,760	5,415	1,429	3,252	.801	.481	.601	.439
Other industries	9,720	3,514	323	3,365	.361	.346	.958	.096
All industries	16,486	8,929	1,752	6,617	.542	.401	.741	.265
Oil and gas/all industries	.410	.607	.816	.492				
1974:								
Oil and gas	32,186	26,668	4,366	15,516	.829	.482	.582	.281
Other industries	14,584	5,040	363	4,740	.346	.325	.940	.077
All industries	46,770	31,708	4,729	20,256	.678	.433	.639	.233
Oil and gas/all industries	.688	.841	.923	.766				
1976:								
Oil and gas	37,459	33,368	3,999	17,820	.891	.476	.534	.224
Other industries	17,955	5,841	655	5,760	.325	.321	.986	.114

All industries	55,414	39,209	4,654	23,580	.708	.426	.601	.197
Oil and gas/all industries	.676	.851	.859	.756				
1978:								
Oil and gas	36,148	31,148	18,270	17,111	.862	.473	.549	1.068
Other industries	29,002	9,504	990	9,235	.328	.318	.972	.107
All industries	65,150	40,652	19,260	26,346	.624	.404	.648	.731
Oil and gas/all industries	.555	.766	.949	.649				
1980:								
Oil and gas	31,515	18,859	3,175	14,080	.598	.447	.747	.225
Other industries	39,026	11,137	1,036	10,801	.285	.277	.970	.096
All industries	70,541	29,996	4,211	24,881	.425	.353	.829	.169
Oil and gas/all industries	.447	.629	.754	.566				
1982:								
Oil and gas	20,670	12,430	15,872	9,022	.601	.436	.726	1.759
Other industries	38,812	10,365	1,598	9,922	.267	.256	.957	.161
All industries	59,482	22,795	17,470	18,944	.383	.318	.831	.922
Oil and gas/all industries	.348	.545	.909	.476				

Sources: U.S. Dept. of the Treasury, Internal Revenue Service, *Statistics of Income*, various publications.

exporting country, port of landing, f.o.b. and landed prices, sulfur and gravity, credit terms, volume, and transaction type for cargoes of crude oil imported into the United States during this period.[4] While some previous analysts have concluded that the absence of a "market price" precludes assessment of transfer-price manipulation (Rugman 1985), we are able to take advantage of this information in the regression analysis, thereby correcting for much of the heterogeneity discussed above.

For our purposes, the most interesting aspect of the data base is the breakdown of imports by type of transaction, whether interaffiliate transfers (designated type A below) or arm's length purchases. The latter is further broken down into purchases directly from host governments (type H), "third-party" purchases (purchases from other firms, designated type T), and arm's length purchases with type of seller unreported (type U). The decline of the major multinational oil companies and the rise of state enterprises in oil-exporting countries is reflected in the falling share over time of interaffiliate transfers relative to arm's length transactions. The breakdown of transaction types for purchases from each oil-exporting country is provided for an illustrative year in table 4.2.

4.2 Hypotheses Regarding Transfer Pricing

The hypotheses about transfer-price behavior are straightforward. Multinational petroleum companies set transfer prices that differ from their arm's length prices when they have the incentive and the ability to do so. Ceteris paribus, firms that produce crude oil in countries with effective marginal corporate tax rates (t_f) that exceed the rate in the United States (t_{US}) will reduce their tax obligations by reporting transfer prices as low as possible. At the margin, the dollar in profit "lost" in the host country will reduce firms' tax obligations by t_f, while increasing their U.S. tax obligation by an amount $t_{US} < t_f$. Similarly, when $t_{US} > t_f$, firms have an incentive to report greater profits in the host country, in order for as much of their revenue as possible to be taxed at the lower rate abroad.

In practice, calculations of tax obligations are complicated by the fact that U.S. MNCs must pay U.S. corporate tax on income earned by their foreign subsidiaries. In order to avoid double taxation, the IRS allows U.S. MNCs to credit foreign taxes paid against their U.S. tax obligations. In terms of this very simple model, the U.S. MNC would owe U.S. tax of $t_{US} - t_f$ on the marginal dollar of profit if $t_{US} > t_f$. If the foreign rate exceeds the U.S. rate, the U.S. MNC owes no tax to the United States at the margin.

When $t_{US} > t_f$, U.S. MNCs nonetheless have an incentive to report profits abroad because the U.S. tax owed is payable only when the profit is repatriated to the United States. By investing their profits abroad, U.S. MNCs can thus defer their U.S. tax obligations. When t_f exceeds t_{US}, the difference is an excess foreign tax credit, which the U.S. MNC can carry

Table 4.2   **Number of Transactions by Type, 1981**

Country	H	T	A	Other	Total
			Type of Transaction		
Abu Dhabi	2	7	60	0	69
Algeria	18	73	150	1	242
Angola	0	10	20	0	30
Brunei	0	11	0	0	11
Cameroon	0	12	14	0	26
Canada	0	13	145	0	158
China	0	2	0	0	2
Congo	0	23	0	0	23
Dubai	5	0	4	0	9
Ecuador	6	5	19	0	30
Egypt	2	1	11	0	14
Gabon	0	5	26	0	31
Indonesia	24	94	196	0	314
Iraq	4	0	0	0	4
Libya	32	55	125	3	215
Malaysia	0	4	15	0	19
Mexico	232	38	342	2	614
Neutral Zone	0	0	25	0	25
Nigeria	26	181	218	4	429
Norway	8	75	60	1	144
Oman	0	13	7	0	20
Peru	3	6	12	0	21
Qatar	3	3	0	0	6
Saudi Arabia	0	162	592	4	758
Sharjah	0	0	6	0	6
Syria	2	1	0	0	3
Trinidad	3	27	97	0	127
United Kingdom	17	56	92	2	167
Venezuela	100	83	117	2	302
Zaire	0	0	23	0	23
Undefined	12	52	66	0	130
Total	499	1,012	2,442	19	3,972
(%)	(13)	(25)	(61)	(1)	(100)

Note: H = host government, T = third party, A = affiliate.

forward against future U.S. tax obligations. Thus, the incentives for transfer-price manipulation described above are present even when foreign taxes are creditable against U.S. taxes.[5]

Because the comparison we undertake is so straightforward, we do not present a formal theoretical model of transfer pricing in this paper. A model that integrates some features of the theoretical literature in this area can be found in Eden (1985), where it is demonstrated that tariff rates, as well as corporate tax rates, can influence transfer-price decisions. Although the

United States has imposed a tariff on crude oil imports since 1973 (when it switched from a quota), the tariff is very small ($0.20/barrel, corresponding to a rate of roughly 1 percent) and is neglected in our analysis.

Transfer prices can also serve purposes other than reduction of tax obligations (e.g., providing signals for managerial incentives within the firm; see Eccles 1985). These other considerations will confound efforts to examine hypotheses regarding tax factors only if they vary systematically with tax rates, which appears unlikely.

The scope for multinational firms to set transfer prices to minimize their tax obligations is constrained by the tax regulations of their home and host countries and by the ability of the tax authorities to enforce these regulations. In the United States, the relevant regulation is Section 482 of the Internal Revenue Code, which requires that transfer prices be set at arm's length prices. The regulations acknowledge the difficulty often involved in the establishment of arm's length prices. Section 482 specifies that, if "comparable" third-party transactions exist, then they must be used in determining arm's length prices. Firms have considerable discretion in deciding what constitutes "comparable," however. In the event that no comparable transaction exist, firms are instructed to choose, in descending hierarchy, the "resale price" method (which uses downstream arm's length prices to impute upstream transfer prices), the "cost-plus" method, or any other pricing method that can be justified to the IRS.[6] Using FTC line-of-business data for 1975, Benvignati (1985) estimated that 24 percent of transfer prices set for goods exported from the United States to affiliates abroad were established using the comparable-third-party and resale-price methods, 57 percent using the cost-plus method, and 19 percent using other methods. Unfortunately, the FTC data do not cover interaffiliate imports into the United States. In contrast, the breakdown for interaffiliate transfers within the United States (where tax considerations do not enter) in 1975 was 49 percent comparable-third-party and resale-price methods, 29 percent cost-plus method, and 22 percent other methods.

The null hypothesis here is that the U.S. tax authorities are sufficiently knowledgeable about the arm's length market in crude oil and sufficiently capable at enforcing transfer-price regulations that MNCs are obliged to set the prices for their interaffiliate transactions equal to prices prevailing for third-party transactions. As noted above, the heterogeneity of the product and third-party contract terms will tend to complicate efforts to establish arm's length prices with which to compare a firm's transfer prices. However, IRS enforcement of the arm's length yardstick need not be perfect to deter the practice of using transfer prices to avoid taxes. As detailed in Robbins and Stobaugh (1973), there are many channels through which MNCs can shift funds between affiliates besides trade transactions, including dividend payments, loans, service fees and overhead charges, and royalties. Depending on the costs of doing so, MNCs may choose one or more of these other channels as a means of shifting profits among tax jurisdictions.

In addition to testing for differences between arm's length and transfer prices, we examine below the hypothesis that MNCs transfer funds between tax jurisdictions by charging themselves above- or below-market rates of interest on their credit transactions. The effective interest rates charged are imputed from the sensitivity of f.o.b. prices to credit terms. The higher the effective interest rate, the more an increase in the number of days credit should raise the purchase price. In other words, the effective interest rate rises with $d(\text{price})/d(\text{credit days})$.

The hypothesis here is that U.S. multinationals would like their affiliates in countries with relatively low marginal corporate tax rates to "charge" high interest rates on their transfers to affiliates in countries where such rates are relatively high, thereby tranferring income to jurisdictions where it is taxed more lightly. Effective interest rates are of course unobservable, but this hypothesis can nonetheless be tested using a two-step procedure similar to the one mentioned above for prices. The first step is a comparison of regression coefficients for $d(\text{price})/d(\text{credit days})$ for arm's length and interaffiliate transactions, in order to locate significant differences. The second is to relate any such differences to tax rates abroad. If MNCs are transferring funds in this manner, the correlation between foreign tax rates and "excess" effective interest rates, as measured by: $d(\text{price})/d(\text{credit days})_{\text{interaffiliate}} - d(\text{price})/d(\text{credit days})_{\text{third-party}}$, should be negative.

The statistical work below constitutes the first systematic test of the effectiveness of transfer-price regulations. Scattered indirect evidence suggests that the IRS is active in attempting to enforce Section 482. Plasschaert (1979) reports that, in 1968–69, the IRS investigated 871 cases of international interaffiliate transactions. The largest number (roughly a third of the total) of potential adjustments concerned transfer prices in trade transactions. Only 26.9 percent of the adjustments were actually implemented, but those that were involved fairly large dollar figures. According to Plasschaert, two-thirds of the firms surveyed by the Conference Board in 1970 and 1971 have been subject to adjustments under Section 482.

4.3 Empirical Tests

Our objectives for the empirical work are three. First, we want to determine whether interaffiliate prices and third-party prices differ significantly, in both an economic and a statistical sense, and whether any such differences vary systematically over time. Second, we wish to identify the exporting countries, if any, that exhibit such differences. Our final desire is to relate any country-specific differences we find to tax rates in oil-exporting countries.

The approach that we adopt is as follows. We conduct OLS regressions with the purchase price as the dependent variable. Crude oil transactions have traditionally been conducted on an f.o.b. basis, and, with a few exceptions, our purchase price data are quoted f.o.b. point of export.[7] To control for any systematic differences in prices caused by factors other than the relation between parties in the transaction, the following explanatory variables are included: gravity, sulfur content, size of shipment, and dummy variables for spot transactions, port of entry into the United States (East and Gulf Coasts, West Coast, Hawaii, Guam, and unknown), and credit terms.

Separate regressions were run for each year, both because the effect of the control variables on price is likely to vary with changing conditions in the oil market over time and because we are interested in changes over time in differences between third-party and transfer prices, for the reasons discussed above.[8] A dummy variable is used for each loading month to control for intrayear fluctuations in oil prices.

To conduct hypothesis tests, we include separate dummy variables for each transaction type (interaffiliate transfer, third-party purchase, host-government purchase) for each country that exported crude oil to the United States in a given year.[9] We test whether the regression coefficients for third-party transactions and interaffiliate transfers are equal for each exporting country. In equation form, the null hypothesis is $t_{ij} - a_{ij} = 0$, $i = 1, \ldots, q_j$, where t_{ij} and a_{ij} are the regression coefficients on the third-party and interaffiliate dummy variables for country i in the regression for year j, and q_j is the number of countries that exported crude oil to the United States in year j through both these transaction types.[10]

The standard technique for testing the null hypothesis that the q_j length vector $t_j - a_j = 0$ is to construct an F-ratio based on the squared errors from the constrained (the constraints being the equality of all the t_j and a_j coefficients) and the unconstrained regressions. Here, we use instead the Bonferroni t-test (as described in Savin 1980), which rejects the null hypothesis at the α-level if any of the q_j t-values for the difference in coefficients exceeds the t_α critical point in absolute value. The reasons for using the Bonferroni t-test are two. First, the standard F-test can reject the null hypothesis at the α-level even when none of the t_j - a_j coefficients differ significantly from zero at the α-level, a result that is not meaningful here because we are primarily interested not in whether the restrictions are accepted universally but rather in where the violations of these restrictions arise. The second reason is that the Bonferroni t-test indicates which of the coefficients in the vector t_j - a_j cause the rejection of the null hypothesis when it is rejected, whereas the F-test does not.

The difficulty with the Bonferroni t-test is that the distribution of the test statistic $B = \max_i |t_{ij}|$ is not easily calculated because the t_{ij}'s are not independent. It should be intuitively clear, however, that rejection of the null hypothesis at the α-level entails using a critical t-value at a level smaller than

α if more than one t-value is being calculated. Although the exact distribution of B will not in general be known, Savin (1980) shows that using a critical level of α/q_j for the q_j individual t_{ij}'s will result in the test's rejecting the null hypothesis at a level $\leq \alpha$.[11] In this paper, we use the levels $\alpha = .05$ and $\alpha = .10$; our q_j's vary from year to year but are around twenty exporters, so that the individual t-statistics must exceed the critical value (for the two-tailed test with a large number of degrees of freedom, so that we use the standard normal distribution to approximate) $t_{.0025} = 3.03, t_{.005} = 2.81$.

Canada is treated separately on the grounds that Canadian crude oil shipments enter the United States via pipeline, primarily in the North Central region (Indiana to Montana), where there is relatively little immediate competition with other foreign sources of crude oil, which are shipped by tanker to the U.S. East, West, and Gulf coasts.[12] Otherwise, the same regression model is applied to Canadian data.

An illustrative example for 1981 of the overall regression results appears in table 4.3. The dummy variables have been chosen so that the constant represents the average price paid to the Venezuelan government for crude oil shipped to the East Coast during the month of January with zero credit days. American Petroleum Institute (API) gravity and sulfur content have the expected positive and negative signs, respectively. This result is quite robust over time. Volume or size of shipment displays an expected negative sign owing to size discount; however, this result is far from robust as the coefficients turn out to be significantly positive for a number of years. As expected, the spot transaction variable yields a mixture of positive and negative signs over the sample period. Although this is not the case in 1981, oil delivered to the West Coast is usually significantly cheaper than oil delivered to the East Coast owing to the added cost of moving oil south of Africa or through the Panama Canal. The dummy variables for loading month display a pattern of falling prices in 1981.

The variable for credit days was introduced in the years for which data are available (1979–84) with the intent of measuring an implicit interest rate across transaction types, as explained above. Unfortunately, no coherent inference can be made, as can be seen from the 1981 result. It was expected that the average purchase price increases with the number of credit days owing to the implicit loan. Furthermore, affiliates may want to charge implicit interest rates different from market interest rates in order to realize money transfers. Unfortunately, the data reveal no definite pattern in this respect, although some coefficients of the variables for credit days are statistically significant.

The last group of explanatory variables is based on transaction type by country. It yields the annual average price differential associated with the type of transaction. Table 4.3 shows that, with two exceptions, crude oil sold by the Venezuelan government was the cheapest crude oil imported into the United States.[13] Using the estimated coefficients reported in table 4.3 and

Table 4.3   OLS Regression Results for 1981

Explanatory Variable	Estimated Coefficients and Standard Errors[a]		
	Estimated Coefficient	Standard Error	t-statistic
Constant	29.738	.462	64.331
Gravity	.152	.011	13.606
Sulfur	-1.610	.076	-21.225
Volume	-.326	.129	-2.533
Spot	-.791	.331	-2.390
Transaction type T:			
Abu Dhabi	6.710	.813	8.252
Algeria	3.298	.468	7.047
Angola	1.198	.714	1.679
Brunei	3.404	.750	4.536
Cameroon	4.547	.654	6.953
China	-2.384	1.551	-1.537
Congo	2.204	.631	3.494
Ecuador	2.627	.948	2.772
Egypt	6.638	2.032	3.267
Gabon	2.648	.990	2.676
Indonesia	1.551	.431	3.601
Libya	3.454	.444	7.780
Malaysia	2.406	1.098	2.192
Mexico	3.736	.514	7.269
Nigeria	4.048	.367	11.020
Norway	3.710	.424	8.759
Oman	4.723	.677	6.980
Peru	4.440	.896	4.955
Qatar	2.994	1.209	2.477
Saudi Arabia	3.657	.331	11.034
Syria	8.557	2.030	4.216
Trinidad	3.240	.480	6.753
United Kingdom	3.060	.437	6.995
Venezuela	2.391	.324	7.370
Transaction type A:			
Abu Dhabi	3.313	.441	7.504
Algeria	3.859	.406	9.496
Angola	3.274	.568	5.763
Cameroon	4.357	.742	5.873
Dubai	5.501	1.059	5.195
Ecuador	2.294	.553	4.146
Egypt	3.095	.693	4.464
Gabon	2.812	.502	5.598
Indonesia	2.262	.378	5.985
Libya	5.481	.374	14.640
Malaysia	5.564	.629	8.852
Mexico	5.047	.286	17.642
Neutral Zone	5.856	.482	12.159
Nigeria	4.894	.348	14.059
Norway	3.718	.534	6.962

Table 4.3 (continued)

	Estimated Coefficients and Standard Errors[a]		
Explanatory Variable	Estimated Coefficient	Standard Error	t-statistic
Oman	4.825	1.452	3.323
Peru	3.806	.651	5.844
Saudi Arabia	2.350	.316	7.448
Sharjah	1.604	1.209	1.326
Trinidad	6.641	.373	17.784
United Kingdom	3.312	.393	8.436
Venezuela	-.316	.444	-.712
Zaire	2.710	.626	4.328
Transaction type H:			
Abu Dhabi	3.272	1.461	2.239
Algeria	3.875	.679	5.707
Dubai	6.576	1.042	6.313
Ecuador	2.342	.867	2.700
Egypt	4.111	1.454	2.827
Indonesia	2.069	.648	3.194
Iraq	8.644	1.057	8.175
Libya	6.850	.508	13.476
Mexico	5.206	.294	17.729
Nigeria	4.753	.575	8.262
Norway	5.160	.962	5.365
Peru	.857	1.199	.715
Qatar	9.943	2.034	4.889
Trinidad	3.179	1.455	2.185
United Kingdom	4.135	.599	6.906
Transaction type U:			
All Countries	4.226	.975	4.333
Port of entry:			
Hawaii	1.358	.381	3.564
Guam	2.206	.401	5.507
United States	.392	.171	2.297
West	-.109	.236	-.461
Unknown	-.773	.471	-1.639
Number of credit days:			
0–9	.504	.598	.842
10	-.191	.229	-.833
11–29	-.936	.272	-3.443
30	-.105	.101	-1.042
31–59	2.575	.407	6.324
60	.773	.583	1.327
61–179	3.060	.467	6.547
180 or more	-.168	.196	-.856
Loading month:			
February	.219	.188	1.170
March	.036	.178	.202
April	-.372	.181	-2.054
May	-.546	.184	-2.969

(continued)

Table 4.3 (continued)

Explanatory Variable	Estimated Coefficients and Standard Errors[a]		
	Estimated Coefficient	Standard Error	t-statistic
June	-1.680	.185	-9.098
July	-1.992	.187	-10.634
August	-2.305	.179	-12.864
September	-2.555	.188	-13.593
October	-2.606	.190	-13.716
November	-2.373	.195	-12.162
December	-2.195	.188	-11.675
	Test for Differences between Third-Party and Affiliate Prices		
Countries:			
Abu Dhabi	3.397	.821	4.135[b]
Algeria	-.561	.361	-1.554
Angola	-2.077	.800	-2.596
Cameroon	.190	.895	.212
Ecuador	.334	1.024	.326
Egypt	3.543	2.112	1.678
Gabon	-.164	1.026	-.159
Indonesia	-.711	.294	-2.416
Libya	-2.027	.362	-5.594[b]
Malaysia	-3.158	1.171	-2.697
Mexico	-1.311	.468	-2.803[c]
Nigeria	-.846	.249	-3.404[b]
Norway	-.008	.485	-.016
Oman	-.102	1.547	-.066
Peru	.634	1.028	.616
Saudi Arabia	1.307	.229	5.715[b]
Trinidad	-3.401	.463	-7.348[b]
United Kingdom	-.252	.396	-.638
Venezuela	2.708	.443	6.117[b]

[a] The dependent variable is purchase price. The number of observations is 2,942. The adjusted R^2 is .787.

[b] and [c] indicate significance levels of 5 percent and 10 percent, respectively, according to the Bonferroni test, i.e., greater than 3.00 and 2.79, respectively, in absolute value.

the estimated variance-covariance matrix, the average price "differential" (defined as the difference, corrected for the control variables) between third-party and affiliate transactions is calculated for each country along with the pertinent standard error and t-statistic. The results are reproduced at the bottom of table 4.3. A positive value implies that prices for transactions through affiliates were lower than those for transactions through third parties. A negative value implies the reverse. Recalling the discussion above, differentials motivated by tax considerations should be positive. Table 4.3 shows that the two prices were statistically different at the 5 percent significance level for Abu Dhabi, Libya, Nigeria, Saudi Arabia, Trinidad, and Venezuela and at the 10 percent level for Mexico but that only three of the significant differentials have the sign predicted by the tax motivation hypothesis.[14]

Table 4.4 provides a summary of the results from the annual regressions. Only the price differentials that are statistically significant at the 10 percent level are shown.[15] No price differential is statistically significant in 1983, so the null hypothesis of no difference is not rejected for that year according to the Bonferroni procedure. The null hypothesis is rejected for all other years. Countries are separated into two groups, with the first including major exporting countries, which contributed 5 percent or more of all U.S. crude oil imports in a particular year and the second, all other smaller oil-exporting countries.

If attention is centered on the major oil-exporting countries only, it is possible to observe specific patterns over time and for individual countries. From 1973 to 1975, when major oil-exporting countries had yet to nationalize completely their oil production, all average price differentials were negative, with one exception, Algeria in 1973. From 1982 to 1984, all price differentials are positive, with Indonesia in 1984 being the single exception. Between these two periods, the results are mixed. At the individual country level, Indonesia shows negative price differentials for all years except 1978. Saudi Arabia has only positive price differentials, while Venezuela has negative price differentials before nationalization, in 1973 and 1974, and positive price differentials from 1979 to 1984 after nationalization. It should be pointed out that average price differentials were unusually large in favor of interaffiliate transactions in 1979.[16] This can be explained by the 1979 oil price surge, with interaffiliate prices being adjusted slowly.

When prices are higher for transactions through affiliates than prices through third parties (assumed to represent market prices), or, in other words, when price differentials are negative, money is transferred from the United States to other countries. The converse occurs with positive price differentials. To get an idea of the relative importance of these money transfers within affiliated parties, the statistically significant differences in prices reported in table 4.4 were multiplied by the number of barrels imported by affiliated parties. The results appear in table 4.5, which also shows the total value of oil imported by affiliated parties, and of all oil imports. With the exception of the first two years and the last one, more money was flowing into the United States than out. The gross money transfer represents less than 2 percent of the value of crude oil imported into the United States by affiliated parties, with 1979 being an exception, and an even smaller percentage of all crude oil imports.

The data base includes information on both the purchase price and the price of oil at the port of entry, the difference being transportation costs. There is no information on the ownership of tankers (or pipelines) carrying crude oil to the American port of entry, nor is there information about which

Table 4.4   Differences between Third-Party and Affiliate Prices

	1984	1983	1982	1981	1980	1979	1978	1977	1976	1975	1974	1973
Major countries exporting oil to the United States:												
Algeria	1.08[a,b]	—	—	—	—	.98[a]	—	-1.38[a]	-1.04[a]	-.37[a]	—	5.12[a]
Canada	.27[b]	—	4.09[a]	-1.02	—	—	—	—	—	—	—	—
Indonesia	-1.13[a,b]	—	—	—	—	—	.13[b]	-.15[a,b]	-.35[a,b]	-.59[a,b]	—	-1.60[a,b]
Iran	—	—	—	-2.03[a,b]	—	2.22[a,b]	—	.12[a,b]	—	—	—	—
Libya	—	—	—	-1.31[b]	—	—	—	—	.29[a,b]	—	—	—
Mexico	—	—	—	—	—	—	—	—	—	—	—	—
Nigeria	—	—	—	-.85[a,b]	.91[a,b]	—	—	-.10[a,b]	.22[a,b]	—	-.62[a,b]	-1.42[a,b]
Saudi Arabia	—	—	—	1.31[a,b]	—	—	.24[a,b]	.51[a,b]	.37[a,b]	—	—	—
United Kingdom	—	—	—	—	—	—	—	—	—	—	—	—
Venezuela	.87[b]	—	1.69[a]	2.71[a]	—	2.23[a]	—	—	—	—	-1.13[a,b]	-.70[a,b]
Other countries exporting oil to the United States:												
Abu Dhabi	—	—	—	3.40[a]	—	6.68[a]	—	—	.23[a,b]	—	—	—
Angola	—	—	—	—	-4.04[a]	—	—	—	—	—	—	—
Bolivia	—	—	—	—	—	—	—	—	—	—	5.56[a]	—
Brunei	—	—	—	—	—	—	—	—	—	—	—	—
Cameroon	—	—	—	—	—	—	—	—	—	—		
China	—	—	—	—	—	—	—	—	—	—		
Congo	—	—	—	—	—	—	—	—	-1.50[a]	—		
Dubai	—	—	—	—	2.92	—	—	—	—	—		

Country												
Ecuador	—	—	—	—	—	—	—	—	—	—	2.42[a]	2.46[a]
Egypt	.90[a]	—	−2.03[a]	—	−3.51[a]	—	—	1.62[a]	—	—	—	—
Gabon		—	—	—	—	—	−.63	.36[a]	—	—	—	—
Iraq						9.33[a]			.73[a]			—
Ivory Coast	—											—
Kuwait									.68[a]			
Malaysia			−7.39[a]			−8.47[a]						
Neutral Zone	—				—						—	
Norway	−.71	—	—	—	—					—		
Oman		—		—	−6.62					—		
Peru				—	−3.35[a]	7.81[a]						
Qatar										—	—	
Sharjah										—	—	
Syria					—	—						
Trinidad	−1.82[a]			−3.40[a]			−.76[a]					
Tunisia			—									
Soviet Union												
Zaire		—	—									
R^2	.85	.85	.88	.79	.80	.74	.81	.85	.83	.73	.47	.71
N	1816	2228	2238	2942	3979	4480	4729	5039	4573	3412	3266	659

Note: A dash indicates that the differential between T and A is not significant at the 10 percent level (according to the Bonferroni test, except for Canada, to which the usual *t*-test is applied); a blank space indicates insufficient data to estimate coefficients for both T and A. [a] indicates a difference significant at the 5 percent level. [b] indicates a country that accounts for at least 5 percent of U.S. imports in the given year.

Table 4.5   Value of Differences between Third-Party and Affiliate Prices (million $)

	1984	1983	1982	1981	1980	1979	1978	1977	1976	1975	1974	1973
Major countries exporting oil to the United States:												
Algeria	11.8											1.6
Canada	10.0		182.7	−35.0		25.3		−41.7	−29.1	−15.4		
Indonesia	−80.0						19.0	−21.1	−56.7	−52.1		−16.6
Iran						119.1		16.4	26.9			
Libya				−138.3								
Mexico				−115.6								
Nigeria				−106.2	170.7		87.1	−17.7	50.0		−99.8	−35.7
Saudi Arabia				526.8				209.1	131.2			
United Kingdom												
Venezuela	1.7		10.3	45.9		73.9					−121.2	−18.2
Other countries exporting oil to the United States:												
Abu Dhabi				119.8		479.1			16.5			
Angola					−51.7						154.8	
Congo									−1.5			
Dubai					12.6							

Ecuador									31.9	1.5
Egypt	11.0	-18.4			150.3					
Gabon							16.4			
Iraq				-37.3	244.7	-12.0	5.8	4.4		
Malaysia					-75.0			4.6		
Neutral Zone		-25.7								
Norway	-8.1			-22.3						
Oman				-27.8						
Peru					55.2	-26.8				
Trinidad	-48.4		-120.2							
Total	-102.0	149.0	177.2	44.3	1,072.5	67.3	167.1	146.3	-34.3	-67.5
Summation (+)	34.6	193.1	692.6	183.4	1,147.5	106.1	247.7	233.6	186.7	3.1
% total type A	.3	.8	1.7	.4	3.6	.5	1.2	1.4	2.0	.4
% total imports	.1	.5	1.2	.3	2.4	.3	.7	.9	1.2	.2
Summation (−)	-136.5	-44.1	-515.4	-139.1	-75.0	-38.8	-80.5	-87.3	-221.0	-70.6
% total type A	1.2	.2	1.3	.3	.2	.2	.4	.5	2.3	8.1
% total imports	.5	.1	.9	.2	.2	.1	.2	.3	1.5	5.3
Total type A	11,073.4	23,769.3	41,198.6	46,180.9	31,870.2	21,214.3	20,360.3	17,142.5	11,446.2	9,490.6
Total imports	29,395.5	38,733.1	57,126.7	62,039.2	48,806.9	32,451.2	34,769.9	26,623.1	17,302.7	14,948.8

Note: + and − indicate the sum of all the positive and negative numbers that are significant at the 10 percent level.

countries ultimately received the money spent on transportation. Nevertheless, transportation fees form another channel that could be used to transfer money into or out of the United States. In spite of the incomplete information, an analysis similar to that described above for crude oil prices was applied to transportation costs in order to test whether the latter differ between third-party and affiliate transactions.[17]

Table 4.6 displays the summary results with respect to differences between transportation costs of third-party and affiliate transactions. No systematic differences over the years seem evident, but some individual countries display definite patterns: Algeria (positive), Iran (negative), Libya (positive), Mexico (positive), Saudi Arabia (negative), Angola (positive), Egypt (negative), and Norway (positive). Table 4.7 shows the money transfers that result from affiliates paying significantly different transportation costs than third parties. These transfers represent less than 1 percent of the value of oil imported into the United States by affiliated parties.[18]

4.4   Tax Effects

As shown in tables 4.4 and 4.6, third-party and interaffiliate purchase price and transportation cost differentials display specific patterns for some countries. What are the relations between these estimated patterns and the host country tax regimes? Oil taxation in each country of interest and its evolution over time are highly complex and cannot easily be summarized in a few general statements (see Kemp 1987). Furthermore, it is difficult to put together a set of statistical information on this matter that displays consistency over time. Since our interest lies in transfer pricing between affiliated parties, our objective is to find an indicator of the fiscal treatment granted to an additional dollar of oil production income by host countries. The higher the marginal oil income tax rate, the greater is the incentive to reduce reported taxable income in a particular country, regardless of whether the marginal tax rate is higher than the home country (U.S.) tax rate.[19] Since marginal tax rates are not readily available, we have to rely on average effective tax rates prevailing abroad. The average effective income tax rate is defined as the ratio of income tax paid or accrued to taxable income based on measures that would normally be acceptable to the IRS. The average effective income tax rate may be a poor indicator of the marginal rate when the latter is increasing (understatement) or decreasing (overstatement). It is possible to have a situation where the average tax rate is high and the marginal rate is nil, as was the case when the income tax paid was based on the posted prices (see U.S. Congress 1977).

Average effective income tax rates are displayed in table 4.8 but should be interpreted with great care. The main statistical sources are as follows. The tax and income data for even years up to 1982 are taken from various issues of *Statistics of Income* put out by the IRS; the data for 1977 and 1982 come from the benchmark survey of the U.S. Department of Commerce on U.S. direct investment abroad. Smith (1987) presents a few figures for 1983, and, finally, some judgment was applied to make interpolations or extrapolations. We are left with a number of missing observations. The salient feature of the average effective tax rates as shown in table 4.8 is that they are high, both in absolute terms and relative to U.S. statutory income tax rates over the same period.[20] Furthermore, the effective income tax rate of U.S. parents of foreign oil affiliates, computed in a similar fashion, was 0.30 in 1982 (U.S. Department of Commerce 1985, table iii.M.1); only Mexico was characterized by a lower figure. No overall time trends are evident; some countries, such as Canada, Egypt, and Nigeria, display upward trends, while others, such as Ecuador, Indonesia and Kuwait, show downward trends.

What is the relation between third-party and interaffiliate purchase price and transportation cost differentials, on the one hand, and the average effective income tax rates, on the other? For purchase price, the transfer-pricing hypothesis states that interaffiliates would like to set a lower price in high-tax host countries relative to third-party transactions, hence generating high positive price differentials. As for transportation cost, a high effective tax rate should induce integrated companies to take income out of the oil-producing host country, possibly into the home country, or more likely into a tax-haven country through a flag-of-convenience shipping affiliate. This would result in more of the oil acquisition cost being in the form of transportation cost and hence increase transportation cost relative to third parties.

Along with these two transfer-pricing hypotheses, our objective is to check whether significant structural breaks occurred between the early part of the sampling period and the latter part, when a number of oil-producing countries had taken over oil production and when the IRS improved its ability to monitor U.S. oil companies operating abroad.

To test for the influence of effective income tax rates on affiliate pricing behavior and for possible structural changes, regressions were run, with average effective tax rate as the explanatory variable and differentials between third-party and affiliate prices (as shown, e.g., at the end of table 4.3) as the dependent variable, for two subperiods, 1975–78 and 1980–84.[21] Each observation is weighted by the inverse of the standard error of the estimated third-party/affiliate differential to take into account the precision of the information. Only observations for which tax rates and estimated price differentials are both available are used.

Table 4.9 presents the summary regression results. The relation between the two sets of variables is at best tenuous. There appears to be no significant relation between third-party and affiliate estimated purchase price differentials and average effective income tax rates in both subperiods. Estimated transportation cost differentials, on the other hand, show the predicted negative relation with tax rates, significantly so in the first subperiod and a

Table 4.6   Differences between Third-Party and Affiliate Transportation Costs

	1984	1983	1982	1981	1980	1979	1978	1977	1976	1975	1974	1973
Major countries exporting oil to the United States:												
Algeria	—	—	—	-.41[a,b]	.32[a,b]	.22[a,b]	.25[a,b]	.26[a,b]	.20[a,b]	—	—	—
Canada	-.15[a,b]	—	.48[a]	.13[a]	—	.48[a]	—	-1.40	-.94[a]	-3.04[a]	—	—
Indonesia	-.44[a,b]	—	.50[a,b]	.45[a,b]	.27[a,b]	—	-.20[a,b]	.15[a,b]	—	—	—	—
Iran	-1.10[a]	-.80[a]	-1.58[a]	—	—	-.88[a,b]	.31[a,b]	—	-.15[b]	-.33[a,b]	—	—
Libya	—	—	—	.44[a,b]	.64[a,b]	.38[a,b]	.23[a,b]	.19[a,b]	—	.37[a,b]	—	—
Mexico	—	.41[a,b]	—	—	.84[a,b]	—	—	—	—	1.11[a]	—	—
Nigeria	-.29[b]	—	—	-.23[a,b]	—	.26[a,b]	.35[a,b]	.25[a,b]	—	.29[a,b]	—	—
Saudi Arabia	-.37[a,b]	-.29[a,b]	—	-.88[a,b]	—	—	—	-.46[a,b]	-.34[a,b]	-.33[a,b]	-.48[a,b]	—
United Kingdom	—	—	—	—	—	—	.44[a]	.45[a]	—	—	—	—
Venezuela	—	—	—	.39[a]	1.00[a]	—	—	-.17[a]	-.15[a,b]	-.73[a,b]	-.31[a,b]	—
Other countries exporting oil to the United States:												
Abu Dhabi	—	—	-1.64[a]	-.78[a]	—	—	.45[a,b]	—	.23[a,b]	-.56[a]	—	—
Angola	—	—	—	—	.77[a]	.46[a]	—	—	—	.95[a]	—	—
Bolivia	—	—	—	—	—	—	—	—	—	—	—	—
Brunei	—	—	—	—	-3.17[a]	—	—	—	—	—	—	—
Cameroon	—	—	—	—	—	—	—	—	—	—	—	—
China	—	—	—	—	—	—	—	—	—	—	—	—
Congo	—	—	—	—	—	—	—	—	—	—	—	—
Dubai	—	—	—	—	—	—	—	—	-1.34	—	—	—

	1	2	3	4	5	6	7	8	9	10	11	12
Ecuador	$.40^a$	—	—					—		—	—	—
Egypt	—	-1.12^a	-1.41^a	-2.61^a	-1.53^a	—	$-.82^a$	-1.93^a	—	—	—	—
Gabon	—	—	—						—	—	—	—
Ivory Coast								$-.50^a$	-1.08^a	—		—
Kuwait			—	—				—				
Malaysia	—	—	—					—	$-.89^a$	—		—
Neutral Zone	—	—					$.34^a$	$.49^a$	$.53^a$	—		
Norway												
Oman	—	—	—				$.51^a$	—	—			—
Peru								$.54^a$		—	—	
Qatar												
Sharjah					-1.43^a							
Syria	—		—	—				—	—	—	—	—
Trinidad												
Tunisia	—	—					—					
Soviet Union												
Zaire									—			
R^2	.51	.46	.49	.47	.49	.44	.50	.42	.47	.29	.54	.49
N	1816	2228	2238	2942	3979	4480	4729	5039	4573	3412	3266	659

Note: A dash indicates that the difference between T and A is not significant at the 10 percent level (according to the Bonferroni test, to which the usual *t*-test is applied); a blank space indicates insufficient data to estimate coefficients for both T and A. [a] indicates a difference significant at the 5 percent level. [b] indicates a country that accounts for at least 5 percent of U.S. imports in the given year.

Table 4.7 Value of Differences between Third-Party and Affiliate Transportation Costs (million $)

	1984	1983	1982	1981	1980	1979	1978	1977	1976	1975	1974	1973
Major countries exporting oil to the United States:												
Algeria				−25.7	21.2	23.0	25.5	19.2	12.6			
Canada	−5.6		21.4	4.5		12.4		−42.3	−26.3	−76.5		
Indonesia	−31.1		41.7	−41.8	28.3		−29.3	21.1				
Iran	−7.8	−17.1	−6.5			−47.2	28.3	24.7	−13.5	−30.2		
Libya					83.2	56.0	33.8			23.9		
Mexico		16.9		38.8	97.1					4.9		
Nigeria	−6.6			−28.7		54.9	69.5	44.4		41.4		
Saudi Arabia	−10.3	−23.0		−353.9				−188.6	−120.5	−54.1	−74.9	
United Kingdom							8.8	5.7				
Venezuela				6.6	16.3			−11.8	−10.4	−87.2	−33.3	
Other countries exporting oil to the United States:												
Abu Dhabi			−30.4	−27.5			43.5		16.5	−20.4		
Angola					9.9	4.0				28.5		
Brunei					−.5							
Dubai									−5.4			

Ecuador	3.6	−1.6	−12.8	−8.8	−16.3	−6.0					
Egypt						−19.6	−8.0				
Iraq									−6.5	−6.1	
Malaysia											
Norway						3.2	5.7		6.2		
Oman						7.9		8.1			
Qatar											
Syria						−1.0					
Total	−57.7	−24.8	13.6	−436.6	239.3	102.1	185.3	−141.4	−153.3	−169.6	−108.2
Summation (+)	3.6	16.9	63.1	49.9	256.0	150.3	220.5	128.8	35.4	98.7	
% imports type A	.0	.1	.3	.1	.6	.5	1.0	.6	.2	.9	
% total imports	.0	.1	.2	.1	.4	.3	.7	.4	.1	.6	
Summation (−)	−61.4	−41.7	−49.6	−486.5	−16.7	−48.2	−35.2	−270.2	−188.7	−268.3	−108.2
% total type A	.6	.3	.2	1.2	.0	.2	.2	1.3	1.1	2.3	1.1
% total imports	.2	.1	.1	.9	.0	.1	.1	.8	.7	1.6	.7
Total type A	11,073.4	14,003.8	23,769.3	41,198.6	46,180.9	31,870.2	21,214.3	20,360.3	17,142.5	11,446.2	9,490.6
Total imports	29,395.5	33,758.6	38,733.1	57,126.7	62,039.2	48,806.9	32,451.2	34,769.9	26,623.1	17,302.7	14,948.8

Note: + and − indicate the sum of all the positive and negative numbers that are significant at the 10 percent level.

Table 4.8   Average Effective Tax Rates for the U.S. Petroleum Industry Abroad (%)

	1984	1983	1982	1981	1980	1979	1978	1977	1976	1975	1974	1973	1972
Abu Dhabi	70[b]	70[b]	70	71[a]	73[a]	75[a]	77[a]	78[a]	80	75[a]	70[a]	66[a]	61
Algeria	..	..	..	..	..	..	..	..	0	..	..	..	56
Angola	93[c]	93	..	..	..	..	..	..	..	..	..	..	..
Bolivia	..	..	..	..	..	..	..	..	0	..	..	..	..
Brunei	..	..	..	..	..	..	..	..	..	..	..	..	..
Cameroon	..	..	..	..	..	..	..	..	..	..	..	..	..
Canada	56[b]	56[b]	56	48[a]	39	41[a]	43[a]	46	35	41[a]	47[a]	34[a]	21
China	81[c]	81	..	..	..	..	..	..	4	..	..	..	..
Congo	..	..	..	..	..	..	..	..	..	..	..	..	..
Dubai	70[b]	70[b]	70	71[a]	73[a]	75[a]	77[a]	78[a]	80	75[a]	70[a]	66[a]	61
Ecuador	89[c]	89	97	101[a]	105[a]	109[a]	112[a]	116[a]	120	106[a]	92	..	0
Egypt	87[c]	87	75	73[a]	71[a]	70[a]	68[a]	66[a]	64	61[a]	59[a]	56[a]	53
Gabon	..	..	..	..	..	..	..	..	0	..	..	..	..
Indonesia	57[b]	57[b]	57	57[a]	56	57[a]	58[a]	59[a]	60	59[a]	58	63[a]	68
Iran	94[b]	94[b]	94	91[a]	88[a]	86[a]	83[a]	80	92	91[a]	89[a]	88[a]	86
Iraq	77[c]	77	..	..	..	..	..	..	0	..	..	..	..
Ivory Coast	..	..	..	..	..	..	..	..	..	..	..	..	..
Kuwait	70[b]	70[b]	70	71[a]	73[a]	75[a]	77[a]	78[a]	80	90[a]	101[a]	111[a]	121

Libya	81[c]	81	83[a]	85[a]	87[a]	89[a]	91[a]	92	90	90[a]	90[a]	90[a]	89
Malaysia	47[b]	47[b]	47	48[a]	48[a]	49[a]	49[a]	50	0	:	:	:	:
Mexico	:	:	29	:	:	:	:	67	76	58[a]	40	33[a]	25
Neutral Zone	:	:	:	:	:	:	:	:	:	:	:	:	:
Nigeria	95[c]	95	86	86[a]	85[a]	85[a]	85[a]	84	80	79[a]	69[a]	64[a]	59
Norway	94[c]	94	71	68[a]	66[a]	64[a]	62[a]	59	86	:	:	:	:
Oman	:	:	:	:	:	:	:	:	:	150[a]	106[a]	92[a]	80
Peru	77[c]	77	:	:	:	:	:	:	194	:	:	:	:
Qatar	:	:	:	:	:	:	:	:	:	:	:	:	:
Saudi Arabia	65[b]	65[b]	65	:	:	:	:	:	96	93[a]	90[a]	88[a]	85
Sharjah	70[b]	70[b]	70	71[a]	73[a]	75[a]	77[a]	78[a]	80	75[a]	70[a]	66[a]	61
Syria	:	:	:	:	:	:	:	:	:	:	:	:	:
Trinidad	80[c]	80	:	:	:	:	:	:	118	116[a]	115[a]	114[a]	113
Tunisia	:	:	:	:	:	:	:	:	:	:	:	:	:
United Kingdom	42[c]	42	58	52[a]	46	54[a]	62[a]	70	0	:	38	42[a]	46
Soviet Union	:	:	:	:	:	:	:	:	:	:	:	:	:
Venezuela	42[b]	42[b]	42	45[a]	48	47[a]	46[a]	45	160	150[a]	139	122[a]	105
Zaire	:	:	:	:	:	:	:	:	:	:	:	:	:

[a]:Linear interpolation.

[b]:Same as the 1982 figure.

[c]:Same as the 1983 figure.

Table 4.9   **Empirical Results: Relations between Third-Party/Affiliate Differentials and Tax Rates**

Variable	Coefficient	Standard Error	t-statistic
1973–78:			
Dependent variable: purchase-price differential:[a]			
Constant	.057	.068	.846
Tax rate	−.039	.077	−.499
Dependent variable: transportation-cost differential:[b]			
Constant	.241	.088	2.746
Tax rate	−.268	.100	−2.668
1980–84:			
Dependent variable: purchase-price differential:[c]			
Constant	.179	.387	.463
Tax rate	−.295	.539	−.546
Dependent variable: transportation-cost differential:[d]			
Constant	.253	.173	1.466
Tax rate	−.402	.253	−1.587

Note: All variables are normalized by the appropriate estimated purchase-price (transportation-cost) differential standard error.

[a]$N = 78.$ $R^2 = .019.$ R^2 (adjusted) $= -.007.$
[b]$N = 78.$ $R^2 = .091.$ R^2 (adjusted) $= .067.$
[c]$N = 66.$ $R^2 = .005.$ R^2 (adjusted) $= -.026.$
[d]$N = 66.$ $R^2 = .039.$ R^2 (adjusted) $= .009.$

weaker relation in the second one. To probe this relation further, attention was centered on the year 1976, which had the most extensive set of information on individual country effective oil income tax rates. Spearman rank correlations between third-party and affiliate estimated purchase price (and transportation cost) differentials and effective income tax rates[22] were computed in an attempt to reduce the influence of measurement errors. As can be seen from table 4.10, the price differential/effective income tax rate rank correlation yields, as predicted, a positive value, 0.34, with a standard error of 0.23, while the transportation cost/effective income tax rate rank correlation is negative, as predicted, and equal to -0.14 with a standard error of 0.23. The first estimated rank correlation coefficient is significantly different from zero at the 10 percent level, while the second is not.[23] Taken together, the regression and rank correlation results provide only very weak support for an influence of effective income tax rate on transfer prices between affiliated parties.

4.5 Conclusion

In general, multinational corporations can reduce their tax obligations by setting transfer prices that differ from arm's length prices. Their ability to do

Table 4.10   **Rank Correlation: Relations between Third-Party/Affiliate Differentials and Tax Rates, 1976**

Variables Correlated	Spearman Rank Correlation Coefficient
Purchase-price differential/tax rate	.339
Transportation-cost differential/tax rate	−.145

Note: The twenty-two observations are normalized by the appropriate estimated purchase-price (transportation-cost) differential standard error.

so is constrained by tax regulations in their home and host countries. The effectiveness of these regulations, however, is not easily determined.

In this paper, we have conducted the first systematic empirical analysis of transfer prices. The industry we have studied, petroleum, has a long history of tax-motivated transfer pricing. Even after the changes in the tax treatment of the industry in the mid-1970s, there have been allegations of transfer-price abuse, but little in the way of hard evidence.

Our findings indicate that there are systematic differences between transfer and arm's length prices for many exporting countries. Some of these countries exhibit consistent patterns over time, but others do not. Moreover, the relation between transfer-price/arm's length–price differentials and corporate tax rates appears to be weak. There are at least four possible hypotheses for this. First, the nature and enforcement of IRS regulations may be so effective that companies are precluded from reducing their tax obligations through transfer pricing. Second, it may be easier to avoid taxes through other channels. Third, transfer prices may serve a primarily managerial role within the firm, as described by Eccles (1985) and Robbins and Stobaugh (1973).[24] Finally, marginal and average effective tax rates may be sufficiently different as to prevent identification of any relation between the former and transfer-pricing behavior. These hypotheses are not all mutually exclusive, and untangling them is unlikely to prove easy. While this study represents a step in the empirical analysis of transfer pricing, it is clear that much work remains to be done in this area.

Notes

1. Briefly, this practice arose out of U.S. foreign policy goals in the Middle East following World War II. The practice began with the establishment of an income tax on petroleum company profits by Saudi Arabia in 1950. The IRS issued a ruling accepting the deductibility of this tax against U.S. income tax in 1955. In the 1960s, market prices for crude oil declined, but transfer prices, called "posted," or

"tax-reference," prices (used in determining petroleum companies taxes paid to oil-producing countries), did not, effectively increasing transfers from the U.S. Treasury to foreign governments (for details, see U.S. Congress 1977; for an economic analysis, see Jenkins and Wright 1975).

In the mid-1970s foreign crude oil reserves (except in Canada) were nationalized, limiting the ability of U.S. multinationals to claim payments to foreign governments as creditable against U.S. income tax. The rules on deductibility of foreign taxes were tightened by the U.S. Tax Reduction Act of 1975 and the Tax Reform Act of 1976. McDaniel and Ault (1977) summarize these changes.

2. The primary use of the data in Anderson (1988) was to adjust crude oil import prices for quality. Weiner (1986) used the data to test hypotheses about contracting and spot trading.

3. Reporting of the data by firms that import crude oil into the United States is mandatory under the U.S. Federal Administration Act (1974) and the U.S. Energy Policy and Conservation Act (1975), which were part of the basis for U.S. domestic crude oil price regulation. We were unable to find out whether these data were the same as those reported to the IRS. However, these regulations did not provide an incentive for misreporting transfer prices of imported crude oil (for a description and analysis of U.S. petroleum regulation in the 1970s, see Kalt 1981), and it appears unlikely that MNCs maintained separate accounting systems for the DOE in addition to their tax and managerial systems. Since the U.S. deregulation of crude oil prices in 1981, the data have been collected for statistical purposes only. The reporting form was not changed until late 1984, after which the information we use here was no longer requested.

4. Firms are not required to report in months in which they import less than 500,000 barrels into the United States. In comparison, crude oil imports into the United States averaged roughly 200 million barrels per month during this period. The data base covers approximately 90 percent of U.S. crude oil imports.

5. The MNC's U.S. tax credits and liabilities are incurred immediately when its foreign affiliates are organized as branches rather than separately incorporated abroad as subsidiaries. Most U.S. petroleum MNCs organize their foreign operations as branches, implying that the transfer-price incentive discussed in the text is relevant only when $t_f > t_{US}$. As indicated below, this is always the case in our data.

6. For a more detailed description, see Plasschaert (1979).

7. The data base contains landed as well as f.o.b. prices. Shipments for which the two prices were equal were assumed to change hands on a c.i.f. basis and were not used in the regressions.

8. Shipments that loaded in one year and landed in the next were counted in the loading year. An alternative to conducting annual regressions would have been to run one regression with interaction terms to allow for changes over time. The data base contains so many observations (see table 4.4 below) that there is little to be gained from pooling years for additional degrees of freedom.

9. Not every country exported through every transaction type every year. Dummy variables are omitted in cases where no transactions from a given country of a given type exist.

10. Transaction type variables could be considered to represent endogenous choice, thus leading to biased coefficient estimates. A logit test using transaction type as dependent variable and effective tax rates, described later on, as explanatory variables was performed, and it showed no significant relation between transaction type and country-specific effective tax rates.

11. Applying the Bonferroni inequality $P(E_1, \ldots, E_m) \leq 1 - \sum_{i=1}^{m} P(E_i^c)$, where E_i stands for event i and E_i^c for the complement of event i, gives this result. As an example, suppose that the events E_1, E_2 are that the t-statistics associated with two

regression coefficients are in the acceptance region for the null hypothesis. Then the $\leq .05$ level test of both being in the acceptance region is that each is in the .025 acceptance region. In comparison, if the two t-statistics are independent, then the exact distribution of B can be calculated; a .025 level test on each coefficient is equivalent to a $1 - (1 - .025)^2 = .0494$ level test of the null hypothesis.

12. The null hypothesis that Canadian data fit the overall regression is rejected at conventional significance levels.

13. The exceptions are China (transaction type T) and Venezuela (transaction type A), but neither is statistically significant at conventional levels.

14. The suggestion has been made that transaction A prices may follow closely transaction H prices, thus indicating that affiliates set oil prices at the level set by their host government. The Bonferroni test leads to a rejection, at the 5 percent level, of the hypothesis of no price differentials between transactions types A and H.

15. In addition, the differences that are significantly different from zero at the 5 percent level are so indicated.

16. Malaysia is the exception.

17. These regressions omit the explanatory variables API gravity, sulfur, and credit days.

18. The result that the United States has received relatively small net inflows differs markedly from that of Jenkins and Wright (1975) for the period before our data start.

19. See the discussion earlier in the paper. For a summary of U.S. taxation of income earned abroad, see Hines (1988a).

20. Average effective tax rates greater than one reflect the fact that the tax base used by the IRS for foreign operations of U.S. companies differs from the tax base as defined by other governments.

21. As can be seen in table 4.4, the price differentials for 1979 are very large. This is in part due to the disruption in the oil market, which resulted in rapid price changes. Since the differentials were almost certainly affected, we have dropped 1979 from the regressions.

22. Taking into account the standard error of the estimated differentials.

23. The approximate distribution for order statistics suggested by Kendall and Stuart (1967, sec. 31.19) is used to obtain the critical value.

24. This hypothesis requires the additional, questionable assumption that it is too costly for the MNC to maintain separate accounting systems for managerial and tax purposes.

References

Anderson, J. M. 1988. Empirical analysis of world oil trade, 1967–1984. In *Responding to international oil crises,* ed. G. Horwich and D. L. Weimer. Washington, D.C.: American Enterprise Institute.

Benvignati, A. M. 1985. An empirical investigation of international transfer pricing by US manufacturing firms. In *Multinationals and transfer pricing,* ed. A. M. Rugman and L. Eden. New York: St. Martin's.

Bertrand, R. J. 1981. *The state of competition in the canadian petroleum industry.* Vol. 3, *International linkages: Canada and the world petroleum market.* Ottawa: Minister of Supply and Services.

Eccles, R. G. 1985. *The transfer pricing problem: A theory for practice.* Lexington, Mass.: Heath.

Eden, L. 1985. The microeconomics of transfer pricing. In *Multinationals and transfer pricing,* ed. A. M. Rugman and L. Eden. New York: St. Martin's.

Hines, J. R. 1988a. Taxation and U.S. multinational investment. In *Tax policy and the economy 2,* ed. Lawrence Summers. Cambridge, Mass.: MIT Press and the National Bureau of Economic Research.

———. 1988b. Where the profits are: On the taxation of transfers by multinational firms. Paper presented to the National Bureau of Economic Research Summer Institute, Cambridge, Mass.

Hubbard, R. G., and R. J. Weiner. 1989. Contracting and price adjustment in commodity markets: Evidence from copper and oil. *Review of Economics and Statistics* 71 (1): 80–89.

Jenkins, G. P., and B. D. Wright. 1975. Taxation of income of multinational corporations: The case of the United States petroleum industry. *Review of Economics and Statistics* 57 (1): 1–11.

Kalt, J. P. 1981. *The economics and politics of oil price regulation.* Cambridge, Mass.: MIT Press.

Kemp, A. 1987. *Petroleum rent collection around the world.* Halifax: Institute for Research on Public Policy.

Kendall, M. G., and A. Stuart. 1967. *The advanced theory of statistics.* Vol. 2. 2d ed. London: Griffin.

Lall, S. 1973. Transfer pricing by multinational manufacturing firms. *Oxford Bulletin of Economics and Statistics* 35(3): 173–95.

LaMont, H. 1975. Multinational enterprise, transfer pricing, and the 482 mess. *Columbia Journal of Transnational Law* 14(3): 383–433.

McDaniel, P. R., and H. J. Ault. 1977. *Introduction to United States international taxation.* Deventer, Netherlands: Kluwer.

Plasschaert, S. R. F. 1979. *Transfer pricing and multinational corporations.* New York: Praeger.

Robbins, S. M., and R. B. Stobaugh. 1973. *Money in the multinational enterprise.* New York: Basic.

Roumeliotis, P. 1977. La politique des prix d'importation et d'exportation des enterprises multinationales en Grèce. *Revue Tiers Monde* 18 (70): 353–65.

Rugman, A. M. 1985. Transfer pricing in the Canadian petroleum industry. In *Multinationals and transfer pricing,* ed. A. M. Rugman and L. Eden. New York: St. Martin's.

Savin, N. E. 1980. The Bonferroni and the Scheffé multiple comparison procedures. *Review of Economic Studies* 47 (146): 255–73.

Smith, J. L. 1987. International petroleum taxation: Reasons for instability. In *World energy markets: Coping with instability,* ed. J. G. Rowse. Calgary: IAEE.

U.S. Congress. House Committee on Government Operations. 1977. *Foreign tax credits claimed by U.S. petroleum companies.* Hearings before the Commerce, Consumer, and Monetary Affairs Subcommittee. Washington, D.C.: U.S. Government Printing Office.

U.S. Department of Commerce. Bureau of Economic Analysis. 1985. *U.S. direct investment abroad: 1982 benchmark survey data.* Washington, D.C.: U.S. Government Printing Office.

Vaitsos, C. V. 1974. *Intercountry income distribution and transnational enterprises.* Oxford: Clarendon.

Weiner, R. J. 1986. Models of contracting, trading, and spot markets. Ph.D. diss., Harvard University.

Williamson, O. E. 1975. *Markets and hierarchies.* New York: Free Press.

Comment   Lorraine Eden

The petroleum industry is an international oligopoly, consisting of four stages: extraction, shipping, refining, and distribution. The purpose of the Bernard and Weiner paper is to test the effectiveness of U.S. transfer price regulation at the extraction and shipping stages. The key variable in their analysis is "transaction type," which consists of three main categories: U.S. imports from foreign affiliates (A), host governments (H), and third parties (T). The authors hypothesize that, over the 1973–84 period, U.S. petroleum multinationals (MNCs) underinvoiced crude oil exports from high-tax source countries into the United States in order to reduce overall tax payments. Thus $P(T) - P(A)$ should be positively related to $t(J) - t(US)$, where imports of A, H, and T come from country J, and $t(J)$ is the marginal income tax rate in country J. In addition, MNCs may have also overinvoiced shipping charges.

In many cases (see table 4.4), the authors do find significant transfer price manipulation (TPM); for example, repeated overinvoicing through Nigeria and Indonesia and underinvoicing through Saudi Arabia. The peak years appear to be 1976, 1977, and 1981. Overall, there is net underinvoicing, equal to less than 2 percent of the total value of affiliate imports into the United States (dominated by the large underinvoicing in 1979 by Adu Dhabi and in 1981 by Saudi Arabia [$527 million]). More significant differences in transport costs occur than in transfer prices (see table 4.6). In general, the reverse occurs: Nigeria, Libya, and Algeria undercharge and Saudi Arabia overcharges; Indonesia is mixed. The total value of net shipping transfers is an overcharge of less than 1 percent of affiliate imports (dominated by a huge overcharge by Saudi Arabia, also in 1981, of $354 million).

The authors conclude that little manipulation of transfer prices and shipping charges occurred and that it was only weakly related to income tax differentials. Three rationales are offered for these results: the effectiveness of U.S. transfer price regulation, MNCs using other channels to avoid taxes, or problems related to using average tax rates to proxy for marginal rates.

Since the authors have an unusually detailed data base and have performed the most rigorous tests of TPM to date, their failure to find significant evidence of transfer pricing in response to tax differentials is an important result and one that may be extensively cited. Their results clearly contradict the widely held view of substantial MNC price manipulation in the petroleum industry (see Jenkins and Wright 1975; Bertrand 1981). Therefore it is important to determine whether their conclusions are robust or confounded by statistical problems.

Lorraine Eden is associate professor in the Norman Paterson School of International Affairs at Carleton University.

Since there are several issues involved, let me deal with them individually. The key issues are (1) how to measure transfer price manipulation, (2) the factors affecting TPM, and (3) the relevant income tax differential.

How Should Transfer Price Manipulation Be Measured?

Transfer price manipulation has a different meaning in the theoretical MNC literature than in government regulations. *Theoretical* transfer price manipulation (TTPM) is measured by the gap between the transfer price $P(A)$ and the shadow price, the marginal cost of the exporting firm (Eden 1985). *Regulatory* transfer price manipulation (RTPM) is measured by the gap between $P(A)$ and $P(T)$, the price at which the same product is sold to or bought from an unrelated buyer (e.g., Sec. 482). There is no reason for TTPM and RTPM to be the same or for one necessarily to imply the other (Eden 1989).

In Bernard and Weiner, while the motivation for transfer pricing is based on theoretical models of TPM, the definition used in the tests is the regulatory one, $P(T) - P(A)$. However, the implicit reference hypothesis in the background must be that such an empirical gap does not also exist between $P(T)$ and $P(H)$ or between $P(A)$ and $P(H)$. If significant differences exist between these other pairs of prices, the evidence on RTPM is much less clear. In fact, the authors do find a significant differential between $P(A)$ and $P(H)$ (see n. 14); however, they do not report calculations for the third price gap.

Related to this is another question as to the role played by firm A in the host country. Prior to this time period, many countries nationalized their oil fields. In these cases, A acts as a middleman, supplying technical expertise in return for crude petroleum, so that $P(H)$ should be related to $P(A)$. In other countries, A extracts the oil from private fields, and $P(H)$ represents an unrelated price like $P(T)$; or, alternatively, $P(H)$ may be a posted price. Given note 14, the latter situation may be the representative one. In the absence of information as to the share of A's exports (or of T's exports) purchased from the host government relative to own production, it is impossible to determine what these price gaps mean. Hence, a significant $P(T) - P(A)$ gap may not indicate RTPM at all.

In addition, the value of price manipulation to the petroleum multinationals depends on the relative shares of their affiliates' purchased versus produced crude oil. Bernard and Weiner find significant underinvoicing equal to 2 percent of the value of affiliate imports; however, if much of this was purchased rather than produced, the relevant denominator is value added, not sales. The underinvoicing percentage would therefore be larger, implying more RTPM than first appears.

What Factors Affect TPM?

Eden (1989) explores the factors that affect TPM in a model of a vertically integrated multinational petroleum company. During the 1973–84 period, most petroleum affiliates were organized as branches in order to take advantage of deductible losses and U.S. percentage depletion. In addition, most were taxed on an overall basis so that surplus and deficit foreign tax credits were pooled. Eden finds that TTPM depends on differences in the statutory tax rates, days of credit, the host country's pricing policy for calculating the income tax, and the importing government's definition of an acceptable transfer price. Under posted prices (mostly prior to 1974, although data are unavailable), the MNC should theoretically overinvoice since a higher $P(A)$ does not affect host taxes. However, after 1978 the U.S. government disallowed crediting posted prices so that underinvoicing would be the preferred route, given high statutory rates abroad. Moreover, if tax credits are pooled, the relevant tax rate is the weighted average statutory rate, not the tax rate where A is located.

Even if MNCs do not theoretically transfer price (i.e., assume that $P(A)$ equals marginal cost), there are several reasons why $P(A)$ would not equal $P(T)$: gravity and sulphur characteristics differ; number of credit days differs; per-unit transport costs vary; the MNC refinery may have monopsony power in the external market; there may be transactions costs associated with the external market; the posted price is different from the transfer price; statutory tax rates and method of foreign tax crediting differ; and royalties are charged by the host country. Bernard and Weiner control for the first three: days of credit, transport costs, and characteristics of oil; but this is not sufficient to guarantee that $P(T)$ equals $P(A)$ even if no TTPM occurs.

What Tax Differential Should Be Used?

Bernard and Weiner use $t(J) - t(US)$, the difference between the average effective tax rate in the host country and in the United States to proxy for the tax differential. This measure is problematic on both theoretical and empirical grounds.

As other papers in this volume show, statutory tax rates affect financial and transfer price decisions; marginal effective tax rates affect real capital investment decisions. The relevant gap between the statutory rates depends on the organizational structure (branch/subsidiary) of the affiliate, deferral, whether the affiliate has a surplus or deficit of foreign tax credits, the per-country or overall limitation, the ability to carry tax credits forward and backward, and the definition of the tax base including the use of posted prices (Eden 1989). Average tax rates on a per-country basis may therefore be a poor proxy for the relevant differential. And, as pointed out earlier, other variables besides a tax gap affect RTPM.

In Bernard and Weiner's empirical work, the tax rates in table 4.8 used to calculate the tax differential are problematic for several reasons. First, most tax rates other than for the years 1976 and 1982 were determined by the interpolations between 1976 and 1982 or were assumed to be constant (e.g., 1983 and 1984). Given that U.S. law changed considerably over this period, using interpolated rates may have confounded the results in table 4.9. A more reliable test (although the number of cases falls substantially) would be to use only 1976 and 1982 data. Additional support for this is shown by table 4.1, where the foreign tax as a percentage of U.S. taxable income falls from .8 to .9 in the 1972–78 period and to .6 in 1980–82. Clearly, what happened was a shift of foreign taxes from creditable to deductible status. This is also reflected in the tax credit as a percentage of the foreign tax, which rises over the period.

A second problem with the tax data is the elimination of years without a tax rate. Unfortunately, most of the transfer pricing was caused by Saudi Arabia, which, owing to absence of tax data, was excluded from the runs. Abu Dhabi, the other large manipulator, has tax rates that were interpolated for all but three years; its tax data are, therefore, not very reliable.

A third problem is that shipping charges are regressed against the same average tax differential as transfer prices. This is problematic because it assumes that the MNCs use shipping affiliates rather than independent firms and that both the shipping and the extraction affiliates are located in the same host country. Data are unavailable on either of these issues. Assuming that the shipping affiliate is located elsewhere, under the overall limitation it is legitimate to use a foreign statutory rate pooled across all affiliates. However, that information is also not available.

Finally, a vertically integrated petroleum MNC can take its profits at any stage; tight regulation of the transfer price at one stage may simply shift profits to another stage or by means of another form (e.g., financial maneuvers). Given that the petroleum MNCs were forced to report prices of shipped crude oil, it is not surprising that the authors find little evidence of RTPM. The authors argue that the limited evidence of RTPM implies the effectiveness of government regulation; however, regulation at one stage does not ensure effectiveness.

Conclusions

In summary, this is a nice paper trying to handle a complex task. The authors have taken a new and rigorous approach to the transfer pricing problem, isolating differences between $P(T)$ and $P(A)$ and relating them to tax differentials. The paper concludes that the petroleum MNCs did *not* substantially manipulate transfer prices between 1973 and 1984. This is a surprising result since it is contrary to theoretical predictions of MNC behavior, conventional wisdom, and previous tests.

My conclusions are somewhat different. Although the Bernard and Weiner approach is clearly superior to earlier tests, both the amount of transfer pricing and the tax differential, as measured in the paper, are problematic on theoretical and empirical grounds. Additional information is needed to determine the actual amount of transfer price manipulation in response to tax differentials.

As explained above, the required information would include the organizational form of the affiliates, the statutory tax rate affecting each affiliate, the foreign tax credit limitation used, the share of affiliate exports produced within the MNC relative to that purchased from the host government, the location of the shipping affiliate, the role of the posted price, and the size of the royalty payment. Clearly, this is a tall order.

My presumption, therefore, in the absence of this additional evidence, is to continue to assume the petroleum MNCs guilty until proved innocent.

References

Bertrand, R. J. 1981. *The state of competition in the canadian petroleum industry. Volume III International linkages: Canada and the world petroleum market.* Ottawa: Minister of Supply and Services.
Eden, Lorraine. 1985. The microeconomics of transfer pricing. In *Multinationals and transfer pricing,* ed. Alan M. Rugman and Lorraine Eden. New York: St. Martin's.
———. 1989. The taxation of U.S. petroleum multinationals and their foreign affiliates. Mimeo.
Jenkins, G. P., and B. D. Wright. 1975. Taxation of income of multinational corporations: The case of the United States petroleum industry. *Review of Economics and Statistics* 57 (1): 1–11

5   Coming Home To America: Dividend Repatriations By U.S. Multinationals

James R. Hines, Jr., and R. Glenn Hubbard

American corporations earn a large and growing volume of after-tax profits through their affiliated foreign companies. The foreign earnings of U.S. corporations are typically subject to taxation both by host foreign governments and by the U.S. government, an arrangement that dramatically complicates the companies' tax returns and the consequences of their international financial transactions. Under these circumstances, obvious questions arise about the extent to which the system of international taxation affects the behavior of multinational corporations.

This paper analyzes the financial flows from foreign subsidiaries of American multinational corporations to their parent corporations in the United States. These flows represent one method by which foreign earnings of American companies are returned ("repatriated") to American investors. Their size generally reflects the size of American investments overseas: in 1984, the last year for which data are available, the controlled foreign corporations of American multinationals earned after-foreign-tax profits of $30 billion, of which they repatriated $11.8 billion in dividends to their American parent companies.[1] These repatriations are of importance not only to U.S. investors, who thereby have access to those funds, but also to the U.S. government, which generally does not tax foreign earnings of

James R. Hines, Jr., is assistant professor of economics and public affairs at Princeton University and a faculty research fellow of the National Bureau of Economic Research. R. Glenn Hubbard is professor of economics and finance at the Graduate School of Business of Columbia University and a research associate of the National Bureau of Economic Research.

The authors are grateful to Daniel Frisch and Timothy Goodspeed for invaluable advice and assistance in using the U.S. Treasury's tax data on U.S. multinational firms and their subsidiaries; to Joann Martens Weiner for outstanding research assistance; to David Bradford, Alberto Giovannini, Trevor Harris, Karl Scholz, and Mark Wolfson for helpful comments and suggestions; and to the National Bureau of Economic Research for financial support. The usual disclaimer applies.

161

controlled foreign corporations until they are repatriated. It is precisely the effect on repatriation behavior of this deferred taxation that we examine.

The paper is organized as follows. In section 5.1, we review the current tax system as applied to multinational firms and consider the incentives it creates for various intrafirm financial transactions (and, in particular, forms of repatriations). We summarize in section 5.2 repatriation patterns from aggregate time-series data on the overseas operations of U.S. multinationals. Our principal findings appear in section 5.3, in which we explore directly the determinants of distributions by foreign subsidiaries to their U.S. parent corporations, using new micro data on 12,041 controlled foreign corporations (and their 453 U.S. parents) collected from tax returns for 1984. This source exposes variations in distribution patterns not detectable in aggregate data. In particular, we find that most subsidiaries paid no dividends at all to their parents and that the U.S. tax system collected very little revenue on their foreign income while distorting their internal financial transactions. Conclusions and some implications for U.S. corporate tax reform are presented in section 5.4.

5.1   The Tax System and Its Incentives

5.1.1   The System

The United States claims tax authority over all persons resident in America, meaning that American individuals and corporations must pay tax to the U.S. government on all their income, whether earned in the United States or abroad. "Residence" is not the only possible criterion for tax authority, and a number of European countries tax their residents on a "territorial" basis, on which only that income earned within the country's borders is subject to tax.[2] The American "residence" system is arguably a more common practice and is used by other important capital-exporting countries such as the United Kingdom and Japan. Hence, an understanding of the international effects of residence taxation by the United States may shed light on the effects of international taxation throughout the world.

In addition to their U.S. tax liabilities, American multinational corporations usually owe taxes to foreign governments on profits earned locally within their borders. In order not to subject Americans earning income abroad to double taxation, U.S. tax law provides a foreign tax credit for income taxes (and related taxes) paid to foreign governments. Thus, in the simplest possible situation, a U.S. corporation earning $100 in a foreign country with a 10 percent tax rate (and a foreign tax obligation of $10) pays only $24 to the U.S. government since its U.S. corporate tax obligation of $34 (34 percent of $100) is reduced to $24 by the foreign tax credit of $10. The foreign tax credit is, however, limited to U.S. tax liability on foreign income; if, in the example, the foreign tax rate were 50 percent, then the firm pays $50 to the foreign government, but its U.S. foreign tax credit is limited to $34. Hence, a U.S. firm receives full tax credits for its foreign taxes paid only when it is in a "deficit credit" position, that is, when its average foreign tax rate is less than its tax rate on domestic operations. A firm has "excess credits" if its available foreign tax credits exceed U.S. tax liability on its foreign income. Since 1976, the law requires American companies to calculate their foreign tax credits on a worldwide basis, so that all foreign income and foreign taxes paid are added together in the computation of the foreign tax credit limit. Furthermore, income is broken into different functional "baskets" in the calculation of applicable credits and limits.[3]

Deferral of U.S. taxation of certain foreign earnings is another important feature of the U.S. international tax system. This deferral takes two forms. The first is very common in income tax systems: unrealized capital gains are usually untaxed.[4] The second is that earnings of foreign subsidiaries of U.S. corporations are not subject to U.S. taxation until repatriated to their American parent corporations. This type of deferral is available only to foreign operations that are separately incorporated in foreign countries ("subsidiaries" of the parent) and not to consolidated ("branch") operations.[5] Multinationals generally can choose the legal form of their foreign operations, and this choice can affect their tax obligations. Parent U.S. firms are generally taxed on their subsidiaries' foreign income only when repatriated and receive "indirect" foreign tax credits ("deemed-paid credits") for foreign income taxes paid (by the subsidiaries) on income subsequently received as dividends. The U.S. government taxes branch profits as they are earned, just as it would profits earned within the United States. On the other hand, organizing as a branch offers to the investor the possibility of deducting from U.S. income foreign branch losses and may involve (in some cases) more lenient foreign regulations.

The deferral of U.S. taxation creates an incentive for firms to delay paying dividends from their subsidiaries to their American parents. In 1962, Congress enacted the Subpart F provisions in part to prevent indefinite deferral of U.S. tax liability on income earned abroad that is continually reinvested merely in order to escape U.S. taxes. Subpart F rules apply to controlled foreign corporations (CFCs), which are foreign corporations owned at least 50 percent by U.S. persons holding stakes of at least 10 percent each. The Subpart F rules include provisions that treat passive income, and income invested in U.S. property, as if that income were distributed to the U.S. parent company, so it is subject to immediate U.S. taxation. Controlled foreign corporations that reinvest their earnings in active foreign businesses avoid the Subpart F restrictions and can continue to defer U.S. tax liability on those earnings. The Tax Reform Act of 1986 further expands the coverage of Subpart F and also makes currently taxable in the United States the income of American investors in passive foreign investment companies that do not qualify as CFCs because they do not meet the 50 percent ownership rule.

"Dividends" to the parent are not the only form of repatriation. "Interest" paid to the parent to service debt capital contributions usually has the additional tax feature of deductibility in the host country. Astute use of transfer pricing can allow the subsidiary to shift earnings to the parent or to other subsidiaries of the parent having more advantageous tax treatment; royalty payments to the parent can serve a similar function. Foreign governments often impose moderate taxes on interest, rent, and royalty payments from foreign affiliates to their American parents; these withholding taxes are fully creditable against foreign tax liabilities of the U.S. taxpayer. We return to a comparison of various repatriation channels later.

5.1.2 Taxes and the Repatriation Decision

At the core of our concern is the effect of the tax rules just described on firms' repatriation decisions. Consider first the tax cost of dividends (D) paid from a foreign subsidiary to its American parent. Assume that the foreign country uses a classical corporate income tax system and imposes no withholding taxes on dividends. Then the dividend payment does not change the foreign tax liability of the firm, but it does produce a U.S. tax liability of (D + FTC) τ − FTC, where τ is the U.S. tax rate and FTC the foreign tax credit generated by the dividend payment. For parent corporations that do not have excess foreign tax credits and their subsidiaries that pay dividends out of current earnings, the foreign tax credit is $\tau^* E^* D/[(1 - \tau^*)E^*]$, where τ^* is the foreign tax rate and E^* is the subsidiary's foreign earnings. Hence, the dividend payment obliges the U.S. parent to pay net U.S. taxes of

(1) $$D(\tau - \tau^*)/(1 - \tau^*),$$

and the parent keeps a net dividend of

(2) $$D(1 - \tau)/(1 - \tau^*).$$

Significant withholding taxes imposed by foreign governments offer a complication, especially for firms in excess credit positions. For U.S. parents with deficit credits, the payment of a dividend increases their foreign tax liability by the withholding tax on the dividend, but their American tax liability is reduced by an equal amount through the foreign tax credit. For U.S. parents in excess credit positions, subsidiary dividend payments trigger withholding tax liabilities with no corresponding reduction in U.S. taxes; in that case, dividends raise total worldwide tax burdens.

Abstracting for the moment from considerations of transfer pricing, alternative repatriation strategies include payments to the parent of interest, rent, or royalties, all of which are generally deductible for tax purposes.[6]

Since foreign corporate tax rates are generally much higher than withholding tax rates,[7] the foreign tax saving offered by deducting repatriations in those forms well outweighs the cost of withholding tax liabilities. Hence, a tax-minimizing firm with excess foreign tax credits should seek to maximize those repatriations.

5.1.3   U.S. Tax Law and the "Dividend Puzzle"

Given the structure of U.S. taxation of multinationals, one might question whether domestic tax revenue is likely to be collected. For example, given the credit for foreign taxes paid, if foreign tax rates are high relative to U.S. tax rates, much if not all of the U.S. tax liability on this income would be eliminated. However, historically (prior to passage of the Tax Reform Act of 1986), foreign tax rates have been lower than the U.S. statutory corporate income tax rate.

Dividends are paid to U.S. parents. As we describe in more detail in section 5.2, the controlled foreign corporations of U.S. multinationals repatriate more than one-third and as much as 60 percent of their foreign earnings each year as dividends. The "dividend puzzle" is the following: why do they pay dividends, given that dividends are often the least favorable (from a tax standpoint) means of repatriating earnings? The same puzzle arises in the analysis of dividend payouts of domestic firms to their stockholders, and analyses of the domestic puzzle suggest three general approaches to this question.

The first view is based on the "trapped equity" or "tax capitalization" model of corporate dividends associated with King (1977), Auerbach (1979), and Bradford (1981)[8] and applied by Hartman (1985) to the analysis of foreign dividends received by multinationals. Suppose that a parent capitalizes a wholly owned subsidiary with an initial transfer of equity capital. When the subsidiary has growth opportunities and desired investment exceeds internally generated funds, the parent transfers additional funds to it. For a mature subsidiary, equity is trapped—earnings exceed profitable investment opportunities, and the subsidiary repatriates the residual funds. Costly repatriations can be delayed as long as the subsidiary has active investment opportunities abroad, but, once these are exhausted, the Subpart F rules prevent the use of passive investments to defer U.S. tax obligations. In the trapped equity view, dividend payouts are unaffected by (permanent) changes in their tax price; they respond only to characteristics of the subsidiary, in particular, the difference between its internally generated funds and its profitable investment opportunities. The characteristics of the parent firm and other subsidiaries are irrelevant.

A second view corresponds to the notion that a multinational chooses financial policy in its subsidiaries in order to minimize the firm's global tax liability. The most preferred tool is transfer pricing across affiliates to locate profits in low-tax "havens." In addition, one portion of income received from subsidiaries is compensation for technology transferred via direct investment—for example, royalties and license fees. There is scope for tax minimization through strategies that trade off royalties for dividends. Kopits (1976) illustrates this point by showing that the tax-minimizing royalty is at least as large as the tax shelter provided by any excess credits from dividends (properly adjusted).

Tax-minimization schemes encounter two stumbling blocks. The first is external: governments are understandably unenthusiastic about such behavior by multinationals and generally limit firms' discretion over pricing and financial decisions. Sales of goods between multinationals and their affiliates are generally required to take place at market, or "arm's length," prices, though in practice this requirement may be difficult to enforce.[9] Similarly, many countries limit multinationals to using arm's length interest rates and have formula restrictions on rent and royalty payments. As a consequence, even tax-minimizing firms may be unable to use nondividend methods to repatriate foreign earnings.[10] The second difficulty that tax-minimization encounters is that, for reasons of corporate control, the parent may prefer to evaluate the subsidiary as an independent profit center; this point is developed below.

In addition to altering the form of payment across repatriation mechanisms at a given point in time, global tax-minimization strategies alter the time-series patterns of dividend repatriations as well. For example, increased dividend payments from subsidiaries during a period in which the parent is making losses at home reduces future tax liabilities. Global tax-minimization behavior is distinguished from "trapped equity" behavior in that subsidiaries' distribution patterns depend not only on their own tax prices but also on their tax prices relative to those for other subsidiaries of the same parent. In addition, parent characteristics are relevant to global tax minimization. To the extent that subsidiaries can, at the margin, alter the composition of their distributions among royalties, interest, and dividends, then whether their parents are in excess credit positions—or, alternatively, losing money domestically—will be important factors in dividend decisions.[11]

A third general view suggests that dividend repatriations are "valued" by the parent. That is, the parent desires a particular pattern of repatriations, and tax authorities have effectively forestalled clever use of royalty payments and transfer pricing at the margin. Alternatively, the parent values dividend distributions per se. In the literature on domestic dividend distributions, models with asymmetric information between firm "insiders" and "outsiders" (in the domestic case, "management" and "shareholders," respectively) figure prominently. Signaling models (see, e.g., Bhattacharya 1979) emphasize that dividend payments convey information about the profitability of the firm; such signals—valuable because of the private information—are sent even given the tax cost of paying dividends. It is hard to believe that private information about capital investment projects is an important problem in majority-owned or wholly owned affiliates of U.S. multinationals.[12]

An alternative information problem stresses "agency cost" considerations.[13] For example, absent substantial equity interest in the venture by a subsidiary's managers—or, alternatively, compensation tied closely to subsidiary profits—subsidiary managers may be tempted to raise costs by investing funds intended for "soft capital" expenditures (such as organizational expenditures or maintenance) in perquisites or projects for personal gain. Such soft capital expenditures are much harder to observe and monitor than spending on "hard capital" (capital investment projects). Monitoring is additionally complicated by differences in local language and custom, the possible involvement of host country nationals (or the host country government) with conflicting objectives, and so on. The optimal contract in such a setting will have less variable payments across project outcomes than would prevail under symmetric information (see the formal model in Gertler and Hubbard 1988). To the extent that direct ownership stakes by subsidiary managers are limited, incentive-compatible financing arrangements will necessarily mitigate the use of tax-minimizing strategies that artificially lower the subsidiary's accounting profits.

Such concerns have been expressed in the management literature as well. The use of complicated schemes for tax avoidance by shuffling profits among subsidiaries has been observed to be mitigated by high administrative costs and the increased difficulty in monitoring managerial performance. The need for internal accounting systems to monitor managerial decision making has been emphasized by Brooke and Remmers (1970) and Greene and Duerr (1970) and in survey evidence for U.S. firms by Burns (1980) and for U.S. and Japanese firms by Tang (1979, chap. 6).

5.1.4 Previous Studies of Dividend Repatriation Patterns

Empirical evidence on the determinants of multinational dividend repatriations and of the importance of tax considerations has been mixed, in part because of problems of data availability. In an early study, Barlow and Wender (1955) hypothesized that a multinational would make an initial infusion of capital and reinvest the earnings in the hope of a large ultimate realization. Such a pattern was not consistent with early empirical evidence, however. Stevens (1969) documented the importance of continuing infusions of capital by parents to established subsidiaries; additional evidence of continuing external finance was provided by Stevens (1972) and Severn (1972). The issue of adjustment of dividend repatriations to changes in profitability was addressed by Mauer and Scaperlanda (1972), who worked within the framework of Lintner's (1956) partial adjustment model of dividend payments. They found much more rapid speeds of adjustment of subsidiary dividend payments to earnings changes than had comparable studies for domestic (U.S.) firm payouts to shareholders; tax effects were not considered.

Perhaps the first systematic evidence incorporating tax effects is found in Kopits's (1972) study of 1962 data on U.S. subsidiary repatriations from a set of selected countries. Kopits finds that "mature subsidiaries" (those with low growth of desired capital stock) have higher payout ratios, ceteris paribus, than do subsidiaries with more rapidly growing desired capital stocks. However, he also finds important "tax price" effects, especially in countries with separate taxes on undistributed profits.[14]

Additional evidence against the view that dividends are only a residual has accumulated. Zenoff's (1966) survey of repatriation patterns within U.S. multinationals found that firms with "young" subsidiaries varied remittance patterns according to the subsidiaries' needs for funds while remittance patterns of "established" subsidiaries were set according to rules of thumb (see also Brooke and Remmers 1970, chap. 6). Using a sample of majority-owned affiliates of U.S. multinationals in 1977 and 1982, Jun (1987) finds that roughly 25 percent simultaneously repatriated dividends to their American parents and received from them new capital infusions. This fact not only seems to belie the trapped equity view of dividends but throws into question the skill of U.S. multinationals in avoiding taxes since two-way flows of funds between the U.S. parent and its more lightly taxed foreign subsidiary are always tax disadvantaged. Finally, Hines (1988b) observes that, even within the Hartman framework, particular features of the calculation of the indirect foreign tax credit should make dividend payouts (and subsidiary reinvestment decisions) sensitive to the tax and financial position of other subsidiaries; evidence for 1982 is consistent with important effects of these features.

Mutti (1981) analyzed repatriation patterns in data drawn from a large cross section of subsidiaries operating in eleven foreign countries in 1977. Dividends were the dominant form of repatriation in seven countries, including West Germany, which has an undistributed profits tax on corporate earnings. He finds a very low rank correlation coefficient between tax cost proxies and the relative role of dividends in total repatriations. When he controlled for industry effects, tax considerations appeared important. Dividend payments relative to earnings were negatively related to levels of interest and royalty payments (treated as predetermined in Mutti's estimating equation).

A number of studies of tax determinants of aggregate foreign direct investment also bear on the repatriation decisions of U.S. multinationals. Hartman (1981) and Boskin and Gale (1987) find the level of foreign direct investment out of retained earnings to be sensitive to rates of return and relative tax rates in the United States and abroad. The corollary of their finding is that repatriations are also sensitive to relative taxes. Newlon

(1987) broadly confirms their results, using adjusted data and a variety of econometric specifications.

5.2 Aggregate Repatriation Behavior

This section examines the pattern of aggregate repatriations by U.S. multinationals over the period 1962–82.[15] As illustrated in table 5.1, payouts from after-tax earnings are substantial, ranging for all industries from 21 percent in 1982 to 47 percent in 1962. The calculated payout rates are in line with those of U.S. domestic corporations reported in Poterba (1987).[16] Dividend payout rates are slightly higher for subsidiaries in manufacturing industries. Within manufacturing, there is significant variation across major industry groups—with, for example, high payout rates for motor vehicles (payouts exceeding current earnings in recession years) and low payouts in electronic equipment. Corresponding dollar volumes of dividends paid are reported in table 5.2. As table 5.2 indicates, the manufacturing industries account for by far the majority of the dividends received by U.S. multinational corporations each year.

Tables 5.3 and 5.4 report CFC dividends by country of their incorporation. The summary data in table 5.3 do not indicate a strong geographic pattern in dividend payout rates, suggesting that any effects that taxes may have on dividend distributions are likely to be operating through the particular circumstances of individual companies rather than a country's statutory tax rate on corporations. Table 5.4 exhibits dividend payout levels by country, illustrating the continuing importance of U.S. multinational operations in Canada, the United Kingdom, West Germany, France, Brazil, Mexico, and the Netherlands.

As noted earlier, dividends are not the only method by which a subsidiary can repatriate funds to its American parent. As shown in table 5.5, interest, rent, and royalty distributions are important as well. In the years for which separate data on the distributions are available, interest, rents, and royalties account for 43 percent of the (sum of the) distributions in 1976, 31 percent in 1974, 30 percent in 1972, and 39 percent in 1968. Here again, there is substantial variation across major industry categories, with interest, rents, and royalties virtually nonexistent in trade and very important in services. Within manufacturing, motor vehicles—an industry with relatively high dividend payouts—distributed little in the form of interest, rents, and royalties, while nonelectrical machinery relied more heavily on nondividend distributions.

Even apart from considerations of transfer pricing, focusing on dividend distributions from subsidiaries to parents directly may seriously underestimate total payments. In particular, dividends are often distributed to domestic subsidiaries of the U.S. parent company or distributed to another one of the parent's foreign subsidiaries. Table 5.6 documents the importance of these indirect distributions for selected years in which detailed data are available. In 1976 and 1982, for example, more dividends were paid indirectly to the parent than directly. In other years for which relevant data are available, direct payments are only about two-thirds of total dividend distributions.

In table 5.7, we reevaluate the magnitudes of dividend distributions (out of after-tax and also out of pre-tax current earnings) for selected years. The payout ratios reported in table 5.7 represent distributions made directly to the U.S. parent and to other U.S (domestic) corporations controlled by the parent. These payout ratios still understate total dividend distributions in the years reported since payments to other subsidiaries of the same parent are not included. Nonetheless, the payout ratios are quite high, exceeding 40 percent for all industries in most years (based on after-tax earnings); payouts are higher in manufacturing industries than average payouts for all industries. The payout rates reported in table 5.7 are substantially higher than those for domestic U.S. corporations noted previously in table 5.1.

As described in section 5.1, distributing dividends is not the only way in which CFCs can generate U.S. tax liabilities with their after-tax foreign earnings; CFCs are subject to the Subpart F rules that treat certain types of passive income and also foreign earnings reinvested in the United States as "deemed distributed" to American parents and hence currently taxable. Table 5.8 documents a dramatic rise in the level of Subpart F income over recent years.[17] Subpart F income rose from $60 million in 1968 (equal to 3 percent of actual dividend distributions [from table 5.7] that year) to $4.5 billion in 1982 (43 percent of actual dividends). Manufacturing industries accounted for the bulk of Subpart F income over this period, particularly the CFCs in petroleum, chemicals, nonelectrical machinery, and electronic equipment industries; motor vehicles CFCs became important sources of Subpart F income in 1982.

Since Subpart F income produces a U.S. tax liability very similar to the liability generated by an actual dividend repatriation, repatriated actual dividends *plus* deemed distributions indicate the fraction of foreign income subject to U.S. taxation each year.[18] From the percentages in tables 5.7 and 5.8, it is clear that the fraction has been rising over time. One likely explanation for the recent increase in Subpart F income is the secular rise in interest rates and the corresponding rise in the returns to CFCs' passive investments. But, more broadly, Subpart F income reflects a pattern of increasing repatriations, with Subpart F one vehicle for those repatriations. Unlike actual dividend distributions, of course, Subpart F income does not make funds directly available to the parent. However, making passive foreign investments and incurring Subpart F liabilities—rather than distributing dividends—allows a CFC's U.S. parent to defer U.S. tax liability on the principal amount reinvested since Subpart F applies only to the return on the reinvested funds. The rise in Subpart F income, then, assuming the primary source of that income to be passive investments, reflects an even larger rise in foreign-earned income that U.S. multinationals have chosen not to reinvest actively abroad.

U.S. multinationals are also required to pay U.S. taxes on the current earnings (and deduct against U.S. income the current losses) of their foreign branches. Since branch income is not eligible for deferral of U.S. taxes, it is clearly not in the interest of tax-avoiding U.S. multinationals to organize their profitable operations in low-tax foreign countries as branches rather than subsidiaries. The literature suggests that two types of firms might benefit from branch rather than subsidiary organization: petroleum firms that can recognize up-front tax losses from the special deductions for dry wells and depletion allowances and banks that can avoid onerous foreign regulations by not incorporating in foreign countries.

Table 5.9 indicates the importance of foreign branch operations of U.S. multinationals for the three years for which separate data on branches are available: 1982, 1980, and 1976. Total branch income (net of foreign taxes) in 1982 and 1980 is roughly equal to subsidiary dividend payments to U.S. parents and their domestic subsidiaries (from table 5.6), while in 1976 branch income is about half of U.S.-taxable dividends. The industry composition of branch income is quite different from that of dividends, however. Finance, insurance, and real estate (FIRE) firms earn more than half of total branch income, and petroleum companies earned more than half of the non-FIRE branch income in 1982 and 1980.[19] The FIRE branches were rather lightly taxed, while manufacturing branches endured foreign tax rates that average 73 percent in 1982, 68 percent in 1980, and 89 percent in 1976. Since parent U.S. companies average their branch income with the dividends they receive from subsidiaries in calculating their foreign tax credits, these highly taxed manufacturing branches may act as "tax cows" for American parents that also have lightly taxed subsidiaries from which they can repatriate dividends to soak up foreign tax credits from their branches.[20] Whether the tax credits from foreign branches can help explain subsidiary dividend behavior requires an examination that only firm-level data can provide.

5.3   Repatriation Behavior in 1984: Evidence from Micro Data

5.3.1   Summary Evidence from the Data

We now analyze the dividend payout behavior of U.S. multinationals in 1984, using subsidiary-level tax information. These micro data argue for a very different interpretation of multinational behavior than one might suppose from the aggregate numbers. In particular, we find strong evidence in favor of the view that multinationals very effectively minimize their U.S. taxes.

Our data were provided by the U.S. Department of the Treasury and consist of information on the tax returns filed by large U.S. multinationals with controlled foreign corporations in 1984.[21] Out of roughly 18,000 controlled foreign corporations in this sample, we excluded firms whose American parents had overall net operating losses and hence were untaxable on their foreign income that year. In addition, exclusions for inactive corporations, corporations filing part-year returns, missing variables, and obviously miscoded data reduce the sample to 12,041 foreign corporations and 453 American parent corporations. While the Internal Revenue Service estimated that a total of 45,000 CFCs would file information returns in 1984 (see Skelly and Hobbs 1986), we believe that our sample captures most of the economically significant CFCs.[22] The sample does not include American multinationals whose only foreign affiliates are branches or those with no controlled foreign corporations among their subsidiaries. Furthermore, the data span only one tax year. While cross-sectional data are not ideal for our purposes, the year 1984 offers a distinct advantage over years such as 1982 and 1980. Recessions in 1982 and 1980 created tax losses for CFCs and their American parents, reducing their chances of filing important tax forms and making their taxable incomes particularly unreliable proxies of permanent incomes. By contrast, 1984 was a year of economic expansion in the United States and abroad.

Most significantly, the micro data enable us to examine whether the summary information on distributions obtained from aggregate data reflect similar patterns among relatively homogeneous CFCs. In fact, we find much the opposite to be true. Most CFCs paid no dividends, though a minority made large payouts. Below, we first report some summary tabulations of the data. We then estimate a simple model of the response of CFC payouts to changes in the tax price of dividends, incorporating features of the domestic tax code that change the tax price regime.

Based on the data for 12,041 CFCs in 1984, the average dividend payout rate (out of after-tax earnings) to U.S. parents and their domestic subsidiaries is 42.1 percent. Including interest, rent, and royalties raises the distribution rate to over 60 percent. At first glance, such average payout figures seem consistent with the Treasury data for earlier years discussed above. However, summary figures for the micro data obscure important heterogeneity in patterns of repatriations. To illustrate this simply and starkly, we decompose (in table 5.10) the sample into four cells, according to whether "dividends" or "interest, rent, and royalties" (added together)[23] distributed to the American parent are greater than zero. For each cell, we report levels of assets, pre-tax earnings, after-tax earnings, dividends, interest, rent, and royalties as well as the numbers of CFCs and U.S. parents involved.

First, we observe that 69 percent of the CFCs—8,277 of them, accounting for 46 percent of total CFC assets and 33 percent of total after-tax earnings—paid *no* dividends and *no* interest, rent, or royalties in 1984.[24] An additional 1,815 CFCs—with 23 percent of the assets and 17 percent of after-tax earnings—paid interest, rent, and royalties but no dividends; their interest, rent, and royalty distributions equaled 65 percent of their after-tax earnings. The 732 CFCs—with 15 percent of the total assets and 19 percent of total after-tax earnings—who paid both dividends and interest, rents, and royalties distributed more than their current after-tax earnings through the two channels. Finally, the 1,217 CFCs—with 17 percent of total assets and 30 percent of after-tax earnings—who paid only dividends had an average payout rate of 86 percent. In short, dividend distributions are highly skewed; 84 percent of the CFCs paid no dividends at all.

It is difficult to reconcile these patterns within a strict agency cost model of multinational dividend behavior. In that framework, the managers of 84 percent of the universe of CFCs are unfettered by the requirement to pay dividends each year. Of course, the use of a single annual cross section may obscure the payout behavior of firms that pay regular dividends on a less than annual basis, and some parent firms may use nondividend payout methods to control their CFCs. More than eight thousand CFCs, however, pay zero dividends, interest, rents, and royalties to their American parents and their domestic subsidiaries.

On the other hand, the data in table 5.10 appear to be quite consistent with a tax-minimization model of multinational firm behavior. Most CFCs avoid current U.S. tax liability on their foreign earnings. And the selection of dividends rather than other forms of repatriation is consistent with tax-minimizing principles: CFCs paying dividends but no interest, rent, and royalties faced on average lower tax rates (34 percent) than those choosing to pay interest, rent, and royalties but no dividends (51 percent).

Some of the complicated financial arrangements used by multinationals can complicate interpretation of the statistics presented in table 5.10. In particular, it is possible that a relatively small number of foreign holding companies (owned by American parents) themselves own the shares of many of the CFCs in our sample; the dividends that they receive from the "second-tier" CFCs they own would not appear as repatriated by those CFCs to American parents and their domestic subsidiaries, even if the holding companies then turned around and sent the profits back to the United States. Those dividends would appear as repatriated by the holding companies, but such schemes would be consistent with small numbers of CFCs making dividend repatriations at the same time that aggregate dividends are large.

In fact, CFCs identified as nonbank holding companies are relatively unimportant in the sample, as are the FIRE industries generally; the sum of dividends paid by FIRE CFCs equals $1.0 billion. Table 5.11 provides further confirmation that financial flows within multinational firms do not greatly complicate the interpretation of table 5.10. Table 5.11 presents a breakdown of CFC financial behavior that includes dividends and interest, rents, and royalties received from other CFCs of the same American parent. As the table indicates, dividend flows from one CFC to another owned by the same parent are very small, grossing only $190 million for the whole sample. Interest, rent, and royalty payments are significantly larger, grossing $3.4 billion, but the majority are received by CFCs that pay nothing to their American parents. With some adjustments, then, it remains true that most CFCs appear to generate no U.S. tax liability on their income each year.

Section 5.2 illustrates the increasing significance of Subpart F income over time both absolutely and as a fraction of U.S.-taxable income of CFCs. Table 5.10 presents information on the Subpart F income of CFCs in different repatriation regimes. Total Subpart F income in 1984 was $3.3 billion, representing a reduction from its level in 1982. In addition, Subpart F income is heavily concentrated in CFCs that pay no dividends, a fact consistent with the view that some CFCs place their foreign earnings in passive foreign investments and incur Subpart F liabilities as a tax-minimizing strategy (relative to paying dividends directly). Use of such a strategy makes little sense, of course, in the presence of significant costs of intrafirm control.

The foreign tax credit status of a parent firm directly affects the tax cost of its CFCs' repatriations. Table 5.12 offers fine detail on parent firms' foreign tax credit positions and the Subpart F payouts of the non-FIRE CFCs described in table 5.10. Several features of these decompositions are of interest. First, sizable shares of total CFC assets (38 percent), after-tax earnings (45 percent), and dividends (53 percent) are accounted for by CFCs of firms with excess foreign tax credits. Second, firms with deficit foreign tax credits account for a disproportionate share (63 percent) of repatriations in the form of interest, rent, and royalties. This pattern is consistent with tax-minimizing behavior by CFCs whose host governments permit them to adjust their interest, rent, and royalty payments to related parties. Third, deficit foreign tax credit firms also account for a disproportionate share (58 percent) of Subpart F income, again in accord with tax-minimizing principles.

Given the small number of CFCs that pay dividends at all and the excess foreign tax credit status of U.S. parents that receive about half the dividends, the question arises of how much tax revenue the U.S. government collects on the profits earned by foreign subsidiaries of U.S. multinationals. Table 5.13 breaks down by foreign tax rate those CFCs that either pay dividends or incur Subpart F liabilities and whose parents have deficit foreign tax credits. The top panel presents data on CFCs whose payout is less than their current-year earnings and profits; the CFCs in the bottom panel have payouts greater than current-year earnings. For the latter, it is unfortunately impossible to identify from tax-form data their deemed-paid credits on that part of their payouts that exceed current-year income; still, current tax rates seem to be reasonable proxies for tax rates in earlier years.

There is substantial variation in foreign tax rates for these CFCs,[25] with about half the dividends coming from CFCs facing tax rates of over 40 percent. In addition, there is some bunching at the lower ranges. For Subpart F income, the pattern is, as one might expect, different; the CFCs earning Subpart F income are lightly taxed by foreign governments. Since American parents receive foreign tax credits for the foreign taxes paid by the CFCs described in table 5.13 (and also receive credits for any foreign withholding taxes paid on repatriation of those dividends), the residual after-credit income taxes paid to the U.S. government on CFC earnings in 1984 are very small. However, these small tax collections are associated with a system that has a large effect on CFC financial transactions generally, as we demonstrate below.

Our finding that U.S. taxation of dividend repatriations from multinationals raises very little revenue for the U.S. government needs to be qualified by the broader context of the tax system. The (potential) U.S. taxation of dividends may prompt CFCs to remit more U.S.-taxable interest, rent, and royalties than they otherwise would. In our sample of non-FIRE CFCs, only one-third of the interest, rent, and royalty payments ($1.5 billion out of $4.5 billion) were received by parents with excess foreign tax credits; the remaining two-thirds were presumably taxable at full rates. In addition, foreign earnings of CFCs may generate U.S. tax revenue through the taxation of domestic U.S. shareholders of parent companies since they are taxed on any added dividends the company pays because of its foreign earnings and they may pay capital gains taxes on share price appreciation from foreign earnings as well.

5.3.2 Estimating the Effects of Taxation on Repatriations

Because so many CFCs in our sample do not pay any dividends, estimating a simple regression model of dividend distributions is clearly inappropriate. In particular, estimated tax price effects in such a regression are biased toward zero. Simple probit models (not reported) reinforce the patterns noted in our discussion of table 5.12. The primary determinants of whether a CFC pays a dividend are the excess credit position of its parent and the amount of distributions in the form of interest, rent, and royalties. Industry effects do not appear to be very important in this respect.

We begin with a basic model of the form

$$(3) \qquad D_i = (\alpha_0 + \alpha_1 TAX_{ij})E_i + \beta'X_j,$$

where j and i index the parent and the CFC, respectively; D and E represent dividends and after-foreign-tax earnings of the CFC, respectively; and both

D and E are deflated by CFC assets.[26] TAX_{ij} represents the tax price to U.S. parent j of distributions from CFC i. X_j is a vector of parent j's characteristics. If the parent is in a deficit credit position, the tax price is given in equation (1).[27] For parents in excess credit positions, we take the U.S. tax price to be zero, [28] though the parent may owe withholding taxes on the dividends that cannot be credited against U.S. tax liabilities.

With panel data, one would incorporate the excess credit/deficit credit position of the parent in a switching-regime model. Indeed, if one could parameterize the transition process (from excess credit to deficit credit position), it would be possible in principle to estimate the average probability of being in one regime or the other. We, of course, have only a single cross section of data in which to observe the two regimes. The credit position is still endogenous. For example, higher payouts from CFCs with low tax prices make the parent firm more likely to have excess foreign tax credits. Indeed, even the location (and hence the foreign tax rate) of a CFC may be endogenous with respect to the tax rates of its parent's other CFCs. Potential instrumental variables to identify the credit regime include branch income, branch taxes, and interest, rent, and royalties (to the extent that they are exogenous). Unfortunately, the tax data do not come in a form that permits one to identify this non-CFC income and foreign taxes (of the parent) in order to employ an instrumental variables procedure. Accordingly, we take the excess credit/deficit credit position of the parent as exogenous to the CFC payout decision.[29]

Given the significance (revealed by the summary of the data) of the discrete choice of whether to pay a dividend, we estimated a Tobit model of dividend distributions. There are two regimes (corresponding to the parent's credit position). To illustrate, we define a dummy variable X equal to unity if the parent is in an excess credit position (and equal to zero otherwise) and estimate:

$$(4) \qquad D_i = (\beta_0 + \beta_1 TAX_i + \beta_2 X_i) + [\beta_3 + \beta_4(1 - X_i)TAX_i]E_i$$
$$\text{if } D_i > 0,$$
$$= 0 \quad \text{otherwise.}$$

That is, we allow the intercept to shift if the parent is in an excess credit position. We also included on the right-hand side of equation (4) major industry dummy variables[30] and the parent firm's ratio of its dividends paid to stockholders to its assets.

The first column of table 5.14 presents estimated coefficients from (4).[31] The principal findings can be summarized as follows. Conditional on the CFC's paying dividends and its parent's having deficit credits, the tax price of CFC dividends has a negative effect on distributions. The response of the payout rate to a 1 percentage point decrease in TAX is an increase of 0.16 percentage points. Evaluated at average values of the tax price, a 1 percentage point decrease in the U.S. corporate tax rate would raise the payout (relative to assets) by 0.28 percentage points, or about 4 percent of the mean CFC payout relative to assets. One cannot necessarily extrapolate such a change to evaluate the effects of a large reduction in corporate taxes such as that enacted in the Tax Reform Act of 1986 since the lower tax rate affects the probability of being in an excess credit position. When the parent has excess foreign tax credits, payout is increased, ceteris paribus.

The ratio of parent dividends to parent assets has a strong and positive effect on CFC distributions. This is consistent with a view that parents for whom agency problems of control (between domestic shareholders and domestic management) are most severe have higher payouts and, ceteris paribus, demand more cash from their CFCs to make these payments. Alternatively, domestic parents receiving dividends from their CFCs find uses for those funds, one of which is to distribute dividends to shareholders. Finally, coefficient estimates are not dramatically changed whether or not industry dummies are included. Table 5.14 does not report coefficients for industry dummies when they are present; breakdowns within manufacturing generally had estimated effects on payouts that were neither statistically significant nor economically important.

In the third column of table 5.14, we report results of estimating the same model, redefining the dependent variable to include Subpart F income. The estimated coefficients are similar to those in the first two columns, a result consistent with behavior by multinationals that treats Subpart F income as similar to dividend income.

5.4 Summary and Implications

Despite the growing importance of activities of overseas affiliates of U.S. firms, relatively little is known about multinationals' decisions to repatriate their foreign earnings. Analyses of aggregate data (and of data disaggregated to the level of major industry categories) on distributions by foreign subsidiaries of U.S. multinationals point to significant levels of repatriations of current earnings. Given the (domestic) tax costs of this activity, it seems at first surprising that subsidiaries should pay so much in dividends. The application of models of domestic firms' dividend decisions to this case is not straightforward, however. First, the aggregate data mask the fact that distributions are skewed; most subsidiaries pay no dividends. Second, the combination of deferral and granting credits for foreign taxes paid implies that many repatriating firms have excess foreign tax credits, so that the tax price of repatriations is not what it appears.

Understanding links between taxation and subsidiary repatriation decisions is important for assessing the effect of "dividend taxes" on the cost of capital. Under the "trapped equity" view of the dividend decision (in which repatriations are residuals in CFC accounts), only the foreign corporate tax rate matters for the cost of capital. Alternatively, when dividend patterns are of concern to the parent (e.g., for agency cost reasons), both domestic and foreign tax rates matter for the cost of capital.

Our results demonstrate that such simple pedagogical cases are likely to be difficult to apply. The relative unimportance of industry effects—as proxies for investment opportunities—within broad industry groups (such as manufacturing) casts doubt on the pure trapped equity view. For firms in deficit credit positions, we do find that shifts in the tax prices of their repatriations matter, in support of the view that parents value some stream of repatriations, trading off perceived benefits with tax costs. However, many firms are in excess credit positions. The interaction of (i) the credit system that adjusts for the burden of foreign taxes and (ii) deferral by taking subsidiary income only when repatriated implies that at any point in time many subsidiaries (most, in our sample) are likely to be at corner solutions, paying no dividends.

One concern stemming from our findings is that—if 1984 is a representative year—many U.S. parents are able to take advantage of intrafirm financial transactions and their abilities to time repatriations in order to reduce their U.S. tax liabilities. That is, the combination of the credit system and deferral can diminish substantially the revenue raised by the United States from the taxation of overseas operations of U.S. multinationals.[32] Given the volume of activity conducted by foreign affiliates of U.S. firms, these revenue consequences of the present system may be important. Of course, the recent reduction in the U.S. statutory tax rate from 46 to 34 percent increases the likelihood that many multinational firms will have excess foreign tax credits.[33] The effect of the rate reduction may be offset somewhat by the introduction of new functional baskets of foreign income and new methods of calculating indirect foreign tax credits introduced by the Tax Reform Act of 1986, but it remains to be demonstrated that the current system of taxing foreign subsidiaries of U.S. multinationals can generate significant amounts of tax revenue.

We believe that our analysis suggests the importance of modeling explicitly the margins on which payments from subsidiaries to parents are accomplished. The present U.S. system of taxing multinationals' income may be raising little U.S. tax revenue while stimulating a host of tax-motivated financial transactions. Whether current U.S. policy is a sensible approach depends very much on what we intend our international tax laws to do.

Appendix
Sources for Dividend Tables

[1] U.S. Department of the Treasury, Internal Revenue Service. Supplemental Report, *Statistics of Income* 1962. "Foreign Income and Taxes Reported on Corporation Income Tax Returns." Washington, D.C.: U.S. Government Printing Office.

[2] _____. Supplemental Report, *Statistics of Income* 1964, 1965, 1966. "Foreign Income and Taxes Reported on Corporation Income Tax Returns." Washington, D.C.: U.S. Government Printing Office.

[3] _____. Supplemental Report, *Statistics of Income* 1968, 1972. *International Income and Taxes.* "U.S. Corporations and Their Controlled Foreign Corporations." Washington, D.C.: U.S. Government Printing Office.

[4] _____. Supplemental Report, *Statistics of Income* 1968–72. *International Income and Taxes.* "Foreign Tax Credit Claimed on Corporation Income Tax Returns." Washington, D.C.: U.S. Government Printing Office.

[5] _____. Supplemental Report, *Statistics of Income* 1974. *International Income and Taxes.* "Foreign Tax Credit Claimed on Corporation Income Tax Returns." Washington D.C.: U.S. Government Printing Office.

[6] _____. Supplemental Report, *Statistics of Income* 1974–78. *International Income and Taxes.* "U.S. Corporations and Their Controlled Foreign Corporations." Washington, D.C.: U.S. Government Printing Office.

[7] _____. Supplemental Report, *Statistics of Income* 1976–79. *International Income and Taxes.* "Foreign Income and Taxes Reported on U.S. Income Tax Returns." Washington, D.C.: U.S. Government Printing Office.

[8] _____. 1985. "Compendium of Studies of International Income and Taxes, 1979–1983." Washington, D.C.: U.S. Government Printing Office.

[9] Barlow, Mary. 1986. "Foreign Tax Credit by Industry, 1982." U.S. Department of the Treasury, Internal Revenue Service, *SOI Bulletin* 5(4): 9–29.

[10] Carson, Chris. 1986. "Corporate Foreign Tax Credit, 1982: A Geographic Focus." U.S. Department of the Treasury, Internal Revenue Service, *SOI Bulletin* 6(2): 21–47.

[11]Simenauer, Ronald. 1986. "Controlled Foreign Corporations, 1982: An Industry Focus." U.S. Department of the Treasury, Internal Revenue Service, *SOI Bulletin* 6(1): 63–86.

[12] States, William. 1986–87. "Controlled Foreign Corporations, 1982: A Geographic Focus." U.S. Department of the Treasury, Internal Revenue Service, *SOI Bulletin* 6(3): 49–80.

Table 5.1   Dividends Paid by CFCs to U.S. Parents as a Share of CFC Post-tax Earnings (%)

U.S. Industry	1982	1980	1976	1974	1972	1968[a]	1966[a]	1965[a]	1962[a]
All industries	21	27	21	31	33	43	33	38	47
Mining	28	8	12	15	31	23	21	17	24
Construction	15	8	9	11	35	33	19	16	20
Manufacturing	24	30	22	32	35	45	34	38	50
Food	21	3238	22	18	30	48	34	29	62
Chemicals	29	26	32	31	33	47	42	34	40
Petroleum	20	27	23	26	44	84	36	49	58
Nonelectrical machinery	10	43	12	36	39	32	32	31	34
Electronic equipment	22	13	18	11	16	24	14	17	38
Motor vehicles	231	97	23	142	43	41	68	60	71
Transportation and public utilities	7	16	13	21	11	24	31	28	35
Trade	19	15	39	33	15	26	29	37	40
FIRE[b]	5	11	4	19	27	39	34	41	46
Banking	2	3	3	42	17	40	25	33	50
Insurance carriers	14	2	5	5	20	50	6	0	0
Services	11	22	10	66	27	36	24	69	23
Total of manufacturing six	22	31	21	32	37	47	38	40	53
Total manufacturing, except six	33	26	33	32	27	38	23	32	40
All U.S. Corporations[c]	69	33	29	29	39	43	37	38	43

Sources: 1982 table 1, pp. 75–80 in [11]; 1980 table 1, pp. 190–95 in [8]; 1976 table 11, pp. 262–85 in [7]; 1974 table 2, pp. 14–33 in [6]; 1972 table 16, pp. 93–97 in [3]; 1968 table 2, p. 17 in [3]; 1966 table 29, pp. 270–73 in [2]; 1965 table 25, pp. 254–57 in [2]; 1962 table 13, p. 86 in [1].

[a]1968 dividends paid to related persons, 1966 payments by directly owned foreign corporation, 1965 payments by directly owned foreign corporation, and 1962 dividends paid to domestic corporation. 1972–82 U.S. corporations with assets of at least $250 million.

[b]Finance, insurance, and real estate.

[c]Figures are adapted from Poterba (1987).

Table 5.2   **Dividends Paid by CFCs to U.S. Parents**

U.S. Industry	1982	1980	1976	1974	1972	1968[a]	1966[a]	1965[a]	1962[a]
All industries	4,829	8,358	3,112	4,095	3,210	1,978	1,512	1,445	1,127
Mining	188	75	36	44	35	13	22	11	5
Construction	40	27	38	22	5	22	15	12	8
Manufacturing	4,224	7,635	2,624	3,747	2,985	1,775	1,345	1,237	968
Food	331	259	198	114	158	121	87	72	79
Chemicals	922	1,004	566	656	399	325	227	173	118
Petroleum	908	2,417	486	1,028	805	493	324	314	293
Nonelectrical machinery	383	1,825	317	655	618	175	179	135	52
Electronic equipment	295	254	182	97	118	107	42	35	42
Motor vehicles	324	196	359	569	345	193	251	269	197
Transportation and public utilities	85	113	36	48	27	21	13	15	13
Trade	187	294	350	178	59	87	71	91	76
FIRE	83	144	20	38	61	45	32	37	36
Banking	18	13	8	24	10	6	2	2	2
Insurance carriers	41	28	5	3	11	1	1	0	0
Services	21	69	8	15	20	20	19	43	24
Total of manufacturing six	3,163	5,956	2,108	3,119	2,443	1,414	1,110	998	780
Total manufacturing, except six	1,061	1,679	516	628	542	361	235	239	189

Sources: 1982 table 1, pp. 75–80 in [11]; 1980 table 1, pp. 190–95 in [8]; 1976 table 11, pp. 262–85 in [7]; 1974 table 2, pp. 14–33 in [6]; 1972 table 16, pp. 93–97 in [3]; 1968 table 2, p. 17 in [3]; 1966 table 29, p. 270–73 in [2]; 1965 table 25, p. 254–57 in [2]; 1962 table 13, p. 86 in [1].

Note: All figures are in millions of current dollars.

[a] 1968 dividends paid to related persons, 1966 payments by directly owned foreign corporation, 1965 payments by directly owned foreign corporation, and 1962 dividends paid to domestic corporation. 1972–82 U.S. corporations with assets of at least $250 million.

Table 5.3   **CFC Dividend Payout Ratios to U.S. Parents, by Country**

Country of Incorporation of CFC	1982	1976	1974	1972	1968[a]	1962[a]
All countries	.21	.21	.22	.33	.30	.39
Canada	.30	.24	.18	.37	.25	.39
Mexico	−.24	.97	.14	.39	.28	.50
Brazil	.17	.15	.19	.20	.46	.06
Bahamas	.10	2.36	.39	.21	.13	.10
France	.89	.23	.13	.23	.42	.25
Netherlands	.17	.13	.05	−.20	.26	.20
United Kingdom	.12	.20	−.64	.27	.47	.56
West Germany	.26	.18	.45	.46	.38	.71
Japan	.21	.11	.20	.17	.12	.07
All others	.20	.20	.19	.30	.27	.30

Sources: 1982 table 1, pp. 63–65 in [12]; 1976 table 16, pp. 310–21 in [7]; 1974 table 7, pp. 61–84 in [6]; 1972 table 23, pp. 133–56 in [3]; 1968 table 8, pp. 43–64 in [3]; 1962 table 22, pp. 130–35 in [1].

[a]Payout ratios are calculated on after-tax earnings of the CFC. 1968 payments to all related persons. 1962 payments to domestic corporations.

Table 5.4   **CFC Payouts to U.S. Parents, by Country**

Country of Incorporation of CFC	1982	1976	1974	1972	1968[a]	1962[a]
All countries	4,829	3,112	4,095	3,210	1,423	1,133
Canada	1,034	797	888	783	325	316
Mexico	125	140	62	56	32	22
Brazil	197	102	94	59	58	3
Bahamas	35	33	171	40	11	5
France	216	113	116	124	54	24
Netherlands	115	57	40	53	18	11
United Kingdom	558	188	274	444	284	271
West Germany	428	414	679	440	172	151
Japan	51	36	80	42	9	1
All others	2,070	1,232	1,691	1,170	460	329

Sources: 1982 table 1, pp. 63–65 in [12]; 1976 table 16, pp. 310–21 in [7]; 1974 table 7, pp. 61–84 in [6]; 1972 table 23, pp. 133–56 in [3]; 1968 table 8, pp. 43–64 in [3]; 1962 table 22, pp. 130–35 in [1].

[a]All figures are in millions of current dollars. Payments to U.S. corporations filing returns. 1962 payments to domestic corporations. 1968 payments to all related persons.

Table 5.5 Distribution Patterns: CFCs of U.S. Parents (Selected Years): Fraction of Pretax Earnings Plus Interest, Rent, and Royalties Distributed to U.S. Parents

U.S. Industry	Dividends				Interest, Rents, Royalties				Both			
	1976	1974	1972	1968	1976	1974	1972	1968	1976	1974	1972	1968
All Industries	.12	.18	.19	.22	.09	.08	.08	.14	.21	.26	.27	.36
Mining	.08	.12	.22	.18	.03	.04	.12	.06	.11	.16	.34	.24
Construction	.06	.09	.21	.18	.10	.12	.11	.17	.16	.21	.32	.35
Manufacturing	.12	.19	.20	.23	.09	.07	.08	.13	.21	.26	.28	.36
Food	.13	.10	.18	.26	.06	.06	.05	.11	.19	.17	.23	.36
Chemicals	.18	.19	.19	.26	.09	.07	.09	.12	.27	.26	.28	.38
Petroleum	.16	.18	.31	.43	.02	.02	.03	.16	.18	.20	.34	.60
Nonelectrical machinery	.06	.17	.20	.14	.17	.18	.15	.18	.23	.35	.35	.32
Electronic equipment	.11	.06	.10	.23	.04	.05	.08	.09	.15	.11	.18	.22
Motor vehicles	.14	.64	.24	.21	.02	.04	.02	.06	.16	.68	.26	.28
Transportation	.07	.11	.07	.14	.12	.11	.08	.20	.19	.22	.15	.34
Trade	.21	.01	.10	.16	.00	.01	.01	.05	.21	.02	.11	.21
FIRE	.02	1.12	.13	.16	.11	.38	.19	.28	.13	1.50	.32	.44
Services	.04	.41	.13	.10	.39	.62	.20	.55	.43	.03	.33	.65
Total of six manufacturing	.12	.19	.21	.24	.09	.07	.08	.13	.21	.26	.33	.65
Total manufacturing, except six	.13	.19	.16	.20	.08	.06	.07	.13	.21	.25	.23	.33

Sources: 1976 table 11, pp. 270–85 in [7]; 1974 table 2, pp. 14–33 in [6]; 1972 table 16, pp. 93–97 in [3]; 1968 table 2, pp. 13–17 in [3].

Note: Figures are for U.S. corporations and their CFCs reported on Form 2952. Data for 1972–76 are for U.S. corporations with assets of at least $250 million.

Table 5.6   Direct and Indirect Dividend Payments by CFCs to U.S. Parents

	1982	1980	1976	1974	1972	1968
Dividends paid ($)	13,762	13,211	6,279	6,570	4,682	1,978
Fraction representing: (%):						
Payments to U.S. parent	35.1	63.3	49.6	62.3	68.6	72.2
Payments to U.S. subsidiaries of U.S. parent	40.3	17.4	26.8 ⎫			
			⎬ 37.7	37.7	31.4	27.8
Payments to foreign subsidiaries of U.S. parent	24.6	19.3	23.6 ⎭			
Interest/dividends	N.A.	.36	.08	.24	.21	.24
Rent and royalties/dividends	N.A.	.34	.64	.30	.30	.39

Sources: 1982 table 1, pp. 75–80 in [12]; 1980 table 1, pp. 190–95 in [8]; 1976 table 11, pp. 262–85 in [7]; 1974 table 2, pp. 14–33 in [6]; 1972 table 16, pp. 93–97 in [3]; 1968 table 2, p. 17 in [3]

Note: Dollar amounts are in millions of current dollars.

Table 5.7   Dividend Payouts by CFCs to U.S. Parents and Their Domestic Subsidiaries (%)

U.S. Industry	Payout Ratios								
	1982	1980	1976	1974[a]	1972[a]	1968[a]	1966[a]	1965[a]	1962[a]
All industries	61	42	43	49	48	43	33	38	47
	(38)	(28)	(27)	(31)	(30)	(26)	(22)	(25)	(30)
Mining	84	36	50	24	31	23	21	17	24
	(45)	(28)	(36)	(21)	(25)	(19)	(17)	(13)	(19)
Construction	79	54	29	15	35	33	19	16	20
	(57)	(45)	(23)	(12)	(24)	(22)	(15)	(14)	(16)
Manufacturing	63	44	44	51	35	45	34	38	50
	(38)	(28)	(27)	(33)	(22)	(27)	(22)	(25)	(32)
Food	60	5375	42	46	30	48	34	29	62
	(38)	(59)	(27)	(28)	(19)	(29)	(23)	(19)	(36)
Chemicals	56	41	49	46	33	47	42	34	40
	(33)	(26)	(32)	(30)	(21)	(30)	(28)	(22)	(26)
Petroleum	74	37	43	51	44	84	36	49	58
	(44)	(25)	(30)	(35)	(32)	(52)	(27)	(34)	(44)
Nonelectrical machinery	43	56	47	50	39	32	32	31	34
	(26)	(36)	(28)	(30)	(23)	(17)	(20)	(18)	(21)
Electronic equipment	61	38	50	43	16	24	14	17	38
	(40)	(26)	(31)	(27)	(11)	(14)	(9)	(11)	(23)

(continued)

Table 5.7 (continued)

U.S. Industry	Payout Ratios								
	1982	1980	1976	1974[a]	1972[a]	1968[a]	1966[a]	1965[a]	1962[a]
Motor vehicles	376 (101)	168 (39)	31 (19)	161 (76)	43 (25)	41 (23)	68 (40)	60 (35)	71 (41)
Transportation and public utilities	39 (31)	50 (35)	47 (31)	35 (24)	11 (8)	24 (17)	31 (23)	28 (18)	35 (27)
Trade	69 (49)	23 (17)	41 (22)	36 (21)	15 (10)	26 (17)	29 (19)	37 (25)	40 (23)
FIRE	37 (26)	32 (23)	37 (24)	48 (27)	27 (16)	39 (23)	34 (25)	41 (32)	46 (31)
Services	49 (27)	38 (23)	25 (16)	83 (43)	27 (17)	36 (22)	24 (16)	69 (47)	23 (12)
Total of manufacturing six	63 (37)	46 (29)	44 (28)	53 (34)	37 (23)	47 (28)	38 (25)	40 (26)	53 (35)
Total manufacturing, except six	65 (41)	40 (26)	42 (25)	41 (26)	27 (17)	38 (23)	23 (15)	32 (21)	40 (25)

Sources: 1982 table 1, pp. 75–80 in [11]; 1980 table 1, pp. 190–95 in [8]; 1976 table 11, pp. 262–85 in [7]; 1974 table 2, pp. 14–33 in [6]; 1972 table 16, pp. 93–97 in [3]; 1968 table 2, p. 17 in [3]; 1966 table 29, pp. 270–73 in [2]; 1965 table 25, pp. 254–57 in [2]; 1962 table 13, p. 86 in [1].

Note: Data are for U.S. corporations and their CFCs reported on Form 2952. Payout ratios based on after-tax earnings appear first; payout ratios based on pretax earnings are in parentheses. 1972–82: U.S. corporations with assets of at least $250 million.

[a] 1968 dividends paid to related persons, 1966 and 1965 payments by directly owned foreign corporation, 1962 dividends paid to domestic corporations, and 1972 and 1974 dividends include payments to foreign subsidiaries of U.S. corporations.

Table 5.8   **Subpart F Income of U.S. CFCs Relative to CFC Dividend Payouts**

U.S. Industry	1982	1980	1976	1974	1972[a]	1968[a]
All industries	$4,466	2,579	823	359	96	60
	(.43)	(.24)	(.17)	(.05)	(.02)	(.03)
Mining	156	58	18	1	4	. . .
	(.33)	(.19)	(.16)	(.01)	(.07)	. . .
Construction	43	108	15	1	6	2
	(.22)	(2.51)	(.31)	(.03)	(.23)	(.13)
Manufacturing	3,498	2,060	736	327	73	39
	(.42)	(.22)	(.18)	(.05)	(.02)	(.02)
Food	151	78	39	9	18	5
	(.22)	(.24)	(.13)	(.03)	(.07)	(.04)
Chemicals	609	518	174	20	13	13
	(.41)	(.44)	(.25)	(.02)	(.02)	(.04)
Petroleum	731	574	278	236	. . .	. . .
	(.33)	(.20)	(.41)	(.12)	. . .	. . .
Nonelectrical machinery	307	234	39	5	6	10
	(.22)	(.12)	(.04)	(.01)	(.01)	(.06)
Electronic equipment	239	185	49	15	11	1
	(.44)	(.33)	(.13)	(.04)	(.04)	(.01)
Motor vehicles	1,112	56	13	5	2	. . .
	(2.79)	(.21)	(.03)	(.01)	(.01)	. . .
Transportation and	348	92	8	6	6	4
public utilities	(.98)	(.41)	(.06)	(.07)	(.09)	(.19)
Trade	146	131	32	11	. . .	4
	(.24)	(.37)	(.09)	(.06)	. . .	(.05)
FIRE	249	97	7	9	5	8
	(.80)	(.32)	(.08)	(.10)	(.05)	(.18)
Banking	198	33	3	5	1	. . .
	(1.35)	(.28)	(.04)	(.16)	(.07)	. . .
Insurance carriers	31	28	2	4	. . .	. . .
	(.38)	(.64)	(.22)	(.44)	. . .	. . .
Services	24	32	5	4	1	3
	(.29)	(.34)	(.26)	(.17)	(.03)	(.15)
Total of manufacturing	3,149	1,645	592	290	50	29
six	(.47)	(.23)	(.18)	(.06)	(.01)	(.02)
Total manufacturing,	349	415	144	37	23	10
except six	(.22)	(.19)	(.20)	(.05)	(.03)	(.07)

Sources: 1982 table 1, pp. 75–80 in [11]; 1980 table 1, pp. 190(N95 in [8]; 1976 table 11, pp. 262–85 in [7]; 1974 table 2, pp. 14–33 in [6]; 1972 table 16, pp. 93–97 in [3]; 1968 table 2, p. 17 in [3]; 1966 table 29, pp. 270–73 in [2]; 1965 table 25, pp. 254–57 in [2]; 1962 table 13, p. 86 in [1].

Note: Dollar amounts in millions are includable (Subpart F) income of CFCs. Figures in parentheses are ratios of Subpart F income to dividends paid by CFCs to U.S. corporations and their domestic subsidiaries.

[a]1972 and 1968 dividend payments include dividends paid to foreign subsidiaries of the U.S. parent.

Table 5.9 Foreign Branches of U.S. Corporations: Income and Foreign Taxes

	1982			1980			1976		
	After-tax Branch Income ($)	Foreign Branch Tax Rate	After-tax Branch Income as a Share of CFC Dividends Paid[a]	After-tax Branch Income ($)	Foreign Branch Tax Rate	After-tax Branch Income as a Share of CFC Dividends Paid[a]	After-tax Branch Income ($)	Foreign Branch Tax Rate	After-tax Branch Income as a Share of CFC Dividends Paid[a]
All industries	8,942	.39	.86	11,783	.46	1.11	2,267	.65	.47
Mining	338	.24	.71	308	.66	1.01	350	.63	3.18
Construction	7	.70	.04	19	.42	.44	14	.22	.29
Manufacturing	1,754	.73	.21	4,229	.68	.45	373	.89	.09
Food	73	.57	.11	99	.46	.30	72	.45	.23
Chemicals	125	.80	.09	490	.49	.41	7	.91	.01
Petroleum	1,194	.76	.54	2,945	.72	1.02	102	.96	.15
Nonelectrical machinery	128	.50	.09	72	.63	.04	86	.46	.10
Electronic equipment	186	.49	.34	255	.38	.46	−11	1.55	−.03
Motor vehicles	54	.29	.14	29	.52	.11	15	.52	.04
Transportation and public utilities	76	.24	.21	33	.46	.15	24	.37	.25
Trade	−7	1.41	−.01	93	.27	.26	28	.33	.08
FIRE	6,789	.08	21.83	7,071	.07	23.18	1,470	.18	15.98
Banking	6,638	.08	45.16	7,024	.06	60.03	1,359	.17	19.41
Insurance carriers	139	.31	1.70	54	.41	1.23	74	.24	8.22
Services	−15	6.00	−2.18	27	.41	.28	7	.36	.37
Total of manufacturing six	1,760	.73	.26	3,890	.69	.54	271	.92	.08
Total manufacturing, except six	−6	1.09	.00	339	.47	.16	102	.53	.14

Sources: 1982 table 1, pp. 19–26 in [9]; 1980 table 1, pp. 51–59 in [8]; 1976 table 2, pp. 92–99 in [7].

[a]Dividends paid include payments to U.S. parent and its domestic subsidiary.

Note: Dollar figures are in millions. Data obtained from Form 1118, U.S. corporation returns.

Table 5.10   Distribution Breakdowns: Micro Data on U.S. CFCs in 1984

	Assets ($)	Pretax Earnings ($)	After-tax Earnings ($)	Average Tax Rate (%)	Dividends ($)	Interest, Rent, Royalties ($)	Subpart F ($)	Number of:	
								CFCs	Parents
Dividends and interest, rent, royalties > 0	55.1 (.15)	7.90 (.19)	4.54 (.19)	42.5	3.8 (.38)	1.95 (.42)	0.33 (.10)	732 (.06)	183
Dividends > 0; interest, rent, royalties = 0	62.7 (.17)	11.1 (.26)	7.3 (.30)	34.2	6.3 (.63)	0 (0)	.63 (.19)	1,217 (.10)	252
Dividends = 0; interest, rent, royalties > 0	83.7 (.23)	8.5 (.20)	4.2 (.17)	50.6	0 (0)	2.73 (.58)	.74 (.23)	1,815 (.15)	288
Dividends and interest, rent, royalties = 0	169.6 (.46)	14.4 (.34)	8.0 (.33)	44.4	0 (0)	0 (0)	1.58 (.48)	8,277 (.69)	433

Source: Authors' tabulations based on U.S. Treasury data described in the text.

Note: Dollar amounts are in billions of dollars. Figures in parentheses are shares of column totals.

Table 5.11   **Financial Flows between Parties Related to U.S. CFCs, 1984 ($)**

	Dividends		Interest, Rent, Royalties	
	Received	Paid to U.S.	Received	Paid to U.S.
Dividends and interest,	.048	3.8	.200	1.95
rent, royalties > 0	(.25)	(.38)	(.06)	(.42)
Dividends > 0; interest,	.075	6.3	.400	0
rent, royalties = 0	(.39)	(.62)	(.12)	(0)
Dividends = 0; interest,	.030	0	.716	2.73
rent, royalties > 0	(.16)		(.21)	(.58)
Dividends and interest,	.037	0	2.129	0
rent, royalties = 0	(.20)		(.62)	(0)

Source: Author's tabulations based on U.S. Treasury data described in the text.

Note: Dollar amounts are in billions of dollars. Figures in parentheses are shares of column totals.

Table 5.12 Distribution Breakdowns: Detail on Credit Position and Subpart F Liabilities, 1984

	Billions of Dollars						Number of:	
	Assets	Pretax Earnings	After-tax Earnings	Dividends	Interest, Rent, Royalties	Subpart F	CFCs	Parents
Dividends and interest, rents, royalties > 0:								
Excess credit; Subpart F = 0	18.6	1.9	1.0	1.4	0.33	0	302	73
	(.35)	(.25)	(.23)	(.38)	(.17)	(0)	(.42)	(.37)
Excess credit; Subpart F > 0	6.7	.2	.05	.2	.044	.103	25	12
	(.12)	(.02)	(.01)	(.05)	(.02)	(.33)	(.04)	(.06)
Deficit credit; Subpart F = 0	25.8	5.1	2.9	1.9	1.46	0	373	104
	(.48)	(.66)	(.67)	(.52)	(.76)	(0)	(.52)	(.53)
Deficit credit; Subpart F > 0	2.4	.5	.4	.2	.08	.208	13	9
	(.04)	(.06)	(.05)	(.05)	(.04)	(.67)	(.02)	(.04)
Dividends > 0; interest, rents, royalties = 0:								
Excess credit; Subpart F = 0	23.1	5.5	3.5	2.9	0	0	439	89
	(.45)	(.54)	(.53)	(.53)		(0)	(.41)	(.33)
Excess credit; Subpart F > 0	4.1	.7	.5	.7	0	.26	75	23
	(.08)	(.07)	(.08)	(.13)		(.76)	(.07)	(.08)
Deficit credit; Subpart F = 0	22.5	3.8	2.4	1.6	0	0	508	133
	(.44)	(.37)	(.37)	(.29)		(0)	(.48)	(.49)
Deficit credit; Subpart F > 0	1.5	.18	.15	.3	0	.08	36	27
	(.03)	(.02)	(.02)	(.05)		(.24)	(.03)	(.10)

(continued)

Table 5.12 (continued)

	Billions of Dollars						Number of:	
	Assets	Pretax Earnings	After-tax Earnings	Dividends	Interest, Rent, Royalties	Subpart F	CFCs	Parents
Dividends = 0; interest, rents, royalties > 0:								
Excess credit; Subpart F = 0	28.1	4.5	1.8	0	.54	0	543	87
	(.40)	(.57)	(.51)		(.27)	(0)	(.32)	(.27)
Excess credit; Subpart F > 0	1.9	.17	.12	0	.58	.09	28	17
	(.03)	(.02)	(.03)		(.03)	(.22)	(.02)	(.05)
Deficit credit; Subpart F = 0	35.9	2.6	1.2	0	1.3	0	1,086	182
	(.51)	(.33)	(.34)		(.65)	(0)	(.64)	(.56)
Deficit credit; Subpart F > 0	4.3	.59	.41	0	.11	.32	48	40
	(.06)	(.08)	(.12)		(.05)	(.78)	(.03)	(.12)
Dividends and Interest, Rents, Royalties = 0:								
Excess credit; Subpart F = 0	52.8	7.8	3.4	0	0	0	2,963	134
	(.45)	(.62)	(.53)			(0)	(.41)	(.25)
Excess credit; Subpart F > 0	5.5	.72	.36	0	0	.21	139	46
	(.05)	(.06)	(.06)			(.40)	(.02)	(.09)
Deficit credit; Subpart F = 0,	53.8	3.6	2.2	0	0	0	3,890	270
	(.46)	(.28)	(.34)			(0)	(.54)	(.51)
Deficit credit; Subpart F > 0	4.6	.52	.44	0	0	.31	156	80
	(.04)	(.04)	(.07)			(.60)	(.02)	(.15)

Source: Authors' tabulations based on U.S. Treasury data described in the text.

Note: Figures in parentheses are percentages of column totals.

Table 5.13   Foreign Tax Rates of CFCs Paying Dividends to Parents with Deficit Foreign Tax Credits, 1984

All Industries	Assets	Earnings and Profits	Earnings and Profits After Tax	Dividends	Interest, Rents, Royalties	Subpart F	Number of CFCS
Payout less than current earnings and profits after tax:							
Total	57,264	9,424	6,299	2,247	1,474	792	794
Foreign tax rate:							
≤20%	24,074	2,594	2,465	389	205	682	284
20–30%	4,093	596	439	101	27	40	82
30–40%	9,951	1,915	1,199	395	362	52	115
40–40%	8,818	2,436	1,362	806	245	7187	
50–60%	7,824	1,538	727	519	517	1	89
>60%	2,502	346	105	43	62	11	37
Payout more than current earnings and profits after tax:							
Total	31,828	2,994	1,942	2,187	264	1,145	645
Foreign tax rate:							
≤20%	18,861	1,155	1,070	1,020	57	897	342
20–30%	3,101	198	144	64	23	121	42
30–40%	1,238	152	99	167	18	7	55
40–50%	2,145	282	151	215	72	37	75
50–60%	2,748	766	365	462	54	8	51
>60%	3,735	440	111	257	38	74	80

Note: Figures are in millions of dollars. Details may not add to totals due to rounding.

Table 5.14   **Tobit Model of CFC Dividend Distributions**

Independent Variable	Dependent Variable			
	Dividends/Assets		Dividends + Subpart F/Assets	
Constant	− 14.6359	− 15.7046	− 10.2714	− 10.8799
	(.4511)	(.3070)	(.3268)	(.2204)
TAX	− .0155	− .0145	− .0101	− .0097
	(.0997)	(.0100)	(.0076)	(.0076
X	1.0229	1.1961	.6281	.8568
	(.3727)	(.3536)	(.2667)	(.2551)
Earnings/assets	.1088	.1145	.0967	.0988
	(.0405)	(.0395)	(.0297)	(.0294)
TAX* (earnings/assets)	− .1606	− .1707	− .1318	− .1367
	(.0943)	(.0924)	(.0697)	(.0692)
Parent dividends/parent assets	34.1940	43.4463	26.2514	31.5056
	(6.1868)	(5.9001)	(4.4807)	(4.3105)
Industry dummies	Present	None	Present	None
Log likelihood	− 8,452.2	− 8,502.7	− 9,437.5	− 9,459.7
Percentage with payout	16.7	16.7	20.2	20.2
Number of observations	10,606	10,606	10,606	10,606

Note: Standard errors are in parentheses.

Notes

1. Controlled foreign corporations also made sizable repatriations out of their pre-foreign-tax income in the form of interest, rent, and royalties paid to their American parents. These data are reported in Goodspeed and Frisch (1989).

2. This list includes France, Belgium, the Netherlands, and Norway; others such as Switzerland and West Germany have complicated systems that are hybrids of territorial and residence systems.

3. For somewhat more detail on the foreign tax credit mechanism and recent changes therein, see Ault and Bradford (in this volume); for more comprehensive treatment of earlier law, see McDaniel and Ault (1981). In order to be eligible for the credit, firms must own at least 10 percent of a foreign affiliate, and only those taxes that qualify as income taxes are creditable. Further, there are some complications in the calculation of deemed-paid credits that are important to the results presented in sec. 5.3

4. This feature may be more important in an international setting since exchange rate variability can create substantial changes in dollar-denominated capital values. For a critical analysis of recent legislative changes in the U.S. taxation of income and capital values affected by foreign exchange movements, see Wahl (1987).

5. The nomenclature is somewhat detailed. All foreign operations take place through affiliates; those that are separately incorporated are subsidiaries. Majority ownership is sometimes very important from a legal, economic, and data-reporting standpoint; much of the U.S. Department of Commerce data on foreign operations of U.S. multinationals is reported for majority-owned foreign affiliates, without dis-

tinguishing branches from subsidiaries. Controlled foreign corporations are the subset of subsidiaries that meet the ownership requirements described in the text; they need not be (but usually are) majority owned by a single parent.

6. It seems reasonable here to assume that there are no fundamental (i.e., not related to taxes) differences between debt and equity contracts, so long as the parent is the sole owner of either claim. Caves (1982) discusses evidence on this point.

7. For a concise survey of OECD withholding rates on various types of remittances, see Alworth (1988, chap. 4). All are well below statutory tax rates. See also various issues of Price Waterhouse's *Corporate Taxes*.

8. For further elaboration of this model, see also Poterba and Summers (1985) and Poterba (1987).

9. Tax-minimizing multinationals have incentives to raise the (recorded) prices of goods sold by affiliates in low-tax jurisdictions to other affiliates in higher-tax jurisdictions. Properly used, transfer pricing can repatriate profits from high-tax foreign countries while generating tax deductions in those countries. Naturally, U.S. and foreign tax authorities discourage tax-minimizing transfer price manipulations and have adopted regulations to deter firms from engaging in them. For the purposes of this paper, we will assume that those rules are binding and that transfer pricing cannot be used for tax avoidance in repatriations. For evidence that transfer prices are sensitive to tax considerations, see Wheeler (1988) and Grubert and Mutti (1989); for contrary evidence, see Bernard and Weiner (in this volume). Of course, in a wide class of circumstances, it is difficult even to know what constitute appropriate transfer prices for goods traded within multinational corporations; Hines (1988a) suggests an approach to this problem.

10. Foreign subsidiaries of multinational firms are unable to use other devices commonly employed by domestic firms to distribute earnings to shareholders without creating a dividend tax liability. For example, share repurchases and liquidating distributions by foreign subsidiaries are treated for tax purposes as if they were dividends.

11. Detailed reviews of tax-minimizing patterns of intrafirm financial transactions in multinationals can be found in Alworth (1988) and Scholes and Wolfson (1988). Scholes and Wolfson consider as well the effects of U.S. taxation on the decision of foreign multinationals to acquire U.S. firms.

12. Even in the case of a domestic firm, signaling models must confront the empirical regularity (in U.S. data) that large, mature firms have high payout rates while small, growing firms (with presumably the greatest need to signal) have very low or zero payout rates (see Fazzari, Hubbard, and Petersen 1988).

13. Agency cost motivations for dividend distributions are considered by Jensen (1986) and Hubbard and Reiss (1988).

14. Some caution must be exercised in interpreting such results. Kopits uses pooled cross-sectional/time-series data on subsidiaries in different countries in 1961 and 1962. Since fixed country effects were not included, we cannot separate co-movements among variables reflecting persistent differences across countries (e.g., in the mix of industries of the constituent subsidiaries) from true within-group variation. Horst (1972) notes that certain (two-digit) industry groups are more likely to invest abroad, so that analyses of payout ratios by country without information on industry composition or comparison of payout ratios of subsidiaries (as a whole) with U.S. firms (as a whole) may not be informative.

15. The period before 1962 remains something of a black box to the tax analyst. The tax system was quite different before 1962, but the reason that we do not include those years in our analysis is that tax data on multinational financial behavior are neither consistently nor comprehensively available for any of those years.

16. The payout ratios reported in Poterba (1987) do not incorporate foreign earnings and retentions of American multinationals, making the comparison somewhat strained. However, adjusted payout ratios reported in Hines (1988b) do not differ greatly from those in Poterba (1987).

17. Data on Subpart F income are available for years prior to 1968 but are not reported in table 5.8. The years before 1968 are very similar to 1968 and 1972 in that Subpart F income is trivial relative to actual dividend distributions.

18. One hesitates to construct a series of such numbers in part because some of the repatriations designated as dividends in the data may represent income that was previously (or possibly even currently) deemed distributed as Subpart F. Hence, there is the possibility of double counting that income. Figures for dividend payments to American parents and their domestic subsidiaries are taken from Form 5471 and its predecessor Form 2952; these forms instruct the taxpayer not to include as dividends the deemed distributions under Subpart F. But it is somewhat ambiguous whether to include as a current-year dividend the current distributions of Subpart F income of prior years. Because Subpart F income is stacked first in the payout inventory rules, this may not be a major problem. And, since firms have little incentive to overstate their dividends on Form 5741, we follow the Treasury in treating dividends and Subpart F income separately.

19. The growth of petroleum firms after 1974 may be responsible for the anomalously low petroleum industry earnings in 1976. Since oil companies can expense for tax purposes part of their exploration and development costs, taxable earnings are likely to be low in a period of rapid growth. This observation should reinforce one's caution in drawing conclusions from simple cross sections of taxable income and tax rates.

20. Certain types of income are kept in separate "baskets" to prevent just such pooling. The Tax Reform Act of 1986 strengthened the functional separation of various income types (see also Ault and Bradford, in this volume). In addition, the creditability of foreign taxes on petroleum income has since 1975 been subject to various limits.

21. This sample is a subset of the sample collected by the Statistics of Income Division of the Internal Revenue Service on the same basis as that used to construct the aggregate statistics described in sec. 5.2. Strictly speaking, the universe for this sample is large U.S. multinationals reporting on their tax forms that they have controlled foreign corporations in 1984. The data of course cannot include corporations that fail to file their tax forms, and there is some evidence that tax noncompliance is a particularly serious problem for corporations earning income in offshore tax havens (see Rice 1989). But the questionable income of this group seems unlikely to be quantitatively significant compared to the corporations we include.

22. Goodspeed and Frisch (1989) analyze data from a larger sample of CFCs in 1984, one that was not restricted in the same way as ours. The CFCs in their sample had after-foreign-tax earnings of $30 billion, while ours had $24 billion; their CFCs paid $11.8 billion in dividends, ours $10.1 billion.

23. We add interest, rent, and royalty payments together in the subsequent analysis because they represent repatriation methods that (usually) share the feature of tax deductibility in CFCs' host countries. We do not claim that they are identical; in particular, the three types of payments are often subject to different withholding tax rates by foreign governments, and their levels may be restricted in different ways. Our focus in any case is on dividend payments; we presume firms to have less year-to-year discretion over interest, rent, and royalty payments than they do over dividend distributions.

24. A potential complication arises in interpreting these data since, prior to the enactment of the Tax Reform Act of 1986, firms were allowed for tax purposes to

treat dividends paid in the first sixty days of their annual accounting period as paid during the previous year. This rule, enacted to permit firms with complicated foreign tax situations the opportunity to calculate their foreign tax obligations before selecting their repatriation strategies for the year, makes it almost impossible for us to know the tax consequences of a year's dividend payouts since firms are not required to indicate on their tax forms to which year dividends paid in the first sixty days are attributed. This problem has not been previously addressed, though it applies to all the published U.S. aggregate data and to all the micro data of which we are aware; the aggregate numbers reported in *Statistics of Income* publications represent dividends paid at any time during the tax year. As it happens, this problem is not quantitatively significant (at least in 1984) since of $9.15 billion paid in dividends (outside FIRE industries) only $1.15 billion were reported to have been paid during the first sixty days.

25. It is interesting to note in table 5.13 that the pretax rate of return (on assets) generally rises with the tax rate, as one would expect. It declines sharply, however, for firms with the highest foreign tax rates, perhaps implying judicious use of transfer pricing to lower reported earnings in such jurisdictions. We are grateful to Mark Wolfson for this observation.

26. There are other reasonable candidates for variables with which to deflate D and E in (3) and subsequently; our discussant Mark Wolfson suggested stockholder's equity rather than total assets. Our choices are, however, tightly constrained by limited data: total CFC assets is the only reliable stock variable we could extract from the tax forms.

27. In our empirical work, we use .46 for τ and the average foreign tax rate of the CFC for τ^*. Since none of the American parents in our sample had domestic tax losses that year and all are large corporations, .46 is a very close approximation of their marginal U.S. corporate tax rates. The average foreign tax rate is the best that one can do for τ^*; without panel data, it is impossible to know exactly the indirectly creditable foreign tax rate on dividends that exceed current-year earnings and profits. Two additional features of foreign tax systems are not included in the tax prices we use. One is that we ignore foreign withholding taxes on dividends. These taxes represent net costs when American parents have excess foreign tax credits. The other is that some countries like West Germany employ split-rate corporate tax systems that tax distributed profits differently (less heavily, in the German case) than reinvested profits. Variations in withholding taxes and corporate tax systems are unlikely to be important enough to change the results reported in table 3.14, but we are currently investigating those effects.

28. This is not fully satisfactory, of course, since excess credits can be carried forward. That is, there is an opportunity cost of suing excess credits in a given period and a potential benefit from generating additional excess credits. These costs and benefits depend on the discount rate and the probability of transiting to a deficit credit state (itself endogenous). Absent longitudinal data on the parent's tax status and foreign income, there is little scope for incorporating this consideration.

29. To the extent that our results are biased, one would expect the estimated tax price effect to be understated.

30. The industries are mining, construction, transportation, trade, services, and the following manufacturing industries: food, chemicals, nonelectrical machinery, electronic equipment, and motor vehicles; the excluded category is other manufacturing industries.

31. This equation is estimated only for non-FIRE CFCs, in order to avoid the potential problem that the dividend payments of a manufacturing CFC to a holding company that owns it would be double counted as income.

32. Modifying these provisions for the taxation of multinationals (say, by removing "deferral" and taxing earnings directly) is difficult within the framework

of the corporate income tax because some attempt would have to be made to measure "profits" of the CFC. One alternative would be to adopt a variant of a corporate "cash flow" tax, which would tax the difference between net revenues and investment expenditures. In such a system, there is no argument for crediting foreign taxes paid; because investment is expensed, the U.S. Treasury is a partner in the firm's equity. Absent the credit, the U.S. parent would get its share (one minus the corporate-cash-flow tax rate) of the net-of-foreign-tax returns from investing. The removal of deferral and the credit system removes much of the incentive to use financial transactions to time tax payments.

33. This is significant, of course, only to the extent that other countries do not follow suit in reducing their statutory tax rates.

References

Adler, Michael. 1979. U.S. taxation of U.S. multinationals: A manual of computation techniques and managerial decision rules. In *International finance and trade,* ed. M. Salant and G. Szego, 2:157–210. Cambridge, Mass.: Ballinger.

Alsegg, R. J. 1971. *Control relationships between American corporations and their European subsidiaries.* Research Study no. 107. New York: American Management Association.

Alworth, Julian. 1988. *The finance investment and taxation decisions of multinationals.* Oxford: Blackwell.

Auerbach, Alan J. 1979. Wealth maximization and the cost of capital. *Quarterly Journal of Economics* 93:433–46.

Barlow, E. R., and J. T. Wender. 1955. *Foreign investment and taxation.* Englewood Cliffs, N.J.: Prentice-Hall.

Bhattacharya, Sudipto. 1979. Imperfect information, dividend policy, and the "bird in the hand" fallacy. *Bell Journal of Economics* 10:259–70.

Boskin, Michael J., and William G. Gale. 1987. New results on the effects of tax policy on the international location of investment. In *The effects of taxation on capital accumulation,* ed. M. S. Feldstein, 201–19. Chicago: University of Chicago Press.

Bradford, David F. 1981. The incidence and allocation effects of a tax on corporate distributions. *Journal of Public Economics* 15:1–22.

Brooke, M. Z., and H. L. Remmers. 1970. *The strategy of multinational enterprise: Organization and finance.* New York: Elsevier.

Burns, J. O. 1980. Transfer pricing decisions in U.S. multinational corporations. *Journal of International Business Studies* 11:23–29.

Caves, Richard E. 1982. *Multinational enterprise and economic analysis.* Cambridge: Cambridge University Press.

Fazzari, Steven M., R. Glenn Hubbard, and Bruce C. Petersen. 1988. Financing constraints and corporate investment. *Brookings Papers on Economic Activity* 1:141–95.

Gertler, Mark L., and R. Glenn Hubbard. 1988. Financial factors in business fluctuations. In *Financial market volatility: Causes, consequences, and policy responses.* Kansas City: Federal Reserve Bank of Kansas City.

Goodspeed, Timothy J., and Daniel J. Frisch. 1989. U.S. tax policy and the overseas activities of U.S. multinational corporations: A quantitative assessment. Washington, D.C.: U.S. Department of the Treasury. Mimeo.

Greene, J., and M. G. Duerr. 1970. *Intercompany transactions in the multinational firm: A survey.* Managing International Business no. 6. New York: Conference Board.

Grubert, Harry, and John Mutti. 1989. Taxes, tariffs and transfer pricing in multinational corporation decision-making. U.S. Department of the Treasury. Mineo.

Hartman, David. 1981. Domestic tax policy and foreign investment: Some evidence. NBER Working Paper no. 784. Cambridge, Mass.: National Bureau of Economic Research, October.

———. 1985. Tax policy and foreign direct investment. *Journal of Public Economics* 26:107–21.

Hines, James R., Jr. 1988a. Multinational transfer pricing and its tax consequences: Where the profits are. Princeton University. Mimeo.

———. 1988b. Taxation and U.S. multinational investment. In *Tax policy and the economy,* ed. L. H. Summers, 2:33–61. Cambridge, Mass.: MIT Press and the National Bureau of Economic Research.

Horst, Thomas. 1972. Firm and industry determinants of the decision to invest abroad: an empirical study. *Review of Economics and Statistics* 54:258–66.

———. 1977. American taxation of multinational firms. *American Economic Review* 67:376–89.

Hubbard, R. Glenn, and Peter C. Reiss. 1988. Corporate payouts and agency problems: Evidence from the undistributed profits tax of 1936–1938. Columbia University. Mimeo.

Jensen, Michael C. 1986. Agency costs of free cash flow, corporate finance, and takeovers. *American Economic Review* 76:323–29.

Jun, Joosung. 1987. Taxation, international investment, and financing sources. Harvard University. Mimeo.

King, Mervyn A. 1977. *Public policy and the corporation.* London: Chapman & Hall.

Kopits, George F. 1972. Dividend remittance behavior within the international firm: A cross-country analysis. *Review of Economics and Statistics* 54:339–42.

———. 1976. Intra-firm royalties crossing frontiers and transfer-pricing behaviour. *Economic Journal* 86:791–805.

Lintner, John V. 1956. Distribution of income of corporations among dividends, retained earnings, and taxes. *American Economic Review* 46:97–113.

McDaniel, Paul R., and Hugh J. Ault. 1981. *Introduction to United States international taxation.* Deventer, The Netherlands: Kluwer.

Mauer, L. J., and A. Scaperlanda. 1972. Remittances from U.S. direct foreign investment in the European Economic Community: An exploratory estimate of their determinants. *Economia Internazionale* 25:33–43.

Mutti, John. 1981. Tax incentives and repatriation decisions of U.S. multinational corporations." *National Tax Journal* 34:241–48.

Newlon, Timothy Scott. 1987. Tax policy and the multinational firm's financial policy and investment decisions." Ph.D. diss., Princeton University.

Poterba, James M. 1987. Tax policy and corporate saving. *Brookings Papers on Economic Activity* 2:455–503.

Poterba, James M., and Lawrence H. Summers. 1985. The economic effects of dividend taxation. In *Recent advances in corporate finance,* ed. E. I. Altman and M. G. Subrahmanyam. Homewood, Ill.: Irwin.

Price Waterhouse. *Corporate taxes—a worldwide summary* (various annual editions and individual country guides). New York: Price Waterhouse.

Rice, Eric M. 1989. The corporate tax gap: Evidence on tax compliance by small corporations. Harvard University. Mimeo.

Robbins, S. M., and R. B. Stobaugh. 1973. *Money in the multinational enterprise: A study of financial policy.* New York: Basic.
Scholes, Myron S., and Mark A. Wolfson. 1988. The effects of changes in tax laws on corporate reorganization activity. Stanford University. Mimeo.
Severn, A. K. 1972. Investment and financial behavior of American direct investors in manufacturing. In *The international mobility and movement of capital,* ed. F. Machlup, W. S. Salant, and L. Tarshis. New York: Columbia University Press for the National Bureau of Economic Research.
Skelly, Daniel F., and James R. Hobbs. 1986. Statistics of income studies of international income and taxes. *SOI Bulletin* 6:1–19.
Stevens, G. V. G., 1969. Fixed investment expenditures of foreign manufacturing affiliates of United States firms: Theoretical models and empirical evidence. *Yale Economic Essays* 9:137–206.
———. 1972. Capital mobility and the international firm. In *The international mobility and movement of capital,* ed. F. Machlup, W. S. Salant, and L. Tarshis. New York: Columbia University Press for the National Bureau of Economic Research.
Stopford, J. M., and L. T. Wells, Jr. 1972. *Managing the multinational enterprise: Organization of the firm and ownership of the subsidiaries.* New York: Basic.
Tang, R. Y. W. 1979. *Transfer pricing practices in the United States and Japan.* New York: Praeger.
Wahl, Jenny Bourne. 1987. Taxation of foreign exchange gains and losses. OTA Working Paper 57. Washington, D.C.: U.S. Department of the Treasury, October.
Wheeler, James E. 1988. An academic look at transfer pricing in a global economy. *Tax notes* (4 July), 87–96.
Zenoff, D. B. 1966. The determinants of dividend remittance practices of wholly owned European and Canadian subsidiaries of American multinational corporations. D.B.A. thesis, Graduate School of Business Administration, Harvard University.

Comment   Mark A. Wolfson

I enjoyed this paper very much, particularly the analysis of the micro data for 1984. The exercise serves to remind us just how much richness can be lost when our inferences about economic behavior are necessarily restricted to economic aggregates.

Hines and Hubbard (hereafter HH) partition the data in particularly informative ways. Like all good descriptive work, the analysis raises as many questions as it answers. And one of the nice things about working with micro data is that the questions raised might actually be answerable. Whereas parsimony in modeling is especially virtuous when the available data afford few degrees of freedom (the typical situation when macro data

Mark A. Wolfson is the Joseph McDonald Professor in the Graduate School of Business at Stanford University, the Thomas Henry Carroll Ford Foundation Visiting Professor of Business Administration in the Graduate School of Business Administration at Harvard University, and a research associate of the National Bureau of Economic Research.

are used), there are returns to more sophisticated modeling when micro data are available, particularly when they offer thousands of degrees of freedom. Before providing some examples of what I have in mind here, let me first make a few more general remarks about the paper.

The claim that there exists a dividend puzzle would seem to be a bit of a red herring in a multinational context in the presence of a foreign tax credit system. So is the fact that the U.S. Treasury appears to collect no corporate-level tax on the profits earned abroad by U.S. multinationals.

Unlike in the domestic context, where a current dividend gives rise to the collection of current tax revenues by the U.S. Treasury, a dividend paid to a U.S. multinational by a profitable subsidiary operating in a country with a tax rate similar to that in the United States will, to a first approximation, yield no current revenues to the U.S. Treasury by design. So we need not resort to a "trapped equity" calculus to remind us that the cost of a current dividend to the declaring firm is less than the immediate tax cost because, to a first approximation, there is not an immediate tax cost, let alone a future one. Indeed, the most interesting aspect of the paper is that U.S. multinational firms appear to be so careful in tax planning that they leave clearly identifiable audit trails that document their attempts to contain even the second-order effects of multinational tax rules on their tax liabilities.

Having said this, it is nevertheless misleading to state that the U.S. Treasury collects no revenues on the foreign profits earned by U.S. multinationals. A component of taxes that HH (and others in this literature) have forgotten is the shareholder-level tax. As U.S. multinationals generate profits abroad, share prices increase, and the resulting increase in domestic dividends and capital gains give rise to U.S. tax revenues. This source of tax revenue may well increase following passage of the Tax Reform Act of 1986 because the reduction in the capital gains tax break increases shareholder-level taxes.

Prior to presenting their data, HH attempt to lay out a framework for understanding (1) the incentives to repatriate foreign earnings in alternative forms (by means of dividends, interest, rent, royalties, transfer pricing, and Subpart F rules) and (2) the incentives to repatriate foreign earnings, rather than to reinvest them locally, as a function of tax rates and foreign tax credit limitation status.

As an aside here, another dimension that they might have considered is the importance of alternative routes (from one controlled foreign corporation to another in different tax jurisdictions) through which repatriations can travel to maximize after-tax repatriations. Some of the accounting firms have developed elaborate software to do just this. Price Waterhouse, for example, has a package that considers up to one hundred routes and allows as many as four intermediate countries to repatriate.

In my remaining comments, I would like to embellish the HH framework somewhat. I will close with some remarks about their data analysis. To begin, HH develop the conventional wisdom that the deferral of U.S. tax on foreign subsidiary earnings of U.S. multinationals provides an incentive for the subsidiaries to postpone the payment of dividends to their U.S. parents. This is basically correct in a wide variety of circumstances, but not in all situations.

For example, HH interpret Jun's evidence (that a significant fraction of multinationals simultaneously receive dividends from their foreign subsidiaries as well as make new capital infusions) as being inconsistent with tax minimization. But in fact the payment of dividends can be a tax-saving strategy in a number of important situations. I will briefly list three cases here.

First, it pays to repatriate, particularly from low-tax countries, when the parent's marginal U.S. tax rate is temporarily low. This may be the result of net operating losses for the parent; the add-on minimum tax prior to 1986, which dropped marginal tax rates from 46 to 39.1 percent; the alternative minimum tax; or investment tax credit carryforwards.[1] With a little calculating, table 5.6 of the paper can be seen as providing evidence consistent with an incentive to repatriate when the parent generates net operating losses. Dividends paid to the U.S. by foreign subsidiaries in 1982 were roughly the same as in 1980 despite a 25 percent reduction in foreign subsidiary earnings. And many firms faced net operating losses in 1982, as we know from the work of Auerbach and Poterba, among others, so firms apparently seized this opportunity to repatriate (see Auerbach and Poterba 1987, 304–42).

A second situation in which it may pay to accelerate dividend payments is when a firm's excess foreign tax credits are about to expire unused. In such a circumstance, it may pay to repatriate profits from a low-tax foreign subsidiary to use up the credits, especially if such profits would eventually be repatriated anyway. This ensures that the low-tax subsidiary profits will escape a repatriation tax. Note that it can be optimal to repatriate from the low-tax country and turn around and make new capital infusions in the same firm, all purely for tax reasons.

As a third example, if repatriation occurs from a low-tax foreign subsidiary for nontax reasons (such as the existence of poor investment opportunities), repatriations from a high-tax country can actually give rise to a net tax refund from the U.S. Treasury. That is, any firm in a deficit foreign tax credit position, repatriating from a country where the tax rate exceeds that in the United States, will receive a foreign tax credit exceeding the U.S. tax on the repatriated dividend.

Related to this last point, let me turn next to the question of the "tax price" of repatriation. HH argue that the tax price of a repatriation when a firm is in an excess foreign tax credit position is zero (or possibly positive if a withholding tax must be incurred to effect the repatriation). This observation is reflected in the design of their Tobit model. But this claim ignores the possibility that excess foreign tax credits, which can be carried forward for five years, might actually get used to offset U.S. tax in the future. Setting the tax price of a dividend repatriation to zero for an excess foreign tax credit firm is akin to arguing that the marginal tax rate of a firm that generates net operating losses is 0 percent, and this can be far from correct. A firm with an excess of foreign tax credits naturally becomes attracted to those investments in low-tax countries for which repatriation of profits is desirable for nontax reasons within a short period of time. Such considerations can make the tax price of repatriation negative even where excess foreign tax credits exist.

Another way to use up excess foreign tax credits not mentioned in the paper is to generate export sales from the United States rather than through a foreign subsidiary, branch, or even a so-called foreign sales corporation. In appropriate circumstances, this permits half the profit on the sale to be allocated to "foreign-source income," thereby allowing, in most cases, an additional foreign tax credit to be taken against U.S. tax liability equal to the U.S. tax rate on half the profit.[2]

A further complication that arises here is that a firm may face an excess foreign tax credit for one income basket but a deficit foreign tax credit for another. In this case, the tax price of repatriation can be positive for a firm reporting excess foreign tax credits.

Trapped Equity

As suggested earlier, I was a bit puzzled by the prominence given the trapped equity ideas in this paper. The trapped equity argument applies when retained earnings are trapped in the corporation and cannot be distributed in any other way than by dividends. Yet a major theme of the paper is alternatives to dividends as a way to deliver retained earnings to the parent. There is one sense, though, in which the trapped equity argument does apply more naturally to the multinational setting than to the domestic one. Shoven's evidence on share repurchases as a tax-favored way of distributing profits to shareholders is sufficient to cast serious doubt on the importance of the trapped equity argument in the United States. In the multinational context, however, share repurchases and liquidations give rise to dividend treatment to the extent of earnings and profits generated since 1962. As a related matter, such transactions (i.e., share repurchases and liquidations) should be counted as dividends for the purposes of the HH study, but I do not believe that they were.

Analysis of the Micro Data

Let me turn next to what I find to be the most interesting part in the paper: the micro data for 1984 presented in tables 5.10–5.14. First, consider table 5.10. Let me begin with a minor quibble. HH indicate that, for firms paying interest, rent, or royalties, but no dividends, to their parents, the amount distributed was 65 percent of after-tax earnings. While this is true, it can be misleading. Interest, rent, and royalties represent a distribution of pretax earnings. Their payment triggers tax in the United States. More meaningfully, these payments represented less than 25 percent of taxable income before interest, rent, and royalties.

Now I will turn to more important matters. Although not calculated directly in table 5.10, it is interesting to compare the average foreign tax rate paid for firms that paid dividends but not interest, rent, or royalties (34 percent) to those that paid interest, rent, or royalties but not dividends (51 percent). For the most part, the benefits of tax deferral exist only in low-tax foreign subsidiary jurisdictions, as HH correctly point out. This, in turn, has implications for the optimal capital structure of foreign subsidiaries.

Because dividends can be delayed for many years but interest on debt, rent on lease contracts, and royalties on licensing agreements cannot be, equity financing is desirable in low-tax environments.[3] Similarly, in high-tax environments, distributions from pretax income in a form that is deductible locally are tax preferred, so debt, leases, and licenses are desirable financing arrangements, although these benefits must be traded off against the cost of precommitment to the timing of repatriation that is not present with dividends. Because of this, capital structure may well differ systematically across foreign subsidiaries as a function of their tax rates.

In the Tobit model run by HH, this possibility is not considered. Their dependent variable is dividends divided by total assets. The arguments I have just made, however, suggest that the ability to explain cross-sectional variation in dividends as a function of the "tax price" of paying them might be improved if dividends were deflated by stockholders' equity rather than total assets to control for capital structure differences. Despite this, their results in table 5.14 fare pretty well on this score.

One final comment about the results in table 5.10 is in order. In interpreting the finding that 84 percent of foreign subsidiaries paid no dividends in 1984, HH note that most controlled foreign corporations appear to generate no U.S. tax liability on their income each year. But, given an average foreign tax rate of nearly 43 percent (and this is before withholding taxes on dividends), repatriations would hardly raise any U.S. tax anyway.

I will skip over table 5.11 other than to mention in passing that it constitutes good detective work to deal with the possible problem of foreign holding companies polluting the results. Moving on to table 5.12, we see that firms with deficit foreign tax credits account for 63 percent of interest, rent, and royalty repatriations. HH claim that this is consistent with tax-minimizing behavior, but I cannot see why. Such repatriations are neutral relative to dividends for deficit foreign tax credit firms. Both can be shown to have a tax price equal to that given in equation (1) of the paper. On the other hand, both are inferior to passive investment that generates Subpart F income.

As to passive income, table 5.12 also reveals that deficit foreign tax credit firms account for a disproportionate share of Subpart F income (58 vs. only 52 percent of total assets). This is consistent with what HH expected to see, but what I find striking is that such a high proportion of Subpart F income is accounted for by excess foreign tax credit firms.

This points to a possible tax motivation for investing in Subpart F income that is not recognized in the paper. Firms with excess foreign tax credits and without good active investment opportunities might wish to postpone repatriations until they can average the large foreign tax credits with income from lower-tax-rate controlled foreign corporations. Another possibility is that, until the Tax Reform Act of 1986, the definition of earnings and profits differed for ordinary dividends and for Subpart F income. Since dividends are taxable only to the extent of earnings and profits, repatriation by way of Subpart F income can be preferred if it results in a larger nontaxable return of capital than does a dividend repatriation.

But table 5.12 reveals much more. With some calculating, one can see that deficit foreign tax credit firms reporting Subpart F income generate an amount of Subpart F income equal to 7.15 percent of total assets. This suggests that a significant fraction of total assets (probably well in excess of half) is invested passively. By contrast, excess foreign tax credit firms reporting Subpart F income generate total Subpart F income equal to only 3.64 percent of total assets, suggesting a percentage investment in Subpart F assets of perhaps half as much. Note that Subpart F investment for deficit foreign tax credit firms is more desirable the lower is the average tax rate of the foreign subsidiary. In this regard, some calculating from table 5.12 reveals that the average tax rate of the deficit foreign tax credit firms reporting Subpart F income is 21.8 percent, whereas those reporting no Subpart F income pay average tax rates of 42.4 percent or nearly twice as much in 1984. At this high rate, deferral is not particularly valuable. Table 5.13 demonstrates this point even more vividly.

Table 5.13 is interesting for another reason that is not discussed in the paper. It may be stretching things some, but table 5.13 can be interpreted as providing evidence that transfer pricing is being used to repatriate profits for controlled foreign corporations that face the highest tax rates. One would expect competition to result in pretax rates of return on investment to be increasing in the level of tax rates across tax jurisdictions.[4] Table 5.13 shows this to be the case except for the firms facing the highest tax rates.

It would be interesting to compare the pretax return on asset numbers in table 5.13 with analogous numbers for excess foreign tax credit firms. Table 5.13 reports data for deficit foreign tax credit firms only. The excess foreign tax credit firms have an even greater incentive to shift income via transfer pricing, so it would be interesting to see whether the positive relation between tax rates and pretax investment rates of return turns negative for these firms at lower average tax rates.

Finally, I will comment briefly on the Tobit model of dividends reported in table 5.14. I like the results here, but a few qualifications are in order. I have already expressed my major experimental design regret, that the model does not control for expected capital structure differences across the subsidiaries. It also does not consider withholding taxes, although this is acknowledged by HH. In addition, the model takes as exogenous factors that are clearly endogenous, although the authors are well aware of this as well.

Although the result that dividends are higher where there is an excess foreign tax credit is sensible (and is consistent with my earlier argument that the tax cost of a repatriation can be negative in a present value sense if foreign tax credits can be carried forward and used to offset U.S. taxes in the future), it is also partially induced by construction. If dividends were the only means to effect repatriation, a necessary condition for generating an excess foreign tax credit would be to pay a dividend.

Finally, table 5.14 considers two dependent variables: dividends divided by total assets and dividends plus Subpart F income divided by total assets. HH claim that the results are similar across the two dependent variable specifications, suggesting that Subpart F income responds similarly to dividend income with respect to the independent variables in the model. But this seems inconsistent with what was shown in tables 5.12 and 5.13. Indeed, on closer inspection, there is no inconsistency: Subpart F income does *not* seem to behave similarly to dividend income. In fact, the estimated coefficient on the foreign tax credit dummy drops 40 percent when Subpart F income is included in the dependent variable despite the fact that Subpart F income is less than 20 percent of dividends. And this makes sense: Subpart F income is desirable the *lower* the tax rate and hence the less likely it is that excess foreign tax credits are present. Similarly, the coefficient on the tax cost variable declines by one-third, which is consistent with the earlier finding that Subpart F income is the preferred repatriation method when tax rates are lower abroad.

To conclude, Hines and Hubbard are to be greatly commended for a fine piece of work. They have provided the best analysis of microdata in the multinational area that I have seen. Their effort deserves to be widely read, for it should stimulate much though on how taxes affect the flow of capital in an increasingly global economy.

Notes

1. The presence of investment tax credit (ITC) carryforwards affects the marginal tax rate since the ability to utilize ITCs is tied directly to the regular tax. Each dollar of regular tax frees up some ITC carryforward.

2. On the other hand, up to 25 percent of the profits from sales through a "foreign sales corporation" may also give rise to "foreign-source income."

3. Two caveats are in order here. First, withholding tax rates often differ among the repatriation alternatives, and this can affect the optional capital structure. Second,

unlike equity financing, debt financing allows the possibility of repatriating principal without triggering a tax even when foreign ''earnings and profits'' are positive.

4. For further elaboration of this point, see Scholes and Wolfson (in press).

References

Auerbach, Alan J., and James M. Poterba. 1987. Tax loss carryforwards and corporate tax incentives. In *The effects of taxation on capital accumulation,* ed. Martin Feldstein. (Chicago: University of Chicago Press).

Scholes, Myron S., and Mark A. Wolfson. In press. *Taxes and business strategy: A global planning approach.* Englewood Cliffs, NJ: Prentice-Hall.

III The Effect of Taxation on Trade and Capital Flows

6 International Spillovers of Taxation

Jacob A. Frenkel, Assaf Razin, and Steve Symansky

Tax policies have profound effects on the temporal composition and on the intertemporal evolution of the macro economy. They influence saving and investment decisions of households and firms as well as decisions governing labor supply and demand. With integrated world markets for goods and capital, the effects of tax policies undertaken by a single country spill over to the rest of the world. Recognition of such international economic interdependence stimulated interest in the international coordination of fiscal policies, in general, and of tax policies and tax reforms, in particular. The purpose of this paper is to highlight key issues pertinent for the understanding of some international effects of domestic tax policies and of international tax harmonization.

The analytical framework used in the paper adopts the saving-investment balance approach to the analysis of international economic interdependence. It thus emphasizes the effects of changes in the time profile of the various taxes on the intertemporal allocations of savings, investment, and labor. These dynamic effects are supplemented by the more conventional effects of the level of taxes on the margins governing labor-leisure choice (such as the negative effect of consumption and income taxes on labor supply). In order to gain some feel for the magnitudes involved, we present in section 6.1

Jacob A. Frenkel is the economic counsellor and director of research of the International Monetary Fund and a research associate of the National Bureau of Economic Research. Before joining the IMF he was the David Rockefeller Professor of International Economics at the University of Chicago. Assaf Razin is the Daniel Ross Professor of International Economics at Tel Aviv University, a research associate of the National Bureau of Economic Research, and a visiting scholar at the International Monetary Fund. Steve Symansky is a senior economist in the Research Department at the International Monetary Fund.

The authors wish to thank Lans Bovenberg, David Bradford, and Martin Feldstein for useful discussions, Ravina Malkani for efficient research assistance, and Willem Buiter for helpful comments.

stylized facts on the time profile of average consumption and income tax rates for the seven major industrial countries. These stylized facts reveal large international diversity of tax rates and tax structures. They also reveal the significant changes that took place over time in some of the countries.

In section 6.2, we present the basic international-intertemporal model. The model, grounded on microeconomic foundations, is neoclassical in nature and is suitable therefore for the analysis of the incentive effects of tax policies. It allows for rich tax structures and contains a detailed specification of public- and private-sector behavior. The various economies are integrated through both goods and capital markets. Our formulation focuses on the roles played by taxes on income and consumption (value-added) as well as by a unified international market for capital.

In section 6.3, we apply the analytical framework to an examination of the international implications of tax harmonization. In this context, we analyze the consequences of revenue-neutral conversions between income and consumption (VAT) tax systems. Reflecting our emphasis on the saving-investment balance, we demonstrate that the effects of such changes in the composition of taxes depend critically on international differences in saving and investment propensities, which in turn govern the time profile of the current account of the balance of payments. The key results are derived analytically and are also illustrated by means of dynamic simulations. In section 6.4, we shift the focus of analysis from the composition of taxes to the timing of taxes. We thus examine the international effects of budget deficits and public-debt management. We demonstrate analytically as well as by means of dynamic simulations that these effects depend critically on whether the government manages its deficit through alterations in income or consumption taxes.

In section 6.5, we combine the analytical framework of section 6.2 with the key elements of the analysis in sections 6.3 and 6.4 to examine the effects of international tax harmonization. The impetus to such an examination is provided by the discussions surrounding the tax harmonization measures (notably the VAT) associated with the move toward the single market of Europe of 1992. The main results conform with those obtained from the analysis of revenue-neutral tax conversions. Accordingly, it is shown that the saving-investment balance approach is useful for the analysis of the effects of international tax harmonization. Specifically, the dynamic simulations demonstrate that these effects depend critically on the intercountry differences in saving and investment propensities. These differences underlie the current account position and its evolution over time. The paper ends with concluding remarks. The appendix that follows the main text presents the details of the simulation model.

6.1 Average Tax Rates in Major Industrial Countries

In this section, we present stylized facts concerning (average) tax rates in the seven major industrial countries: Canada, the United States, Japan,

France, Germany, Italy, and the United Kingdom. Since we focus our theoretical and simulation analysis on changes over time of income and consumption taxes, we attempt to present here some measures of the evolution of these tax rates.

It is important, however, to start with a word of caution: the marginal tax rates relevant for the analysis of investment, savings, and labor supply are relatively clear as a conceptual matter. In practice, however, owing to the complexity of the tax code involving progressivity of taxes, exemptions, tax credits, tax evasion, delays and advances in payments of taxes, and the like, the empirical counterparts to the conceptual marginal tax rates are less clear. Owing to intercountry differences in the tax code in the factors underlying tax collections and in the relative share of state and local governments in total tax revenue, the international comparison of tax rates is even more complex. Keeping these empirical difficulties in mind, we nevertheless attempt to highlight some key features of intercountry differences in consumption and income tax rates. In calculating the various tax rates, we divide the general government tax-revenue data from OECD (1987a) by a corresponding computed tax base from OECD (1987b). We thus generate series of average tax rates for the major industrial countries.[1]

Figure 6.1 exhibits the total tax rate for the period 1973–86.[2] It highlights the international diversity of this measure of the tax burden. While in Japan and the United States the total tax rate is less than 30 percent by 1986, the rest of the OECD are substantially higher, reaching close to 45 percent in

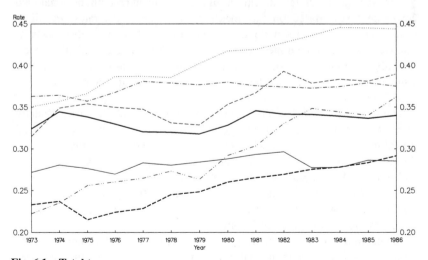

Fig. 6.1   Total tax

——— United States
– – – United Kingdom
·········· France
—·—·— Germany
—··—··— Italy
——— Canada
– – – Japan

France. The other noteworthy feature apparent in figure 6.1 is the different degree of variability of this measure of tax rates over time. For example, while for some countries (e.g., Italy, France, and Japan) this measure of tax rates exhibits a positive trend, for other countries such a trend is less pronounced.

While the total tax rate provides some information regarding the overall tax burden, the key decisions concerning investment, saving, and labor supply depend on the detailed composition of taxes. Our main focus in this paper is on consumption and income taxes. We turn next, therefore, to examine more detailed information. Figure 6.2 exhibits the consumption tax rate. As is evident, the highest measure of the consumption tax rate prevails in France (about 15 percent), while the lowest prevails in Japan and the United States (about 3 percent). The figure also reveals the upward trend (during the 1980s) prevailing in Canada, Italy, and the United Kingdom, whose rate has risen to about 10 percent (the rate prevailing in Germany). In this context, the sharp increase in the U.K. tax rate associated with the decision in 1979 to nearly double the value-added tax rate is especially noteworthy. The intra-European differences in the consumption tax rates are of special relevance in view of the VAT harmonization proposals associated with the plans for Europe of 1992.

Figures 6.3–6.5 exhibit various measures of income tax rates. The personal income tax rates shown in figure 6.3 reveal the international diversity. The highest rate prevails in Canada (about 22 percent), while the lowest rate prevails in France (about 10 percent). Also noteworthy is the upward trend in the Italian personal income tax rate.

The income tax rates shown in figure 6.4 include both personal and corporate taxes. Based on this measure, the highest tax rates prevail in Canada and the United Kingdom. The height of the U.K. tax rate reflects its relatively high corporate income tax. The lowest tax rate (about 10 percent) prevails in France. The significant decline of this measure in 1982 in the United States reflects the sharp fall in the corporate income tax rates associated with the Tax Act of 1981.

The role of the social security and payroll tax rates and the internationally diversity thereof is presented in figure 6.5. We first note the upward trend prevailing in all major industrial countries. A second noteworthy feature is the roles played by these tax rates relative to the income tax rates in Canada and France. While France has the highest social security and payroll tax rate (exceeding one-third), Canada has the lowest rate (below 10 percent). This ranking of Canada and France is the opposite to the one obtained in figure 6.4 pertaining to the personal income tax rate.

In concluding this section, we present in table 6.1 selected summary data on the various tax rates in the major industrial countries and on their changes over time. The international diversity of these rates, notably within Europe, is of special interest in view of the tax harmonization plans for Europe of 1992.

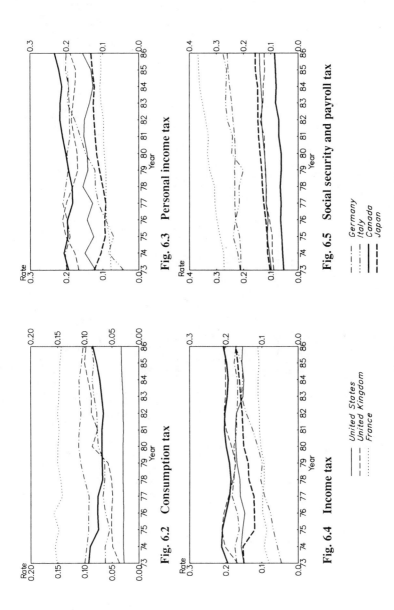

Fig. 6.2 Consumption tax

Fig. 6.3 Personal income tax

Fig. 6.4 Income tax

Fig. 6.5 Social security and payroll tax

—— United States
––– United Kingdom
········ France

––– Germany
–·–· Italy
—— Canada
––– Japan

Table 6.1   Average Tax Rates in the Major Industrial Countries (general government)

	Total Tax Rate				Consumption Tax Rate				Personal Income Tax Rate				Income Tax Rate				Social Security and Payroll Tax Rate			
	1975	1980	1985	1986	1975	1980	1985	1986	1975	1980	1985	1986	1975	1980	1985	1986	1975	1980	1985	1986
Canada	33.8	32.8	33.6	34.0	7.4	6.8	7.7	8.5	19.6	20.1	22.0	23.2	20.9	19.9	19.7	20.6	6.0	6.2	8.3	8.6
United States	27.7	28.8	28.6	28.5	2.9	3.0	3.2	3.3	12.5	14.2	13.2	15.5	15.3	17.2	15.5	15.3	11.3	12.3	14.0	14.1
Japan	21.5	26.0	28.3	29.2	...	...	...	...	9.4	11.6	12.8	13.2	12.0	15.0	16.7	17.2	11.3	13.9	15.7	15.7
France	36.6	41.7	44.5	44.4	14.8	15.0	14.6	14.3	8.3	9.6	10.4	10.6	8.6	10.3	10.8	11.1	28.7	33.4	36.6	36.8
Germany	35.7	38.0	37.9	37.5	9.2	11.1	10.5	10.3	18.9	19.8	20.2	20.0	16.3	17.7	17.6	17.2	21.5	23.0	25.7	26.1
Italy	25.6	29.2	34.0	36.2	5.4	7.5	8.3	8.7	7.0	14.7	19.6	...	6.9	11.2	15.4	17.4	23.9	24.4	26.3	27.7
United Kingdom	35.4	35.3	38.1	39.0	5.1	8.6	10.0	9.7	20.1	17.0	17.4	18.9	21.1	18.4	20.2	20.3	9.5	12.3	12.3	12.4

Source: Computed from OECD (1987a) and OECD (1987b).

Note: Our measure of the *consumption-tax rate* is computed as the ratio of general taxes on goods and services (including value-added taxes, sales taxes, and other general taxes on goods and services) to private final consumption. For income taxes, we use various measures distinguishing between individuals and corporations as well as between social security and the more conventional definition of income taxes. Accordingly, the *personal income tax rate* is computed as taxes on incomes, profits, and capital gains of individuals divided by compensation of employees (a broader internationally comparable tax base is unavailable). The *income-tax rate* is computed as the taxes on income, profits, and capital gains (including individual and corporate taxes) divided by the compensation of employees plus property and entrepreneurial income. The *social security and payroll tax rate* is computed as social security contributions and payroll taxes of the work force divided by compensation of employees. Finally, the *total tax rate* is computed as taxes on income, profits, and capital gains plus social security contributions plus payroll taxes plus property taxes on goods and services, all divided by GNP or GDP. To maintain a consistent use of the OECD data, we have used GNP for the United States, Japan, and Germany and GDP for Canada, France, Italy, and the United Kingdom.

In the subsequent sections, we provide a sketch of a theoretical analysis highlighting the key factors governing the macroeconomic effects of tax restructuring that is then developed further by means of dynamic simulations.

6.2 The Analytical Framework

In developing the analytical framework, we start with a formulation of the budget constraint that serves to focus attention on the key economic variables and tax-policy parameters that play a central role in the subsequent analysis.[3] The home country's private-sector (full-income) budget constraint applicable to period ($t = 0, 1, \ldots, T - 1$) is

$$(1) \quad (1 + \tau_{ct})C_t + (1 - \tau_{yt})w_t(1 - \ell_t) = (1 - \tau_{yt})[w_t + r_{kt}(K_{t-1}$$

$$+ I_{t-1}) - I_t\left(1 + \frac{b}{2}\frac{I_t}{K_t}\right)] + (1 - \tau_{bt})[B_t^P - (1 + r_{t-1})B_{t-1}^P],$$

where τ_{ct}, τ_{yt}, and τ_{bt} denote the cash flow tax rates on consumption (VAT), income, and international borrowing, respectively. The levels of consumption, labor supply, capital stock, investment, and the private-sector international borrowing are denoted, respectively, by C_t, ℓ_t, K_t, I_t, and B_t^P. The wage rate, the capital-rental rate, and the interest rate are denoted, respectively, by w_t, r_{kt}, and r_t. For convenience, we normalize the endowment of leisure to unity and assume costs of adjustment in capital formation of the form $(\frac{1}{2})bI_t^2/K_t$. We note that in the final period (period T) the private sector settles its debt commitments and no new investment or new borrowing occurs. Accordingly, $I_T = B_T^P = 0.$[4]

To simplify the exposition, we assume a linear production function with fixed coefficients. Thus, the competitive equilibrium conditions imply that the wage rate and the capital-rental rates, w and r_k, are constant. To simplify further, we also assume that the historical debt commitment of the private sector, B_{-1}^P, is zero.

The formulation of the periodic budget constraint illustrates the equivalence relation existing among the taxes on consumption, income, and international borrowing. Indeed, the real effects of any given combination of the three taxes can be duplicated by a policy consisting of any two of them.[5] For example, consider an initial situation with a positive consumption tax rate, $\bar{\tau}_c$ and zero income and international borrowing tax rates. If the consumption tax was eliminated and the income and international borrowing taxes were both set equal to $\bar{\tau}_c/(1 + \bar{\tau}_c)$, then the effective tax rates associated with this new combination of taxes are zero income and international borrowing taxes and a positive ($\bar{\tau}_c$) consumption tax. It follows that the real equilibrium associated with the new tax pattern ($\tau_c = 0$, $\tau_y = \tau_b = \bar{\tau}_c/[1 + \bar{\tau}_c]$) is identical to the one associated with the initial tax pattern ($\tau_c = \bar{\tau}_c$, $\tau_y = \tau_b = 0$).

The periodic (full-income) budget constraints specified in equation (1) can be consolidated to yield the lifetime present-value budget constraint. To facilitate the diagrammatic analysis of subsequent sections, we illustrate the lifetime present-value budget constraint for a two-period case ($t = 0,1$). Accordingly,

$$
(2) \quad C_0 + \alpha_c C_1 + \left(\frac{1 - \tau_{y0}}{1 + \tau_{c0}} \right) [w(1 - \ell_0) + \alpha_L w(1 - \ell_1)]
$$

$$
= \left(\frac{1 - \tau_{y0}}{1 + \tau_{c0}} \right) w + \left(\frac{1 - \tau_{y1}}{1 + \tau_{c1}} \right) \alpha_c \, w + \left(\frac{1 - \tau_{y0}}{1 + \tau_{c0}} \right)
$$

$$
\left[r_k K_0 + \alpha_I (a + r_k) K_1 - I_0 \left(1 + \frac{b}{2} \frac{I_0}{K_0} \right) \right],
$$

where

$$
\alpha_c = \frac{(1 + \tau_{c1})}{(1 + \tau_{c0})} \frac{(1 - \tau_{b0})}{(1 - \tau_{b1})} \frac{1}{(1 + r_0)},
$$

$$
\alpha_L = \alpha_I
$$

$$
= \frac{(1 - \tau_{y1})}{(1 - \tau_{y0})} \frac{(1 - \tau_{b0})}{(1 - \tau_{b1})} \frac{1}{(1 + r_0)}.
$$

As indicated, the discount factors α_c, α_L, and α_I are the effective (tax-adjusted) discount factors governing intertemporal consumption, leisure, and investment decisions, respectively.[6] The intratemporal choice between labor supply (leisure) and consumption of ordinary goods is governed by the prevailing effective intratemporal tax ratio $(1 - \tau_y)/(1 + \tau_c)$. We note that in this cash flow formulation the effective discount factor governing intertemporal consumption decisions, α_c, is independent of the income tax whereas the effective discount factors governing investment and leisure decisions, α_I and α_L, are independent of the consumption tax. In addition, the effective discount factors depend on the time path of the various taxes rather than on their levels. Specifically, if the various tax rates do not vary over time, then their time paths are "flat," and the effective discount factors α_c, α_L, and α_I are equal to the undistorted tax-free factor, $\alpha = 1/(1 + r_0)$. In that case, the intertemporal allocations are undistorted while the intratemporal allocations are distorted if the intratemporal tax ratio differs from unity.

Having discussed the formulation of the private-sector budget constraint, we turn next to the specification of the multiperiod utility function. To facilitate the discussion of the simulations reported in subsequent sections, we need to specify its form in some detail. We thus suppose that the homothetic intraperiod utility function between consumption of ordinary goods and leisure is

$$u_t = [\beta C_t^{\frac{\sigma-1}{\sigma}} + (1 - \beta)(1 - \ell_t)^{\frac{\sigma-1}{\sigma}}]^{\frac{\sigma}{\sigma-1}} \tag{3}$$

while the interperiod utility function is

$$\mathsf{U}_0 = \sum_{t=0}^{T} \delta^t \, log(u_t), \tag{4}$$

where σ is the temporal elasticity of substitution between leisure and consumption of ordinary goods, β is the distributive parameter of consumption, and δ is the subjective discount factor.

Maximizing the utility functions in equations (3) and (4) subject to the lifetime present-value budget constraint (the multiperiod analogue to eq. [2]) yields the utility-based real spending, u, its associated price index, P, and the periodic demand functions for the consumption of ordinary goods, C, and leisure, $1 - \ell$, as follows:

$$u_t = \left(\sum_{s=0}^{T} \delta^s \right)^{-1} \frac{W_0 \delta_t}{P_t \alpha_t}, \tag{5}$$

where α_t is period-t present-value factor (i.e.,

$$\alpha_t = [(1 + r_0)(1 + r_1)...(1 + r_{t-1})]^{-1}.$$

$$P_t = \left(\beta^\sigma \left(\frac{1 + \tau_{ct}}{1 - \tau_{bt}} \right)^{1-\sigma} + (1 - \beta)^\sigma \left\{ \left[\frac{(1 - \tau_{yt})}{(1 - \tau_{bt})} \right] w \right\}^{1-\sigma} \right)^{\frac{1}{1-\sigma}}, \tag{6}$$

$$C_t = \frac{\beta^\sigma \left[\frac{(1 + \tau_{ct})}{(1 - \tau_{bt})} \right]^{-\sigma} P_t u_t}{\beta^\sigma \left(\frac{1 + \tau_{ct}}{1 - \tau_{bt}} \right)^{1-\sigma} + (1 - \beta)^\sigma \left[\frac{(1 - \tau_{yt})}{(1 - \tau_{bt})} w \right]^{1-\sigma}}, \tag{7}$$

$$1 - \ell_t = \frac{(1 - \beta)^\sigma \left[\frac{(1 - \tau_{yt})}{(1 - \tau_{bt})} w \right]^{-\sigma} P_t u_t}{\beta^\sigma \left[\frac{1 + \tau_{ct}}{1 - \tau_{bt}} \right]^{1-\sigma} + (1 - \beta)^\sigma \left[\frac{(1 - \tau_{yt})}{(1 - \tau_{bt})} w \right]^{1-\sigma}}, \tag{8}$$

where $t = 1, 1, ..., T$, and where wealth is

$$W_0 = \sum_{t=0}^{T} \alpha_t \frac{(1 - \tau_{yt})}{(1 - \tau_{bt})} \left[w + r_k K_t - I_t \left(1 + \frac{b}{2} \frac{I_t}{K_t} \right) \right] + \alpha_T \frac{(1 + \tau_{yT})}{(1 - \tau_{bT})} a K_T.$$

To complete the description of the private-sector behavior, we maximize the representative individual wealth, W_0, with respect to investment, I_t.[7] This yields

$$(9) \quad -\frac{1 - \tau_{yt}}{1 - \tau_{bt}}\alpha_t\left(1 + b\frac{I_{t-1}}{K_{t-1}}\right) + \sum_{s=t}^{T} \frac{(1 - \tau_{ys})}{(1 - \tau_{bs})}\alpha_s\left[r_k + \frac{b}{2}\left(\frac{I_s}{K_s}\right)^2\right]$$

$$+ (r_k + a)\alpha_T = 0.$$

Equation (9) represents the implicit investment rule. The negative term is equal to the marginal cost of investment in period t, while the positive terms are equal to the marginal benefits consisting of the rise in output resulting from the increased capital stock (the terms with r_k and a) and the fall in the future cost of investment (the terms associated with $[b/2] \cdot [I/K]^2$); all terms are expressed as present values adjusted for taxes. For the two-period case, the investment function implied by equation (9) is

$$(9a) \qquad\qquad I_0 = \frac{1}{b}[\alpha_I(a + r_k) - 1]K_0 .$$

Equation (9a) together with the assumption that $(a + r_k)$ exceeds unity (an assumption necessary for a positive level of investment in the two-period case) implies that the level of investment rises with the initial capital stock, K_0, with the effective (tax-adjusted) discount factor, α_I, with the rental rate, r_k, and with the consumption-coefficient, a, attached to the final-period capital. On the other hand, investment falls with an increase in the cost-of-adjustment parameter, b.

This completes the presentation of the key building blocks of the model. In the subsequent sections, we use the model for the analysis of three issues in tax restructuring: revenue-neutral tax conversions, budgetary imbalances arising from changes in the time profile of taxes, and international tax harmonization.

6.3   Revenue-Neutral Tax Conversions

In examining the effects of tax conversions between income and consumption tax systems, we focus on revenue-neutral reforms. By ensuring that the restructuring of the tax system does not result in budgetary imbalances (which are considered separately in sec. 6.4), we obtain the pure effects of tax conversions. The present section is divided into four subsections. The first lays the groundwork by considering tax conversions in a small open economy, the second extends the analytical framework to a two-country model of the world economy, the third examines tax conversions in this extended framework, and the fourth reports on some dynamic simulations.

6.3.1 Tax Conversions in a Small Open Economy

In considering revenue-neutral tax reforms, we note that such reforms are characterized by a change in the composition of a given tax revenue among different tax bases. It is obtained through alterations in the various tax rates designed to keep total tax revenue in each period intact. In what follows, we focus on a reform that substitutes a consumption tax (VAT) system for an income tax system.[8]

Even though the focus is on consumption and income tax systems, the equivalence relation that exists among the consumption, income, and international borrowing taxes permits us to simplify the exposition. Accordingly, we set the explicit consumption tax rate, τ_c, equal to zero while maintaining the rates of the other taxes, τ_b and τ_y, different from zero so as to assure a constant tax revenue. To simplify further, we consider the two-period case with inelastic labor supply[9] and an international borrowing tax equal to a fixed proportion, θ, of the income tax. Accordingly,

$$(10) \qquad \tau_{ct} = 0, \quad \tau_{bt} = \theta\tau_{yt}, \quad 0 \leqslant \theta \leqslant 1, \quad t = 0, 1.$$

Substituting (10) into the expressions for the effective discount factors (in eq. [2]) yields

$$(11) \qquad \alpha_c = \frac{(1 - \theta\tau_{y0})}{(1 - \theta\tau_{y1})}\alpha, \quad \alpha_I = \frac{(1 - \tau_{y1})(1 - \theta\tau_{y0})}{(1 - \tau_{y0})(1 - \theta\tau_{y1})}\alpha.$$

In the extreme case for which the proportionality factor, θ, is equal to zero, equation (11) implies that the effective-discount factor applicable to consumption decisions, α_c, equals the undistorted tax-free discount factor α. In that case, the tax system amounts to a pure income-tax system. In the other extreme case for which the proportionality factor, θ, is equal to unity, equation (11) implies that the effective discount factor applicable to investment decisions, α_I, is equal to the tax-free discount factor α. In that case, the tax system amounts to a pure consumption tax system.

In figure 6.6, we analyze the effects of revenue-neutral conversions involving consumption and income tax systems.[10] In the figure, we portray combinations of the intertemporal income tax rates, τ_{y1}/τ_{y0}, and the intratemporal (constant) proportionality factor, $\theta = \tau_b/\tau_y$, which generate constant tax revenue. The resulting iso-tax-revenue schedule is denoted by RR. The slope of the schedule depends on the initial-period trade-balance position. For the case drawn, the trade-balance position is in surplus, and the schedule is negatively sloped.

To verify that with a trade-balance surplus the iso-tax-revenue schedule is downward sloping, consider a change from a consumption tax system, in which $\theta = 1$ (e.g., point B), to an income-tax system, in which $\theta = 0$ (e.g., point A). This change can be thought of as consisting of two components. First, it involves a permanent reduction of the prevailing (consumption) tax and a permanent equiproportional rise of the other tax

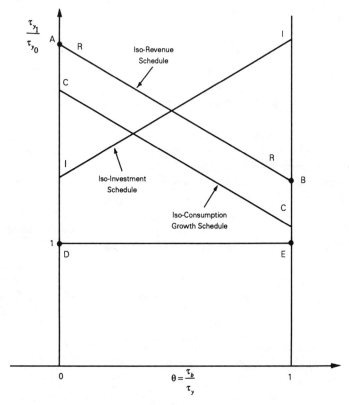

Fig. 6.6   Revenue-neutral tax conversions in a small, open economy

Data: $B_{-1}^{p} = 0, \tau_{c_{f}} = 0, \tau_{b_{f}} = \theta\tau_{y_{t}}, 0 \leq \theta \leq 1,$
The economy runs a current-period
trade balance surplus

(income tax). Second, it involves further adjustments in the newly
introduced tax aimed at restoring the initial level of tax revenue. If the
economy runs a current-period trade-balance surplus so that in the current
period income minus investment (the income tax base) exceeds consumption (the consumption tax base) while in the future, owing to the
intertemporal budget constraint, this pattern is reversed, the first component of the reform results in a budget surplus in the current period and
in a budget deficit in the future. Evidently, the second component of the
reform aimed at restoring the initial level of tax revenue lowers the income
tax rate in the current period and raises the income tax rate in the future.
As a result, the intertemporal income tax ratio, τ_{y1}/τ_{y0}, rises. It follows
that the fall in the proportionality factor, θ, from one to zero, holding tax
revenue intact, must be associated with a rise in the ratio τ_{y1}/τ_{y0}.

In figure 6.6, this is reflected by the negative slope of the iso-tax-revenue schedule connecting points A and B. If, on the other hand, the initial period trade-balance position is in deficit, the iso-tax-revenue schedule is positively sloped.

The II schedule in figure 6.6 portrays combinations of the intertemporal ratio, τ_{y1}/τ_{y0}, and the proportionality factor, θ, along which the level of investment remains intact. As is evident from the definition of the effective discount factor α_I in equation (11), a rise in the proportionality factor, θ, raises the effective discount factor, α_I, and encourages investment if the intertemporal income tax ratio, τ_{y1}/τ_{y0}, exceeds unity. In that case, in order to maintain the initial level of investment intact, the rise in θ (which raises α_I) must be accompanied by a rise in the intertemporal income tax ratio (which lowers α_I). This is the case shown by the positively sloped II schedule in figure 6.6.

The CC schedule in figure 6.6 portrays combinations of τ_{y1}/τ_{y0} and θ that maintain a given growth rate of consumption (indicated by the intertemporal consumption ratio C_1/C_0). Applying a similar reasoning to the analysis of the effects of changes in θ and τ_{y1}/τ_{y0} on the effective discount factor α_c in equation (11), it can be verified that the iso-consumption-growth schedule, CC, is negatively sloped if the intertemporal income tax ratio exceeds unity. The slopes of the II and the CC schedules are reversed if the intertemporal income tax ratio falls short of unity. In the borderline case in which the path of the income tax rates is flat (so that $\tau_{y1}/\tau_{y0} = 1$), the two schedules coincide with the horizontal line DE.[11]

These ingredients can now be used to analyze the consequences of a revenue-neutral tax conversion. As should be evident from the foregoing discussion, the key factor governing the effects of such tax policies is the initial trade-balance position. In terms of figure 6.6, if the economy runs a current-period trade-balance surplus and the intertemporal income tax ratio exceeds unity, then a revenue-neutral tax reform that replaces a consumption tax system (indicated by point B) by an income tax system (indicated by point A) moves the economy to new iso-investment and iso-consumption growth schedules passing through point A (not drawn). These new schedules correspond to lower investment and growth rate of consumption. A similar argument shows that, if the economy runs a current-period trade-balance deficit, the same tax conversion reduces the level of investment and lowers the growth rate of consumption.[12]

If the tax conversion is in the opposite direction so that an income tax system is replaced by a consumption tax system and the economy runs a trade-balance surplus, then such a conversion shifts the equilibrium from point A to point B in figure 6.6. The iso-investment and iso-consumption growth schedules passing through point B (not drawn) indicate that the new equilibrium is associated with a higher level of investment and growth rate of consumption. The opposite results obtain if the initial position is of trade-balance surplus.

6.3.2   The World Economy

We now extend the analysis to a two-country model of the world economy consisting of the domestic and the foreign countries. The economic structure of the foreign economy is similar to that of the domestic economy described in section 6.3.1. The endowments and the parameters of the production and utility functions, however, may differ across countries. Variables pertaining to the foreign country are denoted by asterisks. In contrast with the small-country case, the world rate of interest is endogenously determined in the two-country model. To facilitate the exposition, we assume that initially all taxes are zero. Thus, in terms of equation (2), the domestic discount factors governing consumption and investment decisions, α_c and α_I, respectively, are initially equal to the world discount factor $\alpha = 1/(1 + r_0)$.

In what follows, we carry out the analysis by means of a simple diagrammatic apparatus.[13] The initial equilibrium is portrayed in figure 6.7, in which the upward-sloping schedule, S^w, describes the ratio, z, of current to future world GDP net of investment (denoted by z) as an increasing function of the rate of interest. Accordingly, the world relative supply (evaluated at $r = r_0$) is

$$(12) \qquad z^w = \frac{Y_0 - I_0\left[1 + \frac{1}{2}b(I_0/K_0)\right] + Y_0^* - I_0^*\left[1 + \frac{1}{2}b^*(I_0^*/K_0^*)\right]}{Y_1 + Y_1^*},$$

where Y denotes output.

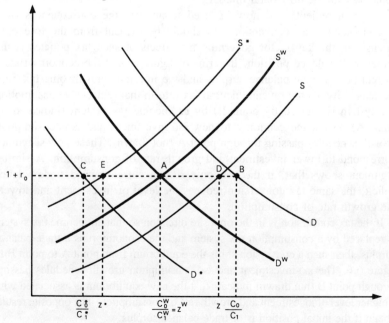

Fig. 6.7   Relative demands, relative supplies and world equilibrium

The positive dependence of z on the rate of interest reflects the fact that a rise in the rate of interest lowers investment. The world relative supply schedule, S^w, is a weighted average of the domestic country relative supply schedule, S, where

$$S = \left[Y_0 - I_0\left(1 + \frac{1}{2}b\,\frac{I_0}{K_0}\right)\right]\Big/Y_1,$$

and the foreign country relative supply schedule, S^*, where

$$S^* = \left[Y_0^* - I_0^*\left(1 + \frac{1}{2}b^*\,\frac{I_0^*}{K_0^*}\right)\right]\Big/Y_1^*.$$

Accordingly,

(13) $S^w = \mu_s S + (1 - \mu_s)S^*,$

where the domestic-country weight is

(14) $\mu_s = \dfrac{Y_1}{Y_1 + Y_1^*}.$

The downward-sloping schedules in figure 6.7 plot the desired ratio of current to future consumption as a decreasing function of the rate of interest. The domestic and foreign relative demands are denoted by D and D^*, respectively, and their values at the point in which $C_0/C_1 = C_0^*/C_1^* = 1$ are one plus the subjective rate of time preference, $1/\delta$ and $1/\delta^*$.

Analogously to the construction of the world relative supply, the world relative demand, $D^w = C_0^w/C_1^w = (C_0 + C_0^*) / (C_1 + C_1^*)$, is a weighted average of the two countries' relative demands, $D = C_0/C_1$ and $D^* = C_0^*/C_1^*$. Accordingly,

(15) $D^w = \mu_d D + (1 - \mu_d)D^*,$

where the domestic-country weight is

(16) $\mu_d = \dfrac{C_1}{C_1 + C_1^*}.$

The initial equilibrium is exhibited by point A in figure 6.7. As shown, the world rate of interest is r_0, and the world consumption ratio (indicating the reciprocal of the growth rate of world consumption) is C_0^w/C_1^w. The domestic and foreign consumption ratios corresponding to this equilibrium are C_0/C_1 and C_0^*/C_1^*, as indicated by points B and C, respectively. We also note that the domestic and foreign relative supplies associated with this equilibrium are z and z^*, as indicated by points D and E, respectively. As is evident, these levels of relative supplies are associated with the equilibrium levels of domestic and foreign investment. Finally, since point B lies to the right of point D while point C lies to the left of point E, the domestic economy runs an initial-period trade-balance deficit while the foreign economy runs a corresponding trade-balance surplus. This pattern of trade imbalances is implied from the assumed zero level of the predetermined initial debt position. Obviously, solvency implies that this configuration of trade imbalances is reversed in the subsequent period. We also note that this pattern of trade imbalances implies that the equilibrium domestic relative demand weight, μ_d, falls short of the corresponding relative supply weight, μ_s.[14]

6.3.3 Tax Conversions in a Two-Country World Economy

Consider a revenue-neutral tax reform that introduces a consumption tax system in place of an income tax system. As before, the tax reform can be divided into two components. We first introduce permanent consumption taxes at the rate τ_c accompanied by the equiproportional reduction in income taxes.[15] As is evident from our previous discussions, this tax shift creates a current-period government budget surplus if the domestic economy runs a current-period trade-balance deficit, and vice versa. Obviously, this pattern of budgetary and trade imbalances is reversed in the subsequent period. The second component of the tax reform aims at restoring revenue neutrality in each period. Since the economy has adopted a consumption tax system, it is assumed that the restoration of revenue neutrality is achieved through appropriate further adjustments in the consumption tax rates.

Suppose that the domestic economy runs an initial-period trade-balance deficit. Under such circumstances, the first component of the tax reform results in an initial-period government budget surplus and in a corresponding future-period deficit. To restore revenue neutrality, the current-period consumption tax rate, τ_{c0}, must be lowered while the corresponding future-period rate, τ_{c1}, must be raised. This pattern of tax rates breaks the initial flatness of the time profile of the consumption tax so that $\tau_{c0} < \tau_{c1}$. The new configuration of the consumption tax rates raises α_c—the effective discount factor applicable to consumption decisions—so that $\alpha_c = [(1 + \tau_{c1})/(1 + \tau_{c0})]\alpha$ exceeds the world discount factor $\alpha = 1/(1 + r_0)$. Since income taxes remain flat, the effective discount factor applicable to investment decisions remains intact, so that $\alpha_I = \alpha$.

Armed with this information, we analyze in figure 6.8 the effects of this tax reform. The initial equilibrium is portrayed by point A at which the world rate of interest is r_0 (as in fig. 6.7). The rise in the effective discount factor applicable to consumption (i.e., the reduction in the corresponding effective rate of interest) induces an intertemporal substitution in domestic demand toward current-period consumption. Thus, for each and every value of the world rate of interest, the domestic (relative) demand schedule shifts to the right from D to D'. The proportional vertical displacement of the schedule equals the proportional tax-induced rise in the effective discount factor. This proportion is $(1 + \tau_{c1})/(1 + \tau_{c0})$. Associated with the new levels of domestic demand, the new world relative demand $(C_0 + C_0^*)/(C_1 + C_1^*)$ also shifts to the right from D^w to $D^{w'}$ in figure 6.8. This shift

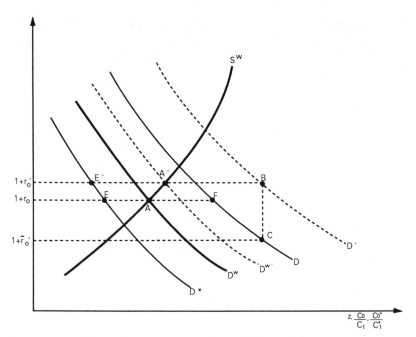

Fig. 6.8   The effects of a revenue-neutral tax shift from income taxes to consumption taxes with an initial-period domestic trade-balance deficit

reflects the substitution from future to current-period consumption in the domestic economy.[16] Furthermore, the proportional displacement of the world relative demand schedule is smaller than the corresponding displacement of the domestic relative demand schedule.[17]

In contrast with the effects of the tax reforms on the relative demand schedules, this reform does not affect the effective discount factor applicable to investment decisions, and it leaves the world relative supply schedule intact. The new equilibrium obtains at the intersection of the (unchanged) world relative supply schedule, S^w, and the new world relative demand schedule, $D^{w\prime}$. This equilibrium is indicated by point A' in figure 6.8, at which the world rate of interest has risen from r_0 to r_0'.

To determine the incidence of this change on the domestic effective rate of interest, we subtract from $1 + r_0$ the distance BC, representing the tax-induced percentage change in the effective discount factor. This yields $1 + \tilde{r}_0'$ in figure 6.8. As is evident, $\tilde{r}_0'$ is lower than the initial world rate r_0 since the vertical displacement of the D^w schedule is smaller than the magnitude represented by the distance BC.

In view of the rise in the world rate of interest, both domestic and foreign investment fall, and the rate of growth of foreign consumption, as indicated by the move from point E to point E' in figure 6.8, rises. On the other hand, the fall in the domestic effective rate of interest applicable to consumption lowers the rate of growth of domestic consumption, as indicated by the move from point F to point C. Thus, this tax reform crowds out both domestic and foreign investment and results in a negative correlation between the rates of growth of domestic and foreign consumption. Using similar reasoning, we can show that, in the presence of an initial surplus in the balance of trade, the tax reform crowds in both domestic and foreign investment, lowers the rate of growth of foreign consumption, and raises the growth rate of domestic consumption. As in the small-country case (discussed in sec. 6.3.1), this analysis also underscores the critical importance of the trade-balance position in determining the domestic and international effects of such a tax reform.

The same reasoning can be used to analyze the opposite tax conversion, from a consumption tax to an income tax system. In that case, the first component of the tax restructuring yields a budgetary deficit if the initial-period current-account position was in deficit (so that income net of investment falls short of consumption). The restoration of revenue neutrality therefore involves a rise in the initial-period income tax rate, τ_{y0}, and a corresponding reduction in the future-period income tax rate, τ_{y1}. These changes in the time profile of income taxes raise the effective discount factor governing investment decisions, α_I, while keeping intact the effective discount factor governing consumption decisions, α_c. In terms of figures 6.7–6.8, the rise in investment induces a leftward shift of the relative supply schedule, resulting in a higher world rate of interest. The rise in the world rate of interest crowds out foreign investment, while the fall in the domestic effective rate of interest applicable to domestic investment decisions crowds in domestic investment. This tax conversion also raises the rates of growth of domestic and foreign consumption. As is evident, in contrast with the case shown in figure 6.8 in which the tax conversion from income to consumption tax system alters the relative demand schedules, in the present case, where the conversion is from a consumption to an income tax system, the reform alters the world equilibrium through its effect on the relative supply schedules. Obviously, these results reflect the assumed initial-period trade-balance deficit. They are reversed if the initial-period trade-balance position is in surplus.

6.3.4 Dynamic Simulations of Tax Conversions

The foregoing analysis identified the key factors determining the domestic and international consequences of revenue-neutral tax reforms. We turn next to highlight these features by means of dynamic simulations. For that purpose, we return to the multiperiod model and allow for a variable labor supply. The detailed specification of the two-country dynamic-simulation model is provided in the appendix.

In performing the simulations, we first computed a baseline equilibrium. This equilibrium was then perturbed by the assumed tax conversion. The various figures presented below show the effects of the tax restructuring measured as percentage deviations from the baseline levels.

As indicated by the theoretical analysis, a key factor governing the effects of such revenue-neutral tax conversions is the time pattern of the trade-balance position. Since the trade-balance position can be expressed in terms of the saving-investment gap, trade imbalances reflect intercountry differences in either saving propensities (induced, e.g., by differences between the subjective discount factors, δ and δ^*) or investment patterns (induced, e.g., by differences between the productivities of capital, r_k and r_k^*). In figures 6.9–6.12, we plot the simulation results for cases distinguished according to the time pattern of trade imbalances. We focus in these simulations on tax conversions from an income to a consumption tax system. Throughout, we assume that the home country reduces permanently its income tax rates by 5 percent and restores its tax revenue by raising consumption tax rates.

Consider first figures 6.9 and 6.10. These figures characterize the situation in which in the early periods the home country runs trade-balance deficits. Obviously, the intertemporal budget constraints imply that in later periods the country runs trade-balance surpluses. The initial domestic trade deficits may arise from either a relatively low saving propensity ($\delta < \delta^*$), shown in figure 6.9, or from a relatively high productivity of capital ($r_k > r_k^*$), shown in figure 6.10. These figures demonstrate the results obtained in the simplified theoretical analysis as well as new results reflecting the multiperiod-variable labor supply model. As seen, the revenue-neutral tax conversion policy from income to consumption taxes raises the world rates of interest, lowers domestic and foreign investment, and worsens the home country's (early-periods) current account of the balance payments. Reflecting the solvency requirement, the simulations show that, in the medium term, the home country's current account improves. Throughout the adjustment process, the home country external-debt position worsens. The changes in the domestic tax structure induce corresponding changes in labor supply and output. As seen, both domestic employment and output decline in the early periods following the tax conversion. In the medium term, the level of domestic employment rises. The medium-term effects of the tax conversion on the level of domestic output reflect the rise in employment and the decline in the capital stock. Figure 6.9 shows a case in which output rises in the medium term, while figure 6.10 shows the opposite case. These results, which correspond to the case in which the home country runs trade-balance deficits in the early period, are reversed in the opposite case, in which the country runs early-periods trade surpluses. Such an opposite pattern is exhibited in figures 6.11 and 6.12, corresponding, respectively, to the cases in which the home country has a high saving propensity ($\delta > \delta^*$) and low investment ($r_k < r_k^*$).

6.4   Budget Deficits under Consumption and Income Tax Systems

The analysis in section 6.3 focused on the effects of changes in the composition of taxes while maintaining in each period a given value of total

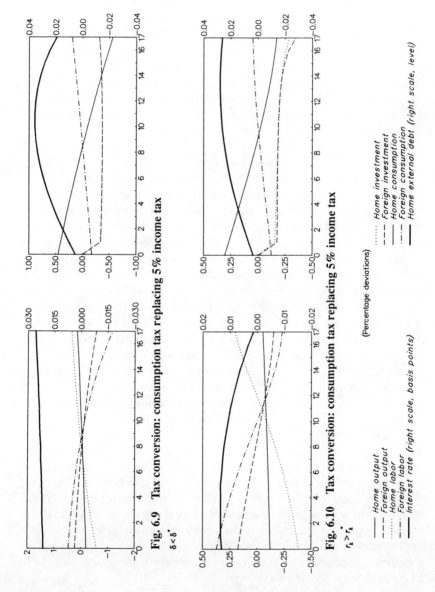

Fig. 6.9 Tax conversion: consumption tax replacing 5% income tax

$\delta < \delta^*$

Fig. 6.10 Tax conversion: consumption tax replacing 5% income tax

$r_k > r_k^*$

(Percentage deviations)

...... Home investment
– – – Foreign investment
– — – Home consumption
– · – · Foreign consumption
——— Home external debt (right scale, level)

——— Home output
– – – Foreign output
...... Home labor
– – – Foreign labor
– · – · interest rate (right scale, basis points)

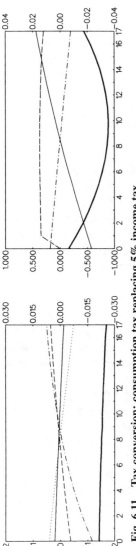

Fig. 6.11 Tax conversion: consumption tax replacing 5% income tax

$\delta > \dot{\delta}$

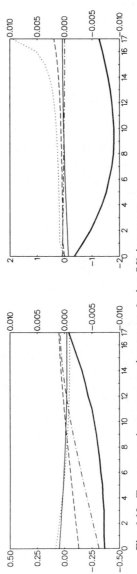

Fig. 6.12 Tax conversion: consumption tax replacing 5% income tax

$r_k < \dot{r}_k$

(Percentage deviations)

———— Home output
— — — Foreign output
·········· Home labor
—··—··— Foreign labor
—·—·— Interest rate (right scale, basis points)

·········· Home investment
— — — Foreign investment
—·—·— Home consumption
—··—··— Foreign consumption
———— Home external debt (right scale, level)

tax revenue. Such revenue-neutral tax restructuring ensures that the tax conversion policies do not affect the budgetary imbalances. In this section, we use the same analytical framework to shed light on the domestic and international macroeconomic consequences of changes in the timing of taxes and provide dynamic simulations.[18]

6.4.1   Budget Deficits in a Two-Country World Economy

Consider the effects of budget deficits arising from a current tax cut. Of course, the intertemporal government budget constraint implies that, as long as government spending remains intact, the current tax cut must be followed by a future rise in taxes. The main conclusion of the analysis is that the effect of budget deficits depends critically on whether it arises from changes in the timing of consumption or income taxes.

Consider first a budget deficit arising from a current-period consumption tax cut (followed by a corresponding rise in future consumption taxes). As is evident from the definitions of the effective discount factors in equation (2), such a tax shift raises the effective discount factor governing consumption decisions, α_c, while leaving the discount factor governing investment decisions intact. These changes induce a substitution of demand from future to current consumption and induce rightward shifts of the domestic (and the world) relative demand schedules in figure 6.7 while leaving the relative supply schedules intact.[19]

Figure 6.8, which was used for the analysis of tax conversion from income to consumption tax systems, is also fully applicable for the analysis of the budget deficit under the consumption tax system. Accordingly, the budget deficit raises the world rate of interest and crowds out domestic and foreign investment. It also lowers the growth rate of domestic consumption while raising the growth rate of foreign consumption.

By the same reasoning, a budget deficit arising from a cut in current income tax rates (and followed by a corresponding rise in future income tax rates) yields results similar to those obtained under a revenue-neutral tax conversion from consumption to income tax systems. Again, as is evident from the definitions of the effective discount factors in equation (2), this change in the timing of income tax rates lowers the effective discount factor governing investment decisions, α_I, and discourages domestic investment while leaving α_c intact. In terms of figure 6.7, these tax changes induce a rightward shift of the domestic (and the world) relative supply schedule while leaving the relative demand schedules intact. As a result, the world rate of interest falls, foreign investment rises, and the domestic investment is crowded out. At the same time, the lower world rate of interest lowers the growth rate of both domestic and foreign consumption.

6.4.2   Dynamic Simulations of Budget Deficits

The simulations that allow for a variable labor supply in a multiperiod model illustrate the key relations implied by the theoretical model: they underscore the critical importance of the underlying tax system in determining the macroeconomic effects of budget deficits. They also provide further insights into the dynamic consequences of budget deficits.

Figures 6.13 and 6.14 contain selected simulations of the dynamic effects of current-period budget deficits under a consumption tax system and under an income tax system, respectively. We assume that the current-period deficit arises from a 10 percent reduction in tax rates, which is made up for by a permanent rise in tax rates in all future periods. By and large, the directions of changes in the various variables in the two figures are opposite to each other. This underscores the key proposition of the theoretical analysis. In addition, the simulations show that the effects of the budget deficit on the qualitative characteristics of the time path of employment and output also depend critically on the underlying tax system. Specifically, under a consumption tax system, a domestic budget deficit exerts recessionary effects on the contemporaneous levels of domestic employment and output and expansionary effects on the corresponding levels abroad. These employment and output effects are reversed in all future periods.[20] In contrast, under an income tax system, the same budget deficit induces a contemporaneous expansion at home and a recession abroad. These changes are reversed in subsequent periods. In general, the international transmission of the effects of budget deficits is shown to be negative in both the short and the medium run.

We also note that the current-period budget deficit exerts opposite effects on the levels of domestic and foreign consumption. Under a consumption tax system, the deficit raises current-period domestic consumption and lowers the corresponding level of foreign consumption. These changes are reversed in subsequent periods. In contrast, under an income tax system, domestic consumption falls in the current period while foreign consumption rises, and, as before, these changes are reversed in subsequent periods. Again, in terms of the correlations between domestic and foreign consumption, the simulations demonstrate the negative transmission of the effects of domestic budget deficits.

The effects of the budget deficits on the time paths of consumption and leisure influence the levels of domestic and foreign welfare. Using the utility function specified in equation (4), our simulations show that the current period budget deficit, arising from a 10 percent reduction in the consumption tax rate, raises the level of domestic welfare (by about 2 percent) and lowers the level of foreign welfare (by about 1.5 percent). In contrast, if the current-period budget deficit arises from a 10 percent reduction in the income tax rate, then the level of domestic welfare falls (by about 3 percent) while the corresponding foreign welfare rises (by about 3.5 percent). These opposite changes in the levels of domestic and foreign welfare reflect the negative transmission of the effects of budget deficits.

The effects of an expected future-period budget deficit are shown in figures 6.15–6.16. These simulations show the consequences of an expected 10 percent tax cut in periods 4 and 5 that is then made up for by a permanent

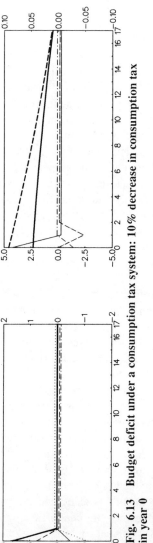

Fig. 6.13   Budget deficit under a consumption tax system: 10% decrease in consumption tax in year 0

$\delta = \delta^*,\ r_t = \dot{r}_t$

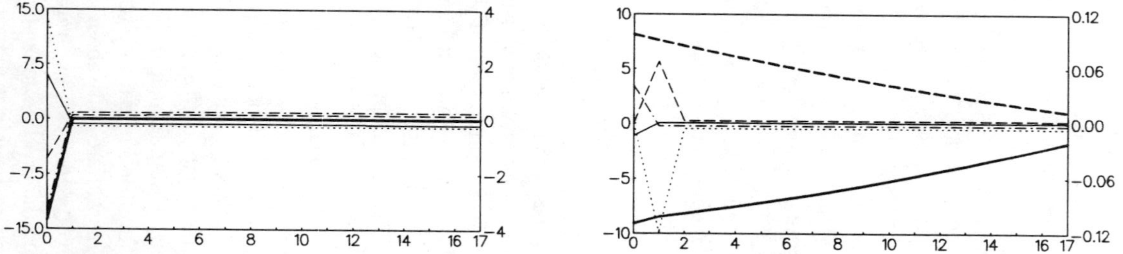

Fig. 6.14   Budget deficit under an income tax system: 10% decrease in income tax in year 0

$\delta = \delta^*,\ r_t = \dot{r}_t$

(Percentage deviations)

——— Home output
– – – Foreign output
········ Home labor
–·–·– Foreign labor

······ Home investment
– – – Foreign investment
–·–·– Home consumption
········ Foreign consumption
——— Home external debt (right scale, level)
– – – Home government debt (right scale, level)

Interest rate (right scale, basis points)

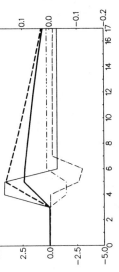

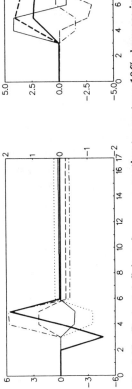

Fig. 6.15 Budget deficit under a consumption tax system: 10% decrease in consumption tax in years 4 & 5

$\delta = \delta^*,\ r_t = r_t^*$

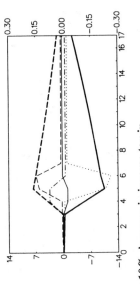

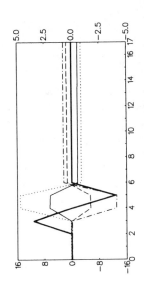

Fig. 6.16 Budget deficit under an income tax system: 10% decrease in income tax in years 4 & 5

$\delta = \delta^*,\ r_t = r_t^*$

(Percentage deviations)

—— Home output
——— Foreign output
·········· Home labor
—·—·— Foreign labor
—— Interest rate (right scale, basis points)

········· Home investment
——— Foreign investment
—— Home consumption
—·—·— Foreign consumption
——— Home external debt (right scale, level)
—— Home government debt (right scale, level)

rise in tax rates in all subsequent periods. As before, they reveal the central role played by the tax system. They also reveal the general feature of a negative transmission. However, since the various changes in tax rates occur only in the more distant future, our simulations show that their effects on the levels of domestic and foreign utility (viewed from the standpoint of the current period) are very small.

6.5   VAT Harmonization

In this section, we examine the dynamic effects of international VAT harmonization. Such policies form an important ingredient of the wide-ranging measures associated with the move toward the single market of Europe of 1992. In the fiscal area, the European Commission has drawn up various proposals on the approximation of the rates and the harmonization of the structures of VAT.

The process of harmonization of the VAT systems has started with the First Council Directive of April 1967 and has proceeded thereafter through consecutive directives. The process involved the adoption of VAT in various member countries and the continuous convergence of rates and structures among members of the community. Much of the discussion surrounding the practical implementation of the approximation of the VAT rates concerned the width of bands within which various VAT rates should be placed, the products to which a reduced rate would be applicable, and the problem of zero-rated products.[21] For 1992, the commission envisaged a standard VAT rate ranging between 14 and 20 percent and a reduced rate (applied to selected categories, such as foodstuffs) ranging between 4 and 9 percent. The commission proposes to abolish the higher rate that presently exists in some member countries on certain categories of goods. In subsequent discussions, an alternative proposal was considered, according to which the standard rate band would be replaced by a minimum rate applicable from 1 January 1993. Each member state would choose a rate at least equal to the minimum rate, with due regard to the budgetary implications and to the "competitive pressures" arising from the rates chosen by other neighboring states and main trading partners. Table 6.2 provides summary information on VAT in the European Community. It illustrates the disparities among the various member-country VAT rates.

One of the central issues that needs to be addressed is the budgetary consequences of the harmonization in the VAT systems. A few member states (notably Denmark and Ireland) would suffer considerable tax revenue losses, while others (notably Spain, Luxembourg, and Portugal) would see their tax revenue go up considerably.

In what follows, we present dynamic simulations of the consequences of international harmonization of VAT. We use our two-country model and presume that, prior to the VAT harmonization, the two countries use very different tax systems. The home country tax revenue stems from high

Table 6.2   **VAT Rates in the European Community (1989)**

	Statutory Rates (%)				
Country (year of VAT introduction)	Reduced Rate	Standard Rate	Higher Rate	Revenue Contribution as % of Total Tax Revenue (1986)	Revenue Contribution as % of GDP (1986)
Belgium (1971)	1, 6, 7	19	25, 33	15.5	7.0
Denmark (1967)	0	22	. . .	19.5	9.9
France (1968)	5.5, 7	18.6	28	19.2	8.5
Germany (1968)	7	14	. . .	15.3	5.7
Greece	3, 6	18	36	. . .	. . .
Ireland (1972)	0, 2.2, 10	25	. . .	20.8	8.4
Italy (1973)	2, 9	18	38	14.5	5.0
Luxembourg (1970)	3, 6	12	. . .	13.3	5.7
Netherlands (1969)	6	19	. . .	16.5	7.5
Portugal (1986)	8	17	30	17.6	5.7
Spain (1986)	6	12	33	. . .	. . .
United Kingdom (1973)	0	15	. . .	15.5	6.9
Commission proposal:					
A:		4 to 9		14 to 20	abolished
B:		4 to 9		minimum rate	abolished

Sources: Table 2.1 in Cnossen and Shoup (1987) and table 3.5.1 in *European Economy* (March 1988); *EC: The Evolution of VAT Rates Applicable in the Member States of the Community* (Inter-tax, 1987/3, pp. 85–88); and OECD, *Revenue Statistics of OECD Member Countries* (Paris, 1988).

income tax, while the foreign country revenue stems from high VAT. The harmonization of VAT entails a rise in the home country VAT rate and an equivalent reduction in the foreign VAT rate.

To avoid the budgetary imbalances consequent on the changes in the VAT rates, we ensure revenue neutrality by adopting the same procedure used in the analysis of tax conversions in section 6.3. Accordingly, the induced budgetary imbalances are corrected through changes in income tax rates. In the home country, the rise in the VAT is accompanied by a reduction in income tax rates, whereas in the foreign country the fall in the VAT rate is accompanied by a corresponding rise in income tax rates. The narrowing of the international disparities between VAT captures the commission's proposal of reducing the disparities of VAT rates among member countries and categories of goods. The maintenance of budgetary balance through appropriate changes in income tax rates makes the analysis of revenue-neutral tax conversion of section 6.2 applicable to the problem at hand.

In performing the simulations, we first computed a baseline equilibrium. This equilibrium was then perturbed by the assumed VAT harmonization.

The various figures presented below show the effects of the tax restructuring measured as percentage deviations from the baseline levels.

As indicated by the theoretical analysis, one of the key factors governing the effects of revenue-neutral tax conversions is the time pattern of the current-account position. Since the current-account positions can be expressed in terms of the saving-investment gap, they reflect intercountry differences either in saving propensities, induced, for example, by differences between the subjective discount factors, δ and δ^*, or in investment patterns, induced, for example, by differences between the productivities of capital, r_k and r_k^*. In figures 6.17–6.22, we plot the simulation results for cases distinguished according to the time pattern of current-account imbalances. In these figures, we assume that the income tax used in both countries is of the case-flow variety. Throughout, we assume that the home country raises permanently its VAT by 6 percent and restores its tax revenue by lowering its cash-flow income tax rates; the foreign country (whose initial VAT rate is assumed to be high) lowers permanently its VAT by 6 percent and restores its tax revenue by raising its cash-flow income tax rates. The figures show the paths of domestic and foreign output, labor supply, savings, investment, and consumption as well as the paths of the world rate of interest and the home country's external debt consequent on the VAT harmonization. All paths are expressed as percentage deviations from baseline (except for the rate of interest, whose deviation is expressed in basis points). The simulations reveal that the international VAT harmonization triggers a dynamic response in all the key macroeconomic variables. The specific nature of the dynamic response reflects international differences in the parameters governing saving and investment patterns.

The key features of the simulation analysis of tax harmonization underlying figures 6.17–6.22 are summarized in table 6.3, which also reports the implied welfare implications of the VAT harmonization. In order to capture the essence of the dynamic evolution of the various variables, we report in table 6.3 the direction of changes for both the short run (SR) and the medium run (MR). In figures 6.17–6.18, we show the time path of the endogenously determined home and foreign income tax rates. These rates are adjusted in each period so as to offset the budgetary implications of the VAT harmonization. The changes in the time profile of income taxes influence the present-value factors governing intertemporal investment and labor-supply decisions. In addition, the level changes in the VAT rates affect intratemporal consumption-leisure choice. In figures 6.19–6.22, we show the corresponding effects on employment, investment, consumption, the current account, and welfare.

In conformity with the tax conversion analysis of section 6.3, the results in table 6.3 demonstrate the key role played by the current-account position. Specifically, if in the early stage the home country runs a current-account deficit owing to low saving or high investment (e.g., if $\delta < \delta^*$ or $r_k > r_k^*$), then the paths of domestic and foreign income tax rates rise over time while

**VAT harmonization: the paths of income tax rates (6% permanent increase in
home country VAT and 6% permanent reduction in foreign country VAT)**

—— $\delta < \delta^*$
––– $\delta > \delta^*$
········ $r_k < r_k^*$
–·–· $r_k > r_k^*$

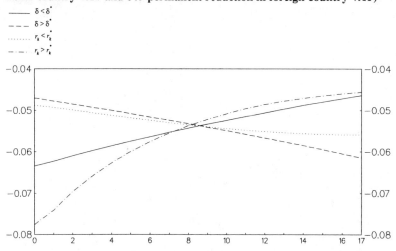

Fig. 6.17   Home country income tax rates   (deviations from baseline)

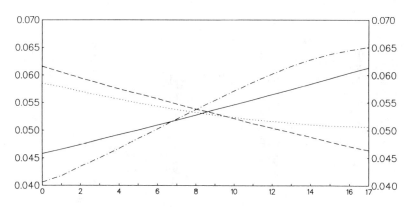

Fig. 6.18   Foreign country income tax rates   (deviations from baseline)

the world rate of interest falls. In that case, the rates of growth of domestic
and foreign consumption (g_c and g_c^* respectively) fall, both in the short and
in the medium runs.

If, on the other hand, the configuration of saving and investment
propensities is such that the home country runs a current-account surplus in
the early stage, then the dynamic effects of the VAT harmonization on these

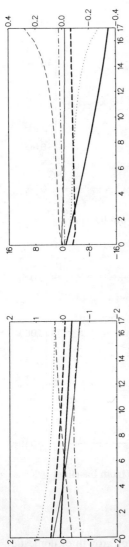

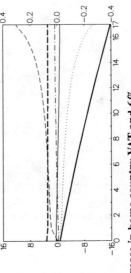

Fig. 6.19 VAT harmonization: 6% permanent increase in home country VAT and 6% permanent reduction in foreign country VAT

$\delta < \delta^*$

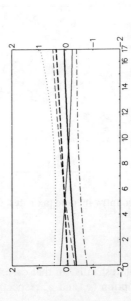

Fig. 6.20 VAT harmonization: 6% permanent increase in home country VAT and 6% permanent reduction in foreign country VAT

$\delta > \delta^*$

(Percentage deviations)

——— Home output
– – – Foreign output
–·–·– Home labor
– – – Foreign labor
——— Home consumption
——— Foreign consumption

········ Home investment
– – – Foreign investment
–·–·– Home saving ratio
——— Foreign saving ratio
——— Home external debt ratio
——— Interest rate (right scale, basis points)

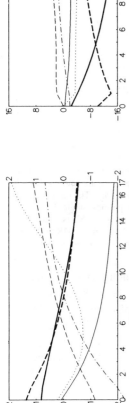

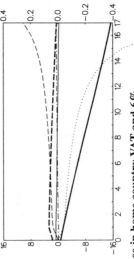

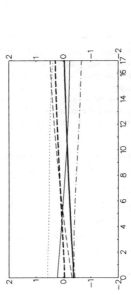

Fig. 6.21 VAT harmonization: 6% permanent increase in home country VAT and 6% permanent reduction in foreign country VAT

$r_k > \dot{r}_k$

Fig. 6.22 VAT harmonization: 6% permanent increase in home country VAT and 6% permanent reduction in foreign country VAT

$r_k < \dot{r}_k$

(Percentage deviations)

——— Home output
- - - Foreign output
········· Home labor
—·—· Foreign labor
——— Home consumption
- - - Foreign consumption

········· Home investment
- - - Foreign investment
——— Home saving ratio
——— Foreign saving ratio
—·—· Home external debt ratio
- - - Interest rate (right scale, basis points)

Table 6.3   **Effects of VAT Harmonization under Alternative Current-Account Positions (deviations from baseline)**

	Home Country Current-Account Deficit				Home Country Current-Account Surplus			
Variable	$\delta < \delta^*, r_k = r_k^*$		$\delta = \delta^*, r_k > r_k^*$		$\delta > \delta^*, r_k = r_k^*$		$\delta = \delta^*, r_k < r_k^*$	
	SR	MR	SR	MR	SR	MR	SR	MR
Path of τ_y	rising		rising		falling		falling	
Path of τ_y^*	rising		rising		falling		falling	
r	−	−	−	−	+	+	+	+
g_c	−	−	−	−	+	+	+	+
g_c^*	−	−	−	−	+	+	+	+
I	−	−	−	−	−	−	−	−
I^*	+	+	+	+	+	+	+	+
L	+	+	−	+	+	+	+	+
L^*	−	−	−	−	−	−	−	−
Y	+	−	−	−	+	−	+	+
Y^*	−	+	−	+	−	+	−	+
C	+	−	+	−	−	+	−	−
C^*	+	−	+	−	−	+	+	+
S	+	−	−	−	+	−	+	−
S^*	−	+	−	+	−	+	−	+
B	−	−	−	−	−	−	−	−
U	−	+	+	+	−	+	−	+
U*	+	−	+	−	+	−	+	−

Note: The VAT harmonization obtains through a permanent reduction in τ_c and a rise in τ_c^*. Budgetary balance obtains through appropriate adjustments in the periodic income tax rates, τ_y and τ_y^*. SR and MR denote, respectively, the short run and the medium run. The tax system is a cash-flow system. In general, the short run pertains to the first few periods, while the medium run pertains to the remaining periods in the simulation. For the utility index, SR pertains to the discounted sum of utilities over the entire periods except for the final one, while MR pertains to the final-period utility (reflecting the entire function beyond the simulation period).

variables are reversed. Specifically, if in the home country saving is high or investment is low (e.g., if $\delta > \delta^*$ or $r_k < r_k^*$), then the paths of domestic and foreign income tax rates fall while the world rate of interest rises. In that case, the rates of growth of domestic and foreign consumption rise. Thus, under the present cash-flow income tax system, the direction of changes in the world rate of interest and in the growth rates of consumption consequent on international VAT harmonization depend exclusively on the paths of the saving-investment gap.

The lower panel of table 6.3 summarizes the corresponding short- and medium-run changes in other key economic variables. As can be seen, in the cases considered, the international VAT harmonization crowds out domestic investment and crowds in foreign investment independent of the current-account positions. These investment responses reflect the induced changes in the domestic and foreign effective discount factors governing investment.

These changes in the effective discount factors reflect two conflicting effects: the effect of the change in the world rate of interest and the opposite effect of the change in the tax wedges induced by the alteration of the time paths of income tax rates. The changes in the tax structure also alter the intraperiod tax ratios governing labor supply and consumption demand. These tax ratios are subject to conflicting forces since the changes in the consumption tax rates and the associated changes in the income tax rates induce opposite effects on both labor supply and consumption demand. In addition to these conventional substitution mechanisms, the simulation results also reflect wealth effects on labor supply and consumption demand induced by changes in the intertemporal terms of trade (the world rate of interest) and by changes in the excess burden associated with the distorted tax system. Finally, the time paths of labor supply and consumption demand are altered by the intertemporal substitution induced by changes in the effective discount factors governing labor supply and consumption demand. The changes in these discount factors arise from the change in the world rate of interest and, in the case of labor supplies, from the changes in the time paths of income taxes. The welfare effects of term-of-trade changes depend on the magnitudeof the change in the terms of trade and on the gap between purchases and sales of the good whose relative price has changed. In our intertemporal context, the terms of trade correspond to the world rate of interest, and the gap between purchases and sales corresponds to the current-account position. As illustrated by table 6.3, in all cases the change in the terms of trade operates in favor of the country that raises its VAT. When the country runs a current-account deficit (i.e., when it borrows in the world economy), its intertemporal terms of trade improve since the rate of interest falls. Likewise, if the country's current-account position is in surplus, its intertemporal terms of trade also improve since the rate of interest rises. As illustrated by the table, this improvement in the home country welfare induced by the changes in the world rate of interest can be mitigated (or even offset) by the excess-burden effects of the VAT harmonization. Similar considerations apply to the welfare consequences of the reduction in VAT in the foreign economy.

A comparison between the effects of the international VAT harmonization on the domestic and the foreign economies reveals that in the two countries the level of foreign employment, investment, output, and some other key macroeconomic indicators change in opposite directions. In fact, in most cases, the utility index indicates that domestic and foreign welfare move in opposite directions. These phenomena suggest the possibility that international VAT harmonization may induce international conflicts of interest. A resolution of such conflicts may necessitate international fiscal transfers from countries benefiting from the VAT harmonization to countries that lose. The potential difficulties arising from international conflicts of interest may be augmented by internal conflicts of interest associated with redistributions of income between labor and capital in the short and medium runs.

The foregoing analysis was confined to the case in which the income taxes used to restore budgetary balance following the international VAT harmonization were of the cash-flow variety. Under such circumstances, in conformity with the analytical results of section 6.2, the current-account positions played the key role in determining the direction of changes in the world rate of interest and the growth rates of domestic and foreign consumption. As indicated by the simulations in figures 6.17–6.22 and in the summary results in the lower panel of table 6.3, the dynamic effects of the international VAT harmonization on the paths of the other key macroeconomic variables do not depend only on the current-account positions. In fact, for the cases shown in these simulations, domestic investment, foreign employment, foreign savings (in the short run), and the level of the domestic country's external debt are reduced independent of the current-account positions, while foreign investment and foreign savings (in the medium run) always rise.

6.6 Concluding Remarks

The increased integration of world goods and capital markets has stimulated interest in the policy implications of international economic interdependence. In this paper, we have analyzed several aspects of such interdependence, focusing on the international transmission of tax policies. For this purpose, we have presented an analytical framework suitable for the examination of the dynamic effects of tax restructuring. In our analysis, we considered the international effects of changes in the composition and the timing of taxes. Accordingly, we have analyzed the consequences of revenue-neutral tax conversions between income and consumption taxes as well as budget deficits that arise under alternative tax systems. Motivated by the various proposals for tax harmonizations associated with the creation of a single market in Europe of 1992, we have also analyzed the effects of international VAT harmonization. Throughout, we have complemented our analytical results with illustrative dynamic simulations. We have identified key factors governing the international effects and transmission of tax policies. These include the intercountry differences in saving and investment propensities. Accordingly, we have shown that the effects of tax policies depend critically on whether the country adopting these policies runs a deficit or a surplus in the current account of its balance of payments. We have also shown that the qualitative and quantitative effects of budget deficits depend critically on whether the deficit arises from changes in income taxes or in VAT. These factors were shown to play a central role in determining the effects of international tax harmonization.

Our analysis focused on a two-country model of the world economy. A useful extension would consider a three-country world and examine the consequences of tax harmonization between two of the three countries. Such an extension would facilitate an analysis of "trade creation" and "trade diversion" in both goods and capital markets in Europe of 1992.

Appendix
The Simulation Model

The model described in this appendix was used in the simulations discussed in the main text. We present below the exact computer printout of the model that is based on the theoretical model described in the text. However, this model was developed to be more general in order to evaluate a wider range of policy questions than are discussed in this paper.

An attempt has been made to use the same notation in the computer model as in the theoretical model. Whenever possible, reference is made to the relevant equations in the main text. There are several additional definitions and specifications in the simulation model, but none of these should alter the theoretical propositions of the paper. First, a number of definitions have been added to the model in order to enhance our understanding of the model's properties or to simplify the presentation of an equation (e.g., the definition of income). In addition, equations have been added in order to examine many possible government policy scenarios (e.g., tax reaction functions). Finally, some equations have been added to account for endpoint and starting point conditions (e.g., consumption of endpoint capital).

A few general notational rules were followed in order to make the reading of the model a little easier. Also $\Sigma_{i=1}^{T} X_i$ is written out as SUM [I = 1 to T: $X(i)$]. In general, all home country variables end with an H and foreign variables with an F. The model is simulated for years 20–40.

Endogenous Variables

BH	= home international borrowing (-BH for the foreign country).
BPH(F)	= home (foreign) private-sector international borrowing.
CH(F)	= home (foreign) private consumption.
EH(F)	= home (foreign) private total expenditures (inclusive of leisure consumption).
INVADJH(F)	= home (foreign) net investment.
INVH(F)	= home (foreign) gross investment.
KH(F)	= home (foreign) capital stock.

LH(F)	= home (foreign) labor supply.
PCH(F)	= home (foreign) tax-adjusted price of consumption.
PH(F)	= home (foreign) price index of utility-based real spending.
PLH(F)	= home (foreign) tax-adjusted price of labor.
R	= rate of interest plus one.
RR	= the inverse of the present-value factor.
RRH(F)	= the inverse of the present-value factor (tax adjusted).
R20(R20F)	= home (foreign) tax-adjusted present-value factor in period T.
SURPH(F)	= home (foreign) cumulative government surplus.
TBH(F)	= home (foreign) tax rate on bonds (τ_b in the text).
TCH(F)	= home (foreign) consumption tax rate (τ_c in the text).
TERKH(F)	= home (foreign) capital stock consumed in period T.
TYH(F)	= home (foreign) income tax rate (τ_y in the text).
UH(F)	= home (foreign) utility-based total expenditure.
WH(F)	= home (foreign) wealth.
YH(F)	= home (foreign) income.
VH(F)	= home (foreign) lifetime utility from $t = 0$ to T.

Exogenous Variables and Parameters

GH(F)	= home (foreign) government spending.
INV0H(F)	= home (foreign) investment in period 0.
TCH(F)BAR	= home (foreign) consumption tax rate when income tax rate is endogenous.
TYH(F)BAR	= home (foreign) income tax rate when consumption tax rate is endogenous.
WAGEH(F)	= home (foreign) wage rate (w in the text).
ALPHAH(F)	= home (foreign) fraction of consumption of end period capital stock (a in the text).
KADJH(F)	= home (foreign) adjustment parameter of the capital stock (b in the text).
BETAH(F)	= home (foreign) distributive parameter of consumption (β in the text).
DELTAH(F)	= home (foreign) subjective discount rate (δ in text).
MPKH(F)	= home (foreign) marginal product of capital (r_k in the text).
SIGMAH(F)	= home (foreign) consumption-leisure elasticity of substitution (σ).
THETAH(F)	= home (foreign) rate of depreciation of capital stock.

TAXDUMH(F)   = home (foreign) tax dummy (1[0] income
                  [consumption] tax is endogenous).
TBTYH(F)   = home (foreign) determines relation between bond
                  and income taxes (θ in the text).
TERSURPH(F)   = home (foreign) value of terminal budget deficit.

Equations

(1) YH   = WAGEH*LH + (MPKH − THETAH)*KH.

(2) YF   = WAGEF*LF + (MPKF − THETAF)*KF.

(3) CH   = (1 − BETAH)**SIGMAH*PCH**(− SIGMAH)*EH/
              ((1 − BETAH)**SIGMAH*PCH**(1 − SIGMAH)
              + BETAH** SIGMAH*PLH**(1 − SIGMAH)).

(4) CF   = (1 − BETAF)**SIGMAF*PCF**(− SIGMAF)*
              EF/((1 − BETAF)**SIGMAF*PCF**(1 − SIGMAF)
              + BETAF**SIGMAF*PLF**(1 − SIGMAF)).

(5) 1 − LH = BETAH**SIGMAH*PLH**(− SIGMAH)*EH/
              ((1 − BETAH)**SIGMAH*PCH**(1 − SIGMAH)
              + BETAH**SIGMAH*PLH**(1 − SIGMAH)).

(6) 1 − LF = BETAF**SIGMAF*PLF**(− SIGMAF)*EF/
              ((1 − BETAF)**SIGMAF*PCF**(1 − SIGMAF)
              + BETAF **SIGMAF*PLF**(1 − SIGMAF)).

(7) PH   = ((1 − BETAH)**SIGMAH*PCH**
              (1 − SIGMAH) + BETAH**SIGMAH*PLH**
              (1 − SIGMAH))**(1/(1 − SIGMAH)).

(8) PF   = ((1 − BETAF)**SIGMAF*PCF**(1 − SIGMAF)
              + BETAF**SIGMAF*PLF**(1 − SIGMAF))**
              (1/(1 − SIGMAF)).

(9) 0   = IF YEAR() EQ 20 THEN INVADJH − INVOH ELSE
              (− (1 − TYH(− 1)))/(RRH(− 1))*
              (1 + KADJH*INVADJH/KH(− 1)) + (1 − THETAH)**
              (20 − TIME) *(MPKH − THETAH + ALPHAH)/R20
              + SUM(I = 1 TO 19 : (1 − THETAH)**(I − 1)*
              (1 − TYH(I − 1))/RRH(I − 1)* IDUM(I)*
              (MPKH − THETAH) + (1 − TYH(I − 1))*KADJH/2*
              (INVADJH(I)/KH(I − 1))**2).

(10) 0   = IF YEAR() EQ 20 THEN INVADJF − INVOF ELSE
              (− (1 − TYF(− 1)))/(RRF(− 1))*(1 + KADJF*INVADJF/

$KF(-1)) + (1 - THETAF)**(20 - TIME)*(MPKF - THETA$
$+ ALPHAF)/R20F + SUM(I = 1\ TO\ 19 :$
$(1 - THETAF)**(I - 1)*(1 - TYF(I - 1))/RRF(I - 1)*$
$IDUM(I)*(MPKF - THETAF) + (1 - TYF(I - 1))*KADJF/2*$
$(INVADJF(I)/KF(I - 1))**2).$

(11) KH $= (1 - THETAH)*KH(-1) + INVADJH.$

(12) KF $= (1 - THETAF)*KF(-1) + INVADJF.$

(13) INVH $= INVADJH*(1 + KADJH/2*INVADJH/KH(-1)).$

(14) INVF $= INVADJF*(1 + KADJF/2* INVADJF/KF(-1)).$

(15) PLH $= WAGEH*(1 - TYH).$

(16) PLF $= WAGEF*(1 - TYF).$

(17) PCH $= (1 + TCH).$

(18) PCF $= (1 + TCF).$

(19) UH $= (1 - DELTAH)*WH/PH/(1 - DELTAH**21)*DELTAH$
$**TIME*RRH.$

(20) UF $= (1 - DELTAF)*WF/PF/$
$(1 - DELTAF**21)*DELTAF**TIME*RRF.$

(21) EH $= PH*UH.$

(22) EF $= PF*UF.$

(23) WH $= IF\ YEAR()\ EQ\ 20\ THEN\ SUM(J = 0\ TO\ 19 :$
$((1 - TYH(J))*(WAGEH(J) + (MPKH - THETAH)*KH(J)$
$- INVH(J + 1))/RRH(J)) + ((1 - TYH(20))*$
$(WAGEH(20) + (MPKH - THETAH)*KH(20) +$
$TERKH(20))/\ RRH(20)\ ELSE\ WH(-1).$

(24) WF $= IF\ YEAR()\ EQ\ 20\ THEN\ WF - R + 1\ ELSE\ WF(-1).$

(25) SURPH $= SURPH(-1)*R(-1) + (TBH*(BPH - R*$
$BPH(-1)) + TCH*CH + TYH*(LH*WAGEH$
$+ (MPKH - THETAH)\ *KH - INVH(1) + TERKH) - GH).$

(26) SURPF $= SURPF(-1)*R(-1) + (TBF*(BPF-R*BPF$
$(-1)) + TCF*CF + TYF*(LF*WAGEF +$
$(MPKF - THETAF)*KF - INVF(1) + TERKF) - GF).$

(27) TYH $= TAXDUMH*(IF\ YEAR()\ LT\ 21\ THEN\ TYHBAR\ ELSE$
$(IF\ YEAR()\ EQ\ 21\ THEN$
$(TERSURPH - SURPH(-1) - SUM(J = 0\ TO\ 19 :$
$1/RR(J)*(TBH(J)*(BPH(J) - R(J)*BPH(J - 1)) + TCH(J)$

    *CH(J) − GH(J))))/SUM(I = 0 TO 19 :
(LH(I)*WAGEH(I) + (MPKH − THETAH)*KH(I)
− INVH(I + 1) + TERKH(I))/RR(I)) ELSE
TYH(− 1))) + (1 − TAXDUMH)*TYHBAR.

(28) TYF   = TAXDUMF*(IF YEAR() LT 21 THEN TYFBAR ELSE
(IF YEAR() EQ 21 THEN
(TERSURPF − SURPF(− 1) − SUM(J = 0 to 19 :
1/RR(J)*(TBF(J)*(BPF(J) − R(J)*BPF(J − 1))
+ TCF(J)*CF(J) − GF(J))))/SUM(I = 0 TO 19 :
(LF(I)*WAGEF(I) + (MPKF − THETAF)*KF(I)
− INVF(I + 1) + TERKF(I))/RR(I)) ELSE TYF(− 1)))
+ (1 − TAXDUMF)*TYFBAR.

(29) TCH   = (1 − TAXDUMH)*(IF YEAR() LT 21 THEN TCHBAR
ELSE (IF YEAR() EQ 21 THEN
(TERSURPH − SURPH(− 1) − SUM(J = 0 TO 19 :
1/RR(J)*(TBH(J)*(BPH(J) − R(J)*BPH(J − 1))
+ TYH(J)*(LH(J)*WAGEH(J) + (MPKH − THETAH)*
KH(J) − INVH(J + 1) + TERKH(J) − GH(J)))))/SUM(I = 0
TO 19 : 1/RR(I)*CH(I)) ELSE
TCH(− 1))) + TAXDUMH*TCHBAR.

(30) TCF   = (1 − TAXDUMF)*(IF YEAR() LT 21 THEN TCFBAR
ELSE (IF YEAR() EQ 21
THEN(TERSURPF − SURPF(− 1) − SUM(J = 0 TO 19 :
1/RR(J)*(TBF(J)*(BPF(J) − R(J)*BPF(J − 1)) + TYF(J)
*(LF(J)*WAGEF(J) + (MPKF − THETAF)*KF(J) − INVF(J +
1) + TERKF(J) − GF(J)))))/SUM(I = 0 TO 19 :
1/RR(I)*CF(I)) ELSE TCF(− 1))) + TAXDUMF*TCFBAR.

(31) TBH   = TBTYH*TYH.

(32) TBF   = TBTYF*TYF.

(33) TERKH = IF YEAR() LT 40 THEN 0 ELSE ALPHAH*KH.

(34) TERKF = IF YEAR() LT 40 THEN 0 ELSE ALPHAF*KF.

(35) BPH   = ((1 + TCH)*CH − (1 − TYH)*(YH + TERKH −
INVH(1))(R(− 1) − 1)*BPH(− 1))/(1 − TBH) + BPH(− 1).

(36) BPF   = ((1 + TCF)*CF − (1 − TYF)*(YF + TERKF −
INVF(1)) + (R(− 1) − 1)*BPF(− 1))/(1 − TBF) +
BPF(− 1).

(37) VH   = SUM(I = 0 TO 19 : DELTAH**I*LOG(UH(I))).

(38) VF   = SUM(I = 0 TO 19 : DELTAF**I*LOG(UF(I))).

(39) R20H   = IF YEAR() EQ 20 THEN RR(20)/(1 − TYH(20)) ELSE
            R20H(− 1).

(40) R20F   = IF YEAR() EQ 20 THEN RR(20)/(1 − TYF(20)) ELSE
            R20F(− 1).

(41) RRH   = EXP(SUM(J = − 19 TO 0 : LOG(1 − TBH(J) + R(J) − 1))).

(42) RRF   = EXP(SUM(J = − 19 TO 0 :
            LOG(1 − TBF(J) + R(J) − 1))).

(43)   GH + GF + CH + CF + INVH(1) + INVF(1) = YH + YF
            + TERKH + TERKF.

(44) RR   = EXP(SUM(J = − 19 TO 0 : LOG(R(J)))).

(45) BH   = CH − YH + R(− 1)*BH(− 1) + INVH(1) + GH − TERKH.

Equations (1) and (2) define home and foreign country income as labor income plus the return on capital. Equations (3)–(8) are the behavioral equations derived by maximizing utility subject to the lifetime present-value budget constraint. Equation (3) is the home consumption equation and identical to equation (7) of the main text. Equation (5) is the leisure equation and (7) the price equation; they represent equations (8) and (6) of the main text. The foreign country equations for these three variables are (4), (6), and (8).

The home and foreign investment equations, (9) and (10), derived by maximizing wealth, differ slightly from equation (9) in the main text in so far as the rate of depreciation (THETA) is included here but omitted from the text. Equations (11) and (12) define the home and foreign capital stocks, and equations (13) and (14) describe investment demands allowing for adjustment costs.

Equations (15)–(19) are definitions of tax-adjusted prices that are then substituted in other equations. For example, a comparison of equation (6) of the text to equation (7) of the simulation model shows that PCH is used in place of $(1 + \tau_{ct})$.

Real utility-based expenditures (eq. [5] of the text) are given in equations (19) and (20), while the values in terms of the consumption good of these expenditures are defined in (21) and (22). Home country wealth is defined by equation (23) and is identical to the wealth equation in the main text. A similar equation could be written for foreign wealth, but, by Walras law, we have dropped this equation from the model and use the relation to solve for the interest rate. Note that these equations solve for W_0 and R_0 in period $t = 0$ (year 20 in the computer model). However, for $t = 1$ to T, these equations set wealth at their previous values (i.e., WH_0 and WF_0) thereafter.

The next eight equations are used to describe government behavior and vary depending on the type of scenario that we are simulating. Equations (25) and (26) define the home and foreign country's cumulated surplus as tax receipts less spending. Various combinations of the next six equations and values for dummy variables are used in the simulations to capture alternative tax and spending policies. For example, in the simulation of a revenue neutral conversion of consumption for income tax, equations (27) and (29) are dropped from the model, and the income tax rate, TYH, and the government surplus, SURPH, are assumed exogenous while the consumption tax rate, TCH, can be thought of as balancing the government's net revenue position. For the budget deficit simulations, the model is altered in a very different way. For example, in order to analyze a current income tax shift, the consumption tax equation, (29), is dropped from the model, and the consumption tax rate is assumed exogenous. Then an exogenous income tax rate is imposed in the relevant years, and equation (27) is used to alter future income tax rates so that the budget is balanced by year T. Analogous assumptions can be made for consumption tax shifts. Equations (31) and (32) define the international borrowing tax rates as described in equation (10) in the main text, and the coefficient, TBTYR (θ in the text), can be set in order to consider a wide variety of tax conversion policies as a result of the tax equivalence relation between the consumption, income, and international borrowing taxes.

Equations (35) and (36) define the privately held home (foreign) stock of international borrowings. The definitions of lifetime utility are given in equations (37) and (38). Note that, since the model is simulated for only twenty years, the only relevant calculation for VH and VF is in the first year. Also, the utility calculation excludes the final year (T) because the arbitrary choice of a time horizon may cause somewhat perverse results at time T. Equations (39) and (40) define period T's tax-adjusted value of the discount factor used in the investment equations, and (41) and (42) define the tax-adjusted discount factor for all other years.

The final three equations do not have home and foreign counterparts. Equation (43) is the equilibrium condition for world output; demand for world output must equal the supply of world output. Equation (44) defines the present-value factor. Finally, the balance of payments for the home country is defined in equation (45). Obviously, the negative of BH defines the foreign country's balance of payment position.

The parameter values used in the baseline simulations are $\beta = \beta^* = .4$, $\delta = \delta^* = .97$, $\sigma = \sigma^* = 0.3$, $r_k = r_k^* = 0.3$, and $\alpha = \alpha^* = 0.2$. For intercountry differences in the parameter values of the discount factor, we use ($\delta = .95$, $\delta^* = .97$) or ($\delta = .97$, $\delta^* = .95$), while, for intercountry differences in the parameter values of the marginal product of capital, we use ($r_k = 0.2$, $r_k^* = 0.3$) or ($r_k = 0.3$, $r_k^* = 0.2$).

Notes

1. We are grateful to Mario Blejer and Jonathan Levin, who assisted us in obtaining the data and the interpretation of the various accounting measures.

2. The definitions of the various statistics are provided in the note to table 6.1.

3. The analytical framework underlying the international-intertemporal approach to open-economy macroeconomics is based on Frenkel and Razin (1987, 1988b). For an analogous approach developed in a closed economy context, see Auerbach and Kotlikoff (1987). The tax systems in many countries include incentives to saving and investment and thereby contain important features of the cash flow income tax system. Suppose that the underlying income tax system is represented by the following modification of the right-hand side of eq. (1):

$$(1 - \tau_{wt})w + (1 - \tau_{kt})((r_k - \theta)K_t) - (1 - \tau_{It})I_t(1 + bI_t/2K_t)$$
$$+ (1 - \tau_{bt})(B_t^p - B_{t-1}^p) - (1 - \tau_{kt})(1 + \tau_{st})r_{t-1}B_{t-1}^p,$$

where τ_{wt} and τ_{Kt} denote the tax rates on labor income and capital income, respectively, and τ_{It} and τ_{st} denote investment-tax credit and saving-tax credit, respectively. Then the tax configuration $\tau_k = \tau_I = \tau_s/(1 + \tau_s)$ yields a cash flow income tax system.

4. Our formulation reflects the assumption that, except for the final period, bolted capital cannot be consumed. However, in the final period, the capital stock, K_T, can be transformed into consumption at the rate equals to aK_T, where $0 \leqslant a \leqslant 1$. This assumption serves to mitigate abrupt changes in the behavior of the economy arising in the final period of the finite horizon model. Accordingly, the budget constraint applicable to the final period (period T) is analogous to the one shown in eq. (1) with an added term on the right-hand side equal to $a(K_{T-1} + I_{T-1}) = aK_T$. For a formulation of a model highlighting the interaction between investment, government spending policies, and international interdependence within an infinite horizon model, see Buiter (1987).

5. A detailed analysis of the various equivalence relations in international macroeconomics and their policy implications is contained in Auerbach, Frenkel, and Razin (1989).

6. Obviously, with more than two periods, these discount factors are replaced by the appropriate present-value factors.

7. The investment behavior could have been generalized to include the depreciation of the capital stock. The simulation model used in this paper and described in the appendix includes capital depreciation.

8. This analysis is based on Frenkel and Razin (1989).

9. In terms of the utility function, this assumption amounts to setting $\beta = 1$ in eq. (3). The simulation analysis relaxes these assumptions by considering multiperiod simulations with a variable labor supply.

10. We are indebted to Alan Auerbach for suggesting this diagram.

11. These considerations imply that, in the neighborhood of a flat path of income tax, if the intertemporal income tax ratio exceeds unity, then the CC schedule is flatter than the RR schedule (assuming an initial-period trade-balance deficit). This is the case shown in fig. 6.6.

12. It can be verified that the quantitative results of the tax conversion remain the same if the intertemporal income tax ratio falls short of unity, though in the latter case the slopes of the CC and the II schedules are reversed (but the II schedule is flatter than the RR schedule in the neighborhood of $\tau_{y1}/\tau_{y0} = 1$).

13. To facilitate the diagrammatic exposition, we continue to assume that labor supply is fixed (so that $\beta = 1$ in eq. [3]). The diagrammatic analysis could also

allow for variable labor supply if leisure and ordinary consumption are separable in the utility function as in Frenkel and Razin (1987).

14. This follows from the fact that in equilibrium the denominators of μ_s and μ_d are equal to each other. Thus, if the domestic economy runs a trade surplus in the second period, then $C_1 + Y_1$, and, since $C + C_1^* = Y_1 + Y_1^*$, it follows that $\mu_d < \mu_s$.

15. In the subsequent analysis, we find it convenient to set the international borrowing tax, τ_b, equal to zero and to use explicitly the consumption and income tax rates rather than using the equivalence relations as in section 6.2.1.

16. Our assumptions that the initial undistorted equilibrium was with a current-account balance imply that the real-income effects induced by the departure from the flat tax pattern and by changes in the world rate of interest are dominated by the substitution effect.

17. To verify this point, we note that

$$\hat{D}^w = [C_0/(C_0 + C_0^*)]\hat{D} + [C_0/(C_0 + C_0^*) - C_1/(C_1 + C_1^*)]\hat{C}_1,$$

where a "hat" denotes a proportional change in the variable. Accordingly, the proportional change in the world relative demand is composed of two components. The first consists of the product of the proportional change of the domestic relative demand and a fraction (the relative share of current-period home consumption in the world consumption), and the second consists of the product of the proportional change in future-period consumption and a term measuring the difference between the relative shares of current and future-period home consumption in world consumption. This latter bracketed term reflects the difference between the domestic and foreign saving propensities. If the current-period trade-balance deficit arises from a relatively low domestic saving propensity, then this bracketed term is positive. We also note that $\hat{C}_1$ is negative since the change in the time profile of consumption taxes induces a substitution away from future-period consumption. It follows that, under such circumstances, $\hat{D}^w < \hat{D}$ and, therefore, the displacement of the D^w schedule is smaller than that of the D schedule.

18. This analysis is based on Frenkel and Razin (1988a).

19. Recall that, in developing fig. 6.7, we have used for simplicity a two-period model with fixed labor supply (so that $\beta = 1$ in eq. [3]). As before, these assumptions are relaxed in the dynamic-simulation model.

20. In performing the simulations, we allow for a variable labor supply. Thus, we assume that $\beta < 1$ in eq. (8). Our simulations are based on the assumption that the elasticity of substitution between consumption and leisure, σ, is smaller than unity. The time path of employment following a current-period cut in consumption tax rates may be reversed if this elasticity was assumed to exceed unity.

21. Zero-rated products involve the reimbursement of taxes levied on inputs with the result that the final good is completely untaxed.

References

Auerbach, Alan J., Jacob A. Frenkel, and Assaf Razin. 1989. Notes on international aspects of taxation. International Monetary Fund.

Auerbach, Alan J., and Laurence J. Kotlikoff. 1987. *Dynamic fiscal policy.* London: Cambridge University Press.

Buiter, Willem H. 1987. Fiscal policy in open interdependent economies. In *Economic policy in theory and practice,* ed. Assaf Razin and Efraim Sadka, 101–44. London: Macmillan.

Cnossen, Sijbren, and Carl S. Shoup. 1987. Coordination of value-added taxes. In *Tax coordination in the European Community.* ed. Cnossen Sijbren. Antwerp: Kluwer Law and Taxation Publishers.

Emerson, Michael, Michel Aujean, Michel Catinat, Philippe Goybet, and Alexis Jacquemin. 1988. Fiscal barrier. *European Economy* (March), 45–107.

Frenkel, Jacob A., and Assaf Razin. 1987. *Fiscal policy and the world economy: An intertemporal approach.* Cambridge, Mass.: MIT Press.

————. 1988a. Budget deficits under alternative tax systems: International effects. *IMF Staff Papers* 35(2):297–315.

————. 1988b. *Spending, taxes and deficits: International-intertemporal approach.* Princeton Studies in International Finance no. 63. Princeton, N.J.: International Finance Section.

————. 1989. International effects of tax reforms. *Economic Journal* 99 (March): 38–59.

OECD. 1987a. *Quarterly National Accounts,* no. 2 (diskettes).

OECD. 1987b. *Revenue Statistics: 1965–1986* (Tape).

Comment   Willem H. Buiter

Working through this interesting paper by Frenkel, Razin, and Symansky was a very useful investment of time and effort. Like Oliver Twist, a typical discussant will always ask for "some more." My comments are no exception.

The paper consists of three parts. Part 1 considers some empirical material on the tax structures of the major seven OECD countries. Part 2 contains a small analytical model that is used to evaluate various changes in the tax structure in a small open economy and in a two-country world. Part 3 goes through the same kinds of exercises using a numerical simulation model that is a generalization of the analytical model of section 6.1. My comments will deal mainly with part 2, the analytical model. Some brief remarks on the data section are, however, in order.

The Data

Figures 6.1 and 6.2 and table 6.1 of the Frenkel-Razin-Symansky paper (henceforth FRS) provide some stylized facts concerning average tax rates (both total and disaggregated) for the seven major industrial countries since the early 1970s. This suggests that there is considerable cross-sectional and time-series variation in the importance of different taxes and in the total tax burden. As regards the latter, the secular increase since World War II came to an end around 1981–82, as can be seen from table C6.1. While there has been no significant reduction in the total tax burden (the sum of direct and indirect taxes and social security contributions paid by employers and employees collected by general government as a percentage

Willem Buiter is professor of economics at Yale University and a research associate of the National Bureau of Economic Research.

Table C6.1   **Total Outlays and Current Receipts of General Government as Percentage of GDP**

	1967	1982	1986
United States:			
Outlays	30.5	36.5	36.9
Receipts	27.1	31.1	31.3
Japan:			
Outlays	18.2	33.7	33.1
Receipts	19.3	29.5	31.3
Germany:			
Outlays	38.6	49.4	46.6
Receipts	36.7	45.4	44.7
France:			
Outlays	39.0	50.4	51.8
Receipts	38.2	45.9	47.1
United Kingdom:			
Outlays	38.2	47.4	46.2
Receipts	36.2	43.3	41.9
Italy:			
Outlays	33.7	47.6	50.5
Receipts	31.0	36.0	38.9
Canada:			
Outlays	31.5	46.6	46.2
Receipts	30.3	39.1	39.2

Source: OECD Economic Outlook 44 (December 1988), tables R14, R15.

of GDP), the roughly stationary shares of general government revenue and expenditure in GDP since the early 1980s represent a major economic and political change.

It is recognized by the authors that the average tax rates bear no obvious relation to the marginal rates that provide the incentives that govern labor demand and supply, saving, capital formation, and portfolio allocation.

These marginal tax rates too are characterized by considerable cross-sectional and time-series variation. For example, in 1986 the top marginal rate of the personal income tax was 38 percent in the United States, 76.5 percent in Japan, 60 percent in the United Kingdom, 56 percent in West Germany, and 65 percent in Italy. The top marginal income tax rate in the United Kingdom had come down from 83 percent (99 percent for unearned income) and was lowered in 1988 to 40 percent.

When there are many different taxes, some of which apply to the same base (e.g., wage income taxes and social security contributions) while others apply to distinct bases, their combined effect on behavior is what matters.

Indeed, for a proper appreciation of the incentive effects and distributional consequences of the budget, we must look jointly at the tax and benefit systems. Some of the most spectacular instances of high effective marginal tax rates (occasionally in excess of 100 percent) come from the interaction of the tax and benefit systems. In many industrial countries, a "poverty trap" exists when at low levels of income a small increase in earned income is effectively nullified by a significant loss of benefits and a high "starting" marginal tax rate. The "Why work?" phenomenon refers to the possibility that the choice between low-paid employment and unemployment is decided in favor of the latter through the combined effect of unemployment benefit, income tax, and social security.

Table C6.2 shows how the "total" marginal tax rate on average wages differed in the seven main industrial countries in 1986.

The marginal tax rates (or tax-net-of-benefit rates) that we can read off the tax and benefit laws and regulations may not represent the relevant economic signals if there is significant scope for tax avoidance.

Finally, even the exhaustive public-spending part of the budget will have potentially important distributional and incentive effects. For instance, public expenditure on health and education, provided free of charge, represents income in kind to private agents and may be a direct substitute for or complement to private spending. Some of this public expenditure may have the characteristics of a national public good, an international public good, a local public good, or a conventional private good. Different income groups benefit differentially from public expenditure on defense and on law and order.

Note that, while the exhaustive expenditure side of the budget will obviously affect private behavior through income (or wealth) effects, it is quite possible that it also affects relevant private static or intertemporal terms of trade.

The empirical material of part 1 is not sufficiently rich to give us a sense of the cross-sectional or time-series variation in the "net" effects of general government budgets on the incentives to work, save, invest, and bear risk or on the distribution of income. In the theoretical parts of the paper, all taxes are assumed to be levied at given proportional or "flat" rates. There is no progressivity or regressivity, no exemptions, tax credits, leads and lags, etc. Even so, the analysis can get rather involved. Modeling descriptively realistic tax-benefit-expenditure structures appears to be a daunting task indeed.

Table C6.2   Marginal Tax Rates on Average Wages under 1986 Tax Systems[a]

United States	40.9
Japan	31.5
Germany	62.7
France	51.2
United Kingdom	43.9
Italy	57.8
Canada	33.7

Source: OECD Economic Outlook 41 (June 1987), table 16.

[a]Overall marginal tax rate for an average (unmarried) production worker, allowing for direct taxes at all levels of government, social security contributions by both employees and employers, and relevant tax concessions.

The Analytical Model

In the small open economy case, there is a single (finite-lived) representative household-worker-producer. There is one traded good that can be used for private consumption, private investment, or export. Public consumption or investment is not considered explicitly. There is a fixed endowment each period of a single nontraded good. This can be either consumed (leisure) or combined with capital to produce the traded good. The production function of the traded good is linear, and the marginal products of labor and capital are fixed at w and r_K, respectively.

A competitive equilibrium with the domestic interest rate, r, fixed by the assumption of perfect international capital mobility and a parametric world rate of interest, would result in corner solutions for the capital stock (unless $r = r_K$). The assumption of quadratic internal adjustment costs to investment guarantees an interior solution for the capital stock, while the competitive wage rate remains independent of the capital-labor ratio.

The multiperiod utility function is time additive and logarithmic, while the single-period utility function is a C.E.S. function of traded goods consumption and leisure.

Without loss of generality, the private sector is assumed to hold no domestic government debt, and (with some loss of generality) the initial external debt is assumed to equal zero.

There are three taxes, each levied at a constant proportional rate in any given period but potentially differing between periods. The taxes are labeled consumption tax (or VAT), (cash flow) income tax, and tax on external private borrowing. These labels are rather misleading.

The ''consumption tax'' is a tax on the private consumption of the traded good only. Leisure, the nontraded good, is not taxed. A comprehensive flat-rate consumption tax would fall equally on the private consumption of traded and nontraded goods and on public consumption. Henceforth, *consumption* denotes private consumption of traded goods only.

The ''cash flow income tax'' is a tax on domestic factor income (GDP) minus investment expenditure. This is of course identically equal to consumption plus exhaustive public spending plus the trade balance surplus. With zero public spending, it is a tax on consumption plus the trade balance surplus.

The tax on private external borrowing is in fact a tax on the private external primary (noninterest) deficit (i.e., private external borrowing minus interest paid on the external private debt). With a balanced government budget, the external primary deficit of the private sector equals the trade deficit. We therefore have (in each period) proportional taxes on consumption, on consumption plus the trade balance surplus, and on the trade balance deficit. The fact that any linear combination of these three taxes can be reproduced by some linear combination of any two of the three is therefore not surprising. I will restrict attention in what follows to the consumption tax and the cash-flow tax.

In the special case of the two-period model with inelastic labor supply, most of the single-country analysis can be obtained directly from the two intertemporal first-order conditions or "Euler equations" governing private consumption and investment.

If the instantaneous utility function is $u(c)$, the optimal intertemporal consumption choice is characterized by

(1)
$$\frac{1}{1 + \tau_{c_0}} u'(c_0) = \frac{(1 + r_0)}{1 + \tau_{c_1}} \delta u'(c_1).$$

In the logarithmic utility case ($u[c] = lnc$), this implies

(2)
$$\frac{c_1}{c_0} = (1 + r_0) \left[\frac{1 + \tau_{c_0}}{1 + \tau_{c_1}} \right] \delta.$$

One plus the growth rate of consumption is increasing in the "consumption interest factor" $(1 + r_0)[(1 + \tau_{c_0})/(1 + \tau_{c_1})]$. In the small open economy, r_0 is exogenous, and the growth rate of consumption increases with $(1 + \tau_{c_0})/(1 + \tau_{c_1})$. A higher value of $(1 + \tau_{c_0})/(1 + \tau_{c_1})$ increases the opportunity cost of consuming today.

For the investment decision, the first-order condition is

(3)
$$(1 - \tau_{y_0}) \left[1 + \frac{bI_0}{K_0} \right] = \left[\frac{a + r_k}{1 + r_0} \right] (1 - \tau_{y_1}),$$

which implies

(4)
$$I_0 = \frac{1}{b} \left[\left(\frac{a + r_k}{1 + r_0} \right) \left(\frac{1 - \tau_{y_1}}{1 - \tau_{y_0}} \right) - 1 \right] K_0.$$

With both r_k and r_0 exogenous and K_0 predetermined, a higher value of τ_{y_1} relative to τ_{y_0} raises the effective (after-tax) investment rate of interest and reduces investment.

If we want c_1 and c_0 separately rather than just c_1/c_0, it is easily checked that

$$(1 + \tau_{c_0})c_0 = \frac{1}{1 + \delta} W_0,$$

$$(1 + \tau_{c_1})c_1 = \frac{\delta}{1 + \delta} W_0(1 + r_0),$$

where

$$W_0 = (1 - \tau_{y_0}) \left[w + r_k K_0 - I_0 \left(1 + \frac{b}{2} \frac{I_0}{K_0} \right) \right] + \frac{1}{1 + r_0} (1 - \tau_{y_1})$$

$$[w + (r_k + a)K_1],$$

and

$$K_1 = K_0 + I_0.$$

Since for consumption growth all that matters is τ_{c_0} / τ_{c_1} and for investment all that matters is τ_{y_1} / τ_{y_0}, the analysis of the consequences of a balanced-budget switch from a consumption tax to a cash-flow tax is straightforward.

If the first-period equilibrium is characterized by a trade deficit, first-period consumption exceeds first-period cash flow, and second-period consumption is less than second-period cash flow. If τ_{c_0} and τ_{c_1} were reduced by a common percentage and τ_{y_0} and τ_{y_1} increased by a common percentage (so as to maintain public-sector solvency over the two-period horizon), there would be a first-period budget deficit and a second-period budget surplus. To maintain period-by-period budget balance, we must reduce τ_{c_0} proportionally by less than τ_{c_1} and increase τ_{y_0} proportionally by more than τ_{y_1}. If follows immediately that c_1/c_0 and I_0 rise. With a little work, it can also be shown that c_0 falls.

In a two-country setting (with a single traded good), the world interest rate becomes endogenous. Assume that the home country, which undergoes the balanced-budget move from a consumption tax to a cash-flow tax, has a first-period trade deficit (say, because it has a higher subjective rate of time preference, a higher marginal product of capital, or a lower adjustment cost coefficient). The single-country analysis showed that, at a given interest rate, the home country wishes to switch resources to the future by increasing saving and investment. In the world economy, this reduces the interest rate, boosting foreign investment and reducing foreign consumption growth. The decline in r_0 further stimulates home country investment and reduces the increase in consumption growth but does not reverse it; that is, $(1 + r_0)$ $[(1 + \tau_{c_0})/(1 + \tau_{c_1})]$ increases. In an overlapping generations model, the decline in r_0 could be strong enough to reduce $(1 + r_0)$ $[(1 + \tau_{c_0})/(1 + \tau_{c_1})]$ despite the increase in $(1 + \tau_{c_0})/(1 + \tau_{c_1})$ (this is an open economy version of the result shown in Diamond [1970]).

An "unbalanced budget" (but solvency consistent) cut in τ_{c_0} followed by an increase in τ_{c_1} can again be analyzed directly from equations (2) and (4). At a given value of r_0, the growth rate of consumption falls, while I_0 is unaffected. In a two-country world, the world interest rate rises, depressing capital formation at home and abroad, raising foreign consumption growth and mitigating the decline in home country consumption growth.

"Tax harmonization" in the two-country model is the sum of two balanced budget tax conversions, in the home country a move toward a lower consumption tax rate and a higher cash-flow tax rate and in the foreign country a move in the opposite direction. No new analytics are involved.

Other Assorted Comments

1. A minor technical problem with the current presentation of the model is that government revenue "disappears." The government's intertemporal budget constraint or solvency constraint is not explicitly substituted into the private sector's intertemporal choice set to obtain the general equilibrium

responses. There is no government spending on goods and services, and the proceeds from the distortionary taxes are not returned (in lump-sum fashion or otherwise) to the private sector. The analysis is therefore strictly valid only for (small) tax rate changes evaluated "at zero."

2. The analysis proceeds as if a cut in tax rates always reduces revenue from the tax in question. This is correct in the FRS model for consumption tax cuts and for equal proportional cuts in cash-flow tax rates in both periods. It is not obviously true if τ_{y_1} alone is cut since this boosts I_0, which might raise cash flow in period 1 by enough to raise cash-flow tax receipts in period 1 despite the cut in τ_{y_1}. With endogenous labor supply (the general case considered in the simulation exercises), the scope for Laffer-style phenomena is enhanced.

3. It would be interesting (and in my view essential for a policy relevant analysis) to extend the analysis beyond the representative agent case with its maintained hypothesis of first-order debt neutrality. Samuelson-Diamond OLG models or the Blanchard-Yaari version of the OLG model are the natural vehicles for carrying out a rich analysis of changes in tax structure with and without balanced budgets. Frenkel and Razin have pioneered the application of these models to international tax questions (see, e.g., Frenkel and Razin 1987), and I hope that in further work on the topics covered in the FRS paper they will take the key step of moving beyond the representative agent paradigm. My own analysis of a proportional tax on the income from labor and capital in open, interdependent economies (Buiter 1989) shows that qualitatively different results can be obtained (even in a balanced budget setting) if we move from a representative agent to an OLG setting.

4. For a policy-oriented analysis, the introduction of endogenous terms of trade (i.e., at least two traded goods) is important. Part of the real-world debate about the switch from conventional income taxes to a VAT concerns the effects of such a change on international competitiveness (see, e.g., Feldstein and Krugman, in this volume). While the model of the FRS paper can be used to analyze the consequences of tax conversions of this kind on the relative sizes of the traded and nontraded goods sectors (in the case where the supply of labor is not exogenous), it cannot be used to address questions concerning effects on the production of exportables and import-competing goods and on the terms of trade. Engel and Kletzer (1987) have demonstrated the importance of the specification of savings behavior for the determination of the effects of a tariff (a tax on the consumption of and an equal proportional subsidy on the production of importables) on the external accounts. A similar sensitivity of the behavior of the external accounts (and of the sectoral allocation of resources) to alternative assumptions about savings behavior can be expected for other changes in the structure of taxation, transfers, and subsidies.

5. The consumption tax of the FRS paper is a reasonable ideal type of a simple VAT with a single rate on traded goods and a zero-rated nontraded

goods sector. The other two taxes, however, cannot be described as reasonable approximations to real-world taxes, nor do they correspond to traditional public finance ideal types such as an ideal consumption tax (equal proportional taxes on the consumption of traded and nontraded goods in all periods) or a Hicks-Simons comprehensive income tax.

Instead of a tax conversion from the FRS cash-flow tax to a consumption tax, it might be more informative to consider switches between conventional taxes on the income from labor and capital (or employers' social security taxes) and a consumption tax. The tax on the external primary deficit of the private sector also has (as far as I know) no close real-world counterpart. It would be useful to analyze changes in the taxation of foreign asset income, perhaps as part of a general review of source- versus residence-based tax systems.

6. Finally, when considering tax harmonization (or the convergence of VAT rates and income tax rates among nations), it is important to realize that the argument in the European Community about this issue is part of a wider debate about the merits of competition between fiscal jurisdictions versus harmonization or uniformity. A proper understanding requires the joint consideration of exhaustive public-spending and tax-transfer-subsidy programs. The right perspective involves extensions of the theories of fiscal federalism, the theory of clubs, and the theory of local public goods. One of the authors of the FRS paper also contributed to this subject at this very conference (Razin and Sadka, in this volume). Issues such as the mobility of factors of production, of owners of factors of production, and of taxpayers and benefit recipients relative to the span of control of national fiscal authorities must be considered when this wider approach to fiscal harmonization is pursued.

The FRS paper is a useful first step toward a dynamic general equilibrium analysis of changes in tax structures in open interdependent economies.

References

Buiter, W. H. 1989. *Budgetary policy, international and intertemporal trade in the global economy.* Amsterdam: North-Holland.

Diamond, P. 1970. Incidence of an interest income tax. *Journal of Economic Theory* 2:211–24.

Engel, C., and K. Kletzer. 1987. Tariffs, saving and the current account. NBER Working Paper no. 1869. Cambridge, Mass.: National Bureau of Economic Research.

Frenkel, J. A., and A. Razin. *Fiscal policy and the world economy: An intertemporal approach.* Cambridge, Mass.: MIT Press.

7 International Trade Effects of Value-Added Taxation

Martin Feldstein and Paul Krugman

There is a well-understood economists' case for a value-added tax (VAT). As a consumption tax, a VAT would not impose the bias against saving that is inherent in income taxation and could therefore help promote capital formation and economic growth. Against this advantage must be weighed possible disadvantages resulting from higher administrative costs and greater difficulty in providing an acceptable degree of progressivity to the overall tax-and-transfer structure as well as the possible political costs (or benefits, depending on one's point of view) of a tax that is relatively invisible and thus easy to raise.

Among many businessmen, however, the case for a VAT is often stated quite differently. They view such a tax as an aid to international competitiveness since VATs are levied on imports but rebated on exports. The case is often stated as follows: an income tax is paid by producers of exports but not by foreign producers of the goods we import, while a VAT is paid on imports but not on exports. Surely, say the proponents of this view, this means that countries that have a VAT have an advantage in international competition over countries that rely on income taxation.

In fact, this argument is wrong. A VAT is not, contrary to popular belief, anything like a tariff–cum–export subsidy. Indeed, a VAT is no more an inherently procompetitive trade policy than a universal sales tax, to which an "idealized" VAT, levied equally on all consumption, is in fact equivalent. The point that VATs do not inherently affect international trade flows has been well recognized in the international tax literature.[1] This point is also

Martin Feldstein is the George F. Baker Professor of Economics at Harvard University and president and chief executive officer of the National Bureau of Economic Research. Paul Krugman is a professor of economics at the Massachusetts Institute of Technology and a research associate of the National Bureau of Economic Research.

familiar to tax policy practitioners; McLure (1987), to take a recent example, dismisses the competitive argument for a VAT as evident nonsense. Yet the belief that VATs are important determinants of international competitiveness persists among laymen.

In large part, the belief that VATs are trade-distorting policies reflects a failure on the part of noneconomists to understand the basic economic arguments. There is also another factor, however: in reality, VATs will *not* be neutral in their effect on trade, for at least two reasons. First, VATs are a substitute for other taxes, especially income taxes, that *do* affect trade. Second, in practice, a VAT will not be neutral; concern over distributional issues, as well as administrative difficulties, inevitably leads to a tax whose rate varies substantially across industries.

To acknowledge that in practice a VAT will indeed affect trade flows is not the same as saying that the lay view is right. In fact, the widespread view that a VAT enhances the international competitiveness (in some sense) of the country that adopts it may well be the reverse of the truth. To the extent that a VAT taxes traded goods more heavily than nontraded, which is normally the case, a VAT in practice probably tends to reduce rather than increase the size of a country's traded goods sector. Against this may be set the favorable effect on saving and hence on a country's trade balance in the short run of substituting a consumption tax for taxes, like the income tax, that distort intertemporal consumption choices.

The purpose of this paper is to lay out a simple analytical approach for thinking about the effects of a VAT on international trade. The paper begins by laying out a simple three-good, two-period model that has the minimal elements necessary to discuss the international trade effects of a VAT. The first section describes the model and shows how equilibrium is determined in the absence of taxation. The second section introduces a VAT and demonstrates in the context of our model the well-known fundamental point that an idealized VAT that is levied on all production is nondistortionary, in particular having no effect on the allocation of resources between tradable and nontradable sectors. We can also show that such an idealized VAT would leave nominal factor prices measured in foreign currency unchanged; this argues, in effect, that even in the short run under fixed exchange rates a VAT should not be expected to have any effect on trade.

We show next that the *absence* of distortionary effects from a VAT depends on precisely the feature that is often alleged to constitute an unfair trade advantage, namely, the rebate of value-added taxes on exports. In the absence of an export rebate, a VAT would act like an export tax—which in general equilibrium is equivalent to an import tariff. Thus, the export rebate is necessary if a VAT is not to be protectionist.

The remainder of the paper is devoted to reasons why in practice the introduction of a VAT may not be neutral in its trade effects. First, a VAT may substitute for an income tax; since an income tax is not neutral in its effects, the substitution will have allocative effects, tending, other things being equal, to improve the trade balance in the short run. Second, and offsetting this effect in the short run and persisting in the long run, a VAT in practice will tend to be levied more heavily on traded than on nontraded output and will therefore tend to shift resources out of the traded goods sectors.

On balance, the substitution of value-added taxation for income taxation is likely to have an uncertain short-run effect on a nation's net exports but is likely to reduce net exports in the longer term. This does not constitute an argument either for or against introducing a VAT; indeed, even if the effect on competitiveness were unambiguous, it is by no means clear what policy moral ought to be drawn. The point of this analysis is more modest; we want to show that the common belief that a VAT is a kind of disguised protectionist policy is based on a misunderstanding.

7.1   A Basic Model

The analysis of the international effect of a VAT has several strands. These strands dictate the necessary content of our model. First, a VAT is often alleged to favor traded goods production over nontraded goods in general; thus, we need to have a model in which some goods are nontraded. Second, the apparent differential taxation of exports and imports resulting from export rebates has been praised and attacked; thus, we need to make the distinction between importables and exportables. Finally, a consumption tax like a VAT differs from an income tax in its effect on the choice between consumption and saving; thus, we need to have a model that allows intertemporal trade-offs. Putting these together, in order to discuss the international economics of a VAT we need at minimum a model with three goods (exports, imports, and nontraded) and with two periods (present and future). At times, it will be helpful to consider more collapsed models, aggregating the two tradable sectors or eliminating the time dimension; however, a three-good, two-period model will be our base in this paper.

Consider, then, a country that produces and consumes three goods: an exported good X, an imported good M, and a nontraded good N. The economy lasts for two periods, 1 and 2. The country will be assumed to be small on both world goods markets and world financial markets, in the sense that it can trade X for M at a fixed relative price in each period and can borrow or lend at a fixed real interest rate in terms of traded goods.

The technology of production is assumed to be standard neoclassical, with perfect competition prevailing. In the first period, the economy's production possibilities may be summarized by a trade-off among the outputs of the three goods:

$$(1) \qquad\qquad T^1(Q_X^1,\ Q_M^1,\ Q_N^1) = 0.$$

Some first-period production may be used to form capital, which expands production possibilities in the second period. It is unnecessary to define a capital aggregate; we can simply define K_I, $I = X, M, N$ as the quantity of each good set aside to enhance second-period production. The second-period transformation function may thus be written

$$(2) \qquad T^2(Q_X^2, Q_M^2, Q_N^2, K_X, K_M, K_N) = 0.$$

Turning next to the demand side, we ignore issues of income distribution and treat the economy in terms of the income and tastes of a representative individual. Preferences of this representative individual may be written in terms of a welfare function,

$$(3) \qquad W = U(C_X^1, C_M^1, C_N^1) + \delta U(C_X^2, C_M^2, C_N^2).$$

Like the production technology, this welfare function is assumed to exhibit all the usual properties.

The country is assumed to be a price taker on world markets. With slight loss of generality, we assume that nominal prices of X and M in foreign currency are constant:

$$(4) \qquad P_I^* = \bar{P}_I^*, \quad I = X, M, \quad t = 1, 2.$$

The loss of generality here lies not in the absence of foreign inflation, which could be introduced without any change in results, but in the assumption that our country's terms of trade are the same in both periods. This assumption could be relaxed without any significant change in our analysis, but it saves on complexity and notation.

We also assume that the country can borrow or lend freely at an interest rate r^*.

Now let us consider the equilibrium conditions of the model. In each period, the consumption of nontraded goods must equal production, less that part of production that (in the first period) is set aside for investment. Thus, we have

$$(5) \qquad C_N^1 = Q_N^1 - K_N,$$

$$(6) \qquad C_N^2 = Q_N^2.$$

For traded goods, the constraint is much looser since the country can both exchange goods within each period and borrow or lend across periods. The only constraint is that the present value of traded goods production that is not invested must equal the present value of traded goods consumption:

$$(7) \qquad P_X^1(Q_X^1 - K_X) + P_M^1(Q_M^1 - K_M) + (1 + r^*)^{-1} [P_X^2 Q_X^2 + P_M^2 Q_M^2]$$
$$= P_X^1 C_X^1 + P_M^1 C_M^1 + (1 + r^*)^{-1}[P_X^2 C_X^2 + P_M^2 C_M^2].$$

To solve the model, we must determine prices. In the absence of taxation, the prices of the traded goods are simply determined by their international prices:

$$(8) \qquad P_I^1 = P_I^2 = P_I^*.$$

The price of the nontraded good is determined in each period by the requirement that supply equal demand. Supply is determined by maximization of the present value of marketed production,

$$(9) \qquad V = P_X^1(Q_X^1 - K_X) + P_M^1(Q_M^1 - K_M) + P_N^1(Q_N^1 - K_N)$$
$$+ (1 + r^*)^{-1}[P_X^2 Q_X^2 + P_M^2 Q_M^2 + P_N^2 Q_N^2].$$

Demand is determined by maximization of (3) subject to the budget constraint.

Equilibrium may be usefully illustrated using figure 7.1. On the axes are the nominal prices of the nontraded good in each period. The curve $N_1 N_1$ represents points consistent with market clearing for N in period 1; it is downward sloping under the usual assumption that excess demand for the good is decreasing in its own price and increasing in prices of substitutes. The curve $N_2 N_2$ similarly represents points consistent with market clearing for N in period 2. We show $N_1 N_1$ steeper than $N_2 N_2$, which will be the case as long as "own" effects are larger than "cross" effects. (This assumption about relative slopes may also be thought of as a stability condition since it is necessary for convergence under most quasi-dynamic stories about price adjustment.) Equilibrium is where the curves intersect, at point E.

We now have a basic model of resource allocation in a trading economy, both across sectors and over time. We can now introduce a value-added tax and examine its effects.

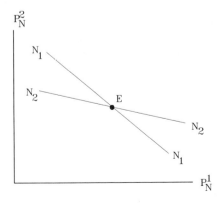

Fig. 7.1

7.2   Effects of an Idealized Value-Added Tax

We now consider the effect of introducing a value-added tax into this economy. This tax will be "idealized," in the sense that it will be assumed to be successfully levied at a flat rate on all production for consumption. In reality, VATs do not meet this ideal, both because of legislated differences in rates and exemptions and because of the impossibility of actually taxing important parts of production. Although these departures from the ideal are of critical importance in evaluating the likely effects of an actual VAT, the idealized VAT is a useful reference point with which to begin our analysis since such an idealized VAT is implicit in most economists' discussions of the effects of a VAT on international trade.

We suppose, then, that any firm selling a good domestically must pay taxes at a rate τ on the value of the good, less any value-added taxation that the firm can demonstrate has been paid on productive inputs. Investment goods are included in this deduction, so that in effect investment is exempt from the VAT. Sales of imported goods must pay the full tax rate. Exported goods, since they are not sold domestically, are not subject to the tax; thus, exporters receive a full rebate. Tax revenue is redistributed to consumers in a nondistorting fashion.

Let us define the prices of goods to domestic consumers as

$$\tilde{P}^t_I, \quad I = X, M, N, \quad t = 1, 2.$$

The price of imported goods is simply the international price plus the tax:

$$(10) \qquad \tilde{P}^t_M = P^*_M(1 + \tau), \quad t = 1, 2.$$

Since a producer of export goods must be indifferent between selling the goods domestically or on the world market, and since tax is paid on domestic but not foreign sales, the internal price of the exported good must also equal the international price plus the tax:

$$(11) \qquad \tilde{P}^t_X = P^*_X(1 + \tau), \quad t = 1, 2.$$

The price of N in each period continues to be determined by market clearing. Supply, however, now reflects the presence of the VAT: firms will maximize the value of output net of taxation,

$$(12) \qquad V = (1 + \tau)^{-1}\{\tilde{P}^1_X(Q^1_X - K_X) + \tilde{P}^1_M(Q^1_M - K_M) + \tilde{P}^1_N(Q^1_N - K_N)$$
$$+ (1 + r^*)^{-1}[\tilde{P}^2_X Q^2_X + \tilde{P}^2_M Q^2_M + \tilde{P}^2_N Q^2_N]\}.$$

We may now assert the following: imposition of a VAT at the rate τ will raise the consumer price of the nontraded good in each period by the fraction τ, thus leaving all relative prices unchanged; as a result, there will be no change either in the allocation of resources or in welfare. Figure 7.2 illustrates what happens: when equilibrium is illustrated in terms of a

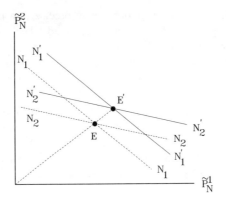

Fig. 7.2

diagram with consumer prices of N on the axes, the effect of a VAT is to shift both N_1N_1 and N_2N_2 out, to $N_1'N_1'$ and $N_2'N_2'$, respectively; the new equilibrium is at E, with the price of the nontraded good increased by a fraction τ in both periods.

To see why this must be true, we first note by inspection of (12) that, if consumer prices of all goods rise exactly in proportion to the VAT, there is no effect on production incentives. So, if all prices rise so as to offset the VAT, there will be no change in the allocation of resources or production.

Second, we argue that under the hypothesized solution there will be no effect on demand. The simplest way to see this is to notice that the welfare function (3) implies a set of compensated demand functions,

$$(13) \qquad C_I^t = H_I^t(p, W), \quad I = X, M, N, \quad t = 1, 2,$$

where p is the vector of present-value consumer prices. The functions $H(\cdot)$ are homogeneous of degree zero in p; so, if all consumer prices rise in the same proportion while welfare is unchanged, then demand will be unchanged. But, if nothing changes, nothing changes, including welfare; so, when all prices rise by τ, the market for nontraded goods continues to clear in each period.

An idealized VAT, then, has no allocative effects. In particular, it is neither procompetitive nor anticompetitive; whatever your definition of competitiveness, it has no effect at all.

Many general equilibrium results, such as the equivalence of a VAT without an export rebate to an import tariff, to which we will refer in the next section, depend on the assumption that nominal price levels do not matter. Thus, their practical relevance depends either on price flexibility or on an appropriate exchange rate adjustment. The assertion that a VAT is neutral with regard to competitiveness does not, however, require even this much defense. Because consumer prices rise precisely in proportion to the tax, the net prices to producers are unchanged. The marginal revenue product of factors of production must also be unchanged. So (to step slightly outside the model), even if factor prices and/or producer prices are sticky and the exchange rate is fixed, a VAT will still have no competitive effect.

Perhaps the surprising point is that this absence of a competitive effect occurs despite the rebate of VAT on exports, which is widely regarded as a kind of export subsidy. In fact, as we show in the next section, in the absence of an export rebate a VAT would distort allocation, definitely reduce export production, and probably shift resources on net away from traded goods sectors.

7.3   The Role of Border Tax Adjustments

The controversy over VATs is largely generated by the impression that the border tax adjustments—the fact that imports are subject to the tax while exports have the tax rebated—constitute a policy favoring a country's traded goods sectors. It is therefore interesting to ask how a VAT would function without these adjustments.

Perhaps the simplest case would be a system with no border adjustments at all—that is, no VAT collected on imports, no rebate on exports. This would in effect shift the tax from a "destination" basis to an "origin" basis. The effects of such a system may be derived immediately by the following observations. First, the prices to consumers of exports and imports will clearly remain unchanged; thus, the price to producers net of taxation must fall in proportion to the VAT rate. Clearly, if the price of the nontraded good also remains the same to consumers, that is, if the price net of taxes to firms falls by the size of the tax, then producers will have no incentive to change their output mix. At the same time, if no relative prices change, then at unchanged utility consumers will also leave their choices unchanged. But, if nothing happens, nothing happens; so the VAT without border tax adjustments is neutral in the same way as a VAT with these adjustments.[2]

The difference in this case is, of course, that the *nominal* marginal product of factors of production in foreign currency falls. Thus, in the case without border tax adjustments, there must be either price flexibility or (more plausibly) a currency depreciation in order for the neutrality of the VAT to hold. This in turn helps explain why in practice VATs do in fact include border adjustments.

It is also true that, given the general preference among authorities for a subtraction method of administration, it would be awkward to exempt imports from the tax. Firms would be given an imputation of taxes paid on imports, as opposed to showing proof of actual payment on domestic inputs; this would raise the odd prospect of firms preferring to use imports because of the lower administrative costs. Partly for this reason, it seems likely that a country pressured into avoiding any border adjustments would end up without an export rebate but would still tax imports. In this case, the VAT would have a distortionary effect on the allocation of resources. Perhaps surprisingly, this effect is essentially protectionist—a VAT without an export rebate is equivalent to an import tariff.

The difference between a VAT with and without an export rebate may be seen in the export pricing condition. Without the rebate, arbitrage will ensure that the consumer price of exportables equals the world price because the producer pays the tax whether the good is exported or sold domestically. Thus,

$$(14) \qquad \tilde{P}_X^t = P_X^*, \quad t = 1, 2.$$

Comparing this with (11), we see that the rebate-less VAT leads to a lower export price. This is not surprising since we have in effect added an export tax to the idealized VAT described before.

The internal price of exports relative to imports is of course lower in this case—or, to reverse the point, the relative price of imports is higher. It is a general proposition, the so-called Lerner symmetry theorem, that an export tax and an import tax are equivalent in their general equilibrium effects. So an ideal VAT without an export rebate is like a protectionist policy.

We should note, however, that the equivalence between import and export taxes is one of those propositions that depends either on nominal prices not mattering or on an appropriate exchange rate adjustment. Note that the effect of a VAT without a rebate is to lower the price to producers of the exported good, when measured in foreign currency; a tariff would of course raise the price of the imported good instead. Thus, these are only equivalent, given either an exchange rate adjustment or sufficient price flexibility.

We see, then, that a VAT without an export adjustment would in effect be a protectionist measure. Will it increase or decrease "competitiveness" as measured by the size of the traded goods sector? The answer is ambiguous, but a presumption may be offered that the size of the traded goods sector as a whole will decrease. To see this, it is helpful to collapse the model into a single period, ignoring the intertemporal aspect (which is in any case unimportant for this question). Equilibrium in the one-period version of the model may be analyzed using a diagram suggested by Dornbusch (1974) and shown in figure 7.3. On the axes are the consumer prices of X and M, relative to the consumer price of N. The curve NN represents a locus of points for which the market for nontraded goods clears: it is downward sloping because a rise in either traded good's relative price will shift demand onto and resources out of the nontraded sector. The ray OT has a slope equal to the consumer price of imports relative to exports, which is determined by world prices and the tax system. Equilibrium occurs where this ray crosses NN, at E.

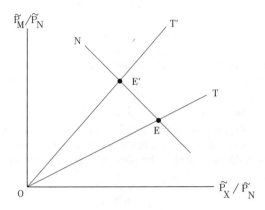

Fig. 7.3

Now suppose that the rebate on exports were to be removed from a VAT. Then the ratio of import to export prices would rise by the fraction τ, corresponding to a counterclockwise rotation of OT to OT'. Equilibrium would shift from E to E'.

Clearly, the resulting rise in P_M/P_N would tend to shift resources out of the nontraded sector, while the fall in P_X/P_N would tend to shift resources into N. The overall effect on the size of N is therefore ambiguous. However, we may offer a presumption that the net effect on N is positive and therefore that the net effect on traded goods sectors as a whole is negative.

The reason for this presumption is the probable relative importance of demand and supply adjustment in the exporting and import-competing sectors. A tariff reduces exports and imports by an equal amount. The reduction comes about through a combined reduction in demand and increase in supply for the importable and on the export side through a combination of increased demand and reduced supply. Initially, however, demand exceeds supply for the importable, while supply exceeds demand for the exportable. Thus, more of the exportable side will tend to come from supply and less from demand than on the import side—that is, we would expect exportable production at world prices to fall more than import-competing production rises. Thus, the size of the tradable sector as a whole will typically fall.

A specific example may make the point. Consider an economy that produces but does not itself consume its export good and that consumes but does not produce its import good—an extreme form of the general proposition that countries must have excess supply for exportables and excess demand for importables. When such an economy imposes a tariff or export tax, the export sector necessarily shrinks, and, since there is no import-competing production, the nontraded sector expands. Thus, in this extreme case, the effect of a tax on trade, such as a VAT without an export rebate, will unambiguously be to shrink the size of the traded goods sector. Adding some import-competing production and some domestic demand for exportables will remove the certainty of this outcome, but it will still be a presumption.

We see, then, that the widespread belief that the use of export rebates in a value-added tax system is questionable and perhaps an unfair protectionist device is very nearly the opposite of the truth. In fact, the export rebate is necessary if the VAT is not to have a protectionist effect, reducing the volume of trade and probably reducing the size of the tradable sector.

7.4   The Idealized VAT as a Substitute for an Income Tax

The best case for arguing that a VAT enhances competitiveness is not what it does but what it doesn't do: a VAT, unlike an income tax, does not place a tax on saving. Thus, to the extent that a VAT substitutes for an income tax, it will tend to reduce the current propensity to consume. As many economists have pointed out (see, in particular, Frenkel and Razin 1988), to the extent that a value-added tax that substitutes for an income tax reduces current consumption, it will in turn will tend to lead to a trade surplus in the short run. A trade surplus, other things equal, tends to increase the size of the traded goods sector.

In order to demonstrate this point, we introduce an income tax into our basic model.

We already know that an idealized VAT does not distort the economy, relative to a no-tax equilibrium. Thus, in making the comparison of a VAT and an income tax, it is sufficient to consider the effects of an income tax. So we now examine the effects of imposing on our economy an income tax at a proportional rate π. Proceeds of this tax, like those of the VAT considered earlier, are assumed to be redistributed in a nondistorting fashion.

It is important to specify how profit income is calculated for tax purposes. The most natural assumption here is that both earnings on foreign investments and earnings on capital are treated as part of second-period income, with profits calculated as the difference between sales and factor costs plus depreciation on capital—but, since the economy only lasts two periods, the whole capital stock is depreciated. There is a potential issue over whether depreciation should be calculated at historical or replacement cost, but our assumption of constant prices on world markets allows us to ignore the issue here.

Income in the first period, then, is the value of production less taxes, plus whatever transfer the government makes:

(15) $$I^1 = (1 - \pi)[P_X^1 Q_X^1 + P_M^1 Q_M^1 + P_N^1 Q_N^1] + L^1,$$

where L_1 is the rebate from the government.

Income in the second period is

(16) $I^2 = (1 - \pi)[P_X^2 Q_X^2 + P_M^2 Q_M^2 + P_N^2 Q_N^2] + (1 - \pi)r^*[P_X^1 Q_X^1$
$- P_X^1 C_X^1 + P_M^1 Q_M^1 - P_M^1 C_M^1 + P_N^1 Q_N^1 - P_N^1 C_N^1] + L^2.$

Here, the first term represents factor income, that is, gross domestic product. The second term represents capital consumption allowances. The third term represents the income from net foreign investment. Finally, the fourth term represents the rebate from the government.

Now consider an individual's budget constraint. In the first period, the individual accumulates wealth equal to the difference between income and consumption expenditures:

(17) $W = I^1 - [P_X^1 C_X^1 + P_M^1 C_M^1 + P_N^1 C_N^1].$

In the second period, the value of consumption equals income plus wealth:

(18) $P_X^1 C_X^1 + P_M^1 C_M^1 + P_N^1 C_N^1 = W(1 + r^*) + I^2.$

From inspection of (16)–(18), it is now immediately apparent that the presence of the tax distorts the incentives of a consumer. An individual who takes the government rebates as given faces a rate of return of r*(1 - π) rather than r* on deferred consumption. For a small income tax, which will have a second-order effect on welfare, the result must be a substitution effect that induces consumers to consume more in the first period and less in the second.

To analyze the trade consequences of this disincentive to save, we turn once again to the diagrammatic analysis of nontraded goods prices. In figure 7.4, the curves $N_1 N_1$ and $N_2 N_2$ represent market clearing for the nontraded goods market in the first and second period, respectively. Imposing an income tax shifts consumption from the second period to the first. Thus, other things being equal, demand for first period N rises, shifting $N_1 N_1$ up to $N_1' N_1'$; other things being equal, demand for second period N falls, shifting $N_2 N_2$ down to $N_2' N_2'$. Thus, the result is to shift the equilibrium from E to E', raising P_N in the first period and lowering it in the second. The initial effect of an income tax is, therefore, to draw resources out of the traded goods sectors and into the nontraded sector, thereby reducing exports and the production of import substitutes.

In passing, it may be worth noting that, in an economy such as this, which, although small in world goods and financial markets, does produce a nontraded good, it is not the case that changes in the saving rate affect only the balance of payments, without affecting domestic real interest rates. It is true that the real rate of interest in terms of traded goods remains fixed at r* by assumption. A real interest rate defined in terms of a basket of either domestic production or domestic consumption will, however, change whenever P_N^1/P_N^2 changes. In particular, the rise in P_N^1/P_N^2 that results from an

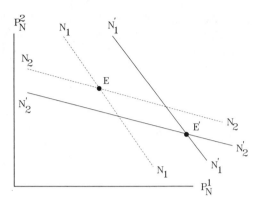

Fig. 7.4

income tax will imply deflation of domestic prices relative to world prices from period 1 to period 2, and will thus be measured as a rise in the real domestic interest rate. In this sense, the income tax produces domestic crowding out as well as a shift toward trade deficit.

We have now seen that an income tax, in contrast to a VAT, does reduce the size of the traded goods sector. It is now straightforward to analyze the effect of introducing a VAT that substitutes for an income tax. The VAT has no competitive effect; the reduction in the income tax expands trade. Thus, the overall effect is to shift resources into tradables.

It is important, however, to note that this is true only in the first period. In the second period, P_N falls, and the traded goods sector is presumably smaller. The point is that the short-term increase in net exports leads to an accumulation of overseas assets that eventually finances an excess of imports over exports.

7.5   Effects of a Selective VAT

We have so far considered only an idealized VAT that succeeds in taxing all consumption at the same rate. In practice, value-added taxation does not fall equally on all activities. In part, this is because of practical difficulties: nonmarketed production, ranging from do-it-yourself repairs to the services of owner-occupied housing and consumer durables, cannot be taxed. Also, social considerations, rightly or wrongly, frequently lead to exemptions for medical care, education, and various other activities that are deemed inappropriate for taxation. As a matter of practice, many other services are frequently exempted from VATs. Among OECD countries with value-added taxes, the VAT typically applies to only about two-thirds of total consumption and often has lower rates for some products than for others.

For the purposes of this paper, the important point is that the de facto and de jure exemptions from a VAT are likely to fall primarily on nontraded rather than traded goods and services. This is necessarily true of nonmarketed production and for one reason or another is also true of most of the marketed areas that are likely to be exempted or subject to reduced taxation.

The effect of a selective VAT is, therefore, to increase nontradable consumption and production at the expense of tradable. Imports and exports are both reduced by the imposition of the typical VAT.

To see this more formally, we return to our basic model. It will simplify matters at no cost if we take advantage of the assumption of an unchanged relative price of exports and imports to aggregate X and M into a composite traded good T. We represent the differential taxation of nontraded and traded goods in extreme form by supposing that, while domestic consumption of T is subject to a value-added tax at a rate τ, consumption of N is nontaxed.

Firms in the economy will maximize the present value of production after taxes,

$$(19) \qquad V = (1 + \tau)^{-1}\tilde{P}^1_T(Q^1_T - K_T) + \tilde{P}^1_N(Q^1_N - K_N)$$
$$+ (1 + r^*)^{-1}[(1 + \tau)^{-1}\tilde{P}^2_T Q^2_T + \tilde{P}^2_N Q^2_N].$$

Clearly, the presence of the tax acts as a disincentive to produce traded goods.

To think about the equilibrium that results, it is helpful once again to start by collapsing the model into a single period. In figure 7.5, the curve QQ represents the economy's production possibility frontier between N and T. In a one-period model, trade must be balanced, implying equality of supply and demand for T as well as N; thus, consumption must lie on this production possibility frontier. The optimum consumption is shown as E, where the

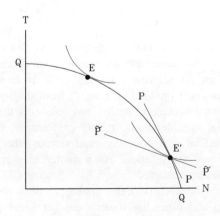

Fig. 7.5

PPF is tangent to the highest possible indifference curve. With a selected VAT on traded goods, however, consumption is distorted; the equilibrium is at a point like E', where $\bar{P}\bar{P}$ represents consumer prices and *PP* the marginal rate of transformation in production. As shown, the relative price of tradable faced by consumers is higher than that faced by firms, and the result is a smaller traded goods sector.

In the two-period model, the basic effect is the same. Figure 7.6 shows initial equilibrium loci at N_1N_1 and N_2N_2, respectively. The effect of the VAT, other things being equal, is to raise the demand for the nontraded good in each period. Thus, both schedules shift out. While it is possible that the net effect could be to lower P_N in one period, ordinarily both prices will rise. Meanwhile, the net price of T to producers will remain unchanged since producers must remain indifferent between producing for the domestic and the world market. Thus, the rise in the price of N will induce a shift of resources out of the traded goods sector.

A selective VAT that falls most heavily on traded goods, then, will tend to hurt the traded goods sectors of an economy—the reverse of the common belief. In addition, there is the effect noted in the last section: to the extent that a VAT substitutes for an income tax, while it will in the short run encourage saving and therefore net exports, in the long run the resulting accumulation of net foreign assets will have the opposite effect on net exports.

7.6 Conclusions

There is a widespread belief that value-added taxation, because it is levied on imports and rebated on exports, acts as a combination of protection and export subsidy, giving the traded goods sectors of countries with VATs an advantage over the corresponding sectors of countries that rely on income taxation. In this paper, we have used a simple model to show that this view is

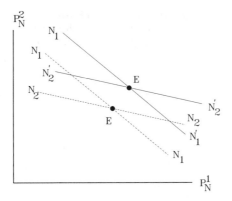

Fig. 7.6

almost completely wrong. A VAT is not a protectionist measure; indeed, the allegedly procompetitive device of export rebates is necessary if the VAT is not to act as an export tax, which in turn is actually a protectionist measure that would reduce both imports and exports. To the extent that a VAT does improve competitiveness, it does so in the short run by offering less bias against saving than an income tax, which, other things being equal, tends to improve the trade balance—but which is far from the common belief about why VATs are helpful in international competition. Moreover, in the longer term, the resulting accumulation of foreign investment would lead to an increase of imports in excess of exports. In practice, moreover, a VAT would almost surely fall more heavily on traded rather than nontraded goods, which would constitute a bias *against* both exports and imports.

Notes

1. An early treatment is Shibata (1967). For a modern and especially neat statement of the point, see Grossman (1980); for a brief statement, see Dixit (1985).
2. Hamilton and Whalley (1986) have pointed out that, given the nonuniformity of tax rates across goods in practice, there is a difference between destination and origin systems. To take an extreme example, imagine a country that places a VAT on importables but not exportables. In a VAT with border tax adjustments, such a system is in effect a consumption tax on the importable, with no tax on domestic producers; without the border adjustments,it becomes a production tax, with no tax on consumers. We abstract from this issue in this paper; Hamilton and Whalley demonstrate that it is relatively unimportant quantitatively.

References

Dixit, A. 1985. Tax policy in open economies. In *Handbook of public economics*, ed. A. Auerbach and M. Feldstein. Amsterdam: North-Holland.
Dornbusch, R. 1974. Tariffs and nontraded goods. *Journal of International Economics* 4:177–85.
Frenkel, J., and A. Razin. 1988. *Fiscal policies and the world economy*. Cambridge, Mass.: MIT Press.
Grossman, G. 1980. Border tax adjustment: Do they distort trade? *Journal of International Economics* 10:117–28.
Hamilton, B., and J. Whalley. 1986. Border tax adjustments in US trade. *Journal of International Economics* 20:377–83.
McLure, C. 1987. *The value-added tax: Key to deficit reduction?* Washington, D.C.: American Enterprise Institute.
Shibata, H. 1967. The theory of economic unions: A Comparative analysis of customs unions, free trade areas, and tax unions. In *Fiscal harmonization in common markets*, ed. C. S. Shoup. New York: Columbia University Press.

Comment   Avinash Dixit

A long line of literature on the value-added tax (VAT) has exposed the fallacy of the common view that, because a VAT is levied on imports and rebated on exports, it constitutes a tariff–cum–export subsidy: an unfair advantage if other nations practice it and something desirable if we do it. McLure (1987, 56) says of the common view, "Although this patently absurd argument is heard less frequently now than in earlier episodes of the continuing debate of the pros and cons of the VAT, it is encountered often enough that it deserves brief discussion." Feldstein and Krugman begin with a lengthy discussion; one would have hoped that a briefer one would have sufficed. Then some of their new contributions could have been discussed in greater depth.

I particularly liked two points that are a very substantial advance over previous work. The first is the treatment of short-run and disequilibrium situations. They examine the consequences of stickiness of nominal prices and exchange rates in a much clearer manner than the catalogs that one finds in the literature. The second is their analysis of a selective VAT. Previous work sets up the benchmark of a uniform VAT and makes some informal remarks about what would happen in the absence of uniformity. Feldstein and Krugman offer a more complete model.

Their focus is on the consumption versus income tax distinction and on production shifts among the export, import, and nontradable sectors. Hence, a two-period, three-sector model. I need hardly say that it is deployed with great skill and elegance; one expects that from these authors. Let me concentrate on what the model leaves out.

First a minor point. In this model, the idealized VAT has no allocative effects at all. This is because labor supply is fixed exogenously. All of net present value of production becomes the rent income of some unspecified fixed factors, and the ideal uniform VAT acts as a tax on pure rent. In a more general model, it would have some distorting effects.

Second, while the nature of capital as a produced input is properly taken into account in the two-period setting, no other produced inputs are recognized. In fact, the treatment of intermediate inputs is a vital aspect of a VAT and deserves more attention. This becomes especially important when tax rates are not uniform across goods and in particular when some sectors are exempt. In the rest of my discussion, I shall extend the Feldstein-Krugman model to handle this issue.

In the usual invoice or credit method of administering VAT, there is a distinction between exemption and zero rating, and the two have different effects. Suppose the production of nontraded goods uses traded goods as

Avinash Dixit is John J. F. Sherrard '52 University Professor at Princeton University.

intermediate inputs. Under zero rating, the producer can claim a refund of the tax paid at the earlier stage. With plain exemption, sometimes called exemption without credit, such a producer is off the VAT register, not liable to pay tax but unable to claim a refund of the tax paid at earlier stages. Both systems are used in practice. In the United Kingdom, for example, food is zero rated, but insurance and finance are exempt. In most systems, exports are zero rated; nonmarketed commodities are by their nature exempt.

The Krugman-Feldstein analysis extends easily to intermediate inputs when nontraded goods are zero rated. But exemption brings new problems. Since the producers of an exempt good pay the tax-inclusive price for their purchases of inputs of taxed goods, a production distortion is introduced. In their figure 7.5, the new production point E' moves into the interior of the feasible set.

If an exempt good is further used in the production of other taxed goods, it breaks the chain of tax credits. Thus, an element of value added is taxed twice, compounding the production distortion. There is also the suspicion that an exempt activity sandwiched between two taxed activities will be at an actual disadvantage (see McLure 1987, 73). This seems to suggest that the tax can lower the outputs of both kinds of goods—traded and nontraded. This is the possibility that I proceed to examine.

The economy produces two kinds of goods, traded (labeled t) and nontraded (labled n). Labor is the only mobile primary factor. Each good is produced using labor, another primary factor that is specific to the sector, and intermediate input of the other good.

The traded good is subject to VAT at rate τ; the nontraded good is exempt (not zero rated). Fix the world price of the traded good at one; then the domestic producer price is one and the domestic consumer price is $(1 + \tau)$. To focus on the production effects, assume a constant domestic marginal rate of substitution in consumption, and normalize it at unity. Then, for the nontraded good, the domestic price (consumer as well as producer) is $(1 + \tau)$. Let w denote the wage rate.

Assume that the cost function for the traded good is

$$Q_t^{1+\mu_t} \, \phi^t(w, \, 1 + \tau),$$

where ϕ^t is the usual increasing, concave, linearly homogeneous cost function, and $\mu_t > 0$ because of the presence of the fixed factor. (This assumes a production function that is Cobb-Douglas in the fixed factor and a labor-nontraded composite. This is a special form, but one that yields results in instructive parametric form.) Similarly, suppose the cost function for the nontraded good is

$$Q_n^{1+\mu_n} \, \phi^n(w, \, 1 + \tau).$$

Note that the tax-inclusive price must be paid for traded good inputs.

In each sector, price equals marginal cost:

(1) $$1 = (1 + \mu_t) \, Q_t^{\mu_t} \, \phi^t(w, \, 1 + \tau),$$

and

(2) $$1 + \tau = (1 + \mu_n) Q_n^{\mu_n} \phi^n(w, 1 + \tau).$$

Finally, suppose the supply of labor is exogenously fixed at L. Then the labor market equilibrium condition is

(3) $$Q_t^{1 + \mu_t} \phi_w^t(w, 1 + \tau) + Q_n^{1 + \mu_n} \phi_w^n(w, 1 + \tau) = L.$$

Equations (1)–(3) determine Q_t, Q_n, and w.

Note that the tax parameter τ affects the equilibrium in three roles. One is by raising the producer price of the nontraded good—the left-hand side of (2). This is the role studied by Krugman and Feldstein. The second is by raising the cost of nontraded inputs for the traded good sector—the right-hand side of (1). The third is the cost of traded inputs for the nontraded good sector—the right-hand side of (2)—which arises because the traded sector is exempt rather than zero rated. It is conceptually useful to separate these roles. Therefore, I shall label the $(1 + \tau)$ occurring in the three places differently when carrying out the comparative statics. Let α, β, γ be the labels for the three roles mentioned above, in that order. Then the equilibrium conditions are

(1') $$1 = (1 + \mu_t) Q_t^{\mu_t} \phi^t(w, \beta),$$

(2') $$\alpha = (1 + \mu_n) Q_n^{\mu_n} \phi^n(w, \gamma),$$

and

(3') $$Q_t^{1 + \mu_t} \phi_w^t(w, \beta) + Q_n^{1 + \mu_n} \phi_w^n(w, \gamma) = L.$$

Total logarithmic differentiation gives

(4) $$0 = \mu_t \hat{Q}_t + \theta_t \hat{w} + (1 - \theta_t)\hat{\beta},$$

(5) $$\hat{\alpha} = \mu_n \hat{Q}_n + \theta_n \hat{w} + (1 - \theta_n)\hat{\gamma},$$

and

(6) $$\lambda_t[(1 + \mu_t)\hat{Q}_t - (1 - \theta_t)\sigma_t(\hat{w} - \hat{\beta})] + \lambda_n[(1 + \mu_n)\hat{Q}_n$$
$$- (1 - \theta_n)\sigma_n(\hat{w} - \hat{\gamma})] = 0.$$

For $i = n, t$, the θ_i are the distributive shares of labor in the labor-intermediate composite, the σ_i are the elasticities of substitution between labor and the intermediate input, and the λ_i are the proportions of labor employed in the sectors.

Substitute for the $\hat{Q}_i$ from (4) and (5) into (6), and simplify. Let

$$v_i = (1 + \mu_i)/\mu_i > 1,$$

and

$$\Delta = \lambda_t[\theta_t \nu_t + (1 - \theta_t)\sigma_t] + \lambda_n[\theta_n \nu_n + (1 - \theta_n)\sigma_n].$$

Then

(7) $$\hat{w} = \frac{1}{\Delta}[\lambda_n \nu_n \hat{\alpha} - \lambda_t(1 - \theta_t)(\nu_t - \sigma_t)\hat{\beta} - \lambda_n(1 - \theta_n)(\nu_n - \sigma_n)\hat{\gamma}].$$

Using this in (4) and (5) gives the solutions for $\hat{Q}_t$ and $\hat{Q}_n$.

The expression (7) clarifies the different roles played by the tax. Most important, the effect of each input-cost-increasing role on the demand for labor is governed by a balance between the diseconomies of scale and the elasticity of substitution parameters. A large ν_i leads to a large reduction in the scale of production and therefore a reduction in labor demand; a large σ_i means a more rapid switch to labor-intensive techniques.

I shall omit further elaboration of these different effects and merely state what happens when we recognize that in fact

$$\hat{\alpha} = \hat{\beta} = \hat{\gamma} = \widehat{1+\tau}.$$

We find

$$\widehat{w/1+\tau} = 1 - \lambda_t \nu_t/\Delta.$$

Then (4) gives

(8) $$\mu_t \widehat{\hat{Q}_t/1+\tau} = -\theta_t[1 - \lambda_t \nu_t/\Delta] - (1 - \theta_t)$$

$$= \theta_t \lambda_t \nu_t/\Delta - 1 < 0.$$

Similarly, from (5) we have

(9) $$\mu_n \widehat{\hat{Q}_n/1+\tau} = 1 - \theta_n[1 - \lambda_t \nu_t/\Delta] - (1 - \theta_n)$$

$$= \theta_n \lambda_t \nu_t/\Delta > 0.$$

Thus, the suspicion that the sector producing an exempt good that both uses and is used in the production of a taxed good might actually be harmed by the tax on the other sector is not borne out. In the limiting case where either of the σ_i goes to infinity, however, the right-hand side of (8) goes to negative one and that of (9) to zero; then the gross output of the traded good is reduced without any increase in that of the nontraded good.

Reference

McLure, Charles E., Jr. 1987. *The value added tax: Key to deficit reduction?* Washington, D.C.: American Enterprise Institute.

8   Tax Incentives and International Capital Flows: The Case of the United States and Japan

A. Lans Bovenberg, Krister Andersson, Kenji Aramaki, and Sheetal K. Chand

The internationalization of financial markets has contributed to the growing interdependence of the world's economies. In particular, policy or other shocks that affect domestic savings-investment balances may set in motion large international capital flows. Accordingly, policymakers increasingly recognize that their macroeconomic policies may have important international ramifications.

Tax rules, especially those regarding the taxation of capital income, potentially have powerful effects on savings-investment balances and, therefore, on external current accounts and international capital flows. Moreover, the integration of financial markets has made tax rules more powerful in affecting the global allocation of investment and savings, thereby potentially distorting the worldwide allocation of resources. Thus, with the capital markets of the major industrial countries now much more integrated, changes in the structure of capital income taxes in one country can have major implications for other countries by affecting international capital flows and global efficiency. This raises important issues of surveillance and coordination in an international context (see Tanzi and Bovenberg 1988). Nevertheless, with only a few recent exceptions (see Alworth and Fritz 1988; Fukao and Hanazaki 1987; Sinn 1987; Tanzi 1988; Sorenson 1987; and Boadway, Bruce, and Mintz 1984, 1987), the

A. Lans Bovenberg is an economist in the Fiscal Affairs Department of the International Monetary Fund. Krister Andersson is an economist in the Western Hemisphere Department of the International Monetary Fund. Kenji Aramaki is deputy director, Office of Investment Trust and Management, Securities Bureau, Ministry of Finance, Tokyo, Japan. Sheetal K. Chand is an advisor in the Fiscal Affairs Department of the International Monetary Fund.

Comments received from Vito Tanzi, Ved Gandhi, George Kopits, Liam Ebrill, Owen Evans, Roger Smith, and other colleagues, together with those from participants of a seminar at the NBER Summer Institute, are greatly appreciated. The authors wish to thank Eric Sidgwick for invaluable research assistance. The opinions expressed in this paper are those of the authors and do not necessarily represent the views of the International Monetary Fund or its staff.

international implications of domestic tax rules have received relatively little attention.

This study explores how tax incentives for investment and savings affect international capital flows as well as national and global welfare. It measures the incentive effects of capital income taxation by using the concept of the tax wedge, which has been developed in the academic literature (see, e.g., King and Fullerton 1984; Auerbach 1983; and Boadway 1985). Most studies using this concept have applied it only to investments financed domestically. A major purpose of this study is to extend the methodology to analyze cross-border investments. This paper also presents some results on how the tax systems in Japan and the United States have interacted over the period 1980–87 in a manner that could affect bilateral capital flows and the efficiency with which resources are allocated between them.

The plan of the paper is as follows. Section 8.1 discusses the scope of the study. Section 8.2 introduces the concept of the tax wedge and describes how it can be used to measure the incentive effects of capital income taxation, both in closed and in open economies. Section 8.3 develops a methodology for summarizing the effects of capital income taxation on international capital flows and welfare. Section 8.4 presents the information on tax parameters and the economic environment needed for the application of the methodology to Japan and the United States and briefly discusses the major tax reforms in recent years in the two countries. Section 8.5 applies the methodology to Japanese and U.S. data for the years 1980, 1984, and 1987, in order to highlight the major tax reforms, and interprets the results. Finally, the concluding section relates the results to the observed movements in savings and investment balances in Japan and the United States and briefly examines the case for coordinating tax policy internationally.

8.1 The Scope of the Study

This study focuses on portfolio rather than direct investment for two reasons. First, portfolio investment can be expected to be more sensitive to after-tax rates of return than direct investment; the latter investments are undertaken for reasons other than temporary higher rates of return, such as avoiding protectionist barriers or entering a market. Second, the share of portfolio investment in private capital flows has increased in recent years, in particular, during the 1980s. Tables 8.1 and 8.2 show the composition of private capital flows from and to the United States during the period 1980–87. In Japan, developments in long-term capital flows are almost entirely determined by movements in portfolio investment (fig. 8.1).

This study does not explicitly consider the role of intermediaries, although tables 8.1–8.3 reveal their importance. Japanese savers in particular show a marked preference for saving through intermediaries (table 8.3). Nevertheless, some of the study's results will continue to hold, even if funds are

Table 8.1   The United States: Private Capital Flows, 1980–87 (in millions of U.S. dollars)

	1980	1981	1982	1983	1984	1985	1986	1987
U.S. private investment abroad[a]	83,382	104,516	95,304	44,265	15,643	43,203	113,891	100,234
Direct investments abroad	27,517	12,973	-20,596	-549	4,277	18,770	29,312	49,318
Foreign securities	5,853	720	12,100	8,353	5,301	23,706	20,385	13,530
Bonds	1,521	2,330	10,890	972	4,134	11,181	8,782	9,240
Corporate stocks	4,332	-1,610	1,210	7,281	1,167	12,525	11,603	4,290
U.S. claims on unaffiliated foreigners reported by U.S. nonbanking concerns	3,175	1,181	-7,270	6,534	-5,061	-1,005	4,219	-3,145
U.S. claims reported by U.S. banks, not included elsewhere	46,794	89,622	111,070	29,927	11,126	1,732	59,975	40,530
Foreign private investment in the United States[b]	68,514	73,503	100,672	91,042	103,268	165,106	240,564	153,985
Direct investments in the United States	28,584	25,668	15,963	12,384	27,522	20,032	35,799	41,513
U.S. securities	17,430	3,363	25,156	28,911	37,810	104,322	110,482	22,482
Bonds	1,179	3,541	13,268	8,833	39,619	75,196	67,503	15,761
U.S. Treasury securities	1,903	2,392	7,253	8,088	24,349	25,441	7,862	-13,108
Corporate and other bonds	-724	1,149	6,015	745	15,270	49,755	59,641	28,869
Corporate stocks	16,251	-178	11,888	20,078	-1,809	29,126	42,979	6,721
U.S. liabilities to unaffiliated foreigners reported by U.S. nonbanking concerns	11,757	180	-3,074	-595	4,087	-1,566	-2,833	2,212
U.S. liabilities reported by U.S. banks, not included elsewhere	10,743	44,292	62,627	50,342	33,849	42,318	97,116	87,778

Source: U.S. Department of Commerce, *Survey of Current Business.*

[a] Changes (including valuation changes) in the year-end balance of U.S. private assets abroad.
[b] Changes (including valuation changes) in the year-end balance of foreign nonofficial assets in the United States.

Table 8.2   The United States: Private Capital Flows, 1980–87 (%)

	1980	1981	1982	1983	1984	1985	1986	1987	1980–87 Average
U.S. private investment abroad[a]	100.0	100.0	100.0	100.0	100.0	100.0	100.0	100.0	100.0
Direct investments abroad	33.0	12.4	-21.6	-1.2	27.3	43.4	25.7	49.2	21.0
Foreign securities	7.0	.7	12.7	18.9	33.9	54.9	17.9	13.5	19.9
Bonds	1.8	2.2	11.4	2.2	26.4	25.9	7.7	9.2	10.9
Corporate stocks	5.2	-1.5	1.3	16.7	7.5	29.0	10.2	4.3	9.1
U.S. claims on unaffiliated foreigners reported by									
U.S. nonbanking concerns	3.8	1.1	-7.6	14.8	-32.4	-2.3	3.7	-3.1	-2.8
U.S. claims reported by U.S. banks, not included elsewhere	56.1	85.7	116.5	67.6	71.1	4.0	52.7	40.4	61.8
Foreign private investment in the United States[b]	100.0	100.0	100.0	100.0	100.0	100.0	100.0	100.0	100.0
Direct investments in the United States	41.7	34.9	15.9	13.6	26.7	12.1	14.9	27.0	23.3
U.S. securities	25.4	4.6	25.0	31.8	36.6	63.2	45.9	14.6	30.9
Bonds	1.7	4.8	13.2	9.7	38.4	45.5	28.1	10.2	19.0
U.S. Treasury securities	2.8	3.3	7.2	8.9	23.6	15.4	3.3	-8.3	7.0
Corporate and other bonds	-1.1	1.6	6.0	.8	14.8	30.1	24.8	18.7	12.0
Corporate stocks	23.7	-.2	11.8	22.1	-1.8	17.6	17.9	4.4	11.9
U.S. liabilities to unaffiliated foreigners reported by									
U.S. nonbanking concerns	17.2	.2	-3.1	-.7	4.0	-.9	-1.2	1.4	2.1
U.S. liabilities reported by U.S. banks, not included elsewhere	15.7	60.3	62.2	55.3	32.8	25.6	40.4	57.0	43.7

Source: U.S. Department of Commerce, *Survey of Current Business.*

[a] Changes (including valuation changes) in the year-end balance of U.S. private assets abroad.

[b] Changes (including valuation changes) in the year-end balance of foreign nonofficial assets in the United States.

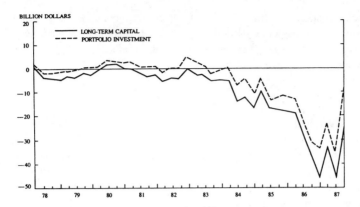

Fig. 8.1   Japan: Long-term capital and portfolio investment (shows changes in the long-term capital balance and in the portfolio investment balance)
Source: Fukao and Okima (1988).

Table 8.3   **Financial Assets of Households (%)**

	Japan 1984	United States 1983
Currency and sight deposit	11.0	5.8
Time deposit	59.7	31.7
Insurance and pension	15.7	25.5
Securities (stocks and bonds)	13.1	35.1
(Stocks)	(1.5)	(22.6)
Total	100	100

Source: Tachibanaki (1988, 23).

channeled through intermediaries, if these institutions are competitive, earning no monopoly profits at the margin. An explicit analysis of the role of intermediaries would require a separate study.

This study examines corporate investments that relate to machinery. Because tax treatments of investments in structures or noncorporate residential assets, especially housing, differ from those of corporate investments in machinery, some modification would be necessary to apply the formulas developed in the study to these investments.

Finally, table 8.1 reveals that part of portfolio investments were in government securities. Although we do not explicitly consider investments in government securities, our calculations can be readily used to infer the effect of taxes on after-tax rates of return to savers, as indicated in section 8.6.1

8.2   Capital Income Taxation in Closed and Open Economies

After introducing the concept of the tax wedge, this section analyzes how capital income taxes influence capital accumulation and welfare in a closed economy. It then turns to an open economy that is integrated in world financial markets. While the initial discussion considers the small open economy, which is conceptually the easiest to handle, the methodology of the paper is developed for the larger open economy, whose policies may influence world market conditions.

8.2.1   The Tax Wedge Concept

An investment project involves a saver sacrificing consumption today by transferring resources to the project. At some point in the future, the saver earns a return on the investment. If taxes are absent, the saver's return coincides with the rate of return earned on the investment. Capital income taxes, however, constitute a wedge between the pretax return on investment and the after-tax return on savings.

The concept of the tax wedge can be explained[1] by defining three rates of return: the required before-tax return on investment p, the market return r, and the after-tax return on savings s. All these returns are measured in real terms.

The market return r represents the price of funds on capital markets and provides the link between the firm carrying out the investment and the saver providing the financing. It is the return that the firm pays to the saver after it has paid corporate tax but before the saver has met personal tax liabilities. The funds may be in the form of either debt or equity. In the case of debt finance, the market return corresponds to the real interest rate. For equity financing, it amounts to the real return on equity (including retained earnings) before personal taxes.

The minimum rate of return that the firm must earn before taxes in order to be able to pay any taxes due and a market rate of return r is denoted by p. This required before-tax rate of return is the conventional user cost of capital measured net of depreciation. The relation between p and r depends both on macroeconomic variables, such as the inflation rate, and on tax provisions, for example, regarding depreciation allowances, investment grants, and the deductibility of interest expenses. The cost of capital function, which links p to r, summarizes these various factors:

$$(1) \qquad\qquad c(r) = p.$$

The cost of capital function generally depends on the type of asset and industry as well as on the form of financing because the tax system typically discriminates between different assets, industries, and types of financing.

The after-tax return function formalizes the relation between the market rate and the after-tax return received by the saver:

$$(2) \qquad\qquad d(r) = s.$$

This relation is typically affected by the inflation rate and the personal tax treatment of the saver. Furthermore, it generally depends on whether the saver provides funds directly or through an intermediary, such as a bank, pension fund, or life insurance company, and on whether the funds are in the form of debt or equity.

The total tax wedge t is defined as the difference between the required pretax rate of return and the posttax return received by the saver:

$$(3) \qquad\qquad t = p - s.$$

One can interpret the tax wedge as the equivalent of a wealth tax rate because it is the difference between two rates of return on an asset.[2]

8.2.2   The Closed Economy

The extensive literature on the effects of capital income taxation in a closed economy summarizes the disincentive effects of capital income taxation by the total tax wedge t. King and Fullerton (1984), for example, calculated these tax wedges for eighty-one different hypothetical investment projects in each of the following four countries: the United States, the United Kingdom, the Federal Republic of Germany, and Sweden. The eighty-one projects combine three types of assets (machinery, buildings, and inventories), three types of industries (manufacturing, commerce, and other), three types of financing (debt, retained earnings, and new share issues), and three types of owners (households, tax-exempt institutions, and insurance companies). The study did not consider international capital flows. Accordingly, firms are assumed to finance their investments by raising funds from savers who reside domestically.

Savings and Investment

Figure 8.2 illustrates how the total tax wedge t affects the capital market equilibrium in a closed economy setting. The investment schedule relates the flow of investment to p. According to the neoclassical theory of investment behavior, which we shall assume here, firms carry out investments until the

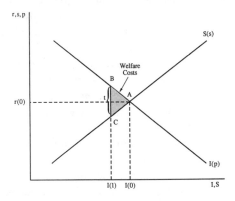

Fig. 8.2   Tax wedge and welfare costs: the closed economy case

before-tax return (i.e., the internal rate of return) equals the required rate of return p. Accordingly, in the absence of externalities, the investment schedule represents the marginal product of investment at different levels of investment. Its downward slope reflects diminishing marginal returns on investment.[3] The slope of the investment curve is inversely related to the elasticity of investment with respect to the required return p.

The savings schedule relates the flow of savings to the after-tax return s. The upward slope of the savings schedule reflects a positive compensated savings elasticity. The smaller the slope is, the larger the savings elasticity becomes.

If taxes are absent and intermediation costs are ignored, both the before- and after-tax returns coincide with the market return:

(4) $$r = s = p,$$

and equilibrium in figure 8.2 is found at the point A where the savings and investment schedules intersect.

Taxes drive a wedge between the before- and the after-tax returns. Given the investment and savings elasticities, the total tax wedge t contains enough information to find the effects of capital income taxes on savings and investment. To illustrate, in figure 8.2 the tax wedge is given by the distance BC. Thus, in this particular case, the wedge is positive, and the required before-tax return on investment exceeds the after-tax return received by the saver.[4] This positive wedge reduces both investment and savings by the distance $I(0)I(1)$. The more elastic savings and investment are, the flatter the curves become, and the more powerful a given tax wedge is in affecting savings and investment.

Welfare

Once the effects of the tax wedge on savings and investment are determined, the welfare effects in a closed economy can more easily be determined. On the savings side, households are assumed to equate the after-tax return on their marginal savings s to the opportunity cost of delaying consumption, which measures the social *costs* of financing the investment.[5] On the investment side, firms equate the required return p to the before-tax return on marginal investment. This latter return includes both the return received by savers and the tax revenues collected by the government. Accordingly, in the absence of externalities, p measures the social *benefits* that a marginal investment earns for society as a whole.[6] The total tax wedge, therefore, captures the difference between the social benefits p and the social costs s associated with a marginal investment. In figure 8.2, the tax wedge reduces capital accumulation by $I(0)I(1)$. The social benefits of these crowded-out units, as measured by the before-tax return p, exceed their social costs, as measured by the after-tax return s. Accordingly, the tax wedge reduces welfare by the triangle ABC. If investment and savings become more sensitive to rates of return, a given tax wedge implies larger welfare losses.

The total tax wedge in the closed economy must be divided into two parts in order to find the effect of capital income taxes on the market return r. The first part is the corporate tax wedge t_c between the before-tax and market returns:

$$(5) \qquad\qquad t_c = p - r.$$

The second wedge, which is called the personal tax wedge t_p, measures the effect of personal taxes and amounts to the gap between the market return and the after-tax return received by the saver:

$$(6) \qquad\qquad t_p = r - s.$$

In a closed economy, if the size of the total tax wedge is kept unchanged, the personal-corporate split affects neither capital accumulation nor welfare. In these circumstances, the composition of the tax wedge affects only the market return. If the personal tax wedge is reduced to zero and the corporate tax wedge is increased so as to account for the whole predetermined wedge between p and s, there would be pressure on investment to decline. Thus, the market rate would be reduced, while savings would be stimulated, further reducing the market rate. It can be readily demonstrated that the market rate would decline by just the amount needed to offset the effects of the changing tax factors on the after-tax return to savings and the costs of investment. It is only by changing the size of the total tax wedge that savings and investment are modified. If the share of the personal tax wedge in the total tax wedge becomes larger, the market rate falls less. The market return rises if the share of the personal tax wedge in the total tax wedge becomes large enough.

8.2.3   The Open Economy

Savings, Investment, and Capital Flows

In an open economy, domestic savings and domestic investment do not necessarily balance because of the possibility of nonzero net capital flows with the rest of the world. The existence of international capital markets has important implications for the analysis of capital income taxation. In particular, it becomes important to distinguish between savings and investment incentives and to attend to the composition of the tax wedge.

Figure 8.3 illustrates the differential effects of savings and investment incentives in the case of a small open economy in which international capital markets fix the domestic market return at the rate of return on world capital markets r^*.[7] If taxes are absent, both the before-tax return on investment and the after-tax return on savings equal the return on world markets:

$$(7) \qquad\qquad p = s = r^*.$$

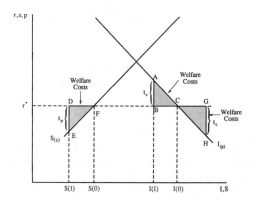

Fig. 8.3   Tax wedge and welfare costs: the small open economy case

In the case depicted in figure 8.3, investment exceeds savings by the distance $I(0)S(0)$ if domestic returns equal the world rate of return. Accordingly, the economy runs a current account deficit of that magnitude.[8]

The introduction of capital income taxes affects investment, savings, and capital flows. Unlike in the closed economy, where the total wedge affects both savings and investment, in the small open economy the corporate tax component of the wedge affects only investment, while the personal tax component affects only savings.

In figure 8.3, a corporate tax wedge of the size AB reduces investment by the distance $I(0)I(1)$ but fails to affect domestic savings. Accordingly, the current account deficit falls by $I(0)I(1)$. It is of interest that the infinitely elastic supply of world savings implicit in the fixed market return r^* makes the corporate tax wedge more powerful in affecting domestic investment than in a closed economy. This is because the market rate would decline in a closed economy, which would cushion the effect of raising the corporate tax component.

The personal tax wedge does not affect domestic investment but reduces domestic savings and, therefore, weakens the external current account. In figure 8.3, for example, a personal tax wedge of the magnitude DE widens the current account deficit by the distance $S(0)S(1)$. As with the effect of corporate taxes on investment, the more open the economy, the more powerful the effects of the personal tax wedge on domestic savings.

National Welfare Effects

The openness of the economy also has important consequences for the effects of capital income taxation on national welfare. In the small open economy in figure 8.3, the rate of return on world markets r^* corresponds to the national cost of financing a marginal investment.[9] The required before-tax rate of return measures the national benefits associated with a marginal investment (see subsec. 8.2.2). Accordingly, the corporate tax wedge, which is the difference between the before-tax and the market returns, measures the gap between the national benefits and the national costs associated with marginal investment. In figure 8.3, the corporate tax wedge AB reduces national welfare by the triangle ABC because this tax wedge crowds out the investment units $I(0)I(1)$ for which national benefits exceed national costs. A given corporate tax wedge imposes larger national welfare losses in an open economy than it does in a closed economy owing to its greater effect on investment.

The personal tax wedge corresponds to the gap between the national benefits and costs associated with a marginal unit of domestic savings. In figure 8.3, a personal tax wedge of the size DE reduces national welfare by the triangle DEF. In a closed economy, a subsidy at the corporate level could have mitigated the welfare losses. In particular, a negative corporate tax wedge equal in absolute value to the personal tax wedge would have avoided the welfare losses altogether. In an open economy, in contrast, such an investment subsidy only adds welfare costs at the investment side to those imposed by the savings tax. For example, in figure 8.3, the investment subsidy implicit in the negative corporate tax wedge $-GH = -DE$ adds welfare losses amounting to the triangle CGH to the welfare costs corresponding to the area DEF imposed by the taxation of savings.[10]

World Welfare Effects

This subsection examines how international differences in investment incentives affect global efficiency. Instead of a small open economy, we now consider a hypothetical world or closed economy consisting of only the United States and Japan. In figure 8.4, the distance between the two vertical

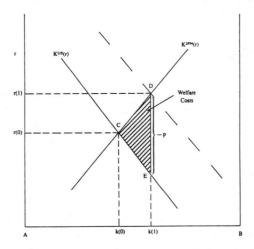

Fig. 8.4   Corporate tax wedges and the international allocation of the capital stock

axes measures the size of the world capital stock, which is assumed to be fixed so as to focus on the international allocation of capital.[11] The solid downward and upward sloping lines represent the marginal product curves in, respectively, the United States and Japan. The schedule for the United States is measured from the left axis and that in Japan from the right axis. If taxes and externalities are absent, these curves coincide with the capital demand curves as a function of the cost of funds. In that case, the intersection of the two solid lines C represents the equilibrium in world capital markets. At this nontax equilibrium, the return on world markets amounts to $r(0)$ while a part $AK(0)$ of the world capital stock is located in the United States.

If the United States provides an investment incentive corresponding to a negative corporate tax wedge equal in absolute value to $-p = DE$, the capital demand curve in the United States shifts upward to the dotted line. As a consequence, the return on world markets rises to $r(1)$ and a part of the world capital stock corresponding to $K(1)K(0)$ gradually moves from Japan to the United States. During the transition to this new long-run equilibrium, net investment in the United States rises relative to that in Japan, and the external current account of the United States weakens.

Conceptually, differential investment incentives distort the global playing field and, if externalities are absent, harm global welfare. With differential investment incentives, equal after-tax returns on assets located in different countries correspond to different before-tax returns on those assets. This violates a necessary condition for efficiency in the allocation of capital, namely, that before-tax returns on different assets should be equal. Overall welfare could be raised by relocating capital from countries with a lower before-tax return to those with higher returns. For example, in figure 8.4, the differential investment incentive corresponding to DE reduces world welfare by the triangle DCE because the capital $K(0)K(1)$ earns a lower before-tax return in the United States than it could earn in Japan.

8.3   Methodology

In this section, the tax wedge concept is extended to cross-border portfolio investments by allowing foreign residents to finance domestic investments and domestic residents to finance foreign investments. In particular, tax wedges are computed for all host-residence (or saver-investment) combinations. A residence country is characterized by a typical saver, while a typical investment represents the host country. Regarding the financing instruments, the study distinguishes between debt and equity finance. New share issues and retained earnings are assumed to account for fixed proportions of total equity financing.

The study disaggregates the total tax wedge for each host-residence combination into three separate wedges corresponding to, respectively, corporate taxes (t_c), withholding taxes (t_w), and residence taxes (t_r) (fig. 8.5). The withholding and residence wedges add up to the personal tax

host B

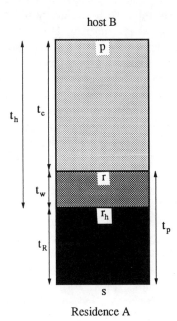

Residence A

Figure 8.5   Tax wedge components

wedge (t_p). Subsection 8.3.1 discusses the measurement of the corporate tax wedge. Subsection 8.3.2 defines international differences in investment incentives and explores how differential corporate tax wedges relate to these differences. It shows that the residence principle cannot be assumed, therefore precluding the easier route considered in the preceding section whereby investment incentives would be identified with corporate tax wedges. The effects of investment incentives on international capital flows and global efficiency are analyzed in subsection 8.3.3. Subsection 8.3.4 defines international differences in savings incentives, and subsection 8.3.5 then explores the corresponding effects of savings incentives. Subsection 8.3.6 defines the host tax wedge (t_h) as the sum of the corporate and withholding tax wedges and explores how the host-residence split affects national welfare. The appendix contains the mathematical expressions for the tax wedges and their components for, respectively, debt- and equity-financed investments.

8.3.1   Corporate Tax Wedges

To compute the corporate tax wedge, two assumptions are made. First, only the host country collects corporate taxes. Second, corporate taxes do not discriminate between domestic and foreign savers. Accordingly, the corporate tax rate on a given investment is the same irrespective of whether the saver financing the investment is residing abroad or domestically.

The two assumptions are generally met for portfolio investments. Even in the case of direct investments, the host country tax system may determine the effective corporate tax wedge on marginal investments. This is the case, for example, if the residence country has a territorial system of corporate taxation or if firms are in an overall excess credit position under a system of worldwide taxation.[12] Moreover, residence countries typically tax income from subsidiaries only on repatriation, unless it is earned in a tax haven. Under these circumstances, host taxes determine marginal investment incentives if firms, at the margin, finance foreign investment by retained earnings, which appears to be a dominant form of marginal financing (see Hartman 1985; and Sinn 1987).

8.3.2   The Measurement of Investment Incentives

Section 8.2 used the corporate tax wedge to measure the effect of capital income taxation on investment incentives in a small open economy. This procedure, which greatly simplifies the analysis, is valid only if international capital markets equalize market returns across different jurisdictions. This, in turn, requires two assumptions. First, assets located in different countries should be perfect substitutes in demand so that savers residing in a given country require the same after-tax return s on all their assets. Second, personal taxes should be collected on the basis of the residence principle. According to this principle, residence governments tax real capital income (after corporate tax) at a personal tax rate that does not depend on the country where the capital income originates. Only if this principle holds does the equalization of after-tax returns by savers correspond to the same market returns (fig. 8.6).

In practice, the residence principle may fail to hold for at least three reasons.[13] First, even if residence countries apply the residence principle to nominal returns, *real* returns are likely to be taxed differently if inflation rates diverge between host countries. In particular, financial instruments denominated in the currency of low-inflation countries tend to benefit from a preferential tax treatment of capital gains because these securities earn a large part of their returns in the form of an exchange rate appreciation (i.e., capital gains), which are typically taxed at lower rates (see, e.g., Gordon 1986; and Sorenson 1986).

Second, withholding taxes on income earned by nonresidents violate the residence principle if savers do not have sufficient residence liabilities against which to credit the foreign withholding taxes. This may be the case if they save through tax-exempt institutions.[14]

A third reason why the residence principle may fail concerns the integration of corporate and personal taxation. Under the numerous methods of integration, residence countries typically impose different tax rates at the personal level depending on whether corporate tax has been levied domestically or abroad (see Sato and Bird 1975). Moreover, host countries may allow corporate credits only if dividends are paid to residents.

host A   host B

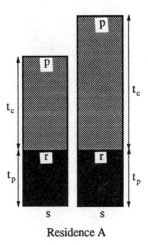

Residence A

Figure 8.6   The residence principle

For these reasons, the residence principle, although it would have simplified the analysis, will not be adopted here. As a consequence, differences in investment incentives cannot be measured simply as differences in corporate tax wedges. Instead, the incentives are measured by comparing, for a given saver, the *total* tax wedges on investments located in different host countries, as illustrated in figure 8.7.

Investment incentives may differ for savers residing in different countries if the residence principle does not hold. In that case, the tax systems provide incentives for tax arbitrage between savers residing in different countries. However, savers do not fully exploit these arbitrage opportunities because assets located in different countries—although easily substitutable—are assumed not to be perfect substitutes in demand.[15]

8.3.3   The Effect of Investment Incentives on International Capital Flows and Global Efficiency

The measure of investment incentives developed here summarizes how personal and corporate income taxes interact to affect international capital flows. If, for example, tax wedges on assets located in country A exceed those on assets in country B, and if all other conditions are equal, the tax system provides incentives for capital flows from A to B.[16]

Such differences indicate how the interaction of capital income taxes in various countries distorts the international allocation of capital by violating

host A   host B

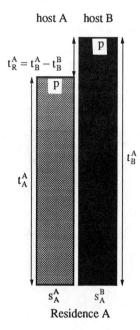

Figure 8.7   **The measurement of investment incentives**

what may be stated as the principle of capital export neutrality. According to this principle, savers should face the same tax rate on assets located in different countries (in the absence of externalities) so that tax systems do not interfere with an efficient global allocation of capital. The principle requires that investors be indifferent between assets located in different countries on both a before-tax and an after-tax basis. If the intercountry tax wedges differ, equal after-tax returns will fail to yield the equal before-tax returns that are required for an efficient allocation of capital. Figure 8.7 illustrates that a higher tax wedge on assets in B compared with that in A causes the before-tax return in B to rise above that in A. Accordingly, in the absence of externalities, moving capital from A to B would raise overall welfare.

8.3.4 The Measurement of Savings Incentives

International differences in saving incentives are measured by comparing, for a given asset, the total tax wedges on savers residing in different countries (fig. 8.8). In this paper, these differences are entirely due to differences in personal tax treatment as a consequence of the assumption (see subsec. 8.3.1) that the corporate tax rate on a given asset is the same whether it is financed abroad or domestically.

host A

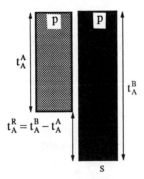

$$t_A^R = t_A^B - t_A^A$$

Residence A   Residence B

Figure 8.8   The measurement of savings incentives

8.3.5   The Effect of Savings Incentives on International Capital Flows and Global Efficiency

International differences in savings incentives, as measured by differences in the tax wedges borne by savers in different countries, will, ceteris paribus, tend to be reflected in lower savings in countries where savers bear the higher tax burden. Accordingly, these differences would contribute to a weaker current account position in those countries, thereby influencing international capital flows.

Differences in savings incentives indicate that capital income taxes violate the so-called principle of capital import neutrality according to which the tax treatment of a given asset should not discriminate between savers residing in different countries (in the absence of externalities). Departures from capital import neutrality are associated with an inefficient allocation of global savings because they drive a wedge between the marginal rates of time preference of different savers. Figure 8.8 illustrates that the cost of postponing marginal consumption for the saver residing in A who faces the lower tax burden exceeds that for the saver who resides in B. Thus, the welfare cost from the allocation of savings to meet a given overall investment level would have been lowered if the less heavily taxed saver were to save less and the more heavily taxed saver were to save more.

8.3.6   Host and Residence Tax Wedges: National Welfare Effects

The personal tax wedge consists of two parts: the withholding tax wedge and the residence tax wedge. The residence country levies the residence tax wedge, while the host country collects, in addition to the corporate tax wedge, the withholding tax wedge. Accordingly, the total host tax wedge is defined as the sum of the corporate and withholding tax wedges. The return after host taxes but before residence taxes is defined as r_h (fig. 8.5). It is the return that the residence country collects from the host country and consists of a part received by the private saver (the after-tax return s) and a part collected by the residence government (the residence tax wedge t_R).

The host-residence split of the total tax wedge provides some insight into the effects of capital income taxation on national welfare.[17] In particular, the host tax wedge captures the difference between, on the one hand, the national return on a marginal investment, which is measured by the before-tax return p, and, on the other hand, the national costs associated with the financing of such an investment by foreign savings, which is represented by the return after host taxes.[18] Therefore, a positive host tax wedge implies that the host country gains from a marginal investment financed by foreign savings. Similarly, the residence tax wedge measures, at the margin, the net national benefit of financing a foreign investment by domestic savings because it corresponds to the difference between the return after host taxes, which measures the national benefits, and the return after all taxes, which represents the national costs of marginal savings (see subsec. 8.2.2).

8.4   Economic Environment and Tax Parameters: The United States and Japan

This study computes tax wedges for the United States and Japan for 1980, 1984, and 1987. Both the macroeconomic environment and tax provisions affect these tax wedges. Subsection 8.4.1 discusses how this study derives the numerical values for the macroeconomic variables in the three years studied. The tax provisions underlying the results are described in subsection 8.4.2.

8.4.1   The Macroeconomic Environment

The tax wedge corresponding to debt instruments can be expressed as a function of tax parameters and of the following variables that describe the economic environment: the nominal interest rate in the host country,[19] expected inflation rates in the host and residence countries, and expected movements in nominal exchange rates. In the case of equity financing, the nominal after-corporate-tax return (including retained earnings) on equity issued in the host country replaces the nominal interest rate as an element in the expressions for the tax wedges.[20]

As regards exchange rate expectations, the study assumes that savers expect movements in nominal exchange rates to reflect inflation differentials.

The expected rate of inflation in the United States is derived from a survey conducted by Drexel Burnham Lambert on expected inflation ten years ahead. The average of the actual inflation rate in the next three years is used as a proxy for the expected inflation rate in Japan.[21]

The study does not assume that real interest rates are necessarily equalized among countries. Instead, it combines observed long-term nominal interest rates with expected inflation rates to find real interest rates in the two countries.[22] Long-term interest rates are measured by the rate of return on government bonds. The maturity of the bonds is ten years for the United States and seven years for Japan.

This paper imposes arbitrage at the firm level to find the return on equity.[23] In particular, it assumes that, for any investment project, the gap between the cost of equity financing and the cost of debt financing is fixed at 5 percentage points. This gap is based on estimates for the costs of equity financing (after corporate tax) during the 1980s that are contained in Hatsopoulos and Brooks (1987). The estimates provided for the 1980s were averaged both over time and over Japan and the United States.[24]

Various other studies link the equity return to the return on debt by imposing an arbitrage condition at the savers' side so that savers earn the same after-tax return on debt and equity.[25] However, in an open economy framework, arbitrage conditions will generally differ for savers residing in different countries because the tax burden on debt relative to that on equity generally differs across countries. Thus, imposing arbitrage conditions for savers residing in different countries typically yields complete specialization in debt or equity, which is inconsistent with empirical observations.[26]

8.4.2   Tax Parameters

Information on key elements of the tax system required for the calculation of the tax wedges is presented in tables 8.4 and 8.5 for the United States and Japan, respectively. (The letters in the columns refer to the sources listed at the end of the tables.)

The corporate tax parameters are based on a typical corporate investment in machinery. The tables reveal that the Japanese tax system has remained relatively stable during the 1980s. U.S. corporate tax provisions, in contrast, have been altered several times during this period. In particular, the Economic Recovery Tax Act of 1981 (ERTA) greatly liberalized depreciation schedules and provided for more generous investment credits. The Tax Equity and Fiscal Responsibility Act of 1982 (TEFRA) tightened some of these investment incentives. The Tax Reform Act of 1986 reduced the marginal tax rate on corporate income but further tightened investment incentives by repealing the investment credit and making the tax provisions governing depreciation somewhat less generous.

On the personal side, the United States gradually reduced the marginal tax rates on interest and dividend income during the 1980s. However, the Tax

Table 8.4   **The United States: Parameters (%)**

	1980	1984	1987
Tax parameters:			
Corporate tax rate	49.5[A]	49.5[A]	38.3[A]
Lifetime for depreciation purposes (in years)[a]	10.5	4.6	6.0
Declining balance rate	200.0	150.0	200.0
Investment grant (rate)	8.7[B]	8.9[B]	. . .[B]
Withholding tax rate on income to nonresidents:			
Interest income	10.0	. . .	. . .
Dividend income	15.0	15.0	15.0
Personal taxes on:			
Interest income	28.5[A]	25.8[A]	22.4[A]
Dividend income	47.5[A]	39.6[A]	32.0[A]
Exchange gains and losses	7.0[A]	5.9[A]	11.0[A]
Capital gains and losses	7.0[A]	5.9[A]	11.0[A]
Portion of foreign withholding tax refunded			
at the personal level	100.0[C]	100.0[C]	100.0[C]
Nontax parameters:			
Fraction of new shares in marginal equity financing	7.4[A]	7.4[b]	7.4[b]
Rate of economic depreciation	12.1[C]	12.3[C]	12.5[C]
Nominal interest rate	11.5	12.5	8.4
Expected inflation rate	8.7	6.2	5.3
Nominal cost of equity[c]	10.8	11.3	10.2

Sources:
[A]Fullerton and Karayannis (1987).
[B]Corker, Evans, Kenward (1988).
[C]Hatsopoulos and Brooks (1987).
[a]Based on a salvage value of 10 percent of purchase value. The most favorable method permitted by the tax code has been used. Accordingly, if after a certain point in time the straight-line method rather than declining balance yields a larger tax deduction, a switch to that method has been assumed.
[b]Assumed to be the same as in 1980.
[c]Based on a gap of 5 percentage points between the costs of equity and debt finance (see main text). The formulas for these costs of finance r_f^* are presented in the second rows in tables 8A.1 and 8A.2.

Reform Act of 1986 raised the tax rate on capital gains. The average marginal tax rate on interest income earned by Japanese residents takes into account various methods of tax-exempt savings, such as the Maru-yu accounts.[27] The marginal tax rate on interest income received from abroad exceeds the marginal rate on interest income from domestic investments because some of the tax-preferred savings, such as postal savings, were not invested abroad. The taxation of dividend income in Japan also favors domestic investment because some tax benefits, such as a 10 percent dividend credit, do not apply to dividends from abroad.

This study focuses on portfolio rather than direct investments (see sec. 8.1). Accordingly, residence countries neither credit nor levy corporate taxes

Table 8.5   **Japan: Parameters (%)**

	1980	1984	1987
Tax parameters:			
Corporate tax rate:			
Retained earnings	52.6	56.1	54.7
Dividends	42.1	45.5	44.2
Lifetime for tax purposes (in years)[a]	11.0	11.0	11.0
Declining balance rate	100.0	100.0	100.0
Investment grant (rate)	. . .	. . .	. . .
Withholding tax rate on income to nonresidents:			
Interest income	10.0	10.0	10.0
Dividend income	15.0	15.0	15.0
Personal taxes on:			
Domestic interest income	8.2	7.1	7.1
Domestic dividend income	25.8	25.8	25.8
Foreign interest income	11.1	10.1	9.8
Foreign dividend income	47.9	47.9	47.9
Exchange gains and losses	. . .	. . .	. . .
Capital gains and losses	. . .	. . .	. . .
Portion of foreign withholding tax refunded			
at personal level	100.0	100.0	100.0
Nontax parameters:			
Fraction of new shares in marginal equity financing	8.7[C]	8.7[b]	8.7[b]
Rate of economic depreciation	15.1[A]	15.3[A]	15.5[A]
Nominal interest rate	9.2	6.8	4.2
Expected inflation rate	5.2	1.6	.9
Nominal cost of equity[c]	9.4	8.1	7.0

Sources:
[A]Hatsopoulos and Brooks (1987).
[B]Kikutani and Tachibanaki (1987).
[C]Shoven and Tachibanaki (1985).
[a]Based on a salvage value of 10 percent of purchase value.
[b]Assumed to be the same as in 1980.
[c]Based on a gap of 5 percentage points between the costs of equity and debt finance (see main text). The formulas for these costs of finance r_f^* are presented in the second rows in tables 8A.1 and 8A.2

(see subsec. 8.3.1). However, savers are assumed to receive full credit for any withholding taxes levied by the host government on their personal income.[28]

8.5   Tax Wedges in the 1980s: The U.S.-Japan Case

This section interprets the empirical estimates for the tax wedges in 1980, 1984, and 1987 contained in tables 8.6–8.8. The two panels in these tables contain the results for, respectively, a debt and an equity-financed investment. Tables 8.6 and 8.7 present the tax wedges on assets located in,

Table 8.6   Taxation of Assets Located in Japan, 1980–87 (in percentage points)

Tax Wedges	Saver Residing in Japan			Saver Residing in the United States			Saver Residing in Japan Relative to Saver Residing in the United States[a]		
	1980	1984	1987	1980	1984	1987	1980	1984	1987
Debt instrument:									
Total	-1.36	-.67	-.34	.75	.87	.78	-2.12	-1.54	-1.12
Corporate	-2.12	-1.16	-.64	-2.12	-1.16	-.64	...	...	...
Personal	.76	.48	.30	2.87	2.03	1.42	-2.12	-1.54	-1.12
Total	-1.36	-.67	-.34	.75	.87	.78	-2.12	-1.54	-1.12
Host	-2.12	-1.16	-.64	-1.20	-.47	-.22	-.92	-.68	-.42
Residence	.76	.48	.30	1.95	1.35	1.00	-1.19	-.86	-.70
Equity instrument:									
Total	6.68	7.77	6.55	7.64	8.56	7.77	-.96	-.79	-1.22
Corporate	6.59	7.63	6.42	6.59	7.63	6.42	...	...	...
Personal	.09	.14	.14	1.05	.93	1.36	-.96	-.79	-1.22
Total	6.68	7.77	6.55	7.64	8.56	7.77	-.96	-.79	-1.22
Host	6.59	7.63	6.42	6.64	7.71	6.50	-.05	-.08	-.08
Residence	.09	.14	.14	1.00	.85	1.28	-.90	-.71	-1.14

Source: Authors' calculations.

[a] The column for each of the three years is computed by subtracting the results for a U.S. saver from those for a Japanese saver.

Table 8.7 Taxation of Assets Located in the United States, 1980–87 (in percentage points)

Tax Wedges	Saver Residing in Japan			Saver Residing in the United States			Saver Residing in Japan Relative to Saver Residing in the United States[a]		
	1980	1984	1987	1980	1984	1987	1980	1984	1987
Debt instrument:									
Total	−4.30	−5.29	−1.67	−2.31	−3.32	−.61	−1.99	−1.97	−1.06
Corporate	−5.57	−6.55	−2.49	−5.57	−6.55	−2.49	...	...	...
Personal	1.27	1.26	.82	3.27	3.23	1.88	−1.99	−1.97	−1.06
Total	−4.30	−5.29	−1.67	−2.31	−3.32	−.61	−1.99	−1.97	−1.06
Host	−4.43	−6.55	−2.49	−5.57	−6.55	−2.49	1.15	...	...
Residence	.13	1.26	.82	3.27	3.23	1.88	−3.14	−1.97	−1.06
Equity instrument:									
Total	1.83	.84	1.98	2.58	1.46	3.01	−.74	−.61	−1.02
Corporate	1.76	.66	1.81	1.76	.66	1.81	...	...	...
Personal	.07	.18	.17	.82	.80	1.19	−.74	−.61	−1.02
Total	1.83	.84	1.98	2.58	1.46	3.01	−.74	−.61	−1.02
Host	1.78	.72	1.87	1.76	.66	1.81	.02	.06	.05
Residence	.05	.12	.12	.82	.80	1.19	−.77	−.67	−1.08

Source: Authors' calculations.

[a] The column for each of the three years is computed by subtracting the results for a U.S. saver from those for a Japanese saver.

Table 8.8 **Taxation of Assets Located in Japan Relative to the Taxation of Assets Located in the United States, 1980–87 (in percentage points)**

Tax Wedges	Saver Residing in Japan			Saver Residing in the United States			Saver Residing in Japan relative to Saver Residing in the United States[a]		
	1980	1984	1987	1980	1984	1987	1980	1984	1987
Debt instrument:									
Total	2.94	4.62	1.33	3.06	4.20	1.40	−.12	.42	−.07
Corporate	3.46	5.40	1.85	3.46	5.40	1.85	. . .	. . .	. . .
Personal	−.52	−.78	−.52	−.39	−1.20	−.45	−.12	.42	−.07
Total	2.94	4.62	1.33	3.06	4.20	1.40	−.12	.42	−.07
Host	2.31	5.40	1.85	4.38	6.08	2.27	−2.07	−.68	−.42
Residence	.63	−.78	−.52	−1.32	−1.88	−.87	1.95	1.10	.35
Equity instrument:									
Total	4.85	6.93	4.57	5.06	7.10	4.77	−.21	−.18	−.20
Corporate	4.83	6.96	4.61	4.83	6.96	4.61	. . .	. . .	. . .
Personal	.02	−.04	−.04	.23	.14	.16	−.21	−.18	−.20
Total	4.85	6.93	4.57	5.06	7.10	4.77	−.21	−.18	−.20
Host	4.81	6.91	4.55	4.88	7.05	4.68	−.08	−.14	−.13
Residence	.04	.02	.02	.18	.06	.08	−.13	−.03	−.07

Source: Authors' calculations.

Note: This table is computed by subtracting the results in table 8.7 from the corresponding results in table 8.6.

[a]The column for each of the three years can be computed by subtracting the results for a U.S. saver from those for a Japanese saver.

respectively, Japan and the United States. The first three columns in tables 8.6 and 8.7 show how a Japanese saver was taxed. The tax treatment of a U.S. saver is presented in the next three columns. The last three columns are computed as the difference between the column for the Japanese saver and the column for the U.S. saver. Thus, the last three columns in tables 8.6 and 8.7 measure relative savings incentives because they reveal how, for a given asset, the tax treatment of a Japanese saver differed from that of a saver residing in the United States (see subsec. 8.3.4 and fig. 8.8). Table 8.8 measures how the tax system may have affected international capital flows through its effect on investment incentives; it compares, for a given saver, the tax treatment of investments in Japan with that of investments in the United States (see subsec. 8.3.2 and fig. 8.6). This table is computed by subtracting the results contained in table 8.7 from the corresponding results contained in table 8.6.

In each column, the total tax burden is broken down in two ways. First, the total tax wedge is the sum of the corporate tax wedge and the personal tax wedge. Second, the total tax wedge consists of the host tax wedge and the residence tax wedge. For investments financed by savers residing in the same country, the distinction between host and residence tax wedges is irrelevant because the host country and residence country are one and the same. For these local investments, the host tax wedge is given by the corporate tax wedge.

The disaggregation of the total tax wedge into host and residence tax wedges provides information on national welfare effects (see subsec. 8.3.6). Moreover, comparing the host tax wedge for a Japanese asset with that for a U.S. asset measures the investment incentive for a saver who does not pay any personal taxes except for those withheld abroad. Savers pay only these personal taxes if they are tax exempt or if they evade taxes.

The rest of this section is organized as follows. Subsection 8.5.1 analyzes tax incentives for international capital flows by investigating, respectively, investment and savings incentives. How capital income taxation affects global efficiency by distorting the international and intertemporal allocation of resources is explored in subsection 8.5.2. Finally, subsection 8.5.3 analyzes national welfare effects.

8.5.1   Tax Incentives for International Capital Flows

Investment Incentives

The positive numbers in (the first six columns of) the first rows of the two panels in table 8.8 indicate that the tax burden on assets located in Japan exceeded the tax burden on assets located in the United States. Accordingly, taxes encouraged capital flows from Japan to the United States by favoring investments in the United States.

The breakdown over the corporate and personal tax wedges reveals which factors are behind the tax incentives for investments in the United States. For the debt case, the corporate-personal split is contained in the second and third rows of the first panel in table 8.8. These rows show that the larger investment incentives in the United States are entirely the consequence of a more favorable corporate tax treatment in the United States, which can be explained by more liberal depreciation rules, more generous investment credits, and, for debt-financed investments, a higher inflation rate that raises the value of the deductibility of nominal interest payments.[29]

Unlike corporate taxes, personal taxes in both Japan and the United States discriminated against debt-financed investments in the United States for two reasons.[30] A major reason is the relatively low expected inflation rate in Japan. Accordingly, under the assumption that exchange rates reflected inflation differentials, the yen was expected to appreciate relative to the dollar. Consequently, Japanese assets yielded part of their expected returns to U.S. savers in capital gains, which the U.S. personal tax system treated favorably relative to nominal interest income. In addition, Japanese savers could not deduct the expected capital losses on U.S. assets from their personal tax liabilities, while they were fully taxed on the higher nominal returns on these assets. A second explanation for the higher personal tax wedge on U.S. assets faced by Japanese residents is that some of the tax-sheltered forms of Japanese savings were not allowed to flow abroad (see subsec. 8.4.2).

The movements of the relative investment incentives over time reveal that international differentials in investment incentives first rose between 1980 and 1984 and then fell in 1987. These developments were due mainly to tax policy in the United States, which first liberalized its investment incentives but later tightened them (see subsec. 8.4.2).

In the case of debt financing, the 1984 increase in the favorable treatment of U.S. investment is particularly dramatic when measured by the change in the relative host tax wedge contained in the fifth row of table 8.8. When the United States repealed the withholding tax on interest income to foreigners in 1984, it became a more attractive investment location for those savers who could not fully credit the withholding tax against their residence tax liabilities.

Savings Incentives

The negative numbers in the last three columns of the first rows of the two panels in table 8.6 reveal that, for an asset located in Japan, the U.S. saver faced the heaviest tax burden, especially on debt instruments. The corresponding numbers in table 8.7 show that this was also the case for an asset located in the United States. Therefore, if higher after-tax returns raise savings, the tax systems harmed the relative savings performance of the United States.[31] Accordingly, in addition to investment incentives, savings incentives may also have encouraged U.S. capital inflows.

Except for an increase in the relatively favorable tax treatment of equity income earned by Japanese savers in 1987, international differences in tax incentives for savings fell during the 1980s. Two main factors explain the increasing harmonization of tax incentives. First, falling inflation rates and nominal interest rates tended to reduce the absolute value of the tax wedges. Second, as regards debt financing, the United States reduced its personal income tax rates during this period.[32]

8.5.2 Global Welfare Effects

This subsection uses the calculated tax wedges to assess how capital income taxation may have influenced the international allocation of savings and investment as well as the intertemporal allocation of resources between the present and the future.

International Allocation of Investment and Saving

The results contained in table 8.8 and discussed above in subsection 8.5.1 revealed that taxes favored investment in the United States over investment in Japan. In the absence of externalities, these differential investment incentives would have interfered with an efficient allocation of the world capital stock. In particular, the relatively favorable treatment of investment in the United States may have caused the social benefit of marginal U.S. investment to fall below the marginal productivity of investment in Japan. Consequently, reallocating capital away from the United States to Japan would have raised world welfare.

The results discussed in subsection 8.5.1 indicated that, compared with Japanese residents, U.S. residents were taxed more heavily on their savings. The less favorable tax treatment of U.S. savings may have contributed to an inefficient allocation of world savings to the extent that world welfare would have risen if the share of U.S. savings in worldwide savings had been larger.

Developments of the tax wedges over time suggest that differential tax distortions in the international distribution of savings fell during the 1980s. The potential tax distortions in the international allocation of capital, in contrast, rose during 1980–84, after which they also decreased.

Intertemporal Allocation of Resources

The global intertemporal distortions from capital taxation depend on the total tax wedge. The first rows in the second panels of tables 8.6 and 8.7 reveal that the total tax wedges levied on marginal equity investments were positive. This implies that the net benefits of a marginal equity investment exceeded the social costs associated with financing such an investment, once again in the absence of externalities. Consequently, a marginal increase in equity investment would have raised global welfare.

In contrast to their treatment of equity investments, tax systems typically subsidized marginal debt investments. The only marginal debt investment carrying a positive tax wedge was one located in Japan and financed by a U.S. saver. The debt investment enjoying the highest subsidy was one located in the United States and financed by a Japanese saver. These results are explained as follows. The personal-corporate split (second and third rows of the first panels in tables 8.6 and 8.7) reveals that debt instruments were subsidized at the corporate level but taxed at the personal level. Whereas assets located in the United States were more heavily subsidized by the corporate tax system, Japanese savers were taxed lightly at the personal level compared to savers residing in the United States. Only if a U.S. saver, who suffered from a relatively high personal tax burden, financed an asset located in Japan, which enjoyed a relatively small subsidy at the corporate level, was the personal tax large enough to offset the subsidy at the corporate level. Thus, a marginal debt investment, in the absence of externalities, would improve world welfare only if it were located in Japan and financed by a U.S. resident.

The total tax wedges indicate that the absolute values of net subsidies to debt financing for assets located in the United States, after remaining broadly constant between 1980 and 1984, decreased during the period 1984–87. Both the falling expected inflation rate and the repeal of some of the investment incentives in the United States played a role in explaining the mitigation of these intertemporal distortions. After rising between 1980 and 1984, the net tax burdens on equity assets located in Japan fell during 1984–87 to levels close to those in 1980 (table 8.6), which is explained in part by movements in the corporate tax rate in Japan. Equity assets located in the United States, in contrast, faced increased tax burdens between 1984 and 1987 after these tax burdens had fallen during 1980–84 (table 8.7).

8.5.3   National Welfare Effects

The host-residence split of the tax wedges (fifth and sixth rows of the two panels in tables 8.6 and 8.7) provides information on how marginal cross-border investments affect national welfare (see subsec. 8.3.6). The fifth rows of the two panels in tables 8.6 and 8.7 indicate that, at the margin, host governments subsidized debt investments. On equity investments, in contrast, they levied taxes. Thus, host countries tended to lose from foreign-financed debt investments but gained from equity capital inflows. The reason is that host countries allow interest expenses to be deducted for corporate tax purposes. Consequently, while the corporate tax acts as a withholding tax for equity income, it fails to withhold interest income on debt.

The net subsidy granted to debt capital inflows was largest in the United States. Whereas the Japanese subsidy fell during the 1980s, that in the United States rose during 1980–84. In 1987, however, the U.S. subsidy dropped below its 1980 level.

8.6   Conclusions

8.6.1   Some Limitations of the Present Study

Tax wedges were estimated separately for investments financed through the issuance of either debt or equity. While this procedure covers the two extremes, it does not address cases where the marginal investment is financed through a mix of debt and equity, which could change some of the results obtained. In particular, a greater preference for debt financing in Japan relative to the United States would reduce the relative incentives to invest in the United States. There is, however, considerable uncertainty as to the actual debt-equity mix of the marginal investment in a particular country. The data are unavailable, and, moreover, the ratio itself could vary depending on the residence of the saver financing the investment. In any event, by presenting the two extremes, this study provides sufficient information to facilitate the computation of the tax wedges for any selected debt-equity ratio.

Another limitation is that the tax wedges were computed only for corporate investments in machinery. The method developed in the study could be employed for a more comprehensive assessment that would also cover other investments, including those in inventories and business structures. However, as many of the qualifications that would be introduced concern the tax treatment of depreciation, and as these were substantially more generous in the United States than in Japan, particularly in the early 1980s, the qualitative ranking of the savings and investment incentives may not change.

A further limitation is the exclusive focus on corporate investment. Other forms of capital flow, for example, investment in government securities, acquisition of real estate, and buyouts of companies, are of increasing importance. While a fuller study is needed to account adequately for the role of tax factors in influencing these capital flows, the information presented in the study permits some inferences for savings through government securities. Income from such securities are subject to a host-withholding tax, if levied, and to the residence personal income tax. As the latter is substantially higher in the United States than in Japan, the U.S. saver was taxed more heavily than the Japanese saver irrespective of whether he invested in U.S. or Japanese government securities. Also in this case, the tax systems hurt the savings performance of the United States relative to Japan. However, the differences in tax incentives for investing in government securities decreased during the 1980s.

8.6.2   Some Implications for Savings-Investment Balances

The tax wedges obtained for Japanese savers investing in Japan can be compared with those for U.S. savers investing in the United States, as has been done in some studies. Such a comparison may be useful if capital is not mobile internationally. This appears to have been characteristic of Japanese capital markets before a major liberalization occurred in the early 1980s. As was noted in section 8.2, in a relatively closed capital market, the composition of the tax wedge needs to be known in order to establish tax effects on real interest rates. Larger corporate tax factors and lower personal tax factors in Japan relative to those in the United States may have contributed to a lower Japanese real interest rate level, although the actual outcome for domestic interest rates may also have been affected by other demands for credit, especially from the public sector. As figure 8.9 demonstrates, the general government fiscal deficit was fairly sizable in Japan up to about 1981 but declined substantially thereafter. Over the same period, real interest rate levels in Japan, which in the years immediately preceding were higher, fell below those in the United States (fig. 8.10). If the Japanese capital market had not been liberalized in the early 1980s, the growing Japanese savings surpluses would have been bottled up within the domestic economy. Accordingly, the equilibrating responses may well have involved greater deflation, with Japanese real interest rates declining further. However, the major liberalization of Japanese capital markets provided a vent for the excess savings by allowing more capital outflows.

Over this period, developments in the United States accommodated the growing Japanese savings surpluses. The U.S. fiscal balance moved into persistent and substantial deficit (see fig. 8.11). If the international capital

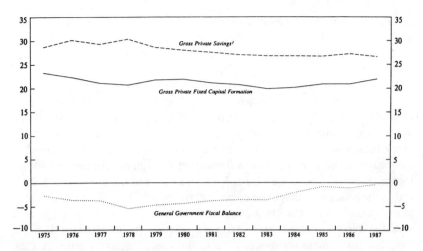

Fig. 8.9   Fiscal balance, private savings, and investment patterns in Japan, 1975–87 (in percentage of GNP)
Source: OECD, National Accounts, and staff calculations.
[1] Private savings defined as the sum of household and corporate savings.

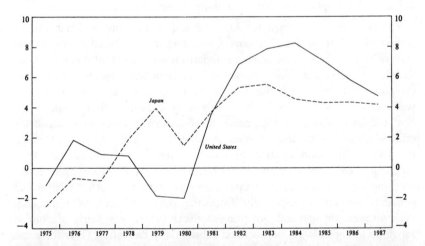

Fig. 8.10   Real long-term interest rates in Japan and the United States, 1975–87 (in percentage per annum; nominal interest rate on long-term government bonds deflated by CPI inflation rate)
Source: IMF, IFS.

market had not become more integrated and resources from abroad had not become available, ensuing adjustments would most likely have added to inflationary pressures in the United States, accompanied by rising real interest rates crowding out investment in the United States in a manner reminiscent of an earlier episode in the late 1960s. The crowding out of

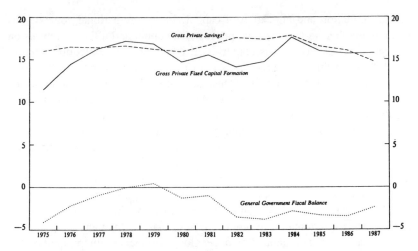

Fig. 8.11   Fiscal balance, private savings, and investment patterns in the United States, 1975–87 (in percentage of GNP)

Source: U.S. Department of Commerce, *Survey of Current Business.*
[1] Private savings defined as the sum of household and corporate savings.

investment was also avoided by the more liberal U.S. investment incentives introduced in 1981, which prevented higher real interest rates from harming investment.

Without a detailed econometric study, it is difficult to assess the contribution of tax factors to capital flows, although some broad inferences can be drawn. In 1982, the net outflow of private capital from the United States was reversed (table 8.1). At the same time, a positive real interest differential in favor of the United States emerged (fig. 8.10), and the value of the U.S. dollar rose. These phenomena are consistent with more generous tax incentives for investment in the United States between 1981 and 1984 (table 8.8). These incentives put upward pressure on the U.S. interest rates, thereby attracting foreign capital and raising the value of the dollar. It is, perhaps, no coincidence that the sharp decline in the tax differential favoring investment in the United States in 1986 is associated with a major reduction in net private capital inflows in 1987, forcing official intervention to finance a much larger share of the U.S. current account deficit, a narrowing of the real interest differential, and downward pressure on the U.S. dollar.

8.6.3   The Role of Tax Coordination

It is interesting to inquire, in the context of the study's findings, whether the systems of capital income taxes were adequately coordinated. A widespread presumption is that tax systems should be neutral and not distort the accumulation and allocation of capital. In an international context, this requires that before-tax marginal products on capital and after-tax returns on savings are equalized across countries. It is a short but contentious step to conclude from this that tax systems in different countries should, therefore, be harmonized. In the context of this study, complete harmonization occurs if the different tax wedges are equalized so that the tax incentives provided are the same for savers and investors in different countries.

However, in practice, complete tax harmonization is elusive, and an attempt to enforce it may well reduce welfare. A greater concern with environmental issues or different perceptions of national contingencies and other externalities may lead to diverse needs for the accumulation of capital and its allocation. Intercountry differences in capital income taxes may, therefore, be necessary to accommodate such needs. There is, nevertheless, a role for tax coordination in order to ensure that the interaction of national tax policies does not unduly damage global efficiency. In particular, tax systems, and the interactions among them, should not excessively bias savings and investment incentives in favor of any one country, thereby misallocating capital. However, the complex considerations involved suggest that circumspection should be used in determining what is an "excessive" bias.

The more generous investment incentives introduced by the United States in 1981 may have acted to offset the adverse effects on investment of the sharp rise in real interest rates. Nevertheless, the reduction in capital income taxes contributed to the decline in income tax collections from 12.9 percent of GDP in 1980 to 9.8 percent in 1986, more than matching the increase in the general government fiscal deficit from 1.3 percent of GDP to 3.4 percent of GDP over the same period. To the extent that the persistent fiscal deficit preempts a significant part of the world's pool of savings and keeps real interest rates high, a vicious circle is generated: cuts in capital income taxes are required to offset the adverse effects on the cost of capital from their deficit-enhancing effects. In increasingly integrated world financial markets, such a policy generates a widening imbalance between domestic savings and investment, resulting in large capital inflows and shifts in exchange rates. Moreover, the required subsidies to investments tend to be inconsistent with the requirements for global and national efficiency. An alternative policy of maintaining 1980 tax levels could have lowered the fiscal deficit and lessened the upward pressures on real interest rates. Such a policy would have protected private investment without having to rely on capital inflows and investment subsidies that were distorting the international allocation of capital. Some adjustment at the margin in the early 1980s, involving an increase in savings incentives for residents of the United States and a decrease in the fiscal deficit, financed by a reduction in the generous investment incentives through increases in corporate taxation (as occurred in 1986) might have been appropriate.

A critical consideration is that, as economies become more integrated, the alleviating role of purely domestic adjustment mechanisms is reduced, for example, through the effect of imbalances on domestic interest rates. Consequently, the distortionary effects of taxes on global and national welfare as well as on international capital flows become more pronounced. If these distortions are to be mitigated, policymakers must pay increasing attention to the international implications of their domestic tax policies.

Appendix
Derivation of the Tax Wedges

This appendix describes how one can derive the real rates of return and the tax wedges introduced in section 8.3 from expected inflation rates, nominal interest rates (for a debt instrument), and nominal equity returns (for an equity instrument).

Tables 8A.1 and 8A.2 present these tax wedges for a debt- and equity-financed investment, respectively. Table 8A.3 defines the different variables and lists the tax parameters required to find the wedges presented in tables 8A.1 and 8A.2.[33] A variable marked with an asterisk refers to the host country. A variable without an asterisk relates to the residence country.[34]

The real market rate of return $r*$, which is contained in the first row of the tables, is the return that is earned after all corporate taxes but before any personal tax. The second row in the tables presents the real cost of finance r_f^*. Investors (usually the firm) adopt this rate as the discount rate at which they compare all receipts and outlays (after corporate tax) occurring at different points in time. The nominal after-tax cost to debt finance is $i*(1 - u_f^*)$, where u_f^* is the effective (corporate) tax rate at which the investor can deduct interest payments in calculating taxable income. In the absence of a split rate system (i.e., $u_s^* = u_k^*$), the real cost of equity finance is simply the market return on equity because, in contrast to interest payments, equity returns are not deductible from taxable income.

The cost of capital $p*$, given in the third row of the tables, is the required real rate of return before corporate income taxes are levied and tax allowances are granted. The expression for $p*$ is derived from the equality between the marginal benefit and the marginal cost on an investment project:

(A1) $$(1 - u_k^*)(p* + \delta*) = (1 - A*)(r_f^* + \delta*).$$

Here, $\delta*$ is the exponential rate of economic depreciation. The left-hand side of (A1) corresponds to the revenues after corporate income tax has been levied on the user cost of capital $p* + \delta*$ at an effective rate of u_k^*.[35] For a marginal investment project, these revenues are equal to the real marginal costs of holding capital, which are represented by the right-hand side of (A1). These costs amount to the after-tax cost of a unit of investment $(1 - A^*)$ times the sum of the after-tax financing costs r_f^* and the costs of depreciation.

Following King and Fullerton (1984, 19), A^* denotes the present value of investment grants and depreciation allowances on a project with a cost (before tax allowances) of unity. This parameter reduces the after-tax cost of a unit of capital. The fourth row in the tables shows that this paper accounts for three forms of grants and allowances: standard depreciation allowances, immediate expensing (or free depreciation) and cash grants.

The fifth row contains the corporate tax wedge t_c^*. This gap between the cost of capital and the market return corresponds to the "investment tax wedge" in Sorenson (1987), Sinn (1987), and Boadway, Bruce, and Mintz (1984, 1987).[36] These papers use the investment tax wedge as a measure for the incentive to invest in a small open economy that takes the real market return r^* as given.[37]

The sixth and seventh rows in the tables contain, respectively, the real return after withholding taxes r_w^* and the withholding tax wedge t_w^*. The withholding tax wedge on dividends includes the effects of provisions to mitigate the double taxation of dividends, such as a split rate or imputation system. Withholding taxes on dividend income influence investment incentives only if the firm uses new share issues to finance marginal investment (see table 8A.2).[38]

The eighth row in the tables aggregates the tax wedges for all host taxes. This host tax wedge t_h^* is important in determining the national welfare effects associated with capital taxation because it corresponds to the wedge between the social return on capital, which at the margin is equal to the cost of capital p^*, and the cost of capital to the host country as a whole, r_w^*.

The after-tax return, which is presented in the ninth row in the tables, affects the incentive to save. The total tax wedge, contained in the twelfth row, reflects the total effect of the tax system on these incentives. This wedge is important in determining the worldwide intertemporal efficiency costs resulting from capital taxation. It corresponds to the wedge between the social return on marginal investment p^* and the social costs associated with the financing of such an investment s.

The residence tax factor for debt instruments, contained in the tenth row in table 8A.1, depends on how the residence country credits foreign withholding taxes on dividend and interest income. The parameters θ_d and θ_i summarize these crediting arrangements for, respectively, dividend and interest income. Relative expected inflation rates may affect the residence tax burden imposed on domestic debt instruments relative to that imposed on foreign debt if the tax rate on interest income exceeds the tax rate on exchange rate gains and losses.[39] In that case, the residence tax burden on domestic debt relative to that on foreign debt generally rises if the expected domestic inflation rate increases relative to the expected foreign rate of inflation.[40]

Table 8A.1   Tax Wedges and Rates of Return: Debt Financing

Real Rate of Return or Tax Wedge	Symbol	Derivation	Expression
(1) Market return	r^*		$i^* - \pi^*$
(2) Discount rate investor	r_f^*		$(1 - u_f^*)\, i^* - \pi^*$
(3) Cost of capital	p^*		$\dfrac{(1 - A^*)}{(1 - u_k^*)}[(1 - u_f^*)i^* - \pi^* + \delta^*] - \delta^*$
(4) Effective subsidy on capital goods	A^*		$f_1^* u_d^* A_d + f_2^* u_d^* + f_3^* g$
(5) Corporate tax wedge	t_c^*	(3) $-$ (1)	$\left[\dfrac{(1 - A^*)}{(1 - u_k^*)}(u_k^* - u_f^*) - A^*\right]i^* + \left[\dfrac{A^* - u_k^*}{(1 - u_k^*)}\right](\pi^* - \delta^*)$
(6) Return after withholding tax	r_w^*		$(1 - w_i^*)i^* - \pi^*$
(7) Withholding tax wedge	t_w^*	(1) $-$ (6)	$w_i^* i^*$
(8) Host tax wedge	t_H^*	(3) $-$ (6) $=$ (5) $+$ (7)	$\left[\dfrac{(1 - A^*)(u_k^* - u_f^*)}{(1 - u_k^*)} + w_i^* - A^*\right]i^* + \left[\dfrac{A^* - u_k^*}{(1 - u_k^*)}\right](\pi^* - \delta^*)$
(9) Return after tax	s		$(1 - m_i)\theta_i(1 - w_i^*)i^* - (1 - z)\pi^* - z\pi$
(10) Residence tax wedge	t_R	(6) $-$ (9)	$[1 - m_i)\theta_i](1 - w_i^*)i^* + z(\pi - \pi^*)$
(11) Personal tax wedge	t_p	(1) $-$ (9) $=$ (7) $+$ (10)	$[1 - (1 - m_i)\theta_i(1 - w_i^*)]i^* + z(\pi - \pi^*)$
(12) Total tax wedge	t	(3) $-$ (9) $=$ (8) $+$ (10) $=$ (5) $+$ (11)	$\left[\dfrac{(1 - A^*)(u_k^* - u_f^*)}{(1 - u_k^*)} + 1 - A^* - (1 - m_i)\theta_i(1 - w_i^*)\right]i^*$ $+\left[\dfrac{A^* - u_k^*}{(1 - u_k^*)}\right](\pi^* - \delta^*) + z(\pi - \pi^*)$

Source: Authors' calculations.

Table 8A.2   Tax Wedges and Rates of Return: Equity Financing

Real Rate of Return or Tax Wedge	Symbol	Derivation	Expression
(1) Market return	r^*		$p^* - \pi^*$
(2) Discount rate investor	r_f^*		$(p^* - \pi^*)[1 - \epsilon^*(u_k^* - u_s^*)]$
(3) Cost of capital	p^*		$\dfrac{(1 - A^*)}{(1 - u_k^*)}(\rho^* - \pi^*)[1 - \epsilon^*(u_k^* - u_s^*)] + \delta^* - \delta^*$
(4) Effective subsidy on capital goods	A^*		$f_1^* u_d^* A_d^* + f_2^* u_d^* + f_3^* g^{**}$
(5) Corporate tax wedge	t_c^*	(3) $-$ (1)	$\left[\dfrac{u_k^* - A^*}{(1 - u_k^*)}\right](\rho^* + \delta^* - \pi^*) - \epsilon^*(u_k^* - u_s^*)\dfrac{(1 - A^*)}{(1 - u_k^*)}(\rho^* - \pi^*)$
(6) Return after withholding tax	r_w^*		$(1 - \epsilon^* w_d^*)(\rho^* - \pi^*)$
(7) Withholding tax wedge	t_w^*	(1) $-$ (6)	$\epsilon^* w_d^*(\rho^* - \pi^*)$
(8) Host tax wedge	t_H^*	(3) $-$ (6) $=$ (5) $+$ (7)	$\epsilon^* w_d^*(\rho^* - \pi^*) + \left[\dfrac{u_k^* - A^*}{(1 - u_k^*)}\right](\rho^* + \delta^* - \pi^*)$ $- \epsilon^*(u_k^* - u_s^*)\dfrac{(1 - A^*)}{(1 - u_k^*)}(\rho^* - \pi^*)$
(9) Return after tax	s		$[\epsilon^*(1 - m_d)\theta_d(1 - w_d^*) + (1 - \epsilon^*)(1 - c)](\rho^* - \pi^*) - [(c - z)\pi^* + z\pi]$
(10) Residence tax wedge	t_R	(6) $-$ (9)	$[\epsilon^*(1 - w_d^*)[1 - (1 - m_d)\theta_d] + (1 - \epsilon^*)c](\rho^* - \pi^*) + (c - z)\pi^* + z\pi$
(11) Personal tax wedge	t_p	(1) $-$ (9) $=$ (7) $+$ (10)	$[\epsilon^*[1 - (1 - m_d)\theta_d(1 - w_d^*)] + (1 - \epsilon^*)c](\rho^* - \pi^*) + (c - z)\pi^* + z\pi$
(12) Total tax wedge	t	(3) $-$ (9) $=$ (8) $+$ (10) $=$ (5) $+$ (11)	$\left(\dfrac{\epsilon^*(1 - A^*)[1 - (u_k^* - u_s^*)] - (1 - m_d)\theta_d(1 - w_d^*)(1 - u_k^*)}{(1 - u_k^*)}\right)(\rho^* - \pi^*)$ $+ \left\{\dfrac{(1 - \epsilon^*)[1 - A^* - (1 - c)(1 - u_k^*)]}{(1 - u_k^*)}\right\}(\rho^* - \pi^*)$ $+ \left[\dfrac{u_k^* - A^*}{(1 - u_k^*)}\right]\delta^* + [(c - z)\pi^* + z\pi]$

Source: Authors' calculations.

Table 8A.3   **Definition of Parameters**

	Description
Host tax parameters:	
u_f^*	Effective income tax rate at which investors can deduct interest expenses.
u_k^*	Effective corporate income tax rate at which retained corporate income is taxed.
u_s^*	Effective corporate tax rate at which dividends are taxed.
A^*	Effective rate of subsidy on capital goods (includes effect of tax credits and depreciation allowances).
u_d^*	Effective corporate income tax rates at which investors can deduct depreciation allowances.
A_d^*	The present value of standard depreciation allowances on a unit of investment.
f_1	The portion of the cost of an asset that is entitled to standard depreciation allowances.
f_2	The portion of the cost of an asset that qualifies for immediate expensing.
f_3	The portion of the cost of an asset that qualifies for an investment grant.
g	The rate of investment grant.
w_i^*	Withholding tax rate on nominal interest income.
w_d^*	Withholding tax rate on dividend income (includes effect of double taxation relief for corporate tax).
Residence tax parameters:	
m_i	Personal tax rate on nominal interest income.
m_d	Personal tax rate on dividend income.
θ_i	Parameter representing relief at personal level for foreign withholding taxes on interest income.
θ_d	Parameter representing relief at personal level for corporate taxes and foreign withholding taxes on dividends.
z	Personal tax rate on exchange rate gains and losses.
c	Personal tax rate on nominal capital gains (excluding exchange rate gains and losses). Other symbols:
ε^*	Fraction of real earnings on equity paid as dividends (or fraction financed by new share issues).
δ^*	Rate of economic depreciation.
i^*	Nominal interest rates.
ρ^*	Nominal return on equity before personal tax.
π^*	Expected inflation rate, host country.
π	Expected inflation rate, residence country.

Source: Authors' calculations.

Notes

1. Auerbach (1983) and Boadway (1985) provide excellent surveys of the literature in this area.

2. Alternatively, the effective marginal tax rate, found by dividing the tax wedge by the before-tax rate of return p, can describe the effects of capital income taxation.

3. Thus, the investment demand curve is in flow terms rather than in stock terms because this section focuses on the short-term equilibrium. These flow demands are derived from a model with adjustment costs, which prevent instantaneous stock adjustment. Alternatively, one could model the long-term capital market equilibrium in stock terms. In that case, a lower p would raise the stock demand for capital. This would imply a higher rate of net investment during the transition, assuming rising short-run adjustment costs.

4. Results below indicate that in some cases the tax wedge is negative. In that case, the government subsidizes marginal investments.

5. Thus, the social costs of postponing consumption equal the private costs. This assumes that private saving does not generate any externalities, which requires that the government can attain the first-best growth path by transferring income between generations in a lump-sum fashion.

6. This assumes that the government can use nondistortionary taxes, such as a lump-sum tax. Otherwise, the social value of one marginal unit of tax revenue may exceed unity.

7. This assumes that assets are perfect substitutes. Moreover, corporate taxes are assumed to be levied on a source basis, while the residence principle governs personal taxation. Subsection 8.3.2 explains and elaborates on these assumptions and relaxes some of them.

8. Over time, the current account deficit may fall as the investment and savings schedules shift in response to the accumulation of capital and wealth.

9. This assumes that the host country collects all corporate taxes, while the residence country collects all personal taxes. Accordingly, withholding taxes on personal income are assumed to be zero. Subsection 8.3.6 discusses and relaxes some of these assumptions.

10. Only if tax wedges do not affect the market return in a closed economy would the welfare costs in a closed economy equal those in an open economy. In all other cases, the welfare costs in an open economy exceed those costs in a closed economy.

11. If savings are elastic with respect to the after-tax rate of return, capital income taxation affects the global capital stock and, therefore, global intertemporal efficiency. In the absence of externalities, the total tax wedges measure the gap between the social benefits of a marginal investment and the social costs of financing it by a marginal unit of saving (see subsec. 8.2.2). Accordingly, they provide information on how marginal changes in the world capital stock affect global welfare.

12. Under a territorial system, the residence country exempts foreign-source income from corporate taxation. Under a system of worldwide taxation, the residence country taxes global income but credits foreign corporate taxes against domestic corporate tax liabilities as long as foreign corporate taxes do not exceed the domestic corporate tax liabilities calculated on the foreign-source income.

13. Differential opportunities for tax evasion are a fourth reason why the residence principle may fail. Savers may find it easier to evade residence taxes on foreign assets than corresponding taxes on domestic assets.

14. Another important case is savings channeled through banks because withholding taxes are imposed on gross interest income so that no deduction is allowed for interest expense and other costs of making the loan. The withholding taxes, therefore, often exceed the residence tax liability on net income from bank loans.

15. Accordingly, this study does not assume that savers necessarily require the same after-tax rate of return s on assets located in different countries. Thus, s_A^A is not necessarily equal to s_A^B in fig. 8.7.

16. Tax wedges provide an unambiguous indicator of the effect of the tax system on investment incentives only if the tax wedge on assets located in country A exceeds that on assets located in B for *all* savers, i.e., both those residing in A and those in B.

17. This discussion of national welfare effects abstracts from optimal tariff type arguments by assuming that countries lack market power to affect the cost of funds on world markets. For an application of such arguments to international capital taxation, see Sinn (1987, chap. 7) and Gordon and Varian (1987). Furthermore, the study does not deal with strategic considerations, which would become relevant if the tax system in one country were perceived to affect tax policy in another country.

18. For a marginal investment financed by domestic savings, the total tax wedge represents the gap between national benefits and costs. For the assumptions underlying this approach, see subsec. 8.2.2 and, in particular, the notes in that subsection. It is assumed, for example, that the government can raise revenue through nondistortionary taxes.

19. This paper assumes that firms do not finance their investments with foreign currency bonds.

20. Projects located in the same country are assumed to pay both a unique nominal interest rate on debt and a unique nominal after-corporate-tax return on equity.

21. Thus, perfect foresight is assumed. The inflation rates in 1988 and 1989 are taken from the projections contained in the *World Economic Outlook* of April 1988.

22. Tax wedges were calculated by using observed rather than uniform nontax parameters in order to capture the interaction between tax provisions and the macroeconomic environment. However, to examine the sensitivity of the results to the values of nominal interest and inflation rates, we also computed tax wedges assuming a constant nominal interest rate of 8 percent and a constant expected inflation rate of 4 percent across countries and over time. The sensitivity analysis revealed that the development of the relative tax wedges was very similar to the results presented in this paper.

23. This construction typically opens up arbitrage opportunities at the savers (or household) level and requires imperfect substitution at the household level between debt and equity.

24. According to the estimates in Hatsopoulos and Brooks (1987) and Ando and Auerbach (1987), the gap between the cost of equity and debt financing was larger in the United States. The current study assumes that the gap is the same in the United States and Japan in order to identify how international differences in tax factors, as opposed to differences in the structure of financial intermediation, affect investment incentives.

25. Some studies allow for an exogenous risk premium on equity. See, e.g., Feldstein (1986). Others measure the return on equity directly by using the inverse of the observed price-earnings ratio on shares. See, e.g., Boadway, Bruce, and Mintz (1987).

26. Even in a closed economy, the tax burden on debt relative to equity can differ among individuals with different marginal tax rates. Moreover, imposing arbitrage conditions on the savers' side is problematic even in a closed economy because it generally implies that a given piece of capital earns a different before-tax rate of return depending on how it is financed (see, e.g., Bradford and Stuart 1984). Therefore, the firm can typically obtain arbitrage profits by specializing in the least expensive type of financing.

Alternatively, one can use the arbitrage condition for only one particular saver. Sinn (1987), e.g., imposes the arbitrage condition only for savers in the host country because he assumes that debt accounts for all international portfolio capital flows and that all equity is held domestically. As an alternative procedure, Alworth and Fritz (1988) average the arbitrage conditions for all savers to arrive at one "world" arbitrage condition.

27. Interest income from small deposits (Maru-yu accounts) with banks and other financial institutions was tax exempt if the total amount of principal did not exceed ¥ 3 million. Tax-exempt savings included holdings of central and local government bonds, not exceeding ¥ 3 million in total face value (special "Maru-yu"), postal savings not exceeding ¥ 3 million, and savings under the Employees' Asset Formation System not exceeding ¥ 5 million. Those tax-exempt savings accounted for about 70 percent of the total balance of personal savings. From April 1988, the tax-exempt systems for Maru-yu, special Maru-yu, and postal savings were abolished, and earnings on these savings are now subject to a 20 percent final tax at source.

28. Thus, if savers channel the funds through a financial intermediary, the intermediary is assumed to have sufficient tax liabilities against which to credit withholding taxes.

29. This effect of inflation dominates the negative effect of inflation on the present value of depreciation allowances.

30. The negative numbers in the third row of the first panel in table 8.8 reveal this. The relatively favorable personal tax treatment of assets located in Japan implies that relative corporate tax wedges overestimated the tax incentives for investment in assets located in the United States.

31. If assets are not close substitutes in portfolios and savers residing in different countries have different preferences for assets, this result may no longer hold. To illustrate, if savers prefer assets located domestically, the higher corporate tax burden on assets located in Japan may have offset the positive incentive effects of the favorable personal tax treatment of Japanese savers. In fact, for both equity and debt financing, the Japanese government taxed locally financed Japanese assets more heavily than the U.S. government taxed local assets. Thus, in the extreme case of savers holding only domestic assets, which is equivalent to a closed economy without any international capital flows, Japanese savers were taxed more heavily than U.S. savers. This result illustrates the important role of more open international capital markets in changing the tax incentives for savings and investment behavior. For an analysis within a closed economy, see Shoven and Tachibanaki (1985) and Makin and Shoven (1987).

32. Following the period of analysis, Japan raised its tax rate on interest income in 1988.

33. In principle, computing the effective tax rate requires expected rather than actual tax parameters. This study, however, uses actual tax provisions to approximate the anticipated provisions.

34. If a saver finances an investment located in his or her own country, the residence and host countries coincide.

35. It is assumed that corporate taxes are not credited in the residence country (see subsec. 8.3.1).

36. The corporate tax wedge does not depend on whether the investment is financed by domestic or foreign savers. In Sinn (1987), the corporate tax wedge depends on the tax treatment of interest and equity income at the personal level in the host country. This is because Sinn (1987) assumes that domestic equity finances a fixed part of domestic investment and that domestic households earn the same after-tax return on equity and debt.

37. For a critical evaluation of this approach, see subsec. 8.3.2.

38. The expressions in table 8A.2 assume that the real return on new share issues is paid in dividends. The purely nominal inflationary gain is reflected in capital gains. This is similar to the procedure in Feldstein (1986) and Boadway, Bruce, and Mintz (1987) but different from that in King and Fullerton (1984).

Sinn (1987) argues, along the lines of the "new" view of dividend taxation, that investors generally adopt profit retentions rather than new share issues as the marginal source of equity finance. In that case, dividend taxes, including withholding taxes on dividends, fail to distort investment decisions and amount to a lump-sum tax on existing rather than a tax on new capital. Dividend taxes affect new investment only when dividends are *not* paid; in that case, internal investment absorbs all profits, and investors are forced to generate new equity capital through new share issues. Hartman (1985) uses similar arguments to argue that home taxation of direct investment is largely irrelevant for direct investment decisions in the presence of deferral provisions.

39. The tax rate on exchange rate gains is generally lower than the tax rate on interest income because it is the rate on accrued gains and losses rather than the statutory rate on realized gains. Moreover, countries often set the tax rate on capital gains, including exchange rate gains, at a rather low level in order to encourage investors to trade their assets and realize their capital gains so as to avoid large efficiency losses and, in some cases, revenue loses.

40. The paper assumes that savers expect nominal exchange rates to adjust fully for the effects of intercountry differences in expected inflation rates. See also Boadway, Bruce, and Mintz (1984) and Gordon (1986).

References

Alworth, Julian S., and Wilhelm Fritz. 1988. Capital mobility, the cost of capital under certainty and effective tax rates in Europe. *Finnish Economic Papers* 1: 25–44

Ando, A., and A. J. Auerbach. 1987. The cost of capital in the U.S. and Japan: A comparison. NBER Working Paper no. 2286. Cambridge, Mass.: National Bureau of Economic Research.

Auerbach, Alan J. 1983. Taxation, corporate financial policy, and the cost of capital. *Journal of Economic Literature* 21; 905–40.

Bernheim, Douglas, and John B. Shoven. 1987. Taxation and the cost of capital: An international comparison. In *The consumption tax: A better alternative?* ed. Charles E. Walker and Mark A. Bloomfield. Cambridge, Mass.: Ballinger.

Boadway, Robin M. 1985. The theory and measurement of effective tax rates. In *The impact of taxation on business activity,* ed. J. M. Mintz and D. Purvis. Kingston, On.: John Deutsch Institute for the Study of Economic Policy, Queens University.

Boadway, Robin M., Neil Bruce, and Jack M. Mintz. 1984. Taxation, inflation, and the effective marginal tax rate in Canada. *Canadian Journal of Economics* 17: 62–79.

———. 1987. *Taxes on capital income in Canada: Analysis and policy.* Canadian Tax Paper, no. 80. Toronto: Canadian Tax Foundation.

Bradford, David, and Charles Stuart. 1984. Issues in the measurement and interpretation of effective tax rates. *National Tax Journal* 39: 307–16.

Brean, Donald J. S. 1984. International issues in taxation: The Canadian perspective. *Canadian Tax Paper,* no. 75.

Corker, R. J., O. Evans, and L. Kenward. 1988. Tax policy and business investment in the United States: Evidence from the 1980s. International Monetary Fund. Typescript.

Feldstein, Martin. 1986. Budget deficits, tax rules, and real interest rates. NBER Working Paper no. 1970. Cambridge, Mass.: National Bureau of Economic Research.

Fukao, Mitsuhiro, and Masaharu Hanazaki. 1987. Internationalisation of financial markets and the allocation of capital. *OECD Economic Studies* (Paris), no. 8, 35–92.

Fukao, Mitsuhiro, and K. Okima. 1988. Balance of payments imbalances and long-term capital movements: Review and prospects. Bank of Japan Research Paper, March.

Fullerton, A. D., and M. Karayannis. 1987. The taxation of income from capital in the United States, 1980–86. NBER Working Paper no. 2478. Cambridge, Mass.: National Bureau of Economic Research.

Gordon, Roger H. 1986. Taxation of investment and savings in a world economy. *American Economic Review* 76 (5): 1086–1102.

Gordon, Roger H., and Hal R. Varian. 1987. Taxation of asset income in the presence of a world securities market. University of Michigan. Mimeo.

Hartman, David G. 1985. Tax policy and foreign direct investment. *Journal of Public Economics* 26 (1): 107–21.

Hatsopoulos, B. G., and S. H. Brooks. 1987. The cost of capital in the United States and Japan. Paper presented to the International Conference on the Cost of Capital, Harvard University.

Kikutani, F., and T. Tachibanaki. 1987. The taxation of income from capital in Japan: Historical perspectives and policy implications. Paper presented to the International Conference on the Cost of Capital, Harvard University.

King, M., and A. D. Fullerton. 1984. *The taxation of income from capital: A comparative study of the United States, the United Kingdom, Sweden, and West Germany.* Chicago: University of Chicago Press.

Makin, John H., and John B. Shoven. 1987. Are there lessons for the United States in the Japanese tax system? In *Contemporary economic problems: Deficits, taxes, and economic adjustments,* ed. Phillip Cagan. Washington, D.C.: American Enterprise Institute.

Sato, Mitsuo, and Richard Bird. 1975. International aspects of the taxation of corporations and shareholders. *Staff Papers* (International Monetary Fund, Washington, D.C.) 22: 384–455.

Shoven, John B., and T. Tachibanaki. 1985. The taxation of income from capital in Japan. Stanford University. Mimeo.

Sinn, Hans-Werner. 1987. *Capital income taxation and resource allocation.* Amsterdam: North-Holland.

Sorenson, Peter B. 1986. Taxation, inflation, and asset accumulation in a small open economy. *European Economic Review* 30: 1025–41.

Sorenson, Peter B. 1987. Reforms of Danish capital income taxation in the 1980s. Paper presented to the Conference on the cost of Capital, Harvard University.

Tachibanaki, Toshiaki. 1988. Government policies, the working of financial markets, saving and investment in Japan. Discussion paper no. 252. Kyoto: Kyoto Institute of Economic Research.

Tanzi, Vito. 1988. Income taxes, interest rate parity, and the allocation of international savings in industrial countries. In *Tax policy and economy,* ed. Antonio Pistone. Padova: Cedam.

Tanzi, Vito, and A. Lans Bovenberg. 1988. Economic interdependence and the international implications of supply-side policies. In *A supply-side agenda for Germany: Stimulation from the United States and Great Britain,* ed. G. Fels and G. Von Furtsenberg. Heidelberg and New York: Springer.

Comment   Alan J. Auerbach

This paper represents a first attempt to introduce an important element of international taxation to the international tax comparison "industry." In the past, authors have followed the lead of King and Fullerton (1984) in calculating the marginal tax rates for domestically financed business investment for different countries and then comparing these results across countries. Absent international capital flows, such comparisons would tell us about the relative tax distortions confronting capital formation and saving in each country, with the saving-investment identity making further distinctions meaningless.

However, such flows are not absent. If domestic saving and investment can move independently (they can, though the controversy continues about how much they do), what do these overall wedges tell us? Not necessarily very much. For example, a large wedge in the United States could primarily discourage domestic investment or domestic saving, depending on how the tax was assessed. The incidence and efficiency effects would turn on this question, as would the direction of induced capital flows. Indeed, if marginal funds for U.S. investment come from Japan, for example, then the "right" overall wedge for U.S. capital formation is the one that combines the investment wedge at home with the saving wedge in Japan. Even that approach is too simple, however, because one cannot generally distinguish separate saving and investment wedges. Japanese savers face different rates of tax on foreign and domestic assets, so we must look at each individual saving-investment country combination to obtain a complete description of the relevant tax incentives.

This is what the paper does admirably well, for a particular class of investments. It leaves open the question of the equilibrium that these distortions generate and the extent to which they are even compatible with capital market equilibrium in the absence of imperfect capital flows or asset substitutability. In considering only portfolio investment, it produces the most straightforward extension of the previous closed economy analysis but leaves aside the empirically more significant and conceptually more complex categories of foreign direct investment and investment by financial intermediaries. We learn from table 8.2 that such portfolio investment represented 20 percent of U.S. investment abroad during the period 1980–87 and 31 percent of foreign investment in the United States. Further whittling down these numbers to account for the fact that only one type of ultimate capital purchase, machinery and equipment, is considered, one finds that this paper's calculations apply to roughly 20 percent of foreign private investment in the United States during the period 1980–87 and, if one

Alan J. Auerbach is professor of economics at the University of Pennsylvania and a research associate of the National Bureau of Economic Research.

assumes the same investment breakdown elsewhere, 13 percent of U.S. private investment abroad.

While the authors do make certain conjectures about how other assets and forms of investment might be affected, one must be fairly cautious in drawing, one might say, global inferences based on the paper's results. Still, there is much of interest here. Before performing their tax wedge calculations, Bovenberg et al. must confront several methodological issues, most of which also arose in the original King-Fullerton international comparisons. These questions do not have simple answers, but little space is devoted to the choices made, even when they diverge from previous approaches. This is primarily a relatively painful collection of index-number problems the details of which the reader might be grateful to be spared, but a brief discussion is worthwhile.

The key problem is how to determine the rate of return to use as a base for each calculation. This leads to problems within each country and problems in comparing the two countries.

Unless a tax system taxes true economic income, the effective tax rate will depend on the rate of return assumed, either before tax or after tax. Even when the effective tax rate is invariant with respect to the assumed rate of return, the *tax wedge* (i.e., the numerator of the effective tax rate calculation) will almost surely increase with the assumed rate of return since part of the tax wedge is associated with the tax rate applied to gross cash flows. Thus, the choice of rate of return influences the estimated tax wedge. One cannot assume that all rates of return, before tax and after tax, are equal, of course, but one can assume that all before-tax rates are equal, all after-tax rates are equal, or all real interest rates are equal, corresponding to the King-Fullerton fixed-p, fixed-s, and fixed-r cases. In my view, any of these would be preferable to the use of observed rates of return in the United States and Japan. Under the current methodology, it would be possible for the two countries to have identical tax systems and even identical inflation experience and yet have systematic tax wedge differences owing to real interest rate differentials. Surely one would not wish to base conclusions about tax policy differences on such results.

Likewise, I do not see the merit in assuming a differential rate of return between debt and equity. It is true that the after-tax return of equity exceeds that of debt, but this is due to risk, a factor not considered in this paper or, to be fair, in most previous efforts either. As has been developed in the literature on risky asset taxation (Auerbach 1983; Bulow and Summers 1984; Gordon and Wilson 1989), one cannot treat an asset with a high expected risky return like one with a high safe return when calculating the asset's tax burden. If assets are to be assumed free of risk, one might as well ignore the risk premia that they actually carry.

A final comment in this vein is that, if one uses ARIMA forecasts of the inflation rate for Japan, consistency would dictate doing so for the United States, even if conceivably better forecasts are available.

Let me turn now to the empirical calculations that are the paper's primary contribution. There are many parameter assumptions necessary to perform these calculations. While one can quarrel with particular choices, I do not see anything unreasonable in them. The results indicate that Japan has taxed investment more heavily and saving less heavily than the United States, a result not unexpected given the previous closed economy calculations of corporate and investor tax wedges reported by Shoven and Tachibanaki (1988). We also learn, from the last three columns of table 8.8, that the lack of formal separability of savings-tax and investment-tax wedges is relatively unimportant: the gap between total tax wedges faced by U.S. and Japanese savers depends very little on where they are assumed to be investing. This could be the result of complete foreign tax crediting but seems here to be due more directly to the unimportance of host country taxes on investor income. It is hard to tell whether this result would also hold for the more complicated ownership patterns excluded from consideration in the paper.

We learn from the last three columns of tables 8.6 and 8.7 that the relative tax advantage of savers in Japan has declined over the past decade and from the first six columns of table 8.8 that the relative tax advantage of investment in the United States rose in the early 1980s and fell in the late 1980s, presumably as the result of the important tax acts of 1981 and 1986. These results suggest that the saving-investment imbalance that has characterized the two countries' bilateral relations may in part have been due to tax policies and that recent policy changes ought to have lessened these imbalances. But, to go further in macroeconomic and welfare analysis, we need not only prices but quantities.

Here, the paper becomes less specific, talking generally about the theoretical welfare and macroeconomic effects but not using the empirical estimates to apply the theory. One could extend the theory a little bit further, by noting, for example, that the deadweight cost due to the distortion of international capital allocation when saving is not fixed would be approximately $-\frac{1}{2} \sum_{i,j} (p_i - s_{ij})K_{ij}$, where $K_{i,j}$ is the capital of type i held by savers of type j, and that the relevant saving elasticity would be a compensated one that would always be positive. It would also be useful to flesh out the conditions under which international asset specialization would occur.

But to do much more welfare analysis than this, one would need a more explicit model of international capital flows, one that would account for the imperfect substitutability that seems present in these asset markets and the more complicated tax rules that apply to foreign direct investment and financial intermediaries. This paper has brought us well beyond the closed economy effective tax rate calculations of the past but shares with previous efforts a focus on the level and dispersion of relative tax rates rather than on the fuller story including a characterization of the associated quantity adjustments and their welfare and macroeconomic consequences. This is not to deny the progress that the authors have made, only to point out the next important step in this line of research. This next step is perhaps even more important in the open economy context; with several alternative ownership structures available for any given underlying real transaction, tax rate dispersion need not be a good indicator of the extent to which capital allocation is distorted, and "representative" overall effective tax rates are hard to come by.

References

Auerbach, Alan J. 1983. Corporate taxation in the United States. *Brookings Papers on Economic Activity* 2:451–505.
Bulow, Jeremy I., and Lawrence H. Summers, 1984. The taxation of risky assets. *Journal of Political Economy* (February), 20–34.
Gordon, Roger H., and John D. Wilson. 1989. Measuring the efficiency cost of taxing risky capital income. *American Economic Review* (June), 427–39.
King, Mervyn, and Don Fullerton, eds. 1984. *The taxation of income from capital.* Chicago: University of Chicago Press.
Shoven, John B., and Toshiaki Tachibanaki. 1988. The taxation of income from capital in Japan. In *Government policy towards industry in the United States and Japan,* ed. John B. Shoven. Cambridge: Cambridge University Press

IV   Implications for Optimal Tax Policy

9   Integration of International Capital Markets: The Size of Government and Tax Coordination

Assaf Razin and Efraim Sadka

International capital market integration has become the subject of major theoretical and practical interest in recent times. Policymakers are becoming more and more aware of the potential benefits accruing from such integration, which allows more efficient allocations of investment and saving between the domestic and the foreign market. In particular, with the prospective comprehensive integration of capital markets in Europe in 1992, some key policy issues arise.[1]

The financial, monetary, and exchange rate management policy implications of capital market integration have been widely discussed in the context of the European Monetary System (EMS) (see, e.g., the survey in Micossi 1988). However, capital market integration also has profound effects on the fiscal branch of each country separately and on the scope of tax coordination among them. These issues have not been dealt with extensively so far. The present paper attempts to contribute to the economic analysis in this area.[2]

The opening up of an economy to international capital movements affects, as expected, the size and the structure of the fiscal branch of its government. Capital flows influence both the optimal structure of taxes, on domestic and foreign-source income, and the welfare cost of taxation. As a result, the optimal size of government (the optimal provision of public goods) and the magnitude of its redistribution (transfer) policies are affected as well. In this context, the paper analyzes the effects of relaxing restrictions on the international flow of capital on the fiscal branch of government.

Assaf Razin is the Ross Professor of International Economics at Tel-Aviv University and a research associate of the National Bureau of Economic Research. Efraim Sadka is professor of Economics at Tel-Aviv University.

The authors would like to thank Alan Auerbach, Jack Mintz, and Torsten Persson for useful comments.

331

The optimal size of government, or, more precisely, the optimal provision of public goods, must be determined by an appropriate cost-benefit analysis. Such an analysis implies that the marginal cost of public funds must be equated to the marginal utility from public goods. Accordingly, in order to find the effect of liberalization in the international capital markets on the optimal quantity of public goods, we study here the effect of such a liberalization on the cost of public funds. This is done in section 9.4, in which we also distinguish between constant and variable internal terms of trade associated with nontradables.

In calculating the cost of public funds, one must take into account the optimal response of the structure of taxation (on incomes from all sources) to the liberalization policy because the cost of public funds is derived from a process of tax optimization. Therefore, we also analyze the effect of liberalization on the structure of taxation. Of course, entangled with the structure of taxation is also the issue of the optimal size of income redistribution. For this reason, we also analyze in section 9.5 the effect of international capital market liberalization on the optimal redistribution (transfer) policy of the government.

Finally, integration of capital markets brings up the issue of international tax coordination. It turns out that perfect mobility of capital necessitates some minimal degree of coordination among the tax authorities. This is discussed in section 9.6.

We present in section 9.1 the analytical framework for our analysis. Sections 9.2 and 9.3 discuss alternative regimes of international capital mobility. Concluding remarks are included in the final section.

9.1 The Analytical Framework

Consider a stylized two-period model of a small open economy with one composite good, serving both for private and public consumption and for investment. In the first period, the economy possesses an initial endowment of the composite good. Individuals can decide how much of their initial endowments to consume in the first period and how much to save. Saving is allocated to either domestic investment or foreign investment. In the second period, output (produced by capital and labor) and income from foreign investment are allocated between private and public consumption. For the sake of simplicity, we assume that the government is active only in the second period. The government employs taxes on labor, taxes on income from domestic investment, and taxes on income from investment abroad in order to finance optimally (taking into account both efficiency and equity considerations) both its (public) consumption and a (uniform lump-sum) subsidy for redistribution purposes.

For simplicity, while still capturing real-world basic features, we assume that government spending on public goods does not affect individual demand patterns for private goods or the supply of labor. That is, only the taxes that are needed to finance these expenditures affect individual demands and supplies, but not the expenditures themselves. Formally, this feature is obtained by assuming that the utility function is weakly separable between private goods and services, on the one hand, and public goods and services, on the other. That is, individual h's utility is

$$(1) \qquad U^h(c_{1h}, c_{2h}, L_h, G) = u^h(c_{1h}, c_{2h}, L_h) + m^h(G),$$

where u^h and m^h are the private and public components of the utility function, respectively; c_{1h}, c_{2h}, and L_h are first-period consumption, second-period consumption, and second-period labor supply, respectively; and G is (second-period) public consumption.[3]

Denote saving in the form of domestic capital by K_h and saving in the form of foreign capital by B_h. The aggregate saving in the form of domestic capital is equal to the stock of capital in the second period since we assume for concreteness, without affecting the results of the paper, that the patterns of capital flows are such that the country is a capital exporter (i.e., $\Sigma_h B_h \geq 0$). Hence, the budget constraints of individual h are

$$(2) \qquad c_{1h} + K_h + B_h = I_h,$$

$$(3) \qquad c_{2h} = K_h[1 + r(1 - t)] + B_h[1 + r^*(1 - t')] + (1 - \theta)wL + S',$$

where:

t = tax on capital income from domestic sources;
t' = tax on capital income from foreign sources;
θ = tax on labor income;
S' = lump-sum subsidy;
r = domestic rate of interest
r^* = foreign rate of interest (net of taxes levied abroad);
w = wage rate; and
I_h = initial (first-period) endowment.

Obviously, in the absence of quantity restrictions on capital flows, individuals must earn the same net return on both forms of investments, that is, $r(1 - t) = r^*(1 - t')$. With restrictions on capital flows, the latter equality does not have to hold. In such a case, there is an inframarginal profit on foreign investment, resulting from the net interest differential. (This differential is equal to the capital export tax rate, which is equivalent to the quota on capital exports.) One possibility is for this profit to accrue to the individual investors. Another possibility is for the government to tax away this profit fully. (This is the equivalent capital-export tax version of the capital-export quota.) We adopt the second possibility, namely, that the government chooses the level of the tax on income from foreign investments (t') so as to eliminate any inframarginal profits. This implies that, whether or not there are restrictions on foreign investment, the government chooses t' so as to maintain the equality $r(1 - t) = r^*(1 - t')$. That is, the rate of tax on income from foreign investment is equal to[4]

$$t' = \frac{r^* - r(1 - t)}{r^*}.$$

Under this tax scheme, the individual is indifferent between investing at home (K_h) or abroad (B_h), caring only about the level of total investment $(K_h + B_h)$. Thus, at equilibrium, the size of the aggregate domestic capital is determined by the demand for capital by domestic firms. The latter is determined by the standard equalization of the marginal product of capital to the domestic rate of interest, r.

We can consolidate the two budget constraints into a single (present-value) constraint:

(4) $c_{1h} + q_2 c_{2h} = I_h + q_L L_h + S,$

where

(5) $q_2 = [1 + (1 - t)r]^{-1}$

is the consumer (after-tax) price of second-period consumption,

(6) $q_L = (1 - \theta)w[1 + (1 - t)r]^{-1}$

is the consumer price of labor, and $S = q_2 S'$ is the present value of the subsidy. Maximization of the utility function u^h, subject to the budget constraint (4), yields the consumption demand functions

(7) $c_{ih} = c_{ih}(q_2, q_L; I_h + S), \quad i = 1, 2,$

the labor supply function

(8) $L_h = L_h(q_2, q_L; I_h + S),$

and the utility obtained from these demand and supply functions, namely, the indirect utility function:

(9) $v^h = v^h(q_2, q_L I^h + S).$

Domestic output (Y) is produced in the second period by capital and labor, according to a constant-returns-to-scale production function

(10) $Y = F(K, L),$

where $K = \Sigma_h K_h$ is the stock of domestic capital, and $L = \Sigma_h L_h$ is the aggregate supply of labor.

The resource constraints of this economy require that

(11a) $I = c_1 + B + K$

and

(11b) $Y + (1 + r^*)B + K = c_2 + G,$

where $I = \Sigma_h I_h$ is aggregate first-period endowment, $B = \Sigma_h B_h$ is aggregate investment abroad, $c_1 = \Sigma_h c_{1h}$ is aggregate consumption in the first period, and $c_2 = \Sigma_h c_{2h}$ is aggregate consumption in the second period.

Substituting (2), (7), (8), (10), and the first-period resource constraint (11a) into the second-period resource constraint (11b) yields the equilibrium condition:

(12) $F[I - C_1(q_2, q_L; I_1 + S, \ldots, I_H + S)$
            $- B, L(q_2, q_L; I_1 + S, \ldots, I_H + S)] + (1 + r^*)B$
            $+ [I - C_1(q_2, q_L; I_1 + S, \ldots, I_H + S) - B]$
            $- C_2(q_2, q_L; I_1 + S, \ldots, I_H + S) - G = 0.$

Observe that aggregate consumptions, C_1 and C_2, depend not only on aggregate income but also on its distribution.

9.2   International Capital Flows: Alternative Regimes

We consider two alternative regimes. In the first regime, the government sets quantity restrictions on capital exports. In the second regime, there are no restrictions on capital exports, and B is thus determined by market clearance.

The optimal tax/transfer policy and provision of public goods are obtained as a solution to the program of maximizing the indirect social welfare function

(13) $W(q_2, q_L; I_1 + S, \ldots, I_H + S) = \Sigma_h \gamma_h v^h(q_2, q_L; I_h + S)$
                                        $+ \Sigma_h \gamma_h m^h(G),$

subject to the resource constraint (12). In this setup, common in the public finance literature, the government operates directly, not on private-sector quantities, but rather on prices (through taxes) that affect these quantities. The government tax policy focuses on q_2, q_L, and S as the control variables. In the first regime, we treat B as a parameter. In the second regime, B is also a control endogenous variable. Notice, however, that this does not mean that the government directly determines the level of investment abroad; rather, the government, through its tax policy, affects total savings $(K + B)$ and domestic investment (K), and B is determined as a residual (the difference between total savings and domestic investment).

Notice that, by Walras law, the government budget constraint is satisfied. Also, the wage rate (w) and the domestic rate of interest (r) are determined by the standard marginal productivity conditions: $F_1 = r$ and $F_2 = w$. Given q_2 and q_L, we can solve for the tax rates, t and θ, by using (5) and (6).

9.3   Efficient Capital Flows

Since there are distortionary taxes as part of the optimal program, obviously the resource allocation is not Pareto efficient: the intertemporal allocation of consumption, the leisure-consumption choice, and the private-public consumption trade-offs are all distorted. Nevertheless, the fully optimal program (namely, the second regime, where no restrictions on B exist) requires an efficient allocation of capital between investment at home and abroad, so that $F_1 = r^*$. That is, the marginal product of domestic capital must be equated to the foreign rate of return on capital (net of foreign taxes).

To see this, observe that the endogenous variable B does not appear in the objective function (13), so that the first-order conditions for optimality require that the derivative of the resource constraint (12) with respect to B, that is, $-F_1 + (1 + r^*) - 1$, be equal to zero. Hence, $F_1 = r^*$. Evidently, this is an open economy variant of the aggregate efficiency theorem in optimal tax theory (see Diamond and Mirrlees 1971; Sadka 1977; and Dixit 1985).

Notice also that this production-efficiency result also implies that there should be no differential tax treatment of foreign and domestic sources of income, namely:

$$t = t'.$$

It might be argued that our investment efficiency result (i.e., equating the return on capital at home to the return on capital abroad by means of free international capital flows) is not valid when the government is concerned about financing its debt. Because, the opening of an economy to international capital flows will raise the domestic interest rate (r) to the world rate (r^*). In such a case, a government that is burdened by an ongoing deficit incurs a higher interest cost of financing this deficit. In fact, it loses some of its monopsony power in the domestic capital market. It can then be argued in this case that the government may not wish to allow residents to invest abroad. To analyze this issue, we extend our model in Appendix A in order to incorporate a meaningful role for a government debt in a non-Ricardian framework. We show that the investment efficiency result is still valid nevertheless. This is because the government can offset the cost of losing its monopsony power by an appropriate tax policy.

However, in the presence of restrictions on capital exports, the production efficiency result does not necessarily hold: the return to capital at home may be lower than the net (after foreign taxes) return on investment abroad. Nevertheless, a small relaxation of this restriction will improve welfare.

We turn next to the study of the effects on the fiscal branch of relaxing the restrictions on investment abroad.

9.4   The Cost of Public Funds in an Open Economy

In the presence of distortionary taxes, the social cost of an additional dollar raised by taxes (namely, the marginal cost of public funds) may exceed one dollar owing to the existence of excess burden (deadweight loss) of taxation. The optimal provision of public goods is determined by equating their marginal benefit with the marginal cost of public funds. In this section, we directly examine the effect of relaxing the restrictions on B on the optimal level of G. Since we have assumed that the marginal benefit from G is diminishing (a concave m), it follows that the optimal G increases if and only if the marginal cost of public funds declines. In this way we indirectly analyze the effect of a liberalization of the international capital markets on the marginal cost of public funds.

For this purpose, we treat B as a parameter and examine the effect of changing B on the optimal quantity of the public good. Specifically, the optimal level of the public good is a function of B, denoted by $\bar{G}(B)$. We then look for the sign of $d\bar{G}/dB$ in the region where $F_1 = r < r^*$, so that increasing B enhances production efficiency and, thus, social welfare.

We proceed as follows. For given levels of G and B, let us maximize the private component of W in (13) (namely, $\Sigma_h \gamma_h v_h[q_2, q_L; I_h + S]$), subject to the resource constraint (12). Denote the value of the maximand by $N(B, G)$. Then, for a given B, the optimal G is determined by solving

$$(14) \qquad \max_{G}\{N(B, G) + M(G)\},$$

where $M(G) = \Sigma_h \gamma_h m^h(G)$.

The first-order condition is

$$(15) \qquad N_2 + M' = 0,$$

and the second-order condition is

$$(16) \qquad N_{22} + M'' \leq 0.$$

Totally differentiating (15) with respect to B yields

$$(17) \qquad \frac{d\bar{G}}{dB} = \frac{N_{12}}{-(N_{22} + M'')}.$$

By (16), the denominator in (17) is positive. Hence,

$$(18) \qquad \text{Sign}\left(\frac{dG}{dB}\right) = \text{Sign}(N_{12}).$$

To proceed further, at this point, we first abstract from redistribution considerations.

9.4.1   Efficiency Considerations

Suppose that all individuals are alike so that we may consider a single representative individual and drop the index h. (Alternatively, we may assume that redistribution can be done by nondistortionary means.) Alleviating the constraint on foreign lending affects the optimal size of government through two channels. First, increasing B generates an additional source of revenues for the government, thereby allowing lower taxes on existing sources. This tends to lower the marginal cost of public funds (and raise the size of government). Second, increasing B may adversely affect the internal terms of trade (associated with nontradable factors or goods) for government expenditures. This effect can raise the marginal cost of public funds (and lower the size of government). To highlight these two effects, we consider first in the next subsection the pure income effect.

Constant Internal Terms of Trade

Assume a linear production function, yielding constant real factor prices: $\bar{r}(\leq r^*)$ and $\bar{w}$, for capital and labor, respectively. In this case, we can unambiguously show that $N_{12} > 0$ and, consequently, that $d\bar{G}/dB > 0$.

The function $N(B, G)$ is defined in this case by

$$(19) \qquad N(B, G) = \max_{\{q_2, q_L, S\}} v(q_2, q_L; I + S)$$

subject to

$$\bar{r}[I - C_1(q_2, q_L; I + S) - B] + \bar{w}L(q_2, q_L; I + S)$$
$$+ [I - C_1(q_2, q_L; I + S) - B] + (1 + r^*)B$$
$$- C_2(q_2, q_L; I + S) - G = 0.$$

Hence, by the envelope theorem, we obtain

$$(20) \qquad N_2(B, G) = - \lambda(B, G) \leq 0,$$

where $\lambda(B, G) \geq 0$ is the Lagrange multiplier associated with the constraint in (19). From (20),

$$(21) \qquad N_{21}(B, G) = -\lambda_1(B, G).$$

Similarly, equation (19) (using the envelope theorem) yields

$$(22) \qquad N_1(B, G) = \lambda(B, G)(r^* - \bar{r}) \geq 0.$$

Therefore,

$$(23) \qquad N_{11}(B, G) = \lambda_1(B, G)(r^* - \bar{r}).$$

One can show (see App. B) that $N(\cdot, \cdot)$ is concave. Hence, $N_{11} < 0$, and it follows from (23) that $\lambda_1 < 0$. Thus, (21) implies that $N_{21} > 0$. Therefore, $d\bar{G}/dB > 0$. That is, the relaxation of international capital controls, in the absence of adjustment in the internal terms of trade, lowers the marginal cost of public funds and increases the optimal size of government.

Variable Internal Terms of Trade

To analyze the effect of variable internal terms of trade on government's expenditures in a simple manner, we assume that labor, the nontradable factor of production, exhibits diminishing marginal productivity and that government's expenditures are used entirely to hire labor. Specifically, we continue to assume constant internal intertemporal terms of trade, that is, that r is constant (at the level $\bar{r}$). However, in the second period, consumption can be provided (in addition to being transferred from the first period) by a concave production function, $f(L)$, using labor alone. The rent (pure profit) generated by such a technology is assumed to be fully taxed by the government. The government hires L_G units of labor in the second period at the prevailing wage, $w = f'$; the government does not purchase any quantity of the consumption good. We thus replace G by L_G.

In this case, the function $N(B, L_G)$ is defined by

(19a) $$N(B, L_G) = \max_{\{q_2, q_L, S\}} v(q_2, q_L; I + S)$$

subject to

$$\bar{r}\,[I - C_1(q_2, q_L; I + S) - B] + f\,[L(q_2, q_L; I + S) - L_G]$$
$$+ I - C_1(q_2, q_L; I + S) - B$$
$$+ (1 + \bar{r})(B - C_2(q_2, q_L; I + S) = 0.$$

Following the same procedure as in the preceding subsection, we conclude that

(21a) $$N_{21}(B, L_G) = -\lambda_1(B, L_G)w - \lambda(B, L_G)\frac{dw}{dB}.$$

The first term in the expression for N_{21} is similar to (21). As before, it is straightforward to show that $\lambda_1 < 0$, so that this term contributes toward making N_{21} positive, that is, toward increasing the size of government in response to alleviating controls on foreign lending (see eq. [17]). However, the second term may work in the opposite direction: the pure income effect of raising B tends to increase the consumption of leisure, thereby increasing the cost of labor that the government hires. Thus, the optimal L_G (namely, the real magnitude of government's consumption) may at the end decline in response to a liberalization of the international capital market. Note, however, that if capital and labor are substitutes in production, capital exports tend to lower the wage rate and thus lower the cost of public funds.

9.4.2 Redistribution Considerations

Now, let us return to the framework of the first subsection of 9.4.1 and reintroduce the redistribution motive.

To simplify the exposition, suppose that the economy consists of two individuals (or two classes of individuals), denoted by indices A and B. We further simplify the analysis by assuming a fixed labor supply (and dropping it altogether from the model). Thus, we are left only with intertemporal decisions and tax-induced intertemporal distortions. Still, to proceed further, we employ a log-linear utility function, in order to keep the analysis tractable.

To emphasize the equity issues, we consider the extreme case of a max-min social welfare criterion; that is, we assume for the social welfare function in (13) that $\gamma_B = 0$ and $\gamma_A = 1$ (where $I_A < I_B$). The function N, the maximized value of the private component in the social welfare function W, is defined in this case by

$$(24) \qquad N(B, G) = \max_{t,S}\{\alpha \, \log[\alpha(I_A + S)] + (1 - \alpha)\log$$
$$[(1 - \alpha)(I_A + S)(1 + \bar{r}(1 - t))]\}$$

subject to

$$(1 + \bar{r})[(I_A + I_B)(1 - \alpha) - 2\alpha S]$$
$$- (1 - \alpha)[1 + \bar{r}(1 - t)](I_A + I_B + 2S)$$
$$+ (r^* - \bar{r})B - G = 0,$$

where the log-linear individual utility function is given by

$$(25) \qquad u(c_1, c_2) = \alpha \log c_1 + (1 - \alpha)\log c_2.$$

Employing the constraint to eliminate S, we can reduce (24) to

$$(26) \qquad N(B, G) = \text{Max}_t\{\log[2I_A(1 + \bar{r}) + t(1 - \alpha)\bar{r}(I_B - I_A)$$
$$+ (r^* - \bar{r})B - G] - \log[1 + \bar{r}(1 - (1 - \alpha)t)]$$
$$+ (1 - \alpha)\log[1 + \bar{r}(1 - t)] + \text{constant}\}$$
$$= \max_t H(t, B, G).$$

The first-order condition for t is

$$(27) \qquad H_1(t, B, G) = 0,$$

while the second-order condition is

$$(28) \qquad H_{11}(t, B, G) \leq 0.$$

By the envelope theorem,

$$N_1(B, G) = H_2(t, B, G);$$

hence,

$$(29) \qquad N_{12} = H_{21}\frac{\partial t}{\partial G} + H_{23}.$$

Total differentiation of (27) with respect to B yields

(30)
$$\frac{\partial t}{\partial G} = -\frac{H_{13}}{H_{11}}.$$

Hence, from (29) and (30), we obtain the expression for N_{12} as follows:

(31)
$$N_{12} = \frac{H_{12}H_{13} - H_{23}H_{11}}{-H_{11}}.$$

Since $H_{11} < 0$ (by [28]), it follows that

(32)
$$\text{Sign}(N_{12}) = \text{Sign}(H_{12}H_{13} - H_{23}H_{11}).$$

Using the definition of H (namely, eq. [26]) to find the partial derivatives H_{ij}, we substitute these derivatives into (32). This substitution yields

(33)
$$\text{Sign}(H_{12}H_{13} - H_{23}H_{11}) =$$
$$\text{Sign}\left\{\frac{1}{[1 + \bar{r}(1 - t)]^2} - \frac{(1 - \alpha)}{[1 + \bar{r}(1 - (1 - \alpha)t)]^2}\right\}$$

(see App. C).

Since $0 < 1 - \alpha < 1$, it follows that (33) is positive and hence that $d\bar{G}/dB > 0.$[5]

9.5   Tax Structure and Redistribution in an Open Economy

In this section, we examine the effects of relaxing some of the controls on international capital flows on the structure of taxation and the size of redistribution. We continue to adopt the simplified framework of subsection 9.4.2. Assume further that the public component in the utility function $m^A(G)$ is equal to $\delta \log G$. In this case, the optimal policy is the solution to the following problem:

(34)
$$\max_{\{t,G\}}\{H(t, B, G) + \delta \log G\},$$

where $H(\cdot)$ is defined in (26).

As before, B is a parameter, and we consider the relations between this parameter and the optimal values of t and G (denoted by $\bar{t}[B]$ and $\bar{G}[B]$, respectively). In doing so, we also find the effect of changing B on t' and S, as will be shown later.

The first-order conditions are

(35)
$$H_1(t, B, G) = 0,$$

(36)
$$H_3(t, B, G) + \frac{\delta}{G} = 0.$$

Total differentiation of (35)–(36) with respect to B yields

(37) $$\frac{d\bar{t}}{dB} = \frac{1}{\Delta}(-H_{12}H_{33} + H_{13}H_{23} + H_{12}\delta/G^2),$$

where Δ is positive by the second-order conditions for the solution to (34).[6] In Appendix C, we show that

(38) $$-H_{12}H_{33} + H_{13}H_{23} = 0$$

and

(39) $$H_{12} < 0.$$

Hence, $d\bar{t}/dB < 0$.

Thus, relaxing the controls on investments abroad reduces the optimal rate of tax on income from domestic investment. This is a natural result in view of the fact that relaxing the controls improves welfare. Since $t' = [r^* - (1 - t)\bar{r}]/r^*$, it follows that t' should be lowered too. That is, the optimal response to relaxing the restrictions on investments abroad is to lower the tax on income from such investments.

To find $d\bar{S}/dB$, recall that the constraint in (24) was employed in order to solve for S in terms of t, B, and G:

(40) $$S = \frac{\bar{r}t(1 - \alpha)(I_A + I_B) + (r^* - \bar{r})B - G}{2\{1 + \bar{r}[1 - (1 - \alpha)t]\}}.$$

We have already concluded that an increase in B raises G and lowers t. These changes have conflicting effects on S, as can be seen from (40). We employed numerical calculations to demonstrate the effect of raising B on the optimal S. These calculations suggest that raising B increases the size of the demogrant S. Again, this result is natural in view of the fact that relaxing the restrictions on international capital flows improves the efficiency of total investment, thereby enabling the economy to devote more resources for redistribution of income. (Note that, if the government does not tax away the inframarginal profits arising from the quota due to the budget constraint, S must decline when G rises and t falls.)

The results of the numerical calculations are given in table 9.1.

9.6   Capital Mobility and International Tax Coordination

Capital market integration between two large countries brings out the issue of tax coordination between them. When residents of one country invest in the other country, one must reckon with the possibility of tax arbitrage that may undermine the feasibility of integration. It is quite obvious that some coordination between countries may in general improve the welfare of both countries. In the case of tax coordination, however, we show that coordination is essential for a sensible world equilibrium (with nonzero interest rates) to exit at all.

Table 9.1   **The Effect of Capital Controls on the Optimal Supply of the Public Good (G), on the Tax Rates (t and t'), and on the Demogrant (S)**

B	G	t	t'	S
0	.191	1.399^a	1.266^a	.381
.25	.193	1.391^a	1.261^a	.402

Note: Parameter values: $\alpha = 0.6$, $\delta = 0.05$, $\bar{r} = 0.50$, $r^* = 0.75$, $I_A = 1.0$, $I_B = 3.0$, $W = U^A = \alpha\log + C_1^A + (1 - \alpha)\log C_2^A + \delta \log G$.

[a]Note that physical investment and foreign lending are the only forms of transferring resources from the present to the future. Hence, t and t' may well exceed one, as long as $1 + (1 - t)\bar{r}$ and $1 + (1 - t')r^*$ are still positive.

To highlight this issue, consider a two-country world with perfect capital mobility. Denote the interest rates in the home country and the foreign country by r and r^*, respectively. In principle, the home country may have three different tax rates applying to interest income:

  i. t_{RD} = the tax rate levied on domestic residents on their domestic-source income;

  ii. t_{RF} = the tax rate levied on domestic residents on their foreign-source income; and

  iii. t_{NRD} = the tax rate levied on nonresidents on their interest income in the home country.

The foreign country may correspondingly have three tax rates, which we denote by t_{RD}^*, t_{RF}^*, and t_{NRD}^*. Furthermore, let us assume that these rates apply symmetrically for both interest earned and interest paid (i.e., full deductibility of interest expenses, including tax rebates).

A complete integration of the capital markets between the two countries (including the possibility of borrowing in one country in order to invest in the other country) requires, owing to arbitrage possibilities, the fulfillment of the following conditions:

$$(41) \qquad r(1 - t_{RD}) = r^*(1 - t_{NRD}^*)(1 - t_{RF})$$

and

$$(42) \qquad r(1 - t_{NRD})(1 - t_{RF}^*) = r^*(1 - t_{RD}^*).$$

The first condition applies to the residents of the home country, and it requires that they be indifferent between investing at home or abroad. Otherwise, they can borrow an infinite amount in the low (net of tax) interest rate country in order to invest an infinite amount in the high (net of tax) interest rate country. The second condition similarly applies to the residents of the foreign country.

Notice that, unless

$$(43) \qquad (1 - t_{RD})(1 - t_{RD}^*) = (1 - t_{NRD})(1 - t_{RF}^*)(1 - t_{NRD}^*)(1 - t_{RF}),$$

the only solution to the linear system of equations (41)–(42) is a zero rate of interest in each country:

$$r = r^* = 0.$$

Since this is impossible, some international tax coordination is needed in order to satisfy (43) and yield a sensible world equilibrium.

Somewhat surprisingly, the two most common polar schemes of source-based or origin-based taxation are examples of workable tax coordinations (although by no means globally efficient arrangements), even when the two countries do not adopt the same scheme. Consider first the case in which both countries adopt the source-based tax scheme. In this case, income is taxed according to its source, regardless of the origin of the taxpayer. This implies that

(44) $$t_{RD} = t_{NRD}, \quad t^*_{RD} = t^*_{NRD}, \quad t_{RF} = t^*_{RF} = 0,$$

so that (43) is satisfied and we can have a world equilibrium with positive rates of interest.

Similarly, consider the case in which both countries adopt the origin-based tax scheme: income is taxed according to the origin of the taxpayer, regardless of its source. This implies that

(45) $$t_{RD} = t_{RF}, \quad t^*_{RD} = t^*_{RF}, \quad t_{NRD} = t^*_{NRD} = 0,$$

so that, again, (43) is satisfied.

Next, consider the case in which one country adopts one tax scheme while the other adopts another one. Suppose, for instance, that the home country adopts the origin-based tax scheme while the foreign county adopts the source-based tax scheme. In this case, we have

(46) $$t_{RD} = t_{RF}, \quad t_{NRD} = 0,$$
$$t^*_{RD} = t^*_{NRD}, \quad t^*_{RF} = 0,$$

and, again, (43) is satisfied.

However, if the two countries do not stick to one or the other of the two polar schemes, then (43) need not hold, and no sensible world equilibrium exists. Suppose, for instance, that each country levies the same tax rate on its residents (irrespective of the source of their income) and also on all nonresidents investing in that country. In this case, we have

(47) $$t_{RD} = t_{RF} = t_{NRD}, \quad t^*_{RD} = t^*_{RF} = t^*_{NRD}.$$

Hence, unless $(1 - t_{NRD})(1 - t^*_{NRD}) = 1$, which is just a sheer coincidence, condition (43) is violated.

Thus, some tax coordination is essential for a full capital market integration. Any mutually beneficial tax coordination must satisfy the tax arbitrage condition (43). In Razin and Sadka (1989b) we found that tax competition among countries leads to each one adapting the residence principle of income taxation.

9.7   Conclusion

In this paper, we analyzed the policy implications of the integration of the international capital markets. Special attention was paid to the effects on the marginal cost of public funds, a crucial factor in the determination of the optimal size of government and the magnitude of income redistribution. Inherent in the determination of the cost of public funds is the design of the structure of taxation (on labor income, domestic-source capital income, and foreign-source capital income).

We show that it is not efficient to impose restrictions on capital exports and that every incremental move toward a more liberalized policy concerning the international flows of capital is welfare improving. This result depends crucially, however, on the assumption that the government can effectively tax foreign-source income. In Razin and Sadka (1989a,b), we consider the case in which the government cannot effectively tax capital income from foreign sources.

In the context of a world economy with integrated capital markets, there arises the issue of international tax coordination. This issue has two aspects. First is the elementary problem of what international tax arrangements are at all viable in the wake of capital market arbitrage possibilities. This issue was dealt with in this paper. A second aspect (dealt with in Razin and Sadka 1989b) is the determination of mutually beneficial international tax arrangements from the set of viable arrangements.

Appendix A

In this appendix, we prove that $N(B, G)$ is concave. Recall that $N(B, G)$ is defined by (19). Since there is only one individual and a lump-sum tax/subsidy is allowed, it follows that the government can choose any bundle (C_1, C_2, L) that is feasible (i.e., that satisfies the resource constraint in [19]). Thus, N may be equivalently defined by

$$\text{(A1)} \qquad N(B, G) = \max_{C_1, C_2, L} u(C_1, C_2, L)$$

subject to

$$\bar{r}(I - C_1 - B) + \bar{w}L + I - C_1 + r^*B - C_2 - G \geq 0.$$

We have to show that

$$N[aB' + (1 - a)B'', aG' + (1 - a)G''] \\ \geq aN(B', G') + (1 - a)N(B'', G'')$$

for all (B', G'), (B'', G''), and $0 \leq a \leq 1$.

Suppose that the bundle (C'_1, C'_2, L') is a solution to (A1) for $(B, G) =$

(B', G') and that the bundle (C''_1, C''_2, L'') is a solution to (A1) for $(B, G) = (B'', G'')$, namely, $N(B', G') = u(C'_1, C'_2, L')$ and $N(B'', G'') = u(C''_1, C''_2, L'')$.

By being solutions to optimum problems, the bundles (C'_1, C'_2, L') and (C''_1, C''_2, L'') satisfy the constraint in (A1), namely,

(A2) $\bar{r}(I - C'_1 - B') + \bar{w}L' + I - C'_1 + r^*B' - C'_2 - G' \geq 0$

and

(A3) $\bar{r}(I - C''_1 - B'') + \bar{w}L'' + I - C''_1 + r^*B'' - C''_2 - G'' \geq 0.$

Hence, on multiplying (A2) by the factor a and (A3) by the factor $(1 - a)$ and adding them together, it follows that

(A4) $\bar{r}\{I - [aC'_1 + (1 - a)c''_1] - [aB' + (1 - a)B'']\}$
$\quad + \bar{\omega}[aL' + (1 - a)L''] + I - [aC'_1 + (1 - a)C''_1]$
$\quad + r^*[aB' + (1 - a)B''] - [aC'_2 + (1 - aC''_2]$
$\quad - [aG' + (1 - a)G''] \geq 0.$

Thus, the bundle $[aC'_1 + (1 - a) C''_1, aC'_2 + (1 - c)C''_2, aL' + (1 - a)L'']$ is feasible for $(B, G) = [aB' + (1 - a)B'', aG' + (1 -a)G'']$. Therefore,

(A5) $N[aB' + (1 - a)B'', aG' + (1 - a)G'']$
$\quad \geq u[aC'_1 + (1 - a)C''_1, aC'_2 + (1 - a)C''_2, aL' + (1 - a)L'']$
$\quad \geq au(C'_1, C'_2, L') + (1 - a)u(C''_1, C''_2, L'')$
$\quad = aN(B', G') + (1 - a)N(B'', G''),$

where the first inequality in (A5) follows from the definition of $N(\cdot, \cdot)$ as the value of the maximand in (A1), and the second inequality follows from the concavity of u. This completes the proof of the concavity of N.

Appendix B

In this appendix we verify the expressions of (33) and (38)–(39). The function H (see [26]) is given by

(B1) $H(t, B, G) = \log[2I_A(1 + \bar{r}) + t(1 - \alpha)\bar{r}(I_B - I_A)$
$\quad + (r^* - \bar{r})B - G] - \log(1 + \bar{r}[1 - (1 - \alpha)t])$
$\quad + (1 - \alpha)\log[1 + \bar{r}(1 - t)].$

The first-order derivatives are

(B2) $H_1 = [2I_A(1 + \bar{r}) + t(1 - \alpha)\bar{r}(I_B - I_A)$
$\qquad + (r^* - \bar{r})B - G](1 - \alpha)\bar{r}(I_B - I_A)$
$\qquad + \{1 + \bar{r}[1 - (1 - \alpha)t]\}^{-1}\bar{r}(1 - \alpha)$
$\qquad - \bar{r}(1 - \alpha)[(1 + \bar{r}(1 - t)]^{-1},$

(B3)
$$H_2 = [2I_A(1 + \bar{r}) + t(1 - \alpha)\bar{r}(I_B - I_A)$$
$$+ (r^* - \bar{r})B - G]^{-1}(r^* - \bar{r}),$$

and

(B4)
$$H_3 = -\frac{H_2}{r^* - \bar{r}}.$$

The second-order derivatives are:

(B5)
$$H_{11} = -(1 - \alpha)^2\bar{r}^2(I_B - I_A)^2[2I_A(1 + \bar{r}) + t(1 - \alpha)\bar{r}(I_B - I_A)$$
$$+ (r^* - \bar{r})B - G]^{-2} + \bar{r}^2(1 - \alpha)^2\{1 + \bar{r}[1 - (1 - \alpha)t]\}^2$$
$$- \bar{r}^2(1 - \alpha)[1 + \bar{r}(1 - t)]^{-2},$$

(B6)
$$H_{12} = \bullet(r^* - \bar{r})[2I_A(a + \bar{r}) + t(1 - \alpha)\bar{r}(I_B - I_A)$$
$$+ (r^* - \bar{r})B - G]^{-2}\bullet(1 - \alpha)\bar{r}(I_B - I_A),$$

(B7)
$$H_{13} = \frac{-H_{12}}{r^* - \bar{r}},$$

(B8)
$$H_{22} = \frac{H_{12}(r^* - \bar{r})}{(1 - \alpha)\bar{r}(I_B I_A)},$$

(B9)
$$H_{23} = \frac{-H_{12}}{(1 - \alpha)\bar{r}(I_B - I_A)},$$

and

(B10)
$$H_{33} = \frac{H_{12}}{(r^* - \bar{r})(1 - \alpha)\bar{r}(I_B - I_B)}.$$

Hence,

$$H_{12}, H_{13} - H_{11}, H_{33}$$
$$= \left(\frac{1}{[1 + \bar{r}(1 - t)]^2} - \frac{(1 - \alpha)}{\{1 + \bar{r}[1 - (1 - \alpha)t]\}^2}\right)(r^* - \bar{r})\bar{r}^2(1 - \alpha)\bullet$$
$$\frac{1}{[2I_A(1 + \bar{r}) + t(1 - \alpha)\bar{r}(I_B - I_A) + (r^* - \bar{r})B - G]^2}.$$

This completes the proof of (33).

Next we prove (38) and (39). Employing (B6), (B7), (B9), and (B10), we find that

$$-H_{12}H_{33} + H_{13}H_{23} = \frac{-(H_{12})^2}{(r^* - \bar{r})(1 - \alpha)\bar{r}(I_B - I_A)}$$
$$+ \frac{(H_{12})^2}{(r^* - \bar{r})(1 - \alpha)\bar{r}(I_B - I_A)} = 0,$$

which proves (38). From (B6), we observe that $H_{12} < 0$, which proves (39).

Notes

1. In a recent paper, Micossi (1988) provides a succinct survey of the proposed institutional arrangements for the 1992 European integration. He writes, "The European integration entails the elimination of restrictions and discriminatory regulations and administrative practices concerning: (i) the right of establishment and acquisition of participations by foreign institutions in domestic financial markets; (ii) permitted operations of foreign-controlled financial institutions; (iii) cross-border transactions in financial services. The first two items basically involve the freedom to supply services in EC national markets, the third, the freedom to move capital throughout the Community."

2. For an earlier discussion of the interaction among taxes, government consumption, and international capital flows, see Razin and Svensson (1983).

3. To ensure diminishing marginal rates of substitution between private and public commodities, we assume, as usual, that u^h and m^h are strictly concave.

4. An equivalent policy to taxing away the inframarginal profits (resulting from the net interest differential) is to auction off the quotas on investment abroad.

5. The reader who is familiar with the optimal income tax literature may realize that the issue of the sign of $d\bar{G}/dB$ is related to the issue of the concavity of the maximized (reduced-form) social welfare function with respect to tax revenues (see Balcer and Sadka 1982; and Stiglitz 1982).

6. The derivative $d\bar{G}/dB$ is negative, as shown in sec. 9.4.2.

References

Balcer, Yves, and Efraim Sadka. 1982. Horizontal equity, income taxation and self-selection with an application to income tax credits. *Journal of Public Economics* 19: 291–309.

Diamond, Peter A., and James A. Mirrlees. 1971. Optimal taxation and public production. *American Economic Review* (March, June), 8–27, 261–78.

Dixit, Avinash. 1985. Tax policy in open economies. In *Handbook on public economics,* ed. Alan Auerbach and Martin Feldstein, 314–74. Amsterdam: North-Holland.

Micossi, Stefano. 1988. The single European market: Finance. *Banca Nazionale del Lavoro Quarterly Review,* no. 165 (June), 217–35.

Razin, Assaf, and Lars E. O. Svensson. 1983. The current account and the optimal government debt. *Journal of International Money and Finance* 2 (2): 215–24.

Razin, Assaf, and Efraim Sadka. 1989a. Optimal incentives to domestic investment in the presence of capital flight. IMF Working Paper no. 90. Washington, D.C.: International Monetary Fund.

————. 1989b. International tax competition and gains from tax harmonization. Foerder Institute Working Paper no. 37-89. Tel Aviv: Tel Aviv University.

Sadka, Efraim. 1977. A note on producer taxation and public production. *Review of Economic Studies* 44 (2): 385–87.

Stiglitz, Joseph. 1982. Utilitarianism and horizontal equity: The case for random taxation. *Journal of Public Economics* 18: 1–33.

Comment   Jack M. Mintz

The paper by Assaf Razin and Efraim Sadka raises an interesting issue for countries that relax capital controls. What effect do such policies have on the optimal fiscal decisions of a benevolent government? Their main result is that a government may reduce the capital income tax rate and, under certain circumstances, expand government expenditures if capital controls are relaxed. With respect to the latter, relaxing capital controls on exported savings reduces the marginal cost of public revenues, thus allowing government expenditure to increase, but it may increase the price of nontraded goods (i.e., labor) used in public production and hence, possibly reduce the expansion of the government sector.

The above results are not intuitively obvious, at least to me, at first glance. In these remarks, I will offer an alternative explanation of the Razin-Sadka results in a simpler version of their model. Despite the simplicity of my own model, I will be able to derive similar efficiency results but with an interpretation that varies from that offered by the authors. Of course, the model can be extended in other ways, as suggested by Razin and Sadka.

In my discussion below, I will also raise a number of other points that are important in determining the effect of capital controls on the fiscal decisions of open economies. Although I agree with the Razin-Sadka analysis, I find that it neglects several important issues that are of interest to policymakers. In particular, they examine a capital exporting country that finances a public consumption good using labor and capital income taxes on residents. No interaction effects with other countries are considered. Savings are invested in domestic and foreign assets that are perfect substitutes, and the international interest rate on foreign assets is exogenous to the small open economy. I wish to extend the Razin-Sadka analysis to consider the effect of the capital controls on fiscal decisions in the following contexts: (i) countries are capital importers as well as exporters, (ii) capital income taxes apply at the firm level and are imposed on nonresidents, and (iii) tax and regulatory policies affect not only the welfare of the country imposing the tax or regulation but also the welfare of other countries. The latter topic may be important for considering the fiscal effect of capital market integration in the European Economic Community.

Capital Importing versus Capital Exporting Considerations

Fiscal decisions often differ considerably for capital exporting and capital importing nations. If the Razin-Sadka analysis is extended to a capital

Jack Mintz is professor of business economics, Faculty of Management and Department of Economics, University of Toronto.
The author is indebted to Ken McKenzie for his comments.

importing framework, what would be the optimal tax decisions, and how would a government react if capital restrictions on imports are relaxed?

To answer these questions, I will consider a simpler form of the Razin-Sadka model. In particular, I shall assume that labor is fixed in supply (so a wage tax is a lump-sum tax). I will also assume that all individuals are identical in the country and that utility is an additive function defined over first- and second-period consumption goods and the public good. In addition, utility is linear in second-period consumption goods (so there are no income effects on savings). I also assume that the capital income tax on foreign and domestic savings is identical, which is a special case of the Razin and Sadka model.

Following the Razin-Sadka analysis, consider an economy that may be (i) a capital exporter facing restrictions on capital exports, $\overline{B}$, or (ii a capital importer facing restrictions on capital imports, $\underline{B}$. Let I denote the endowment of wealth in the first period, c_1 and c_2 first- and second-period consumption, respectively, G consumption of the public good, K domestic capital stock, B net foreign assets ($B = A - c_1 - K$), r^* the international interest rate, t the capital income tax rate, and τ lump-sum taxes. The market equilibrium for the economy can be described as solutions to the following problem:

$$\max_{\{c_1, c_2, K, B\}} U(c_1) + c_2 + g(G),$$

subject to

$$c_2 = K + (1 - t)f(K) + [1 + r^*(1 - t)]B - \tau,$$
$$B = I - c_1 - K \leq \overline{B},$$
$$B = I - c_1 - K \geq \underline{B}.$$

The first-order conditions for this problem yield the familiar results that the marginal rate of substitution would be equal to, less than, or greater than [1 + $r^*(1 - t)$] for the cases of $\overline{B} < B^* < \underline{B}$ (unconstrained capital importer or exporter), $B = \overline{B}$ (constrained capital exporter), and $B = \underline{B}$ (constrained capital importer), respectively. The firm's capital stock decision would be governed by the condition that the marginal productivity of capital, f', equals the (gross of personal tax) "domestic" interest rate, r (which, net of personal taxes, is equal to the time preference rate). In the unconstrained case, this implies $r = r^*$, given the same tax rate imposed on domestic and foreign capital income. For the constrained capital exporter, $r < r^*$ (as suggested by Razin and Sadka), and, for the constrained capital importer, $r > r^*$.

What are the optimal fiscal decisions for the government given the capital controls on net foreign assets B? To obtain the optimal fiscal decisions, t^*, G^*, and τ^*, the government maximizes the indirect utility function, $V(t, \tau, G)$ subject to the second-period budget constraint, $G = t[F(K) + r^* B] + \tau$. The private-sector choices of savings and capital investment depend only on the capital income tax given the absence of income effects. If the country is unconstrained, the capital income tax rate has no effect on the investment decision, K. Only savings and net foreign assets are affected. If the country is a constrained capital exporter, the capital income tax reduces domestic savings and, subsequently, investment. Net foreign assets remain fixed. Finally, if the country is a constrained capital importer, the capital income tax reduces savings and the domestic capital investment since capital imports are fixed (i.e., $\partial c_1/\partial t = \partial K/\partial t$ when B is restricted). Note that, in this formulation, interest on foreign borrowings is fully deducted from the income tax.

The solution for the optimal capital tax rate for this problem is the following:

(i)
$$t^* = \frac{[f(K) + r^* B^*](1 - \lambda/\phi)}{-\partial K/\partial t}$$

for $B^* = \overline{B}$ or $\underline{B}$ with

$$\lambda = 1$$

and

$$\phi = 1 + (r - r^*)(1 - t)\partial c_1/\partial t - (f' - r^*)(1 - t)\partial K/\partial t;$$

(ii)
$$t^* = 0 \text{ for } \underline{B} < B^* < \overline{B}.$$

Note that λ is the marginal utility of the second-period good valued by the private sector and that ϕ is the social marginal value of tax revenue (used to finance public goods in the second period). Conditions (i) and (ii) are readily interpreted by considering the effect of a tax on savings on the allocation of capital in the economy.

The optimal capital income tax rate for the unconstrained economy is zero (given market equilibrium conditions $r = r^*$ and $f' = r^*$ so that $\phi = \lambda$, yielding the result in [ii]). This is quite sensible since a capital income tax is distortionary and only lump-sum taxes should be imposed.

When the economies are constrained by capital controls, then the capital income tax reduces savings and, therefore, investments in domestic assets since net foreign assets are constrained either at $\overline{B}$ or $\underline{B}$. For the constrained capital exporter, this implies that the social value of public revenue is at least as great as the private value $\phi \geq \lambda$ since $r < r^*$ and $f' < r^*$. Thus, given $\partial K/\partial t < 0$, the optimal tax rate is positive. For the capital importing country, the optimal capital tax rate is negative.

Intuitively, these results can be explained as follows (see figs. C9.1 and C9.2). If the country is a capital exporter, capital controls subsidize domestic investment by forcing domestic savings into the domestic asset, causing the gross-of-tax domestic interest to fall. To counteract this effect, a capital income tax can be imposed on savings that causes the gross-of-tax domestic

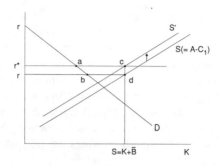

Fig. C9.1   Capital exporting country

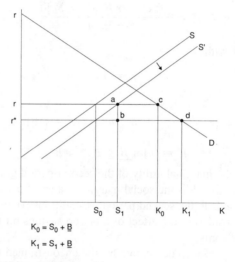

$$K_0 = S_0 + \underline{B}$$
$$K_1 = S_1 + \underline{B}$$

Fig. C9.2   Capital importing country

interest rate to rise, subsequently reducing domestic investment. This tax causes inframarginal returns on capital investment to decline by the area r^*rba in figure C9.1. However, the tax raises revenue equal to r^*rdc, yielding a net gain in welfare indicated by the area $abdc$. In principle, the capital income tax rate, in this model, can be raised until $r = r^*$, which would lead to second-best efficiency.

For a capital importing country, the opposite results hold. Domestic capital investment is discouraged since capital controls cause the domestic interest to rise above the world interest rate. Instead of taxing capital, savings are subsidized since the domestic gross-of-tax interest rate is too high. As shown in figure C9.2, the gain in rents to capital is r^*rcd, and the cost of the subsidy is rr^*ba, yielding a net welfare gain of $abcd$.

This model, although somewhat special, does illustrate the efficiency results obtained in the Razin-Sadka paper. A reduction in capital controls (through a higher $\overline{B}$ in the case of capital exporting country or lower $\underline{B}$ in the case of capital importing country) lowers the optimal corporate tax rate. This can be easily demonstrated by noting that the domestic interest rate, r, moves closer to the international interest rate r^* (in both eq. [i] and [ii] and in the corresponding figures). However, the intuition provided here is different from that explained by Razin and Sadka. In the above model, government expenditures need not be affected by the capital controls (only lump-sum taxes may change). Capital income taxes, however, are imposed since they correct for imperfections caused by capital controls. This is true even though the tax system would otherwise be nondistortionary. In fact, this model would lead to a corner solution—the optimal tax rate is set until $r = f' = r^*$ (this would not necessarily be the case in the Razin-Sadka model).

The above illustrates two issues that would be of interest to explore that are not discussed in Razin and Sadka. The first is that capital controls for a capital importing country imply that a country would subsidize savings and labor if a lump-sum tax could be imposed. The second is that it may be possible for regimes to change in that the use of the fiscal system may move a country from a constrained to an unconstrained equilibrium in capital markets. This could be efficient, suggesting the possibility that the tax system might make capital controls ineffective.

The Role of Corporate and Withholding Taxes

In the Razin and Sadka model, and the one discussed above, the capital income tax can be viewed as personal tax on domestic and foreign-source income. When a personal income tax is imposed in a capital exporting country and net exports of capital are constrained, domestic savings fall, and, as a result of rising interest rates, domestic capital investment also declines. If a corporate tax is imposed on domestic investment of firms (and leaves net foreign assets of households free of tax), domestic investment declines. The demand for foreign assets increases, but households are restricted from purchasing foreign assets. Their consumption of the first-period good thus increases, causing savings to decline and the interest rate to rise. A similar story holds for the capital importing country in that personal and corporate tax/subsidies have a similar effect on the equilibrium. These results suggest that aggregate effects of corporate and personal tax policies in a small open economy can be equivalent when capital controls are binding.

The above result, obtained in the Razin-Sadka paper, is quite interesting since it is well known that the effects of corporate and personal tax policies in a small open economy are not equivalent when there are no capital controls (see Boadway, Bruce, and Mintz 1984; and Bovenberg et al. in this volume). A personal tax on capital income causes domestic savings to decline, but not investment. For a capital exporting country, net foreign assets held by the economy decline, and, for a capital importing country, net foreign borrowings rise. If a corporate tax is imposed, the result is different. A corporate tax causes capital investment to decline, but not domestic savings. A capital exporting country increases its net foreign assets, and a capital importing country reduces its net foreign borrowings. In the presence of lump-sum taxes, neither tax is optimal. A small open economy would "shoot itself in the foot" by taxing capital income either at the corporate or at the personal level. Without lump-sum taxes, a personal tax on capital income may be optimal, but not a corporate tax, since productive efficiency is maintained, a familiar point made by Razin and Sadka in their paper.

The Razin-Sadka model does not address the implications of nonresident withholding taxes imposed by capital importing countries when fiscal decisions are made in the presence of capital controls. This is somewhat unfortunate since withholding taxes may offset the gains that arise from capital taxation when capital controls are imposed. A withholding tax paid by lenders to foreign countries is usually credited against home tax liabilities, which implies that the combined domestic and foreign tax on foreign-source income is equal to the domestic tax on domestic-source income. As a result, the household faces the same budget constraint when withholding taxes are imposed, but the government faces a different budget constraint since savings in foreign assets yield less domestic tax. In terms of national income, savings in foreign assets are of less value than savings in domestic assets for the capital exporting country. This implies that it may not be optimal to impose capital income taxes on savings since the gain in tax revenue may not be sufficient to offset the loss of inframarginal rents earned by domestic capital investments. Thus, capital taxation may not be desirable for the capital exporting country. Similarly, for the capital importing country that taxes interest earned by foreigners, a subsidy for domestic savings may not be desirable.

Capital Controls and Fiscal Policy Coordination

The Razin-Sadka model is a special one in the context of analyzing capital market integration and tax harmonization since tax and regulatory competition problems are not particularly important in their model. Since each country is assumed to be small, they face a perfectly elastic supply of capital from international markets. As a result, fiscal and regulatory policies chosen by one government have no effect on the decisions of others.

This can be explained as follows. Consider capital controls imposed by a capital exporting economy. With no other countries involved, a capital importing economy is also constrained by the capital regulations imposed by the capital exporting country. However, in the small open economy context, the constraint is avoided by the capital importing country since it can obtain capital from other countries at the same interest rate. Thus, capital regulations in one country cannot affect the welfare of the other, and no regulatory competition problem exists between the countries. With capital tax policies, the same argument arises. One country's fiscal regime cannot affect the other since capital can be obtained from international markets without affecting the international cost of funds. Capital tax competition is not a problem either.

If all the above is true, then why should the European nations be at all concerned with regulatory and capital income tax harmonization? Clearly, it is in the best interest of each country to avoid regulatory constraints and choose optimal taxes. Otherwise, they only make themselves worse off. Thus, countries pursuing self-interest would not impose capital taxes or controls anyway. It seems to me that the small open economy assumed by Razin and Sadka may not be a useful characterization of the issues faced by the European Economic Community.

I can think of two cases in which fiscal and regulatory policy competition matters in the sense that one country's action directly affects the interests of another country. The first case is an obvious one: instead of assuming "smallness," one can assume that economies are large relative to each other. In this case, a country that restricts the exportation of capital causes the international interest rate to rise, making its own residents better off but making residents in capital importing countries worse off. Similarly, a capital importing country that restricts the importation of capital forces the world interest down, making the capital exporting countries worse off. Thus, both tax and regulatory competition lead to nonoptimal policies from a worldwide efficiency point of view. It would be interesting to know what type of coordination is needed in this context. If countries only agree to eliminate capital controls, then to what extent would fiscal policies be used to restrict capital imports? As Razin and Sadka note, a country could tax foreign-source income earned by residents as an alternative to capital regulations.

A second source of capital tax competition arises in the context of withholding taxes. As Razin and Sadka implicitly note, withholding taxes imposed by countries are not easy to incorporate in their model. As they show, equilibrium in capital markets holds only if all countries use source-based taxes (taxes imposed on capital income generated at source with foreign-source income of residents exempt from tax) or residence-based taxes (capital income accruing to nonresidents' taxes is exempt, and both domestic and foreign-source income is taxed). Razin and Sadka emphasize the need for harmonization of capital income taxes to ensure the existence of a capital market equilibrium.

Tax competition and harmonization problems, however, are not well understood using models that assume that domestic and foreign assets are perfect substitutes for each country's investors. Instead, tax competition problems would be more interesting if it were assumed that domestic and foreign assets are not perfect substitutes. This would allow for a financial equilibrium in which income generated in different jurisdictions and earned by different investors would be taxed at different rates. For example, many empirical studies suggest that risk is country-specific so that domestic and foreign assets are not perfect substitutes (for an examination of tax policy in this context, see Gordon and Varian 1986). With imperfect substitutability, capital income taxes and capital controls imposed by a country affect the rates of return on individual assets and make savers better off and borrowers worse off.

When assets are not perfect substitutes, withholding taxes, such as nonresident taxes on dividends and interest and corporate income taxes, add another element of tax competition since the tax is paid by nonresident investors or, in the case of crediting, foreign governments. When there is crediting, a capital importing country may obtain a "free lunch" by imposing a withholding tax on nonresidents. This "free lunch" occurs because the capital importing country is able to impose a tax that transfers income from the foreign government treasuries without affect foreign savings. Thus, capital importing countries find it in their favor to export taxes by taxing nonresidents' income particularly if the tax has no distortionary effects. One would find in this type of model that the harmonization of tax bases is important if countries are to reduce the exportation of taxes on nonresidents. This problem goes well beyond the issues of harmonization discussed by Razin and Sadka.

References

Boadway, Robin W., Neil Bruce, and Jack M. Mintz. 1984. Taxation, inflation and the effective marginal tax rate in Canada. *Canadian Journal of Economics* 17: 62–79.
Gordon, Roger H., and Hal R. Varian. 1986. Taxation of asset income in the presence of a world securities market. NBER Working Paper no. 1994. Cambridge, Mass.: National Bureau of Economic Research, August.

10 The Linkage between Domestic Taxes and Border Taxes

Roger H. Gordon and James Levinsohn

Observed patterns of tariffs across countries, and of trade policies more generally, are very puzzling given the clear policy implications of traditional optimal tariff models. These models suggest that countries with little market power should not attempt to distort trade patterns, while those countries that do have market power should attempt to restrict imports and/or exports, relative to the amount that would otherwise occur, in order to take advantage of this monopoly/monopsony power. Yet rich countries, which might plausibly have important market power, are often observed subsidizing exports in various ways. To the degree to which they restrict trade at all, it is often in sectors such as agriculture, where the country clearly has no market power, or it is done through nontariff barriers, where the profits arising from the difference between domestic and world prices are received by foreign firms. Poorer countries often impose tariffs, even in situations where they have no plausible market power.

The objective of this paper is to explore to what degree this pattern of border distortions may simply result from each country's attempt to offset the trade distortions created by their domestic tax structure and by other domestic policies.[1] The basic intuition is as follows. Most countries collect a sizable fraction of their tax revenue through taxation of domestic production, using a variety of tax instruments, including output taxes, property taxes, and capital income taxes.[2] The corporate income tax, used heavily in most

Roger H. Gordon is professor of economics at the University of Michigan and a research associate of the National Bureau of Economic Research. James Levinsohn is assistant professor of economics at the University of Michigan.

The authors would like to thank Gene Grossman, Ray Riezman, John Whalley, and participants at the NBER conference on International Aspects of Taxation for comments, Wei Li for research assistance, Bob Flood and Kellet Hannah for assistance in obtaining the data, and the NBER for financial support.

357

developed countries, is a good example. As a result of these taxes, more domestic taxes are paid on domestically produced goods than on foreign-produced goods.

If the tax rate were the same in all sectors, then the only effect would be a readjustment in the exchange rate. However, effective tax rates vary substantially across industries and tend to be much higher on manufacturing firms, presumably owing to lower administrative costs in enforcing a tax on larger-scale firms. If a country is a net exporter of manufacturing goods, then taxes on domestic production raise the relative prices of these goods. If the country has market power in these goods, it can thereby take advantage of this market power without the need to enact an explicit export tax. If the country has no market power, however, then it can offset the distortion created by domestic production taxes through a rebate of the production tax when goods are exported, as occurs under a VAT, or through an explicit export subsidy.

If a country is a net importer of manufacturing goods, then production taxes discourage the development of a domestic manufacturing industry. To offset this distortion, a country can impose a tariff at a comparable rate on manufacturing imports. In fact, GATT rules allow a country to use import tariffs or export subsidies in this way to offset taxes on the output of domestic firms, as long as the effective tax rate on imports is no higher than that faced on domestic production. GATT rules do not allow taxes on the income of domestic firms to be offset in the same way, however.[3] One alternative response is to impose nontariff barriers to imports. While nontariff barriers do not collect any revenue, unlike explicit tariffs, they still serve to protect domestic production from foreign goods that are artificially cheaper owing to the distorting effects of the domestic tax structure.

Poorer countries tend to be net importers of manufacturing goods and so should be observed imposing tariffs on these imports. Richer countries tend to export manufacturing goods, explaining the pressure toward export subsidies.

Taxes are not the only policy distorting relative domestic prices. Many countries intervene actively in agricultural markets, for example; it is also common for countries to set up state-run enterprises producing tradable goods whose output is unlikely to be sold at marginal cost. The same arguments made above with respect to tax distortions apply with equal force to other distortions.

Nothing in this argument shows that the above policies are optimal for a country. Bhagwati (1971) argued that the first-best response was to eliminate any domestic distortions; only if this failed should tariffs be used as a second-best response. Rather than taking domestic tax distortions as exogenous, however, as did Bhagwati (1971), we will explore the characteristics of a country's optimal use of domestic taxes, tariffs, and nontariff barriers. Since a production tax on a particular industry in combination with an import tariff (or export subsidy) at the same rate has identical economic effects to a tax on domestic consumption of that good, using, for example, a retail sales tax or a VAT, explaining which of these equivalent tax instruments is used leads us to focus on their relative administrative costs. If administrative costs become important, however, then they can have important effects on the characteristics of optimal policy and on the size of any resulting trade distortions. We explore the likely pattern of these trade distortions.

This explanation for the observed use of tariffs has been discussed in a variety of papers since Bhagwati (1971). Corden (1974) explicitly noted that tariffs might well form part of an optimal tax system, once collection costs are taken into account, though he did not attempt to model the optimal domestic and trade tax structures formally. Riezman and Slemrod (1987) provided empirical support for this intuition by showing that tariffs are used most heavily by countries that likely face high administrative costs of alternative taxes. However, little attempt has been made to examine explicitly what optimal tax theory would in fact imply about the optimal use of tariffs. One exception is Aizenman (1987), who examines a particular example with one consumer in which the only available taxes are a consumption tax and a tariff. In his example, only the consumption tax has administrative costs, which are proportional to consumption tax revenues. He finds that tariffs would be part of an optimal tax system.[4] Diamond and Mirrlees (1971) showed that tariffs should not be used by a small open economy if it sets the excise tax rates on all goods optimally. However, Boadway, Maital, and Prachowny (1973) and Dixit (1985), among others, have pointed out that tariffs would almost certainly be used if they were the only source of tax revenue and might well be used if the available set of tax instruments is more limited than assumed in Diamond and Mirrlees (1971). They do not examine the characteristics of an optimal tariff when some but not the full range of domestic taxes are used.[5]

A variety of other explanations have been proposed for the observed use of tariffs and export subsidies. In many political economy models of rent-seeking behavior, tariffs or quantitative restrictions result from the lobbying behavior of economic agents who then compete for the revenue or license premia associated with the protection.[6] This work is summarized in Bhagwati (1982). A very different class of models has found that increasing returns to scale may give rise to welfare-enhancing trade taxes or subsidies. In these models, nicely surveyed by Helpman (1984), a firm produces with increasing returns to scale. If the returns to scale are external to the individual firm, firm output may be suboptimal, and trade policy can address this externality. If, on the other hand, the returns to scale are realized by the firm itself, the resulting market structure tends toward one of large firms with market power. This, in turn, leads to another body of research. The results here often yield welfare-enhancing trade taxes or subsidies. This is the strategic trade policy literature. Here, trade taxes levied by a government act as a credible precommitment and alter the ensuing game played by firms. This literature is well surveyed in Grossman and Richardson (1985).

The objective of this paper is not to question the plausibility of these alternative explanations. Instead, our objective is to reexamine the pattern and characteristics of net trade distortions, taking into account both border taxes and the trade distortions created by internal taxes, to see to what degree the empirical regularities motivating these other papers still seem to exist once the effects of domestic taxes are taken into account.

The outline of our paper is as follows. In section 10.1, we develop a theoretical model of optimal tax and tariff policies in the presence of administrative costs. Numerical simulations of this model will be used to provide a clearer sense of the economic implications of the model. This model will then be used to forecast the pattern of trade distortions across countries and to examine the implications of international agreements banning tariffs.

In section 10.2, we examine IMF data on government financial statistics from a variety of countries in recent years, to see to what degree the forecasts of our model are consistent with the data. In particular, we will attempt to compare average tariff rates and average production tax rates to see to what degree the resulting trade distortions are offsetting.

10.1 Theoretical Analysis of Optimal Taxes and Tariffs

In examining the characteristics of the optimal tax and tariff policy in a small open economy, let us start with the standard optimal tax framework used by Diamond and Mirrlees (1971) and assume that all outputs are tradable but that inputs are not. They showed that, as long as the government has use of excise taxes on all goods, then under the tax policy that minimizes efficiency costs production will occur on the production possibilities frontier. International trading opportunities are in effect another production technology, extending the production possibilities frontier.[7]

As a result, under optimal policies, the value of domestic output, based on world prices, would be maximized conditional on the supplies of all factors. A marginal increase in the output in one industry at the expense of output in any other industry, holding aggregate factor supplies constant, would not affect the value of domestic output in the world market. We will refer to this situation as one in which there are no trade distortions. Note, however, that the optimal taxes will still change trade patterns by changing the pattern of domestic consumption and factor supplies.

We rederive the Diamond-Mirrlees result to provide a formal comparison with other results that we examine below. In particular, assume that a country produces two goods using two factors and constant returns to scale technologies. Assume that the government can collect revenue using excise taxes on the value of goods produced or on the value of factors supplied and using tariffs on imports.[8]

We start by defining notation. Consumption of good i by household h is denoted by C_{hi}, the supply of factor j by the household is denoted by K_{hj}, while its endowment of this factor is K_{hj}^*. The utility of household h is denoted by $U_h(C_{h1}, C_{h2}, K_{h1}^* - K_{h1}, K_{h2}^* - K_{h2})$. Utility functions can differ among the H households. Let the price that consumers pay for good i be denoted by q_i, while the amount they are paid per unit of factor j supplied is r_j. Each consumer's demand for the two goods, and supply of the two factors, depends only on these two output prices and two factor prices. By substituting these demand and factor supply functions into the direct utility function, we obtain the indirect utility function of household h, denoted by $V_h(q_1, q_2, r_1, r_2)$. In order to fix the domestic price level, we assume that the numeraire is the price of good 2, so that $q_2 = 1$.

If K_{ij} denotes the amount of the jth factor used in the domestic production of the ith good, then domestic output of that good, denoted X_i, satisfies $X_i = f^i(K_{i1}, K_{i2})$, where the production function has constant returns to scale. Let p_i denote the price that domestic firms receive for output of good i, and let s_j be the amount that they pay per unit for input j. These prices can differ from the prices that individuals face because of excise taxes on production. If $c^i(s_1, s_2)$ denotes the unit cost function in industry i, then competition implies that

$$(1) \qquad\qquad p_i = c^i(s_1, s_2).$$

Government revenue, denoted R, is used to buy the two goods on international markets to maximize some measure of the welfare of government expenditures. We assume that the country is a price taker on these international markets. Let government purchases of good i be denoted by G_i. Since international prices are taken as given, we can denote the resulting welfare derived from government expenditures by $W(R)$.

If M_i denotes imports of good i, then materials balance implies that

$$(2) \qquad\qquad \sum_h C_{hi} + G_i = f^i(K_{i1}, K_{i2}) + M_i.$$

By assumption, no trade takes place in factor markets,[9] so that

$$(3) \qquad\qquad \sum_h K_{hj} = \sum_i K_{ij}.$$

Let the price, in units of the second good, that must be paid for good i in the international markets be denoted by p_i^*. These prices can differ from domestic consumer prices because of tariffs. Trade balance then requires that

$$(4) \qquad\qquad \sum_i p_i^* M_i = 0.$$

The government's tax and tariff rates are implicit in the above prices. In particular, if we denote the tariff on good i by t_i, then $q_i = p_i^*(1 + t_i)$.[10]

Similarly, if the tax rate on the value of production of good i is denoted by τ_i and the tax on supply of factor j is γ_j, then $q_i = p_i(1 + \tau_i)$ and $r_j = s_j(1 - \gamma_j)$.

In order to have a well-defined set of optimal taxes, we must restrict the set of possible taxes further. Note, for example, that tax revenue from tariffs equals $\Sigma_i t_i p_i^* M_i$. But, given equation (4), the revenue would be exactly the same if the tariff rates were instead $t_i - a$ for any value of a. We therefore assume that there is a nonzero tariff only on good 1. Similarly, revenue from the remaining taxes equals $\Sigma_i [\tau_i p_i X_i + \Sigma_j \gamma_j s_j K_{ij}]$. But competition and constant returns to scale imply that $\Sigma_i p_i X_i = \Sigma_i \Sigma_j s_j K_{ij}$, implying that lowering all the τ_i and raising all the γ_j by some constant b will have no effect on tax revenue or on incentives. Therefore, we can add or subtract a constant from all the other tax rates and again leave revenue unchanged. We normalize by assuming that $\tau_2 = 0$, implying that $p_2 = 1$.

The government is then assumed to choose the tax and tariff rates t_1, τ_1, γ_1, and γ_2, given international prices p_i^*, so as to maximize some measure of social welfare that we denote by $\Sigma_h V_h + W(R)$. It does so subject to equations (1)–(4).

In order to understand the solution to this problem, we start by solving an easier problem and then show that the two problems have the same solution. In particular, assume that the government can control directly the consumer prices, q_1, r_1, and r_2, and all production and international trade decisions, subject to the restriction that consumer markets clear at the chosen prices. With these powers, the government can do at least as well as in the previous case since it can duplicate any solution to the previous problem. However, we will also show that it can do no better.

To begin with, the government fully determines consumer behavior through its choice of the prices q_1, r_1, and r_2. In making production and trade decisions, given its choices on consumer prices, its sole objective would be to maximize R since the consumer prices completely determine each of the V_h. But, by equations (2) and (4), $R = \Sigma_i p_i^* G_i = \Sigma_i p_i^* (X_i - C_i)$, where C_i, $= \Sigma_h C_{hi}$. Since consumer prices determine C_i, production decisions will be made so as to maximize $\Sigma_i p_i^* X_i$ subject to equation (3). Resources will therefore be allocated to maximize the value of output, based on international prices, given factor supplies. Production is therefore efficient.

Note that the resulting optimal allocations are just those that would be produced by a competitive market facing $p_1 = p_1^*$ and facing those s_j that clear the factor markets, given the factor supplies implied by the consumer prices. The desired consumer prices can then be produced by setting t_1 based on the difference between the desired q_1 and p_1^* and setting the γ_j based on the differences between the desired r_j and s_j. This solution is therefore a feasible outcome of the first optimization problem. Since it is the optimal solution to a more general problem, it is the optimal solution to the first problem.

We therefore conclude that, if a country has use of all excise taxes, then it would never choose to distort trade patterns. But, given the proposed tax and tariff system, $p_1 = p_1^*$ only if $t_1 = \tau_1$. Therefore, if excise taxes on output are based on production rather than consumption, then the optimal tariff on imports is at the same rate as is assessed on domestic production of that good. This tax system is equivalent to various other tax systems, requiring care in comparing it to observed tax and tariff systems. For example, we can replace both the production tax on good 1 and the tariff on imports of good 1 with just a sales tax at the same rate on consumption of good 1 without changing the resulting allocation. We can also replace the tax on imports of good 1 with a tax at the appropriate rate on exports of good 2 (e.g., choose a different value of a). This is simply the Lerner symmetry result. Similarly, we can alter the consumer taxes so that all consumer prices change proportionately (i.e. change b,) without changing the resulting allocation. Sales can be taxed either directly or through a VAT. In addition, a proportional income tax could be introduced, with appropriate modifications in the other tax rates, without changing the allocation.

All these results describe the optimal allocation for a small country facing fixed prices on the international market. In order to describe the choice problem faced by a large country, we could replace equation (4) in the above derivation with a more complicated function describing the trading opportunities faced by a large country and redefine the function, $W(R)$, determining the welfare produced by government revenue. Standard types of results concerning the optimal trade distortion would come out of the model. This trade distortion would show up as a difference between the optimal tariff and the production tax rates.

What happens, in this model, if an international agreement were signed forbidding tariffs? Since a tariff along with an equal rate tax on domestic production is equivalent to a sales tax on domestic consumption of that good, a country could simply eliminate the tariff, reduce the tax rate on domestic production by the initial tariff rate, and increase the tax on domestic consumption by the initial tariff rate, leaving the allocation entirely unchanged. In fact, when the Common Market was set up, there was an attempt to shift domestic tax systems away from taxes such as a turnover tax that create trade distortions and toward a destination-based VAT, which does not distort trade patterns.[11] These modifications to domestic taxes on production and consumption would be very hard to prevent by international agreement, given most countries' reluctance to accept restrictions on their choice of a domestic tax structure. But, if the adjustments do occur, then the international agreements forbidding tariffs accomplish nothing.

Why then does so much attention and effort get devoted to these treaties forbidding tariffs? One possible explanation is that the adjustments in the domestic tax system that are necessary to replace tariffs are not so easy and so may not in fact happen. The equivalent domestic taxes may, for example, be much more expensive to administer. But, if we introduce administrative costs, the optimal tax argument given above must be changed to take these costs into account. If these administrative costs are important enough to prevent countries from entirely replacing tariffs with suitable modifications to their domestic tax systems, then these costs should be large enough to have important effects on the characteristics of an optimal tax/tariff system.

Various approaches could be taken to model administrative costs. Aizenman (1987), for example, assumed that the administrative costs from a particular tax were proportional to the revenue raised by that tax, with the proportionality factors differing by tax. This approach does not strike us as entirely satisfactory, however, since the bureaucracy necessary to run a tax system and monitor tax returns should be approximately the same regardless of the tax rate.[12] We therefore explore an alternative approach in which there is some fixed cost to using a given tax base, regardless of the tax rate chosen, with the size of the fixed cost varying by tax base.

How does the previous analysis change if we introduce fixed costs for each tax base? To begin with, when there are alternative taxes that are exactly equivalent, then a country would consider using only that one with the cheapest fixed cost. If, in spite of the fixed costs, the country uses the same set of taxes as analyzed above or their equivalents, then the first-order conditions characterizing the optimal tax structure remain the same, as does the conclusion that there will be no trade distortions.

If the fixed costs are high enough to force a country to restrict its set of tax instruments further, however, then results can change. To take an extreme case, if the fixed costs are too high on all taxes except a tariff on good 1 but government revenue is valuable enough to make it worth paying the fixed cost to use this tariff, then trade distortions certainly exist. In intermediate cases, when some but not all of the other taxes analyzed above are used, trade distortions may still be desired. As Diamond and Mirrlees (1971) point out, production efficiency may not be optimal if the government does not have use of a full set of excise taxes.

Consider, for example, the special case in which, because of fixed costs, a country taxes production of good 1 and taxes imports and exports but does not tax factor incomes. This may provide a crude description of the tax system in a number of poorer countries, if we interpret good 1 to be industrial goods. Industrial production, imports, and exports are quite easy to tax since there are normally few industrial firms and few ports of entry. In contrast, agricultural output and retail sales are much more difficult to tax, given the large number of small firms involved. For mathematical convenience, in the formal analysis of this case we examine the equivalent system of a sales tax on good 1, denoted by σ, and a tax on domestic production of good 1, denoted by τ, ignoring any implications for administrative costs.

In this setting, will a country choose to distort trade patterns by taxing or subsidizing domestic production? If not, then the optimal production tax should be zero. To judge this, let us examine a country's optimal tax rates. Under our assumptions, the country will choose these rates so as to maximize.

(5) $$\sum_h V_h(p_1^*(1 + \sigma), 1, r_1, r_2) + W(\sigma p_1^* C_1 + \tau p_1 X_1),$$

subject to equations (1)–(4). If we let the marginal utility of income to household h be denoted by α_h, let $\bar{\alpha}$ equal the unweighted average value of the α_h, and let ϵ_q represent the uncompensated own price elasticity of C_1, then the resulting first-order conditions can be expressed as follows:[13]

(6a) $$(W' - \bar{\alpha}) + W'\left[-\epsilon_q\left(\frac{\sigma}{1 + \sigma}\right) + \left(\frac{\tau}{C_1(1 + \tau)}\right)\frac{\partial X_1}{\partial \sigma}\right]$$

$$- H \, \mathrm{cov}\left(\alpha_h, \frac{C_{h1}}{C_1}\right) = 0,$$

and

(6b) $$(W' - \bar{\alpha})\frac{p_1 X_1}{1 + \tau} + W'\left[\sigma p_1^* \frac{\partial C_1}{\partial \tau} + \tau p_1 \frac{\partial X_1}{\partial \tau}\right]$$

$$+ \sum_j H \, \mathrm{cov}(\alpha_h, K_{hj})\frac{\partial r_j}{\partial \tau} = 0.$$

In each of these equations, the first term on the left-hand side measures the gain from shifting extra revenue from a representative individual, with marginal utility of income equal to $\bar{\alpha}$, to the government. The second term measures any resulting efficiency loss. This efficiency loss arises owing to changes in C_1 and X_1 since in each case the marginal benefits differ from the marginal costs owing to taxes.[14] The remaining terms measure the distributional gains or losses resulting from the tax change. For example, if the "deserving" individuals, who have a relatively high value of α_h, also have a relatively low value of C_{h1}, then the covariance in equation (6a) is negative, implying that a tax increase is more attractive since it is paid more heavily by those with low α's.

If the optimal tax policy does not distort trade, then at this optimum $\tau = 0$. If, however, the left-hand side of equation (6b) is necessarily positive when evaluated at this point, then we know that the optimal τ is positive, and conversely. In order to shed light on the sign of the left-hand side of equation (6b), when evaluated at $\tau = 0$, we need to know more about the derivative $\partial C_1/\partial \tau = \Sigma_h \, \partial C_{h1}/\partial \tau$. Increasing the tax on production affects consumption of good 1 because it affects factor prices, even though it does not change output prices. In order to simplify the story, let us assume that the utility function is additively separable between consumption and factor supplies, so that each individual's demand curve for good 1 depends only on output prices and factor income, denoted by Y_h, where factor income equals

$\sum_j r_j K_{hj}$. In addition, let β_{h1} represent the fraction of extra factor income spent on good 1 by household h, and let $\bar{\beta}_1$ be the average value of β_{h1}.[15] Under these assumptions,

$$(7) \qquad \frac{\partial C_1}{\partial \tau} = \frac{\bar{\beta}_1}{q_1}\left(-\frac{p_1 X_1}{1 + \tau} + \sum_j r_j \frac{\partial K_j}{\partial \tau}\right) + H \, \text{cov}\left(\frac{\beta_{h1}}{q_1}, \frac{\partial Y_h}{\partial \tau}\right).$$

Here, the first term on the right-hand side equals the average drop in C_1 per dollar drop in income times the aggregate change in income. The drop in income includes both the direct effect of the tax change plus the effects of any resulting behavioral response. The second term captures any effects arising from the income drop being concentrated in households where β_{h1} is particularly large or small.

If we substitute the value of $(W' - \bar{\alpha})$ from equation (6a) into (6b) and make use of equation (7), we find that the value of the left-hand side of equation (6b) equals

$$(8) \qquad \frac{W'\sigma}{1 + \sigma}\left[p_1^* X_1(\epsilon_q - \bar{\beta}_1) + \bar{\beta}_1 \sum_j r_j \frac{\partial K_j}{\partial \tau} + H \, \text{cov}\left(\beta_{h1}, \frac{\partial Y_h}{\partial \tau}\right)\right]$$

$$+ p_1^* X_1 H \, \text{cov}\left(\alpha_h, \frac{C_{h1}}{C_1}\right) + H \sum_j \text{cov}(\alpha_h, K_{hj}) \frac{\partial r_j}{\partial \tau}.$$

In general, this expression can take on either sign, indicating that optimal trade distortions can be either positive or negative. However, if factor supplies are inelastic with respect to uncompensated changes in factor prices, and if the three covariances are small, then this expression is positive as long as $\epsilon_q > \bar{\beta}_1$. If the utility function were Cobb-Douglas, then $\epsilon_q = 1$, and β_1 is the fraction of total income spent on good 1 and so is less than one, implying that the optimal τ is positive. In this special case, trade would be *subsidized*.

The intuition for this result is fairly straightforward. By ignoring the covariance terms, distributional effects are ignored, implying that all that matters are revenue gains and efficiency losses. The efficiency loss from raising a dollar of extra revenue by any means, starting from a situation with only a sales tax on good 1, equals the resulting drop in consumption of good 1 times the sales tax rate. When the sales tax is used to raise extra revenue, the price of good 1 rises, and the resulting drop in consumption of good 1 depends on its own price elasticity, ϵ_q. In contrast, when a production tax is used, the average rate of return to factor supplies drops. If we ignore changes in factor supplies, then this drop in income leads to a drop in expenditures on all goods, where the drop in expenditures on good 1 is proportional to β_1.

If the sum of the remaining terms is sufficiently negative, however, trade may end up being discouraged rather than encouraged. If, for example, the change in factor supplies under a production tax results in a further fall in income, then consumption of good 1 will fall yet more, making a production tax less attractive. Estimating the direction of change in factor supplies owing to a rise in τ is complicated, however. To begin with, the uncompensated price elasticity of a factor can in general be either positive or negative. In addition, while a tax on production of good 1 must lower the return to the factor used relatively more in industry 1 versus industry 2, it must *raise* the return to the other factor.[16] All we can say is that, if the uncompensated price elasticity of the factor used most heavily in industry 1 is large enough and the uncompensated price elasticity of the other factor is not too high, then results could reverse. If good 1 is industrial output and good 2 is agriculture, then an increase in τ would presumably hurt capital owners and skilled workers, while incomes of farmers would necessarily increase since the cost of other factor inputs has dropped while output prices remain unchanged. The supplies of capital and skilled labor are likely to be quite elastic, more elastic than the supply of farmers, so this reversal could well happen.

The third term in brackets may also be negative. This would occur if capital owners and skilled workers spend a larger fraction of their incomes on industrial goods. As a result, the drop in income that arises from an increase in τ would be largest among those most likely to buy industrial goods, resulting in a larger fall in C_1.

The last two terms in equation (8) capture distributional implications of the tax change. If the tax on production of good 1 lowers the incomes of capital owners and skilled workers and raises the incomes of farmers, this may make the tax more desirable because of its distributional effects.[17] Because of these conflicting pressures, in general the optimal trade distortion could be of either sign.

If other subsets of the initial set of tax instruments were used, the analysis is similar, but the conditions determining whether trade is encouraged or discouraged are at least as complicated. Rather than develop these cases explicitly, we provide some numerical examples below to provide some sense of the nature of the resulting optimal tax rates. Given the common use of nontariff trade distortions, however, we thought it useful to discuss the characteristics of the optimal policies when nontariff barriers to trade are used instead of tariffs or the equivalent tax barriers. The particular example we choose to focus on is one in which a country uses a tax on production of good 1 to raise revenue but in addition has the power to restrict imports of good 1. How will the resulting policy compare with one in which explicit tariffs are used instead?

One complication that must be addressed in this situation is who receives the rents that arise from imports that cost less on the international market than they sell for on the domestic market? If the government were to sell import licenses, then the government receives these rents in the form of license fees. With market clearing license fees, quotas have identical economic effects to tariffs.[18] Similarly, if licenses were distributed in proportion to supplies of either or both factors, then the results would again be identical to those found with explicit tariffs—the subsidy to factor supplies created by the distribution rule for the licenses would, under optimal policies, be offset by a surtax that raises as much revenue as is lost through giving away the licenses. If import licenses are distributed without charge, however, then results will differ. We explore two special cases. In the first, licenses are distributed in a lump-sum fashion among domestic residents or perhaps as a function of the exogenous K_{hj}^*. Alternatively, the import licenses could be distributed among foreign firms as, for example, with a voluntary export restraint (VER).

If the nontariff barriers to trade lead to a domestic price for good 1 equal to $q_1 > p_1^*$, rents derived from imports equal $(q_1 - p_1^*)M_1$, which we denote by π_1. Assume that the rents are given to domestic residents and that the fraction θ_h of these rents goes to household h. What will be the nature of the optimal policy? Rather than describing the resulting first-order conditions in detail, we simply point out some important aspects of the problem.

Let us focus first on the policy in which the net distortion to trade is zero, so that $p_1^* = p_1$, implying that $\tau = (q_1 - p_1^*)/p_1$. At any given tax rate τ, the outcome is the same as would occur with a sales tax on good 1 at a rate $\sigma_1 = \tau_1$ along with a lump-sum transfer to each household h equal to $\theta_h(q_1 - p_1^*)M_1 > 0$. In contrast, an explicit tariff in combination with a production tax at the same rate on good 1 is exactly equivalent to a sales tax, without any lump-sum transfers. Therefore, at each possible production tax rate, aggregate tax revenues are lower when nontariff rather than tariff barriers are used, creating pressure to raise tax rates to compensate for this loss in revenue. The marginal efficiency cost of raising tax revenue, at any initial value of τ, may not even be higher when nontariff rather than tariff barriers are present since aggregate lump-sum transfers could well decline as q_1 rises if M_1 drops by enough in response. Another complication that arises in this situation is that distributional benefits (or costs) may result from the lump-sum transfers, making higher tax rates more (less) attractive. Optimal tax rates can therefore be either larger or smaller when nontariff barriers replace tariff barriers.

The same complications arise as previously in determining the nature of the net trade distortions. In addition, however, if we were to increase τ_1, holding q_1 fixed, lump-sum transfers now increase as long as imports increase, whereas previously tariff revenue increased. As a result, protection is more valuable than before.

If rents from the difference between foreign and domestic prices of good 1 go to foreigners, the government may still wish to impose nontariff barriers. By doing so, output of the taxed good increases, allowing government expenditures to expand. As long as these extra government expenditures are valued highly enough, trade restrictions will appear attractive.[19]

This discussion of the effects of nontariff barriers can be applied also to foreign exchange controls. Through administrative control of the exchange rate, domestic prices can differ from world prices. If the resulting controls reduce international trade, then $p_1^*/p_2^* < q_1/q_2$. As a result, while $\Sigma_j \, p_j^* M_j = 0$, under foreign exchange controls $\Sigma_j \, q_j M_j > 0$. With explicit tariffs, $\Sigma_j \, q_j M_j$ simply equals tariff revenue. If the government sells access to foreign exchange or receives all the rents through a government monopoly controlling all international trade, then again the results would be the same as with explicit tariffs. If access to foreign exchange is given away, however, then the analysis would be the same as with nontariff barriers.

10.1.1 Numerical Example

In order to shed further light on the nature of optimal policies, we decided to explore a simple numerical example. Specifically, we assumed that both the production functions and the utility functions were Cobb-Douglas. Let the share of revenue in industry i used to purchase inputs of factor 1 be denoted by λ_{i1}; the rest of the revenue is used to purchase the second factor. Assume that there are two types of households. The first type supplies only the first factor, and the second type supplies only the second factor. The utility function of the hth type is denoted by $U_h = \Sigma_i \, \beta_{hi} \ln C_{hi} + \beta_{h3} \ln (K_h^* - K_h) + \beta_{h4} \ln R$, where $\Sigma_{i=1}^3 \beta_{hi} = 1$. The government chooses its policy so as to maximize $\Sigma_i \, \omega_i U_i$. In interpreting these results, we assume that factor 1 is capital, factor 2 is labor, good 1 is industrial output, and good 2 is agricultural output. Type 1 households are therefore capital owners, while type 2 households are workers. We assume that $\lambda_{11} = .7$ and $\lambda_{21} = .3$, so that industrial production is relatively capital intensive. In addition, we assume that $\beta_{11} = .65$ and $\beta_{21} = .5$, so that capital owners spend relatively more of their income on industrial goods. The compensated own price elasticities of factor supplies are initially set equal to .15, and factor endowments are each initially set equal to 1.0. Finally, we set $p_1^* = .9$ and $\beta_{h4} = .2$. These parameters imply that good 1 will be imported, except under extreme policies.

Several idiosyncratic characteristics of this model should be pointed out. To begin with, uncompensated factor supply elasticities are zero, eliminating this consideration from the analysis. In addition, some care is needed when interpreting distributional effects. We did not build in diminishing marginal utility of income. As a result, the marginal social utility of income to household h equals simply $\omega_h V_h/r_h$, so that a higher utility level in itself implies a higher marginal utility of income. In deciding what value of $\omega \equiv \omega_1/\omega_2$ is reasonable, keep in mind that we report the aggregate, not the per capita, income and consumption levels of each group. To the degree that there are fewer capital owners than workers, then the relative income of individual capital versus labor owners exceeds their relative share of aggregate income, implying that a utilitarian objective would likely assign capital owners less weight. In addition, even if each group faced the same factor price, the resulting utility level of the capitalists would differ because of the differing weight they place on consumption of good 1. If the prices of the two consumption goods were the same, the capitalists would have higher reported utility, given the characteristics of a Cobb-Douglas utility function with differing combinations of weights on different goods. To compensate for this, the social welfare weight on their utility would need to be lower. We therefore focus on utility functions with $\omega \leq 1$.

The resulting optimal tax rates are reported in table 10.1. The first two rows in the table report the optimal tariff rate for two different values of the relative weight, ω, on the utility of the capitalists. When the tariff rate increases, capitalists gain relative to workers because output of the capital intensive industry expands, bidding up the rental price of capital relative to the wage rate. However, a higher tariff rate also raises the consumer price of industrial goods, on which capitalists spend a larger share of their income. Given our parameters, the first effect is more important, and the tariff rate rises as capitalists are given more weight in the welfare function.

The next two rows describe the optimal tax rates when both a tariff and a tax on production of good 1 are available. Notice first that the tax rates and the fraction of GDP used for public goods are much higher than when only a tariff is used—raising revenue is far easier with a somewhat broader tax

Table 10.1   Optimal Tax and Tariff Rates

	Tariff on Good 1	Production Tax on Good 1	Net Tariff	Sales Tax on Good 2	Revenue/ GDP	V_K	V_L
Tariff only:							
$\omega = .5$	.105	. . .	.105	. . .	.017	.107	.097
$\omega = 1.0$	.117	. . .	.117	. . .	.017	.108	.096
Tariff and production tax:							
$\omega = .5$	.333	.527	−.127	. . .	.182	.105	.161
$\omega = 1.0$	.375	.331	.033	. . .	.170	.131	.142
Tariff, production tax, sales tax:							
$\omega = .5$	.246	.437	−.133	.154	.194	.107	.161
$\omega = 1.0$	.252	.184	.057	.291	.186	.140	.136
Production tax:							
$\omega = .5$	. . .	.127	−.113	. . .	.020	.083	.118
$\omega = 1.0$	. . .	.114	−.102	. . .	.020	.085	.117
Production tax, sales tax:							
$\omega = .5$	. . .	.153	−.133	.559	.145	.109	.152
$\omega = 1.0$	. . .	.019	−.019	.692	.144	.130	.138

base. (Seen from a different perspective, the fixed costs associated with domestic taxes must be quite large before it is not worth incurring such costs.) As a result, utility levels are also higher, particularly for workers who consume relatively less of the first good. The optimal tax rates are very sensitive to the distributional weight, ω, however. When ω = .5, so that capitalists get less weight, trade is subsidized, implying that imports occur in spite of the fact that the world price of good 1 exceeds the domestic producer price of good 1. The net tariff rate can be measured by $(p_1 - p_1^*)/p_1^* = (t_1 - \tau_1)/(1 + \tau_1)$, which in this case equals -12.7 percent. When ω = 1.0, however, trade is slightly discouraged.[20] As in the previous case when only a tariff was used, trade distortions have conflicting distributional effects, but tariffs on net aid capitalists by increasing demand for the capital intensive good. When ω = 1.0, aiding capitalists is desired because the marginal social utility of income to capitalists exceeds that for workers, given the algebraic properties of the Cobb-Douglas utility functions being used.

The following two rows describe the optimal tax rates when a tariff, a tax on domestic production of good 1, and a tax on domestic sales of good 2 are used.[21] Again, we find that either trade taxes or subsidies are possible, depending on the distributional weights used. Note, however, that social welfare, and the relative size of the government, increase only slightly when we add a sales tax on good 2 to the available tax instruments, implying that only minor fixed costs would lead a country to use a simpler tax system. Since workers buy relatively more of good 2, their welfare falls when this extra tax is introduced, while the welfare of capitalists increases.

In addition, we examined the effects of eliminating tariffs as a possible tax instrument, as might occur under GATT or IMF pressure. If this left the country with only a tax on domestic production of good 1, social welfare and government expenditures would drop substantially. In spite of the loss of tariff revenue, the production tax rate falls dramatically, in order to keep the trade distortion from becoming too large. The loss is large enough to justify large administrative costs of adding further tax instruments. If the country were left with both a tax on domestic production of good 1 and a tax on domestic sales of good 2, then there would be a major shift toward use of the sales tax—the trade distortions created by the production tax are too large to make its use attractive. Given these readjustments in domestic tax rates, eliminating tariffs does not necessarily reduce trade distortions, though trade subsidies become more likely than trade taxes.

We tried a variety of sensitivity tests to see to what degree these results changed as various parameter values were changed. Changing any of the parameters except for the distributional weights had only minor effects on the size of the optimal trade distortions.

In table 10.2, we explore how nontariff barriers would be used if tariffs are not available and only domestic production of good 1 is taxable. For each value of ω, there are three sets of results, describing how the optimal

Table 10.2   Optimal Production Tax and Nontariff Barriers

	Implicit Tariff Good 1	Production Tax on Good 1	Net Implicit Tariff	Revenue/ GDP	V_K	V_L
Licenses to K:						
$\omega = .5$	.538	.510	.019	.169	.135	.136
$\omega = 1.0$	.482	.398	.060	.161	.138	.134
Licenses to L:						
$\omega = .5$	.620	.776	$-.088$	.148	.097	.164
$\omega = 1.0$	.486	.355	.097	.169	.137	.134
Licenses to foreigners:						
$\omega = .5$	.578	.453	.086	.211	.136	.134
$\omega = 1.0$	.495	.342	.114	.172	.141	.131

policies vary, depending on who receives the profits from the import licenses. There are several striking characteristics of these results. To begin with, the optimal nontariff barriers are very high. For example, when the licenses are given to capital owners and $\omega = .5$, the nontariff barrier leads to a domestic price of good 1 that is 53.8 percent above its price in the world market. The optimal nontariff barriers are more restrictive than the optimal tariff barriers. In fact, when the licenses must be given to foreigners, the optimal nontariff barriers are prohibitive, leading to autarky. These high barriers result in increased tax revenue from domestic production of good 1, which helps offset the lost tariff revenue. This increase in production of good 1, which is capital intensive, also helps capital owners to the point where they would normally prefer nontariff to tariff barriers. In contrast, workers would normally prefer tariff barriers. While social welfare is always higher with tariff than with nontariff barriers, the difference is often very small, implying that a country would not put up much resistance to international pressure to drop tariffs. One other surprising result is that capital owners would rather have foreigners receive the import licenses rather than receiving the licenses themselves. When foreigners get the licenses, the government responds by prohibiting imports, leading to a large enough increase in demand for the capital intensive good that the resulting rise in the rental price of capital more than offsets the loss in license revenue.

Table 10.2 also illustrates a general contribution to the literature on tariff-quota (non)equivalence. This literature has adopted a partial equilibrium focus and has concentrated on the existence of uncertainty, dynamics, or imperfect competition to generate tariff-quota nonequivalence. By explicitly modeling quotas in a general equilibrium setting, we have shown that the presence of distorting taxes in a perfectly certain and static competitive economy gives rise to tariff-quota nonequivalence. A formal and more general treatment of this phenomenon is the subject of forthcoming work by the authors.

10.1.2 Implications for Observed Tax Policies

The above derivations characterize the optimal tax/tariff policies conditional on the set of tax and tariff instruments used. The choice of a set of policies depends on the pattern of fixed costs for different combinations of tax instruments. While theory alone cannot tell us the pattern of these fixed costs, we propose the following simple story. Under any tax system, each taxpayer is monitored to some degree and audited with some probability. To do this requires a certain amount of skilled manpower, which owing to pressures toward factor price equalization costs roughly the same in all countries. The average monitoring cost per taxpayer may vary across categories of taxpayers, however, depending, for example, on the complexity of the transactions involved.[22] While the average monitoring cost for a given category of taxpayer should be roughly the same across countries, however, the tax revenue collected per taxpayer will vary substantially, depending primarily on the income level of the country.

Within a country, the relative importance of monitoring costs, compared with revenue raised, is likely to vary substantially across categories of tax. It seems plausible to presume that border taxes collect a lot of revenue relative to monitoring costs since in most countries relatively few people are sufficient to man the border. Taxation of industrial firms is also likely to collect a lot of revenue compared with monitoring costs, owing to the large size of most industrial firms. In contrast, taxation of retail outlets should be significantly more expensive, while a graduated personal income tax should be even more difficult to administer.

In deciding on the optimal choice of tax bases, a country would compare social welfare under each possible system since the choices are nonmarginal. The per capita efficiency and equity gains from shifting to a more flexible tax system are basically proportional to the GDP per capita of a country, while the per capita increase in monitoring costs should be roughly similar across countries. Therefore, richer countries would be expected to choose more flexible tax systems than poorer countries. Since tariffs plausibly have the lowest monitoring costs relative to revenue raised, this story leads us to expect that the poorest countries would rely primarily on tariffs, somewhat less poor countries would use production taxes as well, while richer countries should use a variety of other tax instruments, such as retail sales taxes and personal income taxes.[23]

Therefore, the poorest countries should be observed discouraging trade, owing to their reliance on tariffs to raise revenue. As seen in table 10.1, however, the cost of using such a narrow tax case can be very high, implying that government revenue will be a small fraction of GNP. Somewhat less poor countries may either encourage or discourage trade on net. The figures in table 10.1 suggest that any distortion is likely to be small, however, in spite of the observed use of tariffs. These countries are likely to have a much larger government sector than the poorest countries. The gain from further broadening of the tax base seems to be quite modest, according to the figures in table 10.1. The richest countries, which use the full complement of tax instruments, have no reason to use tariffs unless they have market power, and they can in principle make use of this market power without relying on tariffs. While other more detailed forecasts can be obtained from the theory, the data at this point are inadequate to test them.

What does this model imply would happen if a country were to agree to eliminate any explicit tariffs? Some countries may not have had tariffs to begin with. Even if a country did have tariffs, in principle it can eliminate the tariff yet duplicate its effects, for example, by cutting the production tax on each good by the original size of the tariff on that good and by raising the sales tax rate on the good by the same amount. However, these changes may create extra administrative costs, which may not be worth the price. For example, if a country initially has a tax on production of good 1 and a tariff on imports of good 1 but no sales tax on good 1, what happens if the tariff is eliminated? Tariff revenue is lost, and in addition production of good 1 will fall since imports are now cheaper, implying a drop in government revenue. This increase in imports can be offset with nontariff barriers, though the revenue from tariffs is still lost. Alternatively, the government can pay the fixed costs to expand its tax system. The net effect of eliminating tariffs on trade distortions will vary, depending on the set of taxes used after tariffs are eliminated. The results in our numerical example suggest that trade distortions are not likely to be reduced significantly as a result of eliminating tariffs and may well get worse.[24]

10.2 Estimates of Actual Trade Distortions

Rather than developing a formal test of the above theory, our intent in this section is to shed light on the actual pattern of trade distortions, taking account of both tariffs and the trade distortions created by the domestic tax systems in various countries. We begin by describing the data and their limitations. We then explain how the data are used to investigate linkages between domestic taxes and border taxes. We conclude with the presentation and discussion of the results.

10.2.1 The Data and Their Limitations

Our primary data source is the IMF's Government Financial Statistics (GFS), which report total tax and nontax revenue collected by the central government in all major countries from 1970 to 1987. Several components of total tax revenue are reported. We use data on revenue from corporate taxes, payroll or manpower taxes, individual income taxes, domestic sales and value added taxes on goods and services, import duties, and export duties. These variables give a rough breakdown of the share of government revenue from different sources but say nothing about the corresponding tax rates.[25]

In order to obtain an estimate of the tax rate associated with each tax, some estimate of the relevant tax base is necessary. We use the data from the IMF's International Finance Statistics (IFS), which provide national data on the levels of imports and exports, private consumption, and GDP (all in the domestic currency). We also obtain data on population, the exchange rate (domestic currency to U.S. dollar), and a GDP deflator from the IFS. Finally, data on the 1980 share of GDP that is industrial output is obtained from the World Development Report (World Bank 1980).

Tax rates are formed for each of the thirty-three countries in our sample as follows.[26] The import tariff rate is given by import tariff revenue divided by value of imports. The export tax rate is analogously defined.[27] Construction of other tax rates is less straightforward.

The production tax rate is intended to measure the degree to which relative domestic output prices are distorted by the domestic tax system, resulting in a trade distortion. Which of the reported taxes distort relative output prices? Presumably, corporate taxes do so because effective rates vary by sector and because parts of the economy are noncorporate. While, in some circumstances, sales taxes may further distort the relative prices of domestic output, we do not have enough information to judge when this is the case.[28] Similarly, personal income tax rates and property tax rates may differ by industry. For example, it is much easier to tax the labor income, capital income, or capital value in the industrial sector than to tax the income or capital of farmers and other self-employed individuals.[29] Since any trade distortions created by sales, personal income, and property taxes likely vary greatly be country and in ways that are unknown given the available data, we chose to ignore any trade distortions created by these taxes. A further question concerns how to treat nontax revenue. This revenue can come from a variety of sources. Our presumption was that a primary source of this revenue was profits from state enterprises in the industrial sector. We therefore chose to define revenue from production taxes to equal corporate tax revenue plus nontax revenue. To the extent that nontax revenue comes from other sources, our results may be misleading.[30] The tax base for the production tax is taken to be industrial output. The resulting figure for the production tax rate, which equals production tax revenue divided by industrial output, is therefore an average tax rate on industrial output.[31]

Industrial output is itself a constructed variable for years other than 1980. We first regress the 1980 industrial share of GDP on real per capita GDP (denoted in 1980 U.S. dollars) and its square.[32] Using the actual 1980 value for the industrial share (I_{80}) as a seed value, we create a time series of I for each country according to the relation:

$$I_t = I_{80} + \alpha_1(\text{GPD}_t - \text{GDP}_{80}) + \alpha_2(\text{GDP}_t^2 - \text{GDP}_{80}^2),$$

where the α's are from the estimated regression. The production tax rate is then set equal to reported production tax revenue divided by the product of GDP and our estimate of the industrial share of GDP.

Given the various strong assumptions that must be made to construct a production tax *rate* from the available data, we also construct two alternative measures of the production tax rate. In one alternative measure, we exclude nontax revenue. Since nontax revenue can come from a variety of sources, we want to check on the role of nontax revenue in our results. We also compute production tax rates using GDP instead of the industrial share of GDP as the tax base. For richer countries, this may yield more accurate rates.

Finally, we compute sales tax rates and individual income tax rates. In each case, we use GDP as the tax base. Revenues from sales taxes are reported on the GFS tape. We take revenues from payroll taxes as well as revenues collected from individuals as the revenue of our income tax. These very gross approximations are presented only to give some feel for the structure of tax rates other than trade or production tax rates.

We made no attempt to measure nontariff barriers (NTBs). Nogues, Olechowski, and Winters (1986) report the percentage of trade affected by NTBs in sixteen industrial countries but say nothing about the implicit tariff rates associated with these NTBs. Leamer (1988) presents a thorough and amusing account of the problems associated with attempting to carefully construct a more satisfactory NTB data base. Countries may differ in their reliance on tariff versus nontariff barriers to trade. As a result, observed differences in the use of tariffs across countries at a given date, or across time for a given country, may provide a very misleading indication of the differences in tariff plus nontariff barriers. Similarly, we know virtually nothing about nontax distortions within the domestic economy. Many countries, for example, have regulations causing agricultural prices to differ systematically from marginal costs, yet we would not know this given the available data.

In addition, from these data alone, we know nothing about which goods are subject to tariffs and production taxes. On the basis of the theory, what we want to measure is the difference between the tariff rate and the production tax rate for each good. Aggregate revenue figures from production taxes and tariffs shed no light on these differences. For example, if production of only industrial goods is taxed and imports of agricultural goods are taxed, the implied distortions are very different than if both taxes and tariffs apply only to industrial goods, yet we cannot tell these two scenarios apart in the data.

10.2.2 Application of the Data to the Model

Even if we knew everything about the domestic tax system, there is a further conceptual question concerning how to measure the size of any trade distortion. All we have claimed so far is that there are no trade distortions if a marginal increase in the output in one industry at the expense of output in any other industry, holding aggregate factor supplies constant, does not affect the value of domestic output in the world market. To the extent that this is not the case, trade patterns are distorted.

There are a variety of ways of measuring the extent to which marginal reallocations of resources can lead to a change in the value of total output, measured at world prices. For example, in a two-good setting, extra output in one industry can be produced with many different combinations of factor movements from the other industry. If production had been efficient, any marginal change has no effect on the value of total output. If production were not efficient, however, then the resulting change in the value of total output would depend on the composition of the factors that are shifted between industries. The approach that we adopt is to measure the change in the value of total output if industry 1 produces one more unit, using its *existing* technology, with industry 2 then using whatever factors are left. We will use this change in the value of total output as an estimate of the size of any trade distortions.

These trade distortions arise from domestic taxes and tariffs in our model. In order to simplify the interpretation of the resulting measure, we use the same normalizations of the tax law described in section 10.1. In particular, we set the tax rate on the output of industry 2 and the tariff on imports of good 2 at zero, making the required adjustments in the other tax and tariff rates. In addition, we now allow for factor taxes at the firm level, with rates varying by firm, in addition to the factor taxes faced by individuals. However, we define the individual tax on each factor to equal the combined firm and individual factor tax rates in industry 2, thereby by construction setting the firms' factor tax rates in industry 2 equal to zero. This normalization then defines the factor tax rates in industry 1. Let the resulting tax rate on inputs of factor j in industry i equal γ_{ij}, and let the resulting required before-tax rate of return on factor j in industry i equal s_{ij}.

If industry 1 expands output by one unit, using its existing technology, and industry 2 loses these inputs, then the change in the value of total output, denoted Δ, equals

$$(8a) \qquad \Delta = \sum_j (p_1^* f_j^1 - p_2^* f_j^2)\left(\frac{K_{1j}}{X_1}\right).$$

But competitive behavior implies that $p_i \partial f^i/\partial K_{ij} = r_j/(1 - \gamma_{ij})$, while competitive pricing implies that $p_i^* = p_i(1 + \tau_i)/(1 + t_i)$. Using these expressions to simplify equation (8a), given the above normalizations, we find that Δ equals

(8b) $$\Delta = \tau p_1 - t p_1^* + \sum_j \gamma_{1j} s_{1j} (K_{1j}/X_1).$$

But this expression simply equals the sum of all the extra taxes due if output of the first good increases by a unit and imports of this good decrease by a unit, with output and imports of good 2 changing as required. Equation (8b) then describes our measure of the extent of any trade distortions. We will need to be careful in using it, however, because of the various normalizations of the tax and tariff rates.

In making use of the available data to estimate the extent of any trade distortions, we make the following assumptions. First, we assume that each economy consists of two sectors, an urban industrial sector and an agricultural sector. We assume that production tax revenue is collected entirely from firms in the industrial sector.[33] To the extent that other sectors are subject to production taxes, our results will be misleading. For example, at least in the richer countries, services and other primarily nontraded goods may well form an important part of the production tax base. A production tax on nontraded goods is equivalent to a consumption tax on these goods and does not distort the efficiency with which the existing output is produced. Therefore, to the extent to which services are subject to the production tax, this part of the revenue should not in principle be included in our measure of the trade distortion created by the production tax.

We measured the average tax rate on imports and the average tax rate on exports as discussed above. Let e denote the export tax rate, so that $(1+e)p_i = p_i^*$ on whatever good i is exported, and let t' denote the tariff rate on imports. Then, when we renormalize the tariff rates to set the export tax rate to zero, the resulting tariff rate, t, equals $t' + e(1 + t')$. We made no attempt to capture the presence of nontariff barriers.

Whether tariffs offset the trade distortion created by the production tax depends on whether the country exports or imports industrial goods. If it imports these goods, then the production tax encourages trade, whereas if it exports these goods, then the production tax discourages trade. In contrast, when tariffs collect positive revenue, they serve to discourage trade. Therefore, the two distortions offset if industrial goods are imported and reinforce if industrial goods are exported. Unfortunately, we have no data on the composition of each country's exports and imports. We therefore made the crude assumption that the countries in the richest two quintiles export industrial goods to countries in the poorest three quintiles.[34] Given our assumption that industrial goods are imported in the countries in the poorest three quintiles, production taxes in these countries encourage international trade, offsetting the effects of any tariffs. Therefore, the net distortion to trade, as shown in equation (8b), is the tariff rate minus the production tax rate. In the countries in the richest two quintiles, however, we assume that industrial goods are exported, in which case the production tax discourages international trade, reinforcing the effects of any tariff. Therefore, the net distortion to trade in these countries equals the tariff rate *plus* the production tax rate.[35]

10.2.3 Data Analysis and Results

In this paper, we simply report our estimates of various average tax rates and the implied net trade distortions and do not attempt a more formal statistical test of the above theory. Given the many weaknesses of the available data, any more ambitious use of the data seemed inappropriate.[36]

Table 10.3 illustrates the structure of tax rates in 1980, reporting results for five groups of countries divided according to their per capita GDP.[37] The table reports the mean tax rate (and its standard deviation) within each group of countries for each tax as well as the implied trade distortion. The cell for the first row and first column, for example, tells us that the countries in our sample that fall into the bottom quintile of per capita income have on average a tariff rate of 21.4 percent. The same tax rate for countries falling in the top quintile of per capita income is only 1.6 percent.

The first row of table 10.3 gives the import tax rate, t'. The second row gives the export tax rate, e, while the third row corresponds to the net border distortion, $t' + e(1 + t')$. The fourth row of table 10.3 give the production tax rate as described above. The fifth row then provides a summary measure of the net trade distortion, based on our assumption that only industrial goods are subject to the production tax and that these goods are imported by countries in the poorest three quintiles and exported by countries in the richest two quintiles. A positive value for the net trade distortion implies that on average the combination of trade and domestic production taxes acts to discourage trade.

The sixth and seventh rows report alternative measures of the production tax rate. The production tax rate reported in the sixth row excludes nontax revenue from the tax revenues, while the rate reported in the seventh row used GDP instead of just industrial GDP as the tax base. The eighth row gives a rough estimate of sales tax rates.[38] The ninth row provides an equally rough estimate of income tax rates. The tenth row gives government revenue as a share of GDP. The bottom row gives the average per capita GDP of the countries in each of the quintiles.

The results tend to support several of the predictions of the theory developed in section 10.1. In particular, we find the following.

1. As countries become richer, import tariff rates in particular and net border distortions in general decline. This is illustrated in the first and third rows of the table 10.3. Import tax rates monotonically decline from a high of 21.4 percent in the poorest quintile of countries to a low of 1.6 percent in the richest quintile. Net border distortions similarly decline (although not quite monotonically) from 26.9 percent to only 1.7 percent. The nonmonotonicity in the decline of net border distortions is due to an unusually high export tax

Table 10.3   The Structure of Tax Rates

			Rank for Variable GDPREAL		
	1	2	3	4	5
Import tariff rate:					
Mean	.214	.153	.083	.039	.016
SD	.103	.053	.027	.035	.018
Export tax rate:					
Mean	.049	.047	.134	.000	.002
SD	.084	.046	.156	.001	.004
Net border distortion:					
Mean	.269	.208	.231	.039	.017
SD	.083	.097	.198	.035	.022
Production tax rate:					
Mean	.196	.150	.126	.171	.127
SD	.106	.062	.086	.147	.059
Net trade distortion:					
Mean	.073	.058	.105	.211	.145
SD	.147	.117	.225	.169	.066
Production tax rate excluding nontax revenue:					
Mean	.087	.061	.075	.089	.068
SD	.059	.029	.073	.137	.024
Production tax rate with GDP as base:					
Mean	.054	.050	.046	.070	.047
SD	.036	.024	.033	.072	.020
Sales tax rate:					
Mean	.026	.021	.021	.035	.054
SD	.022	.018	.019	.022	.032
"Income" tax rate:					
Mean	.015	.029	.019	.048	.070
SD	.009	.030	.008	.044	.030
Government revenue share of GDP:					
Mean	.213	.187	.193	.275	.281
SD	.077	.070	.078	.065	.144
GDP/population in 1980 US$:					
Mean	370.133	976.392	1,905.625	5,862.011	11,288.507
SD	122.401	256.489	505.030	2,338.675	751.764

rate in the third quintile, but this value has a very high standard deviation associated with it. This is consistent with the notion that poorer countries tend to rely more heavily on border taxes to fund public expenditure. Without other sources of revenue, as illustrated, for example, in table 10.1, tariff rates are fairly high. When countries are richer and as a result use a broader range of domestic taxes, border tax rates fall appreciably.

2. Poorer countries seem to have much higher net border distortions than net trade distortions. Net border distortions in the poorest three quintiles of countries appear fairly high (26.9, 20.8, and 23.1 percent, respectively), yet

our estimates of the net trade distortions are significantly lower (7.3, 5.8, and 10.5 percent, respectively). Tariffs are to a large extent simply offsetting the distortions of domestic production taxes (and vice versa). Net border distortions cannot be viewed to be a good approximation to net trade distortions.

3. The richer countries have virtually no border distortions yet still have significant production taxes and so have significant net trade distortions. Since richer countries impose very low border taxes, their taxes on domestic production serve to distort trade patterns. Given our assumption that richer countries export industrial goods, which are subject to the production tax, this production tax discourages international trade, serving the same role as a tariff.

To the degree to which production taxes are assessed on nonindustrial goods, our estimates of the net trade distortion are biased upward. However, our figures also ignore nontariff barriers to trade and to that degree underestimate net trade distortions.

4. Richer countries levy a broader range of taxes and collect more tax revenues as a percentage of GDP. Rows 8 and 9 indicate that effective sales tax and income tax rates generally rise with a country's income. The income tax rate rises from 1.5 percent in the poorest quintile to 7 percent in the richest quintile, while the sales tax rate rises from 2.6 percent to 5.4 percent. Owing to the construction of these tax rate variables, this result is probably due more to the larger tax bases in the richer countries than to their higher tax rates. It is no surprise, then, that government revenue as a share of GDP rises from 21.3 percent in the poorest quintile to 28.1 percent in the richest quintile.

5. Nontax revenues are an important source of revenue for rich and poor countries. We have assumed that nontax revenues are derived from state-owned industrial firms. Without very detailed country-specific information on government fiscal structure, this assumption is difficult to substantiate. Insofar as the assumption is valid, nontax revenue is a quantitatively important part of production tax revenues for countries in every income quintile. Exclusion of nontax revenues from the calculation of the production tax, shown in row 6, reduces the production tax rate by about half for each quintile.

6. Except for the countries in the richest and poorest quintiles, there is much intraquintile variance of net trade distortions. Only in the fifth quintile is the standard deviation of the net trade distortion even as small as half the mean value of this distortion. While comments 1–5 above illustrate some broad trends, one should refrain from assuming too much homogeneity of tax structures within quintiles.

Table 10.4 gives country-specific information about net border distortions, production tax rates, and the resulting net trade distortion. Each entry in the table is the time-series average for a variable across those years in which enough data were available to calculate the net trade distortion.

Table 10.4   The Composition of the Net Trade Distortion

Country	1980 GDP Quintile	Net Border Distortion		Production Tax Rate		Net Trade Distortion		Government Revenue Share of GDP	
		Mean	SD	Mean	SD	Mean	SD	Mean	SD
Argentina	4	.051	.075	.107	.076	.158	.090	.151	.025
Brazil	3	.132	.034	.142	.081	−.010	.100	.214	.027
Cameroon	2	.312	.048	.227	.216	.085	.235	.179	.035
Canada	5	.060	.018	.148	.013	.208	.029	.190	.011
Colombia	2	.197	.033	.103	.025	.094	.054	.116	.010
Egypt	1	.351	.076	.456	.119	−.105	.187	.394	.039
France	5	.002	.002	.103	.009	.105	.008	.377	.030
Germany	5	.004	.008	.050	.010	.054	.009	.275	.018
Ghana	3	.396	.121	.114	.054	.282	.136	.096	.036
Greece	4	.051	.027	.134	.022	.185	.014	.305	.042
India	1	.374	.074	.131	.016	.243	.067	.125	.007
Italy	4	.002	.003	.074	.014	.076	.014	.325	.033
Japan	5	.030	.013	.095	.011	.125	.014	.113	.010
Kenya	1	.122	.022	.365	.071	−.243	.056	.198	.022
Korea	3	.074	.016	.093	.016	−.019	.016	.165	.020
Malaysia	3	.168	.025	.288	.060	−.120	.080	.240	.029
Mexico	3	.263	.156	.099	.016	.164	.155	.140	.027
Netherlands	5	.001	.002	.218	.046	.218	.045	.491	.027
Pakistan	1	.282	.026	.123	.033	.159	.058	.148	.015
Peru	2	.275	.051	.088	.020	.187	.047	.162	.014
Phillipines	2	.167	.044	.074	.012	.093	.040	.118	.016
Portugal	3	.096	.003	.057	.011	.039	.014	.269	.015
Senegal	1	.249	.060	.106	.029	.143	.080	.189	.020
Spain	4	.116	.046	.106	.011	.222	.047	.223	.026
Sri Lanka	1	.263	.087	.131	.029	.131	.101	.198	.026
Tunisia	2	.227	.030	.228	.064	−.001	.065	.295	.042
Turkey	2	.219	.127	.137	.051	.082	.142	.202	.025
United Kingdom	4	.010	.011	.203	.028	.213	.025	.354	.021
United States	5	.037	.008	.111	.008	.148	.009	.193	.011
Venezuela	4	.081	.018	.456	.120	.537	.119	.270	.055

In some cases, there are obvious explanations for why a country's tax patterns differ from those of other countries in the same income quintile. For example, much of the production tax revenue in Venezuela likely comes from the taxation of oil exports, explaining the high calculated value for this production tax. Malaysia is another oil-exporting country with a high production tax rate. Here, the production tax revenue is presumably mainly from a tax on exported rather than imported goods, contrary to our assumptions. It is interesting to note that Brazil, which has a reputation for restrictive policies, has no estimated net trade distortion.[39]

Countries that are members of the EEC have uniformly very small net border distortions.[40] These countries generally have sizable production taxes, however, giving rise to important net trade distortions.

Even for data within a country, there are often high standard deviations, implying significant changes in policy over the period of observation. In future work, we hope to investigate the degree to which changes in net border distortions and changes in net production taxes were coordinated so as to leave net trade distortions relatively unaffected.

10.3 Conclusions

What can optimal tax theory tell us about the optimal trade policy of a country? Diamond and Mirrlees (1971) showed that, if all excise taxes are available, then production will be efficient under an optimal tax system. This implies in a small open economy that there should be no trade distortions if all excise taxes are available. While there may be no net trade distortions, however, tariffs could well be used to offset the trade distortions created by various domestic taxes.

Administrative costs may restrict the set of tax instruments that a country would consider using. If fewer tax instruments are used, however, then trade distortions may well exist under an optimal tax system. We find that the optimal trade distortions in small open economies can be of either sign. Richer small countries would likely use a broader set of tax instruments, however, implying that trade distortions are more likely in poorer small countries as well as in countries with market power in international markets.

We used the IMF financial statistics for thirty countries during the period 1970–87 to examine the size and pattern of net trade distortions. These data suggest that net border distortions are much larger than net trade distortions in countries in the poorer three quintiles. Countries in the richest two quintiles, however, have very small border distortions yet still have significant trade distortions created by their domestic taxes. It is likely that these distortions discourage trade. Our numbers suggest roughly comparable net trade distortions across countries at all income levels, even though border distortions are important in only the poorest countries. The data therefore suggest that the GATT restrictions on border taxes have been relatively ineffective in eliminating trade distortions in richer countries.

It is possible, however, that the net trade distortions in richer countries may not necessarily arise from the exercise of market power and may not result in important reallocations of resources. Our theory forecasts that tax competition between countries with no market power should drive production taxes to zero, assuming that GATT agreements have eliminated border taxes. However, the optimal tax framework examines the Nash equilibrium in which each country chooses its optimal tax policy, taking as given the tax policies elsewhere. As discussed in Gordon (1983), coordination of tax policies across countries would lead to higher welfare. For example, if all countries agreed to impose production taxes at the same rate, then the location of production remains undistorted by taxes, yet countries may find the resulting tax system more attractive on equity or efficiency grounds. Certainly, no explicit agreement exists coordinating production taxes across countries. Recent experience in the EEC shows how difficult it is to convince countries to restrict by international agreement their flexibility in setting domestic tax rates. Yet game theory shows that cooperative outcomes could arise without explicit agreements. Certainly, the observed simultaneous reduction in corporate taxes in many developed countries, around the time of the 1986 tax reform in the United States, suggests such an informal coordination of tax policies. In addition, the characteristics of international tax treaties suggest a concern for world efficiency. It is premature to conclude that these countries are using tariffs to exercise market power.

There is certainly much room for further research on the linkages between domestic and international taxes. We are currently looking more closely at the optimal use of nontariff barriers in the presence of distorting domestic taxes. We also hope to collect much better information about the pattern of net trade distortions, using detailed information on tariff rates versus production tax rates by good in various countries. In addition, we hope to examine what readjustments occurred in domestic taxes in countries that have made major changes in tariff and nontariff barriers to trade. Finally, we hope to learn more about the degree to which production taxes are coordinated among countries in order to minimize trade distortions while still allowing use of this source of tax revenue.

Appendix

The objective of this appendix is to derive equations (6)–(7). This derivation is very similar to those appearing elsewhere in the optimal tax literature.

Equations (6a) and (6b) characterize the values of σ and τ that maximize the expression in equation (5). Differentiating equation (5) with respect to σ, we find that

$$(A1) \quad \sum_h p_1^* \frac{\partial V_h}{\partial q_1} + W' \left[p_1^* C_1 + \sigma p_1^* \frac{\partial C_1}{\partial q_1} \frac{\partial q_1}{\partial \sigma} + \tau p_1 \frac{\partial X_1}{\partial \sigma} \right] = 0.$$

Note that factor prices and the firms' output price, p_1, do not change when σ changes. By Roy's identity, $\partial V_h / \partial q_1 = -\alpha_h C_{h1}$, where α_h is the marginal utility of income of the hth household. Let $\bar{\alpha} = \Sigma_h \alpha_h / H$. If we then substitute the expression $- [\bar{\alpha} + (\alpha_h - \bar{\alpha})]C_{h1}$ for $\partial V_h/\partial q_1$ in equation (A1) and simplify, we get

(A2) $-\bar{\alpha}p_1^*\sum_h C_{h1} - \sum_h (\alpha_h - \bar{\alpha})p_1^*C_{h1} + W'p_1^*C_1$

$$\left[1 + \left(\frac{\sigma}{1 + \sigma}\right)\left(\frac{q_1}{C_1}\frac{\partial C_1}{\partial q_1}\right) + \left(\frac{\tau}{C_1(1 + \tau)}\right)\frac{\partial X_1}{\partial \sigma}\right] = 0.$$

But, by the definition of a covariance, $\Sigma_h(\alpha_h - \bar{\alpha})C_{h1} = H \, \mathrm{cov}(\alpha_h, C_{h1})$. Using this result, equation (6a) follows from equation (A2) by simply dividing through by $p_1^*C_1$ and making use of the definition of ϵ_q.

Differentiating equation (5) with respect to τ, we find that

(A3) $\displaystyle\sum_h \sum_j \frac{\partial V_h}{\partial r_j}\frac{\partial r_j}{\partial \tau} + W'\left[\sigma p_1^*\frac{\partial C_1}{\partial \tau} + \left(\frac{p_1}{1 + \tau}\right)X_1 + \tau p_1\frac{\partial X_1}{\partial \tau}\right] = 0.$

By Roy's identity, $\partial V_h/\partial r_j = \alpha_h K_{hj}$. In addition, however, if we differentiate each of the two cost functions described in equation (1) with respect to τ and sum the total derivatives, we find that

(A4) $\displaystyle\sum_j K_j \partial r_j/\partial \tau = X_1 \partial p_1/\partial \tau.$

Proceeding as above, and making use of this additional result, we quickly get equation (6b).

In order to derive equation (7), note that the assumption that utility is additively separable between consumption and factor supplies implies that

(A5) $\displaystyle\frac{\partial C_1}{\partial \tau} = \sum_h \frac{\partial C_{h1}}{\partial Y_h}\frac{\partial Y_h}{\partial \tau}.$

But, by the definition of β_{h1}, $\partial C_{h1}/\partial Y_h = \beta_{h1}/q_1 = [\bar{\beta}_1 + (\beta_{h1} - \bar{\beta}_1)]/q_1$. After substituting this expression, we find that

(A6) $\displaystyle\frac{\partial C_1}{\partial \tau} = \frac{\bar{\beta}_1}{q_1}\sum_h \frac{\partial Y_h}{\partial \tau} + H \, \mathrm{cov}\left(\frac{\beta_{h1}}{q_1}, \frac{\partial Y_h}{\partial \tau}\right).$

Using equation (A4) and the definition that $Y_h = \Sigma_j r_j K_{hj}$, equation (7) follows quickly.

Notes

1. This basic idea is not new, having been discussed in the literature at least since Bhagwati (1971).
2. Even labor income taxes can distort relative prices of domestic products to the extent that the effective tax rates vary by industry.

3. For a discussion of GATT rules, see Dam (1970).

4. Yitzhaki (1979), Wilson (1988), and Panagariya (1988) also explore the optimal size of the tax base, when a broader base implies higher administrative costs, though in a closed economy setting.

5. Mitra (1987) and Heady and Mitra (1987) also examined some aspects of the linkage between domestic and border taxes.

6. These models try to explain which groups will be favored by government policy, unlike optimal tax models, which simply assume an objective for the government. Conditional on the resulting distributional preferences, the two types of models are likely to make very similar policy forecasts. The optimal tax models simply describe the Pareto-efficient policies, given the desired distribution.

7. Trade theorists will recognize this as the notion that international trade extends the consumption possibility frontier.

8. We ignore taxes on consumption since a tax on the consumption of a good can be duplicated with a production tax and a tariff at the same rate on imports of this good.

9. With trade in both goods and one of the factors, and with factors mobile between industries, a country would almost always specialize production to only one of the two goods, eliminating various effects we wish to focus on.

10. If good i is exported rather than imported and exports are taxed, then it would be more natural to define an export tax rate, e_i, such that $q_i(1 + e_i) = p^*$. Then, $t_i \equiv -e_i/(1 + e_i)$.

11. Article 3 under GATT allows a rebate of indirect taxes, such as a VAT, when a good is exported, thereby eliminating any trade distortions from the tax. Doing the same for a turnover tax is very difficult since the appropriate size of the rebate depends on the degree to which intermediate inputs in a product are transferred between firms in the course of production.

12. To the degree that taxpayers are more aggressive at evading taxes when there is more money at stake, monitoring may become more expensive as rates rise, though higher penalties could substitute imperfectly for extra monitoring.

13. For a derivation of equations (6a), (6b), and (7), see the appendix.

14. The efficiency loss measure therefore takes the form of a tax rate, which measures the difference between marginal benefits and costs for the good, times the change in quantity of the good.

15. In general, the value of β_{h1} will depend on consumer prices and income.

16. Firms in industry 2 must continue to break even. Output prices are unchanged; the cost of one input has fallen, so the cost of the other input must have risen in equilibrium. This is simply a manifestation of the Stolper-Samuelson theorem of international trade.

17. Distributional objectives may differ across countries, however.

18. This equivalence assumes perfect competition, no uncertainty, and a static economic environment. Relaxation of any of these assumptions may result in tariff-quota nonequivalence. The models used in the rent-seeking literature can also lead to this result. For example, if money is used to bribe officials to obtain licenses, then the equilibrium bribe should be the market clearing price for a license, and the official wage rate of officials would in principle adjust to clear the labor market.

19. In fact, we have been able to show in this situation that a prohibitive nontariff barrier is at least a local optimum under plausible assumptions. Reducing the trade barrier slightly from this point reduces tax revenue from domestic production yet does not result in any savings on goods previously purchased from abroad since there were none.

20. When $\omega = 1.5$, the optimal net tariff rate is so high that good 1 is exported rather than imported.

21. The incentive effects of these taxes can be duplicated using a sales tax on each good, at separate rates, along with either a tariff or a production tax on good 1.

22. We have assumed that the cost does not depend on the chosen tax *rate*.

23. For empirical results consistent with these hypotheses, see Tanzi (1987) and Riezman and Slemrod (1987).

24. Judging whether world efficiency improves is very complicated in this second-best setting, given the presence of many tax distortions.

25. A cross-sectional regression analysis relating the share of revenue from each source (relative to GDP and relative to total tax revenue) to a measure of national income is provided in Tanzi (1987).

26. We selected a cross section of countries. The thirty-three countries initially in our sample were Argentina, Brazil, Cameroon, Canada, Chile, Colombia, Egypt, France, Germany, Ghana, Greece, India, Indonesia, Italy, Japan, Kenya, Korea, Malaysia, Mexico, the Netherlands, Nicaragua, Pakistan, Peru, the Philippines, Portugal, Senegal, Spain, Sri Lanka, Tunisia, Turkey, the United Kingdom, Uruguay, and the United States. Owing to lack of data on imports and exports, we dropped Chile, Indonesia, and Uruguay from the sample. The countries were selected as follows. We first included a handful of countries that underwent trade liberalization. These countries are important for future work with the data set. We then randomly selected countries from the list of countries in the World Development Report.

27. For several industrial countries, there were no data on export tax duties. The GFS do not allow us to determine whether this is simply a missing observation or whether zero revenue was collected. Rather than exclude all industrial countries except the United Kingdom from the analysis, we set these missing values to zero.

28. A sales tax would distort relative output prices if it is assessed on the basis of domestic output rather than domestic consumption, if the rate differs by industry, and if no compensating adjustment takes place at the border. In addition, sales of domestic producers and sales of importers might be taxed differently. The European VAT does include compensating border adjustments and so does not distort trade patterns.

29. For a discussion of how sales and income taxes can distort relative producer prices, see Ahmad and Stern (1987).

30. For example, nontax revenue may come from agricultural marketing boards. If the revenue from these boards results from higher prices charged for domestic agricultural output, then this change in relative prices offsets rather than reinforces the distortion created by the corporate income tax. If the revenue comes solely from higher prices on exports of agricultural goods, then this revenue reflects a higher effective tariff rate rather than a higher effective production tax rate.

31. This type of average tax rate is often used to measure tax distortions. See, e.g., Fullerton et al. (1981). However, as emphasized by Auerbach (1983), it has a variety of problems. For example, the size of the tax distortion created by a corporate tax depends on the present value of depreciation deductions and tax credits that result when an investment is undertaken. But the observed use of depreciation deductions and tax credits in a given year depends heavily on the particular timing of investments that occurred in the economy.

32. The resulting regression is IND SHARE $= .2925 + 3.160E - 5 *$ GDP $- 2.136E - 9 *$ GDP $** 2$. Each coefficient is significantly different from zero at the 95 percent level. These coefficients imply that the industrial share of GDP rises with GDP until real (1980) per capita income reaches about U.S.$7,400 and then falls.

33. Our derivation of the measure of trade distortions implies that we need to know only the revenue collected from this tax, relative to output, and not the extent to which it is a tax on output, capital income, or some other tax base, as long as it is not a tax on pure profits.

34. Of course, this crude assumption will be violated in a variety of cases. For example, poorer countries that export petroleum and minerals often impose taxes on these exported goods. In fact, optimal tax theory would support taxation of these goods, even without market power in international markets, since a tax at a constant rate on this output acts as a land tax and to that extent has no efficiency cost and perhaps an equity gain.

35. Since the tariff and the production tax apply to different goods, we implicitly renormalize the production tax rates by setting the renormalized tax rate in the industrial sector to zero and setting the tax in the remaining sector equal to minus the measured production tax rate.

36. We adopt a descriptive approach for two interrelated reasons. First, as sec. 10.1 demonstrates, there are few truly exogenous and observable variables in our analysis. Given this, simple single-equation regression analysis will provide biased and inconsistent estimates. Second, the severe measurement problems with our data make any interpretation of regression results highly problematic.

37. When data needed to calculate the net trade distortion were not available in 1980, which was the case for three countries, we report the data from the latest available year instead.

38. If data were not available in 1980 for one of the following variables, we use data from the latest year available. For four countries, no data were ever available for sales tax revenues. The reported sales tax rate is therefore the average over those countries with available data.

39. The inclusion of NTBs may alter this conclusion.

40. The lack of any border distortion is mildly surprising since, while intra-EEC trade is free, trade between EEC countries and the rest of the world need not be.

References

Ahmad, Ehtisham, and Nicholas Stern. 1987. Alternative sources of government revenue: Examples from India. In *The theory of taxation for developing countries,* ed. David Newbery and Nicholas Stern, 281–332. New York: Oxford University Press.

Aizenman, Joshua. 1987. Inflation, tariffs and tax enforcement costs. *Journal of International Economic Integration* 2:12–28.

Auerbach, Alan J. 1983. Corporate taxation in the United States. *Brookings Papers on Economic Activity* 2:451–514.

Bhagwati, Jagdish. 1971. The generalized theory of distortions and welfare. In *Trade, balance of payments, and growth,* ed. J. Bhagwati, R. Jones, R. Mundell, and J. Vanek. Amsterdam: North-Holland.

———. 1982. Directly unproductive, profit-seeking (DUP) activities. *Journal of Political Economy* 90(5):988–1002.

Boadway, R., S. Maital, and M. Prachowny. 1973. Optimal tariffs, optimal taxes and public goods. *Journal of Public Economics* 2:391–403.

Corden, W. Max. 1974. *Trade policy and economic welfare.* Oxford: Oxford University Press.

———. 1984. Normative theory of international trade. In *Handbook of international economics,* vol. 1, ed. R. W. Jones and P. B. Kenen. Amsterdam: North-Holland.

Dam, Kenneth W. 1970. *The GATT: Law and international economic organization.* Chicago: University of Chicago Press.

Diamond, Peter, and James Mirrlees. 1971. Optimal taxation and public production. I. Production efficiency. *American Economic Review* 61:8–27.

Dixit, Avinash. 1985. Tax policy for open economies. In *The handbook of public economics,* vol. 1, ed. A. Auerbach and M. Feldstein. Amsterdam: North-Holland.

Fullerton, D., A. King, J. Shoven, and J. Whalley. 1981. Corporate tax integration in the United States: A general equilibrium approach. *American Economic Review* 71:677–91.

Gordon, Roger H. 1983. An optimal taxation approach to fiscal federalism. *Quarterly Journal of Economics* 98:567–86.

Grossman, G., and J. D. Richardson. 1985. Strategic trade policy: A survey of issues and early analysis. Special Papers in International Economics no. 15. International Finance Section, Department of Economics, Princeton University.

Heady, C., and P. Mitra. 1987. Distributional and revenue raising arguments for tariffs. *Journal of Development Economics* 26:77–101.

Helpman, Elhanan. 1984. Increasing returns, imperfect markets, and trade theory. In *The handbook of international economics,* vol. 1, ed. R. W. Jones and P. B. Kenen. Amsterdam: North-Holland.

Leamer, Edward. 1988. Notes on estimating nontariff barriers. Typescript.

Mitra, P. 1987. Protective and revenue raising trade taxes: Theory and an application to India. World Bank CPD Discussion Paper no. 1987–4.

Nogues, J., A. Olechowski, and L. A. Winters. 1986. The extent of nontariff barriers to imports of industrial countries. World Bank Staff Working Paper no. 789.

Panagariya, Arvind. 1988. Administrative costs, optimal taxation, and the tax base. Mimeo.

Riezman, Raymond, and Joel Slemrod. 1987. Tariffs and collection costs. *Review of World Economics,* 545–49.

Tanzi, Vito. 1987. Quantitative characteristics of the tax systems of developing countries. In *The theory of taxation for developing countries,* ed. David Newbery and Nicholas Stern. New York: Oxford University Press.

Wilson, John D. 1988. On the optimal tax base for commodity taxation. Mimeo.

World Bank. 1980. *World development report 1980.* Oxford: Oxford University Press.

Yitzhaki, Shlomo. 1979. A note on optimal taxation and administrative costs. *American Economic Review* 69:475–80.

Comment   John Whalley

I enjoyed reading this paper because of the insights that it yields on the role of domestic taxes in shaping the tariff structure of countries, especially poorer and smaller countries. Because of the focus of my own recent research on GATT-related issues, my comments largely relate to the broader factual context within which the paper is set.

Summary of Paper

The focus of the paper is to try to explain why smaller and poorer countries tend to have higher tariffs and associated trade barriers than do larger countries. The paper poses this as something of a paradox since optimal tariff theory

John Whalley is director of the Centre for the Study of International Economic Relations and William G. Davis Professor of International Trade, Department of Economics, the University of Western Ontario. He is also a research associate of the National Bureau of Economic Research.

would suggest that it would be large countries that would have high tariffs and small countries that would have lower tariffs.

The conjectures offered are twofold. The first is that tariffs are administratively more efficient as revenue-raising devices than domestic taxes for lower-income countries, explaining in part why tariffs are used so extensively by them. In turn, administrative considerations, to some extent, determine the form that domestic taxes take in these countries, and, therefore, tariffs become a way of offsetting the trade distortions associated with border taxes.

The paper contains a theoretical section in which the authors lay out the optimal tariff/domestic tax problem for the small open price-taking economy case, demonstrating the well-known and not surprising proposition that the optimal policy for such a country is to have no border distortions. They then proceed to analyze cases with administrative costs and illustrate how this can lead to a presumption for a differential tariff. Moreover, there may be a need for a tariff to offset trade distortions associated with domestic taxes, which may arise from differential administrative costs of taxing different products.

They then proceed to numerical analysis, in which they present an example in which there are Cobb-Douglas production and utility functions and two consumer groups, capitalists and workers, with differing distribution weights in the social welfare function. The government maximizes a social welfare function that includes revenue since this is redistributed to the households. Their numerical results clearly show that the optimal tariff will tend to increase as capitalists are given more weight in the utility function. Also, distorting trade taxes or subsidies may be a desirable arrangement depending on the weights in the preferences. Finally, they show that eliminating tariffs, leaving production taxes in place, does not necessarily eliminate trade distortions.

The authors draw out some of the implications of this analysis for observed tax policies. They suggest that the poorest countries, generally speaking, will adopt policies that discourage trade owing to their need for higher tariffs, a need that is due to the administrative costs. In turn, tariffs may also be needed to offset distorting effects of taxes. They then analyze data from IMF government statistics for 1970–87 and calculate average commodity tax rates for thirty-three countries, emphasizing that little is known about quantitative measures of nontariff barriers, citing the work of Nogues, Olechowski, and Winters.

They conclude by running a series of regressions, emphasizing six major themes from their results. The first is that, as countries become richer, both tariff and border tax rates generally decline. Second, poorer countries seem to have much higher border and trade distortions. Third, richer countries have small if no border distortions yet still have production taxes and so significant trade distortions. Fourth, rich countries use a wider range of taxes and, as a percentage of GDP, collect more tax revenues. Fifth, nontax revenues are an important revenue source for both rich and poor countries.

Finally, there is substantial quintile variance in net trade distortions by country with less for the countries in the richest and poorest quintiles of their data.

Overall Comment

This interesting piece is made all the more so by its strong conclusions. Previous work in public finance and trade by these two authors has tended perhaps to be more analytically focused, but I interpret this paper's primary contribution as helping explain the tariff and border tax structures in poorer countries and relating these to domestic tax structures. I, therefore, will say less about the analytical portion of the paper because my impression is that this is relatively straightforward.

Assumed Determinants of Protection

I begin with the assumed rationale for protection in this paper, namely, that there is a well-defined national welfare function and that revenue needs of government largely drive protection. For people working in the trade policy area at the present time, this view of the world would, I think, be accepted not only as overly simplistic but as potentially misleading, even for smaller poorer countries. For instance, the reasons why we have the Multi Fiber Arrangement and associated trade restrictions in textiles and clothing are not because of national interest. It is because of concerns over adjustment costs, the geographic concentration of industry in protected countries, the high average age of employees, the large fraction of females in the work force, and so on—namely, the particular configuration of industry protectionist pressures. Equally, the reason why agriculture was left out of the GATT in the way that it was in 1947 reflected narrow sectional, not national, interests.

If you look at the recent GATT publication "Review of Developments in the Trading System," you will find a discussion of voluntary export restraints currently in place. These number approximately one hundred thirty in developed and developing countries at the present time, and this is excluding seventy-one measures in textiles outside the coverage of the Multi Fiber Arrangement and another fifty-odd restraint measures in agriculture. Put simply, it is too simplistic to look at the structure of protection in both developed and developing countries and relate it to some notion of national interest in a model where there are revenue needs for protection. While revenue needs from the tariff are undoubtedly there for some of the smaller countries, as a broad generalization over the whole of the trading system this is both inaccurate and simplistic. And, for these smaller countries, it is usually other features of that trade regime (import licensing, foreign exchange rationing, etc.) that have the most influence on trade flows.

The Role of GATT

I found the paper's discussion of the GATT factually somewhat incomplete and thus potentially misleading for the present analysis. It seems to me that the GATT has to be central to any analysis explaining the phenomena that the authors have raised in this paper.

First of all, it is widely agreed in the trade policy community that the GATT's role in shaping the postwar pattern of protection both between developed countries and between developed and developing countries has been central, particularly through MFN under Article 1 of the GATT. Through the seven rounds of multilateral trade negotiations that we have had in the GATT thus far, under MFN (most favored nation) small countries have been able to free ride on tariff negotiations between large countries because any bilateral negotiation between a pair of large countries produces reductions in tariffs that are automatically extended to small countries. In turn, because of the nature of the negotiation process conducted under MFN, large countries typically will not negotiate with small countries because, if they make tariff concessions, these are automatically extended to other countries.

In essence, through its MFN provisions the GATT system has largely removed pressures on smaller and poorer countries to negotiate international agreements to apply discipline to protectionist interests abroad. As a result, forty years on we are left with small countries with high tariff rates and large countries with lower tariff rates. This pattern applies not only between developed and developing countries but also among developed countries. The mid-sized countries (Canada, Australia, New Zealand, and the larger European Free Trade Association countries) generally have significantly higher tariffs than the European Community, the United States, or Japan. They, in turn, have lower tariffs than even smaller developed countries such as Austria and Norway.

In turn, the GATT also provides disciplines that link border taxes and domestic taxes; these are unfortunately ignored in the paper. Article 3 of the GATT, which contains the principle of national treatment and covers indirect taxes, was motivated by the acknowledged need in 1947 that under GATT rules it should not be possible to reduce or eliminate tariffs but achieve the same protective effect through tax or other measures. This, admittedly, is a much more narrowly applied article than the forms of offset that the authors have in mind, but there have been a number of panel cases involving Article 3 measures. These include early tax cases, and, more recently, these same issues have come up again with the border adjustment issues in the value-added tax (VAT).

Beyond Article 3, which constrains the use of domestic taxes in this way, there are other and wider provisions of the GATT that might be used should countries try to use offsets between these instruments as the authors suggest. The key ones are under Article 23:1-B, which provides for nonnullification, violation, and impairment. These provisions, in effect, allow contracting parties to withdraw concessions if a binding on a tariff is offset by the use of some other instrument in a direct and deliberate way. In effect, GATT contracting parties have, in principle, already bound themselves to prevent changes in domestic policies that undo the effects of changes in tariffs.

Therefore, some of the conjectures discussed in this paper, it seems to me, are inappropriate as explanations of the phenomena they pose. The institutional structure of GATT partially limits what the authors suggest, and they also miss the major role that the structure of the GATT has played in generating a trading system with exactly those characteristics that they seek to explain in other ways.

Tax and Tariff Interactions

There are also other problems with the interaction between tariffs and taxes that the paper suggests. Developing countries have a wide variety of trade instruments in place and also an even larger variety of tax structures. Generally speaking, in the lower-income developing countries you will find trade policies that ban imports of consumption goods and have prioritization of imports through foreign exchange licensing schemes, quantitative restrictions, and import licensing of various kinds as well as tariffs that are lower on imports of raw materials and capital goods. On top of that, there are frequently export bans on certain products and, depending on the product or country one is talking about, export-promotion schemes such as duty remissions.

Tax structures are also complex but broadly have a pattern involving light or zero taxation on agriculture and heavy taxes on manufactures (especially through traditional excises and, increasingly, a manufacturing level VAT). This picture, again, is an oversimplification, and there are many complicating features of tax policy of which it is hard to make sense. Generally speaking, however, these patterns of trade and domestic taxes seem to compound one another, not offset one another, as the authors suggest.

A related difficulty is the discussion of tariffs in the foreign trade regime in the paper. In many lower-income developing countries, tariffs coexist with other extensive external sector restrictions, depending on the geographic region one is talking about (quantitative restrictions are heavily in evidence in Africa, they are less heavily in evidence in Latin America, and they seem to be on the decline in the Asian Pacific). A combination of binding foreign exchange rationing and quantitative restrictions, for instance, means that tariffs are not binding instruments in terms of trade distortions. Their role is frequently largely as lump-sum instruments that take rents away from holders of quota and reallocate revenues to the government. Their efficiency as revenue-raising devices is partly because of the nondistorting nature of the tariff.

Tariffs as a Revenue Source

While the emphasis in the paper on the relative heavy reliance on tariffs for revenue in developing countries is quite appropriate, it is only really the case for a subset of developing countries. If one looks at the new *Government Finance Statistics* yearbook published by the IMF, one will find that, for a number of smaller and lower-income developing countries, taxes on international trade and transactions account for a large portion of revenues.

Thus, using data for 1986, in the Gambia they account for 68 percent of revenues, in Uganda 69 percent, and in Benin 53 percent. However, as one goes through the countries by size, even among lower-income countries, these numbers start falling. Bangladesh is 32 percent and India 24 percent. By the time one gets to the NICs, one finds that Korea is around 14 percent of revenues accounted for by trade taxes. In some of the Middle Eastern countries, the numbers can be even smaller, for example, 14 percent in Egypt. In the Latin American countries, the numbers also can become even smaller; Argentina is 13 percent, Brazil only 4 percent, and Jamaica (a much smaller country) only 4 percent. So, while the paper seems right to focus on this crucial feature of trade taxes, it is only really so for a subset of other developing countries.

It is also important to emphasize how quickly things are changing among developing countries since there is now substantial trade liberalization currently under way in these countries. Mexico is a good example of this. When they joined the GATT in 1986, Mexico had bound their tariffs at 50 percent; the average tariff in Mexico is now under 20 percent, and, as liberalization proceeds in the Uruguay Round, Mexico may well bind even lower. In addition, the revenue share of trade taxes will fall.

Determinants of Domestic Tax Structure

Like trade taxes, the basic assumption underlying the analytics of the paper, that administrative costs determine tax structure, is also a little bit too extreme. For instance, the nontaxation of agriculture in many developing countries that I have already referred to in part reflects political pressures on the urban/rural political balance. Thus, rural producers are often subject to price controls on their products, and rural areas are also seen as the poorer segment of the economy. In the absence of a well-defined transfer system, political balance is, in part, restored through the tax structure.

Many other elements of tax structure in these countries cannot be explained by administrative costs alone. India, for instance, still has taxes on transit through major cities, which has substantial effects on the shipment of products across the country. The presence of these taxes reflects the distribution of legislative authority between the national government, the states, and the municipalities and cities.

Empirical Analysis

It is always too easy to criticize empirical work, and I am only too conscious that dealing with this number of countries and trying to extract broad regularities from it opens a project up for criticism.

To my taste, however, the analysis involves an overly mechanical use of IMF data without sufficient recognition of the problems involved. Let me just illustrate a few instances. The definition of a tax in a developing country is a very difficult matter and is not adequately resolved in IMF data. For instance, if you look at the work that Richard Bird and others have done on Colombia on parastatals, the count, I think, is around 160 different parastatal operations. Many of these are revenue-raising entities for government through monopoly purchase and marketing operations of various kinds. Despite the acknowledgments made in the paper, including or excluding these as part of the tax system makes a huge difference for countries such as this.

In calculating tax rates, there are also many pitfalls. For instance, in the Indian case, the black economy is one of the major topics of public policy discussion. There are estimates that as much as 50 percent of income originating in the urban sector may be contained in the black economy. There are rival estimates that it may be as small as 20 percent. These features make a large difference to the effective tax rates used. An element of the black economy is also the misuse of export-promotion schemes through various fungibility arrangements, which are discussed in some of the Indian policy literature.

The border distortions are also a major problem, especially as these enter into the calculations of the authors in such a central way. As I understand the border distortions measure that the authors use, they do not include remission schemes, which have been one of the central components of the Korean export promotion drive in the years since 1962. They do not include foreign exchange allocation schemes, foreign exchange retention schemes, priority credit rationing, and other measures that, in turn, have become significant components of the export-promotion arrangements in many countries in Asia.

Concluding Remarks

In conclusion, despite all the comments above, I would commend the authors for their attempt to focus on what is indeed a central and, to some, a puzzling aspect of the modern-day trading system; namely, why it is that smaller and poorer countries tend to have higher levels of protection?

Having worked recently on these issues, however, I would also inject into the discussion of this paper that central to an understanding of trade policy in the developing world are not only all the issues raised above but also an understanding of the intellectual climate of the developing world. The strong attachment to import substitution and the perceived need for high levels of protection for developmental reasons to aid with industrialization have been central in the postwar years. However, my impression is also that this intellectual climate is now in more of a state of flux than at any time in the postwar years. As I say above, there is a substantial unilateral liberalization under way, and developing countries are beginning to show more willingness to take on disciplines multilaterally in the GATT, in part because of their concerns to keep the trading system open.

Indeed, if these developments accelerate, it may be in ten years' time that we are discussing why smaller and poorer countries have modified their trade policies so quickly. In this event, we would perhaps not be fully convinced by an argument that what caused such rapid change was change in administrative costs.

11   The Optimal Taxation of Internationally Mobile Capital in an Efficiency Wage Model

John Douglas Wilson

The main purpose of this paper is to investigate the optimal system of taxes and subsidies on capital for an open economy in which similar types of workers are paid different wages. Phrased in popular terminology, the question is, What role do capital taxes and subsidies play in the optimal "industrial strategy" for an economy with "good jobs" and "bad jobs," as distinguished by wage levels? Since the answer is found to depend on the availability of other tax instruments, the paper also investigates the optimal choice of these other instruments. Briefly stated, the case for subsidizing capital investment in "good jobs" appears rather dubious. In fact, a model is presented in which informational asymmetries between the government and private firms justify a *positive* marginal tax on capital investment in the high-wage sector.

The basic reason for wage differentials in this paper is that worker productivity and wages are positively related in some firms but not others. This relation is a special case of the general phenomenon of "dependence of quality on price," which has received substantial attention in recent years, not only in labor markets, but also in credit and product markets. Stiglitz (1987a) provides an extensive review of this literature. For the special case of labor markets, "efficiency wage theories" are reviewed by Stiglitz (1986), Carmichael (1988), and Katz (1988). The main explanations that have been given for the dependence of worker productivity on wage levels include worker supervision problems, labor turnover, morale effects, and

John Douglas Wilson is associate professor of economics at Indiana University.

Some of the research reported here was completed during a visit to Queen's University in Canada, under the auspices of the John Deutsch Institute. The author is grateful to Ben Craig, Patricia Wilson, seminar participants at Purdue University and the University of Toronto, and participants at the NBER Conference on International Aspects of Taxation for helpful comments.

nutritional concerns. In their seminal paper, Shapiro and Stiglitz (1984) use the supervision approach to model long-run unemployment as an efficiency wage problem.

Of special relevance here is the work by Bulow and Summers (1986) on industrial policies. They extend the Shapiro-Stiglitz analysis to include two production sectors, one with a supervision problem and one without. Their analysis shows that high-wage firms should receive a production subsidy. Arvan and Schoumaker (1988) dispute the generality of this result by adding a fixed supply of capital to the model and demonstrating that the optimal commercial policy depends on the relative labor intensities of the two sectors. While neither paper analyzes capital tax policies, Bulow and Summers do conjecture that "keeping capital at home, and in the primary sector, may raise welfare by increasing rents created by primary sector jobs" (1986, 397).

I follow Bulow-Summers and others by assuming that the payment of wages above workers' opportunity costs serves as a worker discipline device: high wages make employment termination a genuine punishment for "shirking" on the job. But my model departs from the previous literature in two significant ways. First, I drop the assumption that utilities are linear in income. In the Bulow-Summers paper, a first-best optimum is obtainable through the use of employment subsidies because total economic welfare depends on national income, not on how it is distributed.[1] In the present paper, however, a first-best optimum is not obtainable, even when the government possesses the same information as private firms, because employment subsidies lead to increased efficiency at the cost of a less equitable income distribution. The cause of income distribution problems here is *not* that workers possess innate differences in preferences or endowments. Rather, distributional issues arise because the only way to deal with worker supervision problems is to provide similar workers in different industries with different incomes. This framework allows me to investigate whether the inherently second-best nature of the problem leads to desirable forms of capital market intervention.

The paper's other distinguishing feature is that consideration is given not only to the traditional case where the government knows the relevant characteristics of each firm but also to a case of "asymmetric information." In particular, the government is assumed not to be certain about the identity of those firms with supervision problems. Rather, it assigns a probability to the possibility that a given firm possesses a supervision problem. This specification makes no presumption about the severity of the information problem; nearly complete information could be obtained as a special case of the model where each firm is assigned a probability close to either zero or one. Note finally that the informational asymmetry does not prevent the government from making the employment and capital subsidies that it provides to a given firm depend on the firm's chosen wage. However, the rule for doing so cannot depend on whether the firm has a supervision problem.

To enrich the economic environment along these lines, I work with a full employment model. This allows me to capture in a reasonably simple manner the distinction between "good jobs" and "bad jobs," which has occupied much of the industrial policy debate. In particular, I make use of Calvo and Wellisz's (1978) insightful way of modeling worker supervision problems within a static framework, the main difference being my assumption that workers caught shirking in the "primary sector" obtain an endogenously determined utility by accepting perfectly supervised work in the "secondary sector" rather than becoming "self-employed."

The paper's organization and main results are summarized as follows. In the next section, I present a two-sector model with both international commodity trade and capital mobility. To eliminate obvious market power reasons for capital market intervention, the economy is assumed to be a price taker on world capital and product markets. Section 11.2 investigates the symmetric information case under the assumption that the government is able to make complete use of its information about private firms without being thwarted by limitations on available tax instruments. Here, the case for capital market intervention disappears: each firm should be allowed to equate the value of the marginal product of capital with the interest rate investors can obtain abroad, as it would in the absence of domestic capital taxes.[2] However, worker supervision problems do create a justification for employment and wage subsidies; and Appendix A demonstrates the desirability of excise taxes. In other words, workers should trade at product prices that differ from world prices, and some firms should face tax incentives to increase both the numbers of workers they employ and the wages they pay them. If these other tax instruments are not available, then positive subsidies on capital investment in the high-wage sector may be warranted. Using a simplified version of the model, Appendix B demonstrates the desirability of such subsidies. But the unavailability of other tax instruments is difficult to justify.

Section 11.3 investigates the asymmetric information case described above. Here, capital taxes and subsidies emerge as a desirable tax instrument, but with a rather surprising property: high-wage firms should face a positive tax on capital at the margin, while low-wage firms should face a positive subsidy. The basic reason for this result is that these capital taxes and subsidies lessen the severity of the adverse selection problem in the model. They allow, for example, the government to further raise its subsidization of high-wage employment relative to low-wage employment without causing those firms without worker supervision problems also to raise their wages so as to obtain the employment subsidies. The result is made more understandable by remembering that the low-wage sector is inherently more efficient than the high-wage sector in the sense that it lacks a supervision problem. Simply stated, the optimal tax policy encourages capital investment in the sector with the relatively efficient production process while discouraging capital investment elsewhere. Taken as a whole, the results of this paper call into question the desirability of encouraging capital investment in high-wage firms. Section 11.4 discusses some possible extensions of the analysis.

11.1 The Basic Model

I consider a simple two-sector model of a small open economy. The two goods produced in the economy are perfectly tradeable internationally at exogenously determined world prices. Each good is produced from labor and capital. The economy's total supply of workers is fixed, but each worker's labor effort is variable, making the economy's "effective labor" supply variable. The economy faces an infinitely elastic supply of capital at an exogenously given world interest rate, r (net of taxes levied abroad). In the following subsections, I describe the individual components of the model.

11.1.1 Production and Trade

The economy contains a "primary sector" (x) and a "secondary sector" (y). Each sector is assumed to behave competitively, the meaning of which is fully specified below. For notational simplicity, the economy is modeled as though each sector contains a single firm, but the analysis clearly applies to a model where there are any fixed number of firms in either sector.[3] Each firm possesses a production technology described by a strictly concave production function. Thus, there are decreasing returns to scale. This function is denoted $f^x(E_x, K_x)$ for the primary sector and $f^y(E_y, K_y)$ for the secondary sector, where K_i and E_i denote the capital and "effective labor" used in sector i (superscripts identify functions, and subscripts of functions denote partial derivatives throughout this paper).[4] My main reason for not assuming constant returns to scale is to allow capital to be perfectly mobile internationally without causing the economy to completely specialize in the production of a single good. Incomplete specialization is assumed throughout the paper, for both the laissez-faire equilibria and the social optima. The interpretation of the decreasing returns assumption is that there is a third factor, say, "entrepreneurial talent," that is omitted from the production function as an explicit argument.

The economy's trade balance constraint may be written

(1) $p_x f^x(E_x, K_x) + p_y f^y(E_y, K_y) + r(K^* - K_x - K_y) \geq p_x C_x + p_y C_y,$

where

C_x = total consumption of the primary good;
C_y = total consumption of the secondary good;

K^* = total ownership of capital by domestic residents;
r = world interest rate;
p_i = world price of sector i output.

This constraint states that the total value of domestic output, plus the value of capital exports, must be at least as great as the total value of domestic consumption, calculated at world prices. It is always satisfied with equality throughout the paper. The assumption that the domestic economy is small means that both r and $p = (p_x, p_y)$ are exogenously fixed from its viewpoint.

11.1.2 Workers and Supervision

I now specify the worker supervision problem, which lies at the heart of the model. To isolate efficiency considerations, all individuals are assumed to be ex ante identical. In particular, they possess identical utility functions, identical labor and capital endowments, and identical ownership shares of domestic profits. The common utility function is denoted $u(c_x,\ c_y,\ e)$, where the individual consumption levels, c_x and c_y, contribute positively to utility, and e measures "labor effort," which contributes negatively.[5] If sector i contains N_i workers who each supply labor effort e_i, then its effective labor is $E_i = e_i N_i$.

At the start of the period, the primary-sector firm chooses its desired number of workers. Each chosen worker then makes an irrevocable decision whether to work or to shirk. If he works, he provides the level of labor effort specified by the firm (e_x). In contrast, a shirking worker provides no labor effort and faces a probability $\pi_x < 1$ of being detected. A detected shirker is discharged from the firm and obtains employment in the secondary sector, where supervision is assumed to be perfect. There, he supplies the level of labor effort specified by the firm (e_y) in return for the common wage received by all secondary-sector workers. Undetected shirkers remain in the primary sector and receive the wage given to nonshirkers.

After shirkers have been identified and reassigned jobs, all sector i workers choose their consumption levels to solve the following utility-maximization problem:

$$\max u(c_x, c_y, e)$$

subject to

$$(2) \qquad\qquad q_x c_x + q_y c_y = I_i \,,$$

where $q = (q_x, q_y)$ is the vector of consumer prices ($q = p$ in the absence of excise taxes), e equals e_i for nonshirkers and zero for shirkers, and I_i denotes the total income received by a worker who ends up in sector i after all shirkers have been identified. The income variable I_i satisfies

$$(3) \qquad\qquad I_i = n + w_i \,,$$

where n is the nonlabor income each worker obtains from capital and profits, and w_i is the wage paid to sector i workers.

This utility-maximization problem yields demand functions and an indirect utility function. Excise taxes are eliminated from the analysis until Appendix A because they do not affect the propositions about capital taxation and because their role as an "antishirking device," while theoretically interesting, seems to be of little practical importance. Consumer prices are then fixed at p and can be omitted as explicit arguments in the demand and utility functions. These functions are denoted $c^j(I, e)$ for good j demand and $v(I, e)$ for utility.

To prevent shirking in the primary sector, the utility of nonshirkers must be set at least as high as the expected utility of shirkers. To write this condition mathematically, note first that the assumption of perfect competition means that each firm treats the *utilities* obtained by workers in other firms as exogenously fixed. Thus, the secondary-sector firm chooses w_y and e_y subject to the constraint

$$(4) \qquad v(n + w_y, e_y) \geq \bar{u},$$

where $\bar{u}$ is the utility level at which the firm faces an infinitely elastic supply of workers. Profit maximization obviously requires that (4) hold with equality. The primary-sector firm must then choose w_x and e_x to satisfy the following "no-shirking condition":

$$(5) \qquad v(n + w_x, e_x) \geq \pi_x \bar{u} + (1 - \pi_x)v(n + w_x, 0).$$

This condition also holds with equality under profit maximization (indifference between shirking and not shirking is always resolved in favor of not shirking). Since all primary-sector workers are ex ante identical, either all of them shirk or none of them shirk. In equilibrium, none shirk.

A crucial implication of (5) is that primary-sector workers obtain a higher utility level than secondary-sector workers in equilibrium. While the primary-sector firm can always pay its workers the wage they would get in the secondary sector, it must then require them to provide less labor effort. Mathematically, if the function $e^i(n + w_i, \bar{u})$ relates firm i's chosen effort level to worker incomes and the secondary-sector utility, then

$$(6) \qquad e^x(n + w_x, \bar{u}) < e^y(n + w_y, \bar{u})$$

whenever $w_x = w_y$. This property of the "labor effort functions" is used repeatedly throughout the paper.

11.1.3 Profit Maximization and Taxation

This subsection introduces the tax instruments to be used in the subsequent section and describes the profit-maximizing behavior of firms.

If firm i picks employment N_i, capital K_i, and wage w_i, it obtains revenue $p_i f^i[e^i(n + w_i, \bar{u})N_i, K_i]$ at a cost equal to $rK_i + w_i N_i + T^i(w_i, N_i, K_i)$, where the function T^i gives the firm's tax liability. Until asymmetric information is introduced into the model, I allow these tax functions to be specified in a way that effectively gives the government complete control over each firm's behavior. For concreteness, I work with tax functions with the following form:

$$(7) \qquad T^i(w_i, N_i, K_i) = t_{Ki}K_i + (t_{wi}w_i + \tau_i)N_i.$$

Thus, the firm faces a capital tax, a proportional wage tax, and a per capita employment tax (subsidies are negative taxes). This tax function operates on all the relevant margins: capital is taxed at the marginal rate t_{Ki}, employment is taxed at the marginal rate $t_{wi}w_i + \tau_i$, and the firm's chosen wage is taxed at the marginal rate $t_{wi}N_i$.

To describe the profit-maximizing behavior of firms, it is convenient to write firm i's profits in terms of effective labor, $E_i = e_i N_i$:[6]

$$(8) \qquad p_i f^i(E_i, K_i) - (r + t_{Ki})K_i - \{[(1 + t_{wi})w_i + \tau_i]/e^i(n + w_i, \bar{u})\}E_i.$$

To maximize these profits, the firm chooses the wage to minimize the unit cost of effective labor, given in (8) by the expression in curly brackets. The first-order condition for this minimization problem is[7]

$$(9) \qquad [w_i + \tau_i/(1 + t_{wi})]/e^i(I_i, \bar{u}) = 1/e_I^i(I_i, \bar{u})$$
$$= [-v_e(I_i, e_i)]/[v_I(I_i, e_i) - (1 - \pi_i)v_I(I_i, 0)],$$
$$\pi_x < 1, \quad \pi_y = 1,$$

where $I_i = n + w_i$, subscripts I and e denote partial derivatives, and the second equality follows from implicit differentiation of (4) and (5). The firm then chooses its capital and effective labor to equate values of marginal products to unit costs:

$$(10) \qquad p_i f_K^i(E_i, K_i) = r + t_{Ki}$$

and

$$(11) \qquad p_i f_E^i(E_i, K_i) = [(1 + t_{wi})w_i + \tau_i]/e^i(n + w_i, \bar{u}).$$

First-order conditions (9)–(11) will be used throughout the paper.

The final tax instrument introduced here is a uniform poll tax, collected from each worker. The symbol n then denotes nonlabor income net of this poll tax. Without this tax, the government might not be able to lower the incomes of secondary-sector workers as much as desired. However, its presence adds a fundamental indeterminacy to the model: given any equilibrium, there is an equivalent equilibrium with a higher poll tax. This is easily seen. As the poll tax rises, after-tax incomes can be held constant by raising w_x and w_y by identical amounts. The government budget can then be brought back into balance by using the additional revenue to lower τ_x and τ_y until $(1 + t_{wx})w_x + \tau_x$ and $(1 + t_{wy})w_y + \tau_y$ return to their original values. Thus, neither first-order condition (10) nor (11) is affected by the tax change. Since $w_x + \tau_x/(1 + t_{wx})$ and $w_y + \tau_y/(1 + t_{wy})$ are also clearly unaffected, neither is first-order condition (9) disturbed. Thus, the economy is in a new equilibrium that is identical to the old in all meaningful respects. Essentially, the standard observation about the irrelevance of whether workers or firms pay a tax applies in full force here. In the next section, I shall anchor the tax system without loss of generality by fixing $\tau_y = 0$.

Despite the wide range of tax instruments made available to the government in parts of this paper, I do not allow the government to treat detected shirkers differently than workers who start out in the secondary sector. Without this assumption, the need to use interindustry wage differentials as a worker discipline device disappears, thereby eliminating an essential feature of the economic environment with which this paper is concerned. A possible justification is that significant costs would likely be required to keep track of the past work history of current secondary-sector workers (i.e., did they "shirk"?), especially because these workers would have an incentive to claim those past histories most advantageous to their tax treatment.[8]

11.2 Optimal Government Policy with Symmetric Information

In the absence of taxation, the basic inefficiency in this efficiency wage model may be described as underemployment in the primary sector. To see this, recall that $e^x(n + w_x, \bar{u}) < e^y(n + w\,_y, \bar{u})$ whenever $w_x = w_y$. This means that the minimum unit cost of effective labor is lower for the secondary-sector firm than for the primary-sector firm: $w_y/e_y < w_x/e_x$. The primary-sector firm will therefore set the value of its marginal product of effective labor above the opportunity cost of effective labor, as measured by forgone secondary-sector output.

This reasoning suggests that the government should design a tax system that effectively subsidizes employment in the primary sector relative to the secondary sector. However, account must be taken of the worsening income inequality that may result from doing so. This section shows that such a tax policy is generally desirable, although the form of the subsidies is generally complex in the sense that it involves the use of both the wage and employment taxes described in the previous section. On the other hand, government intervention in the capital market will be shown *not* to be desirable. This and the other results are demonstrated under the assumption that the government has the same information possessed by private firms and can design a tax system that uses this information in any desired way.

11.2.1 The Basic Setup

Social welfare is defined throughout this paper as the sum of utilities:

$$(12) \qquad W = N_x v(w_x, e_x) + N_y v(w_y, e_y).$$

This welfare function can also be thought of as representing a worker's expected utility, assuming that all workers have an equal opportunity of being picked for a primary-sector job. Only nonshirkers appear in W because nobody shirks in equilibrium.

Using its taxing powers, the government effectively exercises complete control over the production and wage policies of all firms. The government's welfare-maximization problem may then be set up with the government treated as though it directly chooses an income-effort vector and input vector for each firm i, denoted (I_i, e_i) and (N_i, K_i). Employment levels N_x and N_y must add up to the total number of workers in the economy, denoted N^*. By using the workers' budget constraints to reexpress the trade balance constraint given by (1), it is then possible to obtain the following formulation of the government's maximization problem:

(P1)   Max $N_x v(I_x, e_x) + N_y v(I_y, e_y)$

subject to

(13) $p_x f^x(e_x N_x, K_x) + p_y f^y(e_y N_y, K_y) + r(K^* - K_x - K_y)$
$$- N_x I_x - N_y I_y \geq 0$$

(14) $v(I_x, e_x) - \pi_x v(I_y, e_y) - (1 - \pi_x) v(I_x, 0) \geq 0,$

(15) $N_x + N_y = N^*.$

After the government solves this problem, it can then decentralize the solution using the tax instruments introduced in section 11.1.3. The properties of this tax system are discussed in detail below.

Let λ and β denote Lagrange multipliers for constraints (13) and (14), and substitute $N^* - N_x$ for N_y to get rid of constraint (15). The Lagrangian for problem (P1) may then be written

(16) $L = N_x v(I_x, e_x) + (N^* - N_x) v(I_y, e_y)$
$$+ \lambda\{p_x f^x(e_x N_x, K_x) + p_y f^y[e_y(N^* - N_x), K_y]$$
$$+ r(K^* - K_x - K_y) - N_x I_x - (N^* - N_x) I_y\}$$
$$+ \beta\{v(I_x, e_x) - \pi_x v(I_y, e_y) - (1 - \pi_x) v(I_x, 0)\}.$$

For the subsequent analysis, both constraints are assumed to bind at the margin, implying that

(17) $\lambda > 0, \quad \beta > 0.$

The first inequality must hold since λ represents the marginal value of foreign exchange, which is necessarily positive in this model. The Bulow-Summers paper has the property that $\beta = 0$, but they assume that workers are risk neutral, in which case there is no social cost to income inequality. The government can achieve a first-best allocation simply by making the difference between primary and secondary incomes large enough to eliminate shirking. In the present paper, positive risk aversion is assumed, so increasing the spread between incomes to prevent shirking has a positive social cost, measured at the margin by the multiplier β.

I describe the solution to this problem in the subsequent subsections. First I take up my main concern, capital taxes. Then I discuss the other taxes and argue that, under the optimal tax policy, the primary sector should indeed be the "high-wage" sector, although this is not always true under laissez faire.

11.2.2 The Case against Capital Taxation

Capital taxes play no role in this model. In particular, the following proposition shows that each firm should be allowed to expand its capital stock to the point where the value of the marginal product of capital equals the world interest rate.

Proposition 1: At the optimum,

$$p_x f^x_K(e_x N_x, K_x) = p_y f^y_K(e_y N_y, K_y) = r.$$

Proof: Differentiate the Lagrangian with respect to K_x and K_y, and set the derivatives equal to zero. The result follows immediately. Q.E.D.

This result is related to Diamond and Mirrlees's (1971) finding that aggregate production efficiency is desirable when all commodities can be taxed at any desired rates. Optimal commodity taxation allows consumer prices to be varied independently of producer prices, thereby eliminating any reason to tolerate production inefficiency. In the present case, however, the small country assumption implies that the world product prices, p, are fixed. Thus, deviations from an efficient capital allocation cannot have a desirable effect on the consumer prices, q, even when the government fails to employ an optimal excise tax system. For this reason, proposition 1 holds regardless of whether the government uses excise taxes.

Proposition 1 does require the use of wage and employment subsidies, however. I analyze these instruments below. If they are assumed not to be available, then examples can be constructed in which social welfare is increased by subsidizing capital in the primary sector or taxing capital in the secondary sector. One such example is given in Appendix B. However, the unavailability of all other tax instruments is difficult to justify. A more reasonable approach would be to limit the use of these other instruments by explicitly incorporating informational problems into the model. Section 11.3 follows this approach.

Although I have not explicitly considered foreign tax systems, their existence need not change the results. Suppose that the domestic economy under consideration is a capital importer, and assume, as commonly practiced, that foreign governments allow a tax credit for taxes paid to the domestic government. Then foreign investors are indifferent about where to invest if and only if

$$g[1 - \max(b, b^*)] = g^*(1 - b^{**}),$$

where b and b^* denote the tax rates imposed by the domestic and foreign governments on foreigners' domestically located capital investments, b^{**} is the tax imposed by foreign governments on foreigners' foreign-located capital investments, and g and g^* denote the before-tax returns that these investors receive on domestically and foreign-located capital investments. As argued by Slemrod (1988), the domestic government maximizes social welfare by setting $b = b^*$ since raising b to b^* merely transfers tax revenue from the foreign government to the home government without affecting private investment incentives. But the tax does affect "public tax incentives" by lowering the social cost of capital from $g^*(1 - b^{**})/(1 - b^*)$ to $g^*(1 - b^{**})$ since foreign investors now pay b^* to the domestic government for every unit of their domestic investment. In other words, $g^*(1 - b^{**})$ now serves as the relevant "world interest rate," r, in both the trade balance constraint (eq. [13]) and proposition 1. As a result, the domestic government now finds it advantageous to provide domestic firms with an investment subsidy, s, that is carefully designed to lie outside the tax crediting system used by foreign governments but is set equal to b^* so that domestic firms expand investment to the point where the values of their marginal products equal $g^*(1 - b^{**})$.[9] The net effect of this domestic tax policy is to lower the social opportunity cost of capital without raising any tax revenue. In other words, the statement that capital should not be taxed still holds in the sense that the optimal $b^* - s$ equals zero. Similarly, the subsequent results about capital taxation may be reinterpreted as results about the optimal $b^* - s_i$ for each firm i when foreign tax crediting is practiced.

11.2.3 The Optimal Tax Policy

With the use of capital taxes having been ruled out, it is useful to ask how the government's other tax instruments should be chosen. My first result is that primary-sector wages are higher than secondary-sector wages under the optimal tax system, given reasonable assumptions about the utility function. This result does not follow immediately from the specification of the model since an alternative way of satisfying the no-shirking condition would be to keep the primary-sector effort level (e_x) relatively low. Indeed, Carmichael notes that "it is simply not obvious what (if anything) efficiency wage models predict about wage differentials in the cross section. The results depend on the precise way in which the firm's . . . characteristics combine to affect the position and shape of the entire wage/productivity relationship" (1988, 27–28). His comment concerns the laissez-faire behavior of firms. If the government is able to pursue the optimal tax policy described here, then a rather strong case can be made for providing primary-sector workers with a higher income than secondary-sector workers. In particular, I now prove the following.

Proposition 2: I_x must exceed I_y at the optimum if the following assumptions hold:

i. $v_I(I, e)$ declines with I and is nonincreasing in e;
ii. $v_I(I_x, e_x) - (1 - \pi_x)v_I(I_x, 0) > 0$.

Proof: Differentiate the Lagrangian with respect to income levels to obtain the following first-order conditions for the optimal income levels:

$$(18) \quad N_x v_I(I_x, e_x) - \lambda N_x + \beta[v_I(I_x, e_x) - (1 - \pi_x)v_I(I_x, 0)] = 0$$

and

$$(19) \quad N_y v_I(I_y, e_y) - \lambda N_y - \beta\pi_x v_I(I_y, e_y) = 0.$$

Combining (18) and (19) gives,

$$(20) \quad v_I(I_x, e_x) - v_I(I_y, e_y) = -\beta N_x^{-1}[v_I(I_x, e_x) - (1 - \pi_x)v_I(I_x, 0)]$$
$$- \beta N_y^{-1}\pi_x v_I(I_y, e_y).$$

Assume now that, contrary to the claim, $I_x \leq I_y$. To satisfy the no-shirking condition, $v(I_x, e_x)$ must exceed $v(I_y, e_y)$. Thus, $e_x < e_y$. By assumption i, it follows that $v_I (I_x, e_x) \geq v_I(I_y, e_y)$. But, under assumption ii, (20) implies that $v_I(I_x, e_x) < v_I(I_y, e_y)$, which is a contradiction. Q.E.D.

Assumption i is quite weak since the marginal utility of income is normally thought of as rising with leisure and an increase in e may be viewed as a reduction in leisure. Assumption ii is also reasonable: although an increase in I_x could increase the incentive to shirk in cases where π_x is near zero and shirking workers possess relatively high marginal utilities of income, such a case is rather extreme. With proposition 2 serving as the justification, I will therefore presume that the primary sector is the high-wage sector throughout this paper.

I now investigate the signs of the optimal per capita employment taxes and proportional wage taxes, τ_i and t_{wi}. Recall that these taxes combine to produce the following *marginal* tax on employment in sector i:

$$(21) \quad T_i = t_{wi}w_i + \tau_i.$$

The marginal wage tax is $t_{wi}N_i$. The next proposition shows that both employment and the wage should be subsidized at the margin in the primary sector but not in the secondary sector. The subsidies are financed with the poll tax.

Proposition 3: There exists an optimal tax system with the following properties:

$$T_x < 0, \quad t_{wx} < 0, \quad T_y = \tau_y = t_{wy} = 0.$$

Proof: To prove that $t_{wx} < 0$ and $t_{wy} = 0$, first differentiate the Lagrangian with respect to e_x and e_y, giving the first-order conditions

$$(22) \qquad N_x v_e(I_x, e_x) + \lambda N_x[p_x f_E^x(E_x, K_x)] + \beta v_e(I_x, e_x) = 0$$

and

$$(23) \qquad N_y v_e(I_y, e_y) + \lambda N_y[p_y f_E^y(E_y, K_y)] - \beta \pi_x v_e(I_y, e_y) = 0.$$

Next use the second equality in (9) to write

$$(24) \qquad v_I(I_x, e_x) + v_e(I_x, e_x)(\partial e^x / \partial I_x) = (1 - \pi_x) v_I(I_x, 0)$$

and

$$(25) \qquad v_I(I_y, e_y) + v_e(I_y, e_y)(\partial e^y / \partial I_y) = 0.$$

If (22) and (23) are multiplied by $\partial e^x / \partial I_x$ and $\partial e^y / \partial I_y$, respectively, and the results are added to the first-order conditions for I_x and I_y (eqq. [18] and [19]), then (24) and (25) can be used to obtain

$$(26) \qquad p_x f_E^x(E_x, K_x)(\partial e^x / \partial I_x) N_x = N_x - \lambda^{-1}(1 - \pi_x) v_I(I_x, 0)$$

and

$$(27) \qquad p_y f_E^y(E_y, K_y)(\partial e^y / \partial I_y) N_y = N_y.$$

On the other hand, combining the first-order conditions for profit maximization given by (9) and (11) yields

$$(28) \qquad p_x f_E^x(E_x, K_x)(\partial e^x / \partial I_x) N_x = \{1 + t_{wx}\} N_x$$

and

$$(29) \qquad p_y f_E^y(E_y, K_y)(\partial e^y / \partial I_y) N_y = \{1 + t_{wy}\} N_y.$$

Equations (26) and (28) then yield $t_{wx} < 0$, while (27) and (29) imply that $t_{wy} = 0$.

As discussed in Section 11.1.3, τ_y may be set equal to zero without loss of generality. With t_{wy} also equal to zero, it follows that $T_y = 0$.

To prove that $T_x < 0$, differentiate the Lagrangian with respect to N_x to obtain the first-order condition

$$(30) \qquad v(I_x, e_x) - v(I_y, e_y) + \lambda\{[p_x f_E^x(E_x, K_x)e_x - I_x]$$
$$- [p_y f_E^y(E_y, K_y)e_y - I_y]\} = 0.$$

Note that

$$(31) \qquad I_x - I_y = w_x - w_y.$$

Since $\lambda > 0$ and the no-shirking condition requires that $v(I_x, e_x) > v(I_y, e_y)$, (30) and (31) give

(32) $\qquad p_x f^x_E(E_x, K_x)e_x - w_x < p_y f^y_E(E_y, K_y)e_y - w_y$.

By the first-order condition for profit maximization given by (11),

(33) $\qquad p_i f^i_E(E_i, K_i)e_i - w_i = t_{wi}w_i + \tau_i = T_i$.

Substituting (33) into (32) and using $T_y = 0$ gives $T_x < 0$. Q.E.D.

Both Calvo (1985) and Bulow-Summers also demonstrate the desirability of employment subsidies on primary-sector jobs, financed by taxes that impose a burden on self-employed workers (Calvo) or secondary-sector workers (Bulow-Summers). Bulow-Summers find that these subsidies should be used to equate the value of a worker's marginal product across sectors (see their fig. 2). Such a use is not generally desirable in the present model because equity considerations eliminate the desirability of satisfying the standard efficiency conditions (my proposition 1 being a major exception). In fact, the relation between the values of the marginal products of labor in the two sectors cannot be signed in general.

An intuitive explanation may be provided for $t_{wx} < 0$ in proposition 3. By (9), the marginal rate of substitution between labor effort and income in the primary sector is less than the additional incomes that workers must receive to induce them to provide another unit of labor effort:

(34) $\qquad -v_e(I_x, e_x)/v_I(I_x, e_x) < (\partial e^x/\partial I_x)^{-1}$.

In the absence of employment and wage taxation, however, (28) implies that

(35) $\qquad p_x f^x_E(E_x, K_x) = (\partial e^x/\partial I_x)^{-1}$.

Thus, we have a situation in which the marginal rate of transformation between effective labor and income exceeds the corresponding marginal rate of substitution; that is, the marginal benefit of additional effort is greater than the marginal cost. For this reason, subsidies should be used to induce the primary-sector firm to raise its wages and thereby induce workers to supply more labor effort without shirking.

In contrast to this result, there is no role for wage subsidies in the Bulow-Summers model because all nonshirking workers are assumed to provide one unit of labor effort, regardless of price incentives. The result also differs from Johnson and Layard's (1986, 963) conclusion that a *positive* proportional tax on a firm's total wage bill is a desirable means of financing a per capita subsidy on employment, the argument being that the combined effect of the two taxes is to lower unemployment in their model. They consider a one-sector efficiency wage model based on labor turnover behavior. The proportional wage tax is completely passed back onto the wage in this model, leaving effective before-tax wages unchanged but lowering all after-tax wages by the same amounts. Such a tax plays the same role as my poll tax: it raises revenue without affecting the marginal behavioral incentives faced by workers and firms.

Note finally that my explanation for wage subsidies in the primary sector does not carry over to the secondary section because the absence of a supervision problem there implies that $p_y f_E^y(E_y, K_y) = - v_e(I_y, e_y)/v_I(I_y, e_y)$ in the absence of taxation.

11.3 Asymmetric Information

I now consider informational asymmetries as a possible justification for positive or negative taxes on internationally mobile capital. My basic assumption about information is that the government possesses incomplete information about the identity of those firms with efficiency wage problems. In other words, the government is not certain about whether a given firm is in the "primary sector" (x) or the "secondary sector" (y). To formalize this idea, I assume that the economy contains a fixed number of firms, indexed by $i = 1, 2, \ldots$; and that the government attaches a probability ψ_i to a firm i being a "type x firm," in which shirking workers are caught with probability $\pi_x < 1$, and a probability $1 - \psi_i$ to the firm being a "type y firm," where the detection probability is $\pi_y = 1$.[10] Thus, a given firm's effort function is either $e^x(I, \bar{u})$ or $e^y(I, \bar{u})$, as previously defined.

To isolate this particular source of uncertainty from uncertainty about production technologies, I continue to assume that each firm's production function is known, $f^i(E, K)$ for firm i.[11] Issues concerning unknown characteristics of production functions are discussed at the end of this section. Note, however, that this specification can be made to handle the empirical observation that capital intensive firms tend to pay high wages simply by making the ψ_i's relatively high for firms with relatively capital intensive technologies. In fact, the model may be transformed back into a symmetric information model by assuming that ψ_i equals zero or one for all i. To avoid obvious qualifications on the results, I henceforth assume that $0 < \psi_i < 1$ for every i.

To make a firm's worker detection probability unobservable, additional assumptions must be made about which of the firm's actions the government can or cannot observe. The government could infer the firm's shirker detection probability from observations of the wage that the firm pays workers and the effort level that it demands in return. To eliminate this possibility, the obvious assumption to make is that the government cannot observe effort levels. But the government could still use its knowledge of production functions to infer effort levels from observations on wages, outputs, employment levels, and capital stocks. Of all these variables, a firm's capital stock is by far the most difficult to measure in practice. Thus, I create an asymmetric information problem by making the capital stock unobservable. Baron and Myerson (1982) follow a similar approach in their seminal article on regulation by assuming that some parameters of a firm's cost function are unobservable. Later, I argue that other choices of the unobservable variable do not affect my results. A natural direction for future research would be to construct a model in which the capital stock is imperfectly observed.

Some readers may now ask, How can you study capital taxation using a model in which the government does not observe capital? The answer is that the government's ability to tax those variables it does observe effectively allows it to tax capital. In particular, the total tax paid by a firm i can be made a function of its wage w, output Q, and employment N: $T^i(w, Q, N)$. The marginal tax on another unit of capital is then $(\partial T^i/\partial Q)(\partial Q/\partial K)$, where $\partial Q/\partial K$ is the marginal product of capital. Under profit maximization, this marginal tax equals $p_i f_K^i(E_i, K_i) - r$ for firm i.

Put differently, there is never any loss of generality in arbitrarily picking a single output or input to be untaxed because only relative prices matter. The limitation placed here on the government's taxation powers is not that capital cannot be taxed directly but rather that the government does not possess the information needed to optimally tailor the tax function to differences between primary- and secondary-sector firms. Instead, it must confront any firm i with a tax function that is independent of its type, $T^i(w, Q, N)$.[12] My main concern is whether the optimal tax system effectively taxes or subsidizes a firm's capital at the margin, as measured by $p_i f_K^i(E_i, K_i) - r$.[13]

11.3.1 The Government's Maximization Problem

To pinpoint the role of the informational asymmetry, it is useful first to pose the government's optimization problem for the case where the government knows each firm's type, but with only those variables that are observable in the asymmetric information case treated as control variables. In particular, capital and effort levels may be omitted as control variables by inverting the production relation for each firm i, $Q = f^i[e^{j(i)}(I, \bar{u})N, K]$ if firm i's type is $j(i)$, to obtain

$$(36) \qquad K = K^i[Q, e^{j(i)}(I, \bar{u})N].$$

This leaves the equilibrium secondary-sector utility, $\bar{u}$, and the income-production vector for each i, (I_i, Q_i, N_i), as the control variables. Problem (P1) may then be rephrased as follows:

$$(P2) \qquad \text{Max} \sum_i N_i v[I_i, e^{j(i)}(I_i, \bar{u})]$$

subject to

$$(37) \qquad rK^* + \sum_i \{p_i Q_i - rK^i[Q_i, e^{j(i)}(I_i, \bar{u})N_i] - N_i I_i\} \geq 0,$$

$$(38) \qquad \sum_i N_i = N^*.$$

The no-shirking condition from problem (P1) does not appear in (P2) because it has been incorporated into the effort functions. Each secondary-sector firm provides workers with the equilibrium utility, $v[I_i, e^y(I_i, \bar{u})]$ $= \bar{u}$, while primary-sector workers receive higher utilities to prevent shirking: $v[I_i, e^x(I_i, \bar{u})] > \bar{u}$. Note that this utility differential will generally differ across firms with different production functions because incomes will differ. For any pair of primary- and secondary-sector firms, however, propositions 1–3 continue to hold. Of greatest interest here is proposition 1, which says that no firm's capital should be taxed or subsidized at the margin.

Now consider the asymmetric information problem. It is again best to proceed indirectly by setting up the optimization problem with outputs, employment levels, and incomes treated as control variables rather than optimizing directly over the set of permissible tax functions. Since the government does not know whether a given firm i is type x or type y, however, it must choose a wage-production vector for both contingencies: (w_{ix}, Q_{ix}, N_{ix}) and (w_{iy}, Q_{iy}, N_{iy}).[14] Furthermore, these vectors will be feasible only if the firm can construct a tax function, $T^i(w, Q, N)$, such that (w_{ix}, Q_{ix}, N_{ix}) gives the firm at least as high a profit level as (w_{iy}, Q_{iy}, N_{iy}) if the firm's type is x and, conversely, if its type is y. Equivalently, there must exist payments T_{ix} and T_{iy} such that the profit function for the type x firm satisfies

$$(39) \quad p_i Q_{ix} - w_{ix} N_{ix} - r K^i[Q_{ix}, e^x(n + w_{ix}, \bar{u}) N_{ix}] - T_{ix} \geq p_i Q_{iy}$$
$$- w_{iy} N_{iy} - r K^i[Q_{iy}, e^x(n + w_{iy}, \bar{u}) N_{iy}] - T_{iy} ,$$

while the profit function for the type y firm satisfies

$$(40) \quad p_i Q_{iy} - w_{iy} N_{iy} - r K^i[Q_{iy}, e^y(n + w_{iy}, \bar{u}) N_{iy}] - T_{iy} \geq p_i Q_{ix}$$
$$- w_{ix} N_{ix} - r K^i[Q_{ix}, e^y(n + w_{ix}, \bar{u}) N_{ix}] - T_{ix} .$$

These are completely new types of constraints, known in the principal-agent literature as an "incentive-compatibility constraints." They can be combined into a single constraint by adding (39) and (40) together, canceling common terms on the two sides of the inequality, and rearranging the result to obtain

$$(41) \quad K^i[Q_{iy}, e^x(n + w_{iy}, \bar{u}) N_{iy}] - K^i[Q_{ix}, e^x(n + w_{ix}, \bar{u}) N_{ix}]$$
$$\geq K^i[Q_{iy}, e^y(n + w_{iy}, \bar{u}) N_{iy}] - K^i[Q_{ix}, e^y(n + w_{ix}, \bar{u}) N_{ix}].$$

This constraint can be understood by observing that the optimal tax problem being considered here is equivalent to the design of an optimal "truth-telling mechanism." The government asks firms to name their types, uses the answers to control their production activities, and ensures that these answers are truthful by awarding the firms with positive or negative subsidies based on their answers. Constraint (41) ensures that such subsidies exist by requiring that the incentive to reveal its type as x rather than y, measured in terms of capital cost savings, is at least as great for an actual type x firm as for an actual type y firm. By the famous "Revelation Principle" from the principal-agent literature, no sacrifice in welfare is incurred by considering only truth-telling mechanisms.

There is no need to include a separate constraint requiring that the tax function allow each firm i to earn nonnegative profits: $p_i Q_{ij} - w_{ij} N_{ij} - r \cdot K^i [Q_{ij}, e^j(n + w_{ij}, \bar{u}) N_{ij}] - T_{ij} \geq 0$ for $j = x, y$, where T_{ij} is again the tax firm i owes if it chooses (w_{ij}, Q_{ij}, N_{ij}). Such constraints would never be binding. To see this, suppose that a given tax function violates one of them. Then the government can lower the total tax owed at every (w, Q, N) by the same amount until profits become nonnegative for both types of firms. This change in the tax function obviously does not affect the profit maximizing (w, Q, N) for either type, and its effect on nonlabor incomes can be offset by a reduction in the poll tax (recall that n is nonlabor income net of this tax).

With (41) representing the only new constraint for the problem, there is no need to include transfers T_{ix} and T_{iy} as explicit variables in the maximization problem. In contrast, the regulator in Baron and Myerson's paper possesses an objective function that contains the subsidies paid to the monopolist. The reason for this difference is that Baron and Myerson treat consumers and the monopolist as separate agents and assume that income in the hands of consumers has a greater social value than income in the hands of the monopolist. This assumption bears a close relation to Laffont and Tirole's (1986) assumption that there is an exogenously determined deadweight loss associated with the transfer of income from consumers to the monopolist. In the present model, however, workers are also owners of the firms, and the transfers provided to the firms can be financed by nondistortionary taxes. Guesnerie and Laffont (1984) also study a class of principal-agent problems in which the income transfers to the agent do not enter the principal's objective function.

The government's maximization problem may now be stated in full. There is no need to include w_{ix} and n as separate control variables in this problem because only their sum matters. Thus, the control variables are the equilibrium utility, $\bar{u}$, and an income-production vector for each firm i, $(I_{ix}, Q_{ix}, N_{ix}, I_{iy}, Q_{iy}, N_{iy})$. With ψ_i denoting firm i's probability of being type x, these variables are chosen to solve

(P3) $$\text{Max} \sum_i \{\psi_i [N_{ix} v(I_{ix}, e^x(I_{ix}, \bar{u}))] + (1 - \psi_i) N_{iy} \bar{u}\}$$

subject to

(42) $$rK^* + \sum_i \{\psi_i [p_i Q_{ix} - rK^i(Q_{ix}, e^x(I_{ix}, \bar{u}) N_{ix}) - N_{ix} I_{ix}]\} +$$
$$\sum_i \{(1 - \psi_i)[p_i Q_{iy} - rK^i(Q_{iy}, e^y(I_{iy}, \bar{u}) N_{iy}) - N_{iy} I_{iy}]\} \geq 0,$$

(43) $$\sum_i \{\psi_i N_{ix} + (1 - \psi_i) N_{iy}\} = N^*,$$

(44)
$$K^i[Q_{iy}, e^x(I_{iy}, \bar{u})N_{iy}] - K^i[Q_{ix}, e^x(I_{ix}, \bar{u})N_{ix}]$$
$$\geq K^i(Q_{iy}, e^y(I_{iy}, \bar{u})N_{iy}) - K^i[Q_{ix}, e^y(I_{ix}, \bar{u})N_{ix}]$$

for all i. As shown, I require only that the trade balance constraint and employment constraint hold in an expected value sense. The assumption underlying this specification is that the number of firms is large enough to eliminate uncertainty about trade and employment in the aggregate.

The major difference between problems (P2) and (P3) is the presence of the incentive-compatibility constraint in the latter. But this difference is irrelevant if the incentive-compatibility constraint does not bind. Appendix C demonstrates that there exist cases where the incentive-compatibility constraint does bind and cases where it does not. Since the example given there assumes that consumers are risk neutral, the analysis demonstrates that the informational asymmetry may by itself prevent the attainment of a first-best optimum. I now discuss the implications of a binding incentive-compatibility constraint for capital taxation.

11.3.2   Capital Taxation

This section presents an argument for taxing primary-sector capital at a positive rate and secondary-sector capital at a negative rate. The driving force behind the result is that the primary sector has an inferior supervision technology. Simply stated, tax policy should discourage investment in firms with inferior production processes.

To prove these results, I need the additional assumption that labor and capital are complements in the sense that an increase in either factor raises the marginal product of the other: $f^i_{EK}(E, K) > 0.$[15] Violations of this assumption would be hard to justify at the current level of aggregation, although they are theoretically possible under my assumption of decreasing returns to scale (but not under constant returns).

The specific proposition is stated as follows:

Proposition 4: If capital and labor are complements in all firms, and if the incentive-compatibility constraint binds at the margin for firm i, then the following conditions hold at the optimum:

i. $p_i f^i_K(E_{ix}, K_{ix}) > r$;

ii. $p_i f^i_K(E_{iy}, K_{iy}) < r.$

Proof: Let λ and α_i denote the Lagrange multipliers on constraints (42) and (44). Omitting i as a subscript or superscript to avoid clutter, I may write the first-order conditions for firm i's outputs, Q_x and Q_y, as follows:

(45)
$$\lambda \psi_i[p_i - rK_Q(Q_x, e^x(I_x, \bar{u})N_x)] + \alpha_i[K_Q(Q_x, e^y(I_x, \bar{u})N_x)$$
$$- K_Q(Q_x, e^x(I_x, \bar{u})N_x)] = 0$$

and

(46) $\lambda(1 - \psi_i)[p_i - rK_Q(Q_y, e^y(I_y, \bar{u})N_y)] + \alpha_i[K_Q(Q_y, e^x(I_y, \bar{u})N_y)$
$- K_Q(Q_y, e^y(I_y, \bar{u})N_y)] = 0.$

Recall that

(47) $e^y(I, \bar{u}) > e^x(I, \bar{u})$

for any given I and $\bar{u}$. It follows that, if both the type x and the type y firms employ the same numbers of workers and pay them the same wages to produce the same output levels, then the type y firm uses more effective labor and less capital than the type x firm to produce this common output. Under the assumption that labor and capital are complements, the marginal product of capital is then greater in the type y firm than in the type x firm, or, since the derivative $K_Q(\cdot)$ is the inverse of this marginal product,

(48) $K_Q[Q, e^y(I, \bar{u})N] < K_Q(Q, e^x(I, \bar{u})N]$

for any $Q, N, I,$ and $\bar{u}$. Conditions (45) and (48) then imply that

(49) $p_i - rK_Q(Q_x, e^x(I_x, \bar{u})N_x] > 0,$

while (46) and (48) give

(50) $p_i - rK_Q[Q_y, e^y(I_y, \bar{u})N_y] < 0.$

Inequalities (49) and (50) are equivalent to i and ii of the proposition. Q.E.D.

The basic idea behind these results may be simply explained using the equivalence between the tax scheme and truth-telling mechanisms. If the government increases the output it wants a given firm i to choose if its type is x (Q_x), then the profits that this firm receives by choosing the wage-production plan (w_x, Q_x, N_x) change by

$$\Delta_x = p_i - rK_Q[Q_x, e^x(I_x, \bar{u})N_x],$$

where $I_x = n + w_x$. On the other hand, if the given firm were a type y but chose the same (w_x, Q_x, N_x), then its profits would change by

$$\Delta_y = p_i - rK_Q[Q_x, e^y(I_x, \bar{u})N_x].$$

But $\Delta_y > \Delta_x$ because (47) and the complementarity assumption imply that capital is more productive in y than in x. This means that the rise in Q_x gives the type y firm a greater incentive to masquerade as a type x firm, relative to the incentive the x firm faces to reveal its type truthfully. The marginal social cost of these incentive changes is determined by the Lagrange multiplier on the firm i's incentive-compatibility constraint. To offset this cost, a rise in Q_x from the optimum must improve the trade balance, implying that the value of the marginal product of capital must exceed the world interest rate. In other words, primary-sector capital should be positively taxed at the margin. By a similar argument, secondary-sector capital should be subsidized.

11.3.3   Alternative Specifications

Using the type of reasoning just given, I may quickly show that alternative specifications of the informational asymmetry either do not change the results or eliminate any role for capital market intervention. Suppose first that the government can directly tax capital, employment, and wages but finds monitoring a firm's output to be prohibitively costly.[16] Let (w_x, N_x, K_x) be the wage-input vector that it wishes to assign a given firm i if its type is x, and consider an increase in K_x. If the type x firm chooses (w_x, N_x, K_x), then its profits change by

$$\Delta_x = p_i f_K[e^x(I_x, \bar{u})N_x, K_x] - r,$$

where again $I_x = n + w_x$. On the other hand, if the given firm i were type y but chose to masquerade as a type x firm by also choosing (w_x, N_x, K_x), then it would experience a change in profits given by

$$\Delta_y = p_i f_K[e^y(I_x, \bar{u})N_x, K_x] - r.$$

Again, $e^y(I_x, \bar{u})$ exceeds $e^x(I_x, \bar{u})$ since only the type x firm has the supervision problem. By the assumption of complementary factors, it follows that $\Delta_y > \Delta_x$. Increasing primary-sector capital therefore increases the incentive for the type y firm to masquerade as a type x firm, relative to the incentive of the type x firm to reveal its type truthfully. Again, this cost must be balanced by an improvement in the trade surplus, implying that $p_i \cdot f_K(E_x, K_x)$ exceeds r at the optimum. By similar reasoning, $p_i f_K(E_y, K_y)$ falls short of r.

The story changes if either wages or employment is made the unobservable variable. In either case, if the government observes both a firm's output and capital stock, then it can infer the firm's effective labor from the production function, $Q = f(E, K)$. Thus, a type y firm cannot hide its true identity unless it chooses the same Q, E, and K as a type x firm (although the two types will use different effort and employment levels to obtain the same $E = eN$). But then the marginal product of capital in a type x firm choosing the (Q_x, K_x) assigned to it will be identical to the marginal production of a y firm choosing the same (Q_x, K_x). Raising K_x can therefore have no desirable effect on the relevant incentive-compatibility constraint for the problem, implying that primary-sector capital should not be taxed or subsidized at the margin. By the same reasoning, neither should secondary-sector capital be taxed or subsidized.

This last argument can be used to analyze the case where the detection probabilities depend positively on unobservable managerial effort, m, with π_y exceeding π_x at any given level of m. Suppose that this managerial effort enters the firm's objective function as an unobservable cost.[17] With both output and capital observable, a type x firm will again have to choose the same effective labor as a type y firm in order to hide its true identity. If wages and employment are also observable, this means that the type x firm will be able to masquerade as a type y firm only if it raises its managerial effort enough to equate π_x with π_y. In any case, the type y and x firms will again possess the same marginal products of capital if they choose the same levels of the observable variables. By the previous argument, neither primary- nor secondary-sector capital should then be taxed or subsidized at the margin.

So far, uncertainty about supervision problems has been analyzed in the absence of production function uncertainty by assuming that the government knows each firm's production function but not the supervision technology. A more general specification might also allow the production function to be uncertain. In this case, if the possibility that a firm has a supervision problem is positively related to the possibility that its marginal product of capital is relatively high at any given (E, K), the results may be reversed. This can be explained intuitively. In the previous model, capital taxation effectively steers investment away from firms with inferior supervision technologies and into firms with superior supervision technologies. High wages in the primary sector basically mask inefficiencies in the production process, thereby making the taxation of primary-sector capital desirable. Differences in production functions may offset this inefficiency, however. Loosely stated, the result is still that the sector with the more efficient production process should receive positive capital subsidies, but the identity of this sector will now depend on both differences in production functions and supervision technologies.

11.4   Concluding Remarks

To summarize, this paper finds little support for policies that subsidize capital investment in high-wage industries. Indeed, the opposite conclusion is obtained under reasonable assumptions about informational asymmetries: a positive marginal tax should be placed on primary-sector capital. The driving force behind this result is that the production processes used by high-wage firms are inferior to low-wage production processes in one particular aspect: the supervision technology.

Thus, informational asymmetries create a role for basing tax policy on efficiency differences between sectors. A useful task for future research would be to examine this role in a variety of different contexts. For example, if efficiency wages are paid to reduce labor turnover rather than shirking, then perhaps investment in high-wage jobs should still be taxed at the margin since high wages may again be viewed as masking an inefficiency in the production process, namely, the relatively severe worker turnover problem. This extension would require a dynamic model.

Another role for a dynamic analysis would be to model the intertemporal process by which a government learns the attributes of various firms. One conjecture is that asymmetric information reasons for distortionary capital taxation are unimportant in the long run since the attributes of different firms can eventually be uncovered. But the government's acquisition of information may be severely hampered by the incentives that firms face to hide those activities that may increase their future tax burdens. A recent paper by Laffont and Tirole (1988) suggests that this consideration may be a serious problem for tax policy.

To conclude, three limitations of the asymmetric information analysis deserve emphasis. First, when interpreting all these results, it is important to keep in mind that only marginal taxes have been considered, not average taxes. In fact, the two are likely to depart quite significantly since a highly nonlinear tax schedule would be required to tax a given firm's capital at a positive marginal rate if its type is x and at a negative marginal rate if its type is y, as defined in the text.

Second, the paper has not addressed the issue of how the incentive-compatibility constraint affects the taxation of employment and wages. I have not obtained clear-cut results on this issue, but it deserves further research.

Finally, the degree to which the results on capital taxation are sensitive to the particular informational asymmetry modeled here needs to be further explored. Section 11.3.3 has noted that there exist additional sources of uncertainty that work against proposition 4. As matters now stand, however, I hope to have convinced readers that it is difficult to justify subsidizing capital investment in high-wage industries with any reasonable degree of confidence.

Appendix A

This appendix discusses the optimal role of excise taxes in the symmetric information case and how this use alters the optimal values of the other tax instruments. To study this role, I must now explicitly include the consumer price vector in the demand and utility functions: $c^i(q, I, e)$ and $v(q, I, e)$. Since only relative prices matter, however, good y may be arbitrarily chosen as the untaxed commodity: $q_y = p_y$.

If $c^x(q, I_x, 0) > (<) \, c^x(q, I_x, e_x)$ in the absence of excise taxes, then placing a small positive (negative) tax on good x raises $v(q, I_x, e_x) - v(q, I_x, 0)$, thereby lessening the shirking problem. This explains the following result.

420   **John Douglas Wilson**

Proposition A1: At the optimum, $q_x \gtreqless p_x$ as $c^x(q, I_x, 0) \gtreqless c^x(q, I_x, e_x)$.

Proof: The Lagrangian expression given by (16) must be reformulated to take account of excise taxes. To do so, I use the workers' budget constraints to write,

(A1) $p_x c^x(q, I_i, e_i) + p_y c^y(q, I_i, e_i) = I_i - (q_x - p_x)c^x(q, I_i, e_i)$.

Using this equality to rewrite the trade balance constraint given by (1), equation (16) may be amended to read

(A2) $L = N_x v(q, I_x, e_x) + (N^* - N_x)v(q, I_y, e_y)$

$+ \lambda\{p_x f^x(e_x N_x, K_x) + p_y f^y[e_y(N^* - N_x), K_y]$
$+ r(K^* - K_x - K_y) - N_x I_x - (N^* - N_x)I_y$
$- (q_x - p_x)[N_x c^x(q, I_x, e_x) + (N^* - N_x)c^x(q, I_y, e_y)]\}$
$+ \beta\{v(q, I_x, e_x) - \pi_x v(q, I_y, e_y) - (1 - \pi_x)v(q, I_x, 0)\}$.

Starting from the optimum, any combination of changes in consumer prices or incomes must have a zero first-order effect on the Lagrangian. Consider an increase in q_x, accompanied by increases in I_x and I_y that leave unchanged the utilities of all secondary-sector workers and nonshirking primary-sector workers:

(A3) $v_q(q, I_y, e_y)dq_x + v_I(q, I_y, e_y)dI_y = 0$

and

(A4) $v_q(q, I_x, e_x)dq_x + v_I(q, I_x, e_x)dI_x = 0$,

where d denotes a differential change. In other words, I am considering compensated changes in q_x for both types of workers. By Roy's Identity, the income compensations must satisfy

(A5) $dI_i = c^x(q, I_i, e_i)dq_x, \quad i = x, y$.

Using (A5), the first-order change in the Lagrangian from these compensated price changes may then be expressed as follows:

(A6) $dL = -\lambda(q_x - p_x)[N_x dc^x(q, I_x, e_x) + N_y dc^x(q, I_y, e_y)]$
$- \beta(1 - \pi_x)dv(q, I_x, 0) = 0$.

Another application of Roy's Identity gives the following expression for the first-order change in the utilities of undetected shirkers:

(A7) $dv(q, I_x, 0) = v_I(q, I_x, 0)[-c^x(q, I_x, 0)dq_x + dI_x]$.

Substituting (A5) into (A7) for dI_x and then substituting the result into (A6) yields

(A8) $dL = \lambda(q_x - p_x)[N_x dc^x(q, I_x, e_x) + N_y dc^x(q, I_y, e_y)]$

$+ \beta(1 - \pi)v_l(q, I_x, 0)[c^x(q, I_x, 0) - c^x(q, I_x, e_x)]dq_x = 0.$

The demand changes in the first bracketed term are necessarily negative because they result from a compensated price increase. The proposition then follows immediately from (A8). Q.E.D.

Thus, the government should place a positive (negative) tax on consumption of the primary-sector good if undetected shirkers possess higher (lower) demands for this good than nonshirking primary-sector workers. In the case of a separable utility function, $u(c_x, c_y, e) = g(c_x, c_y) - h(e)$, proposition A1 implies that the optimal $q_x - p_x$ equals zero.

Remember that no worker actually shirks in equilibrium. The differential tax burden here acts as an additional incentive not to shirk without penalizing any worker.

Proposition A1 offers an interesting contrast to Dixit's (1989) finding that all marginal rates of substitution should equal world prices, although an adverse selection problem in his model constrains the relative utilities of different workers. The crucial difference between the models is easily pinpointed by Dixit's explanation for this result: "The point is that adverse selection imposes incentive-compatibility constraints, but these apply to the utility *levels*, $U_{ij} = U(x_{ij}, y_{ij})$, not to the means by which they are attained. Therefore the usual efficiency argument for minimizing the resource costs of achieving the desired utility levels remains valid" (238). In my model, not only does the no-shirking condition constrain utility levels, but the government is also constrained to give undetected shirkers and nonshirkers in the primary sector the same incomes and consumer prices. This inability to achieve desired utility levels by any means is responsible for the desirability of excise taxes.

I conclude this appendix by describing how the presence of excise taxes affects propositions 2 and 3 in the text.[18] The case of marginal employment subsidies is straightforward. Proposition 3 shows that work in the primary sector should be subsidized relative to work in the secondary sector in the sense that $T_x < T_y$ (the individual values of these taxes were shown to be indeterminate in sec. 11.1.3). This claim remains valid with excise taxes if the definition of the relative subsidies is modified to include differences in the excise tax payments:

(A9) $T_x + (q_x - p_x)c^x(q, I_x, e_x) < T_y + (q_x - p_x)c^x(q, I_y, e_y).$

If poll tax payments are added to both sides of (A9), then the government budget constraint can be balanced only if the right side is positive and the left is negative. As before, secondary-sector workers face a positive total tax burden, while primary-sector workers face a negative total tax burden. The only new feature is that this tax burden includes excise taxes (or subsidies).

The required modification of the wage tax results in proposition 3 is described by the following formulae for the marginal wage taxes:

(A10) $t_{wx}N_x = -\lambda^{-1}(1 - \pi_x)v_l(q, I_x, 0) - (q_x - p_x)N_x[c_l^x(q, I_x, e_x)$
          $+ c_e^x(q, I_x, e_x) \bullet (\partial e^x / \partial I_x)]$

and

(A11) $t_{wy}N_y = -(q_x - p_x)N_y[c_l^x(q, I_y, e_y) + c_e^x(q, I_y, e_y) \bullet (\partial e^y / \partial I_y)]$.

Account must now be taken of the effects of a rise in income and effort levels on the distorted pattern of consumption. For this reason, it may now be undesirable to subsidize wage increases in the primary sector. For the secondary sector, whether consumption becomes more or less distorted in response to a rise in the wage and effort level completely determines the sign of the wage tax. Since proposition A1 shows that the optimal $q_x - p_x$ can be positive or negative, however, there appears to be no general presumption about the direction in which these new considerations push the signs of the wage taxes at the full optimum.

Turn finally to proposition 2, which shows that primary-sector workers receive higher incomes than secondary-sector workers. If aggregate consumption of the commodity with a positive (negative) tax can be increased (reduced) by transferring income from primary- to secondary-sector workers, then this transfer reduces the distortionary effect of the excise tax on consumption patterns. For this reason, proposition 2 may no longer hold in all cases, although it is hard to imagine that this additional consideration would be strong enough in practice to reverse the desirability of setting I_x above I_y.

Appendix B

This appendix considers the case for subsidizing primary-sector capital when employment and wage subsidies are not available. To keep the government budget balanced, a "neutral" tax instrument is used to balance the budget, namely, a uniform poll tax (positive or negative) imposed on each worker. Since such a tax is "lump sum," it creates no incentive effects by itself. Capital taxes and subsidies are then left as the only means of dealing with the multiple distortions described in section 11.2. Concrete results are therefore hard to come by in the general case. For the following analysis, I alter the model in a way that allows me to concentrate on the employment distortion described in section 11.2. Specifically, I now follow the common practice in the efficiency wage literature of assuming that the effort level takes on only two values: zero and one. All workers provide one unit of labor in equilibrium since nobody shirks. Altered in this way, the model is called the "modified model."

My main result uses the assumption that labor and capital are complements in the sense that an increase in either factor raises the marginal product of the other. In this case, an increase in the price of either must lower the demand for both:

(B1)   If $f^i_{NK}(N_i, K_i) > 0$,   then $dN_i/dw_i < 0$ and $dK_i/dw_i < 0$,

and similarly for a rise in $r + t_{Ki}$ (see Silberberg 1978, sec. 4.4).

The main result now may be stated as follows.

Proposition B1: Suppose that $t_{Kx} = t_{Ky} = 0$ initially in the modified model. Then a small fall in t_{Kx} raises social welfare if factors are complements in the primary sector, and a small rise in t_{Ky} raises social welfare if factors are complements in the secondary sector.

Proof. A change in either of the two taxes must leave unchanged the trade balance constraint, given by (13) with $e_x = e_y = 1$:

(B2) $[p_x f^x_K(N_x, K_x) - r]dK_x + [p_y f^y_K(N_y, K_y) - r]dK_y + [p_x f^x_N(N_x, K_x)$
$- p_y f^y_N(N_y, K_y) - (w_x - w_y)]dN_x - [N_x dI_x + N_y dI_y] = 0$,

where a d denotes a differential change, and use is made of the equality, $I_x - I_y = w_x - w_y$. Given the absence of any initial taxes, the profit-maximization conditions given by (10) and (11) can be used to reduce (B2) to the following expression:

(B3) $$N_x dI_x + N_y dI_y = 0.$$

Equation (B3) implies that any change in primary- and secondary-sector worker incomes must take place in opposite directions. But the no-shirking condition, (5), implies that these changes must take place in identical directions. It follows that I_x and I_y do not change:

(B4) $$dI_x = dI_y = 0.$$

Thus, the welfare effects of a tax change are completely determined by the employment change, $dN_x = - dN_y$. Since the no-shirking condition implies that primary-sector workers have higher utilities than secondary-sector workers, welfare rises if and only if the tax change shifts employment from the secondary sector to the primary sector:

(B5) $$dW = (u_x - u_y)dN_x > 0$$

if and only if $dN_x > 0$, where $u_i = v(I_i, 1)$.

Since all workers obtain identical nonlabor incomes, (B4) also implies that any tax-induced changes in the primary- and secondary-sector wages must be identical:

(B6) $dw_x = dw_y$.

This result will be used to sign dN_x.

Suppose that factors are complements in the secondary sector, and consider a rise in t_{Ky}. If N_x fails to rise, then N_y cannot fall, and the assumption of complements implies that w_y must fall to offset the negative effect of t_{Ky} on N_y. Then w_x falls to satisfy (B6), which implies that N_x rises, contradicting the initial assumption.

Suppose that factors are complements in the primary sector, and consider a fall in t_{Kx}. If N_x fails to rise, then the assumption of complements implies that w_x must rise to offset the positive effect of the decline in t_{Kx} on N_x. Then w_y rises to satisfy (B6), which implies that N_y falls, contradicting the assumption that N_x does not rise. Q.E.D.

The basic explanation for this result is that welfare can be improved by undertaking policies that encourage labor to flow from the secondary sector to the primary sector. Given the complementarity assumption, one such policy is to encourage capital investment in the primary sector, while another is to discourage capital investment in the secondary sector. But dropping this assumption leads to ambiguous results and thereby highlights the roundabout nature of capital taxation as a means of encouraging employment in the primary sector.

Appendix C

This appendix shows by way of an example that the incentive-compatibility constraint in section 11.3 is binding in some cases but not in others. Since the example contains risk neutral consumers, it also demonstrates that the asymmetric information problem described in section 11.3 may render infeasible the first-best allocation, even if there is no social cost attached to the income inequality required to eliminate shirking.

By risk neutrality, I mean that utility is linear in income. It is further assumed that the disutility of labor effort is a perfect substitute with income, in which case the indirect utility function may be written

(C1) $v(I, e) = I - h(e); \quad h'(e) > 0, \quad h''(e) \geq 0.$

(The coefficient of I is set equal to one to simplify notation.) Equation (C1) allows the no-shirking condition faced by type x firms (eq. [5]), to be reexpressed

(C2) $I_x \pi_x - h(e_x) \geq \pi_x \tilde{u},$

while the utility requirement faced by type y firms is

(C3) $I_y - h(e_y) \geq \tilde{u}.$

For part of my example, I shall work with the following simple form of the effort disutility function:

(C4) $h(e) = e^{\eta}, \quad \eta \geq 1.$

On the production side of the model, I simplify matters by assuming that all firms produce the same good using identical production functions and that they possess identical probabilities of being a type x firm:

(C5) $f^i(E, K) = f(E, K), \quad \psi_i = \psi$

for all i. Thus, the only difference between firms is their unknown detection probabilities: $\pi_x < \pi_y = 1$.

Following the text, the number of firms is assumed to be large enough for actual aggregate income to be reasonably approximated by expected income. Normalizing the number of firms to equal one, aggregate income may then be written

(C6) $I^A = \psi N_x I_x + (1 - \psi) N_y I_y .$

Social welfare may then be written

(C7) $W = I^A - [\psi N_x h(e_x) + (1 - \psi)(N^* - N_x) h(e_y)].$

This is also social welfare when each firm's type, x or y, is known to the government since the probability ψ simply becomes the known fraction of type x firms.

I now investigate whether the incentive-compatibility constraint is satisfied under the solution to the symmetric information problem and, therefore, whether it is a binding constraint in the asymmetric information problem.

Since only aggregate income enters the social welfare function, no loss of generality is involved in setting $I_y = 0$ and giving all the income to workers in the primary sector since doing so maximizes the set of effort levels that are consistent with the no-shirking condition (eq. [C2]). (Alternatively, if there is a minimum subsistence income greater than zero, I_y may be set equal to its value.) Except for relatively low values of π_x, the no-shirking condition will then fail to bind and can therefore be omitted from the problem. In other words, the first-best solution will be feasible. This is the case I consider.

The control variables for the government's maximization problem are I^A, e_x, e_y, N_x, K_x, and K_y. They are chosen to maximize social welfare, as defined by (C7), subject to the trade balance constraint,

(C8) $\psi p f(e_x N_x, K_x) + (1 - \psi) p f[e_y(N^* - N_x), K_y]$
$$+ r[K^* - \psi K_x - (1 - \psi) K_y] - I^A \geq 0.$$

Given the symmetry of the problem, the solution calls for treating all firms alike along every dimension except income (with $I_x > I_y$ to take care of shirking):

(C9) $e_x = e_y = e'$, $K_x = K_y = K'$, $N_x = N_y = N'$.

Let us now consider whether an allocation with properties (C9) can satisfy the incentive-compatibility constraint for the asymmetric information problem. For the two types of firms both to be willing to choose e', I_x and I_y must be set so that

(C10) $e^x(I_x, \bar{u}) = e^y(I_y, \bar{u}) = e'$, $\bar{u} = I_y - h(e')$.

With incomes so determined, the incentive-compatibility condition ([44] in the text) becomes

(C11) $K[Q', e^x(I_y, \bar{u})N'] - K[Q', e^x(I_x, \bar{u})N']$

$$\geq K[Q', e^y(I_y, \bar{u})N'] - K[Q', e^y(I_x, \bar{u})N'],$$

where Q' is the common output level for both types of firms under (C9).

Whether (C11) holds will depend on the properties of both the production function and the effort functions. For the latter functions, I prove the following fundamental result.

Claim: Under assumptions (C1) and (C4), $e_I^x(I, \bar{u}) < e_I^y(I, \bar{u})$ for all I and $\bar{u}$.
Proof: By definition,

(C12) $h[e^y(I, \bar{u})] = I - \bar{u}$,

and, using (C2),

(C13) $h[e^x(I, \bar{u})] = \pi_x[I - \bar{u}]$.

Since $h'(e) = \eta h(e)/e$ under (C4), (C12) and (C13) give

(C14) $h'(e^y)e_I^y = \eta(I - \bar{u})(e_I^y/e^y) = 1$

and

(C15) $h'(e^x)e_I^x = \pi_x\eta(I - \bar{u})(e_I^x/e^x) = \pi_x$,

where the arguments of functions e^x and e^y have been omitted to simplify notation. Since $e^x(I, \bar{u}) < e^y(I, \bar{u})$, (C14) and (C15) imply that $e_I^x(I, \bar{u}) < e_I^y(I, \bar{u})$. Q.E.D.

Thus, the increase in effort levels that a firm can obtain by increasing worker incomes from I_x to I_y is less for the type x firms than for the type y firms. The crucial implication of this claim is

(C16) $e^x(I_x, \bar{u}) - e^x(I_y, \bar{u}) < e^y(I_x, \bar{u}) - e^y(I_y, \bar{u})$.

By itself, (C16) clearly works against the satisfaction of (C11).

But production considerations work in the opposite direction. In particular, if we assume as before that capital and labor are complements, then it is easily shown that the marginal rate of substitution between effective labor and capital at a given (I, Q, N) is higher for a type x firm than for a type y firm:

(C17) $-K_E[Q, e^x(I, \bar{u})N] > -K_E[Q, e^y(I, \bar{u})N].$

The basic reasoning comes from the inequality, $e^x(I, \bar{u}) < e^y(I, \bar{u})$. When the type x and y firms pay the same numbers of workers the same incomes to produce the same Q, the type x firm uses more capital and less effective labor. As a result, its marginal product of capital is lower and its marginal product of labor higher than those for the type y firm. Thus, the amount of capital needed to compensate for a unit reduction in effective labor is then greater in the type x firm than in the type y firm; that is, (C17) holds.

This production consideration clearly works in favor of (C11), but the assumption of complements implies nothing about the magnitude of the difference in (C17). Indeed, the form of the production function may be varied to make this difference as small or large as desired, thereby producing examples where (C11) holds and examples where it does not. Thus, the first-best optimum is feasible in some asymmetric problems but not in others.

Finally, I demonstrate that, no matter how severely (C11) limits the solution to the asymmetric information, the assumption that the two factors are complements implies that it is never optimal to implement a "pooling equilibrium," where both types of firms are assigned the same (I, Q, N). Under this solution, the equality $I_x = I_y$ would give $E_x = e_x N < e_y N = E_y$, implying that $K_x > K_y$. By the assumption of complements, it would follow that $f_K(E_x, K_x) < f_K(E_y, K_y)$, which violates proposition 4. While this proposition assumes that the incentive-compatibility constraint is binding at the margin, dropping that assumption would imply that $f_K(E_x, K_x) = f_K(E_y, K_y)$, which is again inconsistent with a pooling equilibrium.

Notes

1. Throughout this paper, the term *first best* refers to the allocation that would be socially optimal in the absence of supervision problems.

2. The interest rate referred to here and throughout the paper is, of course, calculated net of taxes levied abroad. The analysis does not depend on whether the given country is a net capital exporter or importer, but in the latter case my formal model ignores foreign tax credits. I argue in sec. 11.2.2 that my results, if properly interpreted, are not affected by foreign tax credits.

3. An economy with many firms is explicitly considered when I model government uncertainty about the identity of firms with worker supervision problems.

4. The production and utility functions in this paper are assumed to be twice continuously differentiable.

5. Labor effort is measured continuously here, although many studies in the literature assume that e takes only two values, zero for shirkers and one for nonshirkers (Sparks 1986 is an important exception). The present specification is needed for the asymmetric information problem in sec. 11.3, and it is responsible for the role of marginal wage subsidies in sec. 11.2.

6. Since the production function is strictly concave, maximum profits will always be positive if the profit-maximizing output level is positive, as assumed throughout the paper.

7. I assume that the effort functions are strictly concave in income, in which case the profit-maximizing wage varies continuously with the tax parameters. This assumption holds under reasonable assumptions about utility.

8. More generally, no utility differences of any type are allowed between workers in the secondary sector, even when different secondary-sector firms are later explicitly included in the model. Examples could presumably be constructed in which welfare is improved by providing workers in these different firms with different utilities, but such examples would be undesirably sensitive to ad hoc assumptions about the rationing mechanism by which detected shirkers get reallocated across these firms. In a related development, the optimal commodity tax literature has already demonstrated the potential desirability of "random taxation" (e.g., Stiglitz 1982; and Chang and Wildasin 1986), but the principle of "horizontal equity" is often invoked to rule out its use.

9. Given that property taxes paid by domestic firms are not credited by foreign governments, property subsidies might serve the stated purpose. If subsidies outside the crediting system were not available, the domestic government would then face incentives to lower the effective cost of capital through various expenditure programs.

10. The results would not change if detection probabilities were allowed to differ across firms in the primary sector.

11. Different firms may produce identical or different goods.

12. The optimal tax functions will generally vary across firms if production functions differ. My results will concern properties that are common to all these functions, suggesting that the same properties would often hold if the government were forced to confront different firms with identical tax functions.

13. Defining the capital tax in terms of this difference has the desirable feature of not requiring that the optimal tax function $T^i(w, Q, N)$ be differentiable, which may not be the case. For a similar procedure with regard to optimal income taxation, see Stiglitz (1987b, 1003).

14. The actual optimization problem contains only total income, I_{ij}, rather than its components, n and w_{ij}, as control variables. In fact, any positive n and w_{ij}'s that sum to the optimal I_{ij}'s are then optimal. (Recall the nonuniqueness of the optimal tax system discussed in sec. 11.1.3.) As a pedagogical device, however, it is useful first to fix the government's choice of n.

15. Paradoxically, the same assumption is also used in App. B to prove that primary-sector capital should be subsidized at the margin while secondary-sector capital should be positively taxed when no other tax instruments are available.

16. For a general analysis of principal-agent problems of this type, with a special application to the optimal regulation of a labor managed firm, see Guesnerie and Laffont (1984).

17. For a detailed analysis of the optimal regulation of a firm when the government can observe both output and costs but where costs can be reduced by means of unobservable managerial effort, see Laffont and Tirole (1986). A particularly exciting feature of their work is that they allow costs to be stochastic at the time the firm chooses output and effort levels.

18. Proofs of the results reported here are available from the author on request.

References

Arvan, Lanny, and Francoise Schoumaker. 1988. Is public opinion right and conventional wisdom wrong about commercial policy? Typescript.

Baron, David P., and Roger B. Myerson. 1982. Regulating a monopolist with unknown costs. *Econometrica* 50 (July): 911–30.

Bulow, Jeremy I., and Lawrence H. Summers. 1986. A theory of dual labor markets with applications to industrial policy. *Journal of Labor Economics* 4 (July): 376–414.

Calvo, Guillermo A. 1985. The inefficiency of unemployment: The supervision perspective. *Quarterly Journal of Economics* 100 (May): 373–87.

Calvo, Guillermo A., and Stanislaw Wellisz. 1978. Hierarchy, ability, and income distribution. *Journal of Political Economy* 87 (October): 991–1012.

Carmichael, H. Lorne. 1988. Efficiency wage models of unemployment: A survey. Typescript.

Chang, Fwu-Ranq, and David E. Wildasin. 1986. Randomization and commodity taxes: An expenditure minimization approach. *Journal of Public Economics* 31 (December): 329–45.

Diamond, Peter A., and James A. Mirrlees. 1971. Optimal taxation and public production I–II. *American Economic Review* 61 (March, June): 8–27, 261–78.

Dixit, Avinash. 1989. Trade and insurance with adverse selection. *Review of Economic Studies* 56 (April): 235–47.

Guesnerie, Roger, and Jean-Jacques Laffont. 1984. A complete solution to a class of principal-agent problems with an application to the control of a self-managed firm. *Journal of Public Economics* 25 (December): 329–69.

Johnson, George E., and Richard Layard. 1986. The natural rate of unemployment: Explanation and policy. In *Handbook of Labor Economics,* vol. 2, ed. Orley C. Ashenfelter and Richard Layard. New York: North-Holland.

Katz, Lawrence F. 1988. Some recent developments in labor economics and their implications for macroeconomics. *Journal of Money, Credit and Banking* 20 (August): 507–22.

Laffont, Jean-Jacques, and Jean Tirole. 1986. Using cost observation to regulate firms. *Journal of Political Economy* 94 (June): 614–41.

———. 1988. The dynamics of incentive contracts. *Econometrica* 56 (September): 1153–75.

Shapiro, Carl, and Joseph E. Stiglitz. 1984. Equilibrium unemployment as a worker discipline device. *American Economic Review* 74 (June): 433–44.

Silberberg, Eugene. 1978. *The structure of economics: A mathematical analysis.* New York: McGraw-Hill.

Slemrod, Joel. 1988. Effect of taxation with international capital mobility. In *Uneasy compromise: Problems of a hybrid income-consumption tax,* ed. H. J. Aaron, H. Galper, and J. A. Pechman. Washington, D.C.: Brookings.

Sparks, Roger. 1986. A model of involuntary unemployment and wage rigidity: Worker incentives and the threat of dismissal. *Journal of Labor Economics* 4 (October): 560–81.

Stiglitz, Joseph E. 1982. Utilitarianism and horizontal equity: The case for random taxation. *Journal of Public Economics* 18 (March): 1–34.

———. 1986. Theories of wage rigidity. In *Keynes' economic legacy: Contemporary economic theories,* ed. J. Butkiewicz, K. Koford, and J. Miller. New York: Praeger.

———. 1987a. The causes and consequences of the dependence of quality on price. *Journal of Economic Literature* 25 (March): 1–48.

———. 1987b. Pareto efficient and optimal taxation and the new welfare economics. In *Handbook of public economics,* vol. 2, ed. A. J. Auerback and M. Feldstein. Amsterdam: North-Holland.

Comment   Lawrence F. Katz

The basic question addressed in Wilson's interesting paper is whether noncompetitive interindustry wage differentials provide a rationale for industrial policies in an economy with internationally mobile capital. This is a particularly important question to analyze given recent concern with U.S. competitiveness in strategic sectors and worries about shifts in employment from sectors that provide high-wage, "good jobs" to sectors that provide low-wage, "bad jobs."

Any economic justification for worrying about the sectoral composition of output must rely on the presence of market imperfections that drive a wedge between the marginal productivities of factors in different sectors. Wilson focuses on a labor market distortion within the context of an efficiency wage model in which a worker supervision problem requiring a wage premium is present in one sector (the primary sector) and absent in the other sector (the secondary sector).

In the first part of the paper, Wilson extends the Bulow-Summers dual labor market model by introducing capital in the production function and making capital perfectly internationally mobile. Wilson concludes that there is no role for the use of sectoral capital taxes and subsidies in the optimal government policy in this model when other instruments are available. This is not surprising since the distortion arises in the labor market (the wage is above opportunity costs in the primary sector) and can be directly solved through policies that serve to subsidize employment in the primary sector. The inclusion of capital and open economy considerations adds little to the analysis of this model. On the other hand, this section of the paper is useful in showing how the exact form of labor market policies (wage vs. employment subsidies and taxes) depends on the exact specification of the monitoring technology in a shirking model. The conclusion of no role for sectoral capital tax and subsidy policies also depends on the choice of model. In models where noncompetitive wage differentials arise from the differential ability of workers to extract product market rents and sunk investments in different sectors, the labor market distortion may take the form of a tax on investment that differs across sectors (Grout 1984; Katz and Summers 1989). In this case, even though the distortion arises in the labor market, its interaction with capital investment decisions means that the optimal policy may involve subsidies to investment in sectors where investments are particularly appropriable by labor.

The second part of the paper adds asymmetric information to a shirking model. The government is assumed not to know the identity of firms with supervision problems requiring premium wages. While there are many

Lawrence F. Katz is assistant professor of economics at Harvard University and a research associate of the National Bureau of Economic Research.

reasons to be skeptical of industrial policies and of the ability of the government to determine whether wage differentials represent "labor rents" rather than competitive differentials, the incentive compatibility issues discussed in the second part of the paper do not seem particularly relevant. The government surely has no problem differentiating firms in high-wage sectors (e.g., steel and auto plants) from those in low-wage sectors (e.g., fast food restaurants and retail stores). The more relevant issue is the political economy issue of how to control rent-seeking activities once significant subsidies become potentially available to potentially affected groups that can commission economists and statisticians to document that their industries provide high-rent jobs that should be subsidized. These political problems, emphasized in critiques of sectoral policies by Aaron (1989) and Schultze (1983), are not well illuminated in the mathematics of truth-telling constraints highlighted by Wilson's asymmetric information model.

The Wilson paper takes as given the existence of noncompetitive wage differentials arising from differences in the importance of supervision problems among firms. Many other discussions of industrial policies presume the existence of identifiable "good jobs" and "bad jobs." In fact, much recent empirical research has examined the nature of interindustry wage differentials (e.g., Dickens and Katz 1987; Krueger and Summers 1988; and Katz and Summers 1989). The basic finding is that there are large, systematic, persistent interindustry wage differentials that remain even after controlling for all observable worker and job characteristics available in micro data sets. For example, workers in autos, aircraft, and petroleum consistently earn 20–40 percent more than workers with the same measured characteristics in apparel, retail trade, and repair services. Interindustry wage differentials are remarkably similar across developed economies and highly correlated over time. The persistence over time suggests they are not just transitory differentials. The similarity across countries means that they reflect something fundamental in the nature of advanced industrial economies rather than particular labor market institutions. The differentials appear even larger when one includes employee benefits in measures of labor compensation.

High-wage industries have lower quit rates and face longer queues of job applicants than low-wage industries. These findings indicate that interindustry wage differentials are not largely compensating differentials. The low quit rates and long job queues in high-wage-differential sectors are easy to explain if these jobs provide labor rents. An alternative view is that industry wage differentials reflect the sorting of workers across industries on the basis of unmeasured ability (Murphy and Topel 1987). Longitudinal studies (reviewed in Katz and Summers 1989) find that the wage changes of industry switchers are quite similar to estimated cross-sectional differentials. This evidence casts doubt on the view that these differentials reflect sorting on time-invariant, unobserved productive ability. Furthermore, industry wage differentials are highly correlated across occupations. Industries that pay their managers wage premia also pay wage premia to their secretaries, laborers, and janitors. It is difficult to believe that industries that need high-ability managers also always need high-ability janitors. This strong correlation across occupations combined with the finding that wage differentials are strongly positively correlated with measures of product market rents per worker and appropriable capital per worker suggests that these differentials may reflect rent-sharing considerations.

The overall evidence does appear to be fairly persuasive that there do exist large noncompetitive interindustry wage differentials. Since profits account for a small share of value added relative to labor compensation, even small noncompetitive differences in wages across industries are likely to have more significant allocative consequences than variations in capital rents. In fact, Katz and Summers (1989) find that even conservative estimates of the variation in labor rents across sectors are substantially larger than the variation in capital rents. This suggests that Wilson's emphasis on labor market distortions rather than on profit shifting considerations in his analysis of industrial policies is well placed. More work on the sources of noncompetitive wage differentials is clearly required before strong policy statements can be made given that different models of differentials can lead to quite different predictions. Furthermore, any economic case for activist policy must be tempered by a recognition of the formidable difficulties likely to be encountered in the implementation of policies that pick "good" and "bad" industries.

References

Aaron, Henry J. 1989. Politics and the professors revisited. *American Economic Review* 79 (May): 1–15.

Dickens, William T., and Lawrence F. Katz. 1987. Inter-industry wage differences and industry characteristics. In *Unemployment and the structure of labor markets,* ed. K. Lang and J. Leonard, 48–89. Oxford: Blackwell.

Grout, Paul A. 1984. Investment and wages in the absence of binding contracts: A Nash bargaining approach. *Econometrica* 52 (March): 449–60.

Katz, Lawrence F., and Lawrence H. Summers. 1989. Industry rents: Evidence and implications. *Brookings Papers on Economic Activity: Microeconomics,* 209–75.

Krueger, Alan B., and Lawrence H. Summers. 1988. Efficiency wages and the inter-industry wage structure. *Econometrica* 56 (March): 259–93.

Murphy, Kevin M., and Robert H. Topel. 1987. Unemployment, risk, and earnings: Testing for equalizing differences in the labor market. In *Unemployment and the structure of labor markets,* ed., K. Lang and J. Leonard, 103–40. Oxford: Blackwell.

Schultze, Charles L. 1983. Industrial policy: A dissent. *Brookings Review* (Fall), 3–12.

Contributors

Krister Andersson
Western Hemisphere Department
International Monetary Fund
700 19th Street, NW
Washington, DC 20431

Kenji Aramaki
Office of Investment Trust and
   Management
Securities Bureau
Ministry of Finance
Tokyo, Japan

Alan J. Auerbach
Department of Economics
University of Pennsylvania
3718 Locust Walk
Philadelphia, PA 19104

Hugh J. Ault
School of Law
Boston College
855 Centre Street
Newton, MA 02159

Jean-Thomas Bernard
Department of Economics
Université Laval
Ste-Foy, Québec G1K 7P4
Canada

A. Lans Bovenberg
Fiscal Affairs Department
International Monetary Fund
700 19th Street, NW
Washington, DC 20431

David F. Bradford
Woodrow Wilson School
Princeton University
Princeton, NJ 08544

Willem H. Buiter
Department of Economics
Yale University
28 Hillhouse Avenue
New Haven, CT 06520

Sheetal K. Chand
Fiscal Affairs Department
International Monetary Fund
700 19th Street, NW
Washington, DC 20431

Avinash Dixit
Department of Economics
Princeton University
Princeton, NJ 08544

Michael P. Dooley
Research Department
International Monetary Fund
700 19th Street, NW
Washington, DC 20431

Lorraine Eden
Norman Paterson School of International
   Affairs
Carleton University
Ottawa, Ontario K1S 5B6
Canada

Martin Feldstein
President and Chief Executive Officer
National Bureau of Economic Research
1050 Massachusetts Avenue
Cambridge, MA 02138

Jacob A. Frenkel
Economic Counsellor and Director
Research Department
International Monetary Fund
700 19th Street, NW
Washington, DC 20431

Daniel J. Frisch
Senior Fellow
Institute for International Economics
11 DuPont Circle, NW
Washington, DC 20036

Roger H. Gordon
Department of Economics
University of Michigan
Ann Arbor, MI 48109

David G. Hartman
Data Resources, Inc.
24 Hartwell Avenue
Lexington, MA 02173

James R. Hines Jr.
Woodrow Wilson School
Princeton University
Princeton, NJ 08544

R. Glenn Hubbard
Graduate School of Business
Columbia University
Uris Hall 609
New York, NY 10027

Joosung Jun
Department of Economics
Yale University
28 Hillhouse Avenue
New Haven, CT 06520

Lawrence F. Katz
Department of Economics
Harvard University
Littauer Center 107
Cambridge, MA 02138

Paul Krugman
Department of Economics
Massachusetts Institute of Technology
E52-383A
Cambridge, MA 02139

James Levinsohn
Department of Economics
University of Michigan
Ann Arbor, MI 48109

Jack M. Mintz
Faculty of Management
University of Toronto
Toronto, Ontario M5S 1V4
Canada

Assaf Razin
Department of Economics
Tel-Aviv University
Ramat Aviv 69978
Israel

Efraim Sadka
Department of Economics
Tel-Aviv University
Ramat Aviv 69978
Israel

Joel Slemrod
Department of Economics
University of Michigan
Ann Arbor, MI 48109

Steve Symansky
Research Department
International Monetary Fund
700 19th Street, NW
Washington, DC 20431

Robert J. Weiner
Department of Economics
Brandeis University
Waltham, MA 02254

John Whalley
Department of Economics
University of Western Ontario
London, Ontario N6A 5C2
Canada

John Douglas Wilson
Department of Economics
Indiana University
Ballantine Hall
Bloomington, IN 47405

Mark A. Wolfson
Department of Economics
Stanford University
Stanford, CA 94305

Author Index

Subject Index